DATABASE SYSTEMS FOR MANAGEMENT

DATABASE SYSTEMS FOR MANAGEMENT

JAMES F. COURTNEY, JR.
DAVID B. PARADICE
BOTH OF TEXAS A & M UNIVERSITY
SECOND EDITION

IRWIN
HOMEWOOD, IL 60430
BOSTON, MA 02116

This symbol indicates that the paper in this book is made from recycled paper. Its fiber content exceeds the recommended minimum of 50% waste paper fibers as specified by the EPA.

Cover photo: George Kamper

© RICHARD D. IRWIN, INC., 1988 and 1992

Senior sponsoring editor: Larry Alexander
Developmental editor: Lena Buonanno
Project editor: Rebecca Dodson
Production manager: Bob Lange
Interior designer: E. Heidi Fieschko
Cover designer: Dolores Wilber
Compositor: Weimer Typesetting Co., Inc.
Typeface: 10/12 Palatino
Printer: Von Hoffmann Press, Inc.

Paradox® is a registered trademark of Borland International.

Library of Congress Cataloging-in-Publication Data

Courtney, James F. (James Forrest), 1944-
    Database systems for management / James F. Courtney, Jr., David B. Paradice. —2nd ed.
        p.   cm.
    Includes bibliographies and index.
    ISBN 0-256-08229-4
    1. Management information systems.   2. Data base management.
I. Paradice, David B.   II. Title.
T58.6.C685   1992
658.4'038—dc20   91–27743

Printed in the United States of America

1 2 3 4 5 6 7 8 9 0 V H 8 7 6 5 4 3 2 1

PREFACE

The Intended Audience for the Book

Database Systems for Management is intended to support a management-oriented first course in database processing concepts. This course is usually taught in the junior or senior year in four-year institutions or in the second year of two-year programs. We recommend that students have taken an introductory computer concepts course, at least one high-level programming course in which basic data structures and access methods have been covered, and a course in systems analysis and design. The systems analysis and design course may be taken concurrently with the database course. Due to the managerial orientation of the book, we recommend that students have completed introductory course work in the major functional areas of business. A course in data structures is not necessary since we provide adequate coverage of this material in appendices. The book can be used for any introductory database management processing course, but is focused on the type of database processing concepts needed in a management information systems program.

Why We Wrote This Book

Many textbooks used in introductory database management classes for management information systems (MIS) students are deficient because of their computer science orientation. This situation occurs because most authors of database textbooks have their foundations in computer science and are currently pursuing careers in that field. Without doubt, their textbooks are excellent presentations of their material. Unfortunately, the material is not in all cases relevant to the ultimate goal of most MIS students (or MIS curricula), which is more oriented toward becoming (or producing) effective decision-making skills than becoming (or producing) top-rate database designers and builders. Specifically:

- Many database management textbooks have a computer science orientation that stresses the "how" aspects of database design but rarely addresses the "why" aspects. When the "why" aspects are addressed in other books, it is rarely from an organizational decision-making perspective. This textbook approaches introductory database design from a distinctly MIS viewpoint. Throughout the text, we emphasize decision-making and the impact of a database environment upon the decision-making process.

- Many database management textbooks motivate examples from a conceptual basis. Our examples are motivated by realistic scenarios. Each example in this text is formulated within the context of a plausible business situation.

- Many database management textbooks provide abstract data in examples. Our examples contain data that simulates the type of data found in most corporate domains.

- Due to their computer science orientation, many books go into great detail on technical topics. Certainly MIS students need to be familiar with the technical aspects of security and transaction recovery. But they also need to understand the managerial implications of choosing one method over another, or the liability of having inadequate technical support. These aspects are unique to our book.

- Due to their computer science orientation, many books do not go into any detail on managerial issues. MIS students need a database management class that will emphasize the database function as a part of the overall information management system of the organization.

We believe you should consider this book because we have developed it with the intention of addressing the inadequacies of other books described above. More than that, however, we have incorporated a number of features in the second edition that we feel instructors of database management systems courses in MIS curricula will find attractive:

- The importance of planning for database design is emphasized. Unlike any other database textbook, we develop the concept of an organizational information systems master plan and the role of the database management system within that plan.

- We present a very thorough coverage of Entity-Relationship modeling techniques. We also demonstrate how to use data structure diagrams.

- The book has a relational model orientation, although we provide thorough coverage of the CODASYL model and provide an overview of IMS to illustrate the hierarchical model.

- The concept of *normalization* is developed early in the text in an intuitive manner without sacrificing the rigor inherent in the definition of the various normal forms. We develop an approach that demonstrates *why* non-normalized data structures are undesirable. Dependencies, presented in this way, become concepts that students are better able to recognize.

- We emphasize the role of organizational assumptions in determining dependencies, making the process practical instead of mechanical. We also emphasize that normalization is a concept to be considered in *all* database systems, not just relational systems.

- Although managerial in orientation, no major technical topic is omitted. Obviously, a manager cannot effectively manage in a database environment when he or she lacks an understanding of these technical issues. Our treatment is different from other textbooks in that, after presenting the basic technical concept, we discuss managerial issues where other textbooks discuss detailed implementation issues.

- The proliferating role of microcomputers in the organizational environment is addressed. We have a chapter devoted to microcomputer database systems issues.

- We have an entire chapter devoted to distributed database systems. All of the major issues of security, concurrency, recovery, and data partitioning are covered in this chapter. We also discuss query optimization in a distributed database environment.

- We provide a chapter that covers several topics that will be important issues in the future. This chapter includes coverage of object-oriented databases, deductive databases and Prolog, implications of computer-integrated manufacturing for database design, and the role of database processing in expert systems.

- We provide a "capstone" chapter on decision support systems. This chapter is also intended to emphasize the database processing function in the overall organizational information management system.

- Our "User's View" section in each chapter emphasizes the view of organizational database systems users. Database users have always presented special managerial issues; as database software increases the accessibility of organizational databases, one must expect database management to become more complex. This section emphasizes user-oriented issues.

- Our "Metropolitan National Bank" scenario provides students with a comprehensive case study. Each chapter introduces new material related to this case study, providing an opportunity for students to apply the concepts of the chapter.

- We have included many, many case examples throughout the text. This is especially evident in our treatment of normalization where we give four separate scenarios. Each chapter contains approximately 20 review questions, with roughly half of these questions requiring the student to *apply* the concepts of the chapter.

- Each chapter contains a brief, annotated reading list where supplemental material may be found.

Our approach immediately reinforces *why* a particular point is being made and *how* the database is supporting the decision-making process. Our approach may be summarized as follows: MIS students are better trained if they understand the managerial impacts of decisions made in designing database systems.

We believe that our practical experience designing and developing database management systems currently in use in businesses, our research in theoretical aspects of the field, and our academic experience teaching various aspects of MIS in colleges of business administration have provided us with some insight into the needs of the undergraduate MIS student of today. We further believe that this text specifically addresses one such need, a need for a truly management-oriented introduction to database management systems, in a rather unique fashion. We are excited about this edition. We hope the features of the book listed above will convince you to consider using our book in your course.

How to Use This Book

Database Systems for Management is presented in five parts. Part One, "Database Fundamentals," introduces the topic of database systems. We begin with an overview of the purpose of using database systems and review the major components of these systems. We also begin our focus on planning and design issues. This part of the book addresses the following questions:

- Why should an organization adopt database management concepts?
- What are the major components of a database system?
- How should the organization plan for the development of a database management system?
- What should be contained in the organization's information systems master plan?

Chapter 1 presents the fundamental concepts and major components of database management systems. Chapter 2 describes planning for database systems and emphasizes that database systems are one part of the overall organizational information management system.

Part Two of this book focuses on design issues. In Chapter 3, we provide an overview of logical design concepts. We provide extensive coverage of Entity-Relationship modeling concepts and show how to convert these to data structure diagrams. Chapter 4 presents the ANSI/X3/SPARC conceptual framework for database management systems and previews the hierarchical, network, and relational models. We feel this glimpse of the models allows students to begin designing databases with some thought of their ultimate implementation goal. But before they can get too far, Chapter 5 presents normalization. We cover the topic first by discussing modification anomalies. These problems are symptomatic of non-normalized designs. Then, we proceed to the normal form criteria. We have found this approach to be a successful one.

- What data should be included in the database system and how is it logically structured?
- How can logical relationships be implemented in data structures?
- What are the primary means for structuring the data in a database system?
- How can one identify potential problems in various database designs?

Part Three of the book examines the relational database model in depth. Three of the four chapters in this part cover relational database issues. We also present the CODASYL model at the end of this part. We include the CODASYL model in our textbook because we believe many of today's students will be involved in conversion projects from CODASYL to relational implementations. Thus, they need a basic knowledge of the CODASYL approach. The issues addressed in this part are:

- What is the relational approach to database management and how can it be used to manipulate data?
- What do the concepts of *essentiality* and *integrity* mean?
- What distinguishes relational systems from systems that merely present data in the form of tables?
- What is SQL and how can it be used to extract data from a relational database?
- What role do microcomputers play in a database environment?
- What special considerations should management have regarding microcomputer-based database systems?
- How is database manipulation different on microcomputers?
- What is a QBE interface and how is it used to access data?
- What is the CODASYL approach to database management and how can it be used to manipulate data?
- What are currency indicators, or cursors, and how are they used to manipulate data in a CODASYL environment?

Chapter 6 reviews the relational model in depth. In Chapter 7, we examine the SQL approach to relational data manipulation. Since SQL has become the official standard in relational data manipulation, we provide extensive coverage of this topic. Chapter 8 looks at microcomputer-based database systems, which are primarily relational systems. We examine managerial issues as well as specific implementations, dBase IV, Paradox, and XQL. Chapter 9 focuses on the CODASYL model. This chapter provides a comprehensive examination of the CODASYL approach.

Part Four emphasizes physical design and implementation issues in database management. Chapter 10 reviews storage methodologies and data structure issues. Chapter 11 provides comprehensive coverage of database issues at the transaction level. We examine the role of data repositories. We address security issues from two viewpoints: database software and managerial responsibility. We present several ways to recover from system failures including logging and memory management techniques. We also cover how problems can arise when multiple users access a data item concurrently, and how to resolve these problems. Some of the specific points covered here are:

- How are logical relationships physically implemented?
- What are the differences in alternative implementations of relationships?
- Under what circumstances is one implementation preferred to another?
- What are data repositories and how do they influence database processing?
- What are the important security considerations in a database environment?
- How does a system recover from a major system failure?
- When should a transaction's effects actually be applied to the database?
- How are problems caused by multiple users resolved?
- How are database systems physically implemented?
- What are the advantages of one physical implementation over another?
- How can the database models be represented at the physical implementation level?
- What technical aspects of database systems are particularly important from a manager's viewpoint?
- How are database transaction failures recovered?
- How can one recover a database after a major system failure?
- How does one prevent problems caused by concurrent access to data by multiple users?
- How are security issues addressed in database systems?
- How is database performance monitored?

Part Five covers advanced database issues. Chapter 12 provides an overview of distributed database management systems. Chapter 13 presents several topics that we feel are the emerging areas for students to learn: database issues in computer-integrated manufacturing systems, object-oriented systems and object-oriented design, deductive database systems and Prolog, and natural language processing. Chapter 14 concludes our coverage of management-oriented database systems by presenting database concepts in a decision support role. Our objective in this part of the book is to answer the following questions.

- What are distributed database systems?
- How is data distributed?
- What are the special issues related to concurrent access, security, and database recovery in a distributed database environment?

- What are the future trends in database systems?
- What are the issues in computer integrated manufacturing that impact database design and implementation?
- What is the object-oriented paradigm?
- What are object-oriented databases and why are they important?
- What is a deductive database?
- How are deductive databases implemented?
- What is the role of natural language processing in a database environment?
- What problems exist in natural language processing?
- What are decision support systems and how do database systems support semi-structured decision-making processes?

Providing a sequencing of chapters that will meet every instructor's needs is difficult at best. The following strategies may be helpful given certain class characteristics and the goals of the instructor:

- Students with strong technical backgrounds may skip Chapter 10 without loss of continuity.
- Students with prior instruction in systems analysis and design may be able to move through Chapter 2 without significant in-class discussion.
- Instructors that wish to get into the relational model quickly may want to give light emphasis to Chapter 1 and skip Chapter 4, thus getting to Chapters 6 and 7 sooner.
- Instructors may wish to substitute coverage of a database package available at their institution for the coverage of SQL in Chapter 7.

Our experience in class testing the book indicates that one must move rather quickly in order to cover all of the topics presented in the text. We have yet to get through an entire semester without feeling that some topic somewhere along the way received a little less attention than we would have liked.

Instructor's Manual

The *Instructor's Manual for Database Systems for Management* has been developed to do what few other instructor's guides do: **guide** the instructor! Of course, we have included an outline of the chapter contents, answers to the review questions that appear at the end of each chapter, over 100 transparency masters, and sample test questions. The test questions will also be available in a computerized test bank (free to adopters). Also included in the instructor's manual are several examples of solutions to the Metropolitan National Bank case. These features are, we think, expected in an instructor's guide. A separate case book with five additional cases is also available.

We have extended the instructor's manual concept, however, in two ways. Since the "cost" of preparation in a course such as this is large, we have included annotated excerpts from our lectures based on the material in the text. These excerpts include emphasis of the major topics in the chapter, suggestions for anticipating students' reactions and pitfalls, and cross references to other textbooks frequently used in this course. We think you'll agree that with this help the transition to our textbook will be much smoother than is typically the case.

Our second extension to the traditional instructor's guide format is the inclusion of small chapter-by-chapter "minicases." These cases are designed to provide instructors with a small amount of extra material that some students need to completely grasp a concept. Additionally, instructors can modify the contents of these minicases to develop a basis for small student projects. These cases also provide an excellent source for comprehensive test questions. We also provide the kernel for another major case study.

We hope you'll agree that our *Instructor's Manual for Database Systems for Management* is a valuable addition to your planning and preparation tools for this class.

ACKNOWLEDGMENTS

This edition of *Database Systems for Management* would not have been possible without the contributions of many people. We would like to express our gratitude to the following reviewers, who contributed greatly to the development of our book:

Boris Baran
Concordia University

John Boggess
Purdue University

Helen Casey
*Sam Houston
State University*

William R. Cornette
*Southwest Missouri
State University*

Annette Easton
*San Diego State
University*

Kevin Gorman
*University of North
Carolina at Charlotte*

W. J. Kenny Jih
*University of Tennessee
at Chattanooga*

Alexis Koster
*San Diego State
University*

Phillip E. Lowry
*University of Nevada
at Las Vegas*

Manohar S. Madan
University of Toledo

Gerard J. Manning
*Cabot Institute of Applied
Arts and Technology*

Saralyn E. Mathis
*West Virginia Institute
of Technology*

Roger Alan Pick
Louisiana Tech University

Jerry Post
Western Kentucky University

Richard G. Ramirez
Arizona State University

Fred Ramos
Oklahoma City University

Laurette Paulos Simmons
Loyola College

Richard T. Watson
University of Georgia

Many corrections and revisions were also driven by recommendations from our students and other teachers using the first edition. We greatly appreciate the efforts these people made to work with us to improve the book. We hope we have gone beyond their expectations in this edition. We certainly remain open to new ideas and suggestions.

Additionally, several persons contributed to the book's development in other ways. Our section on database issues in computer integrated manufacturing environments was drawn from the research of Gabriela Marin. We greatly appreciate her efforts to make that material available to us. Karen Silvermintz worked on initial versions of the Metropolitan National Bank case and helped us refine it. Karen's design work appears in the Instructor's Manual. We would also like to thank Paul Maddock and Josie Ceccoli for contributing design work on this case, which also appears in the Instructor's Manual.

At Irwin, Becky Johnson, Lena Buonanno, and Larry Alexander have worked very hard to bring this edition to the market. We appreciate their efforts to keep our philosophy of teaching database concepts in managerial environments alive.

At home, we must thank our families for their patience and understanding as we tackled the chore of a major revision. As always, their support has been most generous.

Everyone involved tried to find and correct errors, but we as authors must take responsibility for any that managed to get into the final product. As before, any comments, criticisms, suggestions, or improvements are welcomed and appreciated. Write to us in care of Irwin.

Jim Courtney
David Paradice

CONTENTS IN BRIEF

Contents

DATABASE SYSTEMS FOR MANAGEMENT

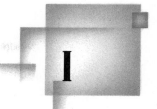

I

DATABASE FUNDAMENTALS

1

INTRODUCTION TO DATABASE SYSTEMS

O rganizations capture and process data for a variety of reasons. Accounting data is used to measure the financial health and vitality of the enterprise: It is useful to internal corporate management in keeping track of how the firm is performing; it is useful to people outside the firm, such as investors interested in the firm's stock and bankers to whom the firm has applied for a loan. Records on a host of other organizational entities, including employees, inventories, customers, and suppliers, are required as well.

One of the main uses of data is in making decisions. A manager must decide, for example, on the price of the firm's product or on how many units of the product to produce. An investor must decide whether to invest in a firm; a banker must decide whether to make a loan. The Federal Reserve Board must decide whether to increase or decrease interest rates, or hold them stable. In all of these cases, it is desirable to have reliable information on which to base the decision. Information and the data on which it is based are valuable organizational assets that warrant careful management.

DATA AS AN ORGANIZATIONAL ASSET

Major functional areas in organizations have evolved from recognition that the function being managed is of vital importance. Financial and accounting departments, for example, manage predominantly monetary assets of an organization. Few would argue that these assets are unimportant to the organization. Marketing departments handle the advertising for new and existing products, carry out research studies, and distribute products. These activities are obviously important. Production, personnel, and other departments also specialize in efficient and effective management of the assets in these areas. Similarly, organizational data and information must be regarded as an asset of vital importance to the organization. A few examples should make clear how important data and information can be.

Consider a company that produces a news magazine with national distribution. It can collect data about its subscribers that can be used in many ways to gain an advantage in the marketplace; it can, for example, use data about personal interests to help select the stories to be printed or to entice organizations to purchase advertising space.

Or imagine an organization that, thanks to a secret formula, manufactures the most popular product in a highly competitive market. In fact, the company maintains the results of hundreds of consumer tests of variations of the formula in a database. These can be analyzed whenever consumer preferences appear to be changing, giving the company the appearance of an uncanny ability to anticipate consumer preferences. Were this data to fall into the hands of competitors, all advantages in the marketplace would be lost.

Or consider such routine information as salary or production schedule data. Salary data in the hands of a competing organization could result in the loss of top employees through offers of higher compensation. Production data could allow a competitor to anticipate an organization's strategy in the near future. Each of these actions could have devastating results for an organization.

These examples are intended to emphasize the point that data is indeed a valuable asset to an organization. You can doubtlessly think of other examples. As with any valuable asset, the organization should have persons and procedures to effectively manage the asset. The management of organizational data is the main topic of concern in this book.

MANAGING ORGANIZATIONAL DATA

Organizations of all sizes now use computers to perform the data processing functions required to provide information for management decision-making. Experience with business applications of data processing has shown that the data itself is a valuable organizational resource that must be carefully managed. The task of managing organizational data and data processing functions is often called **data management** or **information management.**

The data resources of an organization are usually stored in **databases,** which are highly integrated sets of files shared by users throughout the organization. Because it is impractical to store all the data for even relatively small organizations in one database, organizations design **database systems,** which are integrated collections of databases along with users who share the databases, personnel who design and manage databases, techniques for designing and managing databases, and computer systems to support them. These are rather simple definitions of databases and database systems, but they will suffice for now. These definitions are expanded throughout the book.

This book provides an introduction to special technology and techniques for designing and managing organizational database systems. After studying the material in this book, you should have mastered at least the basic principles underlying the technology used to manage databases and the techniques used to design and implement effective database systems.

When reading this chapter, think about what is meant by data as an organizational resource and about how managers use data. Keep in mind the idea that **the main goal of database systems is to provide managers with information so that they can make effective decisions about how to run the organization.** The basic theme of this book is that reliable information and accurate data are required for effective managerial decisions. The objective of the book is to demonstrate how to design and manage effective database systems.

The users of database systems are the customers of the information systems department. If these customers do not use the product (the database system), then the system has not been designed effectively. To emphasize the viewpoint of database system users, each chapter includes a section entitled "The User's View," which discusses the concerns of users as related to that chapter's topics.

DATA VERSUS INFORMATION

Information and data are not the same thing. Information is sometimes defined as processed data, but simply because data has been processed does not mean that it is useful to an organization. The average price of corn in Iowa may be meaningful to thousands of farmers but useless to an automobile manufacturer. For the purposes of this book, **data** is defined simply as numbers, words, names, and other symbols that can be stored in a computer system. **Information** is simply useful data. If a single data value (such as the price of a competitor's product) is useful, then it is information. Several data values may be manipulated or processed to create information (such as in computing the average price of several competing products). If the resulting data value is not useful, then it is not information, no matter how much it has been processed.

ELEMENTS OF DATABASE SYSTEMS

The principal elements in a database environment are people, computer hardware, computer software, databases, and techniques for planning, designing, implementing, and managing databases. Each of these elements is examined in more detail in the next chapter. A brief overview is given here.

People

The people involved with database systems can be divided into two groups: those who use information provided by the system and those who design, develop, and manage the system itself. If a database system is to be of value to the organization, it is imperative that it be designed to support the needs of information users. This point is emphasized repeatedly throughout the book; it cannot be overemphasized. The design of user-oriented database systems is considered in detail in the chapters on system design, implementation, and administration.

Those people responsible for the design, development, and administration of database systems are often referred to as **database administrators.** The position of database administrator is highly challenging and should be a high-level managerial position. Database administrators must possess well-developed skills in both technical and managerial aspects of information management, because they are the primary liaisons between the community of users and the systems development staff.

The personnel responsible for developing database systems are information analysts or database analysts. **Information analysts** work closely with users of information to carefully define information requirements and to structure these requirements into a logical form. **Database analysts** use database technology to design systems satisfying those requirements. This book is aimed primarily at those who seek to develop successful database systems and who may ultimately become database administrators, but it is of interest to users of database systems as well. Thus, the book is concerned with both technical and managerial aspects of information management.

Computer Hardware and Software

Computer hardware and software are two different elements of a database environment, but they are discussed together in this chapter. Hardware and software form the technological foundation for database systems. This book contains a limited discussion of the hardware for database management; hardware is an extensive and complex topic requiring special treatment far beyond the scope of the book.

Software for information management can be separated into two groups: applications software and database management systems. **Database management systems (DBMS)** are commercial software packages designed to provide the basis for building database systems. Many such packages are on the market today, and thousands of organizations use them. The packages are part of the technology of information management and usually depend heavily on the operating system for many of their basic functions.

Organizations acquire database management systems and develop or acquire applications software to satisfy their particular database processing requirements. You are undoubtedly familiar with the way ordinary programming languages such as COBOL describe data files. As is illustrated shortly, this approach may not provide ready access to information. The database approach is intended to overcome these problems.

Databases

As shown in Figures 1–1 and 1–2, database management systems are designed to allow various programs to share the data they have in common. In Figure 1–1, Joe has his files and his data, and Sue has her files and her data. Joe uses the manufacturing budget in his program, but Sue does not. Sue uses salary data, but Joe does not. In fact, Joe is not even allowed to see or access the salary data; it is privileged information. Both programmers use product prices.

In Figure 1–2, the programmers have merged their data into an integrated database ("our" data). The integrated database is defined in the **schema,** which describes all the data items and relationships in the entire database. Note, however, that each programmer still has some data (salary and manufacturing) that is inaccessible to the other, even though it is stored in the integrated database.

Each programmer's individual view of the database is defined in a **subschema.** The use of a database management system to develop an integrated database is discussed later in this chapter. For now, note that a database is an integrated collection of shared files.

FIGURE 1–1   Conventional Programming Environment with Program-File Dependence
Both Joe and Sue have access to product prices. Only Joe has access to the manufacturing budget and only
Sue has access to salary data.

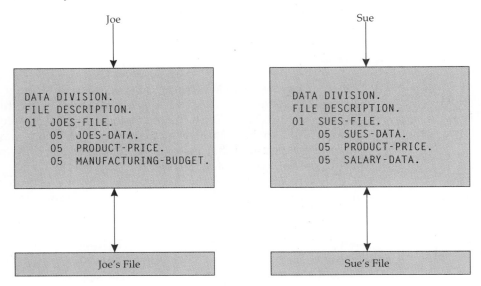

The database management system acts as a sophisticated buffer between applications programs and the data those programs need. This approach separates data from applications programs and makes data management (the treatment of data as an important organizational resource) possible.

Database Planning and Design Techniques

Since database systems involve people from all parts of the organization with a variety of information needs, the development and operation of database systems must be carefully designed to provide efficient access to information required by the various users. The first step in converting to a database approach should be the development of (1) a master plan that specifies in general terms the various applications and data-bases to be included in the overall system and (2) a schedule for detailed design and implementation of these applications and databases.

Detailed database design consists of three major phases: analysis of information requirements, logical database design, and physical database design. **Information requirements analysis** is work done with users to define information needs. **Logical database design** is the development of schema and subschema definitions. **Physical database design** establishes exactly how the data will be organized and stored on the storage devices. Database planning and design are previewed in the next chapter and examined extensively in other chapters of the text.

FIGURE 1–2 An Integrated Database with Both Shared and Private Data
Both Joe and Sue have access to product prices via their respective subschemas, but only Joe can access the manufacturing budget and only Sue can access salary data.

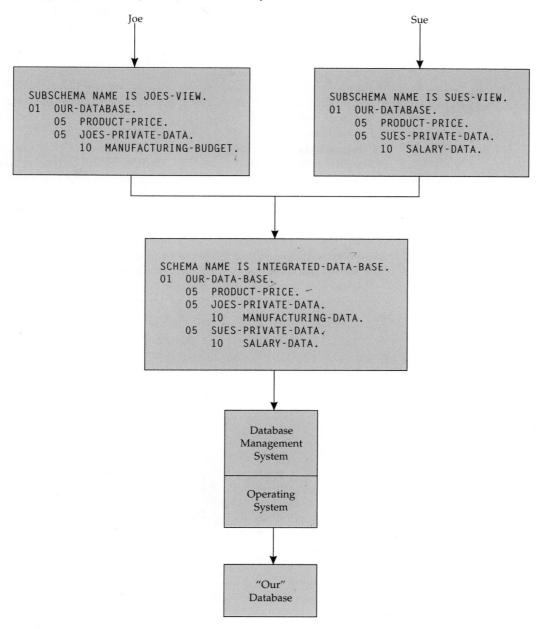

DATABASE SYSTEMS AND OTHER ORGANIZATIONAL INFORMATION SYSTEMS

Databases and database management systems provide the infrastructure on which other organizational information systems are built. Organizational information systems include transaction processing systems (TPS), management information systems (MIS), and decision support systems (DSS). These are applications programs that derive data from the database via the DBMS. The relationships among these various systems are illustrated in Figure 1–3. The entire set of organizational information systems is shown as a pyramid, with the DBMS and databases below the base.

Transaction processing systems form the bottom of the pyramid and are the lifeblood systems of the organization because they support the processing of "production" data—for example, data for inventory maintenance, accounts receivable and payable, and other accounting functions. These transactions provide most of the internal data used as the basis for generating information for managerial decision-making. Transactions themselves are usually well defined; forms displayed on terminal screens can be used to gather and display data. These systems are used primarily by clerical personnel and first-line managers.

Management information systems are in the middle of the pyramid and are used primarily by middle management to control the organization. These systems derive much of their information by summarizing

FIGURE 1–3
The Relationship of Database Systems to Transaction Processing Systems, Management Information Systems, and Decision Support Systems

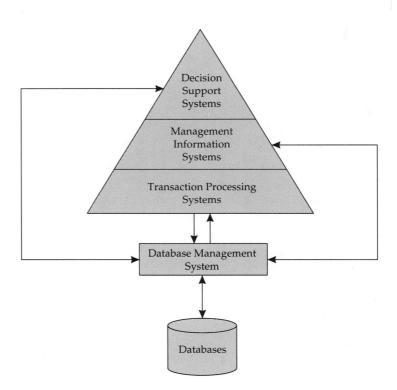

and abstracting data from transaction processing systems. They tend to be report oriented; standard reports are produced periodically (weekly, monthly, or annually) for use by middle managers to support tasks such as budget decisions and personnel assignments.

Decision support systems are designed to provide information for managerial decision-making in cases where the decision is not clear-cut (**ill-structured problems** or **semi-structured problems** in DSS jargon). These problems tend to occur at the apex of the organizational pyramid. DSS often use mathematical and statistical techniques to manipulate and analyze data. It is difficult to anticipate information needs in a DSS environment, so these systems must be flexible and adaptable.

Database management technology has been used as the basis for some DSS. These are referred to as data-oriented DSS. Many of the examples in this book are data-oriented DSS.

At present, most commercial software packages being touted as DSS provide relatively sophisticated mathematical modeling languages, but only simple data management facilities. On the other hand, most database management packages have sophisticated data management facilities, but only very simple mathematical and statistical languages. In the future, these packages may be merged to yield integrated systems providing powerful facilities for both mathematical modeling and data management.

Since DSS have become quite popular and often rely on data extracted from database systems, it is important to understand their relationship to DBMS. Decision support systems are discussed in Chapter 14.

EFFECTIVE SYSTEMS AND EFFICIENT SYSTEMS

It is useful to distinguish between effective database systems and efficient database systems. **Effective systems** provide correct, current information that is relevant to the decision at hand. Ahituv and Neumann (1986) refer to effectiveness as "doing the right thing." To provide effective database systems, analysts must work closely with managers and other users to carefully specify information requirements. The system cannot be effective unless information needs are accurately determined and the database system designed to serve those needs.

Efficient systems, on the other hand, perform a task in a cost-effective manner. A database system must provide the required information at a reasonable cost. Ahituv and Neumann call this "doing the thing right."

Of the two, the concern for effectiveness predominates. If a database system does not provide correct, current, relevant information, it does not matter how efficiently the data is processed—it is still useless. Conversely, if the system is effective, it may contain certain inefficiencies but still be highly useful.

Effective database systems are expensive to develop, and an organization cannot afford to go bankrupt in developing effective systems.

The value of the information provided must exceed the cost of providing that information.

To illustrate some of the concepts already introduced in this chapter and to explain the need for effective data management, two case examples are presented next. The first is that of the Conventional National Bank, which uses the customary file approach to data management. The second contains a portfolio management example that illustrates the database approach.

CASE EXAMPLE
Data Management at the Conventional National Bank

The Conventional National Bank (CNB) acquired a computer in the mid-1960s to automate check processing. The bank soon realized that the computer was useful for many other purposes, such as maintaining information on mortgage loans, auto loans, savings accounts, and portfolios of common stocks, bonds, and other securities. During the late 1960s and early 1970s, the bank converted these applications from manual to computer-based systems. Most of the software to support these applications was written in COBOL. By the mid-1970s, thousands of COBOL programs were in use. Some of these programs were enormous—several thousand lines long. Together, all the programs comprised well over a million lines of COBOL code.

The bank is organized on the basis of the functions it performs: there are departments for checking accounts, savings accounts, auto loans, mortgage loans, trusts, and so on. To reduce the need for inter-departmental communication, separate data files are maintained for each department. Because the bank has several thousand customers, and most customers have several accounts, these files now occupy several billion characters of disk storage.

Tia Fuentes has been a regular customer of CNB for 15 years. Tia began her association with the bank when she graduated from college and moved to Conventional City to begin a position as manager trainee for Silver Flatware Products. Over the years, Tia has accumulated some savings, which she keeps in a passbook savings account with the bank. Two years ago, she purchased a new car with a loan she got at CNB. Three months ago, Tia was promoted to assistant manager, and shortly thereafter she moved into a new home. Tia now resides comfortably in her new estate near the flatware plant.

After an important staff meeting one day, Tia returned to her office to find a telephone message from Gilda Kerr, an auto loan officer at CNB. Tia returned the call only to discover that Gilda was calling to ask why Tia had not made car payments for the past three months. After all, CNB had sent the usual computer-prepared reminder each month with a preprinted return envelope for her convenience.

Tia was stunned! In the excitement of her promotion and move, she had completely forgotten about the car payment. She had called the bank to give them her new address, and she had received her monthly bank statements and notices on the mortgage loan payments. She had not received any notices on the car payments, and they had completely slipped her mind. Gilda knew Tia to be honest and reliable, so she said she would look into the matter.

The manager of information services (IS), Henry Lew, showed Gilda some diagrams (Figure 1–4) and explained that all the departmental files had originally been set up independently and that IS got updates for departmental files from the departments themselves. IS was not at fault because they did not get a notice to change Tia's address from the auto loan department.

Gilda asked why one update form did not suffice, since the system could use the data from that form to change all occurrences of the address. Henry explained that no one in IS had any way of knowing if a person's name and address were in a file. A program could be written to search all the files, but it would be extremely inefficient because so many files would have to be examined.

Gilda wondered aloud why CNB could not just have one file of names and addresses that was shared by all the departments in the bank. Henry replied that they could, but then all the existing programs using names and addresses would have to be changed, and IS did not really even know all the programs that used that data. Just tracking down those programs and the programmers who wrote them (if they were still at CNB) would be a big job.

In desperation, Gilda asked if IS could not at least find each name occurring in more than one file and then compare the addresses to see if they were consistent in all files. Henry said that IS would be glad to do that, but that it would take a special program. IS was already overloaded with a waiting list of two years' worth of programming. With luck, however, they might be able to develop the program in 18 months.

Gilda was flabbergasted! How could it take 18 to 24 months to produce something as simple as a list of people whose names and addresses

FIGURE 1–4   Conventional National Bank Departmental Master File Formats

Checking Account Master File Format

Acct#	Last name	First name	Middle name	SS#	Checking acct. data

Savings Account Master File Format

Acct#	Last name	First name	Middle name	SS#	Savings acct. data

Auto Loan Master File Format

Acct#	Last name	First name	Middle name	SS#	Auto loan data

Personal Loan Master File Format

Acct#	Last name	First name	Middle name	SS#	Personal loan data

appeared in more than one place in the computer system? She left the data processing department more discouraged than ever about computers. Why should the bank waste time putting data into the computer system when it took forever to get it out in a usable form, and even then was wrong half the time? ■

The intent of the preceding scenario is to illustrate some of the problems arising from the conventional file approach to data management. Special programs have to be written for simple tasks. It may be difficult to extract data in the system if it resides in separate files. Users (and data processing personnel) find these problems exasperating and inefficient. The next scenario shows some of the advantages of the database approach.

CASE EXAMPLE
Byer Kaufman's Portfolio Management System

Byer Kaufman was known as the child prodigy of his high school class. While still in high school, he studied the stock market and developed a highly successful investment strategy that he implemented on his personal computer. Using his strategy, Byer had become a teenage millionaire.

Instead of going to college, getting married, or joining the army as most of his friends had, Byer started his own investment counseling firm and was doing extremely well. He had converted his investment software to a larger computer and now maintained data on thousands of securities in his database. In addition, he had added a simple query language that allowed his clients to access the database and his software directly so that they could select their own investments and manage their own portfolios if they chose to do so. His clients could even copy ("download") portions of his database to their own personal computer (PC) and manipulate the data there with a PC version of his query language. Many of his clients, however, were busy with other tasks—they preferred to have Byer manage their portfolios for them.

Byer is presently demonstrating his system to a potential new client, Joan Yasuda. Joan is interested in searching Byer's database for some underpriced stocks: "What would I do to find a stock in the airline industry whose price is less than five times its earnings?"

"That's a good question," Byer replied, "one that requires what database people call an 'ad hoc' query. It's ad hoc because the database designer may not have anticipated that precisely that question would be posed to the system. Nevertheless, the system can still answer it. The name of the stock is FIRM_NAME in the system, and it's stored in a table named STOCK_DATA_TABLE along with current price, earnings, and dividends and the firm's industry [see Figure 1–5a]. We can compute price-earnings ratios just by dividing price by earnings, so you would type in this":

FIGURE 1–5a
Data Elements in Byer's
STOCK_DATA_TABLE

FIGURE 1–5b
Data Elements in Individual Portfolios
By matching Firm Name in the portfolio to Firm Name in the STOCK__DATA__TABLE (in Figure 1–5a), the current price for each stock in a portfolio can be found and the value of the portfolio can be computed by multiplying shares held by the current price and summing over all securities.

```
STOCK-DATA-TABLE

 Firm-Name  Industry    Price    Earnings   Dividends



                           (a)


YASUDA-PORTFOLIO

 Firm-Name  Shares-Held




       (b)
```

```
SELECT FIRM__NAME
FROM STOCK__DATA__TABLE
WHERE INDUSTRY = 'AIRLINE'
AND (PRICE / EARNINGS) < 5.00
```

Almost immediately the system displayed a list of firms meeting these criteria.

"Next," said Byer, "I'll show you how I manage portfolios for my clients who don't have time to do all the analysis and so forth themselves."

"That's a good idea," said Joan.

"Okay," said Byer, "my system works like this. First, I have an enormous database consisting of 20 years of data from financial statements and stock market data on about 5,000 companies. This database is about 2.5 billion characters in size, and it is updated every evening. I have several mathematical models based on sophisticated statistical techniques to analyze market trends and the behavior of individual securities to pick 200 or so that are good investments at any one time. I also have software based on management science models that I use to select and revise portfolios for my clients from the 200 good securities. I developed these models myself and the software is legally protected as a trade secret, so no one else can provide you with my approach.

"Data for individual portfolios is maintained in separate files, so I can manage them separately. These portfolios contain only the name of the securities you hold and the number of shares of each [see Figure 1–5b]. However, they are all integrated into a common database with the stock data, so I can extract prices, earnings, and dividends from the STOCK__DATA__TABLE and send you monthly reports on the value of your account. In other words, I know the firm name from your portfolio file and can relate that to the stock data file to retrieve current prices to compute the current value of your portfolio. The database system makes it easy to do that either on-line or via a program.

"At the end of the year, I send you an annual report to help your accountant prepare your income tax return. This diagram [see Figure 1–6] shows how all the pieces fit together. Let me show you how the portfolio selection system works."

Byer hit the key labeled "MAIN SCREEN," and the main menu appeared on the screen (Figure 1–7). He selected the option to initiate a new portfolio by entering "2," because he wanted the system to continue displaying menus so that Joan could see the options available at that point. He could have entered the word *initiate,* and the system would have entered COMMAND MODE, which is faster for experienced users because it does not display options but expects the user to type in commands without special prompts.

Next the prompt in Figure 1–8 appeared. Byer had developed these menus and prompts to assist in gathering the data for new clients. Byer filled in the blanks as shown in Figure 1–9. Since Joan had plenty of income from other sources, Byer put in growth as the primary objective, meaning Joan wants to maximize the increase in the money invested ($1 million) rather than trying to get immediate cash. Also, because Joan has plenty of money, she can accept high risk in the hopes of getting a high return. The system responded:

FIGURE 1–6
Structure of Byer's Portfolio Management System

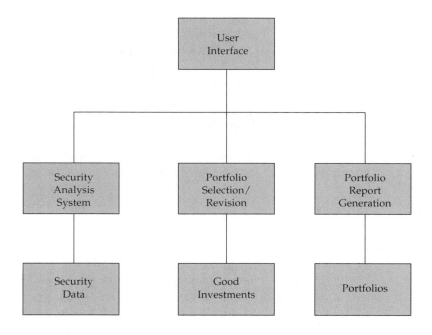

FIGURE 1–7
Main Menu for Byer's Port-folio Management System

```
                          MAIN MENU

YOUR CHOICES ARE:

    1. ANALYZE SECURITIES TO FIND GOOD INVESTMENTS

    2. INITIATE A NEW PORTFOLIO

    3. REVISE AN EXISTING PORTFOLIO

    4. EXAMINE EXISTING PORTFOLIOS

    5. RUN MONTHLY OR ANNUAL REPORTS FOR PORTFOLIOS

    6. HELP ON HOW TO USE THIS SYSTEM

    7. EXIT FROM THE SYSTEM

ENTER A NUMBER FROM 1 TO 7 CORRESPONDING TO YOUR
CHOICE, OR ENTER THE FIRST WORD OF THE LINE TO
ENTER COMMAND MODE.

WHAT IS YOUR CHOICE? 2
```

FIGURE 1–8
Prompts for Data to Initiate a New Portfolio

```
           ENTER THE FOLLOWING:

              CLIENT'S NAME:

             PORTFOLIO NAME:

            RISK ACCEPTABILITY:
            (LOW, NORMAL, OR HIGH)

            PRIMARY OBJECTIVE:
            (GROWTH, INCOME, OR
          PRINCIPAL PROTECTION)

            INITIAL INVESTMENT:
```

```
OK. I'M GOING TO SELECT A HIGH-RISK, GROWTH PORT-
FOLIO FOR YOUR $1.0 MILLION. THAT IS WHAT YOU WANT
ME TO DO, ISN'T IT?
```

Byer typed in "yes," and the system displayed:

```
PLEASE WAIT WHILE I SELECT A GOOD PORTFOLIO FOR YOU.
IT WILL TAKE A FEW SECONDS TO DO ALL THE SEARCHING
AND CALCULATIONS.
```

FIGURE 1–9
**Byer's Responses to the
Prompts of Figure 1–8**

```
                  ENTER  THE  FOLLOWING:

                      CLIENT'S  NAME:   JOAN  YASUDA

                   PORTFOLIO  NAME:   GIGABUCK

              RISK  ACCEPTABILITY:
            (LOW,  NORMAL,  OR  HIGH)   HIGH

                 PRIMARY  OBJECTIVE:
               (GROWTH,   INCOME,  OR
            PRINCIPAL  PROTECTION)   GROWTH

              INITIAL  INVESTMENT:   1,000,000
```

After a brief pause, the following message appeared on the screen, along with a list of securities and the amount to be invested in each:

```
I  HAVE  A  PORTFOLIO  FOR  YOU.  I  EXPECT  IT  TO  INCREASE
YOUR  $  1.0  MILLION  TO  $  1.23  MILLION  IN  SIX  MONTHS.
BUT,  THIS  IS  RISKY.  YOU  COULD  LOSE  YOUR  MONEY.  THE
PORTFOLIO  CONSISTS  OF  THE  FOLLOWING  INVESTMENTS:
```

"This looks great!" said Joan. "Sign me up, and put a million in that portfolio."

"Fine," Byer replied. "I'll draw up a contract." ∎

OBJECTIVES OF DATABASE SYSTEMS

The preceding scenarios may be used to illustrate some problems that occur in traditional file-oriented systems, as well as the objectives of database systems. These objectives are derived from the overriding goal of managing data as an important organizational resource. For each objective, there is a corresponding problem that arises from the use of a file-oriented approach. Database system objectives and problems in file-oriented systems are discussed together. Database objectives include providing flexible access to information, maintaining data integrity, protecting the data from destruction and unauthorized use, providing data shareability and relatability, reducing data redundancy (duplicated data), making data independent of applications programs, standardizing data item definitions, and increasing the productivity of information systems personnel. Each of these objectives is discussed fully in the following sections.

Access Flexibility

Access flexibility allows for easy retrieval of selected items in a database and presentation of that data in a variety of formats. This flexibility is one of the most important reasons for having DBMS in the first place—to have information readily available for managerial purposes. The part of the system that provides for communication with the person using the system is often called the **user interface.**

In conventional programming environments (such as that of the Convention National Bank, where COBOL is in use), the only user interface provided is for programmers. In such environments, special programs must be written to perform even simple tasks such as listing those people whose names and addresses appear in two or more files. Most database packages have a special **query language** designed to perform such tasks with a few simple commands. Query languages are much easier to learn and use than programming languages, and they are suitable for use by many managers and other end-users who have neither the time nor the inclination to learn to program.

Byer's portfolio management system is an example of a system that provides flexible access. The retrieval command given previously is an example of a query in the **Structured Query Language (SQL),** the standard query language for relational database systems.

The portfolio management system also uses menus and fill-in-the-blank operations to guide unfamiliar users through the system. Experienced users can bypass these by entering commands directly. Also, an on-line "help" facility is available to give more complete explanations of system usage.

Although query languages are easy to learn and use, they lack the power and versatility of programming languages. To make up for this deficiency, most database management systems also provide a special **data manipulation language (DML)** consisting of commands that may be embedded in applications programs to add, retrieve, or change data values. Some packages allow SQL statements to be used in programs; others use the data manipulation language designed by various subcommittees of the Conference on Data and Systems Languages (CODASYL). Still other packages have their own proprietary language.

Most database management systems have a language that is intermediate in power between query languages and data manipulation languages. Such languages are called **report generators,** because they are designed to create printed reports. Report generators have special commands for creating headings, titles, rows, columns, sums, and other elements frequently found in reports. The programming of reports is often greatly simplified by using such facilities.

Many database packages also have a **screen generator** to help analysts write routines to create forms on a terminal screen. Users fill in these forms to retrieve, modify, or add data to the database. These facilities simplify the process of capturing data and making it readily accessible to users.

Finally, database management systems usually work closely with the host operating system to provide rapid and flexible access to the database. Some packages have their own access routines, but most rely on the routines of the host operating system.

Data Integrity

Data integrity ensures that data values are correct, consistent, and current. This is a critical aspect of information management. The problem that Tia had in getting notices of payments due is one example of a lack of data integrity. Even more critical to a bank is the need to maintain accurate account balances. How long would a bank survive if it credited deposits to the wrong account or reported incorrect account balances?

Managers insist on accurate data for decision-making, and often they will not use information from a computer system that has produced incorrect data. Such misgivings may be well founded. Suppose you were a portfolio manager using Byer's system and it indicated that the price of a stock was going down, and you sold it—when it was actually still going up. In the future, you would probably be suspicious of the data in that system, if you even used it at all.

One of the best ways to assure data integrity is to make sure that the data values are correctly entered in the first place. This may be done through a variety of methods, such as carefully setting up manual procedures for originally capturing the data, or programming the system to check the reasonableness of data values when they are entered into the machine. For example, you may know that hourly wages in a payroll system never exceed $30 per hour. The data input program should check to see that hourly wages entered never exceed this value.

Data Security

Data security is needed to protect data from unauthorized access and from accidental or intentional damage or destruction. It might be nice (but also illegal) to secretly change one's bank balance or one's grades. Clearly, Byer would not want a person using his portfolio management system to be able to access the portfolios of other clients. Security is a critical aspect of database systems; responsible managers are justifiably reluctant to put sensitive data into computer systems unless every reasonable precaution is made to protect it from unauthorized access.

Another need for security is related to inadvertent destruction of the database by natural disasters such as fires, floods, tornadoes, hurricanes, and volcanoes. Yes, even volcanoes. The fine dust from the Mount St. Helens eruption in Washington wreaked havoc with many computer systems in that area. To provide security from such events, it is customary to keep a log of changes made to the database so that they may be reapplied to "back up" copies of the database that are made occasionally and stored in a safe place. **Recovery** is the process of using logs and backup copies to recreate a damaged database. For critical databases, such as payroll files, it is desirable to store the backup in a different building, perhaps in specially designed rooms.

Other security facilities include passwords for individual users that allow different types of access to the database (for example, read only, or read and write), and passwords for databases, data records, and even individual data items. These measures and others are discussed in Chapter 11.

Data Independence and the ANSI/SPARC Model

Data independence has two dimensions: logical and physical. To explain the difference between logical and physical data independence, it is convenient to use the American National Standards Institute/Standards Planning and Requirements Committee (ANSI/SPARC) three-level architecture of database systems. As illustrated in Figure 1–10, the uppermost level in the architecture is the **external level of data.** The external level is closest to the users of the system and refers to the way users view the data. This may be in terms of printed reports, forms, or other documents that contain information useful to people using the system. Different users may have different, but overlapping, data needs and may view the data differently, as did Joe and Sue in Figure 1–2. The data as thought of by an individual user or group of users with similar needs is called a **user view.**

FIGURE 1–10
ANSI/SPARC Three-level Database Architecture
The external level consists of data as the users view it. The conceptual level is a logical composite of the entire database and is described in the logical schema. The stored data is described in the physical schema at the internal level.

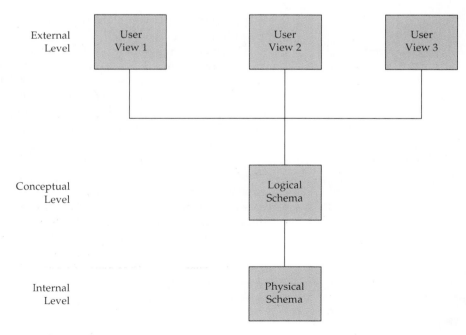

The middle level in the architecture is the **conceptual level of data.** The conceptual level represents the union of all the user views at the external level. Thus, the conceptual representation is an integrated view or schema of the entire database. At this level, the representation of data still reflects human views of data. The database at this level is described in a **logical schema.**

The third level, the **internal level of data,** corresponds to the actual representation of data within the computer system and the methods used to access the data. This may also be referred to as the **physical level of data,** for it specifies how the data is represented physically in the storage devices of the machine.

In a system with **physical data independence,** the conceptual level schema is independent of changes in the internal or physical level; that is, the way the data is actually stored or accessed in the system can be changed without requiring a change in the logical schema. The DBMS is responsible for insulating the conceptual level from changes in the physical level by providing means of translating physical representations into conceptual representations.

In a system with **logical data independence,** the external level is independent of changes to the conceptual level. One user may wish to change or add a user view, which changes the conceptual level, but this should have no impact on other users and their views.

One important result of data independence is that the close link between data files and the programs using those files is weakened. In conventional situations where ordinary programming languages such as COBOL are used, programs and the files they access are very closely associated. When the U.S. Postal Service converted from five- to nine-digit zip codes, for example, a tremendous number of files in the computer systems of organizations throughout the country had to be restructured. Moreover, all of the programs accessing those files had to be modified and recompiled.

Database management systems seek to circumvent problems such as these by making the data independent of applications programs that use the data. This is done by putting the data under the control of the database management software. Applications programs access the data, not directly, but rather via the data manipulation language of the DBMS. The system is responsible for satisfying the requests for data retrievals, changes, and additions.

Data independence is a major objective of database management systems. Separating data files from programs is essential if data is to be managed as an independent resource. Logical data independence is necessary for database systems to provide adaptability to changing user requirements. In an environment where files are shared, it is important to ensure that changes made in response to one user have no major implications for others. Even though it is virtually impossible to achieve absolute logical and physical independence, current database systems provide much more data independence than file-oriented systems, thus enabling better management of organizational data resources.

Reduced Data Redundancy

Data redundancy is storage of the same piece of data in more than one place in the computer system. Another objective of database management is to reduce data redundancy. The master files in the Conventional National Bank scenario (see Figure 1–4) can be used to illustrate some problems that arise when redundancy is allowed. Note that each of the files contains fields for last name, first name, middle name, and social security number. If the same person has several accounts with the bank, then his or her name and social security number are duplicated in several different files. This is clearly a waste of storage space.

When files are updated, data redundancy often leads to problems of data integrity. Because the same data is duplicated in several places, it must be changed in each place it occurs; otherwise, inconsistent data values will arise. In the CNB case, the error of sending Tia's payment notice to the old address would have been avoided if her address had been correctly stored in one location and shared with all necessary departments.

Data redundancy leads to processing inefficiencies as well. Updating the same data in different files requires extra processing time. Because each department generally has its own update programs, several programs contain procedures for updating the same fields and must be run to update files. If the redundant data is stored in only one place, both storage space and processing time for updates can be saved.

Figure 1–11a, referred to as a **data structure diagram** or **Bachman diagram,** shows how CNB's files might be reorganized to reduce data redundancy. Name and social security number are stored only once, in the master record. The master record contains account numbers indicating the type of accounts owned by each person. Data items such as the account numbers in the master file are called **pointers** because they "point to" associated records in other files.

Another representation of CNB's database is shown in Figure 1–11b. This is a **relational model** of CNB's data; data elements are shown in tables called *relations.* Relationships between tables are represented by common data items in different tables: in Figure 1–11b, customer number (Customer#) is shown in each table. Data for any customer can be located by matching common customer numbers in different tables.

In both the data structure diagram and the relational model (two approaches that are examined in detail in this book), some data elements have been reproduced in the reorganized database. (This may or may not result in *actual* data redundancy; the customer number may be stored at one location with pointers in other files to that location.) In designing databases, we seek to *control* data redundancy, since in most cases it is not possible, or even desirable, to totally eliminate it. It may be desirable to allow redundancy, for example, to increase access flexibility and get faster response times.

FIGURE 1–11a   Data Structure for CNB Database
The lines indicate pointers showing relationships between record types in the reorganized database.

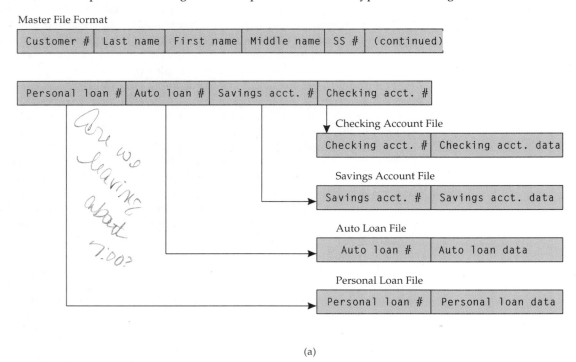

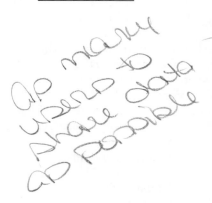

(a)

Data Shareability

Data shareability allows different users or user groups to use the same (nonredundant) data. If data redundancy is to be reduced, then it is necessary to share data among various organizational departments. Tia's address is one example. Byer's security database, which is accessed by several clients, is another. Users are not always enthusiastic about sharing data. Reluctance to share data often arises from fear of unauthorized use of private data or from resistance to making performance data (such as grades) available to others. One who used Byer's portfolio management system would appreciate shared access to public information about securities but would probably not want other users to have access to his or her private portfolios and investment holdings. Likewise, different groups in educational institutions—the registrar's office, advisors, or financial aid officers—need access to student grades, and so it is reasonable that they share grade information. But few others have such needs, and access to such information must be tightly controlled.

Potential providers of data may have legitimate reasons for resisting the placement of data into a shared system. Designers of database systems must be aware of these reasons and be sure to take them into account during system development.

FIGURE 1–11b
**Relational Representation
of the CNB Database**
Relationships between files
are given by including CUS-
TOMER NUMBER as a data
item in each table.

CUSTOMER_DATA

Customer#	Last_Name	First_Name	Middle_Name	SS#

CHECKING_ACCOUNT_DATA

Customer#	Checking_Account#	Checking acct. data

SAVINGS_ACCOUNT_DATA

Customer#	Savings_Account#	Savings acct. data

AUTO_LOAN_DATA

Customer#	Auto_Loan#	Auto loan data

PERSONAL_LOAN_DATA

Customer#	Personal_Loan#	Personal loan data

Data Relatability

Data relatability is the ability to establish logical relationships between different types of records, usually in different files. The pointers in Figure 1–11a, for example, show the relationships between the master files and account files in CNB's database. Because customers have checking accounts, and checking accounts have balances, a relationship exists between the files containing these two data items.

In the case of CNB, it was not possible to perform the simple task of relating names and addresses in various files without writing a special program to do so. In cases where ordinary programming languages alone are used to manage data, such problems arise frequently. If a database system is to achieve the goal of providing flexible access to information, it must also provide the ability to relate data that resides in different parts of the system.

In many instances, some of the most important information in the database must be derived from relationships between database items. Joan's query into Byer's security database, for example, required information on the relationship between price and earnings for each security. Price and earnings data might be kept in different records in the system because price data must be updated more frequently than earnings, and updating could be more efficient if the two were stored separately. But if a query involves a relationship such as price divided by earnings, both records must be retrieved to create the desired information.

As another example, Byer would need information such as current prices, dividends, and earnings to create monthly and annual reports for client portfolios. If these data values were stored every time a security was included in a portfolio, it would result in a great deal of data redundancy because the same security might be held in many portfolios. This data redundancy could be reduced by storing the security data once and providing the ability to relate the information on the relationship between portfolios and securities via the database management system.

Standardization

Standardization refers to the need for common definitions of data items, in terms of both the precise definition of a data item name and its storage format in the database. Most database management systems provide a **data dictionary** or data repository facility to define data item names and to state the internal storage format of the data items in the database. Data dictionaries may be similar to file descriptions in a COBOL program, but they are more powerful and versatile. They may, for example, permit the specification of **synonyms** or **aliases** when more than one name is used to refer to the same data item. This strategy is useful in supporting shareability when different user groups refer to the same data with different names. Thus, *marks* might be an alias for the more common term *grades.*

These repositories may provide means for controlling access to data as well. Some users may be permitted to access certain data items while others are denied access to those items or are not even informed that the items exist in the database. In some cases, it may be desirable to allow selected users to retrieve, but not to change, data in the system; such an approach can prevent inadvertent destruction of data by inexperienced users. Other facilities of data repositories are discussed in Chapter 11.

A related problem in the development of database systems is the tendency of users to have slightly different definitions (or imprecise definitions) of potentially shareable data. In the development of a database system to help manage research proposals submitted by a research and development organization, for example, it was discovered that different departments had different ideas of what constituted a proposal. Most departments thought of a proposal as a formal document spelling out the details of a research project for a potential funding agency. Other departments, however, operated on a much less formal basis, with only a letter or even a telephone call constituting the proposal in some cases. A standardized definition of *proposal* had to be developed as part of the system design effort.

Personnel Productivity

Any organization must deal with constantly changing information needs. Information needs may change as a result of new governmental reporting requirements, tax laws, accounting procedures, or economic conditions. The modification of existing programs to satisfy changing information requirements is referred to as **program maintenance.** Large organizations have discovered that the lack of data independence in file-oriented environments severely hampers the ability to respond to changing information requirements and results in large maintenance expenditures. Martin (1983, p. 48) claims that as much as 80 percent of some corporations' programming budget goes into maintenance, while only 20 percent goes to the development of new systems. The bulk of this maintenance expense is accounted for by personnel time. Another major objective of database systems is to reduce the amount of personnel time it takes to respond to changing information needs.

Database management systems can lead to increased productivity in several ways. Simple requests for data can be handled via the query language, obviating the need to write a program. In many cases, users themselves can use the query facility, circumventing the need for systems personnel entirely.

Even if a more sophisticated report is required, it may be possible to "program" the system using a report generator. This may take far less time than writing an equivalent report in a conventional language. Or, again, users may be able to write their own reports. As new applications are added to the system, the data those applications require may already be in the database. Thus, the time and expense associated with designing file formats and collecting data are bypassed.

DISADVANTAGES OF THE DATABASE APPROACH

Just like any other technology, database systems are not without their costs and disadvantages. An organization may find that a database approach is expensive at first. Database management software is expensive. Some mainframe packages with minimal features may be purchased for $20,000 to $30,000. Full-feature packages, however, may run as much as $300,000. A package with typical capabilities costs around $100,000. Microcomputer packages are available for a few hundred dollars or so. Network versions support data sharing and many of the other objectives described in this chapter. However, single-user versions are not really comparable to multi-user, mainframe packages.

Multi-user packages are complex and often have extensive memory requirements. As new applications are converted to the database system, storage requirements may increase. Thus, new hardware may be required to accommodate the increased memory and storage needs.

If an organization is dependent on an integrated database system, failure of that system may severely disrupt the operation of the entire enterprise. This can be very costly, even disastrous. Thus, it is imperative that back-up systems and procedures be planned carefully.

Additional costs arise because database programming may be more complex than file-oriented programming in some circumstances, and programmers must be trained to use the package. Also, analysts must be trained in database design techniques or experienced analysts must be hired. Careful plans for development of the database system must be developed, and the databases and applications programs must be acquired, designed, or converted. There are, of course, many benefits that offset these costs. As more applications are converted to the database system, costs begin to drop because most or all of the data required are already in the database. Simple applications may be handled with query languages or report generators, resulting in much less programming time. Furthermore, maintenance expenditures are reduced because the independence of data and programs allows programs to be changed without concern for file structures and the effect on other users or programs. It may be possible to cut maintenance expenditures in half, or even more. Management must realize, however, that such results are obtained, not overnight, but only after a period of two years or so. Thus, conversion to a database environment requires a long-term commitment on the part of the organization.

CHAPTER SUMMARY

Data consists of numbers, letters, words, names, and other symbols that may be stored in a computer system. Information is useful data. Organizations now realize that data is a valuable resource that deserves careful management. Information for managing the organization can be derived from data, which resides in integrated collections of shared files called databases.

THE USER'S VIEW

Database systems exist to support the needs of information users. The needs of users are thus paramount in the development of an effective system. Different users of a database system have different needs and different perspectives on the system and the information and data it provides. Different people may refer to the same entity with different terms or, perhaps worse, may use the same term to refer to a different entity. The terms *customer, patron,* and *client,* for example, may all refer to the same entity—people who buy the organization's product or service.

In an integrated database environment, it is unusual for any one user to need access to every item in the database. Thus, the perspective of users is often limited. The primary concern of each user is to get the information he or she needs. Information analysts are concerned with ensuring that the information requirements of users are satisfied. Thus, the objective of information analysts is to provide an effective system—one that does the right thing—by supplying the information required to make decisions.

Database analysts are concerned with designing databases that provide the required information efficiently. Effective, efficient organizational information is best provided through integrated, shared database systems. In database management, the different perspectives of users are referred to as *user views,* hence the name of this section. "The User's View" in each chapter is designed to help you keep in mind why database systems are developed in the first place and to reinforce the main goal as we examine the trees of the database forest. ■

Database management systems are software packages designed to support information management. The major components of database management software, summarized in Figure 1–12, include a query language for simple, ad hoc access to the database; a report generator to create printed reports; a data definition language to describe the data; a data manipulation language for accessing the database via programming languages; facilities for providing security, integrity, backup, and recovery; a data repository facility to catalog all the data items under control of the database system; and access routines for input and output to the database. Each of these major components is examined in detail in the remainder of this book.

Many packages include several other features as well, including screen generators for designing terminal screens, intelligent systems for facilitating application development, and support for databases

FIGURE 1–12
**Components of a Database
Management System**

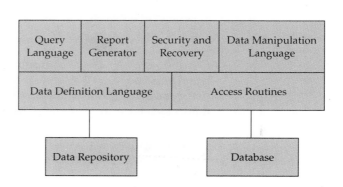

METROPOLITAN NATIONAL BANK

The Metropolitan National Bank scenario is a continuing case study you can work through throughout the text. It provides a general idea of the organizational environment and the type of activities prevalent in the information management field. Each chapter contains a specific project that provides an opportunity to apply the concepts illustrated in that chapter.

The Metropolitan National Bank, or MetNat as it is called, is a large financial institution in the fictitious town of Lincoln, Texas. Lincoln is a moderate-size town of approximately 500,000 people at the base of the Texas panhandle. The rural areas around Lincoln are predominantly ranching and farming areas. MetNat provides checking, savings, and several types of money market accounts to its customers. It also provides a wide range of loan services, from large business loans to small personal loans. MetNat has safe deposit boxes and can access a statewide automated teller network.

MetNat currently services approximately 70,000 checking accounts, 20,000 saving accounts, and 25,000 money market accounts. MetNat has approximately 5,000 commercial loans and 3,000 personal loans outstanding. MetNat also issues a bank credit card. Because the credit card has a low annual fee ($50) and an extremely attractive annual percentage rate (12 percent), the bank has almost 50,000 card holders.

At one time, MetNat performed all of its accounting functions manually. This system was replaced in the early 1960s by the first of many computer-based systems. The most recent system began operation in the early 1980s. MetNat's information processing orientation has always emphasized bank administration efficiency. MetNat's information processing management has never been particularly concerned with using information processing for any type of competitive advantage. However, the competitive nature of the banking industry has caused the board of directors to make some changes in the information processing function. A new position has been created, a chief information officer, and you have been hired to fill the position.

In each of the chapters that follow, you have an opportunity to apply the concepts of the chapter to the scenario at MetNat. Along the way, you will be building, piece by piece, a comprehensive analysis and design of the MetNat information processing system. You should always review prior MetNat assignments before beginning a new one, since the new ones frequently build upon the old ones. By the end of the book, you should have a considerably well-developed project that can demonstrate your information systems design capabilities. Good luck! ■

distributed over several computer systems. These features are described later in the book.

Database administrators are responsible for managing database systems. Database analysts and information analysts are staff members who use database technology to develop database systems.

It is critical that database systems be effective in the sense that they must provide correct, current, and appropriate information for managerial decision-making. A database system should also provide this information efficiently.

The conventional approach to managing data with a close link between applications programs and files often leads to problems of redundant data, processing duplication, lack of data consistency and integrity, and the inability to relate data items stored in different files. Database systems seek to overcome these problems by separating data from applications programs, providing flexible access to the data, protecting the data from unauthorized access and malicious or unintentional damage, controlling data redundancy, improving data integrity, relatability, shareability, and standardization, and increasing programmer productivity.

Questions and Exercises

1. Define the following terms:
   a. data
   b. information
   c. information management
   d. database
   e. database system
   f. database management system
   g. database administrator
   h. database analyst
   i. decision support system
   j. system effectiveness
   k. system efficiency
   l. user view
   m. logical schema
   n. physical schema
2. Explain why data is an important organizational resource.
3. What is the main goal of a database system?
4. If, as a manager in an organization, you needed information to perform your job, would you want your data processing department to emphasize effectiveness or efficiency in its database systems?
5. As a database administrator, would you emphasize effectiveness or efficiency in the development of database systems?
6. List and briefly discuss the objectives of database systems.
7. Describe the three levels of the ANSI/SPARC database architecture.
8. Why might people be reluctant to share data in an organization? How might you convince them to put data into a shared database?
9. Name and briefly describe three applications that are particularly well suited to the database approach. What are some

advantages and disadvantages of the database approach for these applications?

10. Why is planning more important in a database environment than in a conventional file-oriented environment?

11. Determine whether each of the following relates to logical independence or physical independence:
    a. The ability to convert to new storage devices without changing applications programs. *P-ind.*
    b. The ability to provide one user access to additional data items already in the database, without affecting other users.
    c. One user wants a data item displayed with no decimal places; a second user wants the same data item displayed with two decimal places.
    d. The ability to change the access method (see Appendix A) used to retrieve a data record without changing applications programs.

12. Write a short schema and subschema for two users in the following situations: Nassar needs access to customer name, address, and account balance; Jagu needs access to customer name, address, and credit rating.

13. Rodolfo Barella and Chi-Ming Wu both work for the Best Desserts Shop. Rodolfo calls clients of the shop "patrons"; Chi-Ming calls them "customers." Assume that you are developing a database system for Best Desserts. How might you handle the problem of data definition?

14. Name two ways in which use of database systems can lead to increased personnel productivity.

15. Database management systems are expensive. Why do you think so many organizations use them in spite of the expense?

16. Discuss disadvantages of the database approach. What might be done to offset these disadvantages?

17. Indicate whether each of the following examples is a transaction processing system, a management information system, or a decision support system.
    a. A system for entering, maintaining, and distributing student grades at a university. *tran*
    b. A system for reporting differences in budgeted costs and actual costs associated with projects at a software consulting firm. *mis*
    c. A system to help decide whether a potential new product should be manufactured and sold. *DSS*
    d. A system to record data from sales transactions. *tran*
    e. A system that takes data from sales transactions and plugs it into a sales forecasting model to produce information used in deciding on raw material orders. *mis*

18. Give an example of a transaction processing system, a management information system, and a decision support system.

19. What are some unique security problems that might arise in a university system that uses one computer system to support its administrative systems (faculty and staff, student grades, budgets, and so on) and academic systems (teaching programming, software packages, and so forth)? What might be done to control security problems?

20. Indicate whether normal or tight security measures would be justified for each of the following types of data. Briefly explain your answer.
    a. Student names and addresses at a university.
    b. Student grades at a university.
    c. Names and addresses of a firm's employees.
    d. Salary and wage data for a firm's employees.
    e. Travel itinerary of a U.S. senator traveling in the United States.
    f. Travel itinerary of a U.S. senator traveling in countries with known terrorist activities.

For Further Reading

Ahituv, Niv; and Seev Neumann. *Principles of Information Systems for Management.* 2nd ed. Dubuque, Iowa: Wm. C. Brown, 1986. A good explanation of the difference between effective and efficient systems is in Chapter 4.

Cardenas, Alfonso F. *Data Base Management Systems.* 2nd ed. Boston: Allyn & Bacon, 1985. A thorough treatment of database system objectives is found in Chapters 1 and 3.

Kanter, Jerome. *Management Information Systems.* 3rd ed. Englewood Cliffs, N.J.: Prentice-Hall, 1984. The relationship of database systems and management information systems is discussed thoroughly in Chapter 4. Information resource management is treated in Chapter 11.

Martin, James. *Managing the Data-Base Environment.* Englewood Cliffs, N.J.: Prentice-Hall, 1983. One of the first and still one of the best books on the managerial aspects of database systems. The first six chapters provide a very readable view of managerial issues in a database environment.

2

ELEMENTS OF DATABASE SYSTEMS

T he first chapter provided an introduction to database systems, concentrating on three areas: user orientation, data as an organizational resource, and the objectives of database systems. In this chapter, we discuss the organizational environment in which database systems are planned, designed, and used. As we saw in Chapter 1, the elements of the database environment are people, hardware, software, databases, and techniques for planning, designing, and managing databases.

In this chapter, we examine the relationships among three of these elements—people, software, and techniques—and how the database approach can develop systems that effectively support organizational needs. Here, you begin learning to design and structure effective database systems. Remember that an *effective* system means a system that "does the right thing" by providing the information necessary to run the organization. *Structure* refers to the parts of a system and how these parts interact. The objective is to blend the five elements of the database environment into a database system that serves the organization's needs.

Chapter 2 begins with an extended analogy between a database system and the design and layout of a university campus. This provides the background for a discussion of the design and structure of a database system. After the analogy, we present sections on planning and design techniques, software, and people. Even though people are the most important part of a database system, they are discussed last, simply because the tasks performed by various people are easier to describe after the other elements have been presented. After studying this chapter, you should understand how hardware, software, people, procedures, and plans blend to form an effective database system.

HOW A DATABASE SYSTEM IS LIKE A CAMPUS

Whenever a new campus or housing development is planned, a master land-use plan is developed. This plan takes into consideration the special needs of the people who will use the campus or development and the special characteristics of the site related to those needs. Buildings are generally not constructed in floodplains, and architectural styles and placements are intended to provide convenience and accessibility in a way that harmonizes with the environment.

Land is a valuable commodity, so its use is carefully planned. Data, however, may not be recognized as a valuable resource. Often, little planning or coordination is directed toward its use and development. In the next section, we discuss the need for careful database planning.

The Need for Planning and Modular Design

It is not uncommon for one unit of an organization to have databases supported by computer systems that are incompatible with those of other organizational units. This can lead to expensive redundancy of computer systems and to difficulty in maintaining organizationwide information.

The campus analogy illustrates this point. The buildings of a campus are only loosely coupled. The only links between buildings are sidewalks, roads, and perhaps utility tunnels. Because buildings are highly independent, the detailed design and construction of each one may be done independently. Together, however, they should fit into a grand scheme that blends into the natural environment and serves the needs of the entire university community.

A well-designed database system consists of modules or subsystems that can be compared to the buildings of a campus. Here the term *module* describes a major element of the overall database system, not just one piece of programming code. Database system modules are loosely coupled and may be built independently, but they should fit into the grand scheme described in a database system master plan. Like a campus land-use plan, the **database system master plan** lays out the ultimate structure and contents of the database system—and does so before work begins on the system itself. Some similarities between the buildings of a campus and database system modules are illustrated in Figure 2–1.

The analogy can be carried further. Buildings consist of floors, floors contain rooms, and rooms have attributes such as color, number of windows and doors, and type of floor covering. Just as buildings contain floors and rooms, the subsystems of a database system contain data about entities, such as customers and products. An **entity** is any object, tangible or intangible, about which the organization wishes to store data. Entities have **attributes,** such as name, color, and price. Rooms and their attributes must be accessible through stairways and hallways. In some database systems, entities and their attributes must be accessible via navigation paths through the database. A **navigation path** through a database is like a sign in a classroom building showing the direction of rooms. Arrows point left or right to indicate the route to certain rooms. The arrows in databases are pointers indicating where the programs should look on the system's storage devices to find certain records.

FIGURE 2–1
Analogy: Campus and Database System

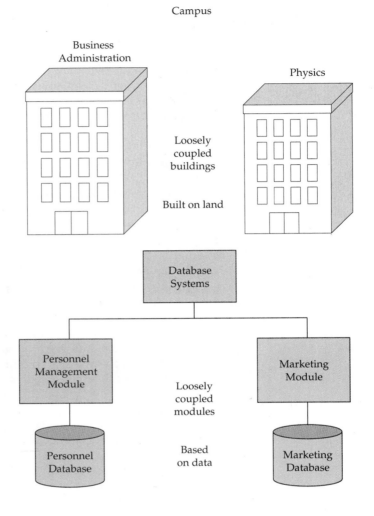

The Need for Access, Security, and Adaptability

Buildings and database systems are designed to be used by people with different characteristics and needs. It may be difficult for handicapped people to access floors and rooms of poorly designed buildings. Likewise, it may be difficult for "computer-handicapped" people (those who have not been trained to use computers) to access information in a poorly designed database system.

Just as someone may break into a building and steal property of value, a database may be broken into and valuable information may be stolen. Buildings are constructed in a logical sequence. Work does not begin on the third floor, and painters do not paint themselves into a corner.

Once a building is constructed, it may not be very expensive to repaint the walls or to put new carpet on the floors. However, it is probably very costly to modify the structure of a building to take out a

TABLE 2–1 Similarities between a Database System and a University Campus

Land-Use Plan	Database System Master Plan
Loosely coupled buildings	Loosely coupled modules
Buildings based on land	Modules based on databases
Shared by different people with different needs	Shared by different people with different views
Buildings designed, then built from the ground up	Top-down design, built from the database up
Structure expensive to modify	Structure expensive to modify
Some features easy to modify	Some features easy to modify
Stairways and halls provide route to rooms	Access paths provide route to data

wall. The same can be said for database systems. Once they are built, it is usually expensive to modify their structure. Thus, the organization should ensure that its buildings and its database system are designed correctly in the first place.

The first thing the organization should do to assure a good database system design is to develop a database system master plan. This plan is discussed in the next section. The similarities between a campus and a database system are summarized in Table 2–1.

THE DATABASE SYSTEM MASTER PLAN

Contents of the database system master plan should include a statement of organizational goals and objectives, an organization chart, entity diagrams showing the major relationships among entities in the enterprise, modules or subsystems to be implemented as part of the database system, the costs and benefits expected to be associated with the system, and a schedule for implementing each module. An outline of the contents of a database system master plan is given in Table 2–2. Each of these elements is discussed separately in the rest of this section, with illustrations from an educational organization called the Professional Training Institute (PTI).

TABLE 2–2 Suggested Outline for the Database System Master Plan

I. Organizational Environment
  A. Goals and Objectives
  B. Organizational Structure and Function
II. Elements of the Database System
  A. Major Entities and Relationships
  B. Entity Groups
  C. Modules
  D. User Groups
  E. Costs and Benefits
  F. Implementation Schedule
III. Summary

Organizational Goals and Objectives

Just as a building should fit into its natural environment, a database system should fit into its surroundings. Two aspects of the organizational environment should be considered in the master plan: (1) organizational goals and objectives, and (2) the manner in which the enterprise is structured. Organizational goals and objectives are important to database system design because many critical information needs may be derived from them. When possible, goals and objectives should be stated in numeric terms, so that progress toward those goals can be measured. Instead of saying that the goal is to increase sales, for example, one might say that the goal is to increase sales by 10 percent.

In the same way, the database system should assist managers of the organization in measuring the level of goal attainment and in steering the organization toward its goals. Thus, the database system master plan should begin with a brief statement of organizational goals and objectives and how the database system will measure progress toward goals.

CASE EXAMPLE
Professional Training Institute

PTI's basic mission is to provide high-quality continuing education in a variety of subject areas to practicing professionals in many industries. This mission is attained through the sponsorship of one-day courses at PTI's facilities in a quiet woodland setting. A goal for the upcoming year is to expand course offerings in computer-related topics. Specific objectives are to offer the standard fare of courses taught the previous year and to add new courses in information management and computer networks. It is expected that 50,000 people will attend the standard course offerings and that 8,000 will attend the new computer courses. These offerings should generate $10 million and $2 million in gross revenues, respectively. PTI's goals and objectives are summarized in Table 2–3. ■

TABLE 2–3   Goals and Objectives for PTI

  I. Continue offering currently viable courses
     A. Attract 50,000 participants
     B. Generate $10 million in gross revenue
 II. Expand course offerings in computer topics
     A. Attract 8,000 participants
     B. Generate $2.4 million in gross revenue

Organizational Structure

The second feature of the organizational environment that should be included in the master plan is the organizational structure. It is important to consider the structure of the organization because the database system will surely be required to support the flow of information between various units or divisions of the enterprise. The information flow usually follows organizational channels between superior and subordinate units. For this reason, the database system is said to be "superimposed" on the structure of the organization. It is convenient to include an organizational chart and a brief description of the function of each of the organizational units in the database system master plan.

CASE EXAMPLE
Professional Training Institute

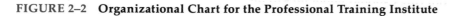

The organizational chart for the Professional Training Institute is shown in Figure 2–2. At the apex of the organization is the director, who is responsible for the general management of the firm. This responsibility includes determining goals, objectives, and the strategies for achieving them. PTI has two major subdivisions: marketing and course management. Each of these is headed by an assistant director who reports to the director.

The marketing department has two major functions: (1) to promote courses already offered by PTI and (2) to develop new marketable courses. To promote courses, marketing maintains extensive mailing lists of prospective participants ("prospects") for the courses being offered. Brochures describing course offerings are developed by the marketing staff and mailed to these prospects. This is an extremely vital function, for, without paying customers, PTI will be out of business. In the past year, over a million brochures were mailed.

The course management department is responsible for organizing and administering courses. Course management involves working with marketing to promote courses, registering participants, collecting fees,

FIGURE 2–2 **Organizational Chart for the Professional Training Institute**

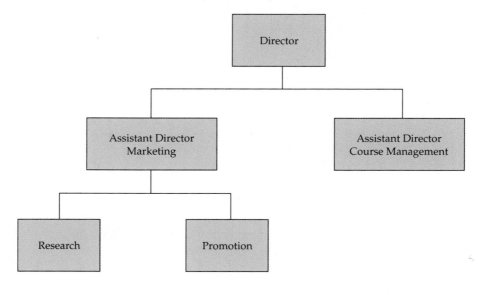

scheduling instructors, ordering textbooks and other materials, administering course evaluations, and maintaining records on participants.

PTI realizes that accurate information on prospects and former participants is vital to its continued success. Satisfied customers are among the most likely prospects for future courses. Thus, PTI has developed a database system to support its information management functions. PTI's system is described throughout the remainder of this chapter.

One of the first tasks in developing a database system for the organization is the identification of relevant entities, attributes, and relationships between entities. In the next few sections, we discuss this process in more detail. ■

Entity Charts

The purpose of the database systems master plan is to guide the organization in its quest to manage its information resources effectively. The master plan views the information needs of the organization at a very broad, general level. It should identify the major information users in the organization and their general information needs. It should also specify the entities to be contained within the database and major relationships between entities. Entities and their relationships are initially defined by working with users, who must be able to specify their information needs.

Specified entities and relationships can be illustrated in an entity chart or diagram, such as that of Figure 2–3 for PTI. Entity charts represent the major entities and relationships among them to give an overall view of the database structure. Detailed database design then fleshes out this general structure, as described in the next chapter.

FIGURE 2–3
Entity Chart for the Professional Training Institute

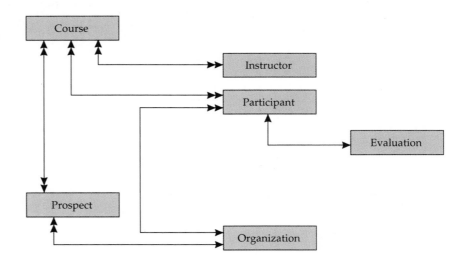

◼ CASE EXAMPLE
Professional Training Institute

PTI decided that the entities of interest were courses, instructors, participants, course evaluations, prospects, and organizations for which prospects work (many times, an organization sends several of its employees to a course). In the entity chart, a box is made for each entity; the lines between boxes represent relationships of interest.

Relationships in the chart are of three types: one-to-one, one-to-many, and many-to-many. In a **one-to-one relationship** (abbreviated 1:1), one entity of a given type is associated with only one member of another type; for example, a participant in a course fills out one evaluation form for the course. Conversely, a given evaluation form was prepared by one participant. Single-headed arrows are used to represent a "one" relationship in the direction of the arrow. In Figure 2–3, a line is drawn between participants and evaluations with single arrowheads on each end to indicate a one-to-one relationship.

In a **one-to-many relationship** (1:M), one type of entity is related to many entities of another type. For example, one prospect works for (is associated with) one organization, so the line emanating from prospect has a single arrowhead where it terminates with the organization. But one organization may have several prospects for a given course. Double-headed arrows are used to represent "many" relationships, so the line emanating from organizations has two arrowheads where it terminates with prospects.

Finally, a **many-to-many relationship** (M:M) is one in which many entities of one type are associated with many instances of another type. For example, an instructor may teach many different courses, and one course may be taught by many different instructors. Thus, the line between courses and instructors has double arrowheads at each end.

Note that the entity chart does not show the details of every user view, entity, or piece of data in its scope. If possible, it should reflect a global or organizationwide perspective of information needs. Unfortunately, even with today's sophisticated technology, such a broad view may be unreasonable for massive organizations such as the federal government or multinational corporations. Nevertheless, the master plan and entity chart should be drawn up for the broadest feasible portion of the enterprise. What is feasible depends on the size of the organization itself, the amount of data it generates, and the resources that management is willing to commit to the project. ◼

Entity Groups, Database System Modules, and Schedules

Because database systems are large and complex, they cannot be designed and built all at once. Rather, they are put together piece by piece over a long period of time—perhaps several years. The master plan should describe the major pieces or modules of the system to be developed, how these modules will fit together into an integrated structure, and a schedule for detailed design and development of each module. It may be possible to define these modules based on the number and strength of the relationships in the entity diagram.

CASE EXAMPLE
Professional Training Institute

PTI's entity groups are shown in Figure 2–4. The COURSE entity group consists of those entities most closely related to the administration of courses. This entity group defines a module that would be most heavily used by personnel in the course management department.

The PROSPECT entity group consists of prospects and organizations and is used most heavily by marketing to promote courses to individuals and organizations. These modules are not totally independent, of course. Note that two lines cross entity group boundaries (these overlaps are more evident when user views are examined). When PTI decided to develop an integrated database system, it already had workable systems in place for course administration. Because the management of the mailing list of prospects was an important task with a simple data structure but large amounts of data, PTI scheduled this as the first database system module to be developed. The simple structure would give PTI personnel a relatively easy problem with which to begin its

FIGURE 2–4　Entity Groups for the Professional Training Institute

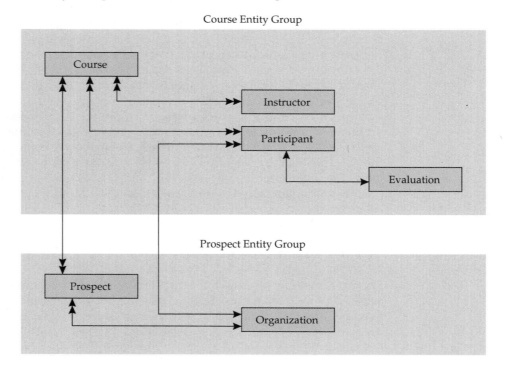

work. The experience gained on the PROSPECT module would be helpful in tackling the more complex COURSE module. ∎

Costs and Benefits

Management of the organization should, and probably will, view the development of a database system as an investment that must pay for itself; that is, the benefits derived from using information provided by the system must outweigh the cost of developing it.

Estimating the cost of developing a database system is not an easy task. If the organization does not already own an appropriate database management package, one must be selected and acquired. Selection must be done very carefully and may take six months to a year of personnel time. Database software itself is expensive, as mentioned in Chapter 1. The cost of installing the package and training systems personnel must be estimated. The master plan must be drawn up and detailed plans for each major module must be made before implementation. Applications software for each module must be developed or acquired, tested, and implemented, and users must be trained. Finally, the system must be operated and maintained.

There is a great deal of uncertainty in determining the cost in time and money of these tasks, but such estimates must be made. The organization must have a realistic picture of the anticipated cost to make sure that funds are available to develop and operate the system. It must also ensure that anticipated benefits outweigh these costs.

This brings us to the other side of the coin, the benefits. The value of benefits of database systems is much more difficult to estimate than costs. Many of the benefits of database systems are difficult to measure in dollars.

CASE EXAMPLE
Professional Training Institute

Suppose, for example, that we are developing a database system for the Professional Training Institute. This system is expected to allow marketing to cut down on postal expenses by eliminating redundancy in current mailing lists and targeting potential course prospects and prospective organizations more effectively. But how much can postal expenses be cut? The system may also reduce the expense of managing courses. But how much will management expenses be reduced?

One way of dealing with such questions is to determine how much expenses would have to be reduced to pay for the system. Is a 5 percent savings in postal and management expenses discounted over each of the next three years enough to pay for developing and operating the database system? Another approach is to estimate how much additional revenue the database system would have to generate to pay for itself. Better targeting of prospects, for example, might lead to larger enrollments for PTI's courses. If enrollments could be increased by 10 percent in each of the next three years, the discounted value might be enough to pay for the system.

Because costs and especially benefits of database systems are difficult to estimate, a great deal of judgment is involved in deciding to institute a new system. This judgment should be based on the best possible estimates from information systems personnel. (For managers, these estimates are a very important form of information concerning the database system, even though they are not derived from the system itself, because it doesn't exist yet.) ■

To summarize, the database system master plan consists of brief descriptions of organizational goals and objectives, structure, entities, modules, costs and benefits, and an implementation schedule. In the next section, techniques for designing and operating each database system module are discussed.

TECHNIQUES AND PROCEDURES IN A DATABASE ENVIRONMENT

Although there are many different techniques and procedures found within a database environment, only one of the more important ones—database design—is previewed here. Other techniques and procedures are discussed in the chapters on database administration. These are more readily understood after other aspects of database systems have been studied.

Database Design Techniques

Once the master plan has been completed, work begins as scheduled on the detailed design of each module and on the database to support that module. The process of database design consists of three major phases: an information-requirements analysis phase, a logical design phase, and a physical design phase. Each of these phases is described below.

 Information-Requirements Analysis and User Views. Information-requirements analysis involves working with users to define their information needs in detail. Information-requirements analysis is concerned with information as users see it; that is, information is viewed in terms of the way it appears in documents, on terminal screens, or even in images in the user's mind. As explained in Chapter 1, representations of information and data at this level are referred to as *user views*.

Example user views for PTI are illustrated in Figure 2–5. Not all views are shown. Figure 2–5a shows the report the instructor gets after the course is over and grades and evaluations have been reported. Figure 2–5b shows the participant's view before the course begins. The

April 29th - Thurs
Exit exam
+ my BD!
PARTY

Do you have a schedule book? phone? ☺

FIGURE 2–5a
PTI Database:
Instructor's View

```
           FINAL GRADE ROLL AND EVALUATION REPORT

     Course: Advanced Database Design

     Date: February 20, 1987

     Instructor: Daniel Wong

     Textbook: Advanced Database Design
               by Lilly Baldwin

     Overall Rating: 4.5

     Participant        Title       Organization        Grade
     ─────────────────────────────────────────────────────────
     Cobb, Ted          Analyst     Sally's Bedding     Pass

     Greise, Fred       Coach       Flatlands High      Pass

     Kaufman, Julie     Manager     Hurts Trucks        Pass

     Solinski, Bill     Chef        Henri's             Pass
```

FIGURE 2–5b
PTI Database:
Participants' View

```
     Participant: Vianelli, Marc

                  Professor of Physics

                  Flatland U.

                  9999 Spaceland Avenue

                  Flatland, California 90001

     Course: Advanced Database Design

     Instructor: Daniel Wong

     Date: February 20, 1987

     Textbook: Advanced Database Design
               by Lilly Baldwin

     Fee: $950

     Grade:

     Rate the Course (Scale of 1 to 5):
```

grade has not been reported and the participant has not yet rated the course. Figure 2–5c shows the course promoter's view. Additional information is provided about the instructor for advertising purposes. The course manager's views are shown in Figures 2–5d and 2–5e. Figure 2–5d shows the course manager's final grade report. The second course manager's view, Figure 2–5e, shows the income statement, since the course manager has financial responsibility for the course.

Note that the course manager's final grade report is similar to the instructor's, except that for reasons of privacy the instructor does not see the rating given by individual participants or the fee each paid. Some participants may be given a discount, but they should not be treated differently by the instructor.

FIGURE 2–5c
PTI Database: Course Promoter's View

```
Course: Advanced Database Design

Instructor: Daniel Wong
            Ph.D., University of Oklahoma, 1944

Date: February 20, 1987

Textbook: Advanced Database Design
          Lilly Baldwin

Standard Fee: $950

_____


PROSPECT MAILING LIST


Mr. Alfred Adams
Systems Analyst
American Business Machines
One Computer Plaza
San Jose, Michigan 87905


Dr. Marc Vianelli
Professor of Physics
Flatland U.
9999 Spaceland Avenue
Flatland, California 90001


Ms. Julie Kaufman
Manager
Hurts Trucks
1212 Detroit Street
Acuff, Texas 78777
```

FIGURE 2–5d
PTI Database: Course Manager's View
This view shows the course rating and fee for each participant.

```
          FINAL GRADE ROLL AND EVALUATION REPORT

Course: Advanced Database Design

Instructor: Daniel Wong

Date: February 20, 1987

Textbook: Advanced Database Design
          by Lilly Baldwin

Standard Fee: $950

Overall Rating: 4.5
_____

Participant        Title      Organization      Grade   Rating   Fee
_____

Cobb, Ted          Analyst    Sally's Bedding    Pass      4      950

Greise, Fred       Coach      Flatlands High     Pass      5      475

Kaufman, Julie     Manager    Hurts Trucks       Pass      5      475

Solinski, Bill     Chef       Henri's            Pass      5      950
```

A great deal of data is shared in these views. The entities, attributes, and relationships contained in user views provide the input necessary for designing a database that supports user needs. Additional information that must be collected in the requirements analysis phase includes specifications for the volume of data within each view, the frequency of each report or query, and requirements for security, integrity, and response time.

Information-requirements analysis is the first and most important phase of the database design process. It is the most important phase because the ultimate effectiveness of the system depends on how accurately the information requirements and user views are specified initially. Specifications of user information requirements feed the entire design process and determine the ultimate form and content of the database system. Poor specifications result in a system that does not satisfy user needs and may lead to costly redesign, or even to cancellation of the project.

Logical Design. Once the various views have been defined and specifications developed, they must be coordinated and organized into an integrated, cohesive system. This process is referred to as *logical design*. Logical design consists of three steps: (1) developing a data model for each user view, (2) integrating the entities, attributes, and relationships into a composite logical schema that describes the database for that module in terms unrelated to the software package being used, and

FIGURE 2–5e
PTI Database: Course Manager's View of the Income Statement

```
                        INCOME  STATEMENT

    Course:  Advanced  Database  Design

    Date:  February  20,  1987

    Instructor:  Daniel  Wong

    Textbook:  Advanced  Database  Design
                by  Lilly  Baldwin

    Overall  Rating:  4.5

    Standard  Fee:  $950

    Income  from  Participant  Fees                        $2850.00

        Expenses:

            Instructor's  Fee          $800.00

            Textbooks                   200.00

            Promotion                   500.00

            Miscellaneous               150.00

    Total  Expenses                                        $1650.00

    Net  Income                                            $1200.00
```

(3) transforming the logical schema into a software schema expressed in the language of the chosen database management package.

Data modeling techniques used to develop a logical schema are described in the next chapter. Software schemas for relational databases and CODASYL databases are described in Chapters 4 and 9. Just to give you some idea as to what a software schema looks like, a portion of a CODASYL schema for PTI's database is shown in Figure 2–6. It is quite COBOL-like in nature and should be easily understood by those familiar with COBOL. Also, part of a relational software schema written in a data description language similar to that used in the product known as ORACLE™ is shown in Figure 2–7. Even though relational systems view data quite differently at the logical level, the software schema is very similar to that of the CODASYL approach.

Physical Design.   The last step of the database design process is physical design. Physical design involves converting the software schema into a form implementable with the organization's particular hardware, operating system, and database management system. Physical design involves designing navigation paths, deciding which records to place in

FIGURE 2–6
Partial CODASYL Software Schema for PTI's Database

```
SCHEMA NAME IS PTI-DATA.

RECORD NAME IS INSTRUCTOR.

    INSTRUCTOR-NAME          CHARACTER          20.

    HIGHEST-DEGREE          CHARACTER           5.

    UNIVERSITY             CHARACTER          20.

    YEAR                   INTEGER             4.

RECORD NAME IS COURSE.

    COURSE-NAME            CHARACTER          20.

    DATE-OFFERED          CHARACTER           8.

    TEXT                  CHARACTER           4.

    RATING                DECIMAL           9.9.

    FEE                   DECIMAL           999.
```

FIGURE 2–7
Partial Relational Software Schema for PTI's Database

```
CREATE TABLE INSTRUCTOR

    INSTRUCTOR-NAME (CHAR [20] NONULL),

    HIGHEST-DEGREE (CHAR [5]),

    UNIVERSITY (CHAR [20]),

    YEAR (NUMBER [4]),

CREATE TABLE COURSE

    COURSE-NAME (CHAR [20] NONULL),

    DATE-OFFERED (CHAR [8]),

    TEXT (CHAR [20]),

    RATING (NUMBER [9.9]),

    FEE (NUMBER [999.]).
```

nearby portions of the storage devices, determining the size of physical records on storage devices and of buffer areas in main memory to hold records, and implementing integrity and security requirements.

Other Database Techniques and Procedures

Many other procedures and techniques, in addition to those for database design, exist in a database environment. These include procedures for analyzing, implementing, and operating systems, designing and documenting programs, and training users. Among the tasks involving these procedures are collecting data to be entered into the system, performing manual edit checks to ensure the integrity of the data before it is entered, actually entering data, running programs necessary to update the database and generate reports from it, logging changes to the databases, making backup copies of the database so that it can be reconstructed if accidentally damaged or destroyed, and assuring that security procedures are followed. Most of these tasks are the responsibility of the database administrator. The role of the database administrator is briefly discussed later in this chapter.

DATABASES

As defined in Chapter 1, databases are integrated, shared collections of files. Databases are stored physically on the storage devices of the organization's computer system. The way the data is organized and stored on these devices is referred to as its **physical organization.**

People think of data in terms of its **logical organization.** There are many different ways that databases can be organized. Several of these are discussed in the next chapter. Many, perhaps most, database management packages use either the CODASYL or the relational approach to represent the logical organization of data. The **CODASYL approach** uses data structure diagrams to portray the logical structure of a database. The **relational approach** describes databases using tables with special characteristics. These tables are called **relations.** Since Part II is concerned with databases, they are not discussed further here.

SOFTWARE

There are three different kinds of software involved in most database systems: database management packages, operating systems, and applications programs. The relationships among these three types of software were illustrated in Chapter 1. As Figure 1–2 illustrates, applications programs gain access to the database through the database management system. Most database management packages use the basic access methods of the host operating system to perform the necessary input-output operations on the data files themselves (some packages support their own access methods). In this section, database management packages are described and then application programming using a DBMS is briefly discussed. Refer to Appendix A for a discussion of access methods and operating systems.

Database Management Systems

The database management packages of interest in this book are complex and expensive. They are complex because many interrelated components are required to support the objectives discussed in Chapter 1. The minimum components of a package that could truly be called a database management system are a data dictionary for cataloging all the data items in the system, a data definition language for further describing the software schema and user views, one or more query languages suitable for end-users as well as programmers, a data manipulation language for use by programmers, a report generator language for efficient programming of management reports, and features to support data integrity, security, privacy, and recovery. Most packages support other functions as well. Some of these features are discussed elsewhere in this book.

Data Dictionary.   The data dictionary is used to maintain standard definitions of all data items within the scope of the database system. The term data repository is being used more and more to reflect the increasingly complex nature of this database system component. We will use data dictionary and data repository interchangeably. The purpose of the data dictionary is to enforce standard definitions of the data resources of the organization. Definitions include a precise description of the meaning of a data item name and a precise description of how values of each data item are stored in the computer system.

Some example data item descriptions are illustrated in Figure 2–8. Descriptions from this figure have been extracted from an actual data dictionary for a database built on Digital Equipment Corporation's (DEC) package called the Common Data Dictionary (CDD). The Common Data Dictionary can be used in Conjunction with DEC database software, such as their Relational Data Base (RDB) package, or it can be used as a stand-alone system to simply catalog and standardize data definitions. Other data repository packages have interfaces to database systems of several vendors.

Some of the functions of a good data repository include (1) maintaining standard user definitions of the precise meaning of data items and standard computer definitions giving formats and data types, (2) maintaining cross-reference lists of data items used by applications programs and applications programs using a given data item, and (3) providing standard definitions of data items to applications programs when requested to do so. As for the latter, some data dictionary

FIGURE 2–8
**Example Data Dictionary
Entry for an Employee
Record Description**

```
DEFINE RECORD CDD$TOP.CORPORATE.EMPLOYEE__LIST
  DESCRIPTION IS
  /* This record contains the master list of all
  employees */
  EMPLOYEE STRUCTURE.
    SS__NUMBER          DATATYPE IS UNSIGNED NUMERIC
                        SIZE IS 9 DIGITS.
    NAME STRUCTURE.
      LAST__NAME        DATATYPE IS TEXT
                        SIZE IS 15 CHARACTERS.
      FIRST__NAME       DATATYPE IS TEXT
                        SIZE IS 10 CHARACTERS.
      MIDDLE__NAME      DATATYPE IS TEXT
                        SIZE IS 1 CHARACTER.
    END NAME STRUCTURE.
    ADDRESS             COPY FROM
                        CCD$TOP.CORPORATE.ADDRESS__RECORD.
    DEPT__CODE          DATATYPE IS UNSIGNED NUMERIC
                        SIZE IS 3 DIGITS.
  END EMPLOYEE STRUCTURE.
END EMPLOYEE__LIST RECORD.
```

systems will generate appropriate COBOL data division statements describing specific data items or groups of data items on issuance of required commands by the applications program.

Data repositories are said to be either "active" or "passive." Passive repositories simply maintain user and computer definitions of data items. Active repositories include an interface to applications programs to support features such as generating record and field (data item) descriptions for application programs. Other properties of active and passive repositories are discussed in the chapters on database administration. Data repositories are discussed more fully in Chapter 11.

Data Definition Languages.   The data definition language is used to translate the logical schema into a software schema for the database management package in use. A standard data definition language (DDL) has been defined by CODASYL committees. Actually, two languages were defined—the schema DDL for specifying the composite schema, and the subschema DDL for specifying user views or data subsets of the schema. The CODASYL schema DDL has already been illustrated in Figure 2–6.

The Structured Query Language (SQL) has been adopted as the industry standard for relational languages. Many relational packages use SQL, which has features for describing the relations of a relational database. Relational data definition languages are discussed further in Chapter 7. A relational definition language was illustrated in Figure 2–7.

Query Languages.   Query languages such as SQL, used in most relational packages, are designed to give end-users direct access to the database. Query languages are one type of **fourth-generation language (4GL).** The first generation is machine (binary) language; the second, assembly language; and the third, programming languages such as COBOL, FORTRAN, PASCAL, or BASIC. Fourth-generation languages are much easier to learn and use than programming languages. Many developers of such languages claim that nonprogrammers can be doing useful work with such languages in a matter of hours and can be proficient in the language in a few days or weeks. However, fourth-generation languages lack the power and versatility of third-generation languages. For example, it would be difficult to write a program to simulate a rocket launch in SQL. Fourth-generation simulation languages are available for this, but it would be difficult to obtain flexible access to a database with a simulation language. A third-generation language could be used to do either job, but not as easily as with languages tailored to the problem.

Report Generators.   Report generators are languages designed for creating management reports. They generally include features for defining report titles, column headings, and row contents. They usually support "control breaks" that facilitate summarizing columns based on a data item such as a department name. Such languages are often simple enough that users are willing to learn them to write their own report programs. They may save many hours compared to what would be required to write the program in a standard programming language.

Security, Integrity, and Recovery Functions.   Database management systems should also include facilities for helping to maintain data integrity and security. Features for security are generally of two types—passwords or procedures for controlling access to the database, and data encryption, which makes the data unusable if it is obtained by an unauthorized user.

One way database management systems help ensure integrity is by providing the ability to specify legitimate values that data items may take. Once such ranges of values are entered, the system checks values at the time of data entry to assure that they are acceptable. Of course, this does not totally eliminate incorrect data, but it helps to reduce the rate of error.

In the complex, multi-user mainframe environments of today, it is almost impossible to totally protect a database system from accidental or intentional damage. Because so many people in the organization depend on shared systems, it is imperative that methods be provided for rapid recovery from damage to the database. Database management systems must provide features to assist in the recovery process. Techniques for doing so are described in Chapter 11.

Database Applications Software

The major difference between database applications software and conventional applications software is the use of special statements for data insertion, removal, retrieval, and modification in database systems. These data manipulation commands are usually embedded in a host language such as COBOL or FORTRAN. Many systems have precompilers that convert these programs with embedded data manipulation language (DML) statements into a program with only standard statements of the host language. The revised program is then compiled and executed.

In CODASYL implementations, this programming can become quite complex at times; the programmer must remain acutely aware of the navigation path being traversed through the database. As can be seen in Chapter 9, traversing navigation paths through a CODASYL database can be rather difficult.

Other differences in database programming and conventional programming in high-level languages include different ways of describing data and data relationships, and the use of report generators. In many cases, these features make the programming much easier than with the conventional file approach.

HARDWARE

The primary hardware components of interest in a database environment are the data storage devices and the central processing unit through which the database is accessed and controlled. Disks remain the most common storage medium for most database systems. Tape is the most common medium for backup. Some systems use faster devices, perhaps with semiconductor memory, to store relatively small amounts of data that are frequently accessed.

Some organizations are beginning to develop distributed database systems that consist of networks of computers, each of which maintains a portion of the total database. This approach may give users better access to and control of local information. It does, however, complicate the operating environment, because networking hardware and software are required. Security procedures become more complex, because the database is scattered among many different machines, which may be at different sites. If so, each machine must have its own security system.

PEOPLE: THE MOST IMPORTANT ELEMENT

Database systems exist to serve the information needs of people, both within and outside the organization. The types of people who use database systems are many and varied. Managers, for example, need information to make decisions. Clerical personnel must enter data from source documents into the system. Customers need information about bills or orders. Government agencies require financial and employment reports. Investors want information about the financial health of companies, and auditors are responsible for expressing an opinion as to whether the firm's financial statements are accurately presented.

The Primary Concerns of Users

Users are concerned with obtaining the information needed to get their jobs done. These jobs are as varied as the users themselves. Some tasks are directly concerned with the system, such as entering data into the database or retrieving data for personal use or for use by others. Even people who do not interact directly with the computer system are important users if the system must satisfy their information requirements. Such is the case for customers of a business or managers whose assistants actually retrieve information.

If the system is to serve end-users effectively and efficiently, it must be easy to learn and easy to use. It must also supply accurate, current data in a format suitable to users.

User Views of Data and Information

It should be noted that in Figures 2–5a through 2–5e no single user requires access to all the data needed by the entire organization. As is usually the case, each user or user group has a limited view of data and information in the system. The course promoter, for example, needs each prospect's name and address to mail out brochures. The instructor needs only the data on participants. The course manager needs information on course income and expenses, which is of no direct concern to the instructor or the promoter (although marketing should know what courses are doing well). All this data can be stored in one integrated database, but no one user needs all the data.

We are taught as children that sharing is a nice thing to do, and this adage applies to data. Unfortunately, just as children may fight over toys or the largest cup of lemonade, users may fight over the rights to data. Users may derive power or prestige through their ability to control data. Logical attempts to share data may fail because of a failure to consider political battles over rights to data.

It may not be possible for the systems development staff to resolve such conflicts. Often they must be resolved at the highest levels in the organization. Many more database projects have run into serious difficulty over organizational issues than as a result of technical problems.

The Role of Top Management

In the development of organizationwide database systems, top management must become actively involved to gain impetus for the project and to resolve conflicts between users, or between users and the systems development staff. Top management must give visible support to the project and provide the resources necessary for successful project completion. Comprehensive database systems are expensive and require a heavy commitment of funds. Top management must be willing to commit the funds necessary for successful completion of the project. Top management may also have to step into frays between users and make unpopular decisions for the benefit of the organization.

The Systems Staff and Its Role

The job of the systems staff is to implement the elements of the database system master plan. This involves working with users to design and develop database system modules that support and integrate multiple end-user views of shared data. Typically, data in the various views is dispersed throughout the organization. Usually, there has been little or no effort to organize this data in any comprehensive fashion. Data in this form is not suitable for computerization, nor can it be effectively managed as an organizational resource.

One major task in database system development is organizing and integrating the data in various views into a logical schema and implementing this schema with the organization's database management system. This is a complex task that may take months and must be carefully managed. Various personnel roles associated with logical database design, development, and operation are discussed next.

The Manager of Information Resources.   The person responsible for the information resources of the organization and for the development of its database systems must have a high-level position in the organizational chart. This position should be just beneath the vice president in charge of all information processing in the enterprise. Titles such as "manager of information resources" and "chief information officer (CIO)" are beginning to appear for this position.

The primary responsibility of the manager of information resources is to work with a steering committee to develop the database system master plan and to oversee the implementation of that plan. The steering committee should be composed of the information resources manager, selected members of the systems staff, and key personnel from user areas. These users should be senior managers who understand the business of the organization and can provide the input necessary for the development of an effective master plan. Systems staff members on the committee must be user oriented and capable of communicating effectively with users.

Information Analyst. The job of the information analyst is to work with end-users of the intended system to implement specific modules and applications of the overall database system. The skills needed by the information analyst include the ability to understand the business of the organization and to communicate effectively with users to determine user views, the information contained within those views, and the data required to support the views. The data must then be logically organized into a logical schema independent of any database management system.

Database Analyst. The task of the database analyst is to transform the information analyst's logical schema into an efficient software schema and physical design for the particular database management system, operating system, and hardware in use. The database analyst must know how to get good performance from the organization's hardware and software. Database processing can be excessively slow with a poor physical design. This job is more technical than that of the information analyst in that it also encompasses physical design of the database required to support the module. The database analyst must be well versed in the particular database management system, operating system, and computer hardware in use.

Database Application Programmers. Database application programmers (or database programmers) write programs in high-level languages such as COBOL or PL/1 to perform the data processing activities required to support the module. These programs use the data manipulation language, the application generator, or the report generator to access the database, so database programmers must be familiar with the database management system and database processing. We touch on aspects of database programming in this book, especially when the CODASYL approach is covered, but we do not give detailed instruction in database programming.

Database Administrator. The jobs of the systems staff described so far involve managing the overall operation or designing or programming part of the database system. Someone must also be responsible for managing the development of specific databases, as well as managing their operation and maintenance once they are put into use.

The database administrator is assigned the responsibility of managing specific databases in the overall database system. Database administration involves such tasks as providing documentation and training, developing security procedures and backup and recovery procedures, performance evaluation, and database reorganization when necessary. The database administrator must be familiar with the organization's DBMS and computer system and must be capable of working with users during the actual operation of the database system. Because the database administrator has such a critical role in successful implementation of database systems in organizations, a more detailed discussion of database administration issues follows this brief note on role sharing.

A Comment on Sharing Roles.   All the roles described in this section must be filled by someone. In many organizations, one person fills more than one role. The same person may, for example, be responsible for information analysis, logical database design, and database programming. Many other combinations of roles are also possible, depending on the size and philosophy of the organization and the management of data processing. Many organizations cannot afford, or are not large enough to require, different people for each role.

KEY ISSUES IN DATABASE ADMINISTRATION

Once a database system has been implemented in an organization, the task of meeting the daily operational challenges of maintaining the system follows. The maintenance function is an extremely complex activity. The essence of database administration is really the ability to adequately address the issues involved in the routine use of the database system without compromising future uses.

The key to effective database administration is twofold. The first step is to be prepared for potentially disastrous events that can affect the database system (discussed in Chapter 11). These are the events that cause the database system to be inoperative for some period of time. The second step is to anticipate and adequately prepare for requests that require changes in either the database system or the database system procedures. Because an organization is dynamic and the needs of users of the database system can be expected to change, requests for changes in the way the database system operates, or in what it produces, are inevitable.

Providing Documentation

The database administrator is the target of continual requests for information regarding effective and efficient use of the database system. In most cases, the requests are straightforward and can be satisfied by directing the person making the request to documentation, *if it exists.* The key is to have documentation available.

What type of documentation should be provided? Documentation can be divided into three types. First, the database system master plan gives users a general context in which to place their specific needs and requirements. The master plan can also educate users who do not understand how their job relates to the operations of the entire organization.

Second, nontechnical documentation can support users who are concerned, not with how the database system operates, but with how to get the information they need to support the decision-making activities of their job. An example of this type of documentation could be an explanation of microcomputer database system interfaces that would explain how to efficiently download data for analysis.

Finally, technical documentation gives detailed explanations of how the database system does what it does. Although this documentation is used predominantly by the database administration staff, it can also be of great use to other database system users who have technical training or are computer literate. Access to some technical documentation may be controlled for reasons of security.

If possible, a central location for documentation should be provided. Even if no more than a bookcase in a particular room, there should be a specified place for documentation. In this way, users can take the first step on their own, without interrupting the database administrator or waiting for the database administration support staff to become available.

Providing Training and Overcoming Resistance

Documentation, however well written, is not enough to entirely support the needs of the organization. The database administrator must also provide periodic training sessions. Although this is an extremely vital function, even initial training is often neglected. Initial training may be required because new users may actually oppose the database system. These users may see the new system as threatening, or they may be unwilling to learn new procedures for a job they have performed for years. In these cases, the database administrator must address these behavioral issues in order to successfully integrate the database approach into the organization.

This resistance, sometimes referred to as *social inertia,* may come about simply because change is stressful and often resisted, but many factors are involved: (1) formal information is only a small component of the organizational decision process; (2) human information processing tends to be simple, experiential, and nonanalytical; (3) organizations are inherently complex, making large changes difficult to implement and institutionalize; (4) many individuals and groups within an organization tend to get their influence and autonomy from their control over information; (5) database systems may restrict lower-management prerogative; (6) database systems may tend to increase a superior's ability to evaluate personnel; (7) information systems and computerization may be expected to lower the employment level in general and threaten job security in particular; and (8) database systems are complex and may be perceived as incomprehensible.

The thread tying these factors together is the observation that database systems are agents of organizational change, with far-reaching effects on many aspects of organizational functioning. Informal information, negotiations, and habits are important factors that are practically impossible to implement in a formal database system. When these factors are overlooked completely or threatened, social inertia may occur because the database system is perceived to have little relevance to or importance for the "real" information flows in the organization.

The complexity of organizations leads to processes of change that are incremental and evolutionary. Large steps are inevitably avoided and resisted. In the case of database systems, this implies that implementation must be phased. Compromise and cooperation are essential.

Many units in organizations get their influence and autonomy from their control over information, so they do not want to lose control of it. When a database system designer is working toward the goal of integrating information controlled by different departments into a system of common databases, groups and individuals naturally view the system as a direct threat and respond accordingly.

Database systems may restrict a manager's prerogative, especially at lower levels of the organization. The degree of standardization and formalization of the role of supervisor may result in a reduction in supervisors' ability to shape their own jobs.

On a more personal note, resistant users may also see the system as a criticism of their own decision processes. In some cases, the integrated database system provides a user's superior with data that makes any mistake highly visible. There is a widespread view that advancing computerization will have a negative effect on job security.

Due to the complexity of these issues and of the database system itself, user training, education, and preparation for change are critical in ensuring successful database implementation. Database administrators must deal effectively with social inertia. One technique for doing so is based on the Lewin-Schien model of organization change. In this model, organizational change is viewed as a process with three stages: unfreezing, changing, and refreezing.

Unfreezing entails the development of a felt need for change in the organization by encouraging users to recognize shortcomings of the existing system and benefits of a new system. Users then become open to trying something new. Instituting the change is the next stage. In this phase, the new database system is introduced and training is initiated. The third stage, refreezing, involves institutionalizing the change by integrating new attitudes and behaviors into existing organizational patterns and relationships.

Education is necessary at all levels of the organization. Top management must have a basic understanding of database concepts to be able to support the information systems department when necessary. Data processing personnel must understand that operating in a database environment is substantially different from conventional operation. And, of course, the end-users of the system at all levels must be trained to prepare them for the transition and to provide a basis for support in the wake of redistributed information flows.

Even experienced users may benefit from additional training. The benefits of advanced training (or even occasional retraining or refresher courses) are not obvious, and hence this type of training is often neglected. Users frequently learn just enough to do what they desire, with little regard for the efficiency of their actions. They may turn to other users for advice and help regarding use of unfamiliar database subsystems. This tendency results in a slow but steady propagation of inefficient techniques throughout the organization. Periodic advanced training of the database system users can therefore help improve the overall efficiency of the database system.

Arbitrating Requested Changes in the Database System

Database administration frequently requires trade-offs among people in the organization. Everyone wants the fastest response time they can have; regardless of the application, users always indicate that they would be able to do a better job if they could get their information faster. Unfortunately, some users must accept slower response times so that other users may have faster response.

A good example is an airline reservation database system. A user in the accounting department may be required to accept slower response times than a ticketing agent. This situation arises because a ticket agent's request for information is probably initiated to handle a prospective sale, whereas the accounting department's request involves a sale that has already been made. The airline could reasonably place higher value on fast response in handling a customer's order than on handling information regarding a sale that has been "sealed."

Another example is computer-based university registration processes. During registration, higher priority is given to requests that service the registration process than to normal student computing services. This situation arises because the administration gives higher value to expediting the registration-related activity during this particular time of the school year. In any organization, there are some users who must accept slower response times than others for the good of the organization as a whole. In many cases, the database administrator must decide which users receive the faster response time.

Response time is not the only issue about which such decisions must be made. Decisions must also be made on resource-related matters such as the amount of secondary storage area that users may have, the number of off-line peripherals (printers, plotters, tape drives) that users may allocate to their applications, the amount of primary memory that a user's application may command, the time of day that particular applications may run, and of course the specific data items in the database system that a user may access.

Users from different parts of the organization frequently propose conflicting requests for changes to the database system. Several requests for increases in primary memory allocation, for example, can add up to too great a decrease in the response time of the database system for all users in the organization. A second common conflict occurs when the database administration function is overloaded with requests requiring the development of new applications within the database system. This happens as users become more aware of what information is available in the database system and how it can be used to help them perform more effectively. Because implementing all requested changes to the database system is typically impossible, some requests must be chosen over others. The database administrator must evaluate the requests and determine how best to resolve conflicts. The following list gives some of the major considerations involved in such decisions:

How important is this request relative to the organization's purposes and goals?

Are the user's claims accurate?

What other alternatives are available for producing the desired result?

Can the modification requested be completed in time to be useful?

Can a short-term solution be implemented while a detailed study is executed?

Would improvement in manual procedures solve the problem?

If work on this request is begun, what other requests will necessarily have to wait?

Is this request technologically feasible? Is it feasible given the organization's resources?

Above all, the database administrator must keep the objectives of the organization foremost and try to resolve disputes in a way that maintains the integrity of the overall database system.

Developing New Applications

The development of new applications of the database system should proceed according to standards specified by the database administrator, or the chief information officer, if one exists. A representative of the information administration function should be included in the design of any new application. This would normally be the person who will ultimately become the database administrator for that application.

The standards for application development should include (1) guidelines for the structure of any new program code and data dictionary entries, (2) the format of supplemental documentation, (3) a full range of tests to determine the reliability of the new application, and (4) a comprehensive review process by members of the organization who have not been involved in the actual development of the application. Access to all parts of the database system at the source code level should be limited to only one or two persons in the organization whose responsibility is to maintain the integrity of the database system at this level. Organizational policy should prevent integration of any new applications programs until all standards have been met.

Controlling Redundancy

Data redundancy leads to inconsistencies in a database system. As we saw in Chapter 1 (at the Conventional National Bank), inconsistencies lead to processing problems. Database design procedures (see Chapter

THE USER'S VIEW

Users are the most important element of an information management system. Without users, there is no need for a database system. Information systems exist to serve the needs of users, so a database system is a success if it satisfies the information needs of its intended users. Many database system projects in the past have met with little success. Martin (1983) lists over 50 reasons for database system failures and corollary requisites for success; most of these relate to management or organizational issues, not to technical problems.

If users are not heavily involved in the planning and design of a database system, there is little chance of its success. Users have their own, limited view of information in the system. As consumers of information, they have their own tastes and preferences, just as consumers of any other commodity do. Their preferences relate to what information is consumed when, and how it is packaged. The only way the information analyst can know the views and preferences of users is to work closely with them during the design process.

Communication between user and analyst should be effective and straightforward. Neither user nor analyst should have hidden agendas or axes to grind—but this is not always the case. Before the database system is considered, users may have control over their own information. They may be hesitant to yield control, especially if the information relate to performance criteria or other sensitive data.

Similarly, people may have developed methods of hiding or masking poor performance data. If so, they surely will not want this data put into a widely accessible database where it might be used against them.

Users are also often concerned about the ownership of data in a shared database. Ownership and the privilege to access and use data may be a source of power, influence, and prestige. If this is the case, it may be necessary for the systems personnel to act as custodians of the data while ownership and other privileges remain in the hands of users.

If the analyst is charged with developing a database system in such an environment, then top management must become involved or the cooperation of users may never be gained. Analysts cannot resolve these issues alone. Only management can make decisions regarding what is best for the organization as a whole. ■

5) complicate this issue because they may result in an increase in redundant data items. Redundancy is also proliferated through inadequate standardization of the data items in a database, as when a data item occurs more than once because different database users have different names for it.

The database administrator must strive to avoid problems of redundancy. A well-developed data repository can help, since it should completely specify the characteristics of a data item, facilitating identification of similar items. However, periodic data repository reviews are still good policy. Knowledge of the applications to the database system is necessary to identify the subtler redundancies.

CHAPTER SUMMARY

The relationships among the five major elements of database systems may be summarized by referring to the ANSI/SPARC architecture in Figure 1–10. Scanning from the top down, the figure depicts an external (end-user) level, a conceptual level, and an internal level. Each of these

METROPOLITAN NATIONAL BANK

The board of directors has given you the mandate to bring MetNat to the forefront in the use of information technology for competitive advantage. In response, you have indicated that you would like to begin a complete and thorough review of all of the information processing systems in the bank: manual and computer-based. You expect that a major reorganization of these systems is necessary, since MetNat does not currently operate with an integrated database system.

As a prelude to your investigation of the bank's information processing systems, you have been reviewing the bank's annual reports for the past few years. Excerpts are provided below:

> Metropolitan National is committed to a complete integration of computing resources into every aspect of the organization's operations. This integration is to entail almost completely automated customer service, account management, human resources management, facilities management, and subsystems for supporting the strategic thrusts of the bank into new areas of competitive advantage, integrated as needed to maintain an accurate description of the entire enterprise.
>
> We have several goals in each of these areas. We want to significantly reduce any amount of time associated with attending to the needs of our customers. Two- to three-day turnaround on customer inquiries is not sufficient. Our customers deserve better.
>
> Account information should be available via telecommunications technology. Checks must be cleared within 24 hours, making funds available for our customers as soon as possible.
>
> We cannot expect our employees to take good care of our customers if we neglect our employees. We intend, therefore, to invest in developing computer-based human resources management systems so that our employees' needs are well maintained.
>
> We will be able to offer competitive services only if we manage our costs well. Therefore, we will look for ways to automate the management of our facilities and physical surroundings. We will investigate means for reducing our inefficiencies in dealing with our suppliers. We expect computer-based systems will provide new methods for creating new efficiencies and for making our management in these areas more effective.
>
> We must begin to put the vast data resources of the bank to work. The data maintained by the bank provides a barometer by which to measure the Lincoln area. We must begin to build computer-based information systems that will help us continue to identify areas where the bank may gain strategic competitive advantage, thus allowing us to provide still better services to our customers.

The bank is functionally organized as follows:

> The president of the bank has the ultimate responsibility for ensuring growth in the bank's assets. He reports to the board of directors, five business leaders who controlled 70 percent of the bank's

original asset base. The president is assisted by an executive vice president. The executive vice president manages the bank's internal operations. Each functional area in the bank is controlled by a vice president who reports to the executive vice president. The president and the executive vice president each has an executive assistant to support their daily activities.

One functional area of the bank provides administrative functions for managing the accounts of typical customers. This department is called the accounts administration department. The head of the department is the vice president of accounts administration. Several account managers oversee the duties associated with opening and closing accounts, monitoring account use for overdrafts, authorizing unusually large withdrawals, wire transfers, and account consolidations. Tellers are employees of this department.

A second functional area of the bank is the loans administration department. This department has two areas: one for business and commercial loans; one for personal loans. The vice president of loan administration is the head of this department. There are two personal loan managers and two commercial loan managers. There are five commercial loan clerks and three personal loan clerks working in these areas.

Approximately 4 percent of the loans made by MetNat end up in default. These accounts are turned over to an external collection agency that has had almost a 50 percent success rate in collecting the loan. The agency receives 33 percent of all loans it ultimately collects.

A third functional area of the bank is called the special services department. Several small areas are housed in the special services department, which has a vice president of special services. The bank maintains a small marketing staff in this department. The customer service area is also a component of this department, as is a financial planning group.

The marketing manager is assisted by three market analysts. The marketing department handles all of the bank's television, radio, and newspaper advertisements. This department conducts market surveys to determine how to best position the bank's services. It develops promotional brochures and, because of this expertise, also handles production of literature that specifies the parameters of bank services. In other words, this department produces the brochures that explicitly outline the bank's responsibilities to customers. The marketing department oversees any promotional campaigns that the bank has, such as contests that occur to increase the number of accounts at the bank.

The customer service area handles inquiries and suggestions that are registered by customers. Inquiries come primarily in the form of questions regarding customers' monthly statements. Prospective customers are directed to the customer service representatives. These representatives determine the needs of the customer and determine which of the bank's services best fill those needs. The customer service area also administers the safe deposit boxes.

The financial planning group provides advice in personal financial services. There are three financial planners in the group. Recently, their primary role has been to establish individual retirement plans for customers. They also provide advice on matters of estate planning, tax-deferred savings plans, and college savings plans. The financial planning group also provides assistance to customers that have exceeded their credit limits or have found themselves overextended on credit. In these cases, the financial planning group will arrange a loan through the loans administration department to consolidate the debt and will work out a plan for repaying the loan.

Another major department at MetNat is the computer services department. This is your department, and your title of chief information officer is considered equivalent to the vice president level. You have a manager of computer operations that oversees the actual day-to-day operation of the computer machinery. He has two employees whose titles are systems programmers. These three employees install and maintain all operating system and purchased software. You also have a manager of applications programming. She has a staff of three programmer analysts who maintain the applications that support the bank's operations.

Finally, a small human resources staff exists at MetNat. There is a vice president of human resources. The manager of human resources has one assistant, human resources clerk.

Employees may arrange to have their paychecks deposited directly into their accounts. Employees have free checking and automatic overdraft protection and pay no annual fee on credit cards issued by the bank.

MetNat's main office building is located in a relatively new office park development in the northwest part of the city. There are five branch offices, one located roughly in each of the north, south, east, and west suburban areas, and one in the downtown business district.

As you have been gathering your information about MetNat's goals and organization, you have learned that some employees are worried about your mandate. For example, the marketing department manager has indicated that her staff cannot understand why a computer-based system might be necessary. The general attitude in marketing is that the manual systems that have been used for years have been quite adequate. Also, these employees really have no computer skills, and they feel that using a computer-based system could cause them to lose touch with their market.

The customer service manager has echoed the marketing department's misgivings. In the past, customer service answered complaints from telephone or walk-in customers. A form was completed noting the customer's complaint, and the form was forwarded to the proper department. For example, if a customer had a complaint about her monthly statement, the form was sent to the demand accounts department. If the problem concerned a loan, the form went to the loan department. The department provided the information requested on the form, usually in two to three working days, and the form was returned to customer service. The customer service department then notified the customer, either by telephone or mail, depending on the customer's choice. Everyone seemed happy with this system. So why change it?

The customer service staff has also raised concerns about being replaced by a computer. After all, they note, when you need a telephone number, it is provided by a computerized voice. What will keep MetNat from replacing them?

The bank tellers were also worried about their jobs. Rumors were spreading that MetNat intended to purchase more automated tellers and terminate some of the employees. Some wondered whether the entire teller operation might become automated. Stories about banks controlled by robots were beginning to spread.

You have decided to prepare and distribute a memorandum addressing these issues. The memorandum will be in the form of a master plan. These "problems" can be solved by providing the correct information to the employees at MetNat, but the information must also provide the "big picture" to the employees.

At this stage, your estimates of costs and benefits will be qualitative at best. Your implementation schedule must also be tentative, since you are not yet familiar with the computing resources. Try, however, to list as many major components as possible. ■

levels deals with information and data at a different degree of abstraction.

The viewpoint of information users is reflected at the highest level of abstraction, that farthest from computerization. At the other extreme is the physical level, the representation of data in the storage devices of the computer system. The level in-between—the conceptual level—serves as a bridge from the user to the hardware. Procedures at each successive level of abstraction make the representation more concrete and hence more suitable for use by computers.

When converting to a database approach, an organization should first develop a database system master plan. The master plan should state the goals and objectives of the organization, describe its structure, list its major entities, entity groups, and relationships between entities, lay out schedules for implementation, and estimate expected costs and benefits to be derived from the database system.

The individual modules and databases themselves must be carefully designed. Information requirements must be specified correctly, for they drive the entire design process. User views are merged into an integrated schema, which is converted to a physical design.

People are the most important element in a database environment. Users need information to perform their jobs. Database administrators and managers must create a climate in which analysts and users can work together to achieve the goals of database projects.

Questions and Exercises

1. Name and briefly describe the five elements of a database system. How do they fit together into an integrated system?
2. Which of the five elements is most important? Why?

3. Why are careful planning and design crucial to the success of a database system?

4. Briefly describe the basic elements of database management software.

5. For whom are data manipulation languages intended? For whom are query languages intended?

6. What are the four generations of software?

7. Describe the basic elements of a database system master plan. Why is this an important document to the organization?

8. Why is it important to design database systems in a modular fashion?

9. What is an entity chart and how is it useful in defining database system modules?

10. What are the three phases of the database design process? Which is the most important? Why?

11. What is meant by *view integration?* What is the output of the view integration process?

12. What is a software schema? How does it differ from a logical schema?

13. What is a data structure diagram? How are data structure diagrams related to logical schemas?

14. What are the primary concerns of users? Why do different users have different views of the same database?

15. What is the role of top management in a database system project? Why is the role of top management important?

16. What is the major role of the information analyst in a database system project? How does this differ from the role of the database analyst?

17. Describe the role of the database administrator and explain how it differs from that of the database analyst.

18. How might you go about treating the estimation of benefits in the following database applications?
    a. A private university developing a database on students interested in attending the university. What if the university were publicly supported?
    b. A database on donors to a public or a private university.
    c. Profiles on expenditure habits, income, preferences, and so on of customers of a large department store.
    d. A reservation system for an airline company.
    e. A reservation system for a hotel chain.

For Further Reading

Barrett, Stephanie. "Strategic Alternatives and Interorganizational Systems." *Journal of Management Information Systems.* 3, no. 3 (Winter 1986–1987), pp. 5–16. Discusses strategies some companies are using to link suppliers and customers directly into their database systems by putting terminals in the offices of other organizations. This is a new and effective information strategy.

Batiste, John; and John Jung. "Requirements, Needs, and Priorities: A Structured Approach for Determining MIS Project Definition." *MIS Quarterly* 8, no. 4 (1984), pp. 215–28. Describes a technique for requirements analysis for MIS projects in general. This technique is useful in database projects as well.

Benjamin, Robert; Charles Dickinson; and John Rockart. "The Changing Role of the Corporate Information Systems Officer." *MIS Quarterly* 9, no. 3, September 1985, pp. 177–88. Describes the position of corporate or chief information officer and how this role relates to database systems in organizations.

Doll, William J. "Avenues for Top Management Involvement in Successful MIS Development." *MIS Quarterly* 9, no. 1 (March 1985), pp. 17–38. Discusses the need for top-management involvement in large-scale MIS projects, such as database systems.

Drury, D. H. "An Evaluation of Data Processing Steering Committees." *MIS Quarterly* 8, no. 4 (December 1984), pp. 257–66. Evaluates steering committees and gives guidelines on how to organize and operate them.

Jackson, Ivan. *Corporate Information Management.* Englewood Cliffs, N.J.: Prentice-Hall, 1986. Thorough discussion of planning and the organizational environment in Chapters 1–4.

Martin, James. *Managing the Data-Base Environment.* Englewood Cliffs, N.J.: Prentice-Hall, 1983. An excellent treatment of normalization and view integration with bubble charts in Chapters 10–14.

Tom, Paul. *Managing Information as a Corporate Resource.* Glenview, Ill.: Scott, Foresman, 1987. Information strategic planning is discussed in Chapter 2, and the relationship of databases to the strategic plan is discussed in Chapter 3.

II

LOGICAL DATABASE DESIGN

3

DATA MODELING

In Chapter 1, we presented broad, fundamental concepts in database systems. In Chapter 2, we discussed planning issues that must be considered in preparing for database systems integration in an organization and presented a general model for database system design. In this chapter, we amplify some of the topics presented thus far and focus on more database design-oriented issues and techniques. In particular, we concentrate on concepts used to describe the data contained in the database.

THE IMPORTANCE OF DATABASE DESIGN

Database design is critical to successful database system implementation and use. Organizations may need data on thousands of items, and these items may be related in complex ways. Database designs must accurately reflect these relationships or risk being inadequate for supporting organizational decision-making.

During the design process, the objectives listed in Chapter 1 (data independence, reduced data redundancy, standardization, and so on) begin to assume a tangible form. The choices made during the database design process determine the degree to which the objectives are met during the actual implementation.

The costs of extensive design activity can be great, and the savings can be difficult to quantify (as observed in Chapter 2). However, the benefits of a clear, correct design are many. A formal design process produces a model of the system that can be evaluated prior to implementation. This model facilitates communication between the system designers and the system users. Clearly, changing the organization of the database is easier and less costly if done during the design phase—before the data is actually entered into records and files. Experience shows that database systems that have been ineffective or particularly difficult to use have been poorly designed.

A general approach to fundamental database design is presented in this chapter. Table 3–1 shows the model of information requirements, logical design, and physical design presented earlier. As you can see, we have added details regarding major activities and goals associated with each phase. Be careful not to be misled by the model's simplicity. Each step is described in more detail shortly.

THE THREE PHASES OF DATABASE DESIGN

Database design occurs in three phases: an information requirements phase, a logical design phase, and a physical design phase. Indeed, many well-planned events follow the same pattern. If an algorithm guaranteed successful results in each phase, database design would be easy. But many aspects of database design require judgment. Therefore,

TABLE 3–1   The Database Design Model (showing the three major design phases and the goals of each)

Phase	Major Activities	Goals
Information requirements	Identify information inputs to decision-making activities	Determine objectives, data availability, data usage, format, and calculations
Logical database design	Identify important entities	Relate entities to specific objectives
		Standardize names and formats
		Identify source of data
	Define attributes that describe the entities	Identify ownership of data
	Identify relationships between entities	Determine nature of relationship (1:1, 1:M, M:M)
	Normalize entity relationships	Reduce redundancy and eliminate anomalies but retain relationships
Physical database design	Implement the database system	Map the logical design to computer devices

we begin with a discussion of the goals of each phase, proceeding on the premise that knowledge of goals make judgments easier.

Recall, from the discussion in Chapter 2, that the information requirements phase consists of determining which data items should be maintained. Logical design is concerned with the logical relationships in the data. Physical design is concerned with how the information is stored physically in the computer.

Frequently, information analysts and database analysts must backtrack a little to incorporate new information requirements specified by the user. Figure 3–1 illustrates that the activities in each phase are executed iteratively, so that distinguishing the end of one phase and the beginning of the next phase is difficult. Rarely is the design process linear.

Goals of the Information Requirements Phase

The information requirements phase focuses on identifying the information needs of the organization. The organization's master plan for information requirements (see Chapter 2) is a good place to begin pinpointing these needs. The master plan enumerates organizational objectives. Some of these objectives require support from the database system.

Objectives supported by the database system are directly related to the needs of the database system users. In some cases, the database system users are not the persons actually interfacing with the system. For example, a manager may assign the preparation of reports to staff

FIGURE 3–1   **Database Design Is an Iterative Process**

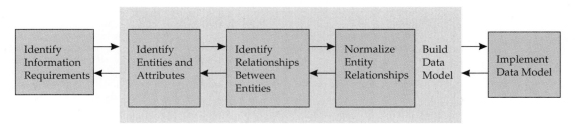

analysts. Database designers must be careful to consider both the needs of the decision-makers who will use the data and the needs of the personnel who actually interface with the system.

After determining objectives to be supported, the next activity in the information requirements phase is to interview users to determine their specific needs. Existing documents and organizational reports are frequently good sources of this type of information, but some objectives require data not currently available in the organization. The information requirements phase must identify these data items so that appropriate action can be taken.

The information requirements phase also involves determining how data will be manipulated. Any calculations required to produce documents and organizational reports should be clarified during the information requirements phase. Such calculations identify data items that must exist in the database in order to generate the needed reports. Finally, any format restrictions should be identified at this time; for example, dollar amounts may be in thousands of dollars, and hours worked may be recorded to the nearest tenth of an hour.

During the information requirements phase, one must also determine the amount of processing activity that will be associated with data items. This activity may be expressed in terms of average number of accesses expected. Critical response times must be determined during the information requirements phase as well. In addition, security and access issues must also be addressed during this phase. All of the information gathered at this time is used in the later phases as the logical and physical aspects of the database evolve.

Goals of the Logical Database Design Phase

The logical design phase focuses on data and data relationships. Characteristics of the data items included in the database system are identified during this phase. Another process that usually occurs during this phase is aggregation of similar data items. Once items have been grouped, determining relationships between them may begin.

A database system must be an accurate model of the organization to adequately support the decision processes of the organization (see Figure 3–2). The database should represent selected aspects of the

FIGURE 3–2
Because the data only exists
for an entire week, answering a question regarding
Wednesday's sales is
impossible.

```
Sales Data

Area    Week    Month       Total Sales

  1       1     January       1532.47
  2       1     January        872.13
  1       2     January       1286.92
  2       2     January       1071.03
```

organization at any time. In the logical design phase, the following steps
are included:

1. Specify the appropriate data items to be included in the database system (that is, identify the important entities).
2. Specify the level of detail to be maintained regarding the data
   items in the system (that is, define attributes that describe the
   entities).
3. Specify the relationships between the data items (that is, identify relationships between entities).
4. Normalize the relationships between these items.

The fourth activity, database design normalization, is discussed in
detail in Chapter 5. In this chapter, we cover only the first three activities in the logical database design phase. Completing all four activities
produces a normalized data model—a representation of the types of
objects about which data will be maintained in the database system.
Data models reflect the relationships between the objects. The data
model produced during this phase of the design process is combined
with the information gathered during the information requirements
phase to form the basis for decisions made in the physical design phase
(discussed next).

Although the database literature increasingly treats information requirements determination and logical database design as distinct (but
not separate) activities, the two are obviously closely related. For brevity
in the rest of this chapter, we use the term *logical database design* (or just
logical design) to refer to both activities.

Goals of the Physical Database Design Phase

As noted in Table 3–1, the physical design phase focuses on the actual
implementation of the database. One goal of this phase is to implement
the relationships defined in the logical database design using efficient
data structures. Database analysts choose appropriate data structures
such as linked lists and trees to implement the logical relationships.
They may also choose an appropriate hashing algorithm for accessing
the data. Database systems often provide a number of such algorithms
that may be used to ensure efficient access to data items. Database

analysts may also determine other system parameters, including the existence of forward and backward pointers between data items.

Another major goal is to develop an efficient mapping of data to the storage devices that will support the database system. Here, the response time requirements (determined during the information requirements activities) are considered to determine the characteristics of the storage devices required to support the processing needs of database users. The choice of storage devices may be based on a cost-benefit analysis that takes into account the fact that faster access typically costs more. These and other aspects of physical database design are presented in Appendix A.

A Note Regarding Prototype Development

A **prototype** is the first version of a system. It is understood to be incomplete or in need of refinement; it is a model on which the finished version of the system is based. Prototype development is called *prototyping*. Prototyping leads to increased communication between the designers and the users of a system, which increases the likelihood that the finished product will meet the needs of the user. Prototyping also focuses on the functions that will be provided, thus emphasizing logical design issues.

A potential problem with prototyping is that the increased communication is ultimately more expensive (because of the time involved) than the benefits warrant. The development process may also be perceived to be harder to control because users may exert greater influence on the final design. Some argue that, instead of emphasizing logical design issues, prototyping actually emphasizes physical aspects of the system too early in the design process. Users will naturally focus on the aspects of the system that can be seen or touched, which are typically physical characteristics.

As in many controversies, the truth probably lies between the extremes. Some aspects of database system development are amenable to prototyping, whereas other aspects probably should not be prototyped. The user interface can be prototyped, for example, to clarify any questions regarding how the user expects information to be accessed or displayed. The actual data accessing methods, however, are probably of little concern to users. Consequently, database developers would not need to prototype this aspect of a system to support a prototype of the user interface.

DATA MODELING USING THE ENTITY-RELATIONSHIP MODEL

The most common approach to logical database specification is the **entity-relationship model (E-R model),** a graphical method of representing entities, attributes, and relationships. Although it may be difficult to incorporate much detailed information in a graphical approach, it is often advantageous to have the relationships between entities explicitly represented. This model of the data items in the system provides one form of system documentation.

When documentation is prepared in text form, there is no question about how it is read. If we write in English that "faculty purchase memberships," we know to read this from left to right. Graphical documentation tools, however, may present problems. One needs to be careful to choose descriptive entity and relationship names so that the relationship is accurately communicated regardless of how the diagram is read.

Graphical modeling approaches are quickly being incorporated into many system development tools. The more sophisticated tools take the graphical models as input and generate the code necessary to support database processing. For example, Electronic Data Systems (EDS) claims their INCA tool can generate over 80 percent of the code necessary for database processing if a complete model is specified. An advantage of this approach is that changes in the system must begin with changes in the data model, since the code for the system is generated from the model. Thus, the model, and therefore the documentation, is always updated.

So, there are many benefits to learning a fundamental data modeling approach. A data model provides a means for discussing system requirements with users. It provides documentation for a system once it is developed. And, many system development tools are being designed to operate on data models as a basic form of input.

Setting Up the E-R Model

The E-R model uses several simple shapes to convey the relationships to be incorporated into the database (see Figure 3–3). Entities are denoted by rectangles labeled with the entity name. Relationships are denoted by diamonds labeled with the relationship name. The existence of a specific relationship between two entities is shown by connecting the entities with a line via the relationship.

In order to illustrate the E-R approach, let's consider the needs of a large university's student recreation center database. A typical student recreation center at a large university will allow students to use the facility only if they have paid their student activity fees. We can consider student activity fees to be analogous to purchasing a "membership" at the recreation center. The recreation center will typically allow faculty to purchase a membership as well.

Members of the recreation center are allowed to check out sports equipment such as basketballs, volleyballs, softball bats and balls, weight-lifting belts, and other equipment that can be used at the facility. When members check out equipment, an equipment-issued form is completed listing the membership number and the equipment being used. This form must list at least one piece of equipment in order to be retained in the file. Otherwise it is discarded. Members must also obtain a clean towel to be used in the shower. Employed personnel monitor the

FIGURE 3–3
Symbols Used in Entity-Relationship Models

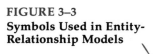

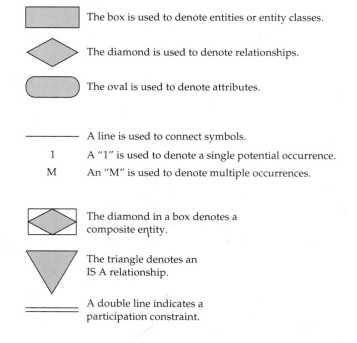

The box is used to denote entities or entity classes.

The diamond is used to denote relationships.

The oval is used to denote attributes.

A line is used to connect symbols.

1   A "1" is used to denote a single potential occurrence.

M   An "M" is used to denote multiple occurrences.

The diamond in a box denotes a composite entity.

The triangle denotes an IS A relationship.

A double line indicates a participation constraint.

checkout and the use of the sporting equipment and do their best to monitor the towel use. Every employee is assigned to one of two departments: maintenance or general staff.

The center has 10 racquetball courts. These courts may be reserved up to one week in advance. Reservations can be made through the equipment check-out window.

The recreation center also operates a small accessory shop where some sporting equipment and clothing is sold. The sporting goods sold are small items such as racquetballs, racquets, bandages, tape, and so forth. In addition, the shop sells assorted sportswear bearing the university emblem and mascot and also handles a limited assortment of name-brand sportswear items.

Finally, the recreation center sponsors a limited number of classes in officiating various sports. Due to budget constraints, instructors often teach a class in more than one sport. However, there are never multiple classes offered in a particular sport.

Step 1: Identify Important Entities

Following the logical database design activities in Table 3–1, our first step is to identify important entities that will be included in the recreation center database.

In a university setting, students are usually important entities. We can begin our list there. In the description above, memberships and members are mentioned, so we'll add them to our list of important

entities. We may decide later to delete these entities or change their names. Such design changes are a normal part of the iterative process of database design. We also note that faculty can purchase a recreation center membership, so let's add faculty to our list.

The recreation center has equipment that is used by the members, so we'll add equipment to our list. There are also racquetball courts and reservations. Also mentioned is an accessory shop that sells two general categories of items: sportswear and sports equipment. These entities go on our list. We are also told that classes are taught in the recreation center, so we'll add that to the list. The classes are taught by personnel, so add personnel to the list, too.

We have now listed most of the explicit entities mentioned in the brief description of our model. You might be surprised by how many entities we've identified. You'll soon see that situations that appear to be quite small can require complex designs in order to be accurately modeled.

Step 2: Define Attributes that Describe the Entities

For each entity that has been identified, we need to determine what characteristics about the entity should be maintained in the database. These characteristics, or attributes, describe the entities in detail. For example, we probably need some way of identifying specific students. So, a student identification number is an attribute that probably should be included in the database. For each student, the student's name, address, and telephone number might also be important for the recreation center to have in the database. While grade point ratio is an important attribute of students in some cases, it may not be relevant to the recreation center. If an attribute is not needed, it should not be included in the database.

Next on our list are memberships and members. Memberships might be characterized by a membership number (so that the recreation center can monitor how many persons might be using the facility), the name, address, and telephone number of the person holding the membership, and the semester in which the membership is valid. There appears to be much overlap in the type of data stored with membership and student. Similarly, we would expect much of the same information for the member entity and the faculty entity. Therefore, perhaps only one of these entities is really necessary. The others would be redundant. Since the members entity seems a little more generic, let's retain it and assume the other entities are not needed.

This elimination process occurs frequently in the early stages of database design. In this case, we began with a general description of a situation and hypothesized its entities. Also you might find that different potential database users refer to an entity by different names. As the design progresses, you can determine that entities that appeared to be different are really the same. Thus, you can eliminate redundant entities and consequently prevent unnecessary data duplication from creeping into your database. Do not be concerned about this process; it is a positive result of the design process.

Attributes of equipment could be an identification number and some type of description. We might also want to know which member is currently responsible for a piece of equipment or whether it is currently in the equipment supply room. Therefore, these attributes also need to be considered for equipment.

Racquetball courts present an interesting case. There is little that needs to be known about the racquetball courts as far as the recreation center is concerned. The attributes of a racquetball court might include the dimensions of the court, when the floor was last resurfaced, and perhaps when the court was last painted. Otherwise, there is little about the court itself that seems too important. Additionally, this information is not very volatile; that is, the values of these attributes remain the same for long periods of time. Consequently, there may be little need for including them in an on-line database.

Information regarding the racquetball court reservations, on the other hand, seems important to the daily decision-making operations of the recreation center. This information is needed to determine who will use the courts and when they will be used. Thus, member names along with the date, time, and some identification of a specific court (perhaps a court number) are probably required.

The accessory shop presents a situation similar to the racquetball courts. The shop itself is not as interesting from a decision-making standpoint as the transactions involving the accessories in the shop. Consequently, the sportswear attributes of size, color, brand, and price seem important. Similar attributes could be specified for sports equipment. Each item in the store might have a unique inventory number assigned to it, which would also be an important attribute.

Finally, we have personnel and classes. Personnel might have many important attributes: name, address, telephone number, salary or wage rate, social security identification number, number of deductions for tax purposes, department assignment, skills, and so forth. We would need more detailed information regarding the decision-making processes supported by this data in order to determine the scope of the important attributes.

The *classes* entity is a little more easily determined. We would expect to need the date, time, and location of the class. We might also want to maintain data regarding the class instructor, any cost associated with the class, and perhaps the number of students allowed in the class. These are typical attributes associated with classes.

In all of these cases, we have made some assumptions about what the important aspects of these entities are. These assumptions should be verified with the database users. The users will identify errors in the designer's assumptions. Again, do not be dismayed if a user finds an error in your design. Since you can't read the user's mind, you are bound to make an errant assumption sooner or later. The important thing for you to remember is that you are in a partnership with the ultimate user, so you need to include the user throughout the design process.

Entity and Attribute Representations. Having identified the entities and the attributes, we need to record our work. Our modeling tool will be the entity-relationship model. The basic modeling unit in the E-R model is the entity. An entity is represented as a rectangle labeled with the entity name. Entity attributes are shown as labeled ovals attached to the entity rectangle. Figure 3–4 shows how the member entity in the recreation center example would be modeled.

Many types of attribute representations exist. A **composite attribute** is formed by combining simpler attributes into a single attribute. For example, the name attribute of the faculty entity could be a composite of first name, middle initial, and last name. Composite attributes are represented by connecting the oval containing the composite attribute directly to the entity. The attributes comprising the composite attribute are then connected to the composite attribute.

A **multivalued attribute** may have more than one value at any time. If we assume that both the home telephone and the office telephone of faculty are maintained in the database, then the telephone attribute is multivalued. Multivalued attributes are diagrammed as double ovals. They can be a source of problems in database designs, but, since they occur naturally and frequently, they must be addressed. Thus, identifying multivalued attributes is critical to the design process. (How to handle multivalued attributes is covered in Chapter 5 when we cover normalization.) Multivalued and composite attributes are illustrated in Figure 3–5.

Some database designers prefer a variation on this approach, one which explicitly incorporates the domain (that is, the set of valid values) of the attribute into the model. When this approach is taken, the oval contains the domain name and the line connecting the oval to the entity

FIGURE 3–4
An Example of an Entity with Attributes

FIGURE 3–5
An Entity with a Multivalued Attribute (telephone number) and a Composite Attribute (name)

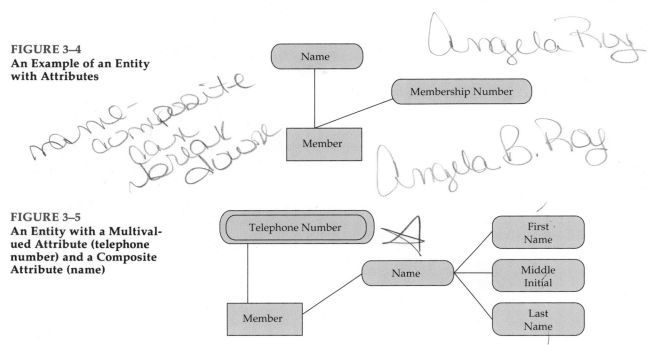

is labeled with the name of the attribute. Frequently, database designers take this approach one step further and place the domain attributes at the bottom of the model, connecting *all* attributes that share a common domain to a single oval showing the domain name as shown in Figure 3–6. This variation makes shared domains explicit and can facilitate identification of implicit relationships between entities.

Step 3: Identify Relationships between Entities

One-to-One Relationships.   Because faculty are allowed to purchase a single membership, the relationship between faculty and memberships is a one-to-one relationship. Using the E-R approach, faculty and memberships are entities, so each would be represented as a labeled rectangle. The relationship between the entities is a purchase: faculty purchase membership. Therefore, a diamond is labeled and placed between the two entities. Figure 3–7 illustrates this relationship. The one-to-one nature of the relationship is signified by placing a 1 over the line located near each entity that connects the entities.

One-to-Many Relationships.   A one-to-many relationship exists between personnel and the officiating classes they teach. The relationship is one-to-many due to the assumptions made earlier: (1) Because budget constraints force the recreation center to limit the number of personnel they hire, the teachers often teach more than one class. (2) Because there are not multiple classes taught for a given sport, anyone teaching a class is the only teacher of the class. Thus, the relationship is one-to-many, not many-to-many. The relationship is modeled using the E-R diagram

FIGURE 3–6
Representing a Domain in the Entity-Relationship Model

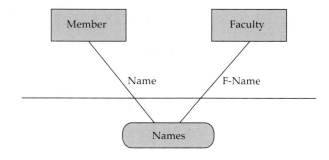

FIGURE 3–7   A One-to-One Relationship in the Entity-Relationship Model

in Figure 3–8. Here, personnel is a labeled rectangle representing the personnel entity, officiating classes is a second labeled rectangle representing the classes entity, and the relationship between them is labeled *teaches*. The 1 over the line near the personnel entity and the *M* (for "many") over the line near the officiating classes entity indicate the cardinality of the relationship.

Many-to-Many Relationships. A many-to-many relationship exists between members and the racquetball courts they may reserve. The recreation center policy allows a member to make up to three reservations, as long as they are no more than a week in advance. The most common way of representing the many-to-many relationship is shown in Figure 3–9a. Again the member and racquetball court entities are shown as labeled rectangles and the relationship (reserve) is shown as a labeled diamond. An *M* is placed over the line near each entity to indicate a "many" relationship.

The relationship in a many-to-many relationship typically has meaning, and intersection relationships are usually constructed to reflect this. Our E-R diagram does not reflect the intersection relationship. A new symbol has been introduced into the E-R approach to correct this oversight, however. A rectangle containing a diamond is used to represent a relationship entity, which is now known as a composite entity. The term **composite entity** denotes that the entity being modeled is composed of characteristics of each of the contributing entities. Using a composite entity symbol, the many-to-many relationship would be drawn as shown in Figure 3–9b. Although the new model follows the formal E-R approach more closely, you will find that the old approach is still used more often in business.

Many different approaches to E-R models have evolved. These approaches differ mainly in how they illustrate multiple occurrences of an entity in a relationship. Some techniques use directed arrows. These

FIGURE 3–8 A One-to-Many Relationship in the Entity-Relationship Model

FIGURE 3–9a The Most Common Way of Representing a Many-to-Many Relationship in the Entity-Relationship Model

FIGURE 3–9b   **One Way of Representing a Many-to-Many Relationship in the Entity-Relationship Model**

FIGURE 3–10   **Alternate Ways of Representing a One-to-Many Relationship in the Entity-Relationship Model**

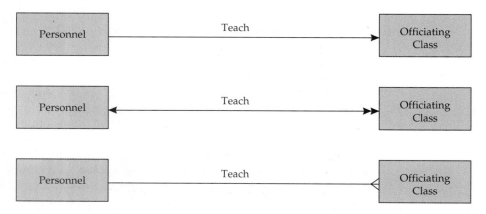

techniques may use an arrowhead pointing to the "many" side of the relationship, with no arrowhead indicating the "one" side. Alternatively, a double arrowhead might be used to indicate "many" and a single arrowhead to indicate "one." Other approaches use a line with multiple branches on the "many" side of the relationship. These variations are shown in Figure 3–10, which all indicate the same one-to-many relationship.

Some database designers prefer to represent only binary relationships (relationships between two entities only) in the E-R model of the database. When many-to-many relationships are converted to relationships containing composite relationships, the diagram automatically converts to binary relationships. We will also advocate representing only binary relationships in our E-R models, as this also facilitates converting the E-R model to data structure diagrams, which we discuss later in this chapter.

Other Relationships.   Relationships may be required between some entities. A **total participation constraint** occurs when an entity cannot exist without being involved in a particular relationship. Otherwise, a **partial participation constraint** occurs. In the recreation center example, the only total participation constraint is the requirement that a record of equipment being issued to someone must contain at least one reference to a piece of equipment. This constraint is designated on the E-R

FIGURE 3–11   Example of a Total Participation Constraint

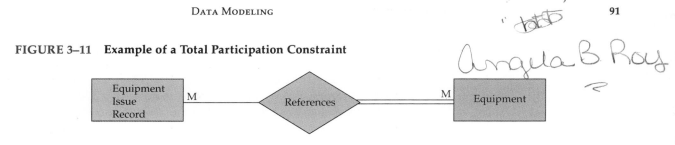

FIGURE 3–12   Representing an Identity Dependency in the Entity-Relationship Model

diagram using a double line to connect the equipment issue entity to the equipment entity via the "references" relationship (see Figure 3–11).

Existence Dependency. There are cases where occurrences of an entity will exist only under certain circumstances. For example, a membership for a faculty member should exist only if the faculty member exists. We want to be sure to constrain the existence of membership records to valid members of the faculty. The memberships are said to be **existence dependent** on the faculty in this case. In other words, the existence of membership information depends on the existence of the corresponding faculty information.

At this point, let us contrast total participation and existence dependency. The total participation constraint is applied in a situation where entities are independent. For example, the equipment exists and the equipment issue forms exist, but we wish to indicate that valid equipment issue forms contain reference to at least one piece of equipment. By contrast, the memberships are not considered to exist until purchased. Thus, they do not exist independently of the faculty. Some approaches refer to the existence dependence relationship as a **characteristic relationship.** The occurrence of the dependent entity acts as an attribute, or characteristic, of the independent entity.

 Identity Dependency. In some situations, an entity cannot be uniquely identified without considering identifying attributes of another entity. For example, when a sale occurs in the recreation center accessory shop, the transaction cannot be uniquely identified without including the identification number of the employee that completed the transaction, or the stock number of the item sold. In these cases, the composite entity class that is diagrammed between the personnel entity and the accessories entity is **ID dependent** on each of these entities. ID dependency is indicated by adding "ID" in the relationship diagram, as shown in Figure 3–12.

Weak Entities. An entity whose existence depends on another entity (existence dependency) or that cannot be uniquely identified without considering identifying attributes of another entity is called a **weak entity.** A weak entity always has a total participation constraint with respect to the relationship in which it participates. Additionally, a weak entity must constrain some attribute values that distinguish it from other weak entities that participate in a relationship with a given (strong) entity.

A weak entity is designated by drawing another rectangle around the rectangle used to designate the entity. The E-R model denotes this dependency by placing an *E* in the relationship symbol, although it is more common to omit the *E* and rely on the double rectangle symbol to indicate the dependency. These conventions are shown in Figure 3–13.

Generalization and Specialization. There are often many different levels at which information is needed in a corporate environment. Even in the recreation center, the manager might want detailed information sometimes and more general information other times. The E-R model provides a method for indicating that some entities are subsets of a more general entity.

The accessories store in the recreation center carries sportswear and sports equipment. The accessories entity is a **generalization** of these two categories of accessories. Or, we can think of sportswear and sports equipment as **specializations** of the category of accessories. The E-R model uses a triangle labeled *ISA* to show this relationship. ISA denotes the words *is a* or *is an,* as in "sportswear *is an* accessory." Figure 3–14 shows the E-R diagram for generalizations and specializations.

Specializations "inherit" the attributes of their general counterparts. In other words, since an accessory entity has the attributes stock number, price, brand, color, and description, the sportswear entity also has these attributes. Specializations may also have attributes that are different from, or in addition to, their general counterpart. The sportswear entity has the attributes material type and size, indicating that this information is required at the specialization level. Similarly, sports equipment is characterized by the additional attributes of weight, length, and equipment specifications (for example, inflation pressure for balls).

Aggregation. In some cases, we want to show that the combination of two or more entities is related to another entity. Combination is accomplished through a method called *aggregation.* Aggregation is a concept similar to generalization, but you should be careful to note the difference. In **aggregation,** *all* of the attributes of each entity are included in the aggregated entity. In generalization, only the *general* attributes exist in the generalized entity.

FIGURE 3–13 **Representing a Weak Entity in the Entity-Relationship Model**

FIGURE 3–14 Generalization and Specialization Using the ISA Relationship

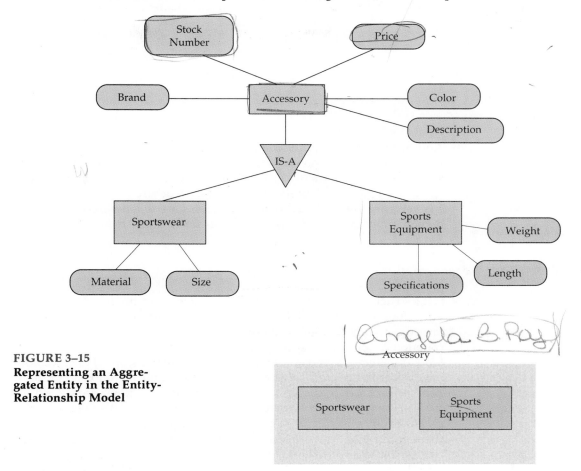

**FIGURE 3–15
Representing an Aggre-
gated Entity in the Entity-
Relationship Model**

Another, but different, way of illustrating the accessories in the recreation center database is shown in Figure 3–15. This figure shows sportswear and sports equipment as being aggregated into accessories. This diagram, however, indicates that *all* of the attributes in each entity would be included in the accessories entity. Figure 3–14, which indicates generalization using the ISA relationship, indicates that only the general attributes would be included in the accessories entity.

Recursive Relationship. Another situation that occurs frequently involves an entity on *both* sides of a relationship. There is a "loop" relationship. A loop is also known as a **recursive relationship.** It is diagrammed in the E-R model by showing a line from the entity to the relationship, *and* a line from the relationship to the entity. A common recursive relationship is shown in Figure 3–16. This diagram illustrates the situation where personnel supervise (other) personnel.

FIGURE 3–16
**A Recursive Relationship
in the Entity-Relationship
Model**

CONVERTING E-R MODELS TO DATA STRUCTURE DIAGRAMS

Another common graphical technique for presenting the entities and relationships in a database is the data structure diagram. These diagrams are also known as Bachman diagrams, after their developer C. W. Bachman. We first illustrated a data structure diagram in Chapter 1 (see Figure 1–11). Data structure diagrams are widely used, so we will demonstrate how to convert E-R models to data structure diagrams.

Entity and Attribute Representations

Data structure diagrams use only rectangles and lines, and represent only one-to-many relationships. (A one-to-many relationship implies one-to-zero, one-to-one, or one-to-more.) Unlike E-R diagrams that illustrate logical entities and relationships, data structure diagrams are intended to illustrate record types and record relationships. Thus, we now have records denoted by labeled rectangles, and record relationships denoted by labeled, directed arrows. Attributes are now record fields.

The simplest data structure diagram shows only the fields in the record. Typically, the key field is underlined. Some variations include the record name in the upper half of the rectangle containing the field names. More information can be incorporated into the rectangle, however. In some CODASYL environments, this data includes field lengths, access modes, and location modes (see Chapter 9).

One-to-One Relationships

One-to-one relationships are typically represented by combining the entities in data structure diagrams. One logical entity in an E-R model one-to-one relationship becomes an attribute of the other logical entity. For example, the recreation center database needs to have access to the names of persons having memberships but does not really need access to detailed faculty information. Therefore, the one-to-one relationship between faculty and membership is combined with membership containing an attribute for the member's name (see Figure 3–17). Similarly, the student attributes could be added to the membership record.

When attributes from different logical entities are combined like this to form a single record type, the attribute names must frequently be changed to adequately represent the new attributes. The membership record could have a field for identification number, for example, which

FIGURE 3–17
**An Example of a Data
Structure Diagram
Component**

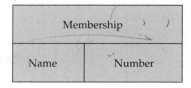

FIGURE 3–18
**A One-to-Many Relation-
ship in a Data Structure
Diagram**

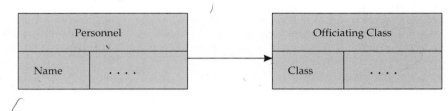

FIGURE 3–19
**A Simple Network in a
Data Structure Diagram**

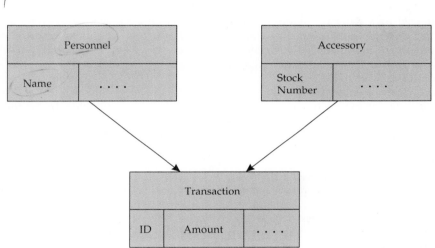

could be either a student's identification number or a faculty member's identification number. Or, the database might keep unique membership numbers and store the identification numbers as an index into other campus databases.

One-to-Many Relationships

One-to-many relationships are the basis of the data structure diagram approach. The entities in the relationship each become record types, represented by rectangles. A directed arrow, pointing toward the "many" side of the relationship, connects the record types. Figure 3–18 illustrates the one-to-many relationship between personnel and officiating classes. Each E-R model rectangle has been converted to the data structure format, and the line points from the "one" side of the relationship to the "many" side.

THE USER'S VIEW

The selection of entities, attributes, and entity classes can be influenced greatly by several factors. Managers' viewpoints differ from those of non-management personnel; the entities of interest to a manager are typically less detailed and more long range in nature. The functional area in which someone works can also have an impact on what entities are considered important. An employee working in a marketing department is quite likely to specify very different entities of interest than an employee working in a production department. A complex organization has many functional areas, each with a unique viewpoint. It is therefore imperative to know what processes are to be supported by a database before any attempt to select and describe entities in an organization is made; otherwise, the database designer is very likely to end up with a large amount of irrelevant data or to omit important data.

When a database is intended to support decision-making across functional areas, it is also important that entities be clearly defined. Different persons in an organization may use different terms for the same concept; they may also use the same terms for different concepts. In the electric utility industry, for example, the meaning of *the date of first operation* of a generating plant varies with different viewpoints.

Financial planners frequently consider the plant to be operating as soon as they begin to depreciate the facilities, whether or not it is generating electricity. Some engineers would say that operation does not begin until electricity is generated, while others hold that it does not begin until the plant is operating smoothly (given the complexity of these plants, this could be as much as two years after the first electricity is generated at the plant).

In some situations, some users may prefer the term *client* to *customer*, or *project* to *assignment*. The terms *revenue, income, fee, charge,* or even *contract value* may be used to refer to the same thing, even though each may actually have a very narrow definition when used appropriately. The term chosen depends on the chooser's background and daily activities. One must be careful to consider the user's orientation when defining entities, attributes, and entity classes. Many database systems allow the user to define aliases or synonyms when several terms are used to refer to precisely the same data item.

Finally, the question of detail must be addressed. One might think that in an ideal situation every detail would be included in the database. Most users tend to indicate that every detail must be included. And while too little detail will certainly result in a failure of the database system to adequately support decision-making, unnecessary detail also causes problems. The more detail included in a database, the more data that must be updated to maintain accuracy. Because the database is a model of an organization, every time a data item in the organization changes the database should also change. When unnecessary detail is maintained in a database, the model quickly begins to lag behind reality. Updating the details fast enough to keep up becomes difficult.

Too much detail may also overwhelm users. Often, as much information may be obtained from a few summary statistics as from all the data. For example, the mean and standard deviations are often much more manageable than a list of 100 numbers. At the heart of this issue is the question, "What information is needed to make the best decision?" The answer to this question is determined by analyzing the information requirements of the decision-making process being supported. The balance between too little and too much detail must be maintained for the good of the user and the database. ■

Many-to-Many Relationships

Many-to-many relationships are modeled directly from the E-R models that have been converted to composite relationships. Each E-R model entity rectangle becomes a data structure rectangle. Directed arrows point toward the record rectangle created from the composite entity rectangle. Figure 3–19 shows how the E-R model in Figure 3–12 illustrating the relationship between personnel and sales transactions has been converted to a data structure diagram.

CHAPTER SUMMARY

Basic concepts of logical database models include attributes, entities, and entity classes. Entities are essentially anything of interest, physical or conceptual. Attributes of entities are characteristics that describe the entity. Entity classes are groups of similar entities, usually distinguished by a particular attribute of interest.

When one builds a logical database model, three steps are taken. First, the entities of interest must be identified. Second, these entities are described by specifying their important attributes. Third, relationships between entities are determined.

Regardless of the relationships in a database, a user rarely needs access to all the data in the database. User views are established to constrain the amount of data a user can access. Sometimes this is done for security purposes.

Tools that aid the production of a logically consistent database design are the entity-relationship model and Bachman diagrams. These approaches have a graphical orientation.

Questions and Exercises

1. Name the three phases of database design. What are the goals of each phase?
2. Define *entity, attribute,* and *entity class.*
3. Give at least three examples of an entity. For each entity, specify at least four attributes. Specify at least three relationships between entities (create new entities if necessary). Justify why you specified the relationships as one-to-one, one-to-many, or many-to-many.
4. Explain the difference between a single valued attribute and a composite attribute. Give an example, and show how each is diagrammed using the E-R model approach.
5. Classify the following relationships as one-to-one, one-to-many, or many-to-many. State any assumptions you are making.
    a. person to driver's license
    b. person to social security number
    c. student to classes taken by a student
    d. employee to dependents
    e. employee to spouse
    f. customer to purchase order
    g. person to hospital admittance record
6. Provide sample data illustrating each of the relationships in Question 5.
7. Describe the major diagram symbols used in the E-R model.
8. How does a single-valued attribute differ from a multivalued attribute? Give an example and show how they are diagrammed using the E-R model approach.

9. Illustrate a one-to-one, one-to-many, and many-to-many relationship using an E-R diagram.

10. Illustrate a many-to-many relationship using an E-R diagram. Include a composite entity with appropriate attributes.

11. Diagram the following relationships using the E-R approach: Cars can have many forms. There are sports cars, trucks, and vans. All of these have wheels. Sports cars have only two seats. Trucks have at least two seats, maybe more. Vans may have many seats. Trucks are characterized by their payload. Vans may be customized for cross-country travel. All cars are characterized by their color and estimated miles per gallon.

12. Convert the E-R diagram for Question 11 into a data structure diagram.

13. Draw an E-R diagram that shows the relationships between faculty, students, departments, and classes at your university. Include several attributes for each entity.

14. Draw an E-R diagram that shows the relationships between customers, bank accounts (checking, savings, and money market), safe deposit boxes, loans, loan managers, deposits, and withdrawals for a banking application. Include several attributes for each entity.

15. Draw an E-R diagram that shows the relationships between airlines, flights, airplanes, and pilots. Include several attributes for each entity.

16. Consider an investment database that contains data items for investor's name, amount invested, stock, broker's name, broker's office address, and broker's telephone. The following assumptions may be made: Investors may invest in many stocks; a broker has only one office; and each broker's office has only one telephone number. Draw an E-R model of this situation. Convert the E-R model to a data structure diagram.

17. Consider a database of transfer-student data intended to maintain data about students transferring into a university. The database contains the following data items: student's name, student's address, student's telephone number, prior university attended, GPA at the prior university, hours earned at the prior university, last date at the prior university, student's sex, student's date of birth, guardian's name, guardian's address, and relationship of guardian to the student. The following assumptions may be made: Students have one address and one telephone number; guardians have one address and one telephone number; and a student may have attended more than one prior university. Draw an E-R model of this situation. Convert the E-R model to a data structure diagram.

18. A database for a local garage is needed. The database contains data items for customer's name, customer's address, customer's work telephone number, customer's home telephone number, date of work done, automobile make, automobile model,

description of work done, parts needed to complete work, charge for parts needed, charge for labor performed, and total charge. For warranty reasons, data must be maintained in the database for at least 90 days; therefore, a customer may have several records in the database at any time. Identical parts have only one cost, but different parts have different costs (e.g., all tires cost the same and all engines cost the same, but a tire and an engine do not cost the same). Draw an E-R model of this situation. Convert the E-R model to a data structure diagram.

19. A small database for a restaurant is needed. The database should contain data for customer's name, reservation date, reservation time, seating preference (booth or table), area preference (indoor or outdoor), number of people dining, and telephone number where the customer can be reached if needed prior to arrival. Assume that a customer makes only one reservation per date, but do not assume that the customer's name will uniquely identify a customer. There may be two John Smiths. Draw an E-R model of this situation. Be prepared to discuss any additional assumptions you make. Convert the E-R model to a data structure diagram.

20. A cable television company desires a database containing data on its customers. The following data items are needed: customer name, customer address, customer telephone number, account number, service provided (basic, movie channel A, movie channel B, movie channel C, and/or children's channel), the charge for each service, equipment used by the customer that belongs to the cable television company (decoder, remote control, etc.), an identifying number for each piece of equipment, and the extra charge (if any) for any equipment used by the customer. Assume that a customer may have more than one account number (some customers have rental properties and use the cable service to make their properties more attractive). Draw an E-R model of this situation. Convert the E-R model to a data structure diagram.

21. Draw an entity-relationship model for the recreation center example in the chapter.

For Further Reading

Data modeling is covered in almost all current textbooks on database design. A classic article outlining the three phases of database design is Teory, T. J., and J. P. Fry. "The Logical Record Access Approach to Database Design," *Computing Surveys* 12, no. 2 (June 1980), pp. 179–210.

For a detailed, very readable explanation of the semantic database model (including a thorough example), the reader is referred to Hammer, Michael, and Dennis McLeod, "Database Description with SDM: A Semantic Database Model," *ACM Transactions on Database Systems* 6, no. 3 (September 1981).

The entity-relationship model is first discussed in Chen, Peter, "The Entity-Relationship Model: Toward a Unified View of Data," *ACM Transactions on Database Systems* 1, no. 1 (March 1976).

For more information regarding the prototyping controversy, the following sources are recommended:

Cerveny, R. "The Application of Prototyping to System Development: A Rationale and Model," *Journal of Management Information Systems* 3, no. 2 (Fall 1986), pp. 52–62.

Huffaker, Debra. "Prototyping Business Applications within the Traditional Life Cycle," *Journal of Information Systems Management* 3, no. 4 (Fall 1986), pp. 71–74.

Licker, Paul S. *Fundamentals of Systems Analysis.* Boston: Boyd and Fraser, 1987.

Whitten, J. L.; L. D. Bentley; and C. Q. Barlow. *Systems Analysis and Design Methods.* St. Louis: Times Mirror/Irwin College Publishing, 1989.

METROPOLITAN NATIONAL BANK

At your request, information has been gathered on the contents of the major computer files, preprinted forms, and reports used most often at the bank. (These documents appear in Appendix B.)

Customer statements. A customer statement, which is made up of a number of sections, is mailed monthly to each customer. The statement contains the customer's name, street address, apartment number, city, state, zip code, and account number. The statement date and the beginning and ending dates for the statement period are in the right corner of the statement. One section of the statement contains the statement summary, which includes the beginning balance, total deposits (including any interest payments), total withdrawals (including any penalties charged), and the ending balance. Another section has a listing of all automated teller transactions. These deposits and withdrawals are annotated with the date, amount, and machine identification number. The final section contains regular deposits (date and amount) followed by regular withdrawals (date, amount, and check number).

Checking account file. The checking account file contains the name, street address, apartment number, city, state, zip code, telephone number, and checking account number. Checking accounts have many monthly transactions. A typical account will have as many as 50 transactions against it per month.

Savings account file. The savings account file contains the name, street address, apartment number, city, state, zip code, telephone number, and savings account number. The fixed interest rate (currently 5.25 percent), which is the same for all savings accounts, is also stored in each record. Historically, savings account transactions are minimal. The average account has two to five transactions per month.

Money market account file. The money market account file contains the name, street address, apartment number, city, state, zip code, telephone number, and money market account number. Money market accounts have a transaction pattern similar to regular checking accounts. The primary difference is that money market accounts require minimum balances of $2,500 to $20,000, depending on the type of money market account owned. The interest rate on these accounts represents the rate on a savings account plus an additional amount. The interest rate schedule for a money market account is as follows:

Average Balance	Rate Added to Basic Savings Rate
$0.00–$2,500.00	0.00%
$2,500.01–$5,000.00	0.50
$5,000.01–$10,000.00	0.75
$10,000.01–$15,000.00	1.00
$15,000.01–$20,000.00	1.25
Over $20,000.00	1.50

This rate schedule, the same for all money market accounts, is also stored in each record.

Checking, savings, and money market accounts have unique account numbers. Therefore, a customer with more than one account will be associated with more than one account number.

Annuity funds file.   MetNat manages several investment funds. These funds provide potential investment opportunities for retirement plans and tax-deferred annuities. Each fund (except the fixed fund) is administered on a per share basis. All investments in a fund are essentially "pooled." An individual investor's portion of the fund is measured in the number of shares that person owns. Share values are determined by the account manager. There are different funds to reflect different investment strategies. The "fixed" fund reflects a very conservative investment strategy. This money is used to invest in safe investments such as municipal bonds. The "managed" fund is slightly more aggressive than the fixed fund. The "market" fund is more aggressive than the managed fund. The "growth" fund is still more aggressive. The "special" fund is the most aggressive (least conservative) fund.

For each investor, each fund is characterized by the share value at the beginning and end of the accounting period and the number of shares that investor owns. If the share value increases, the investor has made money. If it decreases, the investor loses money. The fixed fund is guaranteed, and all other funds are invested at the risk of losing all of the invested amount. The fixed fund earnings rate is the current U.S. government Treasury bill rate. All other earnings rates fluctuate daily with the market conditions.

Loan file.   The loan file contains the name, street address, apartment number, city, state, zip code, telephone number, and the loan account number. It also contains the period of the loan (beginning date and ending date), the principle amount, the total interest amount, the number of months in the loan period, the monthly payment amount, and a description of the collateral securing the loan. Transactions against the loan data typically average only one per month per loan (the monthly payment). Borrowers may pay off the full loan amount at any time.

Safe deposit box file.   The safe deposit box file contains the name, street address, apartment number, city, state, zip·code, telephone number, and the safe deposit box number. The file also contains the box size (3×5, 5×5, 5×10, 10×10), rental period (beginning date and ending date), and the rental rate (specified below). Records of entry to safe deposit boxes are maintained. The pattern is random, but a typical safe deposit box renter enters the box only four to six times per year.

Box Size	Rental Charge per Year
3×5	$10
5×5	$15
5×10	$20
10×10	$25

Certificates of Deposit file.   This file contains the name, street address, apartment number, city, state, zip code, telephone number, and the security identification number. The file also contains the security denomination, the deposit period (beginning date and maturity date), and the interest rate. The only transactions against the securities file are monthly interest credits. Of course, the holder of a security may choose to cash the security before it matures. A 10 percent penalty is assessed for exercising this option.

Account registration form. This form is used by new customers to establish an account. It contains the customer's name, street address, apartment number, city, state, zip code, home telephone number, taxpayer identification number (social security number), and date of birth. If the account is a joint account, the other persons that have access to the account must be listed. The prospective customer must also provide employer's name, street address, city, state, zip code, and telephone number; the name of an immediate supervisor or manager; and the number of years worked for the employer. The preferred account name is also requested (primarily for organizations and joint accounts). The applicant may request an automated teller card when the account is opened. An account number (or account numbers) is provided by someone in the accounts administration department.

Loan application form. This form is used to request a loan. It contains the customer's name, street address, apartment number, city, state, zip code, telephone number, taxpayer identification number (social security number), and date of birth. A preprinted loan number appears on each form. The date the loan is needed, the desired loan period (in months), and the amount requested appear on the form. Also available are places to list current accounts held by the customer, loan numbers of outstanding loans, and loan numbers of prior loans. The form also requests the employer's name, street address, city, state, zip code, and telephone number; the name of an immediate supervisor or manager; and the number of years worked for the employer. Also needed are account numbers of credit card(s) held and the name, street address, city, state, zip code, and telephone number of a personal reference, as well as the relationship to that personal reference. The information on employer and personal reference is used to verify employment prior to approving the loan. It is also used to locate the borrower if a default on the loan occurs. The form also contains the purpose of the loan.

Credit card application form. This form is used to request a credit card. It contains the customer's name, street address, apartment number, city, state, zip code, and telephone number. Also available are places to list current accounts held by the customer, loan numbers of outstanding loans, and loan numbers of prior loans. The form also requests the employer's name, street address, city, state, zip code, and telephone number; the name of an immediate supervisor or manager; and the number of years worked for the employer. Also needed are account numbers of credit card(s) held and the name, street address, city, state, zip code, and telephone number of each credit card holder. The applicant may request a specific credit limit. Credit card applications are approved by loan managers, who set a specific credit limit if the requested limit is considered too high.

Credit card file. The credit card file contains the holder's name, street address, apartment number, city, state, zip code, telephone number, and the credit card number and expiration date. The file also contains the regular charges (date, transaction identifier, store name, amount), cash advances from automated tellers (date, amount, machine number), cash advances from courtesy checks (date, check number, amount), the beginning balance, ending balance, interest charged (where appropriate), payments credited, minimum payment due, credit limit, and cash advance limit.

Credit card statement. A credit card statement (i.e., a bill) is mailed monthly to each customer. It is similar in format to the customer's monthly statement. The bill contains the customer's name, street address, apartment number, city, state, zip code, and credit card number. The billing date and the beginning and ending dates for the billing period are in the right corner of the statement. One major section of the statement is the statement summary, which contains the beginning balance, total payments, total charges, ending balance, and monthly interest rate. The next section contains a detailed listing of all charges. These charges are annotated with a unique transaction identifier (system generated), posting date, store name where the purchase occurred, and the purchase amount. Cash advances, which may be made at automated teller machines using the credit card, are annotated with the date, amount, and machine identification number. The statement also contains the minimum payment due, credit limit, and cash advance limit.

Employee data file. Employee data is collected from a standard employee data form, which is completed when a prospective employee applies for a job. This form contains the employee's name, address (including city, state, and zip code), and telephone number. The name, address, and telephone number of someone to call in case of emergency are also on this form. The employee's education level is on this form, including the degree obtained from any educational institution and the date the degree was awarded. The name and address of three prior employers are also maintained on this form. If a request for employment is denied, the reason is noted in an open area of the form.

Once an employee has been hired, the employee file is updated with payroll and insurance information. The employee's job title and salary are included, as are the department in which the employee will work and the name of the immediate supervisor. MetNat participates in a group insurance plan that provides basic health insurance coverage for all employees. Employees have the option of adding further coverage, including life insurance benefits, dental benefits, accidental death and dismemberment benefits, and life insurance coverage for spouse and dependents. Any insurance options exercised by an employee are noted so that proper payroll deductions can be made. Payroll deductions are contained in the following table:

Coverage	Monthly Deduction
Life insurance	$1.50/$10,000 coverage
Dental insurance	$10.00
Accidental death	$0.25/$10,000 coverage
Dependent coverage	$0.50/$10,000 coverage

Optional life insurance coverage is limited to an amount equal to the employee's current annual salary (rounded down to the nearest $1,000). Dependent coverage is limited to $25,000 per dependent. Dependents include spouse and children under age 18. Accidental death is limited to an amount equal to four times the employee's current annual salary (rounded down to the nearest $1,000).

All employees earn sick leave credit at a rate of eight hours per month of employment. A maximum of 80 hours of sick leave may be carried over from one year to the next. Employees with less than three years of service earn vacation leave at a rate of eight hours per month. Employees with three or more years of service earn vacation at a rate of 10 hours per month. A maximum of 40 hours of vacation time may be carried over from one year to the next. All employees receive (and are required to take) a five-week sabbatical vacation after each five years of service.

MetNat Priorities and Policies

Although MetNat services only about 100,000 accounts, the company may have an opportunity in the near future to expand through acquisition. The economy, poor investment strategies, and mismanagement have caused several smaller banks to encounter difficulties recently. If the current trend continues, MetNat could acquire these smaller operations, eventually doubling the number of MetNat's accounts. In addition, a major university has just completed construction of a research park near MetNat's main office building. Several hundred new residents are expected as the facility becomes staffed. More importantly, this installation could act as a magnet for similar facilities and could result in at least a small-scale housing-development boom. MetNat wants to be in position to service the newcomers to the city. MetNat also wants to be a primary lender for new commercial development to build more research facilities and for new-home construction and sales.

MetNat has always taken great pride in being a service-oriented organization. Consequently, any customer-related aspect of the company has a high priority. MetNat must provide approval on credit card charges as quickly as possible. Studies have shown that customers become irritated when the approval process takes much more than one minute. When customers elect to use some other form of payment, MetNat effectively loses the 6 percent sales revenue associated with the credit card use. MetNat must provide approval information almost instantly to compensate for the manual operations associated with the approval process (that is, the store clerk's operations).

Similarly, credit card billing inquiries are handled as quickly as possible. A customer with a question concerning a credit card bill can initiate a billing inquiry by calling a toll-free number. The customer must provide the account number on the bill so that the customer service operator can access the proper records. This process must be supported through a database system of customer information to which the telephone operator has immediate access. Once the telephone operator verifies that the current mailing address in the database is correct, the customer can request information on any aspect of the bill in question. This information includes the purchase for which the customer is being charged, the posted date, the location where the purchase was made, and the amount billed. Although the cost of mishandling these inquiries is not as easily determined, MetNat recognizes that the customer can choose other forms of payment if not satisfied with the MetNat credit card. Customer service requests regarding customer accounts are also handled as fast as possible.

Of course, not every aspect of an organization can be handled in this way; some areas are given lesser priority. One computing aspect of the organization that does not require extremely fast response time is employee data processing. The employee turnover at MetNat is extremely low, and once an employee record is established it requires little updating. Further, operations involving employee data are typically cyclical: payroll is every two weeks and tax data are processed annually. Accesses involving this data are restricted to the employee's name, social security number, and pay scale. Therefore, there is little need to incur any inordinate expense to support this aspect of the organization's data processing. The payroll, however, must always be processed on time. Employee morale influences customer service dramatically.

Monthly customer statements fall into a category between credit card approvals and employee data processing. On the one hand, these statements must be processed on schedule. On the other hand, they can be processed during off-peak processing times (at night, for example) without significant operator intervention. Thus, they represent a critical, but not urgent, processing requirement.

The time has come for a tangible design for MetNat's information system. At the core of the system will be an integrated bank database. This database will consolidate the information stored in files throughout the current system. The next step in your project is to develop an entity-relationship model for this database. ■

4

A FRAMEWORK FOR DATABASE SYSTEM DESIGN

What do you want?

Part I of this textbook concentrated on developing the fundamental concepts and tools needed to accomplish database design. Part II describes the general environments in which the tools developed in Part I are used.

This chapter presents the characteristics that are expected in all database systems as specified by the American National Standards Institute. It provides an opportunity for you to assimilate the details of Part I and serves as a foundation for Chapters 5, 6, and 7.

THE ANSI/X3/SPARC REPORT ON DATABASE SYSTEM DESIGN

In the early 1970s, concern about database system design was growing among industrial and academic researchers and developers. By that time, several documents had been published advocating competing database system designs and specifying various levels of system requirements. Several questions arose: Did existing and proposed database system implementations meet organizational needs? Were all the designs and requirements that had been specified really necessary? Was one design better than another? Were all the requirements specified by any of the designs economically feasible?

The American National Standards Committee on Computers and Information Processing (ANSI/X3) formed a Standards Planning and Requirements Committee (SPARC) to address these questions. In order to get a better grasp on the situation, SPARC formed an ad hoc Study Group on Data Base Management Systems devoted solely to the objective of "determining which, *if any,* aspects of such systems [were] *at present* suitable candidates for the development of American National Standards" (Tsichritzis and Klug, 1978). The "if any" qualification emphasized the concern that inappropriate specification of standards would constrain technological advances. The "at present" qualification recognized the evolving nature of computer-based systems.

The study group listed the many goals of database systems, including increased data utilization, ease of access by authorized users, enhanced data security, enhanced data integrity, integration of the data processing function with the rest of the organization, and increased control of data redundancy. But it emphasized one objective of database systems specifically and in detail—the ability of databases to evolve by developing systems that provide data independence. Many of the aspects of the ANSI/X3/SPARC framework are related to the concept of data independence.

You may recall from Chapter 1 that there are two types of data independence: logical and physical. A system has logical data independence if one user's access and manipulation of elements in a database are isolated from another user's work with the same database element. A system with physical data independence allows actual implementation of the database with no impact on the logical organization of the database.

Data independence insulates a user from the adverse aspects of the evolution of the database environment. The framework developed by the study group was designed to permit evolution in one part of the database system without affecting other parts of the system, that is, to achieve data independence. "Data independence," the study group report noted, "is not the capability to avoid change; it is the capability to reduce the trauma of change." The study concluded that developing database systems with the maximum degree of data independence was imperative. The rest of this chapter illustrates the results of the ANSI study. A framework for database systems design is presented to provide a global picture of the complicated and complex tasks of successful database system design. As you read this chapter, try to evaluate each component of the database framework in terms of that component's ability to enhance data independence.

THREE VIEWS OF DATA IN DATABASE SYSTEMS

Database processing manipulates symbols that represent entities. In the activities required to accomplish data processing, three views of the data exist. Each view corresponds to a specific aspect of the processing. These views occur at the *conceptual* level, the *external* level, and the *internal* level.

The Conceptual Level View

The conceptual level view is the logical data model of the entire database (see Figure 4–1). This model is maintained for all applications supported by the database system. Only one conceptual level view is maintained in the database system.

The conceptual level view is described by a formal description language, which is called a *logical schema* (or sometimes a *conceptual schema*). No entities or attributes can be referred to in the database system unless they are defined in the logical schema. The conceptual level view is the basis for development of the external and internal level views; as such, it must be particularly stable.

Typical database users cannot access the entire conceptual level view. The logical schema is available only to the database administrator, or more generally to the department charged with database administration.

The planning techniques presented in Chapters 1 and 2 and the model-building methodologies presented in Chapter 3 are designed to support successful conceptual level view development. The planning techniques and information requirements analysis in the earliest stages of the database design process help identify the contents of the logical schema. Modeling techniques help ensure that proper relationships are represented.

FIGURE 4–1 **Logical Schema**
Entities are chosen from the enterprise environment for inclusion in the logical schema.

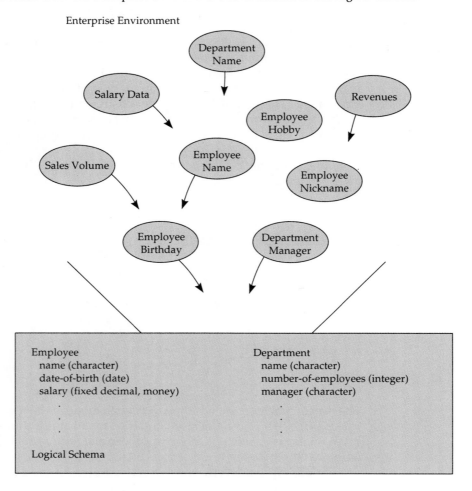

The External Level View

The external level data view focuses on specific data processing applications—or user views (see Figure 4–2). An external level view contains only the subset of the conceptual level view required to support a particular application. Much of the work performed by information analysts is directed toward constructing external level views.

The external level view is described in a description language, one that produces a user view (sometimes known as an *external schema* or a *subschema*). Multiple user views are allowed in a database system because multiple applications are typically supported by the database system. A user view may be a unique subset of the entities in the logical schema or it may be partially or entirely composed of entities that appear in one or more other user views.

FIGURE 4–2   User View

Entities are chosen from the logical schema for inclusion in a user view.

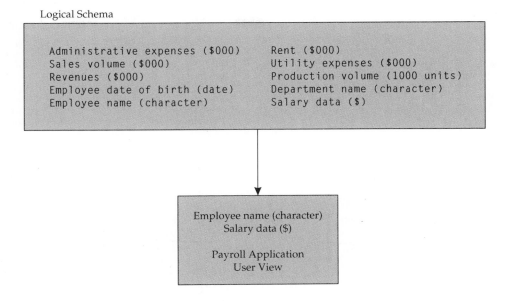

Logical Schema

Administrative expenses ($000)	Rent ($000)
Sales volume ($000)	Utility expenses ($000)
Revenues ($000)	Production volume (1000 units)
Employee date of birth (date)	Department name (character)
Employee name (character)	Salary data ($)

Employee name (character)
Salary data ($)

Payroll Application
User View

A user view need not be composed entirely of entities modeled in the logical schema. Local entities are permitted and are usually defined as temporary storage or as derivations of entities in the logical schema. An average calculated in an application program from data defined in the logical schema is one example of a local entity. Inputs requested by the application are another.

Database users typically have a great deal more latitude in their access and manipulation of a particular user view than with the conceptual level view defined in the logical schema. Ideally, the database system provides a user-oriented, external level schema development language that is easy to use. Such a development language is required to provide proper security and integrity constraints.

The Internal Level View

The internal level view is the data representation maintained for the conceptual view (Figure 4–3). The internal level view defines the internal, physical representation of the database. The internal level view is specified in a *physical schema* (also known as an *internal schema*). The goal of the internal level view is to maximize efficient database system use while meeting the organization's needs.

The physical schema embodies performance strategies. Technical information including the data structures, access paths, and numeric conversion strategies for each entity attribute in the logical schema is specified in the physical schema. All aspects of the physical schema

FIGURE 4–3 Physical Schema
The representation of logical schema entities is described in the physical schema.

Logical Schema

```
Administrative expenses ($000)      Rent ($000)
Sales volume ($000)                 Utility expenses ($000)
Revenues ($000)                     Production volume (1000 units)
Employee date of birth (date)       Department name (character)
Employee name (character)           Salary data ($)
```

Physical Schema

```
Administrative expenses ($000)      Rent ($000)
  floating point, width = 9,          floating point, width = 9,
  decimals = 3                        decimals = 3

Sales volume ($000)                 Utility expenses ($000)
  floating point, width = 9,          floating point, width = 9,
  decimals = 3                        decimals = 3

Revenues ($000)                     Production volume (1000 units)
  floating point, width = 9,          floating point, width = 9,
  chemicals = 3                       decimals = 3

Employee date of birth (date)       Department name (character)
  integer, width = 6                  packed characters, width = 20,

Employee name (character)           Salary data ($)
  packed characters, width = 30       floating point, width = 7,
                                      decimals = 2
```

must, however, work toward representing the conceptual level view. Within this constraint, the internal level view may be altered in any way appropriate for optimization of the database system operation. It may, for example, change to incorporate technological advances that make processing more efficient. Although most database software will generate physical schemas, database analysts are typically employed to fine-tune the system to achieve maximum efficiency. Only one physical schema is maintained in a database system.

Again, typical database users do not generally have access to the physical schema, and, indeed, such access is rarely necessary or desirable. Limited access may be provided when internal data descriptions are absolutely required, but this type of access must be tightly monitored. The database administrator must guard against application development that utilizes knowledge of the internal level view. Such applications are no longer data independent, as explained in the next section.

How the Three Views Achieve Data Independence

The conceptual level view reflects the logical relationships between the database items. Because it is a purely logical description, the conceptual level view is not affected by changes in the physical implementation. Because it always describes all the data in the database, it is also unaffected by changes in external level views.

The placement of the conceptual level view between the internal level view and all external level views provides data independence. Without the logical schema, user views are mapped directly into the physical schema. In such a case, the application supported by the user view becomes dependent on the implementation details reflected in the physical schema. Consequently, changes in the physical schema require changes in the application. Thus, the application is no longer independent of the implementation. This situation is exactly what occurred in traditional file-processing applications. Because physical schema changes are expected (to incorporate technological advances), omitting the logical schema results in an unstable database design. Figure 4–4 repeats Figure 1–10 to show the relationship of the three schemas and the three view levels.

FIGURE 4–4   ANSI/SPARC Three-Level Database Architecture
The external level consists of data as the users view it. The conceptual level is a logical composite of the entire database and is described in the logical schema. The stored data is described in the physical schema at the internal level.

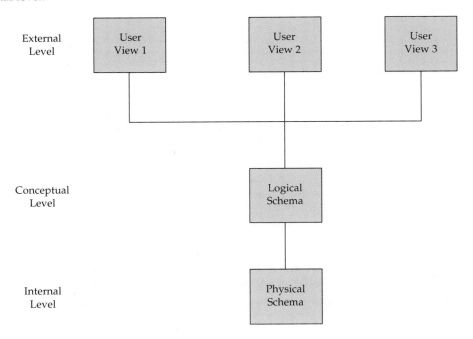

THREE DATA MODELS FOR THE CONCEPTUAL SCHEMA

In the development of the conceptual schema, the database administrator seeks to follow the processes outlined in Chapter 3. The information requirements of the organization are determined, appropriate entities are selected for inclusion in the database, their attributes are defined, and their relationships with other entities are constructed. Three models that are useful as frameworks for the design of the conceptual schema have emerged. These models are alternative ways of picturing the relationships in the database. Each model has implications for implementation in the internal schema. We discuss these models and some of their implementations briefly.

The Hierarchical Model

The oldest of the three models is the hierarchical model. One-to-many relationships are the only logical structure allowed in the hierarchical model. These relationships are often called parent-child relationships, where one occurrence of a record type is associated with many occurrences of a child record type.

A level in a hierarchical model defines how deeply the record type exists in the tree. The root node, or first level, is at level 1. Since other records in a hierarchical model are related to the root node, these records are sometimes referred to as dependent records. Dependent records exist below the root node at levels 2 and 3 and deeper. A hierarchical path is a sequence of records, starting at the root record, in which records alternate from parent to child roles.

In general, any number of record occurrences can exist at levels below the root record—there may be 3 records at level 2, 10 records at level 3, and so on. Each record occurrence at a level below the root node, however, must be related to a record occurrence at a higher level. Only the root node record occurrences are allowed to exist without relation to a higher-level record.

In a hierarchical model, one-to-one relationships are generally replaced by a single record type that combines the data in the two record types in the relationship. This design strategy reduces the relative complexity associated with accessing the hierarchical structure when the structure provides no advantage. One-to-many relationships are modeled naturally in the hierarchical model, since a one-to-many relationship defines a tree. However, a simple network structure, such as the one shown in Figure 4–5a, will require some data redundancy in converting to two trees as shown in Figure 4–5b. Many-to-many relationships must also be decomposed into one-to-many relationships, again incurring some data redundancy.

IMS.　　Perhaps the most widely used database system based on the hierarchical model is IBM's IMS system. Many IMS installations are converting to IBM's relational database product, DB2. However, you

FIGURE 4–5a
Simple Network
An occurrence of a simple
network between pilot, airplane, and flight. Note that
one flight record has two
parent nodes of different
types.

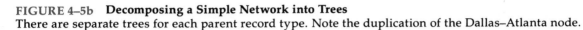

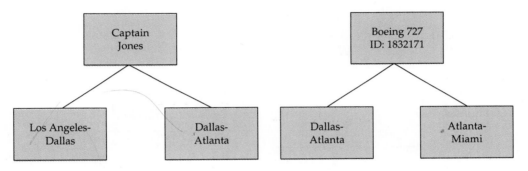

FIGURE 4–5b   Decomposing a Simple Network into Trees
There are separate trees for each parent record type. Note the duplication of the Dallas–Atlanta node.

might encounter an IMS system or be involved in a conversion effort yourself, so we will briefly overview the IMS approach.

In IMS terminology, an attribute is called a *data field*. An occurrence of a data field is called a *data item*. IMS has no explicit domain concept. A record type is called a *segment type,* and an occurrence of a segment type is called a *segment.* Each tree has one segment known as the *root segment.* The root segment is allowed to exist without a parent. A segment that has a parent is called a *dependent segment.* A segment without children is called a *leaf segment.* A tree occurrence is called a *database record,* and a set of database records is called a *database.* One database structure is illustrated in Figure 4–6a. Since an IMS environment may have hundreds of tree structures, there may also be hundreds of "databases."

IMS Access Characteristics. Within a tree occurrence, segments of the same type are called *twins.* Segments of different types but at the same level are called *siblings.* Each segment type exists on one and only one hierarchical path from the root to the segment type. The segments in a tree have an ordering predefined by a **hierarchical sequence.** The hierarchical sequence is a result of both the value of a designated **sequence field** in each segment and the relative positioning of the segment in the hierarchical structure.

FIGURE 4–6a
Hierarchical Structure

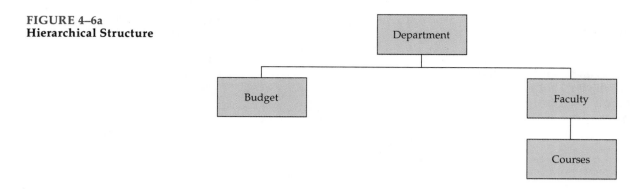

FIGURE 4–6b   **Example Records for the Structure in Figure 4–6a**

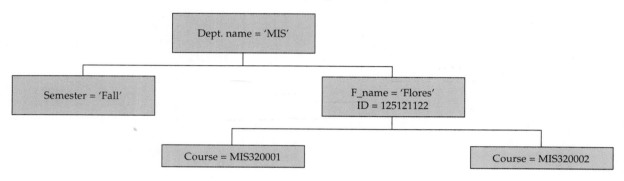

Each segment occurrence in a tree has a unique **hierarchical sequence key** value. A segment's hierarchical sequence key value is a code identifying its segment type code and sequence key value, prefixed by the hierarchical sequence key value for its parent. Figure 4–6b shows the hierarchical sequence key values for example records from the structure in Figure 4–6a. The root segment is required to have unique sequence field values. Dependent segment types may have their sequence fields defined as unique within occurrences of the parent.

The hierarchical sequence mechanisms impart an ordering on the segments. This ordering can then be exploited by the data manipulation language, DL/1. For example, once a BUDGET record has been located in the database, then the next COURSE record can be obtained with a command such as

    GET NEXT COURSE RECORD

If the MIS320001 record was the record being processed prior to executing this command, then the MIS320002 record would be the next processed.

Network Representation in IMS. We mentioned earlier that simple networks would require total decomposition in a database system based strictly on the hierarchical model. Due to the resulting data redundancy, IMS uses logical pointers to represent simple network structures.

Whenever multiple parent segment types are required, multiple tree structures are defined, but only one child segment type actually contains data. The other "redundant" occurrences of the child type contain logical pointers to the segments that contain the data.

Although this approach solves the data redundancy problem, it has some faults. First, the segments actually containing data will be located close to the parent segments to which they are connected. These child segments may not be close to the segments that contain the logical pointers that point to the data. Thus, accessing the trees containing the segments with the pointers may be (in most cases will be) less efficient than accessing the trees with segments that contain the data.

Second, there is little data independence here. Given the efficiency consideration just mentioned, the database designer must determine how the data is most likely to be accessed in order to choose the tree in which the data will actually be stored. Unless one query type clearly dominates all other query types, some types of queries must suffer the inefficiency. And, the types of queries made today may not be the types made tomorrow. Thus, database reorganization may be required when the information requirements change slightly.

User Views. User views are called *logical databases* in IMS. Logical databases may be constructed from physical databases as long as the logical database root is also a physical database root. Thus, there is little data independence in the IMS environment.

Other examples of an overlap of physical and logical schemas exist. For example, a dependent segment occurrence cannot exist without a parent segment type occurrence. In a situation where, for example, there is a one-to-many relationship between managers and employees, the employee record cannot be inserted until it is assigned to a particular manager. This constraint precludes having a new employee record in the database before the employee is assigned to a manager. This situation may not reflect the actual situation, especially if some formal training period exists. Similarly, if a manager quits, the manager record cannot be deleted until the employee records are reassigned to another manager. Deleting the manager record would violate the constraint that dependent segments must have a parent segment.

Although we've pointed out some of the disadvantages, the IMS system has several advantages, too. It has existed for years and has been a relatively stable product, and very many IMS installations still exist. The hierarchical approach is relatively simple and straightforward. Many people adapt quickly to thinking in terms of hierarchical structures. Also, performance prediction is simplified due to the predefined relationships. An IMS database can provide very fast access to data when the underlying relationships are hierarchical.

The Network Models

The next step in data modeling complexity removes the tree structure restriction that a child record have only one parent record. Removing this constraint allows network structures to exist. A simple network structure allows overlapping one-to-many relationships; a complex network structure allows many-to-many relationships.

Most large corporate mainframe DBMS are based on the network model, which is obtained by a simple extension of the hierarchical model. It is quite likely that you may be involved in a conversion project sometime (perhaps very early) in your information systems career. Thus, you need to be familiar with both the network and relational database models. The most widely used network model is the simple network model known as the CODASYL (Conference on Data and Systems Languages) model. The architecture of a CODASYL system is shown in Figure 4–7. Each application program, called a **run unit,** is associated with a subschema. The subschema defines the user view associated with that program. The subschema is a subset of the entire CODASYL database that is defined in the schema.

The CODASYL approach is built upon the concept of a CODASYL *set.* The set resembles a tree structure. There is an **owner record type,** which is similar to a parent record type in a tree structure, and a **member record type,** which is similar to the child record type. A major difference, however, is that member record occurrences can exist in more than one set. Thus, a member record type can be associated with more than one owner record type. Simple network structures are constructed by "overlapping" sets (see Figure 4–8).

FIGURE 4–7
Architecture of a CODASYL System
Run units are executing applications programs. Data is transferred between the database and the run unit via the user work area. The subschema describes the run unit's view of the database. The schema describes the global database in logical terms. Run units B and C share subschema B/C.

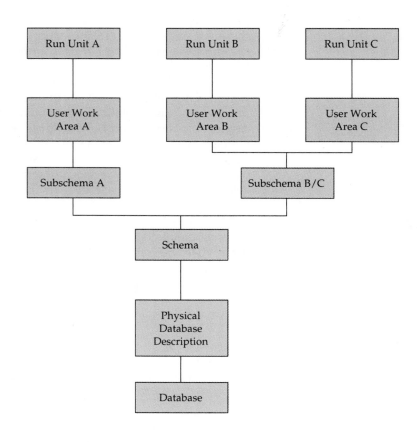

FIGURE 4–8   Example CODASYL Sets for a Portion of the Structure in Figure 4–6

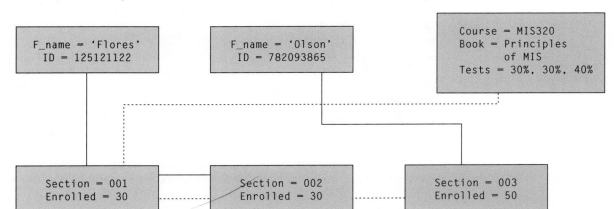

Each run unit is allocated a portion of main memory, called a **user work area (UWA),** for transferring data values between applications programs and the database. The database items under control of the subschema invoked by the run unit are each assigned a location in the work area. The run unit accesses that work area by using the data item names assigned in the subschema. The run unit may use data manipulation commands to instruct the DBMS to move data from the database to the work area, or to move data from the work area to the database.

The CODASYL approach reduces the data redundancy problem inherent in the strictly hierarchical implementation, as well as the potential integrity problems. On the other hand, allowing more than one parent record adds some complexity to the data navigation process. As in the hierarchical approach, the relationships (sets) must be defined ahead of time. Still, the basic owner-member mechanism is easily understood (as is the hierarchical parent-child mechanism), and hence the network models have received widespread acceptance. And network implementation is relatively direct, because here too the relationships are explicitly specified in the schema.

The CODASYL approach has many of the advantages associated with the hierarchical approach. It has existed for years and is now a relatively stable commodity, and very many installations exist. The network approach is relatively simple and straightforward, and most people adapt quickly to thinking in terms of sets, owners, and members. As in the hierarchical model, performance prediction is simplified due to the predefined relationships. A CODASYL database can be very efficient for stable database environments. Chapter 9 is devoted to the CODASYL model, so further discussion is deferred to that chapter.

The Relational Model

The relational model, developed by Dr. E. F. Codd, takes a different approach to relationship representation. The relational model maintains data in tabular form. This is another very familiar data representation.

Most people have worked with data in tabular form since their early elementary school days. The relational model is the only data model that maintains the logical simplicity of flat file structures, that is, file structures in which there are no repeating fields. The data from Figure 4–8 is shown in a relational format in Figure 4–9.

A relation is a two-dimensional table that contains data about an entity class or the relationships between entity classes. Each row of a table contains data about a specific entity, and each column contains data about a specific entity attribute. The intersection of a row and column may contain only atomic, or single-valued, data. Multiple values are not allowed at a row/column intersection.

A major distinction of the relational model, when compared to the hierarchical and network models, is that no explicit reference is made to relationships between entity classes in a relational schema. (A portion of a relational schema is shown in Figure 4–16.) The relationships between entity classes must be implied in the relational model by using pairs of attributes.

The relational approach is based on the well-developed mathematical theory of relations. This rigorous foundation provides a number of advantages not evident in the other approaches. Data manipulation facilities, for example, can be defined much more formally. A theoretical basis also allows a more objective comparison of relational database implementations than is possible with the hierarchical or network approaches.

The relational approach has different advantages than those associated with the hierarchical and network approaches. Albeit younger than the other models, it is becoming widely accepted in database environments. Although many early implementations varied widely from the theoretical basis, relational DBMS software is moving toward the theory. Besides being easy to understand and implement, the relational model provides the most flexible access to data.

Unlike the hierarchical and network models, however, performance prediction is not direct because the relationships are not predefined. In

FIGURE 4–9 **Relational Format for the Data in Figure 4–8**

FACULTY			CLASSES	
F-name	ID		Course	Book
Flores	125121122		MIS320	Principles of MIS
Olson	782093865			

SECTIONS				TESTS		
ID	Course	Section	Enrolled	Course	Test	Weight
125121122	MIS320	001	30	MIS320	1	30
125121122	MIS320	002	30	MIS320	2	30
782093865	MIS320	003	50	MIS320	3	40

fact, the performance of many early relational implementations was simply unacceptable. However, strategies for implementing relational database queries (called query optimization) have evolved that can make relational data manipulation much more efficient. A principal advantage of the relational approach is that the relationships are more flexible. Anywhere that the appropriate pair of attributes exists between entity classes a relationship can be exploited. Thus, the relational approach is very good in dynamic decision-making environments. Because most database installations are moving to the relational approach, we will devote three chapters to the relational model in this book. Chapter 5 addresses database model refinement using relational examples for illustrations. Chapter 6 covers the basic model; Chapter 7 addresses relational data manipulation using SQL.

CONSTRUCTING A SET OF SCHEMAS

To illustrate the general process of constructing conceptual, internal, and external level views, we examine a subset of a hospital database.

Data Model Construction

The first step in the schema generation process is constructing an accurate data model using the techniques discussed in the first three chapters. Tools have been developed in recent years that take some of the drudgery out of this work. These tools are known as computer-assisted software engineering (CASE) tools. You may have studied one or more of these tools in a systems analysis course. One such tool for database design is the E-R Modeler, which is developed and marketed by Chen and Associates. It supports development of E-R diagrams (see Chapter 3), and converts the E-R diagram information into a schema. E-R Modeler can generate schemas appropriate for many popular database management systems.

The E-R Modeler interface is shown in Figure 4–10. The small, solid square in the middle of the grid is a cursor that indicates where a symbol will be placed. A user can select the E-R symbol that is needed by choosing "Icon" from the menu. The symbol will be placed in the grid at the current cursor position. Assume an important relationship in our database is the one between patients and their insurers. We can use E-R Modeler to capture this information. Figure 4–11 shows the contents of the model just prior to adding the insurer entity.

Once entities are placed on the grid, they may be connected by choosing "Conn" from the menu. The cursor is first placed on a grid square containing one of the entities being connected; then "Conn" is selected. Next, E-R Modeler instructs the user to move the cursor to the grid area containing the other entity being connected and select "Conn" again. When these instructions have been carried out, the screen interface shown in Figure 4–12 appears. Here, the user enters information

FIGURE 4–10
E-R Modeler Interface
Empty grid used for E-R diagram construction.

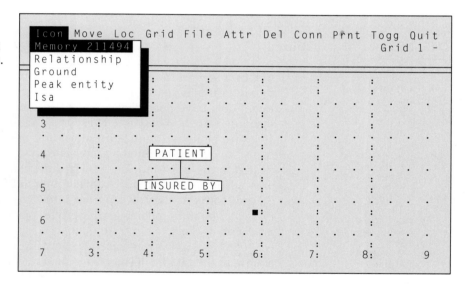

```
Icon Move Loc Grid File Attr Del Conn Prnt Togg Quit
Memory 211494                                  Grid 1 -
```

FIGURE 4–11
E-R Modeler
Sample screen from the E-R model development process.

about the connection, such as whether it is one-to-one, one-to-many, or many-to-many.

Each attribute of an entity or relationship can be described via the interface shown in Figure 4–13. This interface is activated by selecting "Attr" from the menu. This figure illustrates the information that would be entered for the patient entity. Each attribute is described by the attribute name, an abbreviation for the name, the attribute domain (number, character, or date), an indicator whether the attribute is a key attribute (Y for *yes*, N for *no*), and an optional comment describing the attribute.

FIGURE 4–12
E-R Modeler
Sample screen illustrating
the cardinality specification
during entity connection.

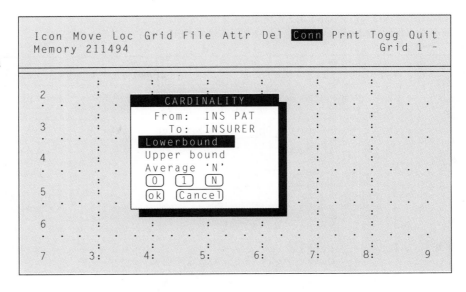

FIGURE 4–13   E-R Modeler Interface
Entity and attribute definition using E-R Modeler.

```
Append  Insert  Delete  Find  Update  Move  Remark  Comments  ruLes  Quit

Cell Name: PATIENT       Cell Type: Entity      #Attr: 9      # Conn: 1
Remark:
```

1	P_MED_REC_NO Patient identification number	P_ID	C,9	Y
2	P_NAME Patient name	P_NAME	C,30	N
3	P_STREET Local street address	P_ADDRESS	C,25	N
4	P_CITY Local city address	P_CITY	C,30	N
5	P_STATE Local state address	P_STATE	C,2	N
6	P_ZIP Local address zip code	P_ZIP	C,9	N
7	P_PHONE Local telephone number	P_PHONE	C,10	N
8	P_SEX Sex code (M/F)	P_SEX	C,1	N
9	P_DATE_OF_BIRTH Date of birth	P_DOB	D	N

FIGURE 4–13   E-R Modeler Interface
Entity and attribute definition using E-R Modeler.

```
Append  Insert  Delete  Find  Update  Move  Remark  Comments  ruLes  Quit

Cell  Name:  INSURER        Cell  Type:  Entity        #Attr:  7        #  Conn:  1
Remark:

1        INSURER_ID                        I_ID              C,3
         Insurer  identification  number                                      Y

2        I_NAME                            I_NAME            C,30
         Insurer  name                                                        N

3        I_STREET                          I_ADDRESS         C,25
         Local  street  address                                              N

4        I_CITY                            I_CITY            C,30
         Local  city  address                                                N

5        I_STATE                           I_STATE           C,2
         Local  state  address                                               N

6        I_ZIP                             I_ZIP             C,9
         Local  address  zip  code                                           N

7        I_PHONE                           I_PHONE           C,10
         Local  telephone  number                                            N
```

```
Append  Insert  Delete  Find  Update  Move  Remark  Comments  ruLes  Quit

Cell  Name:  PAT_INSURER  Cell  Type:  Relationship  #Attr:  3  #Conn:  1
Remark:

1        POLICY_NUMBER                     POL_NO            C,15
         Local  address  zip  code                                           Y

2        PI_MED_REC_NO                     PI_ID             C,9
         Patient  identification  number                                     Y

3        INSURER_ID                        IN_ID             C,3
         Insurer  identification  number                                     Y
```

The information collected during the model-building process can be summarized in report form by E-R Modeler, generating the report shown in Figure 4–14. These reports provide documentation automatically from the E-R diagram. Because documentation often lags behind actual implementations, any system that provides documentation automatically is more likely to have documentation that is current and reliable.

FIGURE 4–14
E-R Modeler
Sample report documenting
E-R model.

```
                    PATIENT-INSURER REPORT

Cell Name: Entity INSURER
Abbreviation: INSURER
Comm:

    Connections List

    Entity INSURER  abbrev: INSURER
    to Entity PATIENT  abbrev: PATIENT
    through Relationship INSURED_BY  abbrev: INS_PAT

    CARDINALITY                 CARDINALITY
    lower  =  1                 lower  =  1
    upper  =  N                 upper  =  N
    lower n  =  1               lower n  =  1
    upper n  =                  upper n  =
    average n  =                average n  =


    Cell Name: Entity PATIENT
    Abbreviation: PATIENT
    Comm:

    Connections List

    Entity PATIENT  abbrev: PATIENT
    to Entity INSURER  abbrev: INSURER
    through Relationship INSURED_BY  abbrev: INS_PAT

    CARDINALITY                 CARDINALITY
    lower  =  1                 lower  =  1
    upper  =  N                 upper  =  N
    lower n  =  1               lower n  =  1
    upper n  =                  upper n  =
    average n  =                average n  =

Cell Name: Relationship INSURED_BY
Abbreviation: INS_PAT
Comm:

    Connections List

    Relationship INSURED_BY  abbrev: INS_PAT
    to Entity INSURER  abbrev: INSURER

    CARDINALITY
    lower  =  1
    upper  =  N
    lower n  =  1
    upper n  =
    average n  =


    Relationship INSURED_BY  abbrev: INS_PAT
    to Entity PATIENT  abbrev: PATIENT

    CARDINALITY
    lower  =  1
    upper  =  N
    lower n  =  1
    upper n  =
    average n  =
```

E-R Modeler also provides a means to enter the business and integrity rules that are associated with a relationship. These rules indicate constraints associated with insertion, deletion, and update procedures that ensure that database integrity is maintained. E-R Modeler also allows a user to specify functional dependencies. Functional dependencies are another type of constraint that, when left unconsidered in database design, can result in unstable designs. Functional dependencies and the assumptions embedded in business and integrity rules are covered in detail in Chapter 5, the chapter on database normalization. At this point, E-R Modeler takes these inputs and generates a "normalized" design, one that is resilient to the problems caused when these rules are not incorporated into the design.

Once this process has been completed, the database designers and the hospital administration would have a set of diagrams similar to the ones shown in Figure 4–15a and 4–15b.

The Conceptual Level View

The Relational Model.   A schema can be generated automatically by E-R Modeler from the normalized design. The conceptual level view reflects the relationships in the E-R diagram. Figure 4–16 shows the logical schema as it would be written in the NOMAD2 schema description language. NOMAD2 has a relational orientation, although it also provides for hierarchical representations. Entity classes are represented as "masters," and attributes are "items" within a master in NOMAD2. We begin with a description of the patient entity.

Patients have a name, address, next of kin, and other attributes. Each attribute's characteristics are given in the logical schema. A patient's name, for example, is a character string up to 30 characters long.

FIGURE 4–15a
E-R Diagram from E-R
Modeler Software for
Hospital Database

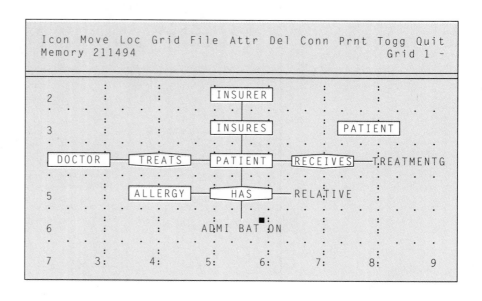

FIGURE 4–15b **Data Structure Diagram for the Hospital Database**

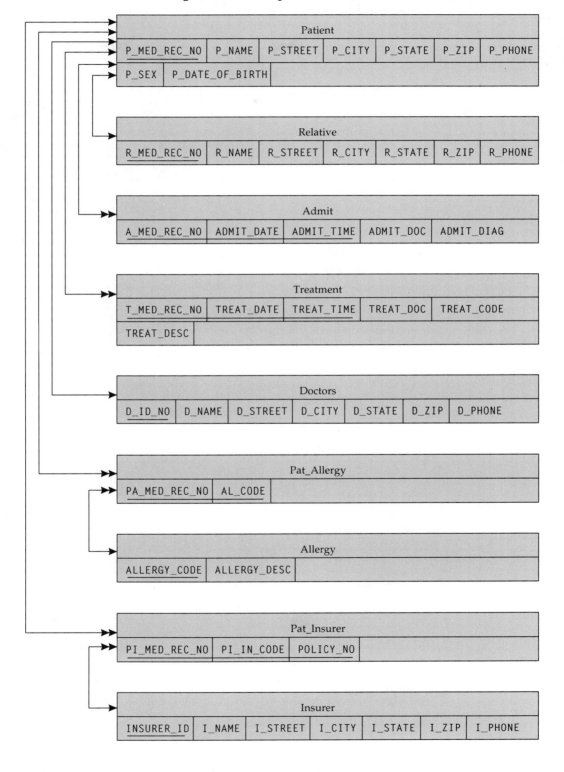

FIGURE 4–16   **A NOMAD2 Logical Schema for the Hospital Database**

```
SCHEMA HOSPITAL;
PASSWORD XYZZY;

MASTER PATIENT KEYED P_MED_REC_NO DISK A ACCESS ALL;
ITEM P_MED_REC_NO AS 9999999 HEADING 'PATIENT: ID';
ITEM P_NAME AS A30 HEADING 'NAME';
ITEM P_STREET AS A25 HEADING 'STREET';
ITEM P_CITY AS A30 HEADING 'CITY';
ITEM P_STATE AS A2 HEADING 'STATE';
ITEM P_ZIP AS 999999999 FORMAT '99999-9999' HEADING 'ZIP';
ITEM P_PHONE AS 9999999999 FORMAT '(999) 999-9999' HEADING 'PHONE';
ITEM P_SEX AS A1 HEADING 'SEX';
ITEM P_DATE_OF_BIRTH AS DATE ALIAS P_DOB HEADING 'DATE OF:BIRTH';

MASTER RELATIVE KEYED R_MED_REC_NO DISK A ACCESS ALL;
ITEM R_MED_REC_NO AS 9999999 ALIAS RELATED_PAT_CODE HEADING 'PATIENT: ID';
ITEM R_NAME AS A30 HEADING 'NAME';
ITEM R_STREET AS A25 HEADING 'STREET';
ITEM R_CITY AS A30 HEADING 'CITY';
ITEM R_STATE AS A2 HEADING 'STATE';
ITEM R_ZIP AS 999999999 FORMAT '99999-9999' HEADING 'ZIP';
ITEM R_PHONE AS 9999999999 FORMAT '(999) 999-9999' HEADING 'PHONE';

MASTER INSURER KEYED INSURER_ID DISK A ACCESS ALL;
ITEM INSURER_ID AS 999 ALIAS I_ID HEADING 'INSURER ID';
ITEM I_NAME AS A30 HEADING 'NAME';
ITEM I_STREET AS A25 HEADING 'STREET';
ITEM I_CITY AS A30 HEADING 'CITY';
ITEM I_STATE AS A2 HEADING 'STATE';
ITEM I_ZIP AS 999999999 FORMAT '99999-9999' HEADING 'ZIP';
ITEM I_PHONE AS 9999999999 FORMAT '(999) 999-9999' HEADING 'PHONE';
ITEM I_MED_REC_NO AS 9999999 ALIAS PAT_INSURED_CODE HEADING 'PATIENT: ID';

MASTER ADMIT KEYED A_MED_REC_NO, ADMIT_DATE DISK A ACCESS ALL;
ITEM A_MED_REC_NO AS 9999999 ALIAS PAT_ADMIT_ID;
ITEM ADMIT_DATE AS DATE FORMAT 'MM/DD/YY';
ITEM ADMIT_TIME AS TIME 'HH24:MM';
ITEM ADMIT_DOC AS A30;
ITEM ADMIT_DIAG AS A500 ALIAS DIAGNOSIS;

MASTER TREATMENT KEYED T_MED_REC_NO, TREAT_DATE, TREAT_TIME DISK A
  ACCESS ALL;
ITEM T_MED_REC_NO AS 9999999 ALIAS PAT_TREAT_ID;
ITEM TREAT_DATE AS DATE FORMAT 'MM/DD/YY';
```

FIGURE 4–16   continued

```
ITEM TREAT_TIME AS TIME 'HH24:MM:SS';
ITEM TREAT_DOC AS A30;
ITEM TREAT_CODE AS MEMBER 'TREAT_TABLE';
DEFINE TREAT_DESC AS
  EXTRACT 'TREATMENT_TEXT FROM TREAT_TABLE USING TREAT_CODE';

MASTER TREAT_TABLE KEYED T_CODE DISK B;
ITEM T_CODE AS A3 HEADING 'TREATMENT: CODE';
ITEM TREATMENT_TEXT AS TEXT HEADING 'TREATMENT';

MASTER DOCTORS KEYED DOC_ID_NO DISK A ACCESS ALL;
ITEM DOC_ID_NO AS 9999999 HEADING 'PHYSICIAN: ID';
ITEM D_NAME AS A30 HEADING 'NAME';
ITEM D_STREET AS A25 HEADING 'STREET';
ITEM D_CITY AS A30 HEADING 'CITY';
ITEM D_STATE AS A2 HEADING 'STATE';
ITEM D_ZIP AS 999999999 FORMAT '99999-9999' HEADING 'ZIP';
ITEM D_PHONE AS 9999999999 FORMAT '(999) 999-9999' HEADING 'PHONE';

MASTER ALLERGY KEYED ALLERGY_CODE DISK B;
ITEM ALLERGY_CODE AS A3 ALIAS AL_CODE HEADING 'ALLERGY: CODE';
ITEM ALLERGY_DESC AS A30 HEADING 'DESCRIPTION';

MASTER INSURE_COMP KEYED INSURER_CODE DISK B;
ITEM INSURER_CODE AS A3 ALIAS IN_CODE HEADING 'INSURER: ID';
ITEM IN_NAME AS A30 HEADING 'NAME';
ITEM IN_STREET AS A25 HEADING 'STREET';
ITEM IN_CITY AS A30 HEADING 'CITY';
ITEM IN_STATE AS A2 HEADING 'STATE';
ITEM IN_ZIP AS 999999999 FORMAT '99999-9999' HEADING 'ZIP';
ITEM IN_PHONE AS 9999999999 FORMAT '(999) 999-9999' HEADING 'PHONE';

MASTER PAT_ALLERGY KEYED PA_MED_REC_NO, AL_CODE DISK A ACCESS ALL;
ITEM PA_MED_REC_NO AS 9999999 ALIAS PAT_AL_ID HEADING 'PATIENT: ID';
ITEM AL_CODE AS MEMBER 'ALLERGY' HEADING 'ALLERGY: CODE';
DEFINE AL_DESC AS EXTRACT'ALLERGY_DESC FROM ALLERGY USING AL_CODE' HEADING
  'DESCRIPTION';

MASTER PAT_INSURER KEYED PI_MED_REC_NO, PI_IN_CODE, POLICY_NO DISK
  A ACCESS ALL;
ITEM POLICY_NO AS A15 HEADING 'POLICY:NUMBER';
ITEM PI_MED_REC_NO AS 9999999 ALIAS PI_IN_ID HEADING 'PATIENT: ID';
ITEM PI_IN_CODE AS A3 HEADING 'INSURER ID';
```

This characteristic is indicated by the AS A30 part of the description of the P_NAME item in Figure 4–16. The admission date (ADM_DATE) and time (ADM_TIME) reflect special data types supported by many database languages.

The logical schema description reflects the relationships between the entity classes. The patient entities are related in a one-to-many fashion to treatments, for instance. This relationship is implied by the choice of the patient's medical record number (T_MED_REC_NO), the treatment date (TREAT_DATE), and the treatment time (TREAT_ TIME) as the key. Patients have a many-to-many relationship with insurers. Thus, the patient–insurer intersection relationship is modeled as another master in the schema (PAT_INSURER). As we noted in Chapter 3, the intersection relationship records typically contain information specific to the relationship. In this case, the policy number for the patient's insurance policy is stored here. This relationship is examined in more detail below.

Sample data for the relational implementation is shown in Figure 4–17. Be careful to note that the relationships between the tables are *implied* by the data attributes; they are not explicitly modeled in the schema. In the hierarchical and network models discussed in the next two sections, explicit links between record types will be defined in the schema. In the relational model, however, relationships between tables are established via data values of attributes established on common domains. The arrows in Figure 4–17 indicate which rows in each table are logically related to rows in another table. *The arrows in Figure 4–17 do not represent explicit links in the database. The arrows are only added to remind*

FIGURE 4–17   Sample Data in a Relational Format for the Hospital Database

Patient

P_MED_REC_NO	P_NAME	P_STREET	P_CITY	P_STATE	P_ZIP	P_PHONE	P_SEX	P_DOB
82173	SMITH	142 MAPLE	ATLANTA	GA	30311	758-1267	M	9/23/56
39721	JONES	192 APPLE	MACON	GA	30340	268-4112	F	2/27/61

Insurer

INSURER_ID	I_NAME	I_STREET	P_CITY	P_STATE	P_ZIP	P_PHONE
301	ALLCITY	421 PECAN	ATLANTA	GA	30339	762-5212
832	CITY & FARM	1010 CAIN	ATLANTA	GA	30338	761-1131
421	BILLCO	8921 STATE	MACON	GA	30340	268-1821

PAT_Insurer

POLICY_NUMBER	PI_MED_REC_NO	INSURER_ID
83-217-9A	82173	301
4271-022-F3	82173	832
29134	39721	421
83-217-9B	82173	301

us that the relationships are maintained in the data. The intersection relationships appear again, this time as a separate table.

The Hierarchical Model.   Figure 4–18 illustrates the general structure for one implementation of the conceptual schema in a (strictly) hierarchical type of database system. In this case, patient records exist in a hierarchy with the other record types. The arrows between the structures represent explicit links that would exist between records in the database. Although IMS is not a strictly hierarchical system, we will use IMS to illustrate the hierarchical schema for the hospital database. We will focus again on just the patient-insurer relationship.

From the E-R diagram in Figure 4–15, we can determine that three entity types are involved: patients, insurers, and the patient-insurer intersection. Because the hierarchical approach is based on one-to-many relationships, the E-R diagram indicates converting to a hierarchical implementation should be a direct process. We need to determine which records will be included in which tree structures and simultaneously determine which record will be the parent and which will be the child.

The relationships in the E-R diagram translate directly into trees. The "one" side of the one-to-many relationship becomes the parent, the "many" side of the relationship becomes the child. In a strictly hierarchical implementation, we would construct two trees, with duplicate child records. IMS provides logical pointers for this purpose.

Figure 4–19a contains just enough of an IMS database description (DBD) to give you a feeling for it. The DBD is roughly equivalent to a physical schema, with exceptions. For example, when a user view that spans multiple tree structures is required, this view is defined in the DBD (see the last DBD definition in the figure). Figure 4–19b contains the program communication block (PCB), which is the IMS version of a user view that does not span multiple trees. As you can see, there is

FIGURE 4–18   General Structure of the Relationships in the Hospital Database for a Hierarchical Implementation

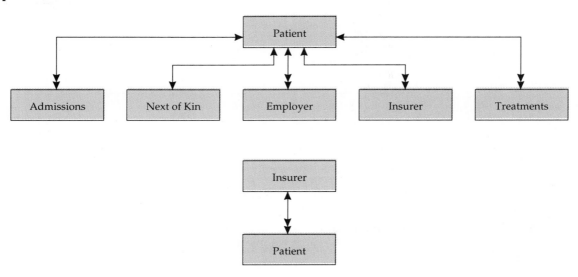

FIGURE 4–19a
IMS DBD
The patient-insurer
relationship in IMS,
internal schema.

```
DBD              NAME=HOSP_PAT
SEGM             NAME=PATIENT, BYTES=100
FIELD  NAME= (P_MED_REC_NO, SEQ), BYTES=7,START=1
FIELD  NAME= P_NAME,BYTES=30,START=8
FIELD  NAME= P_STREET, BYTES=25,START=33
FIELD  NAME= P_CITY,BYTES=30,START=63
FIELD  NAME= P_STATE, BYTES=2,START=65
FIELD  NAME= P_ZIP,BYTES=9,START=74
FIELD  NAME= P_PHONE,BYTES=10,START=84
FIELD  NAME= P_SEX,BYTES=1,START=94
FIELD  NAME= P_DATE_OF_BIRTH,BYTES=6,START=95
SEGM             NAME=PAT_INSURER,BYTES=25
FIELD  NAME= (POLICY_NO, SEQ),BYTES=15,START=1
FIELD  NAME= PI_MED_REC_NO,BYTES=7,START=16
FIELD  NAME= PI_IN_CODE,BYTES=3,START=23

DBD              NAME=HOSP_INS
SEGM             NAME=INSURER,BYTES=95
FIELD  NAME= (INSURER_ID, SEQ),BYTES=3,START=1
FIELD  NAME= I_NAME,BYTES=30,START=4
FIELD  NAME= I_STREET,BYTES=25,START=34
FIELD  NAME= I_CITY,BYTES=30,START=59
FIELD  NAME= I_STATE,BYTES=2,START=61
FIELD  NAME= I_ZIP,BYTES=9,START=70
FIELD  NAME= I_PHONE,BYTES=10,START=79
FIELD  NAME= I_MED_REC_NO,BYTES=7,START=89

DBD              NAME=HOSPINS,ACCESS=LOGICAL
DATASET          LOGICAL
SEGM             NAME=INSURER,SOURCE=(INSURER,HOSP_INS)
SEGM             NAME=PAT_INSURER,PARENT=INSURER,
                 SOURCE=(PAT_INSURER, HOSP_PAT)
DBDGEN
FINISH
END
```

FIGURE 4–19b
IMS PCB
The patient-insurer
relationship in IMS,
user view.

```
PCB              TYPE=DB,DBDNAME=HOSPPAT,KEYLEN=25
SENSEG  NAME= PATIENT,PROCOPT=G
SENSEG  NAME= PAT_INSURER,PROCOPT=G
PSBGEN  LANG= COBOL,PSBNAME=HOSP_PSB
END
```

little data independence in the IMS approach. The database administrator must incorporate user view concepts into the physical schema description. These two concepts together (in a way) represent the schema.

The Network Model.   Figure 4–20 illustrates a general network implementation. The relationship between patient and insurer reflects the only change in this structure from Figure 4–18. Because the CODASYL approach is the most common network model basis, we will illustrate a

FIGURE 4–20   General Structure of the Relationships in the Hospital Database for a Network Implementation

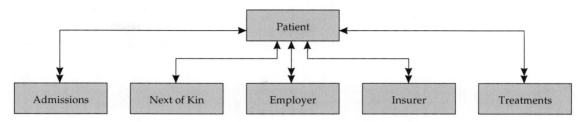

network schema as it would be implemented in the SEED database management system. SEED is a CODASYL-based system developed by the United Telecom Group.

From the E-R diagram in Figure 4–15, we can determine that three entity types are involved: patients, insurers, and the patient-insurer intersection. Like the hierarchical approach, the CODASYL approach is based on one-to-many relationships and the E-R model indicates that converting to a CODASYL implementation should be straightforward. This time, we need to determine which records will be included in which sets, and at the same time determine which record will be the set owner and which will be the set member. Unlike the hierarchical model, however, we are not concerned with how many owners a member might have.

The relationships in the E-R diagram translate directly into sets. The "one" side of the one-to-many relationship becomes the set owner, and the "many" side of the relationship becomes the member. The SEED schema for just the patient-insurer relationship is illustrated in Figure 4–21.

The CODASYL approach specifies all the record types first, followed by all of the set types. The set descriptions provide the only mechanism for relating the data in two record types. Explicit links are maintained between the set owner and the first set member, and between each of the set members (in a linked-list fashion). Other links (for example, backward links) may also be specified. However, if a relationship goes unspecified in the schema, the corresponding link will not be constructed and there will be no way of relating the record types involved in the unspecified relationship.

There are many optional and default constraints that are incorporated into CODASYL schemas. The schema sample presented in Figure 4–21 is minimal. CODASYL databases are covered in detail in Chapter 9.

The External Level View

Two possible external level user views, described again in the NOMAD2 schema description language, are shown in Figure 4–22. Figure 4–22a is a summary of admissions and vital data. It combines name and sex from

FIGURE 4–21
Example CODASYL Schema
This subset of a SEED schema illustrates a typical CODASYL schema language.

```
SCHEMA NAME IS NETWORK.
PRIVACY LOCK IS EXAMPLE.

RECORD NAME IS PATIENT
   LOCATION MODE IS CALC USING PATIENT_ID.
PATIENT_ID IS CHARACTER 9.
P_NAME IS CHARACTER 25.
P_ADDRESS IS CHARACTER 30.

RECORD NAME IS INSURER
   LOCATION MODE IS CALC USING INSURER_ID.
INSURER_ID IS CHARACTER 3.
I_NAME IS CHARACTER 25.
I_ADDRESS IS CHARACTER 30.
I_PHONE IS CHARACTER 10.

RECORD NAME IS POLICY
   LOCATION MODE IS VIA INSURED_BY.
POLICY_NO IS CHARACTER 10.
EXPIRATION_DATE IS INTEGER.

SET NAME IS INSURED_BY
   MODE IS CHAIN LINKED TO PRIOR
   ORDER IS LAST
   OWNER IS PATIENT
   MEMBER IS POLICY MANDATORY
   SELECTION IS THRU CURRENT OF SET.

SET NAME IS CLIENTS
   MODE IS CHAIN LINKED PRIOR
   ORDER IS SORTED
   OWNER IS INSURER
   MEMBER IS POLICY
   SELECTION IS THRU CURRENT OF SET.
```

the patient master, calculates the patients age using the patient's date of birth, and includes allergy data from the allergy master and admission data from the most recent admission occurrence. NOMAD2 defines user views by specifying the masters and data items that are not available to the view. Thus, the items that are not removed are available. The age calculation demonstrates how a local data item may be created. Only items defined in this external level schema are available to an application using this user view. Data regarding a patient's next of kin, for example, is unavailable to the application.

Figure 4–22b view gathers data required for an insurance claim. This view draws on the information stored in the patient, treatment, and insurance masters. The patient-insurance intersection master would be used to determine to which insurance companies a claim should be mailed. As in Figure 4–22a, masters that have been removed are unavailable to an application using this user view.

FIGURE 4–22a
A NOMAD2 User View of Admissions and Vital Data for the Hospital Database

```
PROFILE ADMIT_VIEW
/*
   REMOVE UNNEEDED ITEMS FROM PATIENT MASTER
*/
REMOVE P_STREET P_CITY P_STATE P_ZIP P_PHONE,
/*
   REMOVE UNNEEDED MASTERS
*/



       REMOVE RELATIVE INSURER TREATMENT DOCTORS
   INSURE_COMP PAT_INSURER;

/*
   DEFINE NEW AGE ITEM
*/

DEFINE AGE IN PATIENT AS 999
EXPR=INTERVAL(&DATE,DOB,YEARS);
```

FIGURE 4–22b
A NOMAD2 User View of Insurance Claim Data for the Hospital Database

```
PROFILE INSURANCE_VIEW
/*
   REMOVE UNNEEDED MASTERS
*/

REMOVE RELATIVE DOCTORS INSURE_COMP PAT_INSURER;

/*
   DEFINE AGE FIELD IN PATIENT MASTER
*/

DEFINE IN PATIENT
   AGE AS 999 EXPR=(&TODAY — DOB);
```

The Internal Level View

The internal level physical schema for a NOMAD2 database is generated by "compiling" the conceptual schema and the user views. In NOMAD2, this form is known as the schema internal translation (SIT). This compiled form is used internally by NOMAD2 and is not accessible by the user. The physical schema follows the form of the logical schema, but with additional file and default item information added. Additional NOMAD2 statements can be used by database analysts to modify the schema if the internal level view generated automatically by the NOMAD2 compilation process is unsatisfactory.

THE USER'S VIEW

External schemas define user interfaces with the database system and are the primary views of a database seen by users. In fact, external schemas are sometimes called *user views*. A user may occasionally have an opportunity to examine in detail the conceptual schema in an organization's master plan for database development; rarely does a user see an internal schema.

Each type of schema is important to the user, however. The design of the internal schema deter-mines the efficiency of the database system. The efficiency is reflected in the **response time** of the system, a measure of the speed of the system's response to a user's request. If the internal schema is not well designed, the response time is long. The conceptual schema is also important to users, since it ultimately defines the available data. Users are not very tolerant of circumstances in which they do not have access to required data because it does not exist in the conceptual schema. ∎

A similar compilation process is used by the SEED network database management system. The schema is compiled using a utility known as the file description processor (FDP). The subschema is compiled using SUBFDP. As in NOMAD2, database analysts have commands that can be added to a schema (or subschema) to "optimize" the typical database operations. Although such technological efficiency concerns are important, they are outside the scope of this textbook and thus will not be considered further.

CHAPTER SUMMARY

In response to growing concern from industry and academia, the ANSI/ X3/SPARC Study Group on Database Management Systems was formed to determine which, if any, aspects of database systems should be considered for standardization. In addressing this challenge, the study group outlined a framework for database systems based on three views of data.

The conceptual view of data is the subset of the real world to be maintained in the database system. This view of the organization contains the entities, attributes, and relationships that are important to the organization. The database administrator is responsible for constructing, validating, and maintaining this view. Only one conceptual view exists in a database system.

The external view of data is the subset of the conceptual schema seen by a particular application area. Applications programs and ad hoc user interaction are constructed around external views. There can be many external views in a database system.

The internal view of the data is seen in the implementation of the conceptual view. The internal view is designed by database analysts for efficient operation of the database system. In constructing the internal view, the database analyst considers the information requirements reflected in the conceptual schema. As new technologies emerge, the

Metropolitan National Bank

The next phase of your information system review must consider the database views that need to be implemented. You have asked members of the bank's functional areas to provide you with descriptions of their primary tasks. They have given you the following information.

Accounts Administration Department

The vice president of accounts administration has little need for detailed account information. His primary responsibility is for establishing department policy, marketing the bank's services to prospective customers, and helping the board of directors establish strategic planning objectives. Occasionally, the vice president will get involved in a question on a specific account, but only for very important accounts, such as those held by corporate leaders in the community, or major accounts held by large commercial customers. Even in these cases, the vice president usually has an account manager access the data needed to resolve the problem. The vice president serves primarily as the interface to the community.

Account managers, on the other hand, must have complete access to customer accounts. They may review all activity on checking, saving, and money market accounts. They may update any of the accounts files to add or delete bank charges. In other words, the account manager has the authorization to assess charges or excuse any charges assessed by the bank. Charges are assessed automatically by applications programs when, for example, an account is overdrawn or too many withdrawals are made against a money market account. Account managers may not alter the deposits or withdrawal entries in the account.

Tellers handle the routine deposits into and withdrawals from an account. Tellers have access to all information in an account. They cannot assess or excuse penalties. If a withdrawal or deposit amount is incorrectly posted, a teller can issue a compensatory transaction to correct the balance. The teller cannot delete an incorrect transaction.

The accounts administration department does not access any other files not mentioned here.

Loans Administration Department

The vice president of loan administration serves in a similar role to the VP of accounts administration. This vice president's primary responsibility is as an interface to the community. Lately, the VP has been meeting with companies that are considering expansion into the research park recently built in the city. These companies may require loans to help establish new facilities. Several entrepreneurs have also approached MetNat regarding start-up funds for new research and development companies. And at least two independent home builders are interested in financing the purchase of major tracts of land near the research park to start housing developments. Although the VP rarely gets involved in the details of a specific loan, he may operate as his counterpart in accounts administration: directing a loan manager to access an account to resolve some issue and then acting as the interface to the customer. As with the VP in accounts administration, this type of involvement is reserved for major customers.

Loan managers, on the other hand, require access to all loan file information. Once established, the parameters of a loan are very rarely changed. However, the bank can assess charges for late payments. Thus, the loan managers have the same flexibility as account managers in assessing or excusing penalties. Penalties are assessed automatically by applications programs that process loan payments. However, the loan managers can excuse these penalties under certain circumstances.

Loan clerks handle the routine payments against a loan. They have access to all information about a loan. They cannot assess or excuse penalties. If a payment amount is incorrectly posted, an administrative assistant can issue a compensatory transaction to correct the balance. The loan clerk cannot delete an incorrect transaction.

Because they manage the credit card operations, loan managers and clerks have access to credit card data, too. Only loan managers or the VP can authorize a change in the credit limit of a card holder. Otherwise, the parameters of how employees of loans administration can access the credit card information is analogous to their access privileges for loan information.

The loans administration department does not access any other files not mentioned here.

Special Services Department

The vice president of special services fills many roles, due to the nature of this department. Her primary responsibility is to coordinate the department's areas with the other functional areas in the bank. Her goal is providing accounts administration and loans administration with support services that they require. This vice president feels she has little need to access any of the data files at the bank. She delegates projects to one of the three areas in the department and responds as needed to coordinate these projects.

Marketing. The marketing manager requires summary information about bank customers. This information is primarily demographic. It is used to determine where advertising is needed, which bank services need to be promoted, how the services need to be promoted, and so on. This manager wants her area to have access to all demographic data available at the bank. She does not believe she needs any detailed information regarding bank or credit card transactions. Summary information, such as totals, could be useful in identifying trends however.

The marketing administration assistants perform analyses requested by the marketing manager. Since the area also maintains the brochures that contain information about the bank's services, these assistants are responsible for keeping this documentation current. This documentation is maintained on diskettes. MetNat has invested in desktop publishing software, which is used to develop the brochures. Final versions of brochures are delivered on diskette to a typesetter (who also prints MetNat customer checks and deposit slips), who produces the final brochure.

Customer Service.   The customer service representatives rely on all the other functional areas to provide data they need. Their processes are manual. Customer service representatives complete a form requesting information that is sent to the appropriate department, which supplies the information and returns the form to the customer service representative. The customer service representatives feel this arrangement is satisfactory and prefer not to be bothered with learning new computer-based systems.

Financial Planning.   The financial planners' primary need is data controlled by loans administration, since many of their clients have exceeded their credit card limits or are having difficulty paying back loans. Often, the solution recommended by the financial planner is a loan that is used to pay back all other loans. This effectively consolidates the client's loan payments into a single payment, the one used to pay back the MetNat loan. The financial planner drafts a personal loan plan, which must be authorized by a loan manager, and helps the client establish a living allowance.

The other major service provided by financial planners involves tax-deferred annuities and retirement plans. The financial planners determine the amount to be contributed to the plan and how it will be invested, based on the client's lifestyle and personal goals. In this capacity, the financial planner needs to authorize automatic withdrawals from accounts and automatic contributions toward certificates of deposit and other securities. The financial planner does not have the authority to modify these accounts, however.

Computer Services

As chief information officer, you manage the information systems in the bank. Your primary responsibility is to design, develop, and maintain the computer-based systems required to support all aspects of the bank's operations. Your predecessors have focused on *data processing* and were preoccupied with making the bank's operations more efficient. You have been charged with *information management,* and your mandate is to use information technology to make the bank's operations more effective as well as more efficient. You do not require access to any of the specific data files that exist at MetNat.

Your two managers, the computer operations manager and the applications manager, do not need access to any of the specific files described earlier either. Of course, they manage the utilization of these files, and the programs whose proper functioning the managers must ensure must access these files. However, successful management of these areas does not require an ability to modify any of the bank's files.

The systems programmers and programmer analysts work with simulated data in files that have the same structure as the actual files. They do not have access to the actual data files.

Human Resources

The human resources department requires access to the employee data file. This department has complete access to this data. They can modify the data as necessary to support the human resources function.

Based on this information, you should identify the contents of an integrated database that will support the bank's operations. Begin by identifying the entities that exist in each user view. Integrate the user views into a conceptual schema. State explicitly the relationships (for example, one-to-many) between the entities in the conceptual schema. List the data items that will describe each entity in the conceptual schema. For each attribute in the conceptual schema, describe how the attribute will be represented in the internal schema. (For example, you might determine that customer name requires 25 bytes of characters.) ■

internal view is revised. There is only one internal view in a database system.

The key to understanding the framework designed by the study group is the concept of data independence. The views are constructed in such a way that changes in the internal view do not affect applications or external views, and changes in an external view (or application) do not affect any other external view.

Three data models have evolved to model the relationships in a conceptual schema. The hierarchical model allows only tree structures. The network models allow either simple or complex networks. The most widely used network model is the CODASYL model, a simple network model. The relational model uses tables to structure data relationships.

Questions and Exercises

1. Name and describe the three views of data in a database system.
2. How many external schemas may exist in a database system?
3. What restrictions, if any, exist regarding the database items accessed by different external schemas in a database system?
4. Name and describe each of the data models that are used in describing logical schemas. How are these models alike or different?
5. Give an example of each of the three views of data for a university database system, a police department database system, and a hospital database system.
6. For the user views you described in Question 5, illustrate an implementation using the hierarchical model.
7. For the user views you described in Question 5, illustrate an implementation using the CODASYL model.
8. For the user views you described in Question 5, illustrate an implementation using the relational model.
9. Consider an INVESTMENT database that contains data items for investor's name, amount invested, stock, broker's name, broker's office address, and broker's telephone number. The following assumptions may be made: Investors may invest in many stocks; a broker has only one office; and each broker's office has

only one telephone number. (In Chapter 3, you drew an E-R model and data structure diagram of this situation.) Illustrate an implementation of this situation using the hierarchical, CODASYL, and relational approaches.

10. Consider a database of TRANSFER-STUDENT data intended to maintain data about students transferring into a university. The database contains the following data items: student's name, student's address, student's telephone number, prior university attended, GPA at the prior university, hours earned at the prior university, last date at the prior university, student's sex, student's date of birth, guardian's name, guardian's address, and relationship of guardian to the student. The following assumptions may be made: Students have one address and one telephone number; guardians have one address and one telephone number; and a student may have attended more than one prior university. (In Chapter 3, you drew an E-R model and data structure diagram of this situation.) Illustrate an implementation of this situation using the hierarchical, CODASYL, and relational approaches.

11. A database for a local garage is needed. The database contains data items for customer's name, customer's address, customer's work telephone, customer's home telephone, date of work done, automobile make, automobile model, description of work done, parts needed to complete work, charge for parts needed, charge for labor performed, and total charge. For warranty reasons, data must be maintained in the database for at least 90 days; therefore a customer may have several records in the database at any particular time. Identical parts have only one cost, but different parts have different costs (for example, all tires cost the same and all engines cost the same, but a tire and an engine do not cost the same). (In Chapter 3, you drew an E-R model and data structure diagram of this situation.) Illustrate an implementation of this situation using the hierarchical, CODASYL, and relational approaches.

12. A small database for a restaurant is needed. The database should contain data for customer's name, reservation date, reservation time, seating preference (booth or table), area preference (indoor or outdoor), number of people dining, and telephone number where the customer can be reached if needed prior to arrival. Assume that a customer makes only one reservation per date, but do not assume that the customer's name will uniquely identify a customer. There may be two John Smiths. (In Chapter 3, you drew an E-R model and data structure diagram of this situation.) Illustrate an implementation of this situation using the hierarchical, CODASYL, and relational approaches.

13. A cable television company desires a database containing data on its customers. The following data items are needed: customer's name, customer's address, customer's telephone number, account number, service provided (basic, movie channel A,

movie channel B, movie channel C, and/or children's channel), the charge for each service, equipment used by the customer that belongs to the cable television company (decoder, remote control, etc.), an identifying number for each piece of equipment, and the extra charge (if any) for any equipment used by the customer. Assume that a customer may have more than one account number (some customers have rental properties and use the cable service to make their properties more attractive). (In Chapter 3, you drew an E-R model and data structure diagram of this situation.) Illustrate an implementation of this situation using the hierarchical, CODASYL, and relational approaches.

14. In Chapter 3, you drew an E-R model and data structure diagram of the recreation center example. Illustrate an implementation of this situation using the hierarchical, CODASYL, and relational approaches.

15. How are relationships between data items defined in a CODASYL database system?

16. How are relationships between data items defined in a relational database system?

17. Why is data independence *not* realized in a typical file-based information processing system?

18. Do users need to have knowledge of the internal schema description of a database? What kind of access, if any, should users be given to the internal schema?

For Further Reading

Details of the ANSI/X3/SPARC framework report are presented in: Tsichritzis, Dennis, and Anthony Klug. "The ANSI/X3/SPARC DBMS Framework Report of the Study Group on Database Management Systems," *Information Systems* 3 (1978), pp. 173–91.

5

NORMALIZED DATABASE DESIGN

T his chapter focuses on developing robust database designs. In Chapter 3, we presented tools and methods for designing a database system. Chapter 4 gave an overview of the major models and discussed how to create schemas for each. In this chapter, we provide relational examples that will help us distinguish between good and bad database designs. Although we use the relational model to illustrate concepts, the techniques we present here are also applicable to hierarchical and network models of database implementation.

THE GOALS OF NORMALIZATION

There are many possible designs for the data structures used in a database system. In the long run, some designs are better than others. We consider one design superior to another if it (1) makes the relationships in the database easier to understand and simpler to maintain, (2) is more amenable to processing new requests for data, (3) reflects the semantics, or meaning, of the situation being modeled, (4) prevents the storage of invalid information, and (5) can be represented efficiently using available hardware and software.

Whenever data items (or attributes) have been haphazardly grouped into records (or rows in relations), one or more of the five properties mentioned above is compromised. When data items that are logically unrelated (or logically independent) are aggregated, users become confused. Such groupings also make maintenance difficult because the relationships being maintained are unclear. Finally, new requests for data may require substantial work (1) to determine if the data item being supplied is the one desired, or (2) to create new (possibly more logical) groupings.

When these events occur, the database system may quickly become regarded as ineffective or useless. Experience has shown that most problems can be traced to improper, or unsound, conceptual database designs. Such designs represent monetary losses to management; they require frequent restructuring of the database to accommodate new demands and longer times to implement changes, and they result in ineffective use of the organization's data asset.

Normalization is a technique that structures data in ways that help reduce or prevent problems. The normalization process results in logically consistent record structures that are easy to understand and simple to maintain. Various levels of normalization may be obtained. Criteria that define the levels of normalization are called **normal forms.**

In this chapter, we examine database designs in order to identify their weak and strong points. We present this material as an intuitive approach to the concept of normalization. Consequently, you may find that you have already developed a "sixth sense" for some of the material discussed in this chapter.

Rarely is a manager required to recite the criteria of the various normal forms. Nevertheless, a manager must be familiar with the ramifications of poor database design. As the criteria for higher levels of normalization are met, database system designers are able to say with confidence that certain problems (to be discussed shortly) will never exist.

Several types of problems that may result from poor database design are presented in this chapter. Each of several sources of these problems is examined in detail, and in each case alternative database designs are developed.

MODIFICATION ANOMALIES

To help recognize the differences among alternative database designs, it is useful to examine how mistakes may be inadvertently introduced into a database. Mistakes may occur during insertion, deletion, or modification of data in the database. When the mistake is a consequence of the design of the database, a **modification anomaly** is said to exist. Figures 5–1 through 5–4 will be used to illustrate modification anomalies and the processes that resolve them.

Deletion Anomalies

Consider the relation in Figure 5–1. This table contains data about employees, the department in which they work, the projects on which they are working, and the manager of the project. The primary key of a data structure is underlined. The data structure in Figure 5–1 suffers from a number of problems. If Baker decides to leave the company, and the tuple (row) or record containing the Baker data is deleted from this database, all data recording that Cody is the manager of the project to identify new investment possibilities is lost. The removal of one logical entity that results in the loss of information about an unrelated logical entity is called a **deletion anomaly.** An anomaly (in general) is a deviation from whatever is expected. This deletion has unexpected results: Data regarding a project manager is lost when data about an employee is deleted.

FIGURE 5–1   BUSINESS Relation

ASSIGNMENT E-Number	Name	Department	Project	P-Number	Manager
1001	Adams	Accounting	New billing system	26716	Yates
1001	Adams	Accounting	Mailing list maintenance	23835	Kanter
1002	Baker	Finance	Identify new investments	43873	Cody
1003	Clarke	Accounting	New billing system	26716	Yates
1003	Clarke	Accounting	Purchasing system design	34761	Yates

Another example of a deletion anomaly can be seen in the table in Figure 5–2. This data structure contains data regarding travel plans for members of a private travel club. This organization maintains vacationing facilities worldwide. Notice that if W. Earp decides to cancel the vacation in London and the corresponding tuple is deleted, all data regarding the cost of traveling to London is lost.

A third example can be seen in the medical data shown in Figure 5–3. In this design, the admitting doctor's office address is lost when patient data is deleted. One could argue that this data is no longer needed after a patient's data is deleted. But a reentry of the doctor's office address is highly likely, and thus a data structure that maintains this information is preferable.

A final example is shown in Figure 5–4. This data structure contains data on insurance agents and their clients. As you can see, should policy

FIGURE 5–2   TRAVEL-CLUB Relation

TRAVEL-CLUB Membership Number	Member	Local Address	Destination	Cost	Travel Date
3246	W. Earp	Laramie	London	$1200	7/10
5498	B. Jones	Los Angeles	Madrid	$1500	7/12
8730	R. Steele	Hollywood	Los Angeles	$ 900	6/30
0653	D. Tracy	New York	Madrid	$1500	7/05
6593	J. Friday	San Francisco	Los Angeles	$ 900	7/04

FIGURE 5–3   MEDICAL Relation

MEDICAL-DATA Medical Record Number	Patient Name	Admission Date	Admission Time	Diagnosis	Admitting Doctor	Doctor's Address	Patient's Employer	Employer's Address
76154	Grimes	7/09	6:04	Cardiac Arrest	Barnum	129 Medical Pkwy.	Billco	3562 S. Industrial Blvd.
65429	Robinson	7/09	10:46	Heat Exhaustion	Fraser	104 Medical Pkwy.	P & R Co.	1100 Northcreek, Ste. 200
27635	Lisauckis	7/09	13:20	Stress:Job	Barnum	129 Medical Pkwy.	Gaines HS	1209 Washington Ave.
65283	Hargrove	7/09	18:14	Childbirth	Barnum	129 Medical Pkwy.	N/A	N/A

FIGURE 5–4   INSURANCE Relation

Insurance Policy Owner	Address	Policy Number	Agent	Agent's Address	Premium
Smith	124 Main St.	8906253	Brown	505 Georgia Ave.	$300
Lucas	1704 Hadlock St.	7856253	Jones	818 Enfield St.	$450
Murphy	1210 Marcel Ave.	3482674	Brown	505 Georgia Ave.	$380
Wade	750 Leslie Ave.	6282748	Brown	707 Texas Ave.	$510
Hammock	31 Venetian Dr.	7621938	Jones	818 Enfield St.	$280

owners Lucas and Hammock cancel their policies, all information about insurance agent Jones is lost. As in the medical data example, a data structure that maintains this data is preferable.

Insertion Anomalies

The data structures in Figures 5–1 through 5–4 have a second kind of defect. Suppose that a new project is planned for the organization illustrated in Figure 5–1 and one wants to add data regarding the manager of that project. Because E-Number is part of the primary key and key attributes may not be null, adding this data is impossible until at least one person has been assigned to work on the project.

The insertion of data about one logical entity that requires the insertion of data about an unrelated logical entity is called an **insertion anomaly.** In this case, inserting data about a project manager requires insertion of an unrelated piece of data—a worker assigned to the project.

The same type of insertion anomaly can be seen in Figure 5–2. These designs require that a member of the club be planning to vacation in a particular location in order for cost data about that location to be inserted in the data structure. Consequently, adding cost data about travel to a new location is not possible.

In Figure 5–3, data on a new doctor's office cannot be inserted until a patient is admitted by the doctor. The data about a doctor's office is important even when the doctor has no patients, but the current design precludes maintaining this information. A data structure design that allows insertion of this data regardless of the doctor's current patient load is preferable.

Figure 5–4 shows the same type of problem. An insurance agent's address cannot be inserted until the agent has a client. As with the medical data, this restriction is unacceptable.

Update Anomalies

Refer again to Figure 5–1. Suppose that a project gets a new manager. The design in Figure 5–1 requires a change in several tuples. The modification of the information for one logical entity that requires more than one modification to a relation is called an **update anomaly.**

The same sort of problem exists in Figure 5–2. If the cost of travel to Madrid changes, the modification must be made in more than one place. Similarly, a modification to an admitting doctor's office address (or an employer's address) in Figure 5–3 can require changes in many occurrences. The same problem is evident with an insurance agent's address in Figure 5–4.

In these examples, the update anomaly does not appear to be a costly design error, because very few rows are shown in the figures. The flaw becomes much greater if thousands of occurrences are maintained. Imagine the impact of such a design error in a student information management system for a major university with 30,000 students.

The Role of Assumptions in Identifying Anomalies

To identify modification anomalies, as we have in the examples above, we rely on some unstated assumptions. Such assumptions should be made explicit to avoid inaccurately identifying anomalies. In Figure 5–1, for example, we assume that all employees have one, unique employee number. We also assume that projects have unique project numbers and that each has only one manager. We do not assume that employees have unique names, but we do assume that organizations (that is, employers) have unique names. These are reasonable assumptions.

Consider the data in Figure 5–2. Can we conclude from this relation that the Destination data item always determines the Cost attribute? Although such a conclusion appears evident, we cannot reach this conclusion based on the data in the relation. We must rely on an underlying assumption that the cost for travel to a particular destination is always the same.

Such assumptions depend on the underlying policies of the organization. You should *always* confirm relationships between data items by examining the underlying assumptions. Data structures are time-invariant, but data items assume various values over time. Consequently, as a designer of a database structure, you must consider the underlying (time-invariant) relationships to identify modification anomalies.

AVOIDING PROBLEMS DUE TO DEPENDENCE

The modification anomalies discussed above all stem from the fact that the value of one data item can be determined from the value of a second data item, while the other data items in the data structure are logically independent of this relationship. The name of a project in Figure 5–1, for example, can be determined from the number of the project. The value of the project name data item "depends" on the value of the project number data item.

We introduce here the use of bubble charts to diagram this notion of dependence. To indicate when attributes that compose a key have relationships with non-key attributes, we circle attributes that compose a concatenated primary key. Figure 5–5 shows an arrow from the P-Number data item to the Manager data item. The direction of the arrow indicates which item depends on the other. In this case, Manager depends on P-Number. The diagram also indicates that P-Number determines project name.

In Figure 5–2, there is a relationship between Destination and Cost of traveling to that destination that exists independently of who travels there. Travel to Madrid, for example, always costs $1,500, regardless of who plans to go to Madrid. Travel to Los Angeles is always $900. This is diagrammed in Figure 5–6.

FIGURE 5–5
Dependency Diagram for the Data Structure in Figure 5–1

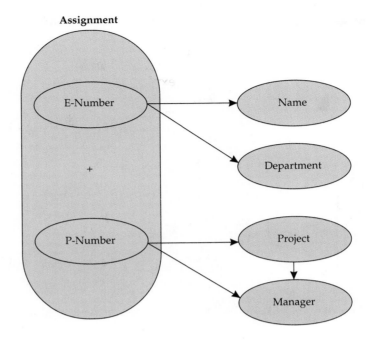

FIGURE 5–6
Dependency Diagram for the Data Structure in Figure 5–2

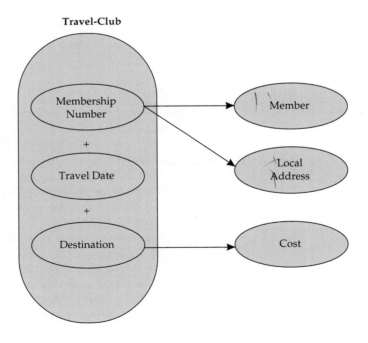

Figure 5–7 shows the dependency diagram for the medical data structures. In this diagram, some of the arrows come from the circle denoting the primary key, indicating that the key determines the data item. Medical Record Number and Admission Date and Admission Time *taken together* determine, for example, Admitting Doctor.

FIGURE 5–7   **Dependency Diagram for the Data Structure in Figure 5–3**

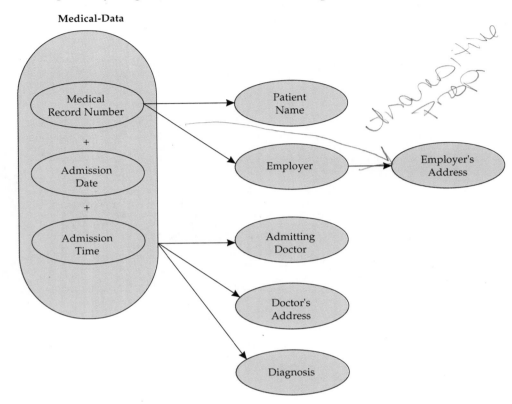

Figure 5–8 shows the dependency diagram for the insurance data structures. Here the primary key is composed of a single data item, so there is no confusion about what is determined by the components of the primary key.

Problems that exist in the data structure in Figure 5–1 can be found by examining the dependency diagrams of data items relative to the primary key. Notice that we must combine two data items (E-Number and P-Number) to form a key for this data structure. The project name, however, can be completely determined if we know just the P-Number. The project name is not dependent on which employee is currently assigned to the project. Whenever such a combination of conditions exists, modification anomalies are also present. In general, a design in which the non-key attributes are dependent on all of the key attributes, and not just any subset of them, is better.

Functional Dependence

From the previous examples, we can introduce the concept of *functional dependence*. **Functional dependence** exists between two data items in a data structure if the value of one data item implies the value of a second

FIGURE 5–8
Dependency Diagram
for the Data Structure
in Figure 5–4

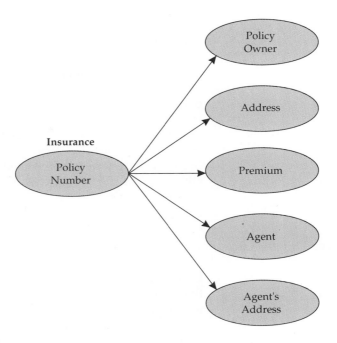

data item. We say that the first data item "determines" the second, and we frequently refer to the first data item as a **determinant.**

Note that there is no requirement for unique values in this discussion. Yates, for example, appears as a manager of two different projects in Figure 5–1. A common misconception about functional dependencies is that the attribute being determined cannot occur more than once in the data. Actually, the important point is that the same manager name appears for every instance of a particular project name. That the manager's name appears more than once is irrelevant.

There is a second common misunderstanding about functional dependence. When a data item (or collection of data items) determines another data item, the second data item does not necessarily determine the first. In the data structures mentioned above, that Yates is a manager does not determine the name of the project Yates manages.

Full Functional Dependence

In cases where the value of a combination of data items determines the value of another data item, we wish to distinguish further between the times when the entire combination of values is required to make the determination and when a subset of the combination of values is adequate. A data item is said to be **fully functionally dependent** on a combination of data items if it is functionally dependent on the combination of data items and not functionally dependent on any proper subset of the combination of data items. A proper subset of a set is any subset of that set except the set itself and the empty set.

If we examine the design in Figure 5–5, we can see that E-Number alone determines employee Name (because an employee has a unique employee number). Because the primary key is the combination of E-Number and P-Number, but a subset of the primary key determines the value of employee Name, employee Name is not fully functionally dependent on the primary key. Figure 5–6 indicates that the Cost of travel to a Destination is dependent only on the Destination and is not influenced by who is traveling or when the trip occurs. Hence, Cost is not fully functionally dependent on the primary key. In Figure 5–7, however, Diagnosis is determined by *all* of the primary key and not by any subset of the key. Therefore, Diagnosis is fully functionally dependent on the primary key.

Transitive Dependence

If the value of one data item determines the value of a second data item that is not a candidate key, and the value of the second data item determines the value of a third data item, then a **transitive dependence** exists between the data items. The dependency diagram in Figure 5–7 can be used to demonstrate transitive dependence. Because Medical Record Number determines Employer and Employer determines Employer's Address (each patient has one employer and each employer has only one address), a transitive dependence exists between Medical Record Number and Employer's Address. Because of this transitive relationship, the first data item determines the third. We note that combinations of data items may be considered, but we'll restrict the consideration to the cases where full functional dependence holds.

Multivalued Dependence

When one value of a data item is associated with a collection of values of a second data item, a **multivalued dependence** exists and we say that the first data item "multidetermines" the second. Functional dependence is a special case of multivalued dependence. We examine multivalued dependencies in greater detail below.

Decomposing Poor Designs

Now that we have developed the concept of functional dependence, we have a firm foundation on which to build our techniques for designing good data structures.

New data structures can be derived from the ASSIGNMENT data structure shown in Figure 5–1. The result is presented in Figure 5–9. These tables do not suffer from the problems identified earlier. New projects can be created without the need to assign employees. Employees can be added without affecting information about the project. Also,

FIGURE 5–9
Normalized Relations for the Data in Figure 5–1

ASSIGNMENT	
E-Number	P-Number
1001	26716
1001	23835
1002	43873
1003	26716
1003	34761

EMPLOYEE		
E-Number	Name	Department
1001	Adams	Accounting
1002	Baker	Finance
1003	Clarke	Accounting

PROJECT		
P-Number	Project	Manager
26716	New billing system	Yates
23835	Mailing list maintenance	Kanter
43873	Identify new investments	Cody
34761	Purchasing system design	Yates

FIGURE 5–10   Revised Dependency Diagrams for the Data Structures in Figure 5–9

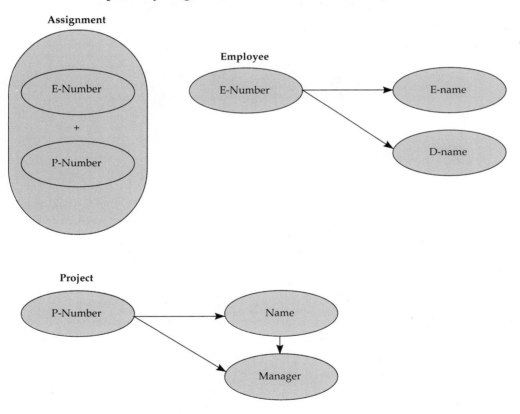

departmental information on employees has been separated into a separate table.

Figure 5–10 shows the dependency diagrams for the revised data structures. These diagrams are much simpler than the diagram in Figure 5–5.

FIGURE 5–11   **Normalized Relations for the Data in Figure 5–2**

```
MEMBER-DATA
Membership                               Local
   Number          Member              Address

    3246        W.  Earp           Laramie
    5498        B.  Jones          Los Angeles
    8730        R.  Steele         Hollywood
    0653        D.  Tracy          New York
    6593        J.  Friday         San Francisco

TRAVEL-PLANS                                                      TRAVEL-COSTS
Membership                          Travel
   Number       Destination         Date           Destination          Cost

    3246        London              7/10           London            $1200
    5498        Madrid              7/12           Madrid            $1500
    8730        Los Angeles         6/30           Los Angeles       $ 900
    0653        Madrid              7/05
    6593        Los Angeles         7/04
```

Figure 5–11 shows the result of decomposing the structures in Figure 5–2. In this design, it is possible to add new destinations before anyone plans to visit them. Altering customer data without affecting data about travel costs is also possible. There are only a small number of updates required to change the cost associated with traveling to a specific location. Figure 5–12 contains the corresponding revised dependency diagrams, which clearly show that the Cost data item is no longer determined by a subset of a primary key.

Figure 5–13 shows a decomposition of the medical data in Figure 5–3. Adding a new doctor's address is now possible. Similarly, data for an employer can now be added without regard to patient data. In this design, many patient records can "share" an employer's data record. This reduces the data redundancy in maintaining an employer record for each patient. The dependency diagrams in Figure 5–14 reflect these changes.

FIRST, SECOND, THIRD, AND BOYCE-CODD NORMAL FORMS

The process of eliminating anomalies results in normalization of the database design. The data structures meet certain criteria known as *normal forms.* There is a sequence of normal forms, each one adding more constraints to a data structure as we progress from the first set of criteria, called **first normal form,** through the highest set, called

FIGURE 5–12   **Revised Dependency Diagrams for the Data Structures in Figure 5–11**

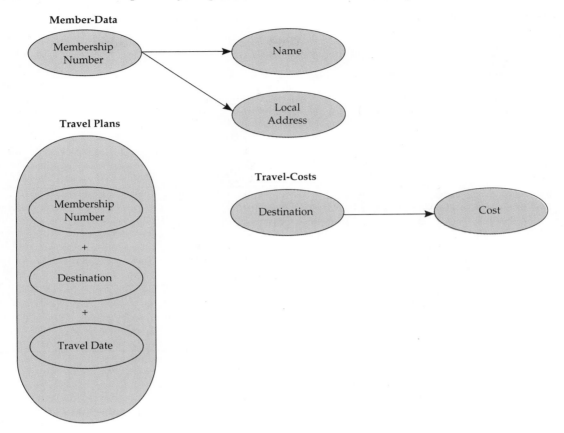

domain-key normal form. The first four normal forms deal with functional dependence.

First Normal Form

A data structure is in first normal form if it can be represented as a flat file structure. Flat files contain no repeating groups. A *repeating group* is a data item that can occur as a collection of values. Figure 5–15a shows a typical nonflat data structure. The data structure in this example contains data for purchase orders and items being ordered. A purchase order can contain any number of items ordered. Hence, "item ordered" is a repeating group. Figure 5–15b shows the equivalent flat data structure.

A benefit gained by converting data structures to first normal form is that the converted structures are much easier to process. Data structures containing repeating groups must also contain either data

FIGURE 5–13　Normalized Relations for the Data in Figure 5–3

ADMISSION

Medical Record Number	Admission Date	Admission Time	Diagnosis	Admitting Doctor
76154	7/09	6:04	Cardiac Arrest	Barnum
65429	7/09	10:46	Heat Exhaustion	Fraser
27635	7/09	13:20	Stress: job	Barnum
65283	7/09	18:14	Childbirth	Barnum

DOCTORS

Admitting Doctor	Doctor's Address
Barnum	129 Medical Pkwy.
Fraser	104 Medical Pkwy.

EMPLOYER

Patient's Employer	Employer's Address
Billco	3562 S. Industrial Blvd.
P & R Co.	1100 Northcreek Suite 200
Gaines HS	1209 Washington Ave.

PATIENT

Medical Record Number	Patient Name
76154	Grimes
65429	Robinson
27635	Lisauckis
65283	Hargrove

EMPLOYED-BY

Medical Record Number	Patient's Employer
76154	Billco
65429	P & R Co.
27635	Gaines HS
65283	N/A

FIGURE 5–14　Revised Dependency Diagrams for the Data Structures in Figure 5–13

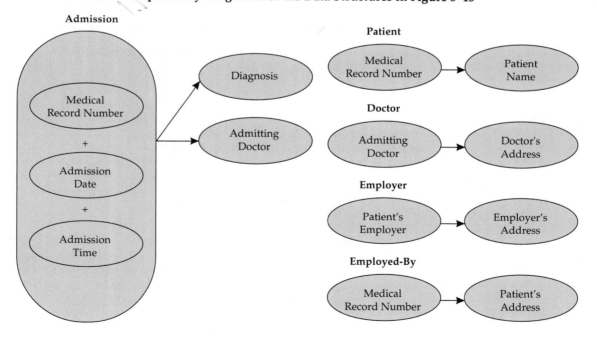

FIGURE 5–15a
A Nonflat File Structure

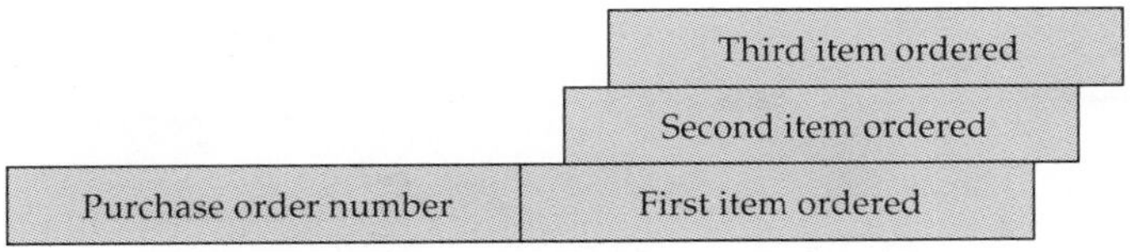

	Third item ordered
	Second item ordered
Purchase order number	First item ordered

(a)

FIGURE 5–15b
The Flat File Equivalent of Figure 5–15a

Purchase order number	First item ordered
Purchase order number	Second item ordered
Purchase order number	Third item ordered

(b)

indicating how many occurrences of the repeating item are contained in the structure or a special mark indicating when the last item occurs. Flat file structures have fixed, or constant, characteristics.

Second Normal Form

If a data structure is in first normal form and all non-key data items are fully functionally dependent on the primary key, then the structure is in **second normal form.** In the design in Figure 5–1, a non-key attribute (employee Name) is determined by a subset of the primary key (E-Number), so this structure is not in second normal form. By comparison, the redesign shown in Figure 5–9 meets the criteria for second normal form. In the ASSIGNMENT relation of Figure 5–9, there are no non-key data items. Therefore, non-key data items cannot possibly be dependent on a subset of the primary key. Consequently, the ASSIGNMENT relation is in (at least) second normal form. The other two tables have primary keys composed of a single data item, so a non-key data item cannot be determined by a proper subset of the primary key. We can therefore conclude that these data structures are also in (at least) second normal form.

Figure 5–12 presents the revised dependency diagrams for the travel club tables from Figure 5–11. MEMBER-DATA and TRAVEL-COSTS contain no multiple-data item keys, so they must be in second normal form. TRAVEL-PLANS contains no non-key data items, so it must also be in second normal form.

The dependency diagrams for the revised medical relations (Figure 5–14) and the insurance relations (Figure 5–8) show clearly that these data structures are in second normal form. In most cases, the primary key is a single data item, thus precluding a violation of full functional dependence. In the ADMISSION data structure (Figure 5–14), the diagram shows that the only determinant is the entire primary key.

Third Normal Form

If a data structure is in second normal form and contains no transitive dependencies, then the structure is in **third normal form.** If we return again to the medical record data structures in Figure 5–3, we now have two reasons why these structures are not in third normal form: They are not in second normal form and we have also identified a transitive dependence. The transitive dependence was that Medical Record Number determined Employer and Employer determined Employer's Address.

From Figure 5–9, we know immediately that if the ASSIGNMENT data structures are in second normal form they must also be in third normal form. The reason is that we need at least three attributes to define a transitive dependence. Because we have only two attributes, no transitive dependence exists. We can conclude that the ASSIGNMENT data structures are in (at least) third normal form.

Observe that all projects have a unique name and that each project has only one manager. P-number determines Project name and Project name determines Manager. However, a transitive dependency does not exist between the data items because Project name is a candidate key. Therefore, the PROJECT relation is in third normal form.

The dependency diagram shown in Figure 5–7 for the MEDICAL-DATA data structure indicates it is not in third normal form because a transitive dependency exists (Medical Record Number determines Employer and Employer determines Employer's Address). This design is not even in second normal form because a subset of the key determines some non-key attributes. To achieve third normal form, the design would require a further decomposition of the MEDICAL-DATA data structure as shown in Figure 5–14.

Figure 5–12 does not expose any transitive dependency in the travel-club data structure. Similarly, Figure 5–8 shows that no transitive dependency exists in the insurance data structure.

Boyce-Codd Normal Form

The original development of the normal forms stopped at third normal form. However, since that time, other normal forms have been identified from research into dependencies when the primary key is composed of a collection of attributes (a concatenated key). The next normal form we will discuss was identified by R. F. Boyce and E. F. Codd, and bears their names.

If a data structure is in third normal form and all determinants are candidate keys, then the data structure is in **Boyce-Codd normal form.** In the design of Figure 5–1, we can identify that P-number is a determinant (of Project name and Manager) but is not a candidate key because P-number will not uniquely determine a tuple. Hence, we could immediately rule out the possibility that the data structure in Figure 5–1 is in

Boyce-Codd normal form. In our alternative design shown in Figure 5–10, the PROJECT data structure is in Boyce-Codd normal form because the Project name determines the Manager and the Project name is a candidate key. The ASSIGNMENT data structure is in Boyce-Codd normal form because there are no non-key data items.

The decomposition of the travel-club data structure shown in Figure 5–12 shows TRAVEL-PLANS in Boyce-Codd normal form because there are no non-key data items. Also, TRAVEL-COSTS and MEMBER-DATA are in Boyce-Codd normal form because the only determinant in each is the primary key.

Similarly, all of the other decompositions have achieved Boyce-Codd normal form. In Figure 5–14, all determinants are primary keys. The same is true in Figure 5–8, the diagram for the insurance data structure.

Boyce-Codd normal form is not a natural by-product of third normal form. Figure 5–16a presents a relation (of travel data) in third normal form that is not in Boyce-Codd normal form. A key assumption in this example is that the airline travels to only one destination. (This is quite reasonable and frequently the case when dealing with commuter airlines in small university towns.)

The relation in Figure 5–16a is clearly in first normal form; it is in second normal form because no subset of the key (Customer and Destination combined) determines Carrier, and no transitive dependency exists. However, Carrier determines Destination (hence Carrier is a determinant) and Carrier is not a candidate key. Therefore, the relation is not in Boyce-Codd normal form.

All of the modification anomalies exist in Figure 5–16a. If the tuple with customer number 6155 is removed, the information that Reliable Airlines travels to Austin is lost. If another Carrier should be added to the table, it cannot be added until it has a customer. If an airline changes its name, the change must be reflected in multiple occurrences in the table. Thus, third normal form still has modification anomalies.

The decomposition in Figure 5–16b resolves these issues. Customer 6155's data can be removed without affecting the database. A new Carrier can be added (to OPTION) without customer data being required. Also, an airline's name can change without requiring multiple updates to the database.

FIGURE 5–16a
A Relation in Third Normal Form But Not in Boyce-Codd Normal Form

| FLIGHT | | |
Customer	Destination	Carrier
1283	Austin	Friendly
2873	Dallas	Speedy
7625	Austin	Friendly
6155	Austin	Reliable
1283	Dallas	Speedy
(Note: Carrier → Destination)		

FIGURE 5–16b
A Boyce-Codd Normaliza-
tion of Figure 5–16a

```
RESERVATION                     OPTION
Customer   Carrier              Carrier     Destination

   1283    Friendly             Friendly    Austin
   2873    Speedy               Speedy      Dallas
   7625    Friendly             Reliable    Austin
   6155    Reliable
   1283    Speedy
```

TABLE 5–1   A Summary of the Normal Form Criteria through
             Boyce-Codd Normal Form (Note that each normal
             form builds on the prior one)

Normal Form	Criteria
First normal form	The data structure is representable as a flat file.
Second normal form	The data structure is in first normal form and all non-key attributes are fully functionally dependent on the primary key.
Third normal form	The data structure is in second normal form and there are no transitive dependencies.
Boyce-Codd normal form	The data structure is in third normal form and every determinant is a candidate key.

The normal forms discussed thus far are summarized in Table 5–1. A general heuristic to follow is that when more than one relationship is represented in a data structure, there is quite likely to be some type of modification anomaly inherent in the structure. In all of these cases, modification anomalies have been resolved by decomposing the original table into smaller tables. When you decompose into smaller tables, you must remember to embed the appropriate part of the primary key from the original table in the new table. (In some cases, the entire primary key must appear in the new table.)

At first glance, it may appear that transforming a database design into a higher normal form requires duplicating data. Actually, although the number of data item *types* in the database may be increased, the number of data item *values* stored in the database is actually reduced. Hence, there is a net savings in storage requirements for the database.

When a data structure is in Boyce-Codd normal form (or higher), it does not suffer modification anomalies due to functional dependence. Boyce-Codd normal form is therefore a desirable database design goal.

AVOIDING PROBLEMS WITH MULTIPLE VALUES

There are also problems in data structure designs that are not due to functional dependence. Figure 5–17 shows a relation containing employee numbers, project numbers, and computer codes. Assume that an

FIGURE 5–17
Relation Containing
Multiple Values

```
                COMPUTER-ACCOUNT
           Employee    Project    User-Code

              100       23796      User100
              100       34548      User100
              102       23487      User102
```

FIGURE 5–18
**A Tuple Has Been Added
to the Data**
Does employee 100 really
use two computer accounts
for project 23796 and only
one account for project
34548?

```
                COMPUTER-ACCOUNT
           Employee    Project    User-Code

              100       23796      User100
              100       34548      User100
              102       23487      User102
              100       23796      User100A
```

FIGURE 5–19
Relation Containing
Multiple Values

```
           MUSIC-AUTO-DATA
                      Music       Automobile
            Name    Preference      Owned

           Clarke     Jazz        Sports car
           Clarke     Rock        Sports car
           Clarke     Jazz        Truck
           Clarke     Rock        Truck
```

employee may use the computer for any project on which he or she is
working, and that there is no restriction on the number of computer
accounts an employee may have. The primary key must be the concatenated key shown in order to reflect these assumptions.

Now suppose that employee number 100 has another computer account authorized. Figure 5–18 shows the modified database. Due to the
initial assumptions, adding one tuple may lead to erroneous inferences.
This data seems to indicate that employee number 100 uses two computer accounts for project 23796 and only one for project 34548. The
problem is caused partially by the fact that the attributes Project and
User-Code can assume multiple values for a given employee. More important, there is no logical dependence between the account numbers
and the projects. As before, the root of the problem is in the attempt to
represent more than one relationship in a data structure.

Figure 5–19 presents another example of the problems that can be
caused by multiple values. This table contains data about a person's
music preferences and the automobiles that the person owns. Clarke
enjoys jazz and rock music and owns a sports car and a truck. Suppose
that Clarke buys a van. If the data is updated as shown in Figure 5–20,
there appears to be an implication that Clarke prefers jazz music while

FIGURE 5–20
An Additional Tuple Occurrence Demonstrates a Problem Caused by Multiple, Independent Values
Does Clarke really enjoy only jazz music only while in the van?

```
        MUSIC-AUTO-DATA
                 Music       Automobile
        Name     Preference  Owned

        Clarke   Jazz        Sports car
        Clarke   Rock        Sports car
        Clarke   Jazz        Truck
        Clarke   Rock        Truck
        Clarke   Jazz        Van
```

FIGURE 5–21
The Relation of Figure 5–20
A second tuple is needed to maintain logical consistency.

```
        MUSIC-AUTO-DATA
                 Music       Automobile
        Name     Preference  Owned

        Clarke   Jazz        Sports car
        Clarke   Rock        Sports car
        Clarke   Jazz        Truck
        Clarke   Rock        Truck
        Clarke   Jazz        Van
        Clarke   Rock        Van
```

driving the van. Two occurrences must be added, as in Figure 5–21, to maintain a logically consistent relationship. The lack of any logical relationship between music preference and automobile type causes these problems.

Note also the deletion and update anomalies in this example. If Clarke sells the sports car, more than one occurrence must be deleted to reflect this. If Clarke's music preference switches from rock to classical, more than one occurrence must be modified to accurately represent this change.

Problems with multiple values arise when there are two or more logically independent relationships within a data structure. In the first example (Figures 5–17 and 5–18), Project and User-Code have logically independent relationships with Employee. An employee may work on many projects and use many computer accounts, but there is no logical relationship between projects and computer accounts. In the second example (Figures 5–19, 5–20, and 5–21), Music Preference and Automobile Owned exist in logically independent relationships with Name. A person may enjoy many types of music and own several automobiles, but there is no logical relationship between music preference and type of automobile owned.

Fourth Normal Form

A comprehensive discussion of the normal forms beyond the Boyce-Codd normal form is beyond the scope of this text. It is instructional, however, to present examples and general definitions for these normal

FIGURE 5–22
**The Multiple Values in
This Data Are Related, So
There Are No Anomalies**

| MUSIC-SKILL | | |
Employee	Skill	Music Type
Borst	Composer	Classical
Borst	Composer	Jazz
Borst	Composer	Rock
Borst	Critic	Classical
Myles	Composer	Classical
Myles	Composer	Jazz

forms. These examples illustrate the potential problems in structures that are in Boyce-Codd normal form.

Fourth normal form addresses the problems caused by multivalued dependence. If a data structure is in Boyce-Codd normal form, and either (1) it contains no multivalued dependencies or (2) all its multivalued dependencies are also functional dependencies, then the data structure is in **fourth normal form.**

Many discussions of fourth normal form include definitions of multivalued dependence. Problems with multivalued dependence arise only when there are three or more *logically independent* data items within a data structure. In our example (Figure 5–18), Project and User-Code are logically independent. Employee multidetermines Project and multidetermines User-Code, but there is no dependence between Project and User-Code. Note that the existence of a multivalued dependence does not imply the existence of a problem. Consider, for example, Figure 5–22, which shows a table containing the Employee, Skill, and Music Type attributes. In this case, we assume that there *is* a relationship between skill and music type. The employee Borst, for example, is a trained critic of classical music and has composed classical, jazz, and rock music. The multiple values do not cause a problem because there is a relationship between skill and music type. Only when the multiple values are independent is there a problem.

AVOIDING PROBLEMS WITH DECOMPOSITIONS

There are problems in relations that have nothing to do with either dependence among attributes or multiple values. Consider the information embodied by the relation in Figure 5–23. At first glance, it may seem that a reasonable alternative design could be as shown in Figure 5–24. But notice the result of combining the two data structures in Figure 5–25 (perhaps by concatenating or "joining" rows of the relations) where EMPLOYEE Manager equals MANAGER Name. New data has been introduced. The combination of values "Adams, Yates, 23438" and the combination "Clarke, Yates, 26197" do not exist in the original data of Figure 5–24. In the relational model, decomposition of a table into subsets of its columns is called projection. Projections that produce spurious information on joining are called **loss projections.** We refer to the

FIGURE 5–23
A Typical Relation Used in Project Management

ASSIGNMENT

Employee	Manager	Project
Adams	Yates	26197
Baker	Kanter	21051
Clarke	Yates	23438
Dexter	Barnes	34687

FIGURE 5–24
An Apparently Harmless Decomposition of the Relation in Figure 5–23

EMPLOYEE

Name	Manager
Adams	Yates
Baker	Kanter
Clarke	Yates
Dexter	Barnes

MANAGER

Name	Project
Yates	26197
Yates	23438
Kanter	21051
Barnes	34687

FIGURE 5–25
The Result of Joining the Relations in Figure 5–24
Note that tuples that did not exist in the original relation have been created.

ASSIGNMENT

Employee	Manager	Project
Adams	Yates	26197
Adams	Yates	23438
Baker	Kanter	21051
Clarke	Yates	23438
Clarke	Yates	26197
Dexter	Barnes	34687

general case as **loss decompositions.** Database designs should strive for nonloss decompositions—decompositions that do not produce incorrect information when recombined.

A nonloss decomposition for this data structure is shown in Figure 5–26. Note that these data structures reconstruct the original data relationships.

Fifth Normal Form

Fifth normal form addresses the issue of loss and nonloss decompositions. In the relational model, this is yet another type of dependence: join dependence. A **join dependence** is a constraint that requires a relation to be the join of its projections. A **constraint** is simply a rule or condition that tuples of a relation must satisfy. Constraints include referential and entity integrity, domain constraints, and functional dependencies. We refer to the general case of join dependence as a **decomposition dependence.**

FIGURE 5–26
A Set of Nonloss Projections of the Data in Figure 5–23

PROJECT-STAFF		PROJECT-MANAGEMENT	
Employee	Project	Project	Manager
Adams	26197	26197	Yates
Baker	21051	21051	Kanter
Clarke	23438	23438	Yates
Dexter	34687	34687	Barnes

FIGURE 5–27a
A Relation in Domain-Key Normal Form

PROJECT Name	P-Number	Manager	Actual Cost	Expected Cost
New billing system	23760	Yates	1000	10000
Common stock issue	28765	Baker	3000	4000
Resolve bad debts	26713	Kanter	2000	1500
New office lease	26511	Yates	5000	5000

```
Key is: P-Number
Domain of Actual cost is {x : x > = 0}
Domain of Expected Cost is {x : x > = 0}
```

A relation is in **fifth normal form** if the data relationships embodied in the data structure cannot be reconstructed from data structures containing fewer data items. If the data structure can be decomposed only into smaller records that all have the same key, then the data structure is in fifth normal form (Kent, 1983). A data structure in fifth normal form also satisfies all lower normal forms.

DOMAIN-KEY NORMAL FORM

The final normal form we discuss is domain-key normal form. Domain-key normal form was defined in 1981 by R. Fagin. Fagin stated that a relation "is in domain-key normal form if every constraint can be inferred by simply knowing the set of attribute names and their underlying domains, along with the set of keys."

An explanation of domain-key normal form requires the definition of two more types of dependence. A **key dependence** implies there can be no changes to the relation that would result in the key no longer being a unique identifier of tuples in the relation are allowed. Figure 5–27a shows an occurrence of a relation with the key dependence (or constraint) explicitly stated.

The second dependence is **domain dependence.** In domain dependence, the values for an attribute must come from a specific domain. In

Figure 5–27a, the domain dependencies for the Actual Cost attribute and the Expected Cost attribute are also stated explicitly.

The tuple "New billing system, 23760, Baker, 1000, 10000" in Figure 5–27b would violate domain-key normal form if added to the PROJECT relation, because P-number would no longer be a key. The tuple "New ad campaign, 34004, Kanter, 0, −1000" in Figure 5–27c would violate domain-key normal form if it were added to the PROJECT relation, because −1000 is not a valid value for Expected Cost (costs should be positive). We also note that any tuple deletion that would result in either a key or domain dependence being violated also violates domain-key normal form.

As you can see, the definition of domain-key normal form is unlike that of the prior normal form definitions in that it says nothing about traditional dependencies (functional, multivalued, and join) but deals instead with the basic concepts of domains, keys, and constraints. Fagin showed that, after modification of the traditional normal forms to consider the consequences of domain sizes, the traditional normal forms are all implied by domain-key normal form.

Domain-key normal form has practical as well as theoretical implications. From a practical viewpoint, it is much easier for database software to deal with domains and keys than to deal with functional, transitive, or multivalued dependencies. Hence, future database sys-

FIGURE 5–27b
A Relation that Violates Domain-Key Normal Form Key Dependence

PROJECT Name	P-Number	Manager	Actual Cost	Expected Cost
New billing system	23760	Yates	1000	10000
Common stock issue	28765	Baker	3000	4000
Resolve bad debts	26713	Kanter	2000	1500
New office lease	26511	Yates	5000	5000
New billing system	23760	Baker	1000	10000

FIGURE 5–27c
Domain-Key Normal Form
A Relation that Violates Domain-Key Normal Form Domain Dependence

PROJECT Name	P-Number	Manager	Actual Cost	Expected Cost
New billing system	23760	Yates	1000	10000
Common stock issue	28765	Baker	3000	4000
Resolve bad debts	26713	Kanter	2000	1500
New office lease	26511	Yates	5000	5000
New ad campaign	34004	Kanter	0	−1000

tems may be able to incorporate checks for normal form consistency based on the domain-key approach to normalization. This could ease the burden of the design phase that is so critical to effective database system use.

SIDE EFFECTS OF NORMALIZATION

By now you may have decided that normalization is without fault. For the most part, we encourage this view. But, as is frequently the case, the solution to one set of problems introduces new problems.

Relationship Constraints

We noted above that the decomposition of data structures into smaller structures of higher normal form results in a duplication of data item types. Every time a data structure is decomposed for the sake of normalization, the determinant data item (or items) ends up in two structures, acting as the primary key in one of them. We saw this in the decomposition of the TRAVEL-CLUB data structure in Figure 5–2 into the TRAVEL-PLANS and TRAVEL-COSTS data structures in Figure 5–12. The determinant data item Destination became the key in the TRAVEL-COSTS relation.

The Destination attribute in TRAVEL-PLANS is now a foreign key—a non-key attribute in one relation that has the same domain as a key attribute in another relation. To ensure that data in a tuple refers to valid data elsewhere after normalization, a concept called referential integrity, then all values of foreign keys must either be null or exist as values of the corresponding primary key. As explained earlier, the decomposition process requires that an appropriate part of the primary key in the original relation (perhaps all of it) be included in the new relations that are formed. Therefore, as primary keys occur in more places, more opportunities exist for referential integrity to be compromised. Consequently, the decomposition process inherently yields a set of referential integrity constraints involving the data structures created in the decomposition.

The overhead necessary to maintain these constraints must be balanced against the ease with which users can interact with the database system. As in many cases, this balance is a design decision that must be made by the information analyst. (Foreign keys and referential integrity are discussed more fully in Chapter 6.)

Retrieval Inefficiency

The increase in data structures inherent in the normalization process can also adversely affect the retrieval efficiency of the database system, especially in a microcomputer-based system. Consequently, a database

THE USER'S VIEW

Issues of normalization and consistency are important concerns for database system designers, and the design decisions made in these areas directly affect database system users. The database is a model of the organization, and as such must change to reflect the changes in the organization. When a database changes, however, preservation of all existing relevant relationships is necessary. This necessity may be at odds with proposed changes to the relationships modeled in the database, as when rearrangement of the data item groupings in the database becomes necessary. When normalization is a goal of database design from the start, the likelihood of changes being required that will have a detrimental effect on existing applications programs is reduced.

One of the most challenging tasks in database system development is to determine an efficient implementation of the database. Conversion to a normalized database results in minimizing the amount of data stored in most (but not all) cases.

One might not expect this, since normalization requires decomposing tables. But whereas some duplication of data *types* may be incurred, there is usually a reduction in the number of occurrences of the data type that must be stored. Hence, there is a net reduction in the total storage required.

The largest advantage to the user is that normalized databases are easier to maintain, due largely to the fact that data relationships in a normalized database are much more clearly and simply represented. This means that new applications will be easier to implement, which the user will see in terms of faster response to requests for changes. On the other hand, users might find that a normalized database is difficult to comprehend. The easiest database for users to understand would consist of a single, universal relation that contained everything. No operations to combine tables would be required, and only one table name is needed! Also, as discussed above, normalization can impact retrieval performance. ■

system designer who knows that the database system will reside on a microcomputer may choose to keep the data structures in less than Boyce-Codd normal form.

In such a case, the data structures are frequently indexed on several keys, allowing access to the data in the structure in many ways. Fortunately, many microcomputer database systems provide a programming-like language that can be used to protect against the modification anomalies inherent in the lower normal forms.

CHAPTER SUMMARY

Modification anomalies are the result of poor database design. These anomalies include deletion anomalies, insertion anomalies, and update anomalies. Deletion anomalies occur when the deletion of a data item in a data structure results in loss of unrelated information from the database. Insertion anomalies occur when one data item cannot be added to a data structure without the addition of an unrelated data item. Update anomalies occur when many updates to a database must occur in order for a single data item to be updated.

The most common source of these problems is dependence among attributes. Modification anomalies are likely to occur when more than one relationship is modeled in a relation. A second source of modification anomalies exists when logically independent attributes occur in a relation and these attributes are allowed to assume multiple values.

METROPOLITAN NATIONAL BANK

You now have some basis for evaluating the preliminary implementation designs that you developed earlier. For each relation in your relational implementaion, identify all functional dependencies and determine the normal form for the relation. Redesign as necessary to achieve Boyce-Codd normal form. If you must redesign, be sure to revise your entity-relationship model as necessary to reflect any changes in *relationships*. In revising your original implementation designs, be careful about the degree to which you allow the normalization process to direct your redesign efforts. You must carefully weigh the trade-offs between resolving anomalies and maintaining a design that supports the priorities outlined in earlier chapters.

Discuss the design decisions you make in a report that accompanies the final design. Compare your normalized design to the performance criteria developed in earlier chapters. Does your normalized design still provide the response times required to adequately support the MetNat decision-making environment? State explicitly how your implementation succeeds or fails in this regard. If you feel that a problem exists, could utility programs be developed to mitigate this problem? State explicitly what these utility programs will provide and when they should be executed. If you feel that the design cannot be adequately adjusted using utility programs, state why you feel the problem cannot be resolved. ■

Both sources of modification anomalies can be avoided by decomposing the data structure into smaller, more logically consistent, data structures.

In some rare cases in a relational database implementaion, improper table decomposition may be a third potential source of problems. These problems occur when recombining the decompositions results in a relation that contains data not in the original relation. Nonloss projections do not have this property. Projection must be used carefully to correct modification anomalies in a relational database design.

Normalization is a process that removes anomalies from data structures. Criteria that define the many levels of normalization are known as normal forms. Each normal form builds on the criteria of the prior forms to construct more stable data structures. Although the normalization process produces more instances of an attribute type, it actually results in a reduction in storage requirements because fewer actual data values must be stored in the database.

Unfortunately, the introduction of normalized data structures increases the need for concern regarding referential integrity between data structures. Also, in microcomputer-based systems, normalization may have to be compromised to increase retrieval efficiency.

Questions and Exercises

1. What is a deletion anomaly? An insertion anomaly? An update anomaly? Why are modification anomalies avoided?
2. Which type of modification anomaly is worse? Why?

3. When might a database designer decide that modification anomalies should not be resolved? What additional burden does this place on users of the database? What additional processing may be required of applications programs that use the database?

4. What is the meaning of *dependence* as used in this chapter?

5. Can a relation with only two attributes ever have problems due to dependence?

6. Can a relation with only two attributes ever have problems due to multiple values?

7. Consider your answers to Questions 5 and 6. Should relational database designers strive to make all relations binary?

8. Give an example of a relation with problems due to multiple values.

9. Show nonloss projections of the relation in Figure 5–16.

10. Join the projections in your answer to Question 9 to demonstrate that your answer is correct.

    NOTE: Many of the following exercises appeared in Chapter 3. In that chapter, the problems called for E-R models and data structure diagrams. Your solutions to those earlier exercises will assist you here. If you did not create E-R models or data structure diagrams, you should do so now.

11. Consider an INVESTMENT database that contains data items for investor's name, amount invested, stock broker's name, broker's office address, and broker's telephone number. The following assumptions may be made: Investors may invest in many stocks; a broker has only one office; and each broker's office has only one telephone number. Design data structures in Boyce-Codd normal form that model these data relationships.

12. Consider a database of TRANSFER-STUDENT data intended to maintain data about students transferring into a university. The database contains the following data items: student's name, student's address, student's telephone number, prior university attended, GPA at the prior university, hours earned at the prior university, last date at the prior university, student's sex, student's date of birth, guardian's name, guardian's address, and relationship of guardian to the student. The following assumptions may be made: Students have one address and one telephone number; guardians have one address and one telephone number; and a student may have attended more than one prior university. Design data structures in Boyce-Codd normal form that model these design relationships.

13. A database for a local garage is needed. The database contains data items for customer's name, customer's address, customer's work telephone, customer's home telephone, date of work done, automobile make, automobile model, description of work done, parts needed to complete work, charge for parts needed, charge for labor performed, and total charge. For warranty reasons, data must be maintained in the database for at least 90 days; therefore, a customer may have several records in the database

at any particular time. Identical parts have only one cost, but different parts have different costs (for example, all tires cost the same and all engines cost the same, but a tire and an engine do not cost the same). Design data structures in Boyce-Codd normal form that model these data relationships.

14. A small database for a restaurant is needed. The database should contain data for customer's name, reservation date, reservation time, seating preference (booth or table), area preference (indoor or outdoor), number of people dining, and telephone number where the customer can be reached if needed prior to arrival. Assume that a customer makes only one reservation per date, but do not assume that the customer's name can alone act as a primary key. Design data structures in Boyce-Codd normal form that model these data relationships. Be prepared to discuss any additional assumptions you make.

15. A cable television company desires a database containing data on its customers. The following data items are needed: customer's name, customer's address, customer's telephone number, account number, service provided (basic, movie channel A, movie channel B, movie channel C, and/or children's channel), the charge for each service, equipment used by the customer that belongs to the cable television company (decoder, remote control, etc.), an identifying number for each piece of equipment, and the extra charge (if any) for any equipment used by the customer. Assume that a customer may have more than one account number (some customers have rental properties and use the cable service to make their properties more attractive). Design data structures in Boyce-Codd normal form that model these data relationships.

16. Consider the following relations and functional dependencies. Assume in part (a) that the key for R1 is AC, the key for R2 is A, and the key for R3 is AC. In part (b), assume that the key for R1 is S and the key for R2 is SU. What normal form are the relations currently in? Convert all relations to Boyce-Codd normal form.

a. R1 (A,B,C,D) $A \rightarrow B$
    R2 (A,B,E) $AC \rightarrow D$
    R3 (A,C,D,F) $A \rightarrow E$
                      $B \rightarrow CD$
                      $D \rightarrow F$

b. R1 (S,T, U,V,W) $S \rightarrow TU$
    R2 (S,U,Y) $S \rightarrow V$
                      $S \rightarrow W$
                      $SU \rightarrow Y$
                      $TU \rightarrow W$
                      $U \rightarrow W$
                      $U \rightarrow S$

17. Suppose you have a data structure for a dance studio. The fields in the data structure are dancer's identification number, dancer's name, dancer's address, dancer's telephone number, class identification number, day that the class meets, and time

that the class meets. Assume that each student takes one class and each class meets only once a week. Assume also that dancer identification number is the key. In what normal form is the data structure currently? Decompose this data structure into at least Boyce-Codd normal form.

18. Consider a database used to support a soccer referees association. Suppose the association schedules referees for games in three youth leagues in the county, for any high school game in the county, and for any college game played at a university in the county. Currently, the database consists of only one data structure that contains the following information: game number (unique), date of game, time of game, location of game, referee assigned to game, telephone number of referee (in case the game is canceled), home team, visiting team, league in which the teams compete, and telephone number of the league office. Data for games for several weeks in advance is maintained in the database. In the case of youth games, a referee may be assigned to more than one game per day. Draw a dependency diagram of this data and decompose the data into data structures in at least Boyce-Codd normal form.

19. Suppose you have been asked to design a database for a company that manages magazine subscriptions. This company mails thousands of advertisements each year to households throughout the country offering hundreds of magazine subscriptions at discount subscription rates. The company also has a sweepstakes each year in which many prizes are awarded to lucky respondents. Design a database that will maintain the following data: subscriber's name and address, magazines subscribed to, expiration dates of subscriptions, prizes awarded to subscriber (if any), date of last advertisement sent to subscriber, addresses of all locations that have received an advertisement regardless of response, and magazines offered and terms of subscription for each magazine.

For Further Reading

Normalization as discussed by the originator of the relational approach is described in: Codd, E. F. "Further Normalization of the Relational Data-base Model." In *Data Base Systems,* Courant Computer Science Symposia 6. Englewood Cliffs, N.J.: Prentice-Hall, 1972, pp. 65–98.

For a very readable (and applied) discussion of the normal forms criteria, see Kent, William. "A Simple Guide to Five Normal Forms in Relational Database Theory." *Communications of the ACM* 26, no. 2 (February 1983), pp. 120–25.

Domain-key normal form was first defined in the following work by Fagin: Fagin, R. "A Normal Form for Relational Databases That Is Based on Domains and Keys." *ACM Transactions on Database Systems* 6, no. 3 (September 1981).

III

RELATIONAL AND CODASYL SYSTEMS

6

THE RELATIONAL DATABASE MODEL

In the previous chapter, we presented an overview of several database models. Here and in Chapter 7, we examine one model, the relational database model, in detail.

BASIC CONCEPTS

The relational database model was originally proposed by E. F. Codd in the early 1970s. This model presents data in the form of tables, a way of picturing data with which almost everyone is comfortable. The relational model has its foundation in set theory, which provides the basis for many of the operations performed on relations. This theoretical basis also allows one to distinguish relational from "relational-like" database systems.

Characteristics of Relations

Figure 6–1 presents an entity-relationship model of a part of a database for employees and projects in a hypothetical organization. The relations shown in Figure 6–2 are derived from this logical description. (For the purposes of this chapter, a *relation* is a two-dimensional table of data about an entity class or the relationships between entity classes.) Figure 6–2 illustrates six relations: EMPLOYEE, PROJECT, ASSIGNMENT, VACATION TAKEN, SICK LEAVE TAKEN, and TIMESHEETS. These relations exhibit the following characteristics:

1. All entries at the intersection of a row and column of the relation are single-valued (there are no arrays or repeating groups).
2. The entries in any column of the relation are all of the same kind.
3. Each column has a unique name (although columns of different relations may have the same name).
4. No two rows of the relation are identical.

The order of rows does not matter, and, in general, the order of the columns does not matter. The data in Figure 6–2 is typical organizational information. Obviously, one would expect an organization to keep much more detailed information than this, but this amount suffices to demonstrate how an organizational database in a relational database model can support decision-making processes.

FIGURE 6–1   E-R Model of Organizational Database (Attributes are not shown)

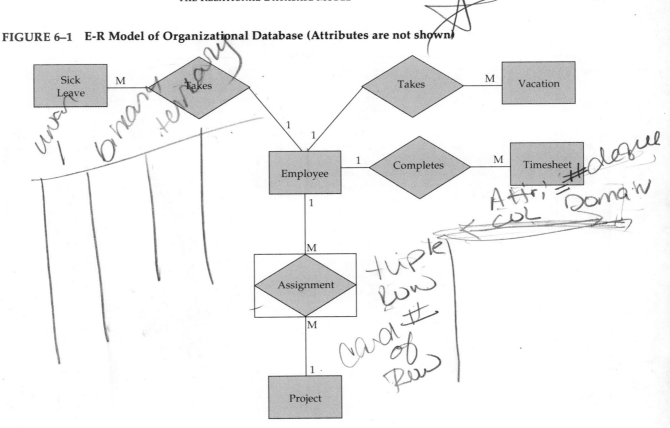

The rows of a relation are called **tuples** (rhymes with "couples"). The row in the EMPLOYEE relation that contains the values 847478599, Clarke, 373 Ave A, Smyrna, 30364, 837-9383, Consultant, 2500, 4, and 5 is one tuple. The number of tuples in a relation determines its **cardinality.** The EMPLOYEE relation has cardinality 8.

The columns of a relation are called *attributes*. NAME is an attribute of the EMPLOYEE relation, as is E-ID. The values an attribute can assume are said to come from that attribute's **domain.** The domain of the E-ID attribute in the EMPLOYEE relation is the set of nine-digit numbers. You may notice that the values for this attribute appear to be social security numbers.

The PROJECT relation has an attribute named P-ID, but it does not appear to be the same as E-ID in the EMPLOYEE relation. Indeed, it is not the same, as it is defined on a different domain. The domain for P-ID in the PROJECT relation is a set of four-digit numbers, perhaps authorized by the company's controller.

The number of attributes in a relation determines the **degree** of the relation. A relation with six attributes, such as the PROJECT relation, is said to be of degree 6. Additionally, a tuple from this relation can be referred to as a *six-tuple*. A relation with only one attribute is called a **unary relation,** one with only two attributes is called a **binary relation,** and one with only three attributes is called a **ternary relation.**

FIGURE 6–2   **Sample Organizational Data in a Relational Format**

EMPLOYEE

E-ID	Name	Address	City	Zip	Phone	Title	Salary	Vacation Available	Sick Leave Available
134572698	Jones	12 Maple St.	Atlanta	30311	758-1267	Programmer	2200	3	8
983749493	Smith	28 Alma St.	Smyrna	30364	748-4847	Programmer	2200	5	8
847478599	Clarke	373 Ave. A	Smyrna	30364	837-9383	Consultant	2500	5	7
252930423	Dexter	3888 6th St.	Smyrna	30364	837-2552	Consultant	2500	4	5
383783993	Hayet	149 Oakside Dr.	Atlanta	30311	758-7399	Programmer	2300	3	7
252928462	Gofman	2333 Briarcrest Dr.	Atlanta	30312	766-6752	Programmer	2350	7	8
262022010	Wray	2911 Windgate St.	Smyrna	30364	837-7288	Manager	3500	7	7
252887324	Bennett	131 Rhodes Dr.	Smyrna	30367	977-0979	Manager	4200	3	8

PROJECT

P-ID	Name	Type	Actual Hours	Expected Hours	Project Leader
6301	Marketing report	E	12	120	252928462
2376	New billing system	E	80	160	252928462
2876	Common stock report	C	12	8	383783993
2671	Bad debt report	D	40	20	252930423
2651	Manpower report bug	C	8	16	983749493

Project types: E = Enhancement, C = Correction, D = Development

VACATION TAKEN

E-ID	Begin Date	End Date	Authorization
134572698	7/1	7/5	252022010
252930423	8/10	8/10	252022010
383783993	9/4	9/7	252022010
983749493	9/4	9/4	252887324
383783993	11/20	11/21	252887324

SICK LEAVE TAKEN

E-ID	Begin Date	End Date	Authorization
134572698	3/2	3/2	252022010
383783993	5/10	5/14	252022010

Two types of relations can be defined. A **base relation** exists independently of all other relations in the database. A **view** (or derived relation) is a relation that can be constructed from other relations in the database. Figure 6–3 illustrates these two concepts. The PAID LEAVE TAKEN relation is formed by combining the VACATION TAKEN and the SICK LEAVE TAKEN relations. The PAID LEAVE TAKEN relation does not actually exist in the database. To have it in the database would be very

FIGURE 6–2 *(continued)*

TIMESHEETS

E-ID	P-ID	Date	Hours
134572698	6301	10/2	3.5
134572698	2376	10/2	5.5
252930423	2671	10/2	8.0
983749493	2376	10/2	8.0
847478599	2876	10/2	5.0
847478599	2671	10/2	3.0
252928462	2376	10/2	3.5
252928462	6301	10/2	4.5
134572698	6301	10/3	7.5
134572698	2376	10/3	0.5
252930423	2671	10/3	8.0
983749493	2376	10/3	8.0
847478599	2876	10/3	4.0
847478599	2671	10/3	4.0

ASSIGNMENTS

E-ID	P-ID	Total Hours	Evaluation
134572698	6301	11.0	On schedule
134572698	2376	6.0	On schedule
252930423	2671	16.0	Slipping - needs analysis
983749493	2376	16.0	Late start - OK now
847478599	2876	9.0	Analysis problems
847478599	2671	7.0	Appears on schedule - Need formal review
252928462	2376	3.5	OK
252928462	6301	4.5	-0-
383783993	2651	-0-	-0-

inefficient and would cause the problems related to data redundancy discussed in Chapter 1.

Whether a relation is a base relation or a view, the relational structure is time-invariant. The relationships between the attributes do not vary with time. Of course, the values assumed by the attributes for a specific tuple can vary with time.

The relational database model terminology is summarized in Table 6–1.

Null Values

Sometimes it is impossible to know all of the data values for an entity. For example, a hospital emergency room patient may be incapable of giving needed data or a crime suspect may be unwilling to give needed

FIGURE 6–3
An Example of a View (or Derived Relation)
This view was derived from the VACATION TAKEN and SICK LEAVE TAKEN relations.

```
PAID LEAVE TAKEN
                    Begin          End
E - ID              Date           Date           Authorization
134572698           7 / 1          7 / 5          252022010
252930423           8 / 10         8 / 10         252022010
383783993           9 / 4          9 / 7          252022010
983749493           9 / 4          9 / 4          252887324
383783993           11 / 20        11 / 21        252887324
134572698           3 / 2          3 / 2          252022010
383783993           5 / 10         5 / 14         252022010
```

TABLE 6–1   Terms Used in the Relational Database Model

Term	Definition
Tuple	A row in a relation.
Cardinality	The number of tuples in a relation.
Attribute	A column in a relation.
Domain	The values an attribute can assume.
Degree	The number of attributes in a relation.
Candidate keys	Attributes or collections of attributes that uniquely identify a tuple.
Primary key	A particular candidate key.
Foreign key	An attribute defined on the same domain as a primary key.
Unary relation	A relation with only one attribute.
Binary relation	A relation with only two attributes.
Ternary relation	A relation with only three attributes.
Base relation	A relation that exists independently of all other relations in the database.
View	A relation that can be derived from base relations (also known as a derived relation).

data. Similarly, future values of data items may be impossible to determine and may only be estimated.

We noted above that the data value at the intersection of a relation row and column must be atomic, or single-valued. Throughout the text, we have generally assumed that data values would exist *and be known* for attributes stored in a database. However, such is not always the case, and because the relational model puts some restrictions on when and where data values may be omitted, we shall consider this point further before continuing.

An unspecified value is a **null value.** Null values are different from zero values or blank values. A zero value represents the numeric quantity *zero.* A null value represents one of two cases: (1) the actual value if unknown or (2) the attribute is not applicable. We will represent a null value with the symbol -0-.

Consider the VACATION-TAKEN relation from Figure 6–4. It contains null entries for the AUTHORIZATION attribute. This value indicates that

FIGURE 6–4
The VACATION TAKEN Relation Modified
A relation with a null value in a foreign key.

VACATION TAKEN E-ID	Begin Date	End Date	Authorization
134572698	7/1	7/5	252022010
252930423	8/10	8/10	252022010
383783993	9/4	9/7	252022010
983749493	9/4	9/4	252887324
383783993	11/20	11/21	-0-

the authorization value (manager's identification number) for vacation taken by employee 383783993 is unknown.

We will see how null values can be manipulated in the section about data manipulation below.

Keys

Since (by definition) no two tuples in a relation are identical, there is always at least one way to identify a particular tuple—by specifying all attributes (data values) of the tuple. Usually, a tuple can be uniquely identified by specifying fewer than all attributes. Attributes or collections of attributes that uniquely identify a tuple are called **candidate keys**. In the PROJECT relation, both NAME and P-ID are candidate keys. Each project has a unique name and a unique project number.

The VACATION TAKEN relation has two candidate keys. E-ID and BEGIN DATE combined form one. E-ID and END DATE combined form the other. Although the combination of E-ID, BEGIN DATE, and END DATE could be considered another candidate key, we will always limit our consideration to the candidate keys with the smallest number of attributes. E-ID alone is not a candidate key if we assume that the relation may contain a record of more than one vacation taken by an employee. The date fields alone are not reasonable choices for candidate keys if we assume more than one employee may begin or end a vacation on the same date. Similarly, the AUTHORIZATION attribute is not a candidate key if a manager can authorize more than one employee's vacation.

When a candidate key is selected to be the key of a relation, it is called the **primary key.** As with candidate keys, we are only interested in primary keys constructed of the fewest number of attributes possible. In the illustrations in this chapter, the attribute names for primary keys are underlined, for example, the E-ID in the EMPLOYEE relation. When two attributes compose a primary key, the values for those two attributes considered together form a combination that is unique to that tuple. The combination of E-ID and BEGIN DATE in the VACATION TAKEN relation form a unique set of values for each tuple, because we would expect only one entry for an employee on a given date. Logically speaking, an employee can begin only one vacation on a given date.

An attribute is frequently defined on the same domain as a primary key in a relation. If this attribute is also logically related to the attribute serving as primary key, then it is called a **foreign key.** The AUTHORIZATION attribute in the VACATION TAKEN relation is a foreign key, since it is defined on the same domain as E-ID in the EMPLOYEE relation.

The two attributes that form this primary key/foreign key relationship may exist in the same relation. Consider the modified version of the EMPLOYEE relation shown in Figure 6–5. Here, MANAGER ID has been added as an attribute. Since a manager must also be an employee, the MANAGER ID attribute is a foreign key to the E-ID attribute in the same relation.

A foreign key establishes a relationship by default between a relation containing the foreign key and the relation in which the primary key related to the foreign key exists. This situation occurs because the existence of a value for the attribute implies that the same value should exist in another relation as a primary key. In the discussion of referential integrity, we explore this situation in more detail.

For example, suppose the VACATION TAKEN relation contained the data shown in Figure 6–6. Here, the last tuple shown contains a value for authorization that does not correspond to an existing manager's identification number. Thus, one must question the validity of the authorization.

FIGURE 6–5 The EMPLOYEE Relation Modified
An example of a foreign key existing in the same relation as the primary key that it references.

EMPLOYEE

E-ID	Name	Address	City	Zip	Phone	Title		Manager ID
134572698	Jones	12 Maple St.	Atlanta	30311	758-1267	Programmer	. . .	252022010
983749493	Smith	28 Alma St.	Smyrna	30364	748-4847	Programmer	. . .	252022010
847478599	Clarke	373 Ave. A	Smyrna	30364	837-9383	Consultant	. . .	252887324
252930423	Dexter	3888 6th St.	Smyrna	30364	837-2552	Consultant	. . .	252887324
383783993	Hayet	149 Oakside Dr.	Atlanta	30311	758-7399	Programmer	. . .	252022010
252928462	Gofman	2333 Briarcrest Dr.	Atlanta	30312	766-6752	Programmer	. . .	252022010
252022010	Wray	2911 Windgate St.	Smyrna	30364	837-7288	Manager	. . .	349942839
252887324	Bennett	131 Rhodes Dr.	Smyrna	30367	977-0979	Manager	. . .	349942839

FIGURE 6–6

An Example of a Questionable Foreign Key Value. The last tuple contains a value that does not correspond to a current manager's identification number.

VACATION TAKEN

E-ID	Begin Date	End Date	Authorization
134572698	7/1	7/5	252022010
252930423	8/10	8/10	252022010
383783993	9/4	9/7	252022010
983749493	9/4	9/4	252887324
383783993	9/10	9/14	837954503

ENTITY RELATIONSHIPS

A relation provides data to a decision-maker about an entity class. Usually, a decision-maker is also interested in *relationships* between data items. If you have a relation containing information about airlines (say airline name and telephone number) and another relation containing information about flights (say destination, departure, and arrival time), but no way of relating flights to the appropriate airlines, you will have a difficult time making a reservation. (Be careful to distinguish between *relation* and *relationship* here and throughout this chapter.)

Relationships within Entities

Two types of relationships can be distinguished in the relational model. The first type is the obvious one that occurs within a tuple due to the existence of data for a particular attribute. The EMPLOYEE relation in Figure 6–2, for example, has been designed so that all of the relevant data about a single employee appears in a tuple. We know that a consultant named Smith, who lives on 28 Alma Street in Smyrna, has five vacation days available because the EMPLOYEE relation contains a tuple for Smith with these values.

Relationships between Entitles

Trees. The second type of relationship occurs between relations. In Chapter 2, we presented the concept of a tree, or a one-to-many relationship. An example of a one-to-many relationship can be seen in the EMPLOYEE and ASSIGNMENT relations (see Figure 6–2): An employee works on many projects.

This relationship is designed into the relations by repeating the primary key for an employee in the PROJECT relation. In fact, all relationships between relations are designed this way. (This aspect of the relational database model is discussed in more detail shortly.) A consequence of this method of building relationships is that the concept of a domain takes on great importance. The domains of the attributes must be the same, not just similar.

Networks. Designing a relational schema to model a more complicated relationship is not too difficult. Our previous example was really a subset of the relationships between projects and employees. This relationship is many-to-many: An employee may be assigned to many projects and a project may engage many employees.

The design reflects the decomposition of this many-to-many structure into two overlapping one-to-many structures. The ASSIGNMENTS relation is the intersection relationship that implements the decomposition. As we noted in Chapter 3, information specific to the intersection relationship can be modeled here as a composite entity. The ASSIGNMENTS relation contains the total number of hours a particular employee has worked on a particular project and the employee's evaluation on that project.

The relationships can be seen by focusing on the key values. As we noted above, the employee's identification number, which is the primary key in the EMPLOYEE relation, appears more than once in the ASSIGNMENTS relation. The project's identification number, which is the primary key in the PROJECT relation, likewise appears multiple times in the ASSIGNMENTS relation. The EMPLOYEE-ASSIGNMENTS one-to-many relationship implements the first one-to-many relationship needed in the decomposition. The PROJECT-ASSIGNMENTS relationship implements the second one-to-many relationship. Notice that the primary key in the intersection relation is the combination of the primary keys for the two relations in the complex network.

Thus far, we have only discussed the superficial characteristics of the relational model. The theory behind this model is much more comprehensive and may be discussed in terms of three distinguishing features of the model. These features describe constraints on the data structures available, relationships that must be maintained, and operations that perform data manipulation in a relational database environment.

Essentiality

We are now in a position to address the first of three distinguishing features of the relational database model. The only data structure that has been discussed thus far is the relation. In fact, the first feature is that the relation is the only data structure provided in the relational database model. There are no links or pointers. To appreciate the significance of this aspect of the model, one must recognize the additional complexity associated with a linking data structure. The data structure in Figure 6–7 is similar to the EMPLOYEE and VACATION TAKEN relations in Figure 6–2, but the employee identification number attribute in the VACATION TAKEN relation has been replaced with links from the EMPLOYEE tuples to the proper VACATION TAKEN tuples. The links represent physical pointers from the employee records to the vacation records. To determine the vacation that has been taken by an employee, the database system must process the link in some manner. Hence, the link is essential to determining the information. This example illustrates the concept of **essentiality**. A data structure is essential if its removal causes a loss of information from the database. A loss of information obviously includes a lost relationship as well as a lost attribute.

In our example, the EMPLOYEE and VACATION TAKEN relations and their attributes are all essential. Each logical unit of information in Figure 6–7 requires two rows and a link, all of which are essential. In the original data structures in Figure 6–2, however, the link is not essential. It adds only complexity to the processing; removing it does not cause any loss of information.

FIGURE 6–7   Explicit Representation of Relationships Using Links

EMPLOYEE

E-ID	Name	Address	City	Zip	Phone	Title	Salary	Vacation Available	Sick Leave Available
134572698	Jones	12 Maple St.	Atlanta	30311	758-1267	Programmer	2200	3	8
983749493	Smith	28 Alma St.	Smyrna	30364	748-4847	Programmer	2200	5	8
847478599	Clarke	373 Ave. A	Smyrna	30364	837-9383	Consultant	2500	5	7
252930423	Dexter	3888 6th St.	Smyrna	30364	837-2552	Consultant	2500	4	5
383783993	Hayet	149 Oakside Dr.	Atlanta	30311	758-7399	Programmer	2300	3	7
252928462	Gofman	2333 Briarcrest Dr.	Atlanta	30312	766-6752	Programmer	2350	7	8
252022010	Wray	2911 Windgate St.	Smyrna	30364	837-7288	Manager	3500	7	7
252887324	Bennett	131 Rhodes Dr.	Smyrna	30367	977-0979	Manager	4200	3	8

VACATION TAKEN

Begin Date	End Date	Authorization
7/1	7/5	252022010
8/10	8/10	252022010
9/4	9/7	252022010
9/4	9/4	252887324
11/20	11/21	252887324

The essentiality concept appears in other aspects of the relational model. Recall that the order of the tuples in a relation does not matter. In fact, requiring tuples to be ordered violates the premise that the relation is the only essential data structure. A required ordering adds complexity to the processing of the model and implies a loss of information should the tuples become unordered.

The fact that the relation is the only essential data structure in the relational model separates this model from all others. All other models explicitly include an essential linking structure. As we have seen above, models that include inessential linking structures can be converted to equivalent relational models.

Integrity Rules

The second distinguishing feature of the relational database model involves integrity rules. *Integrity* is the overall assurance that the content of the database (taken as a whole) is accurate and consistent. Since the content of the database is defined by the base relations, the integrity rules need apply only to the base relations. Two types of integrity are defined in the relational database model: entity integrity and referential integrity.

Entity integrity gives one the ability to uniquely identify each entity in the relational database. This ability guarantees access to all data.

Because each entity is described by a tuple, entity integrity is supported by the requirement that no primary key (or attribute composing a primary key) have a null value. In addition, once the primary key is established, no change may be made that corrupts the ability of the primary key to uniquely identify a tuple.

Entity integrity follows from the fact that the relation models entities that really exist. We have noted earlier in the book that we are only interested in modeling entities that are real and distinguishable. One would not expect any need to specify a null value for the attributes that distinguish one entity from another. A null value would imply either that the attribute does not exist or that it is unknown. It must exist; otherwise, our assumption that the entities are distinguishable is erroneous. If it is unknown, we might be storing redundant data since the data may actually be for an entity already represented in the relation. Also, the primary key provides the only way to access a tuple; hence, the primary key must have a value to support access.

Referential integrity gives one the ability to reference tuples by way of foreign keys. Referential integrity is supported by the requirement that the values assumed by a foreign key either match a primary key that exists in the database or be completely null. This rule ensures that, if another tuple is referenced in the database, then that tuple exists.

Figure 6–6 illustrates the absence of referential integrity. Here, we have introduced a new tuple in the VACATION TAKEN relation. Note that the last tuple in this relation has the value 837954503. This value should reference a valid employee identification number. Specifically, it should reference a manager's identification number. This value, however, does not appear in the EMPLOYEE relation. The VACATION TAKEN relation therefore refers to a nonexistent manager in the EMPLOYEE relation. The validity of this information is questionable, since the authorization appears suspect.

Referential integrity also follows naturally from the assumption that the database models entities that actually exist. We expect that any value for an attribute that can be used to reference a tuple in another relation should be a valid value. Unlike the case for primary keys in entity integrity, however, the value of a foreign key may be null and may not be unique. If, for example, we focus only on the vacations authorized by Wray, we see that the value for AUTHORIZATION in VACATION TAKEN is 252022010 and it appears several times. We could also enter into this relation a tuple in which the AUTHORIZATION attribute contains a null value. This entry would imply that the AUTHORIZATION was unknown. If it is unknown, it does not reference any employee. Thus, it cannot reference a nonexistent employee.

Data Manipulation

The third distinguishing feature of the relational model is data manipulation. A database is of relatively little value unless some means exists to manipulate the data. Data manipulation is a primary way to create information for decision-making. Several types of data manipulation language (DML) have been developed for use with the relational model. Some DMLs are very formal in the way they define mathematical operators for manipulating relations. Others are less formal (at least compared to the rigors of mathematics) and are more like high-level programming languages.

Relational algebra provides a set of operators for manipulating entire relations. Relational algebra is considered a procedural approach to data manipulation because the user must specify the order in which the relational algebra operators will be used. **Relational calculus** is a nonprocedural set of operators that provide great flexibility in manipulating the data in relations. These operators are said to be nonprocedural because the user only specifies what the desired data is, not how to get it. Relational algebra and relational calculus are presented in detail in the following sections.

Transformation languages are high-level languages that transform input relations into the desired output relations. One example of a transformation language is SQL, which is discussed in Chapter 7. **Graphic languages** display pictures of relations; the user fills in the appropriate attribute with an example of the desired data. A graphic language is used in the Paradox database system, discussed in Chapter 9.

RELATIONAL ALGEBRA

Relational algebra operations manipulate entire relations. Relational algebra has **closure**, which means an operation on a relation (or several relations) always produces another relation. Closure is desirable because it reduces the complexity of database processing by eliminating any "special cases." Operations in relational algebra always produce a valid relation, never anything else. Because the relational database model is based on set theory, many of the algebra operations closely resemble set operations. We will review each operation intuitively in the sections that follow. The relational algebra operations are summarized in Table 6–2.

TABLE 6–2   Operations of Relational Algebra

Operation	Usage
Projection	Creates a new relation by selecting attributes from a relation.
Selection	Creates a new relation by selecting tuples from a relation.
Union	Creates a new relation by combining tuples from two relations. The relations must be union-compatible.
Intersection	Creates a new relation consisting of tuples that occur in two relations.
Difference	Creates a new relation consisting of tuples that occur in one relation but not in another.
Division	Creates a new relation by selecting tuples from a relation based on the occurrence of attribute values in the dividing relation.
Join	Creates a new relation based on a relationship between two attributes in different relations.

Projection

Sometimes, a database user needs only one or a few attributes in a relation. The payroll function of our illustrated organization, for example, probably needs only the name and employee number from the EMPLOYEE relation in order to print payroll checks. An operation for choosing specific attributes to be displayed is called **projection**. Because the payroll function requires data only on the names and numbers of employees, EMPLOYEE can be "projected over" E-ID and NAME and the result can be stored in a relation named EMPLOYEE-NUMBER-NAME. The result of such a command is presented in Figure 6–8b. Note that the order of the attributes specified in the command corresponds to the order of the attributes in the new relation.

Closure ensures a projection always produces a relation. Thus, duplicate tuples are always deleted from the result. If PROJECT is projected over the TYPE attribute, the result contains only three tuples. If the specific values for project type were repeated in the result, the table would contain duplicate rows since the value E and C would occur twice. Valid relations, however, do not contain duplicate tuples.

FIGURE 6–8a   Original EMPLOYEE Relation

EMPLOYEE										
										Sick
									Vacation	Leave
E-ID	Name	Address	City	Zip	Phone	Title	Salary	Available	Available
134572698	Jones	12 Maple St.	Atlanta	30311	758-1267	Programmer	2200	3	8
983749493	Smith	28 Alma St.	Smyrna	30364	748-4847	Programmer	2200	5	8
847478599	Clarke	373 Ave. A	Smyrna	30364	837-9383	Consultant	2500	5	7
252930423	Dexter	3888 6th St.	Smyrna	30364	837-2552	Consultant	2500	4	5
383783993	Hayet	149 Oakside Dr.	Atlanta	30311	758-7399	Programmer	2300	3	7
252928462	Gofman	2333 Briarcrest Dr.	Atlanta	30312	766-6752	Programmer	2350	7	8
252022010	Wray	2911 Windgate St.	Smyrna	30364	837-7288	Manager	3500	7	7
252887324	Bennett	131 Rhodes Dr.	Smyrna	30367	977-0979	Manager	4200	3	8

**FIGURE 6–8b
EMPLOYEE Relation
Projected over
E-ID and Name**

EMPLOYEE-NUMBER-NAME	
E-ID	Name
134572698	Jones
983749493	Smith
847478599	Clarke
252930423	Dexter
383783993	Hayet
252928462	Gofman
252022010	Wray
252887324	Bennett

Selection

Occasionally, a user desires only a subset of tuples from a relation. For example, the executive vice president of this organization may wish to have information on projects to answer a question like "What is the status of enhancement projects?" The vice president could select from PROJECT (see Figure 6–9a) all tuples where TYPE has the value *E* and store the result in ENHANCEMENTS. This yields the relation in Figure 6–9b. The **selection** operation is used to obtain this type of result.

The result of selection contains all attributes in the new relation. But why include the TYPE attribute when it is already known that the value is "E" in every tuple? Most users do not want to process more information than they need. Suppose a manager needs only a list of names of all programmers. Selection and projection can be combined to specify exactly this information. The result of selecting from EMPLOYEE all tuples in which TITLE has the value *Programmer* can be projected over NAME to produce the relation PROGRAMMERS as shown in Figure 6–9c.

This example illustrates the procedural aspect of relational algebra. The result in Figure 6–9c was formed by using selection *followed by* projection. In this case, projection followed by selection would not even make sense, because the projection operation would remove the attribute that is the target of the selection.

FIGURE 6–9a   Original PROJECT Relation

PROJECT P-ID	Name	Type	Actual Hours	Expected Hours	Project Leader
6301	Marketing report	E	12	120	252928462
2376	New billing system	E	80	160	252928462
2876	Common stock report	C	12	8	383783993
2671	Bad debt report	D	40	20	252930423
2651	Manpower report bug	C	8	16	983749493

Project types: E = Enhancement, C = Correction, D = Development

**FIGURE 6–9b
Selection from PROJECT
where Type = E**

ENHANCEMENTS P-ID	Name	Type	Actual Hours	Expected Hours	Project Leader
6301	Marketing report	E	12	120	252928462
2376	New billing system	E	80	160	252928462

Project types: E = Enhancement, C = Correction, D = Development

FIGURE 6–9c
**Selection from EMPLOYEE
where Title = Programmer,
Projected over Name**

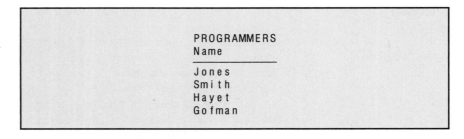

```
                        PROGRAMMERS
                        Name
                        _____
                        Jones
                        Smith
                        Hayet
                        Gofman
```

FIGURE 6–10a
**Original VACATION TAKEN
and SICK LEAVE
TAKEN Relations**

```
VACATION TAKEN
                      Begin          End
E-ID                  Date           Date         Authorization

134572698             7/1            7/5          252022010
252930423             8/10           8/10         252022010
383783993             9/4            9/7          252022010
983749493             9/4            9/4          252887324
383783993             11/20          11/21        252887324


SICK LEAVE TAKEN
                      Begin          End
E-ID                  Date           Date         Authorization

134572698             3/2            3/2          252022010
383783993             5/10           5/14         252022010
```

Union

The preceding examples draw data from a single relation. Frequently, one must combine data from two or more relations to get needed data. Suppose that the data on all paid absences of the organization's personnel is needed. In this case, data is needed from both the VACATION TAKEN and SICK LEAVE TAKEN relations (see Figure 6–10a).

Two relations can be combined vertically to form a third relation by the **union** operation. There are two restrictions: first, the two relations must have the same number of attributes (have the same degree); second, the attributes in the corresponding columns must assume values from the same domain. Two relations that satisfy these criteria are said to be **union compatible.** VACATION TAKEN and SICK LEAVE TAKEN are union compatible. The union of VACATION TAKEN and SICK LEAVE TAKEN produces the relation named PAID LEAVE TAKEN in Figure 6–10b.

You may recall that the PAID LEAVE TAKEN relation was introduced earlier in the chapter (see Figure 6–3). It illustrates a view, or derived relation. Now you know how the view is constructed.

FIGURE 6–10b
Union of VACATION TAKEN **and** SICK LEAVE TAKEN **Relations**

```
PAID  LEAVE  TAKEN
                    Begin         End
E - ID              Date          Date          Authorization
134572698           7 / 1         7 / 5         252022010
252930423           8 / 10        8 / 10        252022010
383783993           9 / 4         9 / 7         252022010
983749493           9 / 4         9 / 4         252887324
383783993           11 / 20       11 / 21       252887324
134572698           3 / 2         3 / 2         252022010
383783993           5 / 10        5 / 14        252022010
```

FIGURE 6–11a
Data to Illustrate an Intersection
Note the identical last tuple in each relation.

```
VACATION  TAKEN
                    Begin         End
E - ID              Date          Date          Authorization
134572698           7 / 1         7 / 5         252022010
252930423           8 / 10        8 / 10        252022010
383783993           9 / 4         9 / 7         252022010
983749493           9 / 4         9 / 4         252887324
383783993           11 / 20       11 / 21       252887324


SICK  LEAVE  TAKEN
                    Begin         End
E - ID              Date          Date          Authorization
134572698           3 / 2         3 / 2         252022010
383783993           5 / 10        5 / 14        252022010
383783993           11 / 20       11 / 21       252887324
```

Intersection

Consider the revised versions of the VACATION TAKEN and SICK LEAVE TAKEN relations in Figure 6–11a. In particular, notice that the data for the last tuple in each relation is identical. Typical accounting principles dictate that the absence should be accounted for as either vacation time or sick leave, but not both. In a large corporate database, examining all entries in relations such as these to find possibly one or two mistakes like this would be very difficult, perhaps impossible.

The **intersection** relational algebra operation can perform this task. Intersection generates a relation that contains only tuples that appear in both relations. Only the tuple for employee 383783993 with a beginning date of 11/20 and an ending date of 11/21 and so on occurs in both VACATION TAKEN and SICK LEAVE TAKEN. Thus, it is the only one in the

FIGURE 6–11b
Intersection of VACATION
TAKEN **and** SICK
LEAVE TAKEN

```
DOUBLE COUNTED ABSENCES
                    Begin        End
    E-ID            Date         Date         Authorization
    383783993       11/20        11/21        252887324
```

resulting relation, shown in Figure 6–11b. As with the union operation, the relations must be union compatible to perform the intersection operation.

Difference

Consider the following problem. A list of all nonmanagers is required. In the small database from Figure 6–12, the problem appears trivial. One might use selection to obtain a relation containing tuples for programmers. Then one might use selection again to form a relation containing tuples for consultants. These relations could be combined using a union operation to obtain the desired result: a relation containing information on the nonmanagers.

Although this approach will work, it is not a feasible approach to use in a complex situation. A typical corporate database might have thousands of employees with dozens of job titles. An approach that required someone to identify each title, create a separate relation for each, and then combine all of the relations would be very tedious. Fortunately, an alternative exists. The **difference** operation identifies tuples that occur in one relation but not in another. Once again, union compatibility is required to perform this operation.

To respond to the need for this data, one would first create a relation containing information for managers. This relation can be created using the selection operation on EMPLOYEE (see Figure 6–12a). Assume the result of this selection forms a relation called MANAGER, as shown in Figure 6–12b. Now, the difference of EMPLOYEE and MANAGER can be taken. This operation produces a relation with the data shown in Figure 6–12c. The difference operation produces a relation containing all tuples in one relation that do not occur in the second relation.

The order in which the relations are specified is significant in the difference operation. The difference of MANAGER and EMPLOYEE is different from the difference of EMPLOYEE and MANAGER. The difference of MANAGER and EMPLOYEE would produce a relation with no tuples. The first difference, EMPLOYEE − MANAGER, answers the question "Which employees are not managers?" The second difference, MANAGER − EMPLOYEE, answers the question "Which managers are not employees?" Since all managers are also employees, one would expect the result of this operation to be an empty relation.

FIGURE 6–12a **Original EMPLOYEE Relation**

EMPLOYEE										
E-ID	Name	Address	City	Zip	Phone	Title	Salary	Vacation Available	Sick Leave Available
134572698	Jones	12 Maple St.	Atlanta	30311	758-1267	Programmer	2200	3	8
983749493	Smith	28 Alma St.	Smyrna	30364	748-4847	Programmer	2200	5	8
847478599	Clarke	373 Ave. A	Smyrna	30364	837-9383	Consultant	2500	5	7
252930423	Dexter	3888 6th St.	Smyrna	30364	837-2552	Consultant	2500	4	5
383783993	Hayet	149 Oakside Dr.	Atlanta	30311	758-7399	Programmer	2300	3	7
252928462	Gofman	2333 Briarcrest Dr.	Atlanta	30312	766-6752	Programmer	2350	7	8
252022010	Wray	2911 Windgate St.	Smyrna	30364	837-7288	Manager	3500	7	7
252887324	Bennett	131 Rhodes Dr.	Smyrna	30367	977-0979	Manager	4200	3	8

FIGURE 6–12b **Selection from EMPLOYEE where Title = "Manager"**

MANAGERS										
E-ID	Name	Address	City	Zip	Phone	Title	Salary	Vacation Available	Sick Leave Available
252022010	Wray	2911 Windgate St.	Smyrna	30364	837-7288	Manager	3500	7	7
252887324	Bennett	131 Rhodes Dr.	Smyrna	30367	977-0979	Manager	4200	3	8

FIGURE 6–12c **The Difference of EMPLOYEE and MANAGER**

E-ID	Name	Address	City	Zip	Phone	Title	Salary	Vacation Available	Sick Leave Available
134572698	Jones	12 Maple St.	Atlanta	30311	758-1267	Programmer	2200	3	8
983749493	Smith	28 Alma St.	Smyrna	30364	748-4847	Programmer	2200	5	8
847478599	Clarke	373 Ave. A	Smyrna	30364	837-9383	Consultant	2500	5	7
252930423	Dexter	3888 6th St.	Smyrna	30364	837-2552	Consultant	2500	4	5
383783993	Hayet	149 Oakside Dr.	Atlanta	30311	758-7399	Programmer	2300	3	7
252928462	Gofman	2333 Briarcrest Dr.	Atlanta	30312	766-6752	Programmer	2350	7	8

Product

The union operation described earlier combines the tuples in two relations *vertically*. It puts the tuples from one relation under the tuples from a second relation. The relational algebra operation known as **product**

constructs a new relation that combines all of the tuples in two relations *horizontally.* It connects each tuple of one relation with all tuples of a second relation, thus combining all of the attributes into the resulting relation.

The product operation is illustrated in Figure 6–13. We have modified the ASSIGNMENTS relation so that it contains only the employee identification number and the project identification number. We have also reduced the number of tuples in ASSIGNMENTS, for a reason that will become evident very soon. The modified ASSIGNMENTS relation has been combined with the PROJECT relation. The result contains 20 tuples, because each tuple in PROJECT is combined with *every* tuple in the modified ASSIGNMENTS relation. In general, if one relation contains *m* tuples and the second relation contains *n* tuples, the result of a product operation will contain *m* times *n* tuples.

The product operation is not too useful alone. However, it can be used to construct a join operation, which is described in the next section.

Natural Join

As we noted above, the product provides one means to combine data in two relations. However, the product is not a very useful operation because the result contains a mixture of tuples, including some that have no logical definition. For example, what meaning can be attached to the second tuple in Figure 6–13b?

Suppose that we wished to know the names of the employees working on each project. Obtaining this result requires that we somehow combine the data in EMPLOYEE and PROJECT. You have learned that the

FIGURE 6–13a   The ASSIGNMENTS (Modified) and PROJECT Relations to Illustrate the Product Operation

```
ASSIGNMENTS
E-ID              P-ID

134572698         6301
134572698         2376
252930423         2671
983749493         2376


PROJECT
                                  Actual    Expected    Project
P-ID    Name              Type    Hours     Hours       Leader

6301    Marketing report    E      12        120        252928462
2376    New billing system  E      80        160        252928462
2876    Common stock report C      12          8        383783993
2671    Bad debt report     D      40         20        252930423
2651    Manpower report bug C       8         16        983749493

Project types: E = Enhancement, C = Correction, D = Development
```

FIGURE 6–13b   The Result of the Product Operation: ASSIGNMENTS - AND - PROJECTS

ASSIGNMENTS - AND - PROJECTS

E-ID	P-ID	PROJECT. P-ID	Name	Type	Actual Hours	Expected Hours	Project Leader
134572698	6301	6301	Marketing report	E	12	120	252928462
134572698	6301	2376	New billing system	E	80	160	252928462
134572698	6301	2876	Common stock report	C	12	8	383783993
134572698	6301	2671	Bad debt report	D	40	20	252930423
134572698	6301	2651	Manpower report bug	C	8	16	983749493
134572698	2376	6301	Marketing report	E	12	120	252928462
134572698	2376	2376	New billing system	E	80	160	252928462
134572698	2376	2876	Common stock report	C	12	8	383783993
134572698	2376	2671	Bad debt report	D	40	20	252930423
134572698	2376	2651	Manpower report bug	C	8	16	983749493
252930423	2671	6301	Marketing report	E	12	120	252928462
252930423	2671	2376	New billing system	E	80	160	252928462
252930423	2671	2876	Common stock report	C	12	8	383783993
252930423	2671	2671	Bad debt report	D	40	20	252930423
252930423	2671	2651	Manpower report bug	C	8	16	983749493
983749493	2376	6301	Marketing report	E	12	120	252928462
983749493	2376	2376	New billing system	E	80	160	252928462
983749493	2376	2876	Common stock report	C	12	8	383783993
983749493	2376	2671	Bad debt report	D	40	20	252930423
983749493	2376	2651	Manpower report bug	C	8	16	983749493

intersection relationship embodied in the ASSIGNMENTS relation provides the key to the solution, since it "connects" to both EMPLOYEE and PROJECT. If we take the result of the product operation from above and keep only tuples where the value for the project identification attribute in ASSIGNMENTS is the same as the project identification attribute in PROJECT, we have the result of a **natural join** operation on ASSIGNMENTS and PROJECT. This operation is typically called simply a *join operation,* as the other types of join operations (described below) are rarely used. The result has combined the employee number for each employee with all occurrences of a project to which the employee is assigned. The P-ID attribute appears only once in the result.

To complete our task of obtaining the *names* of the employees on each project, we would join this result with the EMPLOYEE relation. Our result, shown in Figure 6–14b, retains only the attributes where the value for the employee identification attribute in EMPLOYEE (E-ID) is the same as the value for employee identification attribute in the result from the first join operation. Once again, the result is another relation.

Theta-Join

The most common type of join uses a comparison of equality of two attributes, but any logical comparison can be made. The comparison operation is generically called *theta* and represented by the symbol Θ.

FIGURE 6–14a **The Join of** PROJECT **and** ASSIGNMENTS

| ASSIGNMENTS-AND-PROJECTS | | | | | | |
E-ID	P-ID	Name	Type	Actual Hours	Expected Hours	Project Leader
134572698	6301	Marketing report	E	12	120	252928462
134572698	2376	New billing system	E	80	160	252928462
252930423	2671	Bad debt report	D	40	20	252930423
983749493	2376	New billing system	E	80	160	252928462

FIGURE 6–14b **The Join of** EMPLOYEE **and** ASSIGNMENTS - AND - PROJECTS

| ASSIGNMENTS-PROJECTS-EMPLOYEES | | | | | | |
E-ID	P-ID	Name	Type	Actual Hours	Expected Hours	Project Leader
134572698	6301	Marketing report	E	12	120	252928462
134572698	2376	New billing system	E	80	160	252928462
252930423	2671	Bad debt report	D	40	20	252930423
983749493	2376	New billing system	E	80	160	252928462

E-ID	Name	Address	City	Zip	Phone	Title	Salary	Vacation Available	Sick Leave Available
134572698	Jones	12 Maple St.	Atlanta	30311	758-1267	Programmer	2200	3	8
134572698	Jones	12 Maple St.	Atlanta	30311	758-1267	Programmer	2200	3	8
252930423	Dexter	3888 6th St.	Smyrna	30364	837-2552	Consultant	2500	4	5
983749493	Smith	28 Alma St.	Smyrna	30364	748-4847	Programmer	2200	5	8

In a natural join, "=" is substituted for Θ. When the comparison is equality, the theta-join is called an **equi-join.**

Maybe-Join

In all of the discussions thus far, the existence of a null value would not impact the data manipulation operations described. However, when a null value occurs for a foreign key, the definition of the join operation must be carefully considered. For an example, we will use the data in Figure 6–15a.

FIGURE 6–15a
The VACATION TAKEN Relation Modified
A relation with a null value in a foreign key.

VACATION TAKEN (MODIFIED)			
E-ID	Begin Date	End Date	Authorization
134572698	7/1	7/5	252022010
252930423	8/10	8/10	252022010
383783993	9/4	9/7	252022010
983749493	9/4	9/4	252887324
383783993	11/20	11/21	-0-

FIGURE 6–15b
The True-Join of VACATION TAKEN (Modified) and EMPLOYEE (some attributes from EMPLOYEE are omitted)

VACATION APPROVALS				
E-ID	Begin Date	End Date	Authorization	Name
134572698	7/1	7/5	252022010	Wray
252930423	8/10	8/10	252022010	Wray
383783993	9/4	9/7	252022010	Wray
983749493	9/4	9/4	252887324	Bennett

In this modified VACATION TAKEN relation, we have a null value for one of the authorizations. Suppose we want to resolve a query that asks for the names of the managers that authorized each vacation. We will join VACATION TAKEN with EMPLOYEE to obtain the names of the managers that have approved these vacations. But how should the null value be handled?

Codd (1979) illustrates how this situation is handled by introducing a three-valued logic as defined in the following tables:

AND	F	-0-	T
F	F	F	F
-0-	F	-0-	-0-
T	F	-0-	T

OR	F	-0-	T
F	F	-0-	T
-0-	-0-	-0-	T
T	T	T	T

$$\text{NOT(F)} = \text{T} \quad \text{NOT}(-0-) = -0- \quad \text{NOT(T)} = \text{F}$$

We have now defined two join operations. The *true-join* is the join with which you are familiar. The true-join produces the result that indicates that the operation is true. Figure 6–15b shows the result of the true-join. A second join, called the *maybe-join*, is used with the truth tables to determine the rest of the query (see Figure 6–15c). This join produces the result where the null values are involved. Note that the maybe-join does *not* include the results of the true-join.

FIGURE 6–15c   The Maybe-Join of VACATION TAKEN **(Modified) and** EMPLOYEE **(some attributes from** EMPLOYEE **are omitted)**

VACATION APPROVALS				
E-ID	Begin Date	End Date	Authorization	Name
383783993	11/20	11/21	-0-	Wray
383783993	11/20	11/21	-0-	Bennett

RELATIONAL CALCULUS[1]

Relational calculus is simply an alternative expression of the operations defined in relational algebra. Whereas relational algebra is defined in terms of a set of operations for constructing new relations from existing relations, relational calculus simply specifies the desired result. In many cases, relational calculus can specify in one statement a result that requires several relational algebra statements.

Students are often intimidated by the term *calculus.* One of our goals in writing this section is to remove this intimidation by demonstrating that relational calculus is really quite simple in its operation. On a practical note, data manipulation in a relational database system is occasionally *described* in terms of relational calculus instead of relational algebra. Rarely is data manipulation actually *implemented* in terms of relational calculus, although it certainly could be. Codd (1971) has developed such an implementation, and Date (1990) contains a discussion of implementations. Consequently, we believe an understanding of this notation to be to the student's advantage.

We present a small subset of relational calculus in the following discussion. We illustrate only a few of the many available operations, and the examples are not complex. As you work through the following sections, think in terms of the desired result. This is the fundamental difference between relational algebra and relational calculus. Earlier you were required to think in terms of how a relation was constructed. Now you must think in terms of what the resulting relation contains.

Projection with Relational Calculus

When a projection is performed, the desired result is a relation containing (typically a subset of) attributes arranged in a specified order. Hence, a projection is specified by describing the attributes to be retained in the result, along with their order. If R is a relation containing attributes A, B, and C, and r is a tuple in R, the the projection of R over

---

[1]Note to instructors: This section may be omitted without loss of continuity in the chapter content.

A and *C* is described in relational calculus as the set of all the *r*s such that *r*'s values for *A* and *C* appear in *R*. formally, this is written:

$$R[A,C] = \{r: r \in R \wedge r[A,C]\}$$

In case you are rusty when it comes to reading this type of set notation, the colon stands for "such that" and $\in$ for "is an element of." The $\wedge$ symbol denotes logical conjunction and is read "and." Thus, the statement may be read:

> The projection of the relation *R* over the attributes *A* and *C* is equal to the set of all the tuples (denoted by *r*) such that the tuple comes from (in other words, is an element of) the relation *R* and the tuple containing the attributes *A* and *C*.

The example of relational algebra illustrated in Figure 6–8 projects EMPLOYEE over E-ID and NAME. This would be specified by substituting EMPLOYEE for *R*, E-ID for *B*, and NAME for *C* in the statement above. The *r* has no direct translation, since it represents tuples in general that produce the desired result.

Selection with Relational Calculus

Selection is used to isolate tuples that satisfy a certain constraint or set of constraints. In selection using relational calculus, then, specification of constraints is necessary. Let *R* be a relation containing attributes *A*, *B*, and *C*, and let *r* represent a tuple in *R*. The constraint that the selected tuples must satisfy is Θ. A constant value *v* is also needed.

In relational calculus, two cases of "selection" are distinguished. The first is a selection in which the value of an attribute is compared to a specific value—this is called **restriction.** The term *selection* is reserved for the second case, in which the value of an attribute is compared to the value of another attribute. The example in Figure 6–9 is a restriction; it is defined by selection from *R* of all the *r* tuples where *A* satisfies a constraint specified by Θ on a value *v*. Formally, this is written as:

$$R\,[A \,\Theta\, v] = \{r : r \in R \wedge (r\,[A]\,\Theta\,v)\}$$

Our example requires substitution of EMPLOYEE for *R*, TYPE for *A*, "E" for *v*, and "equals" for Θ.

Selection is formally defined as follows:

$$R\,[A \,\Theta\, B] = \{r : r \in R \wedge (r\,[A]\,\Theta\,r\,[B])\}$$

The only difference between this and restriction occurs in the last term, where the *A* attribute is compared to the *B* attribute instead of to a constant value. This selection can be illustrated with the PROJECT relation in Figure 6–2. If selection of all tuples for projects with ACTUAL HOURS greater than or equal to EXPECTED HOURS is needed, this can be specified by substituting PROJECT for *R*, ACTUAL HOURS for *A*, EXPECTED HOURS for *B*, and "greater than or equal to" for Θ. The result contains the tuples for Projects 2686 and 2671.

Join with Relational Calculus

The join operation can be defined with the definitions used above: Let R be a relation containing attributes A, B, and C, let r represent a tuple in R, and let Θ represent a constraint that the selected tuples must satisfy; in addition, let S be a relation containing tuples represented by S defined on the same domains as R and let ▶◀ define the concatenation of two tuples, so that r ▶◀ s constructs a tuple consisting of all the attributes of r followed by all the attributes of s. The join operation is defined in relational calculus by:

$$R\,[A\,\Theta\,B]\,S = \{(r \blacktriangleright\blacktriangleleft s) : r \in R \wedge s \in S \wedge (r[A]\,\Theta\,s\,[B])\}$$

In other words, the join of R and S over the attributes A and B is defined by the concatenated tuples r and s such that r is in R, s is in S, and the values of A in r and B in s satisfy a constraint specified by Θ.

The join illustrated in Figure 6–14 can be obtained by substituting ASSIGNMENTS for R, PROJECT for S, ASSIGNMENTS P-ID for A, PROJECT P-ID for B, and "equals" for Θ. As above, Θ could be any other conditional operator specifying a constraint.

CASE EXAMPLE:
Relational Models of the Omega Company Database

This section is devoted to more examples of operations in relational algebra. The two relations in Figure 6–16 are used as the basis for these examples. One, ENVIRONMENT, contains typical data from the economic environment of a business organization. The other, ACCOUNTING-DATA, contains some accounting information for several quarters for two firms. Note that these relations are not union compatible; some relational algebra operations are not applicable. Examples of selection, projection, and join, however, can still be given.

These examples illustrate how a user may "browse" through a database, searching for answers to specific questions. The information retrieved may lead to new questions and additional queries. On-line browsing is extremely valuable in searching for information in a database.

Formulating a Forecasting Model

Suppose that you are an executive in one of the illustrated firms and you are interested in formulating a sales forecasting model. Desiring to look at some historical data, but not too much, you select from ENVIRONMENT tuples in which Year is greater than 81, producing the relation RECENT-DATA (Figure 6–17).

After looking at this relation, you decide to examine the Economic Index for the first quarter of every year for which you have data, because, in the first quarter of last year, sales for your firm, the Omega Company, were a little lower than expected. You select from

FIGURE 6–16
**Sample Relations from the
Omega Company Database**

ENVIRONMENT

Quarter	Year	Stock Market Index	Economic Index	Short Term Bill Rate
4	80	95	105	12.5
1	81	98	109	14.0
2	81	102	115	18.0
3	81	97	110	16.5
4	81	96	108	15.0
1	82	97	109	14.5
2	82	100	111	15.0
3	82	99	111	15.0
4	82	97	108	15.0
1	83	99	108	15.5
2	83	101	105	14.5
3	83	97	103	15.0
4	83	98	105	14.5

ACCOUNTING-DATA

Quarter	Year	Firm	Accounts Receivable	Accounts Payable	Sales
4	80	ALPHA	150	70	380
1	81	ALPHA	140	60	350
2	81	ALPHA	170	90	400
3	81	ALPHA	160	95	380
4	81	ALPHA	200	100	450
1	82	ALPHA	165	105	400
2	82	ALPHA	180	110	500
3	82	ALPHA	175	105	480
4	82	ALPHA	170	105	470
1	83	ALPHA	170	110	470
2	83	ALPHA	175	110	480
3	83	ALPHA	160	115	450
4	83	ALPHA	165	105	455
4	80	OMEGA	130	75	350
1	81	OMEGA	125	80	340
2	81	OMEGA	120	90	350
3	81	OMEGA	150	100	360
4	81	OMEGA	170	110	400
1	82	OMEGA	135	110	350
2	82	OMEGA	140	105	360
3	82	OMEGA	140	100	360
4	82	OMEGA	150	110	370
1	83	OMEGA	150	110	370
2	83	OMEGA	140	100	375
3	83	OMEGA	155	110	375
4	83	OMEGA	145	105	380

ENVIRONMENT tuples in which Quarter is equal to 1 and project that result over Year and Economic Index to produce ECON-INDEX.

This data (Figure 6–18) does not seem to indicate any reason for sales to have been slow. You decide, therefore, to compare Sales with Economic Index on a quarterly basis. This could be a first step in deciding if a more sophisticated statistical technique should be considered.

FIGURE 6–17
**Selection from
ENVIRONMENT where
Year > 81**

```
RECENT-DATA
                        Stock Market    Economic     Short Term
   Quarter    Year         Index          Index       Bill Rate
      1        82           97             109          14.5
      2        82          100             111          15.0
      3        82           99             111          15.0
      4        82           97             108          15.0
      1        83           99             108          15.5
      2        83          101             105          14.5
      3        83           97             103          15.0
      4        83           98             105          14.5
```

FIGURE 6–18
**Selection from
ENVIRONMENT where
Quarter = 1, Projected
over Year and
Economic Index**

```
        ECON-INDEX
                      Economic
          Year         Index
           81           109
           82           109
           83           108
```

This manipulation requires a join of ENVIRONMENT with ACCOUNTING-DATA where ENVIRONMENT Quarter is equal to ACCOUNTING-DATA Quarter and ENVIRONMENT Year is equal to ACCOUNTING-DATA Year, with the result projected over Quarter, Year, Firm, Economic Index, and Sales. COMPARISON (Figure 6–19) is the result.

After examining the resulting relation, you recall that the stock market was unusually depressed in that quarter—or was it the year before? What are the values for the STOCK MARKET INDEX for each quarter in the database? To find out, you project ENVIRONMENT over YEAR, QUARTER, and STOCK MARKET INDEX to obtain SMI-VALUE (Figure 6–20). There does not seem to be anything significant in the stock market indices. But now you remember that quarter was the second quarter of the big advertising campaign mounted by your competitor, Alpha Incorporated. What accounting data is available for Alpha Incorporated? You can select tuples from ACCOUNTING-DATA where FIRM = ALPHA, resulting in ALPHA-DATA (Figure 6–21).

While you were busy working on this mystery of Omega's sluggish performance, you did not notice that Jose Garza, one of your best employees in the finance department, had come in and was watching over your shoulder. Jose thinks that there may have been a problem in securing a short-term loan for the company during the time you are analyzing and suggests that you look for some relatively extreme short-term bill rates. You decide to retrieve the Year, Quarter, and Short Term Bill Rate for quarters in which the bill rate exceeded 15 percent. This query is

FIGURE 6–19

Join of ENVIRONMENT and ACCOUNTING-DATA over Quarter and Year, Projected over Quarter, Year, Firm, Economic Index, and Sales

COMPARISON

Quarter	Year	Firm	Economic Index	Sales
4	80	ALPHA	105	380
1	81	ALPHA	109	350
2	81	ALPHA	115	400
3	81	ALPHA	110	380
4	81	ALPHA	108	450
1	82	ALPHA	109	400
2	82	ALPHA	111	500
3	82	ALPHA	111	480
4	82	ALPHA	108	470
1	83	ALPHA	108	470
2	83	ALPHA	105	480
3	83	ALPHA	103	450
4	83	ALPHA	105	455
4	80	OMEGA	105	350
1	81	OMEGA	109	340
2	81	OMEGA	115	350
3	81	OMEGA	110	360
4	81	OMEGA	108	400
1	82	OMEGA	109	350
2	82	OMEGA	111	360
3	82	OMEGA	111	360
4	82	OMEGA	108	370
1	83	OMEGA	108	370
2	83	OMEGA	105	375
3	83	OMEGA	103	375
4	83	OMEGA	105	380

FIGURE 6–20

Projection of ENVIRONMENT over Year, Quarter, and Stock Market Index

SMI-VALUE

Year	Quarter	Stock Market Index
80	4	95
81	1	98
81	2	102
81	3	97
81	4	96
82	1	97
82	2	100
82	3	99
82	4	97
83	1	99
83	2	101
83	3	97
83	4	98

FIGURE 6–21
Selection from
ACCOUNTING-DATA
where Firm = "ALPHA"

| ALPHA-DATA | | | | | |
Quarter	Year	Firm	Accounts Receivable	Accounts Payable	Sales
4	80	ALPHA	150	70	380
1	81	ALPHA	140	60	350
2	81	ALPHA	170	90	400
3	81	ALPHA	160	95	380
4	81	ALPHA	200	100	450
1	82	ALPHA	165	105	400
2	82	ALPHA	180	110	500
3	82	ALPHA	175	105	480
4	82	ALPHA	170	105	470
1	83	ALPHA	170	110	470
2	83	ALPHA	175	110	480
3	83	ALPHA	160	115	450
4	83	ALPHA	165	105	455

FIGURE 6–22
Projection of ENVIRONMENT
over Year, Quarter, and
Short Term Bill Rate, Fol-
lowed by Selection with
Short Term Bill Rate > 15

| STBR-OVER-15 | | |
Year	Quarter	Short Term Bill Rate
81	2	18.0
81	3	16.5
83	1	15.5

obtained by first projecting ENVIRONMENT over Year, Quarter, and Short Term Bill Rate and then selecting tuples in which the Short Term Bill Rate is greater than 15 from the intermediate result. The final result, STBR-OVER-15 (Figure 6–22), shows something worth noticing. The short-term bill rates were a little higher than 15 percent in the first quarter of 1983. You make a note of this and decide to pursue the matter in more detail later.

Formulating a Complex Query

Because Jose is such a conscientious worker, you know he has come into your office for a reason. Jose has been working on a model that he believes will tie the company's sales to the current stock market activity. He is having some trouble getting the data needed to test his model, however. He knows he needs the data for Quarter, Year, Firm, and Sales for all quarters in which the Stock Market Index was less than 97. Extracting this information requires a selection, a projection, a join, and another projection. You decide to break this query into steps (Figure 6–23a–d).

You first select tuples from ENVIRONMENT where Stock Market Index is less than 97 and store the result in STEP–1. Next, you project STEP–1

FIGURE 6–23a
Selection from ENVIRONMENT where Stock Market Index < 97

STEP-1 Quarter	Year	Stock Market Index	Economic Index	Short Term Bill Rate
4	80	95	105	12.5
4	81	96	108	15.0

FIGURE 6–23b
Projection of STEP-1 over Quarter and Year

STEP-2 Quarter	Year
4	80
4	81

FIGURE 6–23c
Join of STEP-2 and ACCOUNTING-DATA over Quarter and Year

STEP-3 Quarter	Year	Firm	Accounts Receivable	Accounts Payable	Sales
4	80	ALPHA	150	70	380
4	81	ALPHA	200	100	450
4	80	OMEGA	130	75	350
4	81	OMEGA	170	110	400

FIGURE 6–23d
Projection of STEP-3 over Quarter, Year, Firm, and Sales

END Quarter	Year	Firm	Sales
4	80	ALPHA	380
4	81	ALPHA	450
4	80	OMEGA	350
4	81	OMEGA	400

over Quarter and Year, producing STEP–2. You then join ACCOUNTING-DATA with STEP–2 where ACCOUNTING-DATA Quarter is equal to STEP–2 Quarter and ACCOUNTING-DATA Year is equal to STEP–2 Year, thus generating STEP–3. Finally, you project STEP–3 Quarter, Year, Firm, and Sales, producing END. This gives Jose the information he needs. He is confident his model will have a positive impact on the operation of the company.

This short scenario demonstrates how a manager can interact with a database in an exploratory fashion, seeking data that might provide information. This exploratory aspect of data retrieval is one of the greatest advantages of the database environment.

Managers are able to get data from the database as fast as the proper query can be formulated. No programs have to be written, run, debugged, rerun, debugged again, and so on. Also, a manager need not know anything about the physical nature of the data. These characteristics of database management systems free managers to do what they have been hired to do—manage. ■

DISTINGUISHING RELATIONAL FROM RELATIONAL-LIKE SYSTEMS

We conclude this chapter with a brief discussion of methods for distinguishing relational from relational-like database systems. As you are probably aware, many systems are advertised as relational database systems. Following Codd (1982), we can define four categories of relational systems. A **tabular system** supports only tables as data structures and does not support any of the operations defined in relational algebra. A **minimally relational system** is tabular and supports only the selection, projection, and join operations of relational algebra. A system that is tabular and supports all the operations of relational algebra is **relationally complete.** Finally, a system that is relationally complete and also supports entity and referential integrity is **fully relational.**

Codd (1985a, 1985b) outlines 12 rules that define a fully relational database management system. These rules emphasize and extend the basic premise that a DBMS must be able to manage databases entirely through its relational capabilities. At the time he wrote these articles, Codd was unable to find a single system claiming to be relational that satisfied all 12 rules. These 12 rules should be considered guidelines for making a rough distinction in relational database systems. Codd (1990) has recently published a set of 333 "features" of the relational model (Version 2).

All of the rules below are based on what Codd calls "Rule Zero":

> For any system that is advertised as, or claims to be, a relational database management system, that system must be able to manage databases entirely through its relational capabilities.

This rule must hold regardless of whatever nonrelational features the DBMS might have. If this rule is not met, Codd believes there is no justification in calling the system a relational system. We list and briefly explain the 12 rules below.

Rule 1, the information rule. All information in a relational database is represented explicitly at the logical level and in exactly one way— by values in tables.

This rule requires that system-related information, such as table names, column names, and domain information, must be maintained as data in relations. There are no special structures for maintaining any of the data in a relational database. Therefore, the database administrator's job is executed by using the same relational data manipulation techniques that any other database user uses. Codd argues that this approach should lead to increased productivity for database administrators.

> **Rule 2, the guaranteed access rule.** Each and every (atomic) value in a relational database is guaranteed to be logically accessible by resorting to a combination of table name, primary key value, and column name.

This rule guarantees that all data in the database can be accessed in at least one way. This rule exists because the relational model does not incorporate any of the traditional methods of accessing data, such as looping through successive memory locations. Therefore, a rule that guarantees that every data value is accessible is important. We mentioned this concept earlier in our discussion of primary keys.

> **Rule 3, the systematic treatment of null values rule.** Null values (distinct from the empty character string, a string of blanks, a zero, or any other number) are supported in fully relational DBMSs for representing missing information and inapplicable information in a systematic way, independent of data type.

Database integrity is closely related to this rule. The database administrator should be able to specify that null values are not allowed for primary keys and for certain foreign keys (as determined by the organization's specific database processing requirements). Also, the *systematic* treatment of nulls leads to increased productivity. The implication here is that a common null value is used regardless of the domain. This approach implies database users need to learn only one null value representation, which is more efficient than learning, for instance, one null value for numeric data, another null value for character data, and so on. Additionally, nulls should be treated in a consistent fashion when functions (sum and average) are applied to data.

> **Rule 4, the dynamic on-line catalog based on the relational model rule.** The database description is represented at the logical level in the same way as ordinary data, so that authorized users can apply the same relational language to its interrogation as they apply to the regular data.

This rule implies database users need learn only one data model. Also, users can extend the on-line catalog into a repository (see Chapter 11) if the vendor of a system does not offer one. Rules 1 and 4 allow database administrators to access the database easily to determine what information is stored in the database.

> **Rule 5, the comprehensive data sublanguage rule.** There must be at least one language whose statements are expressible, per some well-defined syntax, as character strings and that is comprehensive in supporting *all* of the following items:

- data definition
- view definition
- data manipulation (interactive and by the program)

- integrity constraints
- authorization
- transaction boundaries

The intent of this rule is to provide for a single database language that addresses all of the actions required against a database, without requiring the database to be taken off-line for any reason. Other database approaches provide these functions in separate languages. Codd (1990) states that the ANSI/SPARC/X3 model discussed in Chapter 4, with over 40 separate interfaces defined, could have over 40 different languages associated with it. SQL, discussed in Chapter 7, is a comprehensive data manipulation language.

Rule 6, the view updating rule. All views that are theoretically updatable are also updatable in the system.

A view is "theoretically updatable" if there exists a time-independent algorithm for making changes in the base relations so that a desired effect occurs in a user's view. This rule states that changes in a view are reflected in the base relations used to create that view. Logical data independence, discussed in Chapter 4, is closely related to this rule.

Rule 7, the high-level insert, update, and delete rule. The capability of handling a base relation or a derived relation as a single operand applies not only to the retrieval of data but also to the insertion, update, and deletion of data.

This is another user productivity rule. This rule provides a means for users to manipulate data at the table level, rather than requiring separate subqueries to handle data in each row of a table. Also, in distributed database environments (see Chapter 12), the data for a single table may be partitioned and reside at different locations. This rule implies a user need not be concerned with the location of the rows in a table.

Rule 8, the physical data independence rule. Application programs and terminal activity remain logically unimpaired whenever any changes are made in either storage representations or access methods.

We discussed this concept in Chapter 4. Codd states it to emphasize that applications in a relational environment deal strictly with the logical representation of data, not the physical implementation.

Rule 9, the logical data independence rule. Application programs and terminal activities remain logically unimpaired when information-preserving changes of any kind that theoretically permit unimpairment are made to the base tables.

This rule implies that changes in base tables are allowed as long as the original information is preserved. Key preserving decompositions and nonloss joins, both illustrated in Chapter 5, are two ways of altering the base tables. Consequently, the database design may be changed *dynamically* without incurring major reorganization costs.

Rule 10, the integrity independence rule. Integrity constraints specific to a particular database must be definable in the relational data sublanguage and storable in the catalog, not in the application programs.

There is a need to record all integrity constraints related to a database in one place, outside of application programs. The constraints mentioned in this rule include any business policy, governmental regulation, or other constraint including the entity integrity and referential integrity rules discussed earlier in this chapter. This approach allows changes in these constraints to be made without interrupting applications.

Rule 11, the distribution independence rule. A relational database management system has distribution independence.

This rule ensures that applications are unaffected by a decision to distribute data (if it is originally centralized) or redistribute data (if it is already distributed). Note than an existing relational DBMS that does not operate in a distributed environment may still be considered relational. This rule does not impact nondistributed systems. Distributed DBMSs are covered in Chapter 12. Rules 8 through 11, all independence rules, protect against the problems discussed in Chapters 1 and 5.

Rule 12, the nonsubversion rule. If a relational system has a low-level (single-record-at-a-time) language, that low level cannot be used to subvert or by-pass the integrity rules and constraints expressed in the higher-level (multiple-records-at-a-time) relational language.

The intent of this rule is to preserve the integrity aspects of the relational model in a manner that is independent of logical data structures. According to Codd, many systems that have been converted from a different underlying database approach to the relational approach have difficulty satisfying this rule because the prior approach was tightly coupled to low-level implementation details. If low-level languages are allowed to subvert the independence aspects of the relational model, administrators will soon lose control of the database.

As we stated at the beginning of this section, these 12 rules are meant as rough guidelines for how well a system meets the criteria for relational database management systems. Codd's recent work (1990) describes over 300 criteria in 18 categories to define the relational model in detail. No other approach to database management is so thoroughly defined.

CHAPTER SUMMARY

The relational database model presents data in a familiar form, that of two-dimensional tables. This model has its foundation in set theory.

There are two ways of building a relationship in a relational database environment. One type of relationship is constructed by the

THE USER'S VIEW

The relational database model has been presented here in much more depth than those many users encounter. Most DBMSs claiming to be relational do not adhere to even the most basic relational terminology. Relations are frequently referred to as "tables," tuples as "rows," and attributes as "columns." These terms are less threatening to many users, especially those without technical background.

Similarly, the operations of relational algebra are often defined in less formal terms than those given here. Projection, selection, and join operations are typically variations of one basic command, as can be seen in Chapter 7 in the SQL discussion. Furthermore, the operations are frequently simply explained in terms like *retrieving a column* (for projection) or *retrieving a row* (for selection). The fact that data in the relational database model can be pictured as two-dimensional tables facilitates these types of explanations.

Users may be tempted to think that the way they picture data in the database is the way it is actually stored. It is not. Complicated list structures may be required to manage additions and deletions from the database. Logical pointer fields may be implemented to reduce redundancy. Whatever internal data structures are used, however, the result must conform to the characteristics of relations specified earlier.

A great deal has been written regarding the "performance myth," according to which relational database systems are inherently inefficient. Many experienced database systems users remember early implementations of the relational model that may have been inefficient. However, optimization techniques exist that improve the efficiency of relational systems. As more vendors develop relational systems, the efficiency of relational systems is expected to increase. As with any software package, issues such as efficiency and response time should be examined using benchmark tests representative of the normal operating conditions under which the database system is expected to operate. ■

---

existence of data within a single relation. In this case, an entity has a specific property because a value for an attribute corresponding to that property exists in the relation. The other type of relationship is constructed by replicating primary key values from one relation in another relation.

The relational database model can be used to represent all the relationships defined in earlier chapters—one-to-one, one-to-many, and many-to-many. These are all cases of relationships between entities.

Three major aspects of the relational model are data structure, rules for integrity, and methods for data manipulation. Relations are the only data structures provided by the relational model; the relational model requires entity and referential integrity; and data may be manipulated using relational algebra.

There are at least four ways of manipulating data in a relational database management system: relational algebra, relational calculus, transform languages, and graphic languages. The basic operations available in relational algebra are projection, selection, union, intersection, difference, division, and join. These operations are much like those for manipulating sets. Relational calculus differs from relational algebra in that the desired result is specified instead of constructed.

Database systems that claim to be relational systems may be categorized as tabular, minimally relational, relationally complete, or fully relational. These categories require increasingly closer adherence to the relational model. Tabular systems need only represent data in a tabular

METROPOLITAN NATIONAL BANK

The next step in your project is designing a relational implementation of the integrated MetNat database. The entity-relationship model and the conceptual designs developed in earlier chapters provide starting points for your implementation. However, you should be very careful about translating either *directly* into a relational design. Be sure that your implementation meets the criteria for constructing valid relations. Use the sample reports provided in Appendix B for data to illustrate your implementation.

Be sure you consider the goals you outlined in the master plan that you developed earlier in the project. If response time should be fast, for example, what is implied about the number of operations that should be performed (projects, selections, and joins) in accessing a particular data item? Include a brief discussion for each relation that describes how your implementation supports aspects of the master plan and/or the typical operating procedures described in earlier chapters.

You should prepare a report on the relational approach to MetNat's database system that includes complete schema and view descriptions. Specify all tables and attributes that appear in the conceptual schema. Specify all tables and attributes that exist in individual user views. Identify the attributes that compose the candidate, primary, and foreign keys in your relations. Also identify derived tables and attributes. Finally, distinguish between the relatively stable tables that represent account and employee information and the relatively volatile tables that represent transactions on accounts and credit cards. ■

format, but fully relational systems follow all of the specifications of the relational model. As we stated at the beginning of this chapter, it is the theoretical foundation of the relational model that allows one to make distinctions between truly relational database systems and database systems that are "relational-like." No other database system model has this characteristic.

Questions and Exercises

1. Define the following terms: relation, tuple, cardinality, attribute, domain, degree.
2. What is the difference between a candidate key and a primary key?
3. Does a relation always have a primary key? Why or why not?
4. Should a primary key in a database ever be allowed to have a null value?
5. Why might it be a bad idea to have an employee's last name as a primary key in a relation?
6. Consider a relation called SALES with attributes Date, Amount, and Salesperson. Assume that a tuple exists in the relation for Boisvert. How does one determine what amount Boisvert sold on a particular date?

7. How are relationships between relations derived?

8. Name three types of relationships that can exist between relations. Define each and give examples.

9. Consider the following relations: EMPLOYEE has attributes E-Number, Name, and Spouse's name; SPOUSE has attributes Name and Child's-name.

EMPLOYEE			SPOUSE	
E-Number	Name	Spouse's-name	Name	Child's-name
1010	Fraser	Barbara	Barbara	Robert
1003	Clarke	Lisa	Barbara	Kathy
1012	Mason	Robert	Lisa	John

There are at least two major problems with this database design. List all of the problems you can find.

10. What is a data manipulation language? Name four types of data manipulation language that have been developed for use with the relational database model.

11. What is closure?

12. What mathematical operations does relational algebra closely resemble? Why?

13. When would you want to perform a union operation on two relations?

14. What must be true of two relations in order to perform a union operation on them?

15. Compare the difference operation and the intersection operation of relational algebra. How are they similar? How do they differ?

16. Is the difference of two relations the same regardless of the order in which the difference is specified? Give an example to support your answer.

17. What is the difference between the selection operation and the projection operation?

18. Describe the join operation in relational algebra. When would one want to perform a join operation?

19. What is the difference between an equi-join and a natural join?

20. Can one perform a join operation over two attributes when the comparison between the two attributes is something other than equality? If the answer is yes, construct two relations for which such a join makes sense. If the answer is no, explain why.

21. Consider these two relations: SALE has attributes Invoice-number, Salesperson, and Amount (of sale); QUANTITY has attributes Invoice-number, Item-number, and Amount (ordered). Assume that Invoice-number is a unique number assigned to each invoice processed, and that many items can be ordered on a single invoice. Create sample data for these relations.

22. For the relations created in Question 21, show the result of a selection on the SALE relation for Amount greater than some value in your data.

23. For the relations created in Question 21, show the result of a join operation over Invoice-number. What does this represent?

24. What type of relationship is modeled in Question 21?

25. Show relational calculus constructions for the queries formulated in the case example titled "Relational Models of the Omega Company Database."

For Further Reading

The relational model was first presented in: Codd, E. F. "A Relational Model of Data for Large Shared Data Banks." *Communications of the ACM* 13, no. 6 (June 1970).

Dr. Codd (and others) have refined, extended, and in some cases clarified the relational approach in numerous articles since the original publication. See, for example, Codd, E. F. "Extending the Database Relational Model to Capture More Meaning." *ACM Transactions on Database Systems* 4, no. 4 (December 1979), pp. 397–434.

See also: Date, C. J. *An Introduction to Database Systems Volume I.* Reading, Mass: Addison-Wesley Publishing, 1990.

More recently, Dr. Codd authored two somewhat controversial articles in *Computerworld:* Codd, E. F. "Is Your DBMS Really Relational?" *Computerworld* 19, no. 41 (October 14, 1985); and Codd, E. F. "Does Your DBMS Run by the Rules?" *Computerworld* 19, no. 42 (October 21, 1985).

Version 2 of the relational model is described in: Codd, E. F. *The Relational Model for Database Management—Version 2.* Reading, Mass.: Addison-Wesley Publishing, 1990.

As mentioned in the text, there are few detailed descriptions of a data manipulation language for the relational model that is based on relational calculus. However, one of the best treatments is given in an early paper by Dr. Codd: Codd, E. F. "A Data Base Sublanguage Founded on the Relational Calculus." *Proceedings of the ACM SIGFIDET Workshop on Data Description, Access and Control,* 1971, pp. 35–68.

For a very theoretical treatment of the relational model, the reader is referred to: Yang, Chao-Chih. *Relational Databases.* Englewood Cliffs, N. J.: Prentice-Hall, 1986.

7

THE STRUCTURED QUERY LANGUAGE

The previous chapter laid the foundation for understanding the relational database model. This chapter builds on that foundation by describing the Structured Query Language (SQL) for relational databases. SQL has been adopted by the American National Standards Institute (ANSI) as the standard relational database language. Numerous implementations of SQL exist for machines ranging from personal computers to mainframes. It is perhaps the most widely used database language. SQL may be used either interactively or it may be embedded in a host programming language. Most of this chapter is devoted to the interactive use. A section at the end of the chapter deals with embedded SQL.

SQL is a relational transformation language. It provides ways to construct relations and manipulate the data in them. The result of a transformation operation is always another relation (which may have only one row and column).

SQL was developed in IBM research labs during the 1970s. It was the outgrowth of a previous language called SEQUEL (Structured English Query Language). Many people still pronounce the acronym SQL as "sequel." IBM did not release a commercial product supporting the language until 1981. At that time, Oracle Corporation had been marketing a relational system with an SQL interface for several months. Another widely used IBM package, DB2, was released for the MVS environment in 1983.

ANSI developed specifications for SQL and in 1986 adopted SQL as its official relational language. Standard SQL had an immediate impact on the database marketplace. As early as 1987, over 50 implementations of SQL were available commercially. In addition to those mentioned above, some of the more popular packages include XDB from Software Systems Technology, INGRES developed by Relational Technology, XQL now marketed by Novell, Ashton Tate's dBASE IV, and R:base of MicroRim.

Standard SQL is important because it allows training of both programmers and end-users in a language that is common to many computer systems and organizational environments. Also, database applications can be ported much more easily to different environments, and databases in different computer systems can be accessed more readily. Standards also facilitate the development of portable application packages (such as accounting systems) that operate in different database environments.

Unfortunately, as any other standard language, SQL is not without its problems. As you will see in the examples, many queries are readily expressible in SQL, but some are very difficult to express. We will illustrate SQL queries using the database shown in Figure 7–1. First we will show how the relational algebra operations of selection, projection, and join are performed. More extensive features of the query language are presented after that, including how SQL is embedded in host language programs.

PROJECTION

Projection in SQL is accomplished using the command keywords SELECT and FROM. The use of the word *select* for projection may seem confusing, since it seems to suggest the selection operation of relational algebra. In fact, selection is performed using a variation of this command.

To perform a projection, one follows the SELECT keyword with the desired attributes. The order in which the attributes are listed determines the order in which they appear in the result. The FROM keyword is then followed by the name of the relation from which the attributes should be taken.

The projection of EMPLOYEE over NAME and E_NUMBER is specified as:

```
SELECT NAME, E_NUMBER
FROM EMPLOYEE
```

(The indentation above is to improve readability. The entire statement could be placed on one line.)

The result of this command is shown in Figure 7–2a. Not all implementations of SQL include the relation name in the result as in Figure 7–2a. We include the name, however, to help clarify how the result is formed.

The projection of EMPLOYEE over DEPARTMENT is:

```
SELECT DEPARTMENT
FROM EMPLOYEE
```

The result of this command is shown in Figure 7–2b.

FIGURE 7–1   Organizational Data in Relations
Key attributes are underlined.

```
ASSIGNMENT                        SKILL
E_NUMBER    P_NUMBER              AREA

1001        26713                Stock market
1002        26713                Taxation
1003        23760                Investments
1003        26511                Management
1004        26511
1004        28765
1005        23760
```

PROJECT

NAME	P_NUMBER	MANAGER	ACTUAL_COST	EXPECTED_COST
New billing system	23760	Yates	1000	10000
Common stock issue	28765	Baker	3000	4000
Resolve bad debts	26713	Kanter	2000	1500
New office lease	26511	Yates	5000	5000
Revise documentation	34054	Kanter	100	3000
Entertain new client	87108	Yates	5000	2000
New TV commercial	85005	Baker	10000	8000

EMPLOYEE

NAME	E_NUMBER	DEPARTMENT
Kanter	1111	Finance
Yates	1112	Accounting
Adams	1001	Finance
Baker	1002	Finance
Clarke	1003	Accounting
Dexter	1004	Finance
Early	1005	Accounting

TITLE

E_NUMBER	CURRENT_TITLE
1001	Senior consultant
1002	Senior consultant
1003	Senior consultant
1004	Junior consultant
1005	Junior consultant

PRIOR_JOB

E_NUMBER	PRIOR_TITLE
1001	Junior consultant
1001	Research analyst
1002	Junior consultant
1002	Research analyst
1003	Junior consultant
1004	Summer intern

EXPERTISE

E_NUMBER	SKILL
1001	Stock market
1001	Investments
1002	Stock market
1003	Stock market
1003	Investments
1004	Taxation
1005	Management

The DISTINCT Keyword

Note that the result in Figure 7–2b contains duplicate tuples. SQL does not automatically impose the closure property. In order to remove duplicate tuples from the result of a SELECT command, one must include the DISTINCT keyword. The command

```
SELECT DISTINCT DEPARTMENT
FROM EMPLOYEE
```

results in only one occurrence of each department name, giving the result in Figure 7–2c.

FIGURE 7–2a
Projection of EMPLOYEE **over**
NAME **and** E_NUMBER

```
                              SELECT NAME, E_NUMBER
                              FROM DEPARTMENT

                              EMPLOYEE
                              NAME                E_NUMBER

                              Kanter              1111
                              Yates               1112
                              Adams               1001
                              Baker               1002
                              Clarke              1003
                              Dexter              1004
                              Early               1005
```

AVG = AVERAGE

FIGURE 7–2b
Projection of EMPLOYEE **over**
DEPARTMENT

```
             SELECT DEPARTMENT
             FROM EMPLOYEE

             EMPLOYEE
             DEPARTMENT

             Finance
             Accounting
             Finance
             Finance
             Accounting
             Finance
             Accounting
```

FIGURE 7–2c
Another Projection of EM-
PLOYEE **over** DEPARTMENT
This time the DISTINCT key-
word is used to remove
duplicate tuples.

```
             SELECT DISTINCT DEPARTMENT
             FROM EMPLOYEE

             EMPLOYEE
             DEPARTMENT

             Finance
             Accounting
```

Computed Values

Projection may also be carried out on the basis of values computed from
numeric database items, using the operators $+$, $-$, $/$, and $*$. As in other
languages, multiplication and division are performed before addition
and subtraction. This order may be controlled by using parentheses. To

illustrate, suppose we want a list of the difference between actual and expected cost for each project. The appropriate query is:

```
SELECT NAME, ACTUAL_COST — EXPECTED_COST
FROM PROJECT
```

The result is shown in Figure 7–3a.

If we wanted to compute percent of actual to expected, the query would be:

```
SELECT NAME, ACTUAL_COST / EXPECTED_COST * 100.0
FROM PROJECT
```

See Figure 7–3b for the result.

SELECTION

Selection is performed with combinations of the keywords SELECT, FROM, and WHERE. The simplest selection is a retrieval of all attributes from a relation.

FIGURE 7–3a
Projection Based on Actual Cost Less Expected Cost

```
SELECT NAME, ACTUAL_COST — EXPECTED_COST
FROM PROJECT

NAME                        ACTUAL_COST — EXPECTED_COST

New billing system                  -9,000
Common stock issue                  -1,000
Resolve bad debts                      500
New office lease                         0
Revise documentation               -2,900
Entertain new client                3,000
New TV commercial                   2,000
```

FIGURE 7–3b
Projection Based on Percent of Actual to Expected Cost

```
SELECT NAME, ACTUAL_COST / EXPECTED_COST * 100.0
FROM PROJECT

NAME                              ACTUAL_COST /
                                  EXPECTED_COST * 100.0

New billing system                     10.00
Common stock issue                     75.00
Resolve bad debts                     133.33
New office lease                      100.00
Revise documentation                    3.33
Entertain new client                  250.00
New TV commercial                     125.00
```

Retrieving an Entire Table

Retrieving an entire relation, such as the EMPLOYEE table, can be accomplished by using the command:

```
SELECT *
FROM EMPLOYEE
```

The asterisk (*) indicates that all attributes in the relation should be retrieved.

The WHERE Keyword

The WHERE keyword is used to specify conditions for selecting tuples from a relation. To retrieve the tuples for all employees in the finance department, one would use the following command, producing the result in Figure 7–4:

```
SELECT *
FROM EMPLOYEE
WHERE DEPARTMENT = 'Finance'
```

COMBINING PROJECTION AND SELECTION

Combining projection and selection is straightforward in SQL. To retrieve only the names of the employees in the finance department (as shown in Figure 7–5a), one would specify:

```
SELECT NAME
FROM EMPLOYEE
WHERE DEPARTMENT = 'Finance'
```

To select finance employee names and numbers, the query is (Figure 7–5b gives the result):

FIGURE 7–4
Selection from EMPLOYEE where DEPARTMENT = 'Finance'

```
SELECT *
FROM EMPLOYEE
WHERE DEPARTMENT = 'Finance'

EMPLOYEE
NAME                        E_NUMBER              DEPARTMENT

Kanter                      1111                  Finance
Adams                       1001                  Finance
Baker                       1002                  Finance
Dexter                      1004                  Finance
```

FIGURE 7–5a
**Selection of Employees in
the Finance Department
Projected over NAME**

```
SELECT NAME
FROM EMPLOYEE
WHERE DEPARTMENT = 'Finance'

EMPLOYEE
NAME

Kanter
Adams
Baker
Dexter
```

FIGURE 7–5b
**Selection of Employees in
the Finance Department
Projected over NAME and
E_NUMBER**

```
SELECT NAME, E_NUMBER
FROM EMPLOYEE
WHERE DEPARTMENT = 'Finance'

EMPLOYEE
NAME            E_NUMBER

Kanter          1111
Adams           1001
Baker           1002
Dexter          1004
```

```
SELECT NAME, E_NUMBER
FROM EMPLOYEE
WHERE DEPARTMENT = 'Finance'
```

Finally, suppose we want to list employee number before name in the previous query. All we do is interchange the position of NAME and E_NUMBER, as follows (see Figure 7–5c):

```
SELECT E_NUMBER, NAME
FROM EMPLOYEE
WHERE DEPARTMENT = 'Finance'
```

Other examples of combining projection and selection will be given throughout the chapter.

JOIN

A join can be performed in SQL by using more detailed SELECT, FROM, and WHERE clauses. To illustrate, suppose we want a list of employee names and titles. To associate employee names with employee titles,

FIGURE 7–5c
Selection of Employees in the Finance Department Projected over E_NUMBER and NAME
This is the same result as in Figure 7–5b, but the column order is reversed.

```
SELECT E_NUMBER, NAME
FROM EMPLOYEE
WHERE DEPARTMENT = 'Finance'

         EMPLOYEE
         E_NUMBER        NAME

          1111          Kanter
          1001          Adams
          1002          Baker
          1004          Dexter
```

FIGURE 7–6
Join of EMPLOYEE and TITLE over E_NUMBER
This is a natural join because the redundant attribute has been removed.

```
SELECT*
FROM EMPLOYEE, TITLE
WHERE EMPLOYEE.E_NUMBER = TITLE.E_NUMBER

EMPLOYEE
NAME          E_NUMBER      DEPARTMENT      CURRENT_TITLE

 Adams         1001         Finance         Senior consultant
 Baker         1002         Finance         Senior consultant
 Clarke        1003         Accounting      Senior consultant
 Dexter        1004         Finance         Junior consultant
 Early         1005         Accounting      Junior consultant
```

we must join the EMPLOYEE and TITLE relations. The SQL command for this is:

```
SELECT *
FROM EMPLOYEE, TITLE
WHERE EMPLOYEE.E_NUMBER = TITLE.E_NUMBER
```

The FROM keyword is followed by the names of the relations to be joined. The WHERE keyword is followed by the attributes over which the join is to occur. The attribute names are prefixed ("qualified") with the name of the relation that contains the attribute so that all attribute names are uniquely identified. The relation and attribute names are separated by a period. The result of this command is shown in Figure 7–6.

The AND Keyword

To illustrate a slightly more complex join, suppose we want to know the names of all the senior consultants. This requires data from both the TITLE and EMPLOYEE relations, joined over E_NUMBER. This is done in SQL as follows:

```
SELECT NAME
FROM EMPLOYEE, TITLE
WHERE EMPLOYEE.E_NUMBER = TITLE.E_NUMBER
AND CURRENT_TITLE = 'Senior consultant'
```

The results of the query above are shown in Figure 7–7a. Note the use of the AND keyword to link the two conditions in the WHERE clause. AND is discussed further below. There is no need to qualify NAME in the SELECT clause because NAME is not an attribute of TITLE, so there is no ambiguity. Of course, qualifying NAME as EMPLOYEE.NAME would cause no problems.

Finally, for an example that draws on three tables (a "3-way" join), suppose we want the names and skills of all senior consultants. To do this, the previous query may be extended as shown below (results are shown in Figure 7–7b):

```
SELECT NAME, SKILL
FROM EMPLOYEE, TITLE, EXPERTISE
WHERE EMPLOYEE.E_NUMBER = TITLE.E_NUMBER
AND CURRENT_TITLE = 'Senior consultant'
AND EXPERTISE.E_NUMBER = TITLE.E_NUMBER
```

FIGURE 7–7a

Selection of Senior Consultants from TITLE Joined with EMPLOYEE over E_NUMBER and Projected over NAME

```
SELECT NAME
FROM EMPLOYEE, TITLE
WHERE EMPLOYEE.E_NUMBER = TITLE.E_NUMBER
AND CURRENT_TITLE = 'Senior consultant'

NAME

Adams
Baker
Clarke
```

FIGURE 7–7b

The Same Result as in Figure 7–7a Except also joined with EXPERTISE over E_NUMBER and Projected over NAME and SKILL

```
SELECT NAME, SKILL
FROM EMPLOYEE, TITLE, EXPERTISE
WHERE EMPLOYEE.E_NUMBER = TITLE.E_NUMBER
AND CURRENT_TITLE = 'Senior consultant'
AND EXPERTISE.E_NUMBER = TITLE.E_NUMBER

NAME        SKILL

Adams       Stock market
Adams       Investments
Baker       Stock market
Clarke      Stock market
Clarke      Investments
```

The IN Keyword

WHERE clauses can contain other more powerful keywords. One example is the keyword IN. IN is used to specify a list of values an attribute can assume. To retrieve the employee numbers for the employees whose skill is either taxation or management, one could specify:

```
SELECT E_NUMBER
FROM EXPERTISE
WHERE SKILL IN ('Taxation', 'Management')    Domain
```

The result is shown in Figure 7–8.

Joins via Subqueries

The IN keyword can also be followed by another SELECT-FROM-WHERE keyword combination (called a *subquery* or *nested query*). To obtain the skills of employees that have had the prior job title "research analyst" requires data from two tables (a join). The following command demonstrates how to achieve this result, which is shown in Figure 7–9a.

FIGURE 7–8
Selection from EXPERTISE where SKILL Is in the Set of Values (Taxation, Management, Projected over E_NUMBER)

```
SELECT E_NUMBER
FROM EXPERTISE
WHERE SKILL IN ('Taxation', 'Management')

EXPERTISE
E_NUMBER

1004
1005
```

FIGURE 7–9a
Selection from EXPERTISE where the Prior Job Title Is Research Analyst

```
SELECT SKILL
FROM EXPERTISE
WHERE E_NUMBER IN
     (SELECT E_NUMBER
      FROM PRIOR_JOB
      WHERE PRIOR_TITLE = 'Research analyst')

EXPERTISE
SKILL

Stock market
Investments
Stock market
```

```
SELECT SKILL
FROM EXPERTISE
WHERE E_NUMBER IN
  (SELECT E_NUMBER
   FROM PRIOR_JOB
   WHERE PRIOR TITLE = 'Research analyst')
```

Think of the execution of this statement in terms of two loops in a program, one embedded in the other. In the inner loop, employee numbers are selected for employees whose prior job title is "research analyst." In the outer loop, the employee numbers provided by the inner loop are used to select the skills shown in the result. Some people find it easier to think of the clause after the IN keyword as a subroutine that returns a set of values (in this case, the employee numbers).

NOT IN

The NOT keyword can be used to negate the IN clause by specifying NOT IN. The skills of the employees who have not had a prior "research analyst" title are found by using:

```
SELECT SKILL
FROM EXPERTISE
WHERE E_NUMBER NOT IN
  (SELECT E_NUMBER
   FROM PRIOR_JOB
   WHERE PRIOR_TITLE = 'Research analyst')
```

This gives the result shown in Figure 7–9b.

Other Examples of Joins

To illustrate other joins with subqueries, consider the joins given previously with WHERE and AND. The results in Figure 7–7a may be produced by using:

FIGURE 7–9b

Selection from EXPERTISE where Prior Job Title Is *Not* Research Analyst

```
SELECT SKILL
FROM EXPERTISE
WHERE E_NUMBER NOT IN
      (SELECT E_NUMBER
       FROM PRIOR_JOB
       WHERE PRIOR_TITLE = 'Research analyst')

EXPERTISE
SKILL

Stock market
Investments
Taxation
Management
```

```
SELECT NAME
FROM EMPLOYEE
WHERE E_NUMBER IN
  (SELECT E_NUMBER
   FROM TITLE
   WHERE CURRENT_TITLE = 'Senior consultant')
```

To produce the results in Figure 7–7b with a subquery, use:

```
SELECT NAME, SKILL
FROM EMPLOYEE, EXPERTISE
WHERE EMPLOYEE.E_NUMBER = EXPERTISE.E_NUMBER
AND EXPERTISE, E_NUMBER IN
  (SELECT E_NUMBER
   FROM TITLE
   WHERE CURRENT_TITLE = 'Senior consultant')
```

The choice of using ANDs or subqueries to perform joins is really a matter of personal preference. A third way of performing joins, with the keyword EXISTS, is discussed later in the chapter.

WHERE clauses can contain more complex specifications using the connectors AND and OR, and the comparison operators =, >, <, <> (not equal), <=, and >=. For example, suppose one needs to know which projects managed by Kanter are over budget. To achieve the results shown in Figure 7–10, one would specify the following SQL command:

```
SELECT NAME
FROM PROJECT
WHERE MANAGER = 'Kanter' AND ACTUAL_COST >
EXPECTED_COST
```

To gain an understanding of the power SQL provides the user, consider what would be necessary to program this example. Figure 7–11 shows a pseudocode program to perform this retrieval. Obviously, the SQL version is much simpler to construct, especially for the novice user.

MORE-COMPLEX WHERE CLAUSES

The WHERE clause can be made as specific as needed by using the connective keywords AND and another keyword, OR.

FIGURE 7–10
A More Complicated WHERE Clause
Selection from PROJECT where the manager is Kanter and actual cost exceeds expected cost.

```
SELECT NAME
FROM PROJECT
WHERE MANAGER = 'Kanter'
AND ACTUAL_COST > EXPECTED_COST

PROJECT
NAME

Resolve Bad Debts
```

FIGURE 7–11
A Pseudocode Program to Achieve the Result Shown in Figure 7–10

```
PROGRAM OVER-COST/This program retrieves the names
of projects for specified project manager that are
over expected cost/
BEGIN
     Reset Project File
     Display "Please enter Manager name:"
     Accept Mgr-Name
     While not EOF DO
          Begin Loop Read Project File: Project,
          Number Manager, Actual-Cost, Expected-Cost
     If Mgr-Name = Manager and Actual_Cost >
                         Expected_Cost
     Then
          Display project
     End Loop
END PROGRAM
```

FIGURE 7–12a
Selection from PROJECT where Actual Cost > Expected Cost and MANAGER = 'Kanter' or 'Baker,' Projected over NAME

```
SELECT NAME
FROM PROJECT
WHERE ACTUAL_COST > EXPECTED_COST
AND (MANAGER = 'Kanter') OR (MANAGER = 'Baker')

PROJECT
NAME

Resolve bad debts
New TV commercial
```

The OR Keyword

The following command retrieves the names of all projects over budget that are managed by either Kanter or Baker:

```
SELECT NAME
FROM PROJECT
WHERE ACTUAL_COST > EXPECTED_COST
   AND (MANAGER = 'Kanter') OR (MANAGER = 'Baker')
```

Figure 7–12a shows the result of this command.

BETWEEN and LIKE

Standard SQL also supports the keywords BETWEEN and LIKE. BETWEEN is used to specify a range of values for a condition. Suppose we want a

FIGURE 7–12b
Projects with Expected Cost between 4,000 and 8,000

```
SELECT NAME
FROM PROJECT
WHERE EXPECTED_COST BETWEEN 4000 AND 8000.

PROJECT
NAME

Common stock issue
New office lease
New TV commercial
```

list of all projects where the expected cost is $>=4,000$ and $<=8,000$. Using BETWEEN, we have:

```
SELECT NAME
FROM PROJECT
Where EXPECTED_COST BETWEEN 4000 AND 8000.
```

Results are shown in Figure 7–12b. Notice that the lower value (4,000) precedes the upper value and that values equal to the lower or upper limit are included in the result.

LIKE is used to indicate a pattern to match, instead of an exact character string, when searching textual items. The % symbol is used to indicate a string of any characters of arbitrary length (including zero length), and the underscore symbol (__) is used to indicate one arbitrary character. So if we want a list of all employees whose names begin with A, the query is:

```
SELECT NAME
FROM EMPLOYEE
WHERE NAME LIKE 'A%'
```

The result would be Adams. If we want employees' names that begin with A and are 3 characters long, we would substitute 'A__ __' for 'A%' above. If we want employees whose name ends in r, we would use '%r'.

WHERE Clauses with Computed Values

WHERE clauses may also be based on computed values. Suppose we want a list of projects that are 20 percent or more over budget (expected cost). The query is:

```
SELECT NAME
FROM PROJECT
WHERE (ACTUAL_COST — EXPECTED_COST)/
   EXPECTED_COST * 100.0 > 20.0
```

Results are shown in Figure 7–12c.

FIGURE 7–12c
**Projects that Are at Least
20 Percent over Budget**

```
SELECT NAME
FROM PROJECT
WHERE (ACTUAL_COST — EXPECTED_COST) / EXPECTED_COST
* 100.00 > 20.0

PROJECT
NAME

Resolve bad debts
Entertain new client
New TV commercial
```

FIGURE 7–13
Sorting Results
Use of ORDER BY to alphabe-
tize Finance employees.

```
SELECT NAME
FROM EMPLOYEE
WHERE DEPARTMENT = 'Finance'
ORDER BY NAME

EMPLOYEE
NAME

Adams
Baker
Dexter
Kanter
```

SORTING RESULTS

SQL provides an ORDER BY clause to sort results on one or more columns called *sort keys*. Output is displayed in ascending (ASC) order, unless descending order is specified by using DESC.

Ascending Order Sorts

For example, to display the results in Figure 7–13 in alphabetical (ascending) order, one would use:

```
SELECT NAME
FROM EMPLOYEE
WHERE DEPARTMENT = 'Finance'
ORDER BY NAME
```

Descending Order Sorts

If we wanted these names in inverse alphabetical order, the last line in the query would be replaced with:

FIGURE 7–14
Output alphabetized by department **and** name **within** department

```
SELECT DEPARTMENT, NAME, E_NUMBER
FROM EMPLOYEE
ORDER BY DEPARTMENT, NAME

EMPLOYEE
DEPARTMENT        NAME            E_NUMBER

Accounting        Clarke          1003
Accounting        Early           1005
Accounting        Yates           1112
Finance           Adams           1001
Finance           Baker           1002
Finance           Dexter          1004
Finance           Kanter          1111
```

```
ORDER BY NAME DESC
```

To illustrate the use of two sort keys, suppose we want to rearrange the employee table so that department names are alphabetized, employee names are listed alphabetically within departments, and the column order is department, name, e_number. The appropriate query is (results are shown in Figure 7–14):

```
SELECT DEPARTMENT, NAME, E_NUMBER
FROM EMPLOYEE
ORDER BY DEPARTMENT, NAME
```

Finally, rather than using column names to specify sort keys, the relative position of the key in the select list may be used. Thus, the following query produces the same result as the query above.

```
SELECT DEPARTMENT, NAME, E_NUMBER
FROM EMPLOYEE
ORDER BY 1,2
```

AGGREGATE FUNCTIONS

SQL includes a set of built-in functions for computing aggregate values of numeric columns. Aggregate functions (sometimes called *column functions*) include sum, avg, max, min and count. With the exception of the special case count (*), these functions operate on one, numerically valued column of a table and return a single number (a "scalar") as the result. count (*) is a special case because it operates on all columns of a table.

COUNT

The count function provides the number of tuples in a relation that satisfy the conditions (if any) specified in a where clause. In the simplest case, there are no conditions. The command:

```
SELECT COUNT (*)
FROM PROJECTS
```

gives the result 7, the number of projects currently in progress at the company.

Because SQL does not automatically suppress duplicate tuples, the command

```
SELECT COUNT (DEPARTMENT)
FROM EMPLOYEES
```

gives the result 7. Determining the number of unique department names requires use of the DISTINCT keyword. The proper command for this information is:

```
SELECT COUNT (DISTINCT DEPARTMENT)
FROM EMPLOYEES
```

This command produces the result 2.

SUM

The remaining aggregate functions operate on numeric values only. To see how these functions operate, consider the PROJECT relation. The SQL SUM function can be used to provide a total of the cost values. To calculate the total expected cost of the projects in progress, for example, the following command is used:

```
SELECT SUM (EXPECTED_COST)
FROM PROJECT
```

This produces the result $33,500.

AVG

The average expected cost can be computed by using the AVG function:

```
SELECT AVG (EXPECTED_COST)
FROM PROJECT
```

This command gives the result $4,785.71 (to the nearest cent). In order to find the projects with above-average expected cost, one could use:

```
SELECT *
FROM PROJECT
WHERE EXPECTED_COST > (SELECT AVG (EXPECTED_COST)
            FROM PROJECT)
```

This produces the result shown in Figure 7–15a.

MAX and MIN

Maximum and minimum values can be calculated using MAX and MIN functions, respectively. The project with the maximum actual cost accrued can be obtained using:

FIGURE 7–15a   Comparison of Expected Cost to Average Expected Cost to Find the Projects with Above - Average Expected Cost

```
SELECT *
FROM PROJECT
WHERE EXPECTED_COST >
    (SELECT AVG (EXPECTED_COST)
    FROM PROJECT)

PROJECT
NAME                     P_NUMBER   MANAGER   ACTUAL_COST   EXPECTED_COST

New billing system       23760      Yates        1000          10000
New office lease         26511      Yates        5000           5000
New TV commercial        85005      Baker       10000           8000
```

FIGURE 7–15b   The Project with the Maximum Actual Cost

```
SELECT *
FROM PROJECT
WHERE ACTUAL_COST =
    (SELECT MAX (ACTUAL_COST)
    FROM PROJECT)

PROJECT
NAME                 P_NUMBER      MANAGER      ACTUAL_COST      EXPECTED_COST

New TV commercial     85005         Baker         10000             8000
```

```
SELECT *
FROM PROJECT
WHERE ACTUAL_COST = (SELECT MAX (ACTUAL_COST)
            FROM PROJECT)
```

The result is shown in Figure 7–15b. Similarly, the project with the least Actual Cost can be determined by using:

```
SELECT *
FROM PROJECT
WHERE ACTUAL_COST = (SELECT MIN (ACTUAL_COST)
            FROM PROJECT)
```

The result of this query is shown in Figure 7–15c.

Finally, these functions may be combined. For example, the number of projects with expected costs that exceed the average expected cost can be found as follows:

```
SELECT COUNT (*)
FROM PROJECT
WHERE EXPECTED_COST > (SELECT AVG (EXPECTED_COST)
            FROM PROJECT)
```

FIGURE 7–15c   **The Project with the Least Expected Cost**

```
SELECT *
FROM PROJECT
WHERE EXPECTED_COST =
      (SELECT MIN (EXPECTED_COST)
      FROM PROJECT)
```

PROJECT NAME	P_NUMBER	MANAGER	ACTUAL_COST	EXPECTED_COST
Resolve bad debts	26713	Kanter	2000	1500

The result would indicate that there are three projects with expected cost exceeding the average expected cost.

GROUPING RESULTS

Suppose we want to know the total amount spent (actual cost) on projects managed by each person in the PROJECT relation. We could do this for Baker, for example, by using:

```
SELECT SUM (ACTUAL_COST)
FROM PROJECT
WHERE MANAGER = 'Baker'
```

This is very cumbersome because we would have to perform a SELECT for each manager.

GROUP BY

SQL provides a GROUP BY clause to aggregate data on the basis of categories such as different managers' names. To group the output by manager, the following command would be used (the manager's name is also retrieved):

```
SELECT MANAGER, SUM (ACTUAL_COST)
FROM PROJECT
GROUP BY MANAGER
```

The results of this query are shown in Figure 7–16a.

GROUP BY with ORDER BY

If we want the results of the GROUP BY clause sorted, we would use the ORDER BY clause as follows:

FIGURE 7–16a
Use of the GROUP BY Clause to Sum Actual Costs of Projects Managed by Each Person

```
SELECT MANAGER, SUM (ACTUAL_COST)
FROM PROJECT
GROUP BY MANAGER

MANAGER              SUM (ACTUAL_COST)

Yates                      11,000
Baker                      13,000
Kanter                      2,100
```

FIGURE 7–16b
Use of the ORDER BY Clause to Sort the Results in Figure 7–16a

```
SELECT MANAGER, SUM (ACTUAL_COST)
FROM PROJECT
GROUP BY MANAGER
ORDER BY MANAGER

MANAGER              SUM (ACTUAL_COST)

Baker                      13,000
Kanter                      2,100
Yates                      11,000
```

```
SELECT MANAGER, SUM (ACTUAL_COST)
FROM PROJECT
GROUP BY MANAGER
ORDER BY MANAGER
```

Notice that GROUP BY precedes ORDER BY, which is a requirement of SQL. Results are shown in Figure 7–16b.

HAVING

There may be situations where we would like to specify conditions on groups (rather than on *rows* as the WHERE clause does). We might want the information on the managers above, only if total expenditures exceed $5,000, for example. The HAVING clause is used with the GROUP BY to specify group conditions similar to the way WHERE is used to specify tuple conditions. The appropriate query for managers who have spent more than $5,000 is:

```
SELECT MANAGER, SUM (ACTUAL_COST)
FROM PROJECT
GROUP BY MANAGER
HAVING SUM (ACTUAL_COST) > 5000
ORDER BY MANAGER
```

Results are illustrated in Figure 7–16c.

FIGURE 7–16c
Managers Who Have Spent More Than $5,000
HAVING has been used to restrict the output to managers spending more than $5,000. ORDER BY was used to sort results.

```
SELECT MANAGER, SUM (ACTUAL_COST)
FROM PROJECT
GROUP BY MANAGER
HAVING SUM (ACTUAL_COST) > 5000
ORDER BY MANAGER

    MANAGER          SUM (ACTUAL_COST)

    Baker                 13,000
    Yates                 11,000
```

FIGURE 7–16d
Use of WHERE to Restrict Results to Rows in which Actual Cost Exceeds Expected Cost, and GROUP BY to Organize Results by Manager

```
SELECT MANAGER, SUM (ACTUAL_COST — EXPECTED_COST)
FROM PROJECT
WHERE ACTUAL_COST > EXPECTED_COST
GROUP BY MANAGER

        MANAGER          SUM (ACTUAL_COST)

        Kanter                500
        Yates               3,000
        Baker               2,000
```

WHERE can be used *before* GROUP BY and HAVING to restrict rows that qualify. Suppose we want the total amount by which actual cost exceeds expected cost by manager, but only on those projects that are over-budget. The query is:

```
SELECT MANAGER, SUM (ACTUAL_COST — EXPECTED_COST)
FROM PROJECT
WHERE ACTUAL_COST > EXPECTED_COST
GROUP BY MANAGER
```

Figure 7–16d shows the results of this query.

OTHER FUNCTIONS

Another set of functions, sometimes called *table functions*, operate on more than one column. DISTINCT is actually a table function that takes a table as input and returns a table with any duplicate rows removed.

UNION

UNION is a table function that performs a relational algebra union operation. The syntax is *X* UNION *Y* where *X* and *Y* are union-compatible tables. DISTINCT and UNION both return entire tables.

EXISTS

EXISTS is a logical operator that returns the value *true* or *false*. The EXISTS keyword usually follows a SELECT-FROM-WHERE combination. This function returns the value *true* whenever a row satisfying the WHERE clause exists; otherwise, it returns the value *false*.

As an example, consider a situation in which one wishes to determine which employees have more than one skill. The following SQL query can be used to achieve the relation shown in Figure 7–17.

```
SELECT DISTINCT E_NUMBER
FROM EXPERTISE FIRST
WHERE EXISTS
  SELECT *
  FROM EXPERTISE SECOND
  WHERE FIRST.E_NUMBER = SECOND.E_NUMBER
  AND FIRST.SKILL NOT = SECOND.SKILL
```

Here the FROM keyword is followed by a relation name and another word. The word following the relation name can be used as an alias or synonym for the relation name. This is done to allow the relation to be referenced in two different ways.

You may find that imagining two identical occurrences of the EXPERTISE relation is helpful in understanding this command. Refer to the first occurrence as FIRST and to the second as SECOND. The query above takes each tuple from FIRST and compares it to every tuple in SECOND. When there is a match on the employee number and the skills are not the same, then the tuple from SECOND satisfies the condition in the second (lower) WHERE clause. This sets the value of EXISTS to *true.* Because the value of EXISTS is *true,* the employee number from the FIRST relation is included in the result.

Thus far, we have assumed that the database in Figure 7–1 has already been defined and that the data has been entered into it. The next section describes the database definition features of SQL, how data

FIGURE 7–17
Logical Operations with
EXISTS
Employee numbers of employees with two skills.

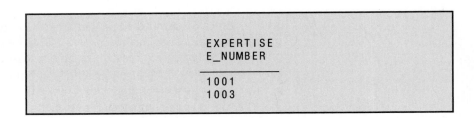

```
           EXPERTISE
           E_NUMBER

           1001
           1003
```

is entered and maintained, and security features including views and access privileges.

DEFINING DATABASES IN SQL

Defining a database in SQL is a rather straightforward process. The command CREATE TABLE is used to name each relation in the database, to name each attribute in the relation, to define the data type for each attribute, and to express certain integrity constraints. For example, the EMPLOYEE relation in Figure 7–1 would be defined as follows:

```
CREATE TABLE EMPLOYEE
    (NAME CHAR (12),
    E_NUMBER SMALLINT NOT NULL UNIQUE,
    DEPARTMENT CHAR (12))
```

In the command above, the indentation is to improve readability and is not required. CHAR means *character data*, and the number in parentheses following CHAR is the maximum number of characters. SMALLINT stands for an integer in the range − 32,768 to 32,767. The key words NOT NULL and UNIQUE associated with E_NUMBER are used because this is the key attribute for the relation and means that E_NUMBER must have a unique value for any tuple inserted into the database.

For another example, consider the EXPERTISE relation, which would be defined as follows:

```
CREATE TABLE EXPERTISE
    (E_NUMBER SMALLINT NOT NULL,
    SKILL CHAR (15) NOT NULL,
    UNIQUE (E_NUMBER, SKILL))
```

Here, E_NUMBER and SKILL appear at the end of the command and form a concatenated key, so both are NOT NULL, and their combination must be unique.

Finally, consider the PROJECT relation, which would be specified with the statement:

```
CREATE TABLE PROJECT
    (NAME CHAR (25),
    P_NUMBER INTEGER NOT NULL UNIQUE,
    MANAGER CHAR (12),
    ACTUAL_COST INTEGER,
    EXPECTED_COST INTEGER)
```

Above, Actual Cost and Expected Cost have been defined as INTEGER, permitting values in the range −2,147,483,648 to 2,147,483,647. Suppose we wanted to express these attributes in dollars and cents, then the DECIMAL data type could be substituted as follows:

```
ACTUAL_COST DECIMAL (12,2),
EXPECTED_COST DECIMAL (12,2)
```

This statement allows a total of 12 digits, with 2 to the right of the decimal point. One other SQL data type is FLOAT, to specify floating point numbers given in exponential notation.

The CREATE TABLE command results in establishing an empty base table. In SQL, base tables have a physical representation in storage, although they may not be stored exactly as files with record occurrences as described in the table format. Use of the terms *file* and *record* are thus discouraged because they may be misleading. However, users can always *think* of base tables as physically existing without worrying about representation details.

Inserting and Deleting Data

The command INSERT INTO is used to add data to base tables. For example, the first row of EMPLOYEE relation could be added with the statement:

```
INSERT INTO EMPLOYEE
VALUES (Kanter, 1111, Finance)
```

SQL also provides basic capabilities for modifying relations. To insert a new tuple into a relation, one specifies the INSERT INTO keywords followed by the name of the relation; this is followed by the data belonging in the new tuple, for example,

```
INSERT INTO EMPLOYEE
VALUES (Farmer, 1006, Accounting)
```

adds a tuple for a new employee to the EMPLOYEE relation. If the department in which the new employee will be working is unknown, an alternate form of the update can be used:

```
INSERT INTO EMPLOYEE (NAME, E_NUMBER)
VALUES (Farmer, 1006)
```

This results in a null value for the Department attribute.

It is also possible to insert tuples from another relation. This is accomplished by specifying a SELECT-FROM-WHERE block after the INSERT INTO keywords. To combine all prior job titles with the current titles, one can use:

```
INSERT INTO TITLE
   SELECT *
   FROM PRIOR_JOB
```

A WHERE clause can also be specified to select particular employee numbers. Of course, the relations must be union compatible for this operation to be valid.

The DELETE and WHERE keywords are used to remove tuples from a relation. The DELETE keyword is followed by the name of the relation containing the tuple to be deleted. The WHERE keyword is used in its normal manner—to specify a condition that selects a tuple or set of tuples from a relation.

To delete Adams from the EMPLOYEE relation, one can use this command:

```
DELETE EMPLOYEE
WHERE NAME = 'Adams'
```

SQL is not a particularly difficult language to master; however, in some cases queries can be rather tricky. Since good relational designs often end up separating the data into numerous tables, it is often necessary to join several tables to get the desired result. This can be quite cumbersome. One way of avoiding this problem is through the use of user views, which are discussed next.

Modification

Existing tuples may also be modified using SQL. The keywords required for this are UPDATE, SET, and WHERE. The relation containing the tuple or set of tuples to be modified follows the UPDATE keyword. The SET keyword precedes the specification of the new value for an attribute. This specification may contain one of the computational functions described earlier, such as MAX or AVG. As usual, the WHERE keyword is followed by a condition that identifies the particular tuple to be modified. As an example, suppose Baker transfers from the finance department to the accounting department:

```
UPDATE EMPLOYEE
SET Department = 'Accounting'
WHERE Name = 'Baker'
```

specifies the update. If there were more than one occurrence of tuples for Baker, then the entire set would have been modified.

Defining Views

User views, which have no physical analog in the stored database, may be defined over one or more base tables, or previously defined views. Views may involve relational algebra projection, selection, or join. They may be used as a form of security device to hide data from certain users, or they may be used to simplify access to the database.

Suppose we have a user who needs only to know project names and numbers. This requires a projection operation on the PROJECT table. A view can be created for this user with the following command:

```
CREATE VIEW PROJECT_LIST AS
  SELECT NAME, P_NUMBER
  FROM PROJECT
```

Users authorized to use this view (see the section on security for a discussion of authorization) may access a virtual relation called PROJECT-LIST with the attributes NAME and P_NUMBER. If we want to name the attributes NAME and NUMBER, the appropriate statement is:

```
CREATE VIEW PROJECT_LIST (NAME, NUMBER) AS
    SELECT NAME, P_NUMBER
    FROM PROJECT
```

Any SELECT clause may be used in defining a view, including GROUP BY and HAVING, which were discussed earlier. If, for example, the user above were only allowed to access projects managed by Baker or Kanter, we would have:

```
CREATE VIEW PROJECT_LIST AS
SELECT NAME, P_NUMBER
FROM PROJECT
WHERE MANAGER = 'Baker'
OR MANAGER = 'Kanter'
```

Equivalently, WHERE MANAGER IN ('Baker', 'Kanter') could be substituted for WHERE and OR above.

To illustrate a join, suppose a user needs access to employee names and projects to which that employee is assigned. This requires a join of the ASSIGNMENT and EMPLOYEE tables and a projection over employee name and project number, as follows:

```
CREATE VIEW NAME_PROJ (NAME, P_NUMBER) AS
    SELECT EMPLOYEE. NAME, ASSIGNMENT. P_NUMBER
    FROM EMPLOYEE, ASSIGNMENT
    WHERE ASSIGNMENT. E_NUMBER = EMPLOYEE. E_NUMBER
```

If this user is really alphabetically inclined and wants both project names and associated projects, the statement would be:

```
CREATE VIEW ALPHA_VIEW (EMPLOYEE, PROJECT) AS
    SELECT EMPLOYEE. NAME, PROJECT. NAME
    FROM EMPLOYEE, ASSIGNMENT, PROJECT
    WHERE EMPLOYEE. E_NUMBER = ASSIGNMENT. E_NUMBER
    AND ASSIGNMENT. P_NUMBER = PROJECT. P_NUMBER
```

Note that this is a 3-way join.

Security Features

Views can be used as a security device in that certain data can be hidden from selected users. The GRANT key word is used to specify privileges to users on the basis of an **authorization identifier** that identifies users who have access to the database. (We will use the term user ID instead of *authorization identifier*.) Privileges may be granted on base tables or views and include the following: SELECT, INSERT, DELETE, MODIFY, and ALL. The creator of a view or base table holds all privileges on that table.

Let's say we want to allow the person holding user ID YAHOO to retrieve data from the PROJECT table but not to change, add, or remove data. The appropriate GRANT statement is:

```
GRANT SELECT ON PROJECT TO YAHOO
```

Other self-explanatory examples are:

```
GRANT SELECT, UPDATE ON EMPLOYEE TO JAGU
GRANT ALL ON ASSIGNMENT TO ADMIN
GRANT INSERT ON SKILL TO PERSONNEL
GRANT SELECT ON ALPHA_VIEW TO ALPHAGUY
```

The last GRANT above applies to a previously defined view.

The special user ID PUBLIC may be used to grant privileges to any user having access to the database. So, for example, we might:

```
GRANT SELECT ON EXPERTISE TO PUBLIC
```

In a database with student grades, we would probably *not*

```
GRANT UPDATE ON GRADES TO PUBLIC
```

All of the examples that have been given thus far have assumed that the user is interacting directly with the database via the SQL processor. The next section shows how SQL statements can be embedded in programs so that the user interacts with the program, which then interacts with the SQL database to retrieve or update the necessary data.

EMBEDDED SQL

SQL statements can also be embedded in a host programming language, such as COBOL, FORTRAN, PL/1, or C. Examples will be given in COBOL. However, they have been designed to be simple enough to understand even if you are unfamiliar with that language.

The first example program is shown in Figure 7–18. All this program does is accept an employee number from the user and fetch and display that employee's title as given in the CURRENT_TITLE table. Note that this program deals with only one row of an SQL table at any one time. An example of retrieving multiple rows is given next.

A few preliminary comments are in order before the program is described. The line numbers in the left-most column are just to make it easier to describe the program. They are *not* part of the program. COBOL programs are divided into divisions, sections, paragraphs, and sentences. There are always four divisions—identification, environment, data, and procedure. The identification division names the program and possibly the programmer. The program in Figure 7–18 is named EMPLOYEE-TITLE. The environment division is used to name the host computer system on which the program is to be run. The statement ENVIRONMENT DIVISION must be present, but everything is optional here and has been omitted in this program.

FIGURE 7–18   An Embedded SQL Program to Retrieve an Employees Current Title

```
   1.      IDENTIFICATION DIVISION.
   2.      PROGRAM-ID. EMPLOYEE-TITLE.
   3.      ENVIRONMENT DIVISION.
   4.      DATA DIVISION.
   5.      WORKING-STORAGE SECTION.
   6.          EXEC SQL BEGIN DECLARE SECTION END-EXEC.
   7.      01    COBOL-TITLE.
   8.            03    COBOL-E-NUMBER                  PIC 9(5).
   9.            03    COBOL-CURRENT-TITLE            PIC X(20).
  10.          EXEC SQL END DECLARE SECTION END-EXEC.
  11.          EXEC SQL
  12.              DECLARE TITLE TABLE
  13.              (E_NUMBER SMALLINT NOT NULL,
  14.              CURRENT_TITLE CHAR (20))
  15.          END-EXEC.
  16.          EXEC SQL INCLUDE SQLCA END-EXEC.
  17.      PROCEDURE DIVISION.
  18.      MAIN-PROCEDURE.
  19.          PERFORM ACCEPT-ENUMBER.
  20.          PERFORM FETCH-TITLE.
  21.          STOP RUN.
  22.      ACCEPT-ENUMBER.
  23.          DISPLAY 'ENTER EMPLOYEE NUMBER:'.
  24.          ACCEPT COBOL-E-NUMBER.
  25.      FETCH-TITLE.
  26.          EXEC SQL
  27.              SELECT CURRENT_TITLE
  28.              INTO:COBOL-CURRENT-TITLE
  29.              FROM TITLE
  30.              WHERE E_NUMBER=:COBOL-E-NUMBER
  31.          END-EXEC.
  32.          IF SQLCODE = 0
  33.              DISPLAY 'CURRENT TITLE IS:' COBOL-CURRENT-TITLE
  34.          ELSE
  35.              PERFORM SQL-ERROR-PROCEDURE.
  36.      SQL-ERROR-PROCEDURE.
  37.          DISPLAY 'ERROR NUMBER', SQL CODE, 'HAS OCCURRED.'.
  38.          DISPLAY 'PLEASE CONTACT YOUR DATABASE ADMINISTRATOR.'.
  39.          STOP RUN.
```

Declaring Host Variables

The data division requires some explanation. It is used to describe any files and variables used in the program. In the case of embedded SQL, "host variables" (COBOL variables in this case), which will hold data retrieved from or sent to the database, must be described first. This is done in a DECLARE SECTION in lines 6–10. Notice that each SQL sentence begins with EXEC SQL and ends with END-EXEC. There are two COBOL host variables in this program, COBOL-E-NUMBER, and COBOL-CURRENT-TITLE. The *COBOL* has been prefixed to these variables as a convenience to remind the programmer that these are variables in the host language, and not SQL names. Putting *COBOL* in front of host variables is not required.

Declaring Tables

After the host variables have been declared, any tables used in the database must be declared. This is done in lines 11–15. The declaration of tables is very similar to the CREATE TABLE statement in SQL.

The Communication Area

Line 16 contains a sentence that must be included in every COBOL program using embedded SQL. It results in the creation of a "communication area" (SQLCA) between the program and the database system. The communication area automatically contains a variable called SQLCODE that is used to indicate the result of SQL operations performed by the program. If, after the execution of an SQL statement, the value of SQLCODE is zero, then the statement executed normally. If the value is negative, then an error occurred and the value of SQLCODE contains the error number.

Retrieving One Row

The actual algorithm of the program begins in the procedure division starting at line 17. The MAIN-PROCEDURE causes paragraphs ACCEPT-ENUMBER and FETCH-TITLE to be run in that order. ACCEPT-ENUMBER (lines 22–24) displays the message "ENTER EMPLOYEE NUMBER:" on the user's screen, and accepts that number into the host variable COBOL-E-NUMBER. The FETCH-TITLE paragraph in lines 25–35 contains an executable SQL statement that retrieves the current title for that employee. Notice that between the EXEC SQL in line 26 and the END-EXEC in line 31, there is an embedded SQL SELECT. The only difference in this and an interactive SELECT is that the host variables to receive the data are named in the INTO clause following SELECT. Also notice that the host variable names are prefixed with a colon (:) to distinguish them from SQL names.

At line 32, SQLCODE is tested. If it is 0, the current title is displayed by line 33; otherwise, an error has occurred and an error message is displayed. In either case, the program terminates at that point.

Using a Cursor to Fetch Multiple Rows

The example program in Figure 7–19 demonstrates a situation in which more than one row qualifies as a result of an SQL operation. This program accepts a manager's name, determines which projects are over budget for that manager, and displays a list of those projects. Since one manager is responsible for more than one project, several rows may qualify for retrieval. In such an event, the programmer must use a "cursor" to iterate through the processing of each row. A *cursor* is a pointer or index to the next row to be processed (it has nothing to do with the cursor on the screen). An SQLCODE of 100 is used to indicate that there are no more rows to be processed.

In the program, we have the identification and environment divisions as before. Five host variables are declared in the DECLARE section (lines 7–14). These variables correspond to those in the PROJECT table. The PROJECT table itself is declared in lines 15–22. Line 23 sets up the communication area, and a new type of entry starts at line 24. Here, the cursor is declared (named) and the SQL statement with which it is associated is given. The SQL statement starts at line 26 and, when invoked in the procedure division, finds all data in the PROJECT table for the manager whose name is stored in the host variable COBOL-MANAGER. It also sets the cursor to the first row for that manager.

The main procedure starts at line 31, and first accepts the manager's name in the ACCEPT-MANAGER paragraph. Next, the cursor is invoked in the OPEN-CURSOR paragraph by using the statement in line 41. The PROCESS-MAN paragraph actually retrieves and processes the data, one row at a time. At line 43, PROCESS-MAN retrieves the first row of data (the program assumes that at least one row exists for the given manager), then tests SQLCODE to see if it is zero. If so, paragraph TEST-COST is run until all rows have been processed (SQLCODE = 100), and, if not, the error routine is performed.

Paragraph TEST-COST compares actual to budgeted cost, and for any projects over budget, displays the project name, manager name, and amount of overrun. Then, the next row is fetched and processed. When all rows have been processed, control returns to the main routine, the cursor is closed, and the run is terminated.

An Update Example

The final program (Figure 7–20) is an example of an update operation. Here, an employee has been promoted and has a new job title, which must be updated in the CURRENT_TITLE table. In addition, the old title must be added to the list in the PRIOR_JOB table. Since only one row is involved in each of these tables, a cursor is not necessary.

Again, after the identification and environment divisions, the host variables are declared, this time in lines 6–11. The TITLE and PRIOR_JOB tables are declared in lines 12–21, and the communication area is established in line 22.

The procedure division starts at line 23. The employee number for the employee who has been promoted is accepted, along with the new title, in the ACCEPT-DATA paragraph in lines 33–37. The employee's old title is found by the GET-OLDTITLE routine in lines 38–44. After the old title is retrieved, SQLCODE is checked in the main procedure at line 27 to make sure everything is OK; then, the PRIOR_JOB table is updated in the

FIGURE 7–19   **An Embedded SQL Program to Retrieve All Projects Over Budget for a Given Manager**

```
 1.      IDENTIFICATION DIVISION.
 2.      PROGRAM-ID. COST-OVER-RUN-LIST.
 3.      ENVIRONMENT DIVISION.
 4.      DATA DIVISION.
 5.      WORKING-STORAGE SECTION.
 6.      01    COST-OVER-RUN                   PIC S9(6) VALUE ZERO.
 7.            EXEC SQL BEGIN DECLARE SECTION END-EXEC.
 8.      01    COBOL-PROJECT.
 9.            03 COBOL-PNAME                  PIC X(20).
10.            03 COBOL-PNUMBER               PIC 9(5).
11.            03 COBOL-MANAGER               PIC X(20).
12.            03 COBOL-ACTUAL-COST           PIC 9(6).
13.            03 COBOL-EXPECTED-COST         PIC 9(6).
14.            EXEC SQL END DECLARE SECTION END-EXEC.
15.            EXEC SQL
16.                DECLARE PROJECT TABLE
17.                (NAME                      PIC X(20),
18.                 P_NUMBER                  PIC 9(5) NOT NULL,
19.                 MANAGER                   PIC X(15),
20.                 ACTUAL_COST               PIC 9(6),
21.                 EXPECTED_COST             PIC 9(6))
22.            END-EXEC.
23.            EXEC SQL INCLUDE SQLCA END-EXEC.
24.            EXEC SQL
25.                DECLARE PROJECT-CURSOR CURSOR FOR
26.                      SELECT *
27.                      FROM PROJECT
28.                      WHERE MANAGER =:COBOL-MANAGER
29.                      END-EXEC.
30.      PROCEDURE DIVISION.
31.      MAIN-PROCEDURE.
32.            PERFORM ACCEPT-MANAGER.
33.            PERFORM OPEN-CURSOR.
```

UPDATE-PRIOR-JOB paragraph. Lines 46–48 give an example of an embedded INSERT operation. Notice that the values to be inserted are given in host variables that are embedded in parentheses following the keyword VALUES.

Control returns to the main procedure, and SQLCODE is tested again (line 29). Then, UPDATE-CURRENT-TITLE is performed. The update operation is performed in lines 51–55, which is similar to an interactive update, except that the new value and employee number are given in host variables. Finally, SQLCODE is checked again, and the program terminates.

While these three examples don't give all the details of using embedded SQL, they do provide enough information to give you an idea of how host programs interface to SQL databases. You should be able to write simple programs such as these after studying the examples carefully.

FIGURE 7–19 **continued**

```
34.          PERFORM PROCESS-MAN.
35.          PERFORM CLOSE-CURSOR.
36.          STOP RUN.
37.      ACCEPT-MANAGER.
38.          DISPLAY 'ENTER NAME:'.
39.          ACCEPT COBOL-MANAGER.
40.      OPEN-CURSOR.
41.          EXEC SQL OPEN PROJECT-CURSOR END-EXEC.
42.      PROCESS-MAN.
43.          PERFORM FETCH-DATA.
44.          IF SQL CODE = 0
45.              PERFORM TEST-COST UNTIL SQL CODE = 100
46.          ELSE
47.              PERFORM SQL-ERROR-PROCEDURE.
48.      FETCH-DATA.
49.          EXEC SQL
50.              FETCH PROJECT-CURSOR
51.              INTO:COBOL-PNAME,:COBOL-PNUMBER,:COBOL-MANAGER,
52.              :COBOL-ACTUAL-COST,:COBOL-EXPECTED-COST
53.          END EXEC.
54.      TEST-COST.
55.          SUBTRACT COBOL-EXPECTED-COST FROM COBOL-ACTUAL-COST
56.              GIVING COST-OVER-RUN.
57.          IF COST-OVER-RUN > 0
58.              DISPLAY COBOL-PNUMBER, COBOL-MANAGER,
59.              COST-OVER-RUN.
60.          PERFORM FETCH-DATA.
61.      CLOSE-CURSOR.
62.          EXEC SQL CLOSE PROJECT-CURSOR END-EXEC.
63.      SQL-ERROR-PROCEDURE.
64.          DISPLAY 'ERROR NUMBER', SQLCODE, 'HAS OCCURRED.'.
65.          DISPLAY 'PLEASE CONTACT YOUR DATABASE ADMINISTRATOR.'.
66.          STOP RUN.
```

CASE EXAMPLE:
Example SQL Queries for the Omega Company

To further illustrate SQL and its power relative to the relational algebra and calculus discussed in Chapter 6, we will show SQL queries to perform the sales forecasting analysis for the Omega Company. The database for the Omega Company is given in the previous chapter in Figure 6–16. The first query simply reduced the number of rows that you have to deal with, perhaps to reduce the "information overload" associated with all the data in the original table. To select the rows for years after 1981, the SQL query is:

```
SELECT *
FROM ENVIRONMENT
WHERE YEAR > 81
```

This query produces the results shown in Figure 6–17.

FIGURE 7–20   An Embedded SQL Program to Update Current Title and Prior Job

```
1.      IDENTIFICATION DIVISION.
2.      PROGRAM-ID. CHANGE-TITLE.
3.      ENVIRONMENT DIVISION.
4.      DATA DIVISION.
5.      WORKING-STORAGE SECTION.
6.          EXEC SQL BEGIN DECLARE SECTION END-EXEC.
7.      01 COBOL-TITLE.
8.          03 COBOL-ENUMBER                PIC 9(5).
9.          03 COBOL-NEWTITLE               PIC X(20).
10.         03 COBOL-OLDTITLE               PIC X(20).
11.         EXEC SQL END DECLARE SECTION END-EXEC.
12.         EXEC SQL
13.             DECLARE TITLE TABLE
14.             (E_NUMBER SMALLINT NOT NULL,
15.             CURRENT_TITLE CHAR (20))
16.         END-EXEC.
17.         EXEC SQL
18.             DECLARE PRIOR_JOB TABLE
19.             (E_NUMBER SMALLINT NOT NULL,
20.             PRIOR_TITLE CHAR (20) NOT NULL))
21.         END-EXEC.
22.         EXEC SQL INCLUDE SQLCA END-EXEC.
23.     PROCEDURE DIVISION.
24.     MAIN-PROCEDURE.
25.         PERFORM ACCEPT DATA.
26.         PERFORM GET-OLDTITLE.
27.         IF SQLCODE NOT EQUAL 0 PERFORM SQL-ERROR-PROCEDURE.
28.         PERFORM UPDATE-PRIOR_JOB.
29.         IF SQLCODE NOT EQUAL 0 PERFORM SQL-ERROR-PROCEDURE.
30.         PERFORM UPDATE_CURRENT_TITLE.
31.         IF SQLCODE NOT EQUAL 0 PERFORM SQL-ERROR-PROCEDURE.
32.         STOP RUN.
33.     ACCEPT-DATA.
34.         DISPLAY 'ENTER EMPLOYEE NUMBER:'.
35.         ACCEPT COBOL-ENUMBER.
36.         DISPLAY 'ENTER NEW TITLE:'.
37.         ACCEPT COBOL-NEWTITLE.
38.     GET OLD_TITLE.
39.         EXEC SQL
40.             SELECT CURRENT_TITLE
41.             INTO:COBOL-OLDTITLE
42.             FROM TITLE
43.             WHERE E_NUMBER=:COBOL-ENUMBER
44.         END-EXEC.
45.     UPDATE-PRIOR-JOB.
46.         EXEC SQL
47.             INSERT INTO PRIOR-JOB
48.             VALUES (:COBOL_ENUMBER,:COBOL_OLDTITLE)
49.         END-EXEC.
50.     UPDATE-CURRENT-TITLE.
51.         EXEC SQL
52.             UPDATE TITLE
53.             SET TITLE=:COBOL-NEWTITLE
54.             WHERE E_NUMBER=:COBOL-ENUMBER
55.         END-EXEC.
56.     SQL-ERROR-PROCEDURE.
57.         DISPLAY 'ERROR NUMBER', SQLCODE, 'HAS OCCURRED.'.
58.         DISPLAY 'PLEASE CONTACT YOUR DATABASE ADMINISTRATOR.'.
59.         STOP RUN.
```

This didn't seem to help you understand what was happening in the economy, and how that was affecting sales. You knew that sales had been low in the first quarter of last year, so you decided to look at only the first quarter's economic index in each year to see if a pattern was evident. The query to choose the desired attributes and tuples is:

```
SELECT YEAR, ECONOMIC_INDEX
FROM ENVIRONMENT
WHERE QUARTER = 1
```

The query above generates the output in Figure 6–18.

Since this data was not much help in understanding the situation, you decided to compare sales with the economic index on a quarterly basis. This involves a join and a projection, which produce the results in Figure 6–19, and is done in SQL with the query:

```
SELECT QUARTER, YEAR, FIRM, ECONOMIC_INDEX, SALES
FROM ENVIRONMENT, ACCOUNTING_DATA
WHERE ENVIRONMENT.QUARTER = ACCOUNTING_DATA.QUARTER
AND ENVIRONMENT.YEAR = ACCOUNTING_DATA.YEAR
```

This data reminded you that the stock market had been quite low during this period of time, so you retrieved the stock market index for each quarter in the database. The SQL query is:

```
SELECT YEAR, QUARTER, STOCK_MARKET_INDEX
FROM ENVIRONMENT
```

When this failed to shed much light on the problem, you finally remembered that your major competitor, Alpha Company, had mounted a major advertising campaign about that time. To confirm your belief, you looked at the accounting data you have for Alpha, which is shown in Figure 6–21. You can do this in SQL with:

```
SELECT *
FROM ACCOUNTING_DATA
WHERE FIRM = 'ALPHA'
```

At that point, your associate, Jose Garza, suggested that the company had been unable to obtain a short-term loan at that time because of rather extreme short-term bill rates. You retrieved the year, quarter, and short-term bill rate for all quarters in which the rate was greater than 15 percent. The SQL query is:

```
SELECT YEAR, QUARTER, SHORT_TERM_BILL_RATE
FROM ENVIRONMENT
WHERE SHORT_TERM_BILL_RATE > 15.0
```

producing the result in Figure 6–22.

Jose had actually come to get your help in obtaining some data he needed. He wanted data on quarter, year, firm, and sales for all quarters in which the stock market index was less than 97. In relational algebra, this required a four-step process described in Figure 6–23. The same data can be retrieved with the single SQL statement:

THE USER'S VIEW

In The User's View in Chapter 6, we hinted that implementations of relational database languages are user oriented. This chapter provides an example of that orientation.

In SQL, we see that only a small number of keywords need be learned to retrieve data from relational databases. Many of the relational algebra operations of Chapter 6 are variations of the SELECT-FROM-WHERE keyword combination. A small number of commands to learn obviously facilitates the learning process. The choice of keywords also helps users to remember them because they are descriptive of the actual operations performed.

In some cases, however, SQL can be rather complex and verbose. The IN key word and nested queries can be quite lengthy. Joins can require complex and lengthy syntax. The last example of SELECT, for example, is not one that most users would be willing to spend the time to master.

Thus, in most cases, users cannot be left to themselves after a database has been designed and implemented, even if SQL is available. They still may need assistance in performing some queries. ∎

```
SELECT QUARTER, YEAR, FIRM, SALES
FROM SALES, ENVIRONMENT
WHERE STOCK_MARKET_INDEX < 97
AND ENVIRONMENT.QUARTER = ACCOUNTING_DATA.QUARTER
AND ENVIRONMENT.YEAR = ACCOUNTING_DATA.YEAR ∎
```

CHAPTER SUMMARY

This chapter has presented features of SQL for retrieving data from relational databases. SQL is a relational transformation language. As such, it provides a user interface consisting of a set of keywords and a basic structure. The basic keyword set consists of SELECT, FROM, and WHERE. The keywords are used in conjunction with relation and attribute names to specify the desired results of relational data manipulation. SQL performs the appropriate relational operations to achieve the desired results, thus insulating the user from the need to learn or even be aware of relational algebra operations such as projection, selection, and join.

Other aspects of SQL for retrieving data include the keywords IN, BETWEEN, and LIKE. IN is used to specify a set of values, which may be defined by a nested subquery (another SELECT-FROM-WHERE combination). BETWEEN is used to specify a range of values in a WHERE clause. LIKE is for specifying character patterns, instead of exact character strings to match in a text search.

The ORDER BY clause in SQL is used to sort output. GROUP BY is available for grouping results, and HAVING may be used with GROUP BY to specify conditions on group results. The functions COUNT, SUM, MIN, MAX, and AVG provide the ability to compute aggregate values. The EXISTS function returns the value *false* or *true*; DISTINCT returns only the

METROPOLITAN NATIONAL BANK

One way of evaluating a database design is to verify that the design supports the decision-making processes that revolve around the database. If you can implement typical queries related to the decision-making process, you have a good chance that your design supports those processes. Listed below are typical queries that must be supported by MetNat's integrated database system. Use your implementation from the last chapter to construct SQL commands that implement each query. If an SQL command alone is inadequate, indicate how the query could be processed using an application program. If you find a query particularly difficult to implement, you may need to revise your implementation from the prior chapter.

Sample Queries

What is the current balance of an account?

Has a recent deposit been credited to an account?

Has a recent check cleared?

When was the last interest amount credited to my savings account?

What is the current interest rate on money market accounts?

How much interest has been credited to an account?

What is the remaining balance on a loan?

How many more payments are outstanding on this loan?

What accounts does a particular customer hold?

What is the maturity date on a particular certificate of deposit?

What is the address of a particular customer?

When was the current balance on an account last calculated?

What penalties have been charged to a particular account?

What are the loan numbers of loans that have been paid back by a particular customer?

What are the loan numbers of outstanding loans held by a particular loan applicant?

What is the credit limit of a particular credit card holder?

How much available credit does a particular credit card customer have?

What is the average monthly balance on a particular credit card account?

How many sick leave days does an employee currently have?

How many vacation days does an employee currently have? ■

---

unique rows of a table; and UNION performs a relational algebra union operation.

Together, these features of SQL provide a powerful set of operators for accessing data in relational databases.

· User views, defined with the CREATE VIEW operation, may be used to restrict the portion of the database available to a user and may also be used to simplify access by joining tables in a way that is transparent to the user. Additional security features are provided with the GRANT operation, which is used to specify the type of access permitted to a user. Finally, SQL may be embedded in host programming languages to provide for batch updates, formatted screens, and so forth.

Questions and Exercises

1. What are the characteristics of a relational transformation language?

2. List the SQL keywords discussed in this chapter. Explain how each is used. What usually follows each?

3. Show the SQL commands to perform the following operations on the EMPLOYEE relation in Figure 7–1.
   a. List the employee names.
   b. List the employee numbers.
   c. Retrieve all data on the employee named Clarke.
   d. Retrieve all data on employee number 1005.
   e. List employee names beginning with C.
   f. List employee names with the second letter d.
   g. List employee names between B and K.

4. Show the SQL commands to perform the following operations on the PROJECT relation in Figure 7–1.
   a. List the project names.
   b. List the managers of projects.
   c. Provide all data for the projects managed by Yates.
   d. Provide a list of the projects with actual cost less than the expected cost.
   e. Display project names in alphabetical order.
   f. Display project names in inverse alphabetical order.
   g. Display managers and project numbers, with managers in alphabetic order and their corresponding projects in descending numeric order.
   h. Display project name and the ratio of actual to expected cost.
   i. Display project names with actual costs more than twice expected costs.

5. Show the SQL commands to perform the following operations on the EMPLOYEE and ASSIGNMENT relations in Figure 7–1.
   a. List the employee names and numbers for employees in the accounting department.
   b. Find the department in which Dexter works.
   c. List the employee numbers for employees assigned to project 23760.
   d. List the names of finance employees assigned to project 26511.

6. Show the SQL commands to perform the following operations on the ASSIGNMENT, PROJECT, and EMPLOYEE relations in Figure 7–1.
   a. List the actual costs of projects managed by Yates.
   b. Provide all information on the project managed by Kanter.
   c. Provide data on the actual and expected costs of project 28765.
   d. Provide data on the project with the minimum expected cost.
   e. Provide the names of the employees working on the project to secure a new office lease.

7. Show the SQL commands to perform the following operations on the EMPLOYEE and ASSIGNMENT relations in Figure 7–1.
   a. Count the number of employees.
   b. Count the number of projects.
   c. Count the number of departments.
   d. Count the number of employees in each department (use GROUP BY).
   e. Limit the results in Question 7d to only those departments with more than three employees.

8. Repeat Questions 7a–c, counting only unique tuples.

9. Show the SQL commands to perform the following operations on the EXPERTISE relation in Figure 7–1.
   a. Count the number of employees.
   b. Count the number of unique skills.
   c. Count the number of employees with stock market training.

10. Show the SQL commands to perform the following operations on the PROJECT relation in Figure 7–1.
    a. Find the project with the maximum cost.
    b. Find the projects where actual cost is less than expected cost.
    c. Find the projects with actual costs less that the average actual cost.

11. Create the following:
    a. A view that shows employee names and associated skills.
    b. A view that shows employee names and current titles.
    c. A view that shows employee names, current titles, and skills.

12. Use GRANT to establish the following privileges:
    a. Allow user JOE read access on the PROJECT relation.
    b. Allow anyone who has access to the database to read the CURRENT-TITLE table.
    c. Allow DAVID to have all privileges on the EMPLOYEE relation.
    d. Allow JOE to add data to the PROJECT table.

13. Write COBOL programs to perform the following tasks:
    a. Accept an employee number and a project number to which that employee has been assigned. Check to see that the project number exists in the PROJECT relation.

    b. Accept data from the user to add a new row to the EMPLOYEE table.

    c. Accept a project number from the user and delete all information about that project from the PROJECT table and the ASSIGNMENT table.

14. Give the CREATE TABLE statements necessary to define the Omega Company database in Chapter 6.

For Further Reading

Early papers on SQL are:

Chamberlin, D. D. and R. F. Boyce. "SEQUEL 2: A Unified Approach to Data Definition, Manipulation, and Control." *IBM Journal of Research and Development* 20, no. 6 (November 1976).

Chamberlin, D. D., and R. F. Boyce. "SEQUEL, A Structured English Query Language." *Proceedings of the ACM SIGMOD Workshop on Data Description, Access, and Control.* 1974.

For critical review of SQL, see: Date, C. J. "Where SQL Falls Short." *Datamation* 33, no. 9 (1987), pp. 83–86.

Descriptions of more recent implementations may be found in: *SQL/Data System Terminal Users' Guide.* White Plains, N.Y.: IBM Corporation. 1982. *Oracle Users' Guide.* San Francisco: Oracle Corporation, 1983.

For the formal SQL standards, see: American National Standards Institute. "Database Language SQL." *Document ANSI X3,* 135–1986 (1986).

For more on specific implementations and a very readable presentation, see: Ageloff, Roy. "A Primer on SQL." St. Louis: Times Mirror/Mosby College Publishing, 1988.

8

MICROCOMPUTER DATABASE SYSTEMS

One of the most important managerial subjects in a database environment is the recent influx of microcomputing power into organizations. The increase in desktop computing has been driven by several factors. These, as well as some of the major issues of managing this latest revolution in computing capabilities, are discussed in this chapter.

THE EVOLUTION OF ORGANIZATIONAL COMPUTING RESOURCES

In the early days of business computing, the main computing resource for the organization was typically a large mainframe computer. In many cases, this was the only computing resource. Frequently, only a select group of highly trained people had any idea how to make the computer operate effectively, which led naturally to centralized information system structures (see Figures 8–1 and 8–2).

With time, computer hardware power increased and computer hardware cost decreased, making it cost-effective for more areas in the organization to begin more-specialized computing activity. At the same time, computer literacy was becoming more widespread. College graduates outside of the engineering disciplines brought computer skills to organizations, which supported the new applications being developed with the powerful, lower-cost computer hardware. These developments led to decentralized organizational structures, such as the one illustrated in Figure 8–3. The early applications of computers in specialized roles tended to bring great returns. But as the need for interorganizational interfaces grew, so did problems resulting from poor interface designs. In many cases, the systems that had been developed were never intended to either supply or accept new or increasing amounts of data.

Functional areas began to duplicate important data items in an attempt to solve interface problems. This led in turn to all of the problems related to data redundancy, consistency, and integrity that we have

FIGURE 8–1
Progression of the Division Structure of Information Systems in Recent History

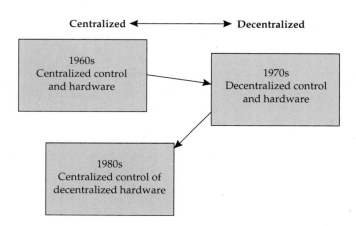

FIGURE 8–2   **A Centralized Division of Information Management Systems**

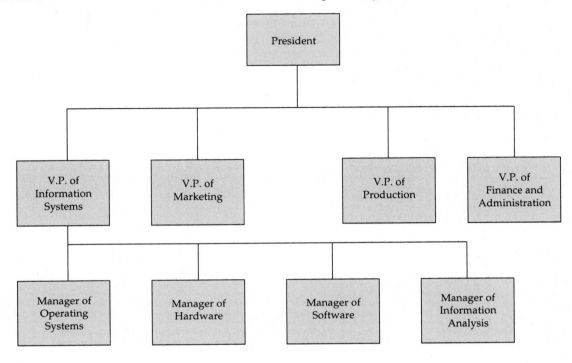

FIGURE 8–3   **A Decentralized Division of Information Management Systems**

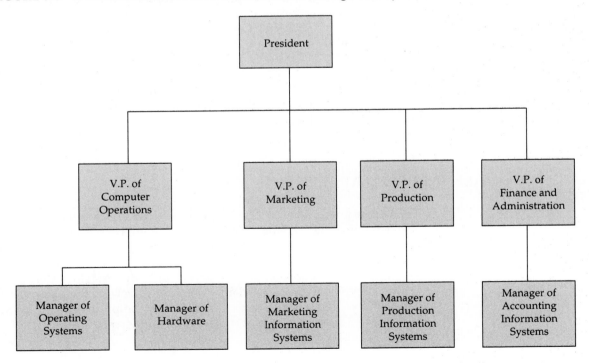

examined earlier in this book. Control of the data resources of the organization was lost.

The response to these problems has been the development of techniques in structured analysis and design, database management, and structured programming. These techniques attempt to bring the standardization inherent in a centralized structure into the decentralized environment.

THE PROLIFERATION OF MICROCOMPUTERS

History is currently repeating itself with the recent proliferation of microcomputers in the workplace. Managers have been careful not to repeat the mistakes of the past, however; they have accurately perceived the microcomputer as another means of increased computer power with decreased cost. Many organizations have adopted a policy of encouraging microcomputer usage throughout the organization.

At the same time, managers remember when powerful minicomputers were introduced and have taken steps to prevent repeating the difficulties associated with them. Specific problems encountered when microcomputers are used in an organization include (1) a tendency by users to "reinvent the wheel" by programming frequently needed routines already programmed by someone else in the organization, (2) an expensive learning period that results from a lack of formal training, (3) recurring exposure to major disasters due to inadequate data management, and (4) uneconomical solutions to technical problems due to the user's unfamiliarity with the microcomputer hardware.

Because microcomputers are so inexpensive, their purchase may not even require an explicit organizational approval process. This makes education about the proper use of this computing resource particularly important. In order to adequately address the need for such education, as well as other problems like the ones just mentioned, many organizations have concentrated a special collection of expertise in a small organizational unit known as the **information center.**

FUNCTIONS OF AN INFORMATION CENTER

The primary functions of an information center are to provide consulting, training, and technical assistance to computer users (especially microcomputer users). Technical assistance may be either hardware- or software-oriented. A user may need help, for example, in selecting among software packages or evaluating disk drives. The information center is typically part of a larger function, such as the information systems division, but interfaces with all other computing resources (see Figure 8–4). The number of people that actually compose the informa-

FIGURE 8–4 Organizational Placement of an Information Center

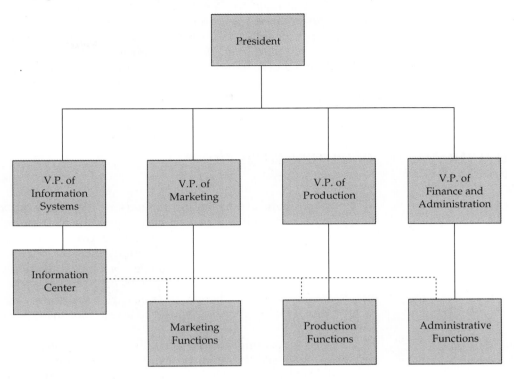

tion center depends on the number of microcomputer users requiring support in the organization. The most important characteristic of the information center staff is that they have both hardware and software expertise and are user-oriented. Business knowledge is also essential, as is an attitude that information systems are not worthwhile unless they are useful to decision-makers.

The information center exists to meet all the needs of the users of the information systems in the organization. Typical services provided by the information center include high-level management overviews of proposed information system enhancements, information-requirements analysis for new database system demands, evaluation and selection of microcomputer hardware and software, and installation, training, and minor maintenance of microcomputer equipment. Training classes are typically formalized to the extent of standardizing the training material and course content.

In cases where the information center personnel act as consultants, the process is usually formalized to a point where standardized analyses are performed. Recommendations resulting from the consultation will likely be reviewed at higher levels in the organization, so standardization is to the organization's advantage. Standardized formats expedite this type of review process.

Whereas training and consulting activities tend to be formalized, many of the other services of the information center are supplied on an ad hoc basis. Once a user has the basic tools, most of the interaction with the information center involves resolution of problems that can usually be handled in a telephone conversation. All employees in the information center should have some expertise in many areas; any one of them could be called on to handle a telephone request for information.

INTERFACING MICROCOMPUTERS WITH THE DATABASE SYSTEM

With the growing use of microcomputers in the organizational workplace, a new challenge has been presented to database administration. That challenge involves the interface between the organization's database systems and the microcomputer. Microcomputers are being used as desktop workstations at all levels of organizations. Portable microcomputers are being used by salespeople to process data (using telephone modems) when on sales trips in other cities and by service personnel to process data when away from the office on a service call.

The microcomputer interface problem can be controlled *within* the organization, if purchases made by the organization include a strong constraint that the microcomputer be compatible with the organization's database system hardware. The problem comes when employees of the organization wish to interface their own microcomputers within the database system.

Management certainly does not want to discourage an employee from having home access to information in the database system if such access makes the employee more productive. Some organizations currently subsidize the purchase of microcomputers for their employees if the employee agrees to purchase a particular brand.

When an employee already has a microcomputer not currently supported by the database administration's procedures, a problem arises. In such a case, the database administrator must decide whether the new microcomputer type is likely to have widespread use by other employees in the organization. If so, specialized interface systems must be developed to support this microcomputer (see Figure 8–5).

Even when a particular microcomputer is supported through the communication aspects of the database system interface, problems usually occur. Although communication between the microcomputer and the database system may be possible, this process may be too difficult for the person using the microcomputer to direct. Users who do not have extensive computer backgrounds typically have little insight into the procedures required to transfer information from the database system to the microcomputer and vice versa. This situation may be alleviated when the database administration provides documentation and training (see below).

FIGURE 8–5   **The Database Administrator Is Responsible for Defining the Interface that Supports Different Types of Computers**

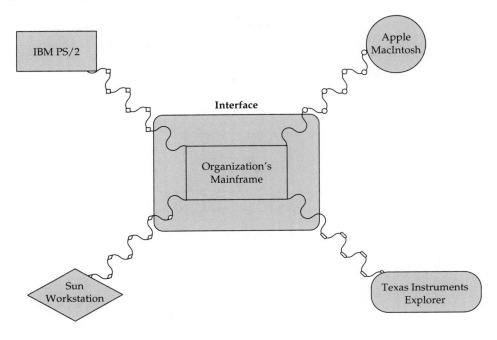

MAINTAINING INTEGRITY WITH MICROCOMPUTERS

A serious problem arising with increased microcomputer use concerns the integrity of the data in the database system. In this context, *integrity* refers to the consistency of the values of data items residing in the organization's database system *and* in a user's microcomputer. Again, integrity is very closely related to the concept of redundancy.

Once a user has transferred data values from the database system to a microcomputer, he or she can easily forget that the data value in the database system may change (see Figure 8–6). Users tend to get deeply involved in their particular application of the data. When several users are manipulating the same data, each of them may be working with different values for the same data item. When different values are being used for a single database item, the overall decision-making process may lead to inconsistent decisions. Clearly, ineffective decisions may result from using inaccurate data.

SECURITY IN MICROCOMPUTER ENVIRONMENTS

Another problem related to the ability to download data concerns security. Disks used with microcomputer systems are small and can be concealed easily. These disks have more than enough capacity to support the theft of enough data to cause a major problem for an organization.

FIGURE 8–6   **Maintaining Integrity in a Microcomputer Environment Can Be Difficult**

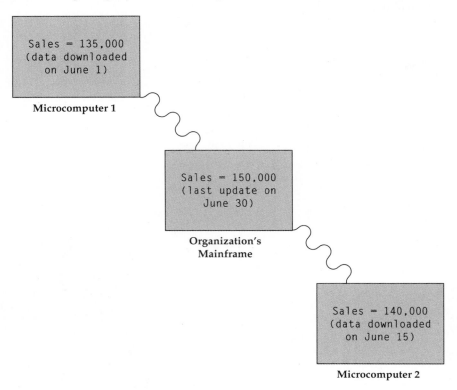

The first line of defense against such theft is to limit access to data through the database system security mechanisms. Of course, there may be cases requiring a wide range of access. Because the physical removal of the data is the issue here, one way to reduce the risk of theft is to remove the floppy disk drives from microcomputers where possible. If the disk cannot be written, the data cannot be removed. This approach has been implemented in organizations in which access to volatile data is the crux of the organization's operations; executive placement services and brokerage services are examples.

The database administrator takes responsibility for any problems arising in the areas of integrity and security. To fulfill such a responsibility, he or she must provide adequate education to the users so that they are aware of how these problematic situations develop. Distribution of periodic messages (either manually, or through the database system, or both) reminding users of pitfalls is recommended.

EVALUATING MICROCOMPUTER DATABASE SYSTEMS

The microcomputer revolution has resulted in the development of thousands of software packages, each vying for the dollars that must be spent to realize the productivity increases promised by the microcomputer industry. Some of these software products are advertised as database management systems. Obviously, with prices ranging from under $50 for some of these packages to several hundred dollars for others, a wide range of so-called database capabilities is being offered. In this section, we address some of the issues unique to microcomputer database systems.

The evaluation of a microcomputer database system can be approached in much the same manner as any software package evaluation, but the microcomputer environment provides a few special issues that should be considered as well. Identification of decision-making processes to be supported by a microcomputer database system is imperative. Hardware requirements for microcomputer database systems may require additional hardware purchases and upgrades to the existing microcomputer system. Still, these upgrades may not be sufficient. Any characteristics of the task to be supported that exceed the constraints of a microcomputer system probably preclude such an approach.

Because most microcomputer-based systems are used by single users away from the organizational database system, ease of learning and documentation become major issues. Many microcomputer users do not have extensive training in using computer-based systems. The package should be evaluated with this point in mind. A microcomputer package should be well supported by its documentation, including written and on-line help and tutorial facilities.

Finally, a database package alone may not be sufficient. The output of the database system may need to be integrated into text documents, requiring word processing software. Also, the data may need further manipulation by either a spreadsheet system or a more sophisticated modeling package. Resolution of these issues may indicate the need for a different type of package.

TYPES OF MICROCOMPUTER DATABASE SYSTEMS

The expected usage of data may indicate the need for a particular type of database system. In the following, we deviate from the concept of database systems developed throughout this text to consider three types of packages that can be used for data management in a microcomputer environment.

A **spreadsheet system** is a simple data management tool. Spreadsheet packages maintain a tabular representation of data. Data is entered into columns and can be manipulated to almost any extent within the confines of the spreadsheet. Such data manipulation is typically restricted to simple arithmetic processes involving data entries in the columns; a column of numbers may be added, for example, or one subtotal may be subtracted from another. In more-sophisticated spreadsheet systems, spreadsheets themselves can be related. This characteristic obviously provides for more-complex relationships between the data in the spreadsheets.

Database packages constitute the second category of microcomputer data management systems. Many packages advertising as database systems are not database systems in the sense presented in this book. These systems would be more accurately named *file management systems.* As noted in Chapter 1, there are a number of objectives that should be supported by a database system, and few microcomputer database packages satisfy all of them. Recovery concerns have already been mentioned. Few packages support any facility for maintaining data integrity. Some packages do not even provide a minimal level of data relatability of data shareability. These packages are "database systems" for the purpose of advertising only.

Most microcomputer database systems are based on a tabular representation of data, similar to that of the relational database model. If these packages are truly relational systems, they support essentiality, integrity constraints, and relational data manipulation.

A final class of microcomputer data management system is the integrated system. The term **integrated system** implies the existence of some combination of data management, data modeling, and word processing capabilities. Integrated systems provide all of the capabilities normally found in each individual component and also support some mechanism for sharing the outputs of one component with another. In many cases, an integrated system is required to meet the needs of an organizational decision-maker.

Packages advertised as microcomputer database systems may be vastly different in their characteristics and capabilities. These characteristics must be carefully considered in light of the needs of the organization before a package is selected. On the positive side, even several hundred dollars is not much for a large organization to spend to purchase and test a package being considered. In this way, an organization can thoroughly evaluate one copy of a microcomputer package before committing to purchase software in large quantities.

To give you a better feel for some existing microcomputer database packages, a few of these products will be described briefly. First, two implementations of SQL will be discussed. Then a relational graphics language called *Query By Example (QBE)* will be presented, followed by a description of two QBE implementations. The database in Figure 7–1 will be used to illustrate these packages.

MICROCOMPUTER DATABASE IMPLEMENTATIONS OF SQL

In this section, some of the more popular implementations of SQL on microcomputers will be presented. The SQL interfaces of two packages, XQL and dBase IV, are described.

XQL

XQL is offered by Novell, Inc. It runs on IBM and IBM-compatible personal computers. The interactive SQL interface is close to the standard SQL described earlier. However, the CREATE TABLE statement in

XQL is somewhat different from the definition in the standard. Views, nested queries, multiple tables, and so on are supported.

The initial screen one gets when XQL is invoked is shown in Figure 8–7. Notice that the functions at the top of the screen include Enter, Go, Clear, Recall, Store, Delete, Options, and Quit. Initially, the cursor will be highlighting Enter. To input a statement, Enter is selected by pressing the return or enter key on the keyboard. The cursor moves into the blank window just below the options menu. Next, the desired SQL statement is entered in that window. An example is shown in Figure 8–8. This statement will retrieve all rows in the PROJECTS relation. The statement itself may be entered in upper- or lowercase, except for character strings in WHERE clauses, which are, of course, case sensitive.

When the statement has been keyed in, you must press the ESC key to return to the menu. Then Go must be selected to execute the query. If the statement runs successfully, output is displayed in the lower window. If more columns are retrieved than the screen will accommodate, the tab key may be used to move to the right or left to view data. If more rows are retrieved than will fit on the screen, then the down arrow key may be used to move down. However, you cannot go back up. Once a screen is left by moving downwards, the statement must be rerun to see the data again. Statements do stay in the upper window until either typed over or erased by using the Clear function.

FIGURE 8–7
The Initial XQL Screen

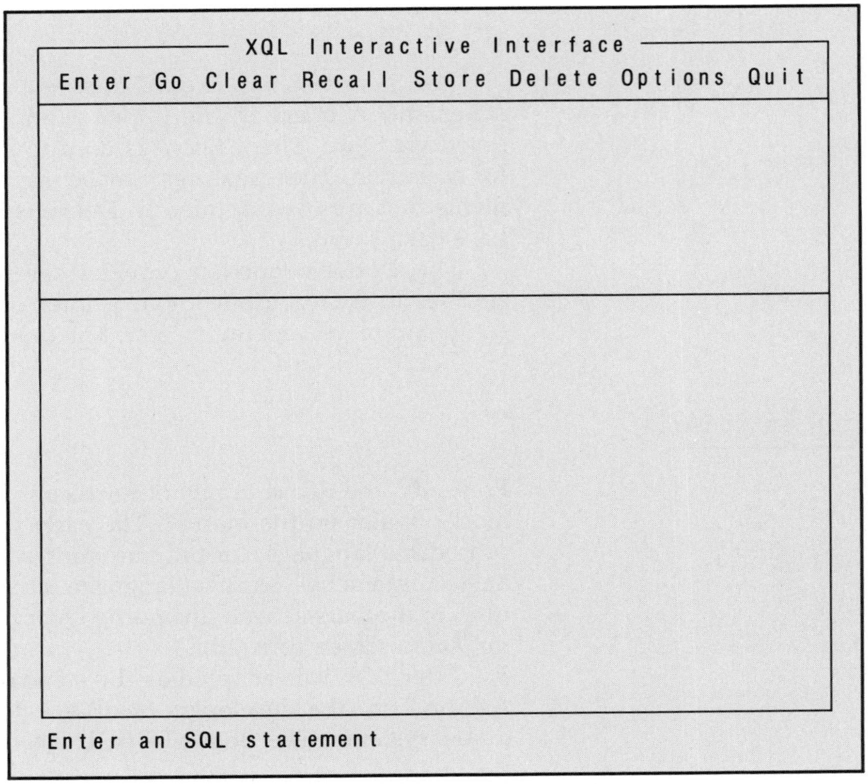

```
┌─────────────────────────────────────────────────────────┐
│  ┌──────────── XQL  Interactive  Interface ──────────┐   │
│  │ Enter  Go  Clear  Recall  Store  Delete  Options  Quit│
│  │                                                    │   │
│  │                                                    │   │
│  │                                                    │   │
│  ├────────────────────────────────────────────────────┤   │
│  │                                                    │   │
│  │                                                    │   │
│  │                                                    │   │
│  │                                                    │   │
│  │                                                    │   │
│  │                                                    │   │
│  │                                                    │   │
│  └────────────────────────────────────────────────────┘   │
│  Enter  an  SQL  statement                               │
└─────────────────────────────────────────────────────────┘
```

FIGURE 8–8
**XQL Screen with an SQL
Statement Entered**

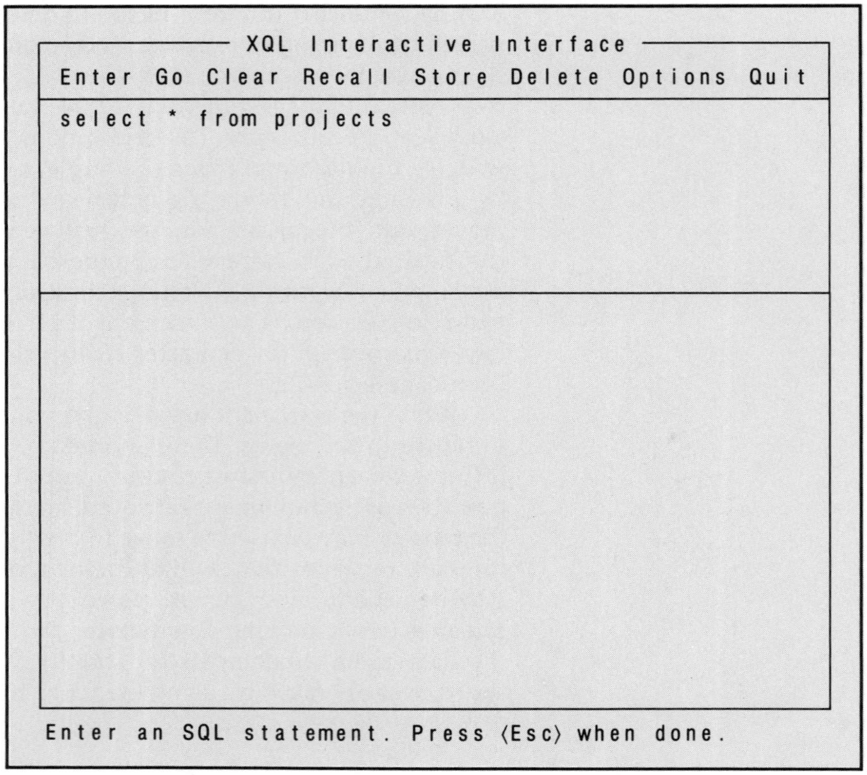

```
┌─────────────────────────────────────────────────────────────┐
│              ── XQL Interactive Interface ──                  │
│   ┌─────────────────────────────────────────────────────┐    │
│   │ Enter  Go  Clear  Recall  Store  Delete  Options  Quit│   │
│   ├─────────────────────────────────────────────────────┤    │
│   │ select * from projects                              │    │
│   │                                                     │    │
│   │                                                     │    │
│   │                                                     │    │
│   ├─────────────────────────────────────────────────────┤    │
│   │                                                     │    │
│   │                                                     │    │
│   │                                                     │    │
│   │                                                     │    │
│   │                                                     │    │
│   │                                                     │    │
│   │                                                     │    │
│   │                                                     │    │
│   │                                                     │    │
│   └─────────────────────────────────────────────────────┘    │
│   Enter an SQL statement. Press ⟨Esc⟩ when done.             │
└─────────────────────────────────────────────────────────────┘
```

The Store function is used to save a statement, *not* the output of a statement. A query in the upper window may be given a name and saved via Store. Then, Recall is used to bring it back into the window for execution. These features may be used to avoid keying in long statements that are used frequently. Delete is used to erase statements that have been saved.

The Options function provides several capabilities, including the abilities to route output into a printer or disk file and to change the setup parameters for the system. The function of Quit is obvious.

SQL in dBase IV

Presently, the dBase family of microcomputer database products is the most popular on the market. The early versions of dBase supported a procedural language, for programming relatively complex applications, and an interactive retrieval language. Later versions support these features and others as well, including Query By Example, a report generator, and a screen generator.

After SQL was adopted as the standard relational query language, Ashton-Tate (the developers of dBase) designed an SQL interface for dBase systems. The dBase IV SQL interface is consistent with many features of the other elements of the product. For example, about 100 dBase commands and 100 dBase functions may be used in the dBase IV SQL mode.

When dBase IV is invoked, the system starts in 'assist' mode (a screen-driven interface). To access SQL, one must be in 'command mode.' To get into command mode, press the Esc key, and answer *Yes* to the prompt "Are you sure you want to abandon operation?" To enter dBase IV SQL from command mode, type SET SQL ON. The SQL command "CREATE DATABASE ⟨database name⟩;" (all SQL commands end with a semicolon) is used to define tables with a syntax similar to that of ANSI standard. SELECT, INSERT, UPDATE, and DELETE are also similar to standard, with the major exceptions being that strings are specified somewhat differently, and column names, when used with table names, are put in parentheses to suffix them, rather than separating the two with a period. Subqueries, GROUP BY, HAVING, ORDER BY, and functions are all supported.

SQL statements may also be embedded in dBase IV programs, but the system must be informed of this and the programs are stored in a special format. It is also possible to mix features of dBase language into SQL statements. Of course, this reduces the portability of programs that do so, as those features would have to be removed if the program were to be ported to a standard SQL environment.

Databases defined in the SQL mode in dBase IV are stored in a format different from those defined in other dBase interfaces. However, data may be imported into SQL databases and exported to dBase databases, thus alleviating this problem somewhat.

To summarize, the SQL mode in dBase IV conforms reasonably well to ANSI standards. However, in order to make the SQL mode compatible with existing dBase features, compromises were necessary. The inclusion of many dBase features in the SQL interface extends the power and compatibility of this interface with dBase environments, but reduces its compatibility with external environments.

DATA MANIPULATION USING QBE: A RELATIONAL GRAPHICS LANGUAGE

Query By Example (QBE), first proposed by Zloof in 1975, is an interesting and different approach to data manipulation in a relational database management system. When first invoked, QBE presents a picture of a relation (without data) to the user. The user then enters QBE commands under the attribute names in order to retrieve data.

There are no true "standards" for QBE, and several microcomputer database packages offer QBE-like interfaces. Ashton-Tate's dBase IV and Paradox from Borland International are two popular microcomputer packages that have QBE interfaces. Paradox was the first microcomputer package with an interface close to the one described in Zloof's original paper. IBM offers QBE on its mainframe computers. A trend that seems to be developing is to offer a user-oriented interface such as QBE on a microcomputer workstation and then translate QBE queries into SQL for processing on a mainframe or file-server in a networked microcomputer environment. Unlike SQL, QBE may not be embedded in an applications program. We present only the basics of QBE.

Initiating a QBE Session

When a session using QBE is initiated, the user is presented a relational structure similar to the one shown in Figure 8–9. Once the relation from which the data is to be drawn is specified, the cursor must be positioned under the proper attribute name. If the user does not know the names of the relations in the database, the cursor can be positioned under the leftmost column on the screen and a P. entered. P. is the "print" command. Whenever the user types P. in an area of the relation, QBE fills the proper values for this query.

The leftmost column is reserved for commands that involve entire relations. When P. is entered in this column and no relation is currently being examined, QBE responds by displaying the names of all the relations in the database.

To begin working with a particular relation, the user must indicate which relation to use. The relation is specified by moving the cursor to the area where the leftmost attribute name could appear. The relation name is entered in this area, followed by P. If one wants to work with the data from the PROJECT relation, for example, one enters PROJECT P., as shown in Figure 8–10a. After execution of this command, the screen appears as in Figure 8–10b.

A user who knows an attribute name but not the relation name can enter the attribute name in one of the attribute heading areas; QBE fills in the appropriate relation name. If Expected Cost is entered in an attribute heading, for example, the relation name PROJECT is supplied by QBE in the leftmost heading area. If, in this example, the PROJECT relation has a different number of attributes than are in the empty structure first presented to the user, QBE adds or removes columns as necessary to accommodate the specified relation. A user can also further

FIGURE 8–9   QBE Graphic Display
The structure presented when a QBE session is initiated shows no data.

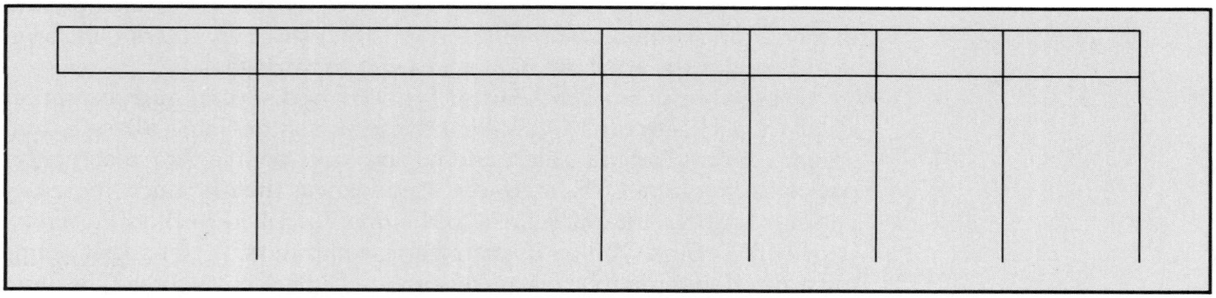

FIGURE 8–10a   Initiating a QBE Session to Work with the PROJECT Relation

PROJECT P.					

FIGURE 8–10b   QBE's Response to the Command in Figure 8–10a
Note that QBE has supplied the attribute names.

PROJECT	Name	P-Number	Manager	Actual Cost	Expected Cost

modify the attributes displayed by blanking out the attribute names that are of no interest. In subsequent commands, these attributes are not displayed.

Projection

Determining the names of the projects currently in progress is now possible. This is done by entering P. under the Name attribute, as shown in Figure 8–11a, producing the result shown in Figure 8–11b. Similarly, a print command under the Manager attribute (Figure 8–12a) produces the projection of the PROJECT relation over Manager, as shown in Figure 8–12b.

Note that, unlike SQL, QBE removes duplicate tuples. To retrieve all tuples, one must use the command ALL after the print command, as shown in Figure 8–12c. This produces the output shown in Figure 8–12d, which includes multiple occurrences of manager names. More than one attribute can be printed by entering print commands under all attributes of interest. Figure 8–13a shows the commands to retrieve both project name and manager, as shown in Figure 8–13b. If ordering the result of the query is necessary, QBE provides ways of doing this. In

FIGURE 8–11a   **Directing QBE to Provide a List of PROJECT Names**

PROJECT	Name	P-Number	Manager	Actual Cost	Expected Cost
	P.				

FIGURE 8–11b   **QBE's Response to the Command in Figure 8–11a**

PROJECT	Name	P-Number	Manager	Actual Cost	Expected Cost
	New billing system Common stock issue Resolve bad debts New office lease Revise documentation Entertain new client New TV commercial				

FIGURE 8–12a   **Directing QBE to Provide a List of Project Managers**

PROJECT	Name	P-Number	Manager	Actual Cost	Expected Cost
			P.		

FIGURE 8–12b   QBE's Response to the Command in Figure 8–12a
Note that QBE removes duplicates.

PROJECT	Name	P-Number	Manager	Actual Cost	Expected Cost
			Yates Baker Kanter		

FIGURE 8–12c   QBE Commands to Provide a List of *All* Entries for Project Manager

PROJECT	Name	P-Number	Manager	Actual Cost	Expected Cost
			P.ALL		

FIGURE 8–12d   QBE's Response to the Command in Figure
Note that specifying ALL forces duplicates in the result.

PROJECT	Name	P-Number	Manager	Actual Cost	Expected Cost
			Yates Baker Kanter Yates Kanter Yates Baker		

FIGURE 8–13a   **QBE Commands to Obtain Data from More Than One Attribute**

PROJECT	Name	P-Number	Manager	Actual Cost	Expected Cost
	P.		P.		

FIGURE 8–13b   **QBE's Response to the Command in Figure 8–13a**

PROJECT	Name	P-Number	Manager	Actual Cost	Expected Cost
	New billing system		Yates		
	Common stock issue		Baker		
	Resolve bad debts		Kanter		
	New office lease		Yates		
	Revise documentation		Kanter		
	Entertain new client		Yates		
	New TV commercial		Baker		

FIGURE 8–14a   **QBE Commands to Produce a List of Project Names and Numbers**

PROJECT	Name	P-Number	Manager	Actual Cost	Expected Cost
	P.	P.AO			

order to obtain a list of projects in order by project number, one makes the entries shown in Figure 8–14a. The AO in the entry under the P-Number attribute heading indicates that the output should be in ascending order (see Figure 8–14b). A DO directs QBE to put the result in descending order.

FIGURE 8–14b QBE's Response to the Command in Figure 8–14a
AO sorts the result in ascending order.

PROJECT	Name	P-Number	Manager	Actual Cost	Expected Cost
	New billing system	23760			
	New office lease	26511			
	Resolve bad debts	26713			
	Common stock issue	28765			
	Revise documentation	34054			
	New TV commercial	85005			
	Entertain new client	87108			

FIGURE 8–15a
QBE Commands to List the Employees in the Finance Department

EMPLOYEE	Name	E-Number	Department
	P.		Finance

FIGURE 8–15b
QBE's response to the Command in Figure 8–15a
Notice that there are no duplicates.

EMPLOYEE	Name	E-Number	Department
	Kanter		
	Adams		
	Baker		
	Dexter		

Selection

Retrieval of particular tuples from a relation requires a variation of the print command. In order to retrieve the names of all employees in the finance department, one enters "Finance" under the Department attribute for the EMPLOYEE relation and the print command under the Name attribute (Figure 8–15a). This produces only the names of the employees in the finance department (Figure 8–15b).

Arithmetic conditions can be demonstrated using the PROJECT relation. Retrieval of project names with expected costs less than $3,000 is done by placing this condition under the Expected Cost attribute and

FIGURE 8–16a   **QBE Commands to List the Projects with Expected Costs Less than $3,000**

PROJECT	Name	P-Number	Manager	Actual Cost	Expected Cost
	P.				<3000

FIGURE 8–16b   **QBE's Response to the Command in Figure 8–16a**
Note that the values for expected costs are not shown.

PROJECT	Name	P-Number	Manager	Actual Cost	Expected Cost
	Resolve bad debts Entertain new client				

FIGURE 8–16c   **Additional Entries Necessary in the Commands in Figure 8–16a**

PROJECT	Name	P-Number	Manager	Actual Cost	Expected Cost
	P.				P.<3000

the print command under the Name attribute (Figure 8–16a). Note that the data printed in the result (Figure 8–16b) is the project name only. To get the expected cost values, one must include a print command with the condition, as shown in Figure 8–16c. This produces both the project names and expected costs, as shown in Figure 8–16d.

FIGURE 8–16d   **QBE's Response to the Command in Figure 8–16c**
Note that the expected cost values are now shown.

PROJECT	Name	P-Number	Manager	Actual Cost	Expected Cost
	Resolve bad debts Entertain new client				1500 2000

FIGURE 8–17a   **A QBE Query with an Unnecessary Example**

PROJECT	Name	P-Number	Manager	Actual Cost	Expected Cost
	P.PROJECT				>2000

Queries Using Examples

Projection and selection operations are performed on single relations. QBE provides facilities for manipulating data in more than one relation when this is necessary to retrieve the data required to answer a question. A QBE query can contain an **example** that helps specify the data to be retrieved. The example is an underlined entry under an attribute name. The entries under the Name and Expected Cost attributes in Figure 8–17a, for instance, mean print names for projects with an expected cost greater than $2,000, which gives the result in Figure 8–17b.

Examples may be very flexible. Since the entire entry is underlined in Figure 8–17a, anything can be a valid value. If an example has the form of G*ATSBY*, then only values beginning with a G are valid. The G is considered a value that should be matched by the result; the *ATSBY* part is an example. Similarly, an example like 5000 allows only values that end in two zeros to be considered in the result.

The power of an example can be seen in a more complex query. Suppose that one wants to know which projects have an expected cost between $2,000 and $6,000. Then the example can be used as in Figure

FIGURE 8–17b   QBE's Response to the Command in Figure 8–17b
The same response would have been made without the example.

PROJECT	Name	P-Number	Manager	Actual Cost	Expected Cost
	New billing system Common stock issue New office lease Revise documentation New TV commercial				

FIGURE 8–18a   A Useful QBE Example
This use requires PROJECT to assume the same value for both conditions.

PROJECT	Name	P-Number	Manager	Actual Cost	Expected Cost
	P. <u>PROJECT</u> <u>PROJECT</u>				>2000 <6000

FIGURE 8–18b   QBE's Response to the Command in Figure 8–18a
These projects satisfy both specified conditions.

PROJECT	Name	P-Number	Manager	Actual Cost	Expected Cost
	Common stock issue New office lease Revise documentation				

8–18a. Because the same underlined example is used in two places, whatever data is retrieved must satisfy both conditions associated with that example. Only the "Common stock issue," "New office lease," and "Revise documentation" projects fulfill this requirement.

FIGURE 8–19a
Using a QBE Example to
Join Data in Two Relations

EMPLOYEE	Name	E-Number	Department
	P.	1234	

TITLE	E-Number	Current title
	1234	Senior consultant

FIGURE 8–19b
QBE's Response to the
Command in Figure 8–19a

EMPLOYEE	Name	E-Number	Department
	Adams Baker Clarke		

Examples are useful when data is needed from two (or more) relations. To determine which employees are senior consultants, one could make the entries shown in Figure 8–19a. Because the example is repeated, it must assume the same value everywhere it is used. The process followed is this: first, the numbers associated with the title "Senior consultant" are determined. Then the employee names associated with those numbers are printed. The result is shown in Figure 8–19b.

Queries Using a Condition Box

QBE provides another area in which the user can specify conditions for retrievals, the **condition box.** When used with examples, the condition box provides a convenient way for a QBE user to specify, only once, conditions that can be used repeatedly.

The query for determining which projects have expected costs between $2,000 and $6,000 can be reformulated using a condition box. The example in the condition box specifies the conditions "greater than 2000 and less than 6000." The complete query is shown in Figure 8–20. Of course, this produces the same result as is shown in Figure 8–18b.

FIGURE 8–20   QBE Condition Box
This is an alternative way to get the data in Figure 8–18b.

PROJECT	Name	P-Number	Manager	Actual Cost	Expected Cost
	P.				EC

CONDITIONS
EC = (>2000 AND <6000)

FIGURE 8–21a   QBE Command to Count the Projects

PROJECT	Name	P-Number	Manager	Actual Cost	Expected Cost
	P.CNT				

Special Functions in QBE

QBE also provides computational functions similar to those of SQL. The CNT function gives the number of tuples in a relation that satisfy the specified conditions. As before, in the simplest case there are no conditions. The command in Figure 8–21a shows how to determine the number of projects in progress at the company.

Note that QBE functions, like those of SQL, do not automatically suppress duplicated tuples. Therefore, the command shown in Figure 8–21b would indicate that seven departments exist, just as the SQL command using the COUNT function does. Determining the number of unique department names requires use of the UNQ function. The proper command for this information is shown in Figure 8–21c. This command produces the result two.

The arithmetic sum and average functions of SQL also exist in QBE. Following the SQL presentation, consider again the PROJECT relation

FIGURE 8–21b
QBE Command to Count the Departments
This command will count duplicates.

EMPLOYEE	Name	E-Number	Department
			P.CNT

FIGURE 8–21c
The Command to Count Departments in Figure 8–21b Modified so that Duplicate Department Names Are Not Counted

EMPLOYEE	Name	E-Number	Department
			P.CNT.UNQ

FIGURE 8–22a   Project Data for the Organization

PROJECT	Name	P-Number	Manager	Actual Cost	Expected Cost
	New billing system	23760	Yates	1000	10000
	Common stock issue	28765	Baker	3000	4000
	Resolve bad debts	26713	Kanter	2000	1500
	New office lease	26511	Yates	5000	5000
	Revise documentation	34054	Kanter	100	3000
	Entertain new client	87108	Yates	5000	2000
	New TV commercial	85005	Baker	10000	8000

(reproduced in Figure 8–22a). The QBE SUM function can be used to provide a total of the cost values. To determine the total expected cost of the projects in progress requires the command shown in Figure 8–22b. This produces the result $33,500.

The average expected cost can be computed by using the AVG function, as in Figure 8–22c. This command gives the result $485.1 (rounded to the nearest cent). To find the projects with expected costs above average, one can use the approach shown in Figure 8–22d. This produces the same result as the SQL function: there is one project that meets this criteria. As with SQL, maximum and minimum values can be calculated using MAX and MIN functions. The project with the maximum actual cost accrued thus far can be obtained using the commands in Figure 8–22e. The result is, of course, the same as produced by SQL.

FIGURE 8–22b   QBE Command to Print the Sum of the Expected Costs

PROJECT	Name		P-Number	Manager	Actual Cost	Expected Cost
						P.SUM

FIGURE 8–22c   QBE Command to Print the Average of the Expected Costs

PROJECT	Name		P-Number	Manager	Actual Cost	Expected Cost
						P.AVG

FIGURE 8–22d   QBE Command to Print the Project Names and Expected Costs of Projects with Expected Costs Exceeding the Average

PROJECT	Name		P-Number	Manager	Actual Cost	Expected Cost
	P.					P.EC>AVG

Similarly, the project with the least expected cost can be determined by using the command in Figure 8–22f.

Finally, these functions can be combined, just as can the SQL functions. The number of projects with expected costs exceeding the average, for example, can be found as shown in Figure 8–22g.

FIGURE 8–22e   QBE Commands to Print the Project with the Maximum Actual Cost

PROJECT	Name	P-Number	Manager	Actual Cost	Expected Cost
	P.			P.MAX	

FIGURE 8–22f   QBE Commands to Print the Project with the Minimum Expected Cost

PROJECT	Name	P-Number	Manager	Actual Cost	Expected Cost
	P.				P.MIN

FIGURE 8–22g   QBE Commands to Print the Number of Projects with Expected Costs
Exceeding the Average

PROJECT	Name	P-Number	Manager	Actual Cost	Expected Cost
					P.CNT. EC>AVG

Insertion

Relations can also be modified in QBE. To insert a new tuple into a relation, one must specify the I. command under the name of the relation. This is followed by the data that belongs in the new tuple. An example is shown in Figure 8–23.

FIGURE 8–23
Insertion
QBE commands to insert
data for a new employee
named Farmer.

EMPLOYEE	Name	E-Number	Department
I.	Farmer	1006	Accounting

FIGURE 8–24
**QBE Commands to Delete
Data for the Employee
Named Adams**
This command also deletes
all tuples with the employee
name Adams.

EMPLOYEE	Name	E-Number	Department
D.	Adams		

Deletion

Tuples can also be deleted. The D. command is placed under the name of the relation containing the tuple to be deleted. To delete Adams from the EMPLOYEE relation, use the command shown in Figure 8–24.

To remove all tuples from the ASSIGNMENT relation with a project number of 26713 following completion of the project "Resolve bad debts," the entries shown in Figure 8–25 are appropriate.

Modification

Tuples can also be modified in QBE. The U. command (for "update") is placed under the name of the relation to be modified. Earlier, we modified the value for employee Baker's Department attribute using SQL. To change that value from Finance to Accounting in QBE, one makes the entries in Figure 8–26.

The QBE interface is an alternative to SQL. Like SQL, it requires very few commands to perform a wide range of retrievals. The commands presented here are summarized in Table 8–1.

MICROCOMPUTER IMPLEMENTATIONS OF QBE

Again, so that you will have a somewhat better understanding of how languages are implemented in a microcomputer environment, we will describe two implementations of QBE: those of Paradox and dBase IV.

FIGURE 8–25 QBE Commands to Delete Data for Employees that Worked on the "Resolve Bad Debts" Project
Note the use of an example to link the data in the two relations.

ASSIGNMENT	E-Number	P-Number
D.		1234

PROJECT	Name	P-Number	Manager	Actual Cost	Expected Cost
	Resolve bad debts	1234			

FIGURE 8–26
Tuple Modification
QBE commands to update an employee's data.

EMPLOYEE	Name	E-Number	Department
	Baker		U.Accounting

TABLE 8–1 QBE Commands and Their Usage

QBE Command	Usage
P.	Used to specify the attributes to be presented in the result
I.	Used to insert new data
D.	Used to delete data from a relation
U.	Used to modify (update) existing data
XYZ	Underlined variables are "examples"
UNQ	Used to specify that only unique values should be considered in the result
CNT	Used to determine a count of tuples that satisfy a condition
SUM	Used to determine the total of the values in the result
AVG	Used to determine the average of the values in the result
MAX	Used to determine the maximum value of an attribute
MIN	Used to determine the minimum value of an attribute
AO or DO	Used to specify the order of the values in the result (use AO for ascending, DO for descending)

QBE in dBase IV

Ashton-Tate hired Zloof to be in charge of the development of the QBE interface for their dBase products. Thus, it is not surprising that QBE in dBase IV is quite faithful to the original design. Specifying retrieval operations is very similar to Zloof's original paper. Updating is different, however. To create a new database, choose CREATE from the CONTROL CENTER in ASSIST mode. A blank table with the column headings shown in Figure 8–27 will be displayed. Fill in the field name, type, width, decimal places (for floating fields) and index (*Y* or *N*, to indicate whether an index is to be maintained for the field). Six data types are supported: character, numeric, floating, date, logical (True or False), and memo. Memo fields are for short documents, up to 4,096 characters. When entry is complete, move the cursor to a blank line and press the ENTER key. dBase IV will prompt for a name. Key in a name and press ENTER, and the table structure (which dBase refers to as a database) is saved.

dBase IV will then prompt you to determine if you want to enter data. If you say *yes,* then a blank form will be displayed in which you enter data. Key in the data for each record. When the last field is filled in, press ENTER and the record will be saved. To exit the DATA ENTRY mode, press RETURN at the beginning (in the first field) of a record.

To query a database, choose "Queries" from the CONTROL CENTER. Choose "Add file to query" and choose the tables desired from the list that is displayed. Columns to be displayed are indicated in a "view." A blank view (table) will be displayed if none has been chosen. To mark a column for inclusion in the view, move to that column, and choose "Add field to view." The field name will appear in the view.

Query conditions are specified in a manner very similar to that originally described by Zloof. A condition box may be used for specifying complex conditions. Columns may be sorted simply by typing ASC or DESC in the appropriate field. Functions are also supported.

The database may be updated in different ways. Individual records may be updated in BROWSE or EDIT modes (accessed via F2 from the CONTROL CENTER screen). BROWSE displays a screen full of records in the familiar row and column format of relational databases. To change a value, simply move the cursor to that field and enter the new value.

FIGURE 8–27

dBase IV Screen for Designing a New Table

NUM	Field Name	Field Type	Width	Dec	Index

Layout Organize Append Go To Exit

EDIT mode displays one record at a time with a row for each data item. Field names are given on the left followed by the data value for the selected record. Again, you simply move to the field to be updated and enter the new value.

To update more than one record, QBE update queries may be used. The following operations are available:

Append: Bring in records from another file.
Mark: Tag records to be deleted.
Unmark: Undo previously set deletion marks.
Replace: Overwrite existing data in chosen fields.

The appropriate command from the list above is placed in the field underneath the database name. Record selection criteria are placed in the appropriate columns. Then the query is executed by choosing "Perform the update" from the menu, which appears when an update operation has been specified.

QBE in Paradox

Paradox is a database package developed by Borland International, Inc. It uses a QBE type of interface for querying databases. The interface is somewhat different from that originally defined by Zloof. Since there are no formal standards for QBE interfaces, it is difficult to say that this is a shortcoming.

The initial screen (main menu) that one sees when Paradox is invoked is shown in Figure 8–28. The options on the main menu include **View, Ask, Report, Create, Modify, Image, Forms, Tools, Scripts, Help,** and **Exit.** View displays a selected table on the screen. Ask permits retrieval of data via the QBE interface. Report is used to create, design, change or print a report. Create is used to create a new table. Modify allows one to revise the structure of a table (add or delete columns), or to add, change, or sort data in a table. Image is used to rearrange information on the screen or display a graph. Forms is chosen to create, display, or change a screen form or enter data into a form. Tools has options for importing and exporting data, and to manage tables, forms, and other objects. Scripts refer to queries or sequences of actions that may be saved and 'replayed.' Help and Exit are self-explanatory.

When Create is chosen to define a new table, the screen in Figure 8–29 is displayed. To define a table, one just fills in the two columns, giving the attribute name and data type. As shown in the box on the Create screen, Paradox supports only four data types, Alphanumeric (denoted A), Numeric (N), Currency ($), and Date (D). Key fields must be defined first and are indicated by placing an asterisk (*) after the abbreviation for field type. For example, in Figure 8–30, which defines the Project table of Figure 7–1, P_Number is defined to be the key. Once all columns have been defined, F10 is pressed and a "pop-up" menu appears, from which "Do It!" is chosen to save the table structure.

FIGURE 8–28   Paradox Main Menu

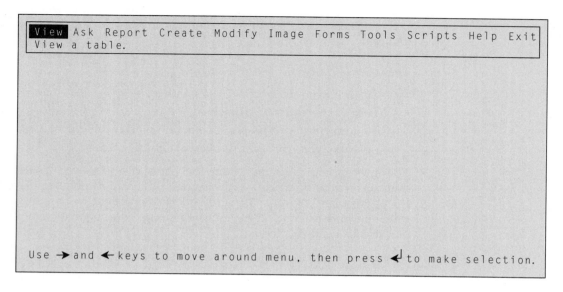

FIGURE 8–29   Paradox Screen for Defining a New Table

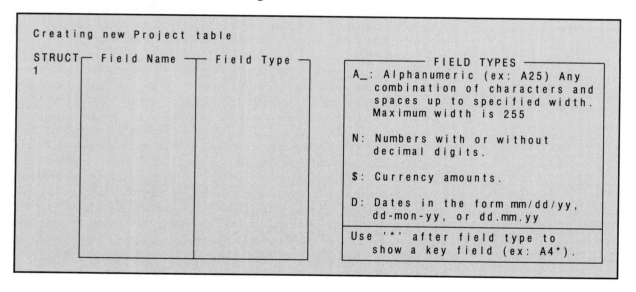

To enter data into a table, choose Modify. Then, from the next menu, choose DataEntry. Paradox prompts you for a table name and can give a list of tables if you don't remember the table name. A blank table will be displayed, with the appropriate column headings. Data items are simply typed into their columns. When done, press F10 and choose "Do It!" Figure 8–31 shows a Paradox table with project data.

To retrieve data, choose Ask from the main menu. Again, Paradox will prompt for a table name or give a list of tables. After a table is

FIGURE 8–30   Paradox Screen with Entries Defining the Project Table

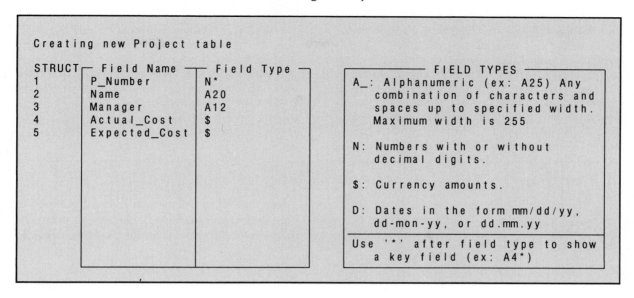

```
Creating new Project table

STRUCT ┬─ Field Name ──┬─ Field Type ─┐      ┌──────── FIELD TYPES ────────┐
1        P_Number         N*                  A_: Alphanumeric (ex: A25) Any
2        Name             A20                     combination of characters and
3        Manager          A12                     spaces up to specified width.
4        Actual_Cost      $                       Maximum width is 255
5        Expected_Cost    $

                                                N: Numbers with or without
                                                   decimal digits.

                                                $: Currency amounts.

                                                D: Dates in the form mm/dd/yy,
                                                   dd-mon-yy, or dd.mm.yy

                                                Use '*' after field type to show
                                                a key field (ex: A4*)
```

FIGURE 8–31   Paradox Data Entry Screen with Project Data

```
DataEntry for Project table: Record 8 of 8                    DataEntry

ENTRY ─┬─ P_Number: ─┬──────── Name ────────┬─ Manager ─┬─ _Actual Cost

   1        23760      New billing system      Yates          1,000.00
   2        28765      Common stock issue      Baker          3,000.00
   3        26713      Resolve bad debts       Kanter         2,000.00
   4        26511      New office lease        Yates          5,000.00
   5        34054      Revise documentation    Kanter           100.00
   6        87108      Entertain new client    Yates          5,000.00
   7        85005      New TV commercial       Baker         10,000.00
   8
```

named, a skeleton of that table (called an *image*) appears. More than one table may be chosen and an image will appear for each one.

Selecting data is similar to that described above for QBE. F6 is used to mark a column for display (rather than P.). F5 is used to enter an example. F3 moves the cursor up to the next higher image on the screen. F4 moves the cursor down to the next lower image. F8 erases the image under the cursor. F2 is Do It!, which executes the query. The specification of conditions conforms very closely to our description of QBE above.

To update existing data in a table, choose Modify. Then choose Edit from the next menu. Indicate the table to be edited, and it will be displayed. (Alternatively, choose View from the main men, indicate the table, then press F9 for Edit.) To delete a record, move the cursor to the

THE USER'S VIEW

In "The User's View" in Chapter 6, we hinted that implementations of relational database data manipulation languages are user-oriented. This chapter provides several examples of this orientation. Psychologists have found that QBE's graphic representation and absence of a rigorous command structure are helpful in training inexperienced users. QBE queries seem to be representative of the way people naturally manipulate data.

QBE represents an approach to developing a friendly user interface to a database management system. The user interface is the part of a database management system with which the user interacts—an important part that must not be neglected in database system design. ■

record to be deleted and press the Del or Delete key. To change a record, move to the field to be changed, use Delete or Backspace to erase the existing data, then key in the new data. To save the changes, press F2 for Do It!

CHAPTER SUMMARY

Microcomputers are increasing in processing speed and storage capacity, but most micros in use at the present time still pose limitations on database management software. Many versions of SQL are available in microcomputer packages, however. Some of these are capable of operating in a networked environment and can direct a query from a micro to a mainframe running a compatible version of SQL.

A unique approach to data manipulation in a relational database environment is demonstrated in the QBE language, which is supported by some microcomputer packages, as well as some mainframes. QBE provides a graphic presentation, or picture, of a relation. As in SQL, there is only a small set of commands to be learned. Users of QBE position the cursor under the name of the attribute (or attributes) of interest and enter commands and conditions to specify the data desired.

QBE also has *examples,* which act like variables, and an area called a *condition box* that can be used to help specify data retrieval requests. These features accomplish what the SQL language accomplishes: They let the user specify data without specifying exactly how to get it, but in a format which many users find more desirable.

Questions and Exercises

1. What are the characteristics of a relational graphics language?
2. List the QBE keywords discussed in this chapter. Explain how each is used. What usually follows each?
3. Show the QBE commands to perform the following operations on the EMPLOYEE relation in Figure 7–1.

METROPOLITAN NATIONAL BANK

In Chapter 7, you were given some queries that were to be applied to Metropolitan National's database system in SQL. Apply QBE to answer the same queries posed in that chapter. ■

    a. List the employee names.
    b. List the employee numbers.
    c. Retrieve all data on the employee named Clarke.
    d. Retrieve all data on employee number 1005.

4. Show the QBE commands to perform the following operations on the PROJECT relation in Figure 7–1.
    a. List the project names.
    b. List the managers of projects.
    c. Provide all data for the projects managed by Yates.
    d. Provide a list of the projects with actual costs less than the expected cost.

5. Show the QBE commands to perform the following operations on the EMPLOYEE and ASSIGNMENT relations in Figure 7–1.
    a. List the employee names and numbers for employees in the accounting department.
    b. Find the department in which Dexter works.
    c. List the employee numbers for employees assigned to project 2360.
    d. List the names of finance employees assigned to project 26511.

6. Show the QBE commands to perform the following operations on the ASSIGNMENT, PROJECT, and EMPLOYEE relations in Figure 7–1.
    a. List the actual costs of projects managed by Yates.
    b. Provide all information on the project managed by Kanter.
    c. Provide data on the actual and expected costs of project 2865.
    d. Provide data on the project with the minimum expected cost.
    e. Provide the names of the employees working on the project to secure a new office lease.

7. Show the QBE commands to perform the following operations on the EMPLOYEE and ASSIGNMENT relations in Figure 7–1.
    a. Count the number of employees.
    b. Count the number of projects.
    c. Count the number of departments.

8. Repeat Question 7, counting only unique tuples.

9. Show the QBE commands to perform the following operations on the EXPERTISE relation in Figure 7–1.
    a. Count the number of employees.

      b. Count the number of unique skills.

      c. Count the number of employees with stock market training.

10. Show the QBE commands to perform the following operations on the PROJECT relation in Figure 7–1.

      a. Find the project with the maximum cost.

      b. Find the projects where actual cost is less than expected cost.

      c. Find the projects with actual costs less than the average actual cost.

11. Show the QBE commands to perform the following operations on the EMPLOYEE relation in Figure 7–1.

      a. Add a tuple for an employee with your name.

      b. Delete the data for Baker.

      c. Update the relation to indicate that Clarke works in the finance department.

12. Show the QBE commands to perform the following operations on the PROJECT relation in Figure 7–1.

      a. Add a tuple for a new project, managed by Clarke, to develop a new advertising campaign.

      b. Delete the tuple for the project managed by Kanter.

      c. Update the relation so that Yates's new billing system project has $500 more in actual cost.

13. Explain in detail the advantages and disadvantages of a graphics language interface. Be sure to include cost in your analysis.

14. Think of other possible interfaces to a database management system. Include some ideas for implementing the interface, such as the hardware needed and whether some existing interface could be extended to implement your idea.

15. Do you think that microcomputer databases will ever replace mainframe databases completely? Explain your answer.

16. If your computer center has microcomputer database packages, use at least two to enter the tables in Figure 7–1. If the packages have QBE interfaces, use them to perform the queries in this chapter. How similar are these interfaces to the original Zloof definition of QBE?

For Further Reading

For an introduction to dBase IV, see: Senn, James A. *The Student Edition of dBase IV.* Reading, Mass.: Addison-Wesley Publishing, 1990.

QBE is defined in: Zloof, M. M. "Design Aspects of the Query-by-Example Data Base Query Language," *IBM Systems Journal,* Vol. 16, No. 4, 19.

Zloof, M. M. "Query-by-Example." *Proceedings of the National Computer Conference AFIPs* 44, May 1975.

9

THE CODASYL MODEL

I n Chapters 2 and 3, we pointed out that most database management packages are built on either the relational model or CODASYL specifications. In Chapters 6 and 7, we described the relational model and its languages. In this chapter, we describe the basic concepts underlying the CODASYL approach.

THE CODASYL COMMITTEES

The Conference on Data and Systems Languages (CODASYL) consists of individuals from private industry and government who have an interest in developing and standardizing languages and techniques for data systems analysis, design, and implementation. A CODASYL committee was responsible for developing the initial standards for COBOL. The early database activities of the CODASYL organization are described in "CODASYL Data Description Language" in its *Journal of Development* published in 1973.

CODASYL's first formal report describing database specifications was published by its Data Base Task Group (DBTG) in 1971. Several vendors subsequently developed database management packages based on these specifications, although not necessarily conforming to them to the letter. These products include IDMS, offered by Cullinet software; DMIV-IDS/II, developed by Honeywell Information Systems; DBMS from Digital Equipment Corporation; PHOLAS, a product of Phillips Electrologica of Holland; and SEED, originally developed by International Data Base Systems but now marketed by the United Telecom Group. In addition, the data manipulation language of SYSTEM 2000, originally developed by MRI Systems of Austin, was based on the DBTG specifications, although its data definition language is quite different. SYSTEM 2000 is now marketed by SAS Institute, Inc., of Chapel Hill, North Carolina.

After 1971, the Data Base Task Group was renamed the Data Description Language Committee (DDLC) and given specific responsibility for the schema definition languages. The intent was to develop an approach to data definition that was independent of programming languages. The CODASYL Programming Language Committee (PLC) was given responsibility for the data manipulation language and the COBOL subschema definition language. The PLC has issued reports in 1976 and 1978 revising the data manipulation language. The DDLC issued updated specifications for the data description language in 1978. Other parties have also entered the specification fray, including the American National Standards Institute, which issued its own report in 1981.

We need not belabor the point further: numerous parties have been involved in developing specifications, and it seems that too many cooks have spoiled the broth. The numerous reports and revisions make it difficult to decide what to cover in a textbook. Many packages are based on the 1971 specifications; yet later updates have some desirable features including better separation between logical and physical constructs. The material in this chapter is based primarily on the 1978 specifications.

This provides a good basis for an understanding of the CODASYL model and how it differs from the relational approach.

Because several different CODASYL committees have been involved in developing the specifications over the years, we simply refer to these specifications collectively as the CODASYL approach. When appropriate, we refer to the specific committee, such as the Data Base Task Group or the Data Description Language Committee.

THE CODASYL ARCHITECTURE AND FUNDAMENTAL CONCEPTS

The basic elements of the CODASYL system architecture and the fundamental concepts underlying its approach to representing relationships between entities were previewed in the first three chapters. In this section, we consider this architecture and the concepts of data items, records, sets, subschemas, and schemas in more detail. An example of a database system for a chain of hair styling salons is used to illustrate these concepts. But first we discuss the architecture of a database system as envisioned by the CODASYL committees.

The Architecture of a CODASYL System

The architecture of a CODASYL system as pictured in various CODASYL reports is shown in Figure 9–1. You may recall that the only access to CODASYL databases for which specifications have actually been developed is via data manipulation language statements embedded in applications programs (although many vendors have developed their own interactive query language). As shown in Figure 9–1, each executing application program, referred to as a *run unit,* is associated with a subschema that expresses the user view associated with that program.

The global database is reflected in the schema, which describes all the data items, records, and sets within the scope of the corresponding database. A CODASYL database is actually defined as all the records and sets controlled by a particular schema. The DBMS uses the schema and subschemas to determine what data a run unit may access.

Each run unit is allocated a portion of main memory, called a *user work area (UWA),* for transferring data values between applications programs and the database. The data items under control of the subschema invoked by the run unit are each assigned a location in the work area. The run unit accesses the work area by using the data item names assigned in the subschema. The run unit may use DML statements to instruct the DBMS to fetch data from the database and place it in the user work area or to move data from the work area to the database (which updates the database).

The relationships between user work areas, subschemas, and the DBMS are illustrated in Figures 9–2 through 9–4. This trivial "database" consists of only one record type consisting of Customer-Name,

FIGURE 9–1 Architecture of a CODASYL System
Run units are executing applications programs. Data is transferred between the database and the run unit via the user work area. The subschema describes the run unit's view of the database. The schema describes the global database in logical terms. Run units B and C share subschema B/C.

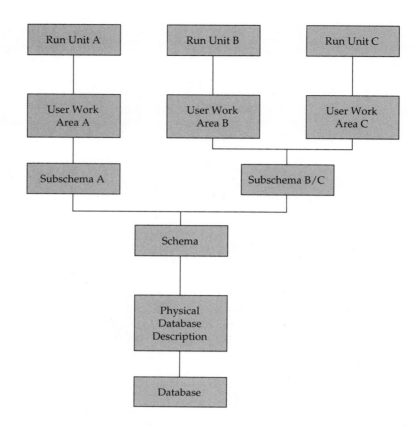

Customer-Number, and Customer-Address. The subschema accesses all three data items. The user work area has memory locations reserved for each data item. Before any data has been retrieved, the DBMS sets memory locations in the work area to null values (Figure 9–2). The FIND statement in Figure 9–3 locates the first customer record occurrence in the database (Alfredo's), but does not move data values to the work area. Transfer of values from the database to the work area is done in response to the GET statement in Figure 9–4.

CASE EXAMPLE
CODASYL Application at TJ's Hair Salons

Tina Jurado Valenzuela (TJ) is the proprietor of a chain of (two) hair styling salons in the towns of Brownlee and Flatland. The shop in Brownlee is named Hair Wranglers, and the shop in Flatland is the Hackin' Shack. TJ is planning to expand her operations in the next few years, and she thinks it is important to have information on how her shops are doing and what factors seem to make them successful.

TJ's husband, Roberto (Rob), works as an information analyst for the local office of a major software vendor. In his spare time, Rob has

FIGURE 9–2
**User Work Area and
Database Before
Execution Begins**

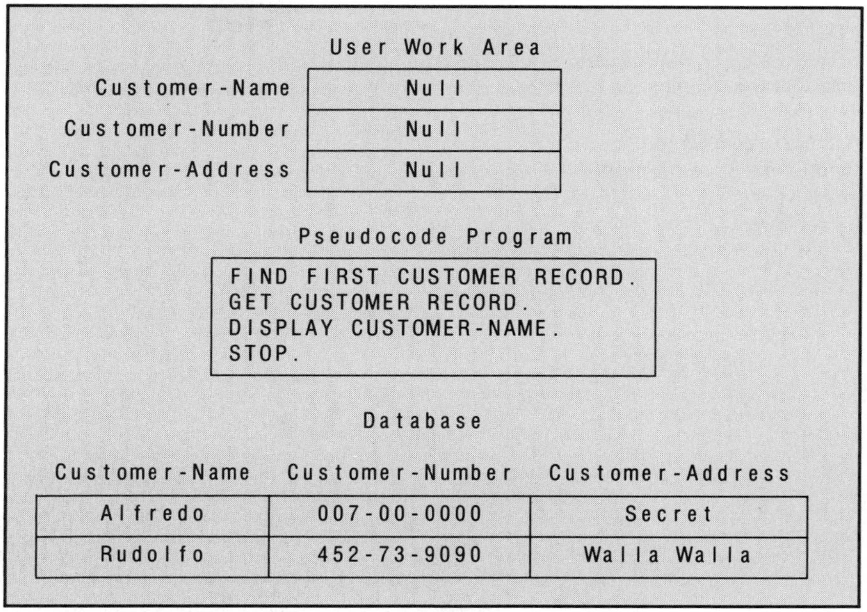

User Work Area

Customer-Name	Null
Customer-Number	Null
Customer-Address	Null

Pseudocode Program

```
FIND FIRST CUSTOMER RECORD.
GET CUSTOMER RECORD.
DISPLAY CUSTOMER-NAME.
STOP.
```

Database

Customer-Name	Customer-Number	Customer-Address
Alfredo	007-00-0000	Secret
Rudolfo	452-73-9090	Walla Walla

FIGURE 9–3
**Status of User Work Area
and Database After FIND
Statement Has Been
Executed**
The FIND Statement
establishes the pointer
to Alfredo's record but
does not place it in the
user work area.

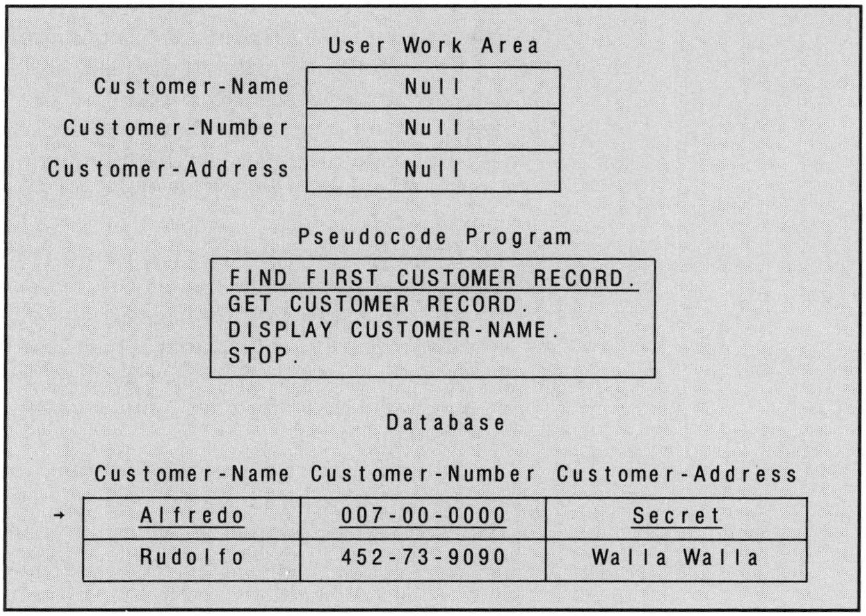

User Work Area

Customer-Name	Null
Customer-Number	Null
Customer-Address	Null

Pseudocode Program

```
FIND FIRST CUSTOMER RECORD.
GET CUSTOMER RECORD.
DISPLAY CUSTOMER-NAME.
STOP.
```

Database

	Customer-Name	Customer-Number	Customer-Address
→	Alfredo	007-00-0000	Secret
	Rudolfo	452-73-9090	Walla Walla

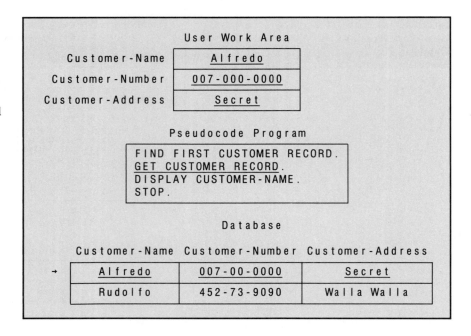

User Work Area

Customer-Name	Alfredo
Customer-Number	007-000-0000
Customer-Address	Secret

Pseudocode Program

```
FIND FIRST CUSTOMER RECORD.
GET CUSTOMER RECORD.
DISPLAY CUSTOMER-NAME.
STOP.
```

Database

Customer-Name	Customer-Number	Customer-Address
Alfredo	007-00-0000	Secret
Rudolfo	452-73-9090	Walla Walla

developed a database system for TJ's shops. Each shop has a minicomputer where records for that shop are maintained on a daily basis. An integrated CODASYL database is maintained at TJ's office.

To ensure integrity and avoid accidental damage to the central database by inexperienced users at the hair salons, Rob is the only person who updates the database. The managers at the two shops have been taught how to access the minicomputer over dial-up phone lines, and each day they copy the day's data from the shop into a file at the central site.

Rob has developed a program to read these files and perform the appropriate updates to the central database. Shop managers can print updated reports or do ad hoc retrievals (but no updates) the next day. Weekly, monthly, and annual reports are also available. The entities in Rob's database system are shops, hair stylists who work in TJ's shop, patrons who visit the shop, and services performed (perms, haircuts, and styles).

Stylists pay TJ a commission for a booth in her shop and act as independent business persons, setting their own prices, hours, days off, and so on. Stylists must be able to do perms, haircuts, and hair styling for both men and women. Patrons usually visit the same stylist, but they will occasionally use another if their customary stylist is on vacation or ill.

To model this situation, note that the relationship between shops and stylists is one-to-many. However, there are three many-to-many relationships between entities: between stylists and patrons, between stylists and services, and between patrons and services.

The many-to-many relationships among stylists, patrons, and services can be eliminated by forming a data group with a concatenated key.

FIGURE 9–5   Rob's Data Structure Diagram for TJ's Database

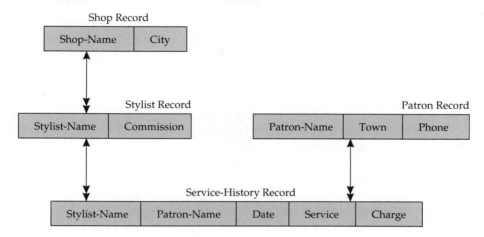

FIGURE 9–6
The SHOP-STYLIST Set Type in TJ's Database

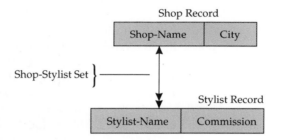

A concatenated key consisting of Stylist-Name, Patron-Name, and Service, however, is not sufficient to form a unique identifier for Date and Charge (because a patron may visit a different stylist on different dates and get different services on the same date, possibly from different stylists). For now, assume that the concatenated key Stylist-Name + Patron-Name + Date + Service will be used. ∎

Data Items

A **data item** in the CODASYL model corresponds to an attribute of an entity. A data item is the smallest unit of named data represented in the database. Examples of data items in TJ's database include the city in which a shop is located and the commission rate that a stylist pays.

The CODASYL reports also define **data aggregates** as named collections of data items. These may be arrays or groups of attributes that occur more than once for an entity. Because accepted database design procedures remove such items from the resulting data structure diagram, data aggregates are not discussed further.

Record Types and Record Occurrences

The CODASYL approach distinguishes between record types and record occurrences. A **record type** is a collection of logically related data items. A **record occurrence** is the set of data values for one instance of a record type.

Record types in TJ's database correspond to records in Rob's data structure diagram. Four record types can be derived from this diagram: a shop record type, a stylist record type, a patron record type, and an intersection record type associating stylists and patrons with a given service on a given day.

The intersection record type has a concatenated key consisting of patron, stylist, and date. This does not necessarily mean that patron and stylist names must be duplicated in the intersection record and the other record types in which they occur. Relationships between record types are maintained via the set concept, which can reduce the need for redundance, as illustrated below.

Database Keys

Each record occurrence in the database is automatically assigned a **database key** by the DBMS when it is entered into the system. The database key is unique and is used to determine the location of each record on the storage devices of the system. Do not confuse database keys with key data items. Database keys are usually *physical* pointers used by the DBMS to locate record occurrences.

Applications programmers seldom use database keys directly; rather, they use key data items to *logically* locate or sort record occurrences.

Set Types and Set Occurrences

One of the fundamental characteristics distinguishing the database approach from a conventional file approach is the ability to handle relationships between records. The CODASYL committees developed the concept of set types to represent hierarchical relationships between records.

A **set type** is a named, two-level, hierarchical relationship between record types. The parent node in the hierarchy is called the *owner record type,* and the child nodes are called *member record types.* A set type can have only one owner record. In the 1978 specifications, a set could have many member record types; however, several CODASYL packages restrict sets to only one member record type. Of course there can be many owner and member record *occurrences.* This discussion is limited to situations with one member record type.

Because sets represent only hierarchical relationships, network relationships are specifically excluded *within* a given set. However, several different sets can be used to model networks. The intersection record

FIGURE 9–7   **The STYLIST-HISTORY and PATRON-HISTORY Sets in TJ's Database**
The SERVICE-HISTORY record has two parents, STYLIST and PATRON, so it is a simple network. In the CODASYL model, it is modeled as two sets, STYLIST-HISTORY and PATRON-HISTORY.

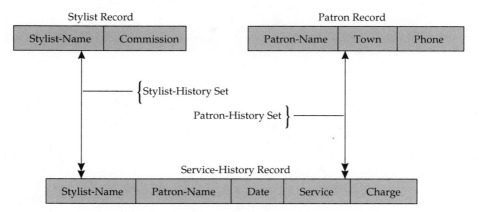

has two parent records (STYLIST and PATRON). These two relationships must be modeled with two separate sets, STYLIST-HISTORY and PATRON-HISTORY, as illustrated in Figure 9–7.

Singular Sets: Representing Sequential Files.   Thus far, we have shown no way to perform the very common data processing function of accessing all occurrences of a record type in sequential order. This operation is performed by defining the desired record type as a **singular set.** Singular sets have a special owner record called SYSTEM, and the desired sequential record as member.

Recursive Sets.   In a **recursive set,** the owner record type and the member record type are the same. Many implementations, however, do not support this feature; in these, multiple sets must be used.

A Skeletal Schema for TJ's Database.   In Figure 9–8 a stylized form of the CODASYL schema data description language (DDL) is used to describe the aspects of TJ's database that have been discussed thus far. This might be viewed as a "skeletal schema" to be fleshed out as the chapter proceeds.

A subschema providing access to all items in the schema is given in Figure 9–9. This (along with the example data given next) is used to illustrate how some data manipulation commands provide access to the database.

Example Set Occurrences and Navigation Paths.   Example record and set occurrences are shown in Figure 9–10. Selected set occurrences are shown via links between record occurrences participating in the set. To avoid cluttering the diagram, we have not shown all links. Links represent navigation paths through the database. Arrows indicate only the direction of ownership; links can be traversed logically in either

FIGURE 9–8
**A Partial Schema for
TJ's Database**

```
SCHEMA NAME IS TJS-DATA.
RECORD NAME IS SHOP RECORD.
  SHOP-NAME           TYPE CHAR 14.
  CITY                TYPE CHAR 10.
RECORD NAME IS STYLIST.
  STYLIST-NAME        TYPE CHAR 20.
  COMMISSION          TYPE DECIMAL 4,2.
RECORD NAME IS PATRON.
  PATRON-NAME         TYPE CHAR 20.
  ADDRESS             TYPE CHAR 50.
  PHONE               TYPE CHAR 8.
RECORD NAME IS SERVICE-HISTORY.
  STYLIST-NAME        TYPE CHAR 20.
  PATRON-NAME         TYPE CHAR 20.
  DATE                TYPE CHAR 8.
  SERVICE             TYPE CHAR 5.
  CHARGE              TYPE DECIMAL 4,2.
SET NAME IS SHOP-STYLIST.
  OWNER IS SHOP.
  MEMBER IS STYLIST.
SET NAME IS STYLIST-HISTORY.
  OWNER IS STYLIST.
  MEMBER IS SERVICE-HISTORY.
SET NAME IS PATRON-HISTORY.
  OWNER IS PATRON.
  MEMBER IS SERVICE-HISTORY.
```

FIGURE 9–9
**Subschema Providing
Access to All Data Items
in TJ's Database**

```
SUBSCHEMA IDENTIFICATION DIVISION.
  SUBSCHEMA NAME IS WHOLE-THING OF SCHEMA TJS-DATA.
SUBSCHEMA DATA DIVISION.
  RECORD SECTION.
    COPY ALL RECORDS.
  SET SECTION.
    COPY ALL SETS.
END SUBSCHEMA.
```

direction. The arrow pointing from the Hair Wranglers record occurrence to the occurrence for stylist Debi, for example, indicates that Debi's record is a member of the SHOP-STYLIST set for Hair Wranglers; that is, Debi works at the Hair Wranglers shop. We can trace these links down the hierarchy or navigation path to determine that Debi has performed two services, as indicated by the links from Debi's record to the SERVICE-HISTORY record occurrence indicating that a $65.00 perm was given on 3/21/88, and from that record to the style given on 3/22/88. The links from the PATRON RECORD indicate that Waylon got the perm and Zeke the style.

Database keys (DB Key) have been included at the beginning of each record occurrence. These are normally "transparent" to the programmer. They are used later to illustrate the data manipulation language.

FIGURE 9–10 Example Record and Set Occurrences for TJ's Database
The link from Hair Wranglers to Debi means that Debi works at the Hair Wranglers shop. This is an occurrence of the SHOP-STYLIST set. The occurrence of the STYLIST-HISTORY set indicates that Debi gave a perm on 3/21/88 and charged $65.00, and a style on 3/22/88, and charged $25.00. By the links to the PATRON-RECORD via the PATRON-HISTORY set, it is known that Waylon got the perm, and Zeke got the style. An example database key is given at the beginning at each record to illustrate currency indicators in the DML.

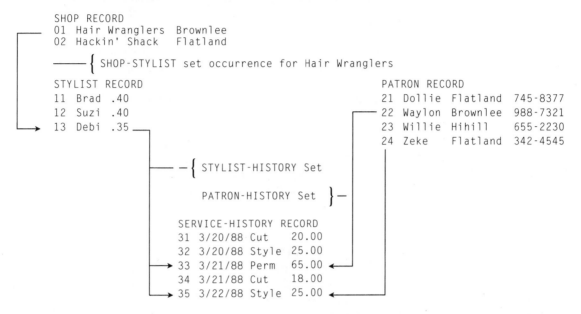

Retrieving Data in a CODASYL Database

The example data in Figure 9–10 can be used to illustrate access path navigation and data retrieval in a CODASYL database. Here we use only simple forms of the FIND and GET commands for illustrations. Details of other aspects of the DML are discussed later in the chapter. Before we discuss data retrieval, it is convenient to present currency indicators and error status variables, which are used in conjunction with DML statements.

Currency Indicators.   The notion of currency indicators is fundamental to an understanding of how the DML is used to navigate through logical access paths in a CODASYL database. **Currency indicators** contain the *database keys* of the most recently accessed record occurrences for each record type and set type in the subschema invoked by the run unit. Currency indicators are stored in the user work area and are accessible to the run unit.

The following currency indicators are maintained by the DBMS and available to the run unit via the user work area.

1. A current of record type indicator for each record type included in the subschema contains the database key of the most recently accessed record occurrence for the corresponding record type.

2. A current of set type indicator for each set type included in the subschema contains the database key of the most recently accessed occurrence of a record in the corresponding set type. The record occurrence may be an owner or a member record.
3. The current of run unit indicator contains the database key of the most recently accessed record occurrence, regardless of the record type or set membership. This is the most frequently used indicator, and thus the most important.

Currency indicators are used by the applications programmer to follow logical navigation paths or access paths in a CODASYL network.

Error Status Variables.   The DBMS is responsible for maintaining values for several error status variables in the user work area, indicating various conditions that may arise in the processing of a DML statement (some of which may not be "errors"). The Data Base Task Group specified several error status codes. A 0 (zero), for example, indicates that the previous function has executed successfully.

We assume here that only one error status variable exists (ERROR-STATUS-CODE), and we use it to test for such things as the last member record occurrence in a set occurrence.

Fetching Data with the FIND Command.   The FIND command is used to locate a record occurrence (determine its storage address), but it does not actually retrieve data values. It does, however, perform a disk access to get the pointers for the specified record occurrence (unless it is already in the work area). FIND is used to set currency indicators to the appropriate record occurrences, and GET is used to actually fetch data into the work area.

FIND has several different formats. Three of these are discussed here and examples given after the general formats are described. A format 1 FIND, which uses key data items for a record type to locate a record occurrence, has the simple form:

```
FIND record-name USING key-data-item-name.
```

where key-data-item-name has been defined as a key for the record type specified in the record-name.

A format 2 FIND has the form:

```
FIND OWNER IN set-name CURRENT OF (record-name | set-name | RUN-UNIT).
```

The items in parentheses and separated by bars (|) indicate options, only one of which must be chosen by the programmer in any one statement.

A format 3 FIND is based on the current of set and the order specified for *member* records in that set. It has the form:

```
FIND (FIRST | NEXT | PRIOR | LAST) record-name RECORD
OF set-name SET.
```

FIND is used to locate records (retrieve pointers or indexes), whereas GET is used to retrieve data, as described next. It is important to remember that FIRST, NEXT, PRIOR, and LAST refer to member records of the selected set, not to other owner records of that set type.

Fetching Record Occurrences: The GET Command.   GET fetches the record occurrence corresponding to the current of run unit indicator and places its data values in the user work area. GET is often used in conjunction with FIND. FIND is used to set the current of run unit indicator to the appropriate record occurrence, and GET is used to fetch the data values from the database. GET has a very simple format:

```
GET record-name.
```

To illustrate the use of GET and FIND, suppose that TJ wants to know Brad's commission. The DML algorithm in Figure 9–11a fetches this information and makes it available to the run unit via the user work area. (The algorithm's effect on currency indicators is shown in Figure 9–11b). Statement 1 in Figure 9–11a is a COBOL MOVE that stores "Brad" in the location reserved for STYLIST-NAME in the user work area. (Statements in the figure have been given numbers to make it easy to describe the algorithm. Numbers would not be used in an actual program.) The second statement is a format 1 FIND that locates the storage address for the STYLIST record with "Brad" as the key value for STYLIST-NAME and updates the currency indicators for the current of run unit, the STYLIST record type, and the sets in which Brad's record (database key 11) participates as either owner or member, that is, the SHOP-STYLIST set and the STYLIST-HISTORY set. The GET statement retrieves the data, and the COBOL DISPLAY statement outputs the data.

FIGURE 9–11a
A DML Algorithm to Retrieve Brad's Commission

```
1. MOVE "Brad" TO STYLIST-NAME IN STYLIST RECORD.
2. FIND STYLIST RECORD USING STYLIST-NAME.
3. GET STYLIST RECORD.
4. DISPLAY STYLIST-NAME, COMMISSION.
```

FIGURE 9–11b   The Algorithm's Effect on Currency Indicators
The FIND statement in Figure 9–11a makes Brad's record the current of run unit, and current of STYLIST record, SHOP-STYLIST set, and STYLIST-HISTORY set. Numbers on the left correspond to statement numbers in the algorithm.

	Records					Sets		
Run-unit	Shop	Stylist	Ser.	Hist.	Patron	Shop/ Styl.	Stylist/ History	Patron/ History
1. No effect								
2. 11		11				11	11	
3. 11		11				11	11	
4. 11		11				11	11	

Here is another example. Suppose that Waylon calls the shop and says, "Hey TJ, the last time I was in your Hair Wranglers shop I got a great perm from one of your stylists, but I don't remember her name. Can you tell me who it was?" An algorithm to retrieve the name of the stylist who gave Waylon the perm is given in Figure 9–12a. In Figure 9–12b, the algorithm's effect on currency indicators is displayed. The MOVE and first FIND in Figure 9–10a establish Waylon's PATRON record (database key 22) occurrence as the current of run unit, current of record type PATRON, and current of set type PATRON-HISTORY. The FIND LAST command gets the SERVICE-HISTORY record for the last time Waylon had his hair done (the $65 perm on 3/21/88 with database key 33) and establishes it as the current of run unit and current of both the PATRON-HISTORY set and STYLIST-HISTORY set. Recall that the PATRON-HISTORY set was defined so that member (SERVICE-HISTORY) record occurrences would be maintained in chronological order. The LAST record occurrence in Waylon's PATRON-HISTORY set therefore corresponds to the last time he had his hair done. Finally, the third FIND illustrates format 2 and establishes Debi's STYLIST record (13) as the current of run unit, the current of record type STYLIST, and the current of set types SHOP-STYLIST and STYLIST-HISTORY.

FIGURE 9–12a

An Algorithm to Determine Which Stylist Gave Waylon His Last Perm

```
1. MOVE "Waylon" TO PATRON-NAME IN PATRON RECORD.
2. FIND PATRON RECORD USING PATRON-NAME.
3. FIND LAST SERVICE-HISTORY RECORD OF PATRON-
   HISTORY SET.
4. FIND OWNER RECORD IN STYLIST-HISTORY SET CURRENT
   OF RUN-UNIT.
5. GET STYLIST RECORD.
6. DISPLAY STYLIST-NAME.
```

FIGURE 9–12b   The Algorithm's Effect on Currency Indicators

	Records					Sets		
Run-unit	Shop	Stylist	Ser. Hist.	Patron		Shop/ Styl.	Stylist/ History	Patron/ History
1. No effect								
2. 22				22				22
3. 33			33	22			33	33
4. 13		13	33	22		13	13	33
5. 13		13	33	22		13	13	33
6. 13		13	33	22		13	13	33

To illustrate a format 3 FIND, suppose that TJ wants the name and commission for each stylist working at the Hair Wranglers shop. The algorithm in Figure 9–13 fetches and displays this information. The algorithm's effect on currency indicators is shown in Figure 9–13b. The first FIND (format 1) in Figure 9–13a establishes the Hair Wranglers record occurrence (01) as the current of run unit and current of set for the SHOP-STYLIST set. The UNTIL statement sets up a loop that continues until all member record occurrences (STYLIST records) of the Hair Wranglers set have been processed. The second FIND statement uses format 3 to locate the storage address of the next STYLIST record occurrence. On the first execution of this FIND, the first record occurrence is located. Subsequent executions of the statement locate records in the sequence specified in the schema.

Thus far, we have given a general overview of the CODASYL approach, including a discussion of data retrieval and access path navigation. Numerous details of the CODASYL specifications have been omitted. Some of these are discussed in the remainder of the chapter. Those wishing only a general overview may disregard the rest of the chapter without loss of continuity in the text.

FIGURE 9–13a

An Algorithm to List the Stylists in the Hair Wranglers Shop

```
1. MOVE "Hair Wranglers" TO SHOP-NAME IN SHOP
   RECORD.
2. FIND SHOP RECORD USING SHOP-NAME.
3. UNTIL ERROR-STATUS-CODE = (code for no more
   member records).
4. FIND NEXT STYLIST RECORD OF SHOP-STYLIST SET.
5. GET STYLIST RECORD.
6. DISPLAY STYLIST-NAME, COMMISSION.
7. END UNTIL.
```

FIGURE 9–13b   **The Algorithm's Effect on Currency Indicators**

	Records					Sets		
Run-unit	Shop	Stylist	Ser.	Hist.	Patron	Shop/ Styl.	Stylist/ History	Patron/ History
1. No effect.								
2. 01	01					01		
3. 01	01					01		
4. 13	01	13				13	13	
5. 13	01	13				13	13	
6. 13.	01	13				13	13	
7. 13	01	13				13	13	

SOME DETAILS OF SCHEMA DEFINITIONS

In this section, we discuss schema data description language features for describing records, data items, and sets, as well as features for security, integrity, and privacy that are critical in database applications.

One form of security in a CODASYL database system is provided through privacy locks and keys. A **privacy lock** is a password or user-written procedure applied to a schema, subschema, record, set, or data item. For a user to gain access to the database or a portion thereof, the appropriate **privacy key** must be supplied to "unlock" the desired data. If a privacy lock requires a password, the privacy key is simply that password.

Another form of security is available for user-selected data items—data encoding/decoding. In **data encoding,** data values are encrypted by a user-written procedure before being written into the database. If an unauthorized person gains access to the database, that person must also discover how to decipher the data before it has any meaning. Clearly the data values must be decrypted for authorized users before it is of any use.

To help maintain data integrity, edit checks may be defined for data items. The DBMS is responsible for applying these checks at the time of data entry and rejecting illegitimate data values. This approach prevents at least some erroneous data from ever getting into the database.

The schema in a CODASYL database consists of three different types of entry, in the following order:

1. An entry to identify the schema (give its name, privacy lock, and so on).
2. Entries to define records and their data items.
3. Entries to define sets.

Earlier versions of the specifications included entries for areas, which were named portions of the storage space. This concept was criticized as being a physical construct that should not be included at the logical data description level. It has since been dropped from the specifications, although many implementations still use it. Because the concept is no longer included in the specifications, we do not discuss it further.

The syntax of the entries above is described in the schema DDL, the topic of this section. The syntax of the DDL, which is rather straightforward, is presented via the example of Rob's database for TJ's hair salons.

Schema Entries and the General Format for Commands

The schema entry gives the name of the schema and, optionally, one or more privacy locks for controlling access to the schema. Separate privacy locks may be specified for update and read (ALTER) and read-only (COPY) privileges. The general format for a schema entry is:

```
SCHEMA NAME IS schema-name
[;PRIVACY LOCK [FOR ALTER | COPY] IS privacy-lock].
```

The notation used here requires explanation. Words in uppercase type are CODASYL reserved words, used in commands. Items in lowercase are user-supplied names. Items inside square brackets are optional. Brackets containing a series of reserved words separated by bars (|) indicate that a user must choose one or more of the reserved words in the series. Thus, the PRIVACY LOCK clause is optional. If the PRIVACY LOCK option is chosen, the FOR clause within it is optional. If the FOR clause is chosen, the user must choose between ALTER or COPY or choose both ALTER and COPY. The semicolon is used to separate clauses, and the period terminates a statement.

The following is an example schema entry for TJ's database:

```
SCHEMA NAME IS TJS_DATABASE;
PRIVACY LOCK FOR ALTER IS "BOBBYCURL";
PRIVACY LOCK FOR COPY IS "TJ".
```

The example assigns update and copy privileges to run units supplying the password "BOBBYCURL" but read-only privileges to suppliers of the password "TJ." Any user wishing to access the schema must supply a privacy key authorized for the operations to be performed.

Record Entries and Data Item Subentries

A record entry consists of a **record subentry** describing the record name and the record's privacy locks, if any, and a **data subentry,** for each data item in the record. Individual data items may have one or more privacy locks associated with them. As before, the privacy locks may be passwords or procedures, and different access privileges may be granted to different locks. These privacy locks specify the DML commands that may be used on the record or data item when the associated privacy key is supplied.

Record Subentries.   The general format for the record subentry is

```
RECORD NAME IS record-name
[;PRIVACY LOCK [FOR CONNECT | DISCONNECT | STORE |
| RECONNECT | ERASE | MODIFY | FIND | GET] IS privacy-
lock [OR privacy-lock]].
```

The words CONNECT, STORE, ERASE, DISCONNECT, RECONNECT, and MODIFY are data manipulation verbs for adding, removing, or changing record occurrences. The words FIND and GET are used to determine the location of a specific record occurrence and to fetch its data values, respectively. An example assigning update privileges to the privacy lock ROBMOD and read privileges to both ROBMOD and TJ for the STYLIST record is:

```
RECORD NAME IS STYLIST RECORD;
PRIVACY LOCK FOR CONNECT, STORE, DISCONNECT, ERASE,
RECONNECT, MODIFY IS "ROBMOD";
PRIVACY LOCK FOR GET, FIND IS "TJ" or "ROBMOD".
```

Data Item Subentries.　Data items contained within each record are described as subentries to the record. Data items may be given a level number (as in COBOL programs), but this is primarily to support data aggregates and is not discussed here.

The general format for data subentries is:

```
DATA-ITEM-NAME [PICTURE format]
[;CHECK IS (PICTURE | VALUE literal [THRU
literal])]
[;FOR ENCODING CALL procedure-name]
[;FOR DECODING CALL procedure-name]
[;PRIVACY LOCK [FOR GET | STORE | MODIFY IS
privacy-lock [OR privacy-lock] ] ].
```

The only required part of the data subentry is the data item name. Each data subentry may optionally specify the format for the data item in a PICTURE clause (as in COBOL), a CHECK clause for editing purposes, an ENCODING clause, and a PRIVACY LOCK. Very briefly, the PICTURE clause A(20) means a 20-character alphabetic item (blanks are allowed, but not special characters or digits), and the clause 9.99 means a decimal number with one digit to the left of the decimal (which is embedded in the field) and two to the right.

Data Integrity: The CHECK Clause.　The CHECK clause is used to help maintain data integrity. This clause provides for automatic editing of data item values by the DBMS whenever the database is updated. This keeps some erroneous data from ever entering the database. Because Rob wants to be certain that the commission rates are entered accurately and he does not expect commissions to go below 30 percent or above 40 percent, he has defined the following CHECK clause for COMMISSION:

```
COMMISSION PICTURE 9.99;
CHECK IS 0.30 THRU 0.40;
FOR ENCODING CALL ENCODER-PROC;
FOR DECODING CALL DECODER-PROC;
PRIVACY LOCK IS "CBCOMM".
```

Describing Security at the Data Item Level.　Data encoding and decoding and privacy locks and keys are used to provide security at the data item level. To illustrate, assume that Rob is concerned with keeping each stylist's commission private. At the present time, TJ is paying a higher commission in Brownlee, because it is difficult to get stylists to work there. She does not want this widely known; it might cause dissension among the other stylists.

In the CHECK clause above, Rob has protected the commission with both a privacy lock and encoding/decoding procedures. Rob wrote a procedure called ENCODER-PROC to encode the data, and one called DECODER-PROC to decode the data. These procedures are automatically called by the DBMS whenever authorized access to COMMISSION has been granted. The privacy lock CBCOMM has also been specified. To gain access to a COMMISSION data value, the privacy key for the record must be supplied, along with the privacy key (CBCOMM) for the data item.

Set Entries

Once the record types and their data items have been defined, the relationships between record types are described by using the set construct. A set entry consists of a **set subentry** and a **member subentry** for each member record type participating in the set. The components of a set subentry are clauses to name the set type and to specify the logical order in which member records are to be maintained in each set occurrence. Privacy locks may be defined for access to the set. Because privacy locks for sets are described in the same manner as those for other schemas, records, and data items, we do not discuss them further.

Logical Ordering of Member Record Occurrences.   The CODASYL specifications include features for maintaining logical orderings for *member* record occurrences within a given set occurrence. Notice, for example, that the links for Debi's service-history record occurrences in Figure 9–12 are in chronological order. The general format for the set subentry is:

```
SET NAME IS set-name;
OWNER IS (record-name | SYSTEM)
[;ORDER IS SORTED BY DEFINED KEYS].
```

The order is sorted clause refers to the order in which *member record occurrences* are to be maintained within a set occurrence. Rob wants member record occurrences to be maintained in ascending order by stylist-name, so he defines stylist-name as the key in the member subentry discussed next.

The set subentry for the shop-stylist set is:

```
SET NAME IS SHOP-STYLIST;
OWNER IS SHOP RECORD;
ORDER IS SORTED BY DEFINED KEYS.
```

order is sorted by defined keys means that member record occurrences within a set occurrence are to be maintained in sorted order by the key (stylist-name) defined in the member subentry.

There are three required components for a member subentry of a set entry, as shown in the general format for a member subentry:

```
MEMBER IS record-name RECORD
;INSERTION IS (AUTOMATIC | MANUAL)
;RETENTION IS (MANDATORY | OPTIONAL | FIXED)
[;KEY IS (ASCENDING | DESCENDING) data-item]
[;DUPLICATES ARE [NOT] ALLOWED]
;SET SELECTION IS BY VALUE OF data-item IN record-
name.
```

First, there is a clause to identify member record types, then a clause specifying set membership class, and third, a clause for set selection that defines how a specific set occurrence is to be located. Two optional clauses are included above for member subentries: first, the clause to specify sort keys for member record occurrences within a given set occurrence, and second, the clause indicating whether duplicate sort key values are to be allowed in a set occurrence. Whenever the optional ORDER IS SORTED clause is used in the set subentry, the KEY IS clause *must* be used in the member subentry:

```
MEMBER IS STYLIST RECORD;
INSERTION IS AUTOMATIC; RETENTION IS MANDATORY;
KEY IS ASCENDING STYLIST-NAME; DUPLICATES ARE
NOT ALLOWED;
SET SELECTION IS BY VALUE OF SHOP-NAME IN
SHOP RECORD.
```

The INSERTION and RETENTION clauses above refer to the set membership class of member records. The INSERTION clause refers to the rules that apply when member record occurrences are added to the database. The RETENTION clause refers to rules that apply when member record occurrences are removed from the database.

Membership Class.   The **membership class** of a record type in a set determines whether the DBMS or the applications program is responsible for maintaining the proper owner-member relationships when records are added to or removed from the database. A member's **insertion class** determines what happens when the record is added to the database, and the **retention class** determines what happens when the record is removed or moved to another set occurrence. These constructs work in conjunction with the DML functions STORE, ERASE, CONNECT, DISCONNECT, and RECONNECT, which are briefly described in the paragraphs that follow.

Insertion class may be automatic or manual. **Automatic insertion status** for a record type in a set means that, whenever a record occurrence of that type is added to the database with a STORE command, the DBMS establishes the record occurrence as a member of a set occurrence that has been preselected by the run unit; that is, the applications program is responsible for selecting the proper set occurrence *before* the record is transferred to the DBMS for addition to the database.

Automatic insertion works as follows: The applications program (1) moves the appropriate data values for the record occurrence into the user work area, (2) selects the appropriate set occurrence into which the record is to be placed, and (3) instructs the DBMS to perform a STORE function, which adds the record occurrence to the database. The DBMS (1) adds the record to the database, (2) checks the schema to determine the insertion class of the record in any sets in which the record participates as a member, and (3) if the insertion class is automatic, inserts the record occurrence into the set occurrence previously selected by the applications program.

Manual insertion status means that the applications program is responsible not only for selecting the appropriate set occurrence but also for establishing membership in that set occurrence by instructing the DBMS to perform a CONNECT function. The procedure works as described for automatic insertion, except that the applications program must specify a CONNECT function after the DBMS has stored the record.

The CONNECT function establishes membership for the record in the selected set.

Retention class for a record in a given set is either optional, mandatory, or fixed. If retention class is **optional,** then membership may be canceled for the record by means of a DISCONNECT function. The record occurrence still exists in the database and may participate as a member (or owner) in a different set from the one from which it has been removed.

If retention class is **mandatory,** then, once the record occurrence is connected to an occurrence of a set type, it must be a member of *some* occurrence of that set as long as it exists in the database. It may be switched to a different set occurrence with a RECONNECT operation or deleted from the database, but it cannot be the target of a DISCONNECT function.

If retention class is **fixed,** then, once a record occurrence has been connected to or stored in an occurrence of a set, it must remain a member of *that* set occurrence as long as it exists in the database; that is, it may not be a target of a DISCONNECT or RECONNECT, but ERASE may be used to delete the record entirely from the database.

In the example above, STYLIST record occurrences are AUTOMATIC members of SHOP-STYLIST sets. If the current set for the run unit corresponds to the Hair Wranglers shop in Brownlee, then any STYLIST record occurrences added to the database via a DML STORE command are associated with (automatically made members of) the set occurrence for Hair Wranglers.

The retention class for STYLIST record occurrences in the example above is MANDATORY. Any STYLIST record existing in the database must either be associated with the SHOP-STYLIST set for Hair Wranglers or for the Hackin' Shack. The complete schema description for TJ's database is given in Figure 9–14. Some of the optional clauses shown previously have been eliminated for simplicity.

SUBSCHEMAS

A *subschema* is a subset of a given schema and cannot overlap schemas. Subschemas are used to represent the user views associated with applications programs, and the only way a program can access the database is through a subschema. The declaration of a subschema has no effect on the declaration of any other subschema, and subschemas can overlap. An arbitrary number of subschemas can be defined over a given schema, and an arbitrary number of applications programs can reference the same subschema. A subschema can vary from the schema over which it is defined in the following ways:

1. Privacy locks can be changed, if the user is so authorized.
2. The order of data items within records can be changed.
3. PICTURE clauses for data items can be changed.
4. Unnecessary data items can be omitted from records.

FIGURE 9–14   Complete Schema for TJ's Database

```
       SCHEMA NAME IS TJS-DATA;
         PRIVACY LOCK FOR ALTER IS BOBBYCURL;
         PRIVACY LOCK FOR COPY IS TJ.
       RECORD NAME IS SHOP RECORD.
         SHOP NAME       PICTURE A(14);
           CHECK IS "HAIR WRANGLERS", "HACKIN' SHACK".
         CITY            PICTURE A(10);
           CHECK IS "FLATLAND", "BROWNLEE".
       RECORD NAME IS STYLIST RECORD.
         STYLIST-NAME PICTURE A(20);
           CHECK IS PICTURE.
       COMMISSION       PICTURE 9.99;
           CHECK IS 0.30 THRU 0.40.
       RECORD NAME IS PATRON RECORD.
         PATRON-NAME    PICTURE A(20).
         ADDRESS        PICTURE X(50).
         PHONE          PICTURE X(8).
       RECORD NAME IS SERVICE-HISTORY.
         DATE           PICTURE 999999;
           CHECK IS 010188 THROUGH 123188.
         SERVICE        PICTURE A(10);
           CHECK IS "CUT", "PERM", "STYLE".
         CHARGE         PICTURE 999V99;
           CHECK IS 0.00 THROUGH +150.00.
       SET NAME IS SHOP-STYLIST;
         OWNER IS SHOP RECORD;
         ORDER IS SORTED BY DEFINED KEYS;
         MEMBER IS STYLIST RECORD;
           INSERTION IS AUTOMATIC, RETENTION IS MANDATORY;
           KEY IS ASCENDING STYLIST-NAME, DUPLICATES ARE NOT ALLOWED;
           SET SELECTION IS BY VALUE OF SHOP-NAME IN SHOP RECORD.
       SET NAME IS STYLIST-HISTORY;
         OWNER IS STYLIST RECORD;
         ORDER IS SORTED BY DEFINED KEYS;
         MEMBER IS SERVICE-HISTORY;
           INSERTION IS AUTOMATIC, RETENTION IS MANDATORY;
           KEY IS ASCENDING DATE, DUPLICATES ALLOWED;
           SET SELECTION IS BY VALUE OF STYLIST-NAME IN STYLIST RECORD.
       SET NAME IS PATRON-HISTORY;
         OWNER IS PATRON RECORD;
         ORDER IS SORTED BY DEFINED KEYS;
         MEMBER IS SERVICE-HISTORY;
         INSERTION IS AUTOMATIC, RETENTION IS MANDATORY;
           KEY IS ASCENDING DATE, DUPLICATES ARE NOT ALLOWED;
           SET SELECTION IS BY VALUE OF PATRON-NAME IN PATRON RECORD.
```

5. Unnecessary record types can be omitted from sets.

6. New record types can be defined based on descriptions of two or more record types in the schema.

7. Unnecessary set types can be omitted.

Omission of unnecessary data items, records, and sets can be used as an additional security feature; private data can simply be left out of subschemas for users not needing access to such data. Some brief examples are used here to illustrate selected aspects of the subschema DDL; it is not described in its entirety.

Subschema descriptions are designed for use with a host programming language, such as COBOL or FORTRAN. The following DDL is the one described for COBOL environments. A knowledge of COBOL is not necessary to understand the discussion.

COBOL subschemas have an Identification Division and a Data Division. The **Identification Division** names the subschema, the schema from which it is derived, and the privacy key to unlock the schema if necessary. The **Data Division** can have an optional Renaming Section to specify aliases for records, sets, and data items. It must have a Record Section specifying records to be accessed. A Set Section giving the sets to be used is also generally included.

The subschema for Rob's view of TJ's database is:

```
SUBSCHEMA IDENTIFICATION DIVISION.
SUBSCHEMA NAME IS CB-VIEW OF SCHEMA TJS-DATA;
PRIVACY KEY IS "BOBBYCURL";
PRIVACY LOCK IS "CBKEY".
SUBSCHEMA DATA DIVISION.
RECORD SECTION.
COPY ALL RECORDS.
SET SECTION.
COPY ALL SETS.
END SUBSCHEMA.
```

Rob can read and update any record, data item, or set in the database. This subschema provides that access.

Suppose that TJ has asked Rob to prepare a report showing the services performed, dates, and charges for each stylist. TJ wants to be able to run the report herself, so Rob writes the following subschema to support the view needed by a program to generate such a report:

```
SUBSCHEMA IDENTIFICATION DIVISION.
SUBSCHEMA NAME IS STYLIST-HISTORY-REPORT OF SCHEMA
TJS-DATA; PRIVACY KEY IS "TJ"; PRIVACY LOCK IS
"TJSUB".
SUBSCHEMA DATA DIVISION.
RENAMING SECTION.
DATA NAME STYLIST-NAME CHANGED TO STYLIST.
RECORD SECTION.
COPY SERVICE-HISTORY RECORD.
STYLIST RECORD.
STYLIST PICTURE A(20).
SET SECTION.
COPY STYLIST-HISTORY.
END SUBSCHEMA.
```

Note that only the STYLIST-HISTORY and its constituent records (STYLIST record and SERVICE-HISTORY) are required to generate the report. The commission rate is not required, so Rob wants to omit it. After writing his program, Rob realized that he called STYLIST-NAME simply STYLIST in many places. Instead of changing his program, he changes the data item name in the Renaming Section of the subschema.

THE 1978 CODASYL DATA MANIPULATION LANGUAGE

The 1978 CODASYL specifications for the DML define commands that are to be embedded in a host programming language. These statements allow for adding, changing, accessing, or deleting record occurrences. The DML is designed for use with COBOL as the host language, but a knowledge of COBOL is not necessary to understand the following discussion. Several vendors have integrated essentially the same data manipulation commands into languages other than COBOL.

Many CODASYL packages have **precompilers,** vendor-developed programs that convert programs with embedded DML commands into programs with only standard statements of the host language. The output of the precompiler is a program that can be compiled with a standard host language compiler. IDMS, SYSTEM 2000, and SEED use this approach. This process is illustrated in Figure 9–15.

To understand the COBOL DML, you need to know that any COBOL program is divided into four divisions: (1) an Identification Division, which names the program and the programmer who wrote it, (2) an Environment Division, which specifies the computer for which the program was written, (3) a Data Division, which contains a File

FIGURE 9–15

The Precompiler Approach to Compiling DML Statements

The precompiler converts DML statements to standard COBOL statements, which are compiled by the standard COBOL compiler.

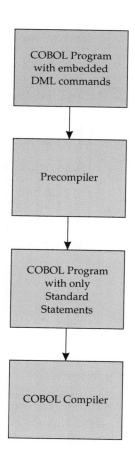

Section describing each record and its data items and a Working Storage Section describing each variable used by the program not already defined as a data item, and (4) a Procedure Division, which contains the executable statements constituting the algorithm the program implements.

Most DML statements are intermixed with standard COBOL statements in the Procedure Division. No DML statements are defined for the Environment Division. An INVOKE statement must be included in the Data Division to name the schema and subschema to be used by the program. Privacy keys are specified in the Identification Division, as described next.

Identification Division Statements: Specifying Privacy Keys

Any privacy keys necessary to access the schema and subschema, or its records, sets, and data items, are placed in the Identification Division. The somewhat curious DML statement

```
PRIVACY KEY FOR COMPILE IS subschema-privacy-key.
```

is used to provide the privacy key for the subschema invoked in the Data Division. For example, Rob would put the following statement in the Identification Division of any COBOL program he wrote using the subschema in Figure 9–9:

```
PRIVACY KEY FOR COMPILE IS "BOBBYCURL".
```

Use of the word COMPILE stems from the fact that the host language compiler (or precompiler) must have access to the subschema invoked by the program to provide the data-flow linkages between the DBMS and the run unit. The other statements for specifying privacy keys are straightforward. Their general form is illustrated below:

```
PRIVACY KEY OF record-name RECORD IS privacy-key.
PRIVACY KEY OF data-item DATA-ITEM IS privacy-key.
PRIVACY KEY OF set-name SET IS privacy-key.
```

The applications programmer must exercise care in handling program listings that may contain printouts of privacy keys. Password security is not effective if users do not protect their passwords.

INVOKE: The Only Data Division DML Statement

The Data Division of a COBOL program accessing a CODASYL database must have a special Schema Section in the Data Division identifying the subschema the program is to use (perhaps "Subschema Section" would have been more descriptive). The only DML statement occurring in the Schema Section has the following general form:

```
INVOKE SUB-SCHEMA subschema-name OF SCHEMA schema-
name.
```

For example, Rob's INVOKE statement would be:

```
INVOKE SUB-SCHEMA CB-VIEW OF SCHEMA TJS-DATA.
```

If a precompiler approach is taken, the precompiler can expand this one line into several pages of statements describing the records and data items in the subschema. This step alone can save the applications programmer a great deal of laborious, time-consuming work. The skeleton of a COBOL program's Identification Division, Environment Division, and Data Division for Rob's subschema are as follows:

```
IDENTIFICATION DIVISION.
PROGRAM-ID. STYLIST-REPORT.
PRIVACY KEY FOR COMPILE IS "TJSUB".
PRIVACY KEY FOR STYLIST RECORD IS "TJSTYLE".
ENVIRONMENT DIVISION.
SOURCE-COMPUTER. CRAY-1.
OBJECT-COMPUTER. NEC-SX2.
DATA DIVISION.
SCHEMA SECTION.
INVOKE SUB-SCHEMA STYLIST-HISTORY-REPORT OF TJS-
DATA.
standard COBOL statements. . .
```

Procedure Division Statements: The Programmer's DML

The heart of a CODASYL applications program consists of DML statements intermixed with standard COBOL statements in the Procedure Division. The statements we discuss in this section include STORE, CONNECT, DISCONNECT, ERASE, and MODIFY. The function of each command is briefly described in Table 9–1.

Adding Record Occurrences: STORE and CONNECT. The STORE command adds a new record occurrence to the database and establishes it as a member in any sets in which it has AUTOMATIC status. It also establishes this record occurrence as the current of run unit, record type, and set type(s) in which it is an owner or AUTOMATIC member. The following algorithm adds a new stylist record to the set occurrence for the Hackin' Shack. The new stylist's name is Judy, and her commission rate is 35 percent:

```
MOVE "Judy" TO STYLIST-NAME IN STYLIST RECORD.
MOVE 0.35 TO COMMISSION IN STYLIST RECORD.
MOVE "Hackin' Shack" TO SHOP-NAME IN SHOP RECORD.
FIND SHOP RECORD USING SHOP-NAME.
STORE STYLIST RECORD.
```

If the insertion class for the STYLIST record in the SHOP-STYLIST set had been MANUAL, then the record occurrence would not automatically be made a member of the set. The run unit would have to perform a CONNECT function after the STORE function to establish membership for the new stylist in the Hackin' Shack shop. The appropriate algorithm is shown here:

TABLE 9–1   Brief Description of the DML Command Functions

Command	Usage
FIND	Locates, but does not retrieve, a record occurrence. The located record becomes the current of run unit, record type, and set(s) in which it participates.
GET	Retrieves the record occurrence corresponding to the current of run unit.
STORE	Adds a new record occurrence to the database by copying its values from the user work area to the storage medium. Establishes membership for the record occurrence in any sets in which it has AUTOMATIC membership. Updates currency indicators for run unit, record type, and set(s) in which the record has AUTOMATIC membership.
ERASE	Makes the current of run unit unavailable for further processing. Deletes all FIXED and MANDATORY record occurrences it owns. Optionally deletes OPTIONAL record occurrences it owns.
CONNECT	Establishes the current of run unit as member of selected set occurrences, provided that its insertion class in the sets is MANUAL. Also permitted with AUTOMATIC OPTIONAL membership class.
DISCONNECT	Cancels membership of the current of run unit in selected sets, provided it has OPTIONAL retention status.
RECONNECT	Performs a DISCONNECT and a CONNECT to another set occurrence.
MODIFY	Changes the values of all or selected data items in the current of run unit by copying values from the user work area to the database.

```
MOVE "Judy" TO STYLIST-NAME IN STYLIST RECORD.
MOVE 0.35 TO COMMISSION IN STYLIST RECORD.
MOVE "Hackin' Shack" TO SHOP-NAME IN SHOP RECORD.
FIND SHOP RECORD USING SHOP-NAME.
CONNECT STYLIST RECORD TO SHOP-STYLIST SET.
```

Suppose TJ interviews Judy and offers her a job with a 35 percent commission. Judy accepts but wants a few days to decide whether to work in Brownlee or Flatland. TJ asks Rob to add Judy's name to the database. But because STYLIST records in Rob's schema are defined as AUTOMATIC, MANDATORY members of the SHOP-STYLIST set, Judy's record must become a member of *some* SHOP-STYLIST when the STORE function is performed and must always be associated with some occurrence of the SHOP-STYLIST set. Thus, the desired operation cannot be performed with the current schema definition.

To allow for such situations, Rob must define STYLIST records as MANUAL, OPTIONAL members in the SHOP-STYLIST set. Assuming that MANUAL, OPTIONAL membership has been declared, the following algorithm adds Judy's record to the database. The record is not associated with any SHOP-STYLIST set:

```
MOVE "Judy" TO STYLIST-NAME IN STYLIST RECORD.
MOVE 0.35 TO COMMISSION IN STYLIST RECORD.
STORE STYLIST RECORD.
```

Suppose that Judy decides to work at the Hackin' Shack. The following algorithm establishes membership for Judy's record in the Hackin' Shack set:

```
MOVE "Judy" TO STYLIST-NAME IN STYLIST RECORD.
FIND STYLIST RECORD USING STYLIST-NAME.
MOVE "Hackin' Shack" TO SHOP-NAME IN SHOP RECORD.
FIND SHOP RECORD USING SHOP-NAME.
CONNECT STYLIST RECORD TO SHOP-STYLIST SET.
```

Allowable operations with the possible combinations of insertion and retention status are summarized in Table 9–2.

Deleting Record Occurrences: The ERASE Command. The ERASE command makes selected record occurrences unavailable for further processing. They can actually be purged or simply flagged for later deletion. ERASE has several formats:

1. ERASE record-name: Deletes the current occurrence of the named record only if it owns no member record occurrences. If it has member record occurrences, an error status condition occurs and no action is taken.

2. ERASE record-name ALL: Deletes the current occurrence of the named record and all member records it owns, regardless of their retention status.

3. ERASE record-name SELECTIVE: Deletes the current occurrence of the named record and any of its member records *not* owned by another set of occurrences. Its OPTIONAL members are deleted, *unless* they are owned by some other record.

4. ERASE record-name PERMANENT: Deletes the current of run unit and its MANDATORY or FIXED members. OPTIONAL members are disconnected from the run unit's set but are not entirely removed from the database regardless of possible ownership by other records.

To illustrate ERASE record-name, assume that Judy changes her mind and does not go to work for TJ after all. The following algorithm deletes Judy's STYLIST record occurrence only if she has performed no services:

```
MOVE "Judy" TO STYLIST-NAME IN STYLIST RECORD.
FIND STYLIST RECORD USING STYLIST-NAME.
ERASE STYLIST RECORD.
```

TABLE 9–2   Effects of Possible Insertion-Retention Combinations

	AUTOMATIC	MANUAL
MANDATORY	STORE creates membership. RECONNECT may be used. DISCONNECT may not be used.	CONNECT creates membership. RECONNECT may be used. DISCONNECT may not be used.
OPTIONAL	STORE creates membership. May exist without an owner. DISCONNECT, CONNECT, and RECONNECT may be used.	CONNECT creates membership. May exist without an owner. DISCONNECT, CONNECT, and RECONNECT may be used.
FIXED	STORE creates membership. Must always have an owner. DISCONNECT, CONNECT, or RECONNECT may not be used.	CONNECT creates membership. Must always have an owner. DISCONNECT or RECONNECT may not be used.

```
IF ERROR-STATUS-CODE = 0 THEN
DISPLAY "RECORD DELETED."
ELSE
DISPLAY "***ERROR CONDITION: RECORD NOT DELETED***".
```

To illustrate the ALL option, assume that TJ sells the Hackin' Shack but wants to keep the names of her patrons so that she can send them an invitation to the Hair Wranglers in Brownlee. The following algorithm deletes the record occurrence for the Hackin' Shack, all its stylists, and all their service histories. Because PATRON records are not descendants (children) of SHOP records, none of them is deleted:

```
MOVE "Hackin' Shack" TO SHOP-NAME IN SHOP RECORD.
ERASE SHOP RECORD ALL.
```

Canceling Set Membership: The DISCONNECT Command. DISCONNECT cancels membership of the named record in specified sets, but it does not purge the record from the database. It can still exist in other sets or can exist independently of any sets. The format of the DISCONNECT statement is:

```
DISCONNECT record-name FROM set-name(s) SET.
```

DISCONNECT can be used only when OPTIONAL membership has been declared for the named record.

To illustrate, assume that Brad has quit. TJ wants to cancel his membership in the Hackin' Shack set occurrence but keep his data to prepare reports at the end of the year for the Internal Revenue Service. This requires that membership for STYLIST records be declared OPTIONAL in the schema definition for the SHOP-STYLIST set, which can be done with:

```
MOVE "Brad" TO STYLIST-NAME IN STYLIST RECORD.
DISCONNECT STYLIST RECORD FROM SHOP-STYLIST SET.
```

Changing Data Values: The MODIFY Command. The final DML command to be discussed, MODIFY, is used to change data values or to change membership from one set occurrence to another. Its format is

```
MODIFY record-name [;USING data item(s)].
```

The optional USING phrase is used when changing ownership to another set. In the following example, Suzi's commission is changed to 35 percent:

```
MOVE "Suzi" TO STYLIST-NAME IN STYLIST RECORD.
FIND STYLIST RECORD USING STYLIST-NAME.
MOVE 0.35 TO COMMISSION IN STYLIST-NAME.
MODIFY STYLIST.
```

Some Comments on the CODASYL Approach

The CODASYL approach is obviously much more complex to learn and to use than the relational approach. The DML, especially, is more complicated. Programmers must be very careful to ensure that their

THE USER'S VIEW

The CODASYL approach and its data definition languages were designed for use by professional data processing personnel, not by end-users. The intent was to make it easier for data processing personnel to support the needs of end-users, and not necessarily to provide hands-on access to users.

Curiously enough, after a three-hour introduction to the CODASYL and relational approaches to modeling data, participants in a continuing education course for non–data processors were about equally split in their preference for viewing data models in tables or in data structure diagrams. Many felt that the relational approach actually masked relationships that should have been highlighted. This was an unscientific survey, and it proves nothing except that different people do have different tastes and preferences. But it does seem reasonable to provide different views of data to different users.

Even though no CODASYL standards exist for a query language, many implementors of CODASYL systems have developed fourth-generation query languages suitable for end-users. The SEED package, for example, has a query language that is limited to retrieval of data. The query language does not provide features for updating, but under certain operating systems it is possible to use standard data manipulation commands to perform updates interactively. Other vendors are adding relational-like interfaces to their packages based on the SQL language. ■

programs perform as expected, particularly during updates. It is easy to forget something amidst all the elements that must be kept in mind when navigating the paths of a large network. Doing so during updates can result in unintended consequences with disastrous effects on the database.

The CODASYL approach is often more efficient than the relational approach in terms of machine time. It has proven to be effective, for example, in relatively well defined, high-volume, transaction-oriented applications—such as payroll processing, sales transaction systems for department stores, and inventory systems for intermediate distributors of products. Queries in these systems can be well defined in advance and based on a few keys, such as part numbers and customer names. Standardized queries permit the development of form-oriented entry and retrieval of data, which may be highly desirable in circumstances where high volumes can overwhelm relational systems.

In some organizations, the need arises for many transactions and many ad hoc queries on the same database. Often in such situations, the ad hoc retrievals are for managers or other users who may not need up-to-the-minute information. Some firms use dual systems to support these separate needs—a CODASYL system to support the transaction-oriented users, and a relational system to support ad hoc queries.

The database for the query-oriented system can be copied from the transaction-oriented system overnight, or perhaps on demand.

CHAPTER SUMMARY

In this chapter, we described the 1978 CODASYL approach to representing hierarchies and networks. The concept of a set is fundamental to describing and processing CODASYL databases. A set is simply a named

METROPOLITAN NATIONAL BANK

The time has come for your *second* implementation of the MetNat database system. This time, a CODASYL implementation is required. You may want to reread the Metropolitan National Bank sections in prior chapters to refresh your memory on the important aspects of the task at hand.

As with your relational implementation, be sure you consider the goals you outlined in the master plan that you developed earlier in the project. If response time should be fast, for example, how does this impact your selection of owner and member record types? Be sure to indicate retention and insertion status for each set. Give a brief explanation for each choice. Include a brief discussion for each set that describes how your implementation supports aspects of the master plan and/or the typical operating procedures described in earlier chapters.

You should prepare a report on a CODASYL approach to MetNat's database system that includes a complete schema description and major subschema descriptions. You should also be able to provide a comparison of the relational and CODASYL approaches. Does either approach seem to address the needs of the organization better than the other? ■

two-level hierarchy. The parent node is called the *owner record type,* and children of that node are called *member record types.*

The schema data description language is used to describe all data items, records, and sets in the database. The subschema data description language is used to describe user views. Applications programs access the database through subschemas, which are subsets of the database. Data manipulation language statements are embedded in host language programs to access or update data in the database. Data values are communicated between the database and the applications programs via the user work area.

Several implementors have developed DBMS packages around the CODASYL specifications. Some are based on the 1971 report, others on the 1978 specifications. These implementations have proven to be highly efficient for transaction-oriented, high-volume processing. Numerous CODASYL databases are in operation today.

The CODASYL DDL and DML commands are summarized in Figures 9–16 and 9–17 respectively.

Questions and Exercises

1. Define the following terms:
   a. CODASYL database
   b. CODASYL schema
   c. CODASYL subschema
   d. run unit
   e. user work area
   f. database key
   g. CODASYL set
   h. owner record type
   i. member record type
   j. singular set
   k. recursive set
   l. currency indicator
   m. error status variable
   n. privacy lock
   o. privacy key
   p. insertion status
   q. retention status
   r. precompiler

FIGURE 9–16
General Format for the
Schema DDL Entries

```
SCHEMA NAME IS schema-name
[;PRIVACY LOCK [FOR (ALTER | COPY)] IS privacy-lock].
RECORD NAME IS record-name
  [;PRIVACY LOCK [ FOR (CONNECT | DISCONNECT | STORE |
  | RECONNECT | ERASE | MODIFY | FIND | GET)] IS privacy-
  lock [OR privacy-lock]].
DATA-ITEM-NAME          [PICTURE FORMAT]
  [;CHECK IS (PICTURE | VALUE literal [THRU
  literal] ) ]
  [;FOR ENCODING CALL procedure-name]
  [;FOR DECODING CALL procedure-name]
  [;PRIVACY LOCK [FOR (GET | STORE | MODIFY) IS
  privacy-lock [OR privacy-lock] . .] ].
SET NAME IS set-name;
  OWNER IS (record-name | SYSTEM);
  ORDER IS SORTED BY DEFINED KEYS.
  MEMBER IS record-name RECORD;
      INSERTION IS (AUTOMATIC | MANUAL)
      ;RETENTION IS (MANDATORY | OPTIONAL | FIXED)
      [;KEY IS (ASCENDING | DESCENDING) data-item]
      [;DUPLICATES ARE [NOT] ALLOWED)
      ;SET SELECTION IS BY VALUE OF data-item IN
      record-name.
```

FIGURE 9–17   General Format of the DML Commands
Note: In most cases, the key words RECORD and SET are optional.

```
FIND record-name USING key-data-item-name.
FIND OWNER IN set-name CURRENT OF (record-name | set-name | RUN-UNIT).
FIND (FIRST | NEXT | PRIOR | LAST) record-name RECORD OF set-name SET.
GET record-name.
STORE record-name.
CONNECT record-name RECORD TO set-name SET.
DISCONNECT record-name RECORD FROM set-name SET.
RECONNECT record-name RECORD TO set-name SET.
MODIFY record-name RECORD ;[ USING data item(s)].
ERASE record-name RECORD [PERMANENT | SELECTIVE | ALL].
```

2. What is the relationship between CODASYL schemas and sub-schemas? How may a schema and subschema differ?

3. What is a database key?

4. What is a CODASYL set? How is the set construct used to model simple networks? Complex networks?

5. What is a singular set, and how is it useful?

6. Assume that Rob wants to access SERVICE-HISTORY records as a regular sequential file in chronological order with Date as the key. Write the necessary set entry to support that function.

7. Develop a data structure diagram for TJ's hair salon, and write a CODASYL schema description for this diagram.

8. Write a DML pseudocode algorithm that would retrieve and display Dollie's phone number using the data in Figure 9–10.

9. The first record occurrence in Figure 9–10 indicates that a $20 haircut was given on 3/20/88. Write a DML algorithm to determine who gave the cut and in what shop it was given.

10. Write a CODASYL subschema that would grant a user read access to SHOP records, STYLIST records, and the SHOP-STYLIST set. Order stylist names alphabetically in set occurrences.

11. Show how a singular set may be used to provide access to SHOP records in alphabetical order by shop name.

12. Integrate the singular set in Question 11 into the subschema in Question 10 and write a DML pseudocode algorithm to display shops and their associated stylists in alphabetical order. With the data in Figure 9–10 and assuming that Brad and Suzi work at Hackin' Shack, the output would be:

```
Hackin' Shack
Debi
Hair Wranglers
Brad
Suzi
```

Note: Use the schema in Figure 9–14, the subschema in Figure 9–9, and the data in Figure 9–8 to write DML pseudocode algorithms for Questions 13 to 20.

13. Add a new patron, Carmen, who lives in Quitman and whose phone number is 555-6876.

14. Add a new stylist, Francine, who works in the Hackin' Shack and has a 40 percent commission.

15. Add the information that Carmen got a perm from Francine on 3/25/88 and paid $50.

16. What must you do to modify the algorithm in Questions 14 and 15 if membership status for STYLIST records and SERVICE-HISTORY records was MANUAL in all sets in which they participate as members?

17. Delete the Hair Wranglers record and all its descendants.

18. Delete Zeke's record, but *retain* his SERVICE-HISTORY records.

19. Change Francine's commission to 35 percent.

20. Zeke and Carmen got married, so change Zeke's phone number to 555-6876 and his address to Quitman.

For Further Reading

For the original CODASYL specifications see: Report of the CODASYL Data Base Task Group of the Programming Language Committee. Association for Computing Machinery, April 1971.

The DDL specifications described in this text are contained in: Secretariat of the Canadian Government EDP Standards Committee. "CODASYL Data Description Language," *Journal of Development,* January 1978.

The COBOL DML specifications described in this text can be found in: CODASYL COBOL Committee. "CODASYL COBOL Data Base Facility." *Journal of Development,* January 1978.

IV

IMPLEMENTATION AND PHYSICAL DATABASE DESIGN

10

PHYSICAL IMPLEMENTATION ISSUES

In previous chapters, we have been primarily concerned with the objectives of database systems, elements of the database system environment, database system planning techniques, and data modeling. These concepts have tended to be rather abstract and are closely related to information analysis and logical database design.

This chapter moves into the arena of physical design to discuss data structures. The term **data structure** refers to the manner in which relationships between data elements are represented in the computer system. As Chapter 3 illustrates, relationships between data elements are fundamental concerns in a database environment. Some systems (for example, those based on CODASYL specifications) give the analyst a choice of data structures to use. Thus, an understanding of data structures is important in gaining an understanding of the technology of database management systems. The material in this chapter helps explain *how* relationships are maintained in the approaches to database management described in the previous part of the book.

Three major types of data structures are discussed: linked lists, inverted lists, and B-trees. Query-processing efficiency (in terms of number of disk accesses) is also considered.

SECONDARY KEYS AND INTERRECORD RELATIONSHIPS

In this chapter, we assume a familiarity with disk storage devices and access methods, such as sequential (SAM), indexed sequential (ISAM), and direct (DAM), that provide access to records on the basis of a primary key. Sequential organization provides access to records in sequential order by primary key. Indexed sequential organization provides access in either sequential or random order by primary key. Direct access permits fetching in random order by primary key. These topics can be reviewed in Appendix A.

In a database environment, the need also arises to access records via secondary keys and to represent relationships between records. One example of the need for secondary keys is in processing the WHERE clauses of SQL statements. Any attribute, not just a primary key, may be included in a WHERE clause. Efficient processing requires that the database system be able to locate target records quickly, even if the data item in the WHERE clause is not a primary key.

An example of the need to represent relationships between records is the association between records in data structure diagrams (which are used in the hierarchical and network models and in the CODASYL approach). In this chapter, we are concerned with data structures that are useful in representing secondary keys and relationships between records.

The design of data structures that provide rapid, flexible data access depends on knowledge of data items used as primary keys and secondary keys and the frequency with which they will be used. Assuming that the database is stored on disk (which is almost always the case at present), the time it takes to respond to a query is heavily dependent on the number of disk accesses that must be made to satisfy the query. This is due to the fact that disk devices are so much slower than main memory. The efficiency of the physical design depends on how well the requirements were specified during information requirements analysis and logical design.

CASE EXAMPLE
Using Pointers to Process SQL Queries on Byer's Stock Data

Some sample queries may help to illustrate the need to provide access to records via secondary keys. Suppose we have the stock data in Figure 10–1 for Byer's portfolio management system. The Symbol is a unique identifier assigned to each security traded on the major exchanges. It is used by stockholders to retrieve price data and other information. Byer has assigned a numeric ID number to each stock to be used as the primary key. (The securities industry has developed similar identification numbers called CUSIP numbers.) The records are in numeric order by ID number.

   Accessing these records sequentially by ID number is no problem. But suppose that the Organization of Petroleum Exporting Countries (OPEC) has announced oil price decreases and Byer wants to examine all the companies in the oil industry to see what impact this event has had on stock prices. He can make the following SQL query:

```
SELECT *
FROM STOCKS
WHERE Industry = "Oil"
```

But if the only access to this file is via a primary key such as ID number, the only way to find oil industry stocks is through a sequential search of the file. This would be quite inefficient if there were just a few oil stocks in a large file. Or suppose that clients frequently wish to find information about a particular stock for which they know the company name but not the ID number. This would also require a sequential

FIGURE 10–1 A One-Table Database for Byer's Stock Data

Table Name: STOCKS

ID	Company	Industry	Symbol	Price	Earnings	Dividends
1122	Exxon	Oil	XON	46.00	2.50	0.75
1152	Lockheed	Aerospace	LCH	112.00	1.25	0.50
1175	Ford	Auto	F	88.00	1.70	0.20
1231	Intel	Computer	INTL	30.00	2.00	0.00
1245	Digital	Computer	DEC	120.00	1.80	0.10
1323	GM	Auto	GM	158.00	2.10	0.30
1378	Texaco	Oil	TX	230.00	2.80	1.00
1480	Conoco	Oil	CON	150.00	2.00	0.50
1767	Tony Lama	Apparel	TONY	45.00	1.50	0.25

FIGURE 10–2   A Simple Linked List for Oil Industry Stocks
Members of the oil industry have been blocked off to highlight them. Arrows point from one member of the list to the next. The head of the list is 1122 (Exxon). The entry in Exxon's Next Oil Stock column points to Texaco (1378), Texaco points to Conoco (1480), and the null value (0000) in Conoco's record ends the chain.

Oil Industry Head: (1122)

ID	Company	Industry	Symbol	Price	Earnings	Dividends	Next Oil Stock
1122	Exxon	Oil	XON	46.00	2.50	0.75	(1378)
1152	Lockheed	Aerospace	LCH	112.00	1.25	0.50	
1175	Ford	Auto	F	88.00	1.70	0.20	
1231	Intel	Computer	INTL	30.00	2.00	0.00	
1245	Digital	Computer	DEC	120.00	1.80	0.10	
1323	GM	Auto	GM	158.00	2.10	0.30	
1378	Texaco	Oil	TX	230.00	2.80	1.00	(1480)
1480	Conoco	Oil	CON	150.00	2.00	0.50	0000
1767	Tony Lama	Apparel	TONY	45.00	1.50	0.25	

search, unless a cross-index was maintained matching company names to ID numbers.

An alternative method is to add another field to each oil industry record, one that gives the ID number of the next oil industry stock, as in Figure 10–2. With this sort of structure, a program that reads Exxon's record can immediately issue a read instruction such as "get record with primary key 1378," thereby moving to the next oil stock. When data items are used in this fashion, they are said to be **logical pointers;** they "point to" the next item in a list. In other words, a logical pointer is a data item in one record that is used to locate an associated record. Logical pointers must be transformed into actual physical addresses before the associated record may be fetched. Logical pointers are discussed in Appendix A in the section on ISAM.

Relative pointers indicate the position of a record in a file by giving its position relative to the beginning of the file. Perhaps the simplest type of relative pointer is a **relative record number.** In relative record numbering, records are numbered from 1 to n as they are entered into the system. When a record is retrieved, the program issues an instruction such as "get record number m." The system must be able to convert m to a physical address before the record can be fetched. An example is given in Appendix A in the section on direct access. Other relative pointers may indicate a certain byte, sector, or block of the disk space.

A **physical pointer** gives the actual address of the associated record in the storage system. Physical pointers require no conversion, but they are difficult to maintain because they must be changed whenever the associated record is moved to a new location.

Pointers, whether they are logical, relative, or physical, are used in locating records in database systems. They are an essential feature of the techniques we discuss next—linked lists, inverted lists, and B-trees—which provide efficient access to records via secondary keys such as industry or stock name. ■

LINKED LISTS

A simple **linked list** is a chain of pointers embedded in records; it indicates either a record sequence for an attribute other than the primary key or all records with a common property. Linked lists are also referred to as *chains,* the term used in CODASYL documents. The structure in Figure 10–2 is a linked list connecting all the companies in the oil industry. Arrows are used to illustrate the relationships between pointers graphically (of course, arrows do not exist in computer files). This list may be used to process such queries as the following:

```
SELECT Company, Current Price
FROM STOCKS
WHERE Industry = "Oil"
```

The first record in the list is referred to as the **head** of the list. A separate pointer is maintained to indicate the head of the list. In Figure 10–2, Exxon is the head of the oil industry list. The **tail,** the last record in the list, is marked by storing a null value (here indicated by 0000) as its pointer value.

To process the list, a program first reads the record containing the pointer to the head of the list, which might be the first record in the file. Assuming that this pointer is read into a variable called OIL-LIST-HEAD (and that at least one oil stock exists in the file), the program then issues a read to the STOCKS file giving OIL-LIST-HEAD as the index for the record to be fetched. When the pointer to the next oil company in the list is read into NEXT-OIL-STOCK, this variable is tested for the null value to see if the end of the list has been reached. If not, another read instruction is issued to the STOCKS file with the index in NEXT-OIL-STOCK.

Numerous types and variations of linked lists have been developed to satisfy special processing needs. These are described below.

Rings

A **ring** is simply a linked list in which the pointer in the tail points to the head of the list. This method permits processing of the entire list beginning from any record, not just from the head. The linked list for oil stocks has been converted into a ring in Figure 10–3 by changing Conoco's pointer from null (0000) to 1122, Exxon's primary key. Exxon is the head of the list.

FIGURE 10–3   A Ring Structure for Oil Industry Stocks
The pointer for Conoco has been changed from a null value marking the end of the list to point back to Exxon (1122), the head of the list.

ID	Company	Industry	Symbol	Price	Earnings	Dividends	Next Oil Stock
			Oil Industry Head:	1122			
1122	Exxon	Oil	XON	46.00	2.50	0.75	1378
1152	Lockheed	Aerospace	LCH	112.00	1.25	0.50	
1175	Ford	Auto	F	88.00	1.70	0.20	
1231	Intel	Computer	INTL	30.00	2.00	0.00	
1245	Digital	Computer	DEC	120.00	1.80	0.10	
1323	GM	Auto	GM	158.00	2.10	0.30	
1378	Texaco	Oil	TX	230.00	2.80	1.00	1480
1480	Conoco	Oil	CON	150.00	2.00	0.50	1122
1767	Tony Lama	Apparel	TONY	45.00	1.50	0.25	

FIGURE 10–4   A Sorted Linked List Alphabetizing Company
This list allows access to records in alphabetic order. It is a dense list: An entry occurs for each record in the file.

Company List Head (Alphabetic Order): 1480

ID	Company	Industry	Symbol	Price	Earnings	Dividends	Next Company
1122	Exxon	Oil	XON	46.00	2.50	0.75	1175
1152	Lockheed	Aerospace	LCH	112.00	1.25	0.50	1378
1175	Ford	Auto	F	88.00	1.70	0.20	1323
1231	Intel	Computer	INTL	30.00	2.00	0.00	1152
1245	Digital	Computer	DEC	120.00	1.80	0.10	1122
1323	GM	Auto	GM	158.00	2.10	0.30	1231
1378	Texaco	Oil	TX	230.00	2.80	1.00	1767
1480	Conoco	Oil	CON	150.00	2.00	0.50	1245
1767	Tony Lama	Apparel	TONY	45.00	1.50	0.25	0000

Dense Lists and Sorted Lists

The oil industry list is said to be **nondense** because only a few of the records in the file are part of the list. A **dense list** is one with a pointer for most or all of the records in the file. Figure 10–4 illustrates a dense list that allows processing of Byer's stock records in alphabetic order by company name (arrows are not used to avoid cluttering the diagram). This is also a **sorted list** because it is maintained in a particular order (alphabetic by company name). This list may be used to process queries of this form:

```
SELECT *
FROM STOCKS
ORDER BY Company ASC
```

Here the ORDER BY clause indicates that the user wants stocks displayed in ascending (ASC) order by company name.

Two-Way (Bidirectional) Lists

The sorted list for company names in Figure 10–4 can be used to access stocks in alphabetic order; but suppose we have this query:

```
SELECT *
FROM STOCKS
ORDER BY Company DESC
```

The DESC option means that the records are to be provided to the user in inverse alphabetic order. Since the list we have is in alphabetic order, we have no way of satisfying this query short of sorting by company name in descending order. Obviously, the problem can be solved by maintaining pointers in descending order. These pointers are illustrated in Figure 10–5. Together, the alphabetic list and inverse alphabetic list provide the ability to process stocks in either direction. Such lists are said to be **two-way** or **bidirectional**.

Relative to the alphabetized list, the pointers in the inverse alphabetic list point to the previous or prior record in the chain and are called **prior** or **backward** pointers. The alphabetic pointers are then referred to as **forward** or **next** pointers. Prior pointers may increase the speed of list updating, but they make it more complicated. To illustrate, assume that a record for Gulf with ID number 1201 is to be inserted into the file. Logically, it should go in the file between Ford and Intel (Figure 10–6), because 1201 is greater than 1175 and less than 1231. But in the

FIGURE 10–5   A Two-Way Linked List for Company
Pointers to the prior record in the list have been added, facilitating updates and providing access to records in inverse order.

ID	Company	...other data...	Next Company	Prior Company
1122	Exxon		1175	1245
1152	Lockheed		1378	1231
1175	Ford		1323	1122
1231	Intel		1152	1323
1245	Digital		1122	1480
1323	GM		1231	1175
1378	Texaco		1767	1152
1480	Conoco		1245	0000
1767	Tony Lama		0000	1378

Company List Head: 1480
Company List Tail: 1767

FIGURE 10–6   Two-Way Linked List for Company with Gulf Inserted
Gulf has been inserted into its physical position by primary key between Ford and Intel. Pointers in Intel's and GM's records have been updated to maintain logical order in the lists for Company.

ID	Company	...other data...	Next Company	Prior Company
	Company List Head (Alphabetic Order): 1480			
	Company List Tail (Alphabetic Order): 1767			
1122	Exxon		1175	1245
1152	Lockheed		1378	1231
1175	Ford		1323	1122
1201	Gulf		1231	1323
1231	Intel		1152	1201
1245	Digital		1122	1480
1323	GM		1201	1175
1378	Texaco		1767	1152
1480	Conoco		1245	0000
1767	Tony Lama		0000	1378

alphabetic company list, Gulf fits between GM and Intel. Thus, GM's pointer must be changed to point to Gulf (1201) and Gulf's must be set to GM's old pointer, which points to Intel (1231). Prior pointers must be similarly updated.

To make the list insertion, we first search the list comparing Gulf to each successive company name until the company name is higher than Gulf in the alphabet. This occurs when we get to Intel. Gulf's forward pointer is set to 1231, Intel's ID number, and its backward pointer is set to Intel's old backward pointer, 1323. Next, Intel's backward pointer is updated to Gulf's ID number, 1201. Finally, Gulf's backward pointer to GM is used to fetch GM's record and update its forward pointer to Gulf's ID number, 1201. Without the backward pointer to GM, we would have to initiate a search at the head of the list to get to GM's record—a much lengthier process.

Multilists

In a **multilist,** several lists are defined over the same file. This situation is also referred to as a **threaded list,** because the lists weave or thread through the records in the file. Figure 10–7 shows a multilist consisting of one-way lists for Company and Symbol. These are both dense lists, and a pointer field is reserved for each of the two attributes.

Figure 10–8 shows a multilist (one-way) for the Industry attribute of Byer's stock file. Here, we have a list for each industry value—Aerospace, Apparel, Auto, Computer, and Oil. We need only one pointer field for each record because each company is defined in only one industry.

FIGURE 10–7   **A Multilist Consisting of One-Way Linked Lists for Company and Symbol**
Two fields have been added to each record to store the pointers for the Company and Symbol lists. If prior pointers had been maintained, two more pointer fields would be necessary.

ID	Company	Symbol	...other data...	Next Company	Next Symbol
Company List Head (Alphabetic Order): 1480					
Symbol List Head (Alphabetic Order): 1480					
1122	Exxon	XON		1175	0000
1152	Lockheed	LCH		1378	1767
1175	Ford	F		1323	1323
1231	Intel	INTL		1152	1152
1245	Digital	DEC		1122	1175
1323	GM	GM		1231	1231
1378	Texaco	TX		1767	1122
1480	Conoco	CON		1245	1245
1767	Tony Lama	TONY		0000	1378

FIGURE 10–8   **A Multilist Consisting of a List for Each Industry**
Only one pointer field has been added because each company is associated with only one industry.

Aerospace Head: 1152
Auto Head: 1175
Apparel Head: 1767
Computer Head: 1231
Oil Industry Head: 1122

ID	Company	Industry	Symbol	Price	Earnings	Dividends	Next Stock
1122	Exxon	Oil	XON	46.00	2.50	0.75	1378
1152	Lockheed	Aerospace	LCH	112.00	1.25	0.50	0000
1175	Ford	Auto	F	88.00	1.70	0.20	1323
1231	Intel	Computer	INTL	30.00	2.00	0.00	1245
1245	Digital	Computer	DEC	120.00	1.80	0.10	0000
1323	GM	Auto	GM	158.00	2.10	0.30	0000
1378	Texaco	Oil	TX	230.00	2.80	1.00	1480
1480	Conoco	Oil	CON	150.00	2.00	0.50	0000
1767	Tony Lama	Apparel	TONY	45.00	1.50	0.25	0000

The Query-Processing Efficiency of Linked Lists

Lists provide the capability of accessing records with similar characteristics or in various logical sequences without sorting or physically rearranging a file. Thus, they provide more-flexible access to data by supporting access by secondary keys. To illustrate, consider this query:

```
SELECT  *
FROM  STOCKS
WHERE  Industry  =  "Oil"
AND  Earnings  >  2.50
```

If a linked list is maintained for oil industry stocks, its pointers can be followed by successively fetching records in the chain and testing the Earnings value. Since only a few records correspond to companies in the oil industry, this would be more efficient than a sequential search through the file.

Unfortunately, lists must be updated; this complicates processing, increases processing time, and consumes storage space. Accessing records via lists often necessitates considerable movement of the access assembly of disks, because pointer chains may lead into widely separated cylinders, thereby slowing response times. Lists also suffer one of the deficiencies of sequential files: Though only a few records on the list must be accessed, many records may still have to be fetched to satisfy a query. To illustrate, consider this query:

```
SELECT  *
FROM  STOCKS
WHERE  Company  =  "Texaco"
```

If a sorted (alphabetized) list is maintained on Company name (as in Figure 10–4), then it can be used to search the file for Texaco's record. This is done by following the pointer to the head of the list, Conoco. Conoco's record is fetched and its pointer followed to Digital, Digital's record is fetched and its pointer followed, and so on until Texaco is found. This process requires several fetches and may involve several movements of the access assembly.

Next, consider this query:

```
SELECT  *
FROM  STOCKS
WHERE  Earnings  >  2.00
```

If a one-way sorted list (ascending order) is available for Earnings, it can be followed to find the first record satisfying the condition Earnings > 2.00. It is known that all subsequent records in the list satisfy the condition, but this does not save anything over a sequential search because all the records in the list must be accessed to follow the pointer chain. It may be even worse than a sequential search, if following the list results in considerable movement of the access assembly. Processing this query would be more efficient via a two-way list (or a one-way list in descending order). Backward pointers could be followed from the stock with the highest Earnings down to the first stock with Earnings of 2.00 or less.

Note that the efficiency of processing the list from highest to lowest depends on the data. What would happen, for example, if the query had given the condition Earnings > 1.00? Every stock qualifies, and again the entire list must be traversed to satisfy the query.

Consider this query:

```
SELECT *
FROM STOCKS
WHERE Earnings > 2.00
OR Dividends < 0.60
```

As before, searching backward pointers of a two-way list for Earnings would provide efficient processing for the first condition. Searching forward (ascending order) pointers of a list for Dividends would provide efficient processing for the OR condition. Why? Because this is an OR, and any records satisfying either condition satisfy the query.

Finally, suppose that we have two-way lists for Earnings and Dividends and the OR in the previous query is changed to AND:

```
SELECT *
FROM STOCKS
WHERE Earnings > 2.00
AND Dividends < 0.60
```

There are at least three different ways that this query can be processed: (1) a sequential search, testing each record to see if both conditions are satisfied; (2) following the forward pointers in the Dividend chain and testing each record to see if Earnings are greater than 2.00; (3) following backward pointers in the Earnings chain with a test of whether Dividends are less than 0.60. With our data in this example, the third alternative results in the fewest number of record accesses; only Texaco and Exxon have Earnings greater than 2.00, so there is no need to search the Earnings chain beyond that point (except that one more record must be accessed to terminate the search). A database management system, of course, must decide which of the three approaches to use in order to satisfy the query. One of the challenges in the design of database software is to give it the capacity to make such choices efficiently.

INVERTED LISTS

In this section, we show how inverted lists can be used to overcome some of the deficiencies associated with linked lists, especially the problem of having to fetch records in order to follow pointer chains. **Inverted lists** may be viewed simply as index tables of pointers stored separately from the data records (much like ISAM indexes) rather than embedded in pointer fields in the stored records themselves. Processing for unique secondary keys (those having a 1:1 association with primary keys) is somewhat different than for those with 1:M associations with primary keys. In the former case, dense indexes are the result; 1:M associations produce nondense indexes.

Dense Inverted Lists

The simplest type of inverted list occurs for dense indexes, in which case the table is just a cross-reference table matching a secondary key field with its corresponding primary key. The inverted list consists of two columns: a **values table** (column) containing the data item that has been "inverted" or rearranged and an **occurrences table** (column) containing the primary key for the record in which that value occurs. Dense inverted lists for Company and Symbol are given in Figure 10–9. The lists are said to be inverted because Company names and Symbols have been alphabetized and corresponding primary keys have been inverted, or rearranged accordingly.

As we illustrated in the previous section, queries such as

```
SELECT *
FROM STOCKS
WHERE Company = "Texaco"
```

may necessitate many disk accesses if a linked list is used to fetch company names in alphabetic order. To process this query with inverted lists, one need only read the list for Company into main memory and search it for Texaco and then issue a read instruction for the record with Texaco's primary key, 1378.

This approach eliminates the need to fetch numerous records to search lengthy pointer chains, as is the case with linked lists. It has the disadvantage of requiring accesses to fetch index tables, which may become quite lengthy themselves in the case of files with many records. In such a case, several accesses may be required to fetch indexes. The trade-off is accesses to indexes for reduced accesses to data records. Conversely, if the file index table is small, one may be able to copy the whole table into memory in one read and then directly fetch the desired record. Also, index tables may be much smaller than the data records and may be manipulated more easily and efficiently.

FIGURE 10–9
Dense Inverted Lists for Company and Symbol
The inverted lists are dense: There is a one-to-one relationship between both Company and primary key and Symbol and primary key.

Values Table Company	Occurrences Table Primary Key	Values Table Symbol	Occurrences Table Primary Key
Conoco	1480	CON	1480
Digital	1245	DEC	1245
Exxon	1122	F	1175
Ford	1175	GM	1323
GM	1323	INTL	1231
Intel	1231	LCH	1152
Lockheed	1152	TONY	1767
Texaco	1378	TX	1378
Tony Lama	1767	XON	1122

Nondense Inverted Lists for 1:M Relationships

The data item Industry has a one-to-many relationship with primary key values because many primary key values are associated with one industry value. One-to-many relationships produce nondense indexes, which have a slightly different form than dense indexes. In dense lists, only one primary key value occurs for each secondary key value, because the relationship is one-to-one. In nondense lists, many primary key values occur for one secondary key value.

The nondense inverted list for Industry is shown in Figure 10–10. To search for all oil industry stocks, for example, we read the oil index into memory, search it for "oil," and issue read instructions for records with the primary keys given in the occurrences table.

In this case, processing the inverted list results in the same number of accesses as would linked lists because in both cases each record containing an oil industry stock must be fetched.

The Query-Processing Efficiency of Inverted Lists

In analyzing the query-processing efficiency of linked lists, we examined this query:

```
SELECT *
FROM STOCKS
WHERE Industry = "Oil"
AND Earnings > 2.50
```

We found that a linked list for oil industry stocks provides a rather efficient approach when only a few oil stocks reside in the database. In this situation, using an inverted list would be comparable in processing time to a linked list. If there were many oil stocks, however, the index for the inverted list would become large, so that reading and searching it could become time-consuming. In that event, a linked list might do just as well as an inverted list.

If oil records constituted more than about 15 percent of the records in the file, sequential access would probably be superior to a search via secondary keys because movement of the access assembly would be minimized. Recall, however, that when we examined the query:

FIGURE 10–10
Nondense Inverted List for Industry
This inverted list is nondense: The relationship between Industry and primary key is many-to-one.

Values Table	Occurrences Table
Aerospace	1152
Auto	1175, 1323
Apparel	1767
Computer	1231,1245
Oil	1122, 1378, 1480

FIGURE 10–11
Primary Keys of Companies with Earnings > 2.00 or Dividends < 0.60
The only key on both lists (the intersection of the lists) is 1323 (General Motors), so it satisfies the query to list stocks with Earnings > 2.00 **and** Dividends < 0.60. The companies on the two lists combined (the union of the lists) satisfy the condition Earnings > 2.00 **or** Dividends < 0.60.

Earnings > 2.00	Dividends < 0.60
1323	1231
1122	1245
1378	1175
	1767
	1323
	1152
	1480

```
SELECT *
FROM STOCKS
WHERE Earnings > 2.00
AND Dividends < 0.60
```

we found processing by linked list to be only modestly efficient. If inversion tables are maintained for both Earnings and Dividends, inverted lists can provide much better efficiency in this case. The Earnings list can be searched for companies with Earnings > 2.00 and the Dividend list can be searched for companies with Dividends < 0.60. Primary keys for these companies are shown in Figure 10–11.

The companies listed in Figure 10–11 satisfy the query with an OR instead of AND. To find the companies satisfying both conditions (AND) of the query, find any primary key occurring in both lists. The only value common to both lists is 1323 (GM). Notice that we have not yet fetched *any* data records. The only stock record that will actually be fetched is that of General Motors. Thus, for complex queries that result in the selection of few qualified records, inverted lists may provide much greater processing efficiency than linked lists, because we can manipulate index tables instead of fetching record occurrences to follow pointer chains.

Binary Search Techniques for Inverted Lists

A technique called **binary searching** can be used to substantially lessen the time required to search the indexes of lengthy inverted lists. In this technique, the value sought is first compared to the value in the middle of the list. This indicates whether the value sought is in the top or the bottom half of the list. The value sought is then compared to the middle entry of the appropriate half. This indicates which fourth the value is in. Then the value is compared to the middle of that fourth, and so on until the desired value is found.

A pseudocode algorithm for a binary search is shown in Figure 10–12, and again in much greater detail in Figure 10–13. A binary search

FIGURE 10–12
A Pseudocode Algorithm for a Binary Search
This assumes data is sorted in ascending order.

```
1. Find middle element.
2. If middle element value is value sought, stop.
   2.1 Else, if middle element value is > value
       sought, then search top half of list.
   2.2 Else, search bottom half of list.
```

FIGURE 10–13
A Detailed Algorithm for Conducting a Binary Search

```
1. Let SEARCH-VALUE be the value sought.
2. Let LIST(I) be the list to be searched.
3. Let FIRST = 1 be the index number of the first
   element in the list.
4. Let LAST = N be the index number of the last
   element in the list.
5. Find middle element of the list using the index
   MIDDLE = (FIRST + LAST) / 2.
6. Until LIST(MIDDLE) = SEARCH-VALUE or all elements
   searched,
   6.1 if LIST(MIDDLE) > SEARCH-VALUE, value sought
       is in top half of list, so let FIRST = 1 and
       LAST = MIDDLE.
   6.2 Else, value sought is in bottom half of list,
       so let FIRST = MIDDLE and LAST = N.
   6.3 Let MIDDLE = (FIRST + LAST) / 2.
7. End.
```

FIGURE 10–14
Using a Binary Search to Find Texaco's Record
The first comparison, with GM, indicates that Texaco is in the bottom half of the list. The second comparison, with Lockheed, indicates that Texaco is in the bottom fourth. The third comparison finds Texaco.

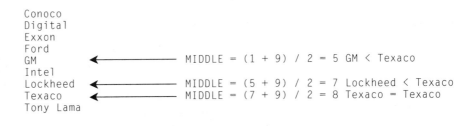

```
Conoco
Digital
Exxon
Ford
GM        ◄──────────── MIDDLE = (1 + 9) / 2 = 5 GM < Texaco
Intel
Lockheed  ◄──────────── MIDDLE = (5 + 9) / 2 = 7 Lockheed < Texaco
Texaco    ◄──────────── MIDDLE = (7 + 9) / 2 = 8 Texaco = Texaco
Tony Lama
```

for Texaco's entry using this algorithm is shown in Figure 10–14. The first step involves comparing Texaco to the entry in the middle of the list, GM. Texaco is (alphabetically) greater than GM, so we know that its entry is in the bottom half of the list. Next, Texaco is compared to Lockheed, the middle entry in the bottom half of the list. Lockheed is less than Texaco, and the next comparison finds Texaco's entry.

This small example involves three comparisons. A sequential search of the list would require seven comparisons. In general, if the list contains n elements, a sequential search takes an average of $n/2$ comparisons and a binary search takes an average of about $\log_2(n)$. For example, a sequential search of a list of 100,000 entries will take an average of 50,000 comparisons, but a binary search will take an average of less than 17 comparisons!

B-TREES

As the name implies, **B-trees** are a form of data structure based on hierarchies. Some authors claim that the B stands for Bayer, the originator; others say it stands for *balanced*. B-trees are **balanced** in the sense that all the terminal (bottom) nodes have the same path length to the root (top) node. Algorithms have been developed for searching and maintaining B-tree indexes efficiently, which have become quite popular for representing both primary and secondary indexes. B-trees provide both sequential and indexed access and are quite flexible.

The Form of B-Tree Indexes

The **height** of a B-tree is the number of levels in the hierarchy. In a simple two-level hierarchy, the B-tree has a height of 2. If there are four levels, the height is 4.

Three kinds of data occur in the nonterminal nodes of a B-tree: (1) pointers to indexes at the next lower level of the tree, (2) values for the data item being indexed, and (3) pointers to record occurrences of the value in (2). Because no indexes occur below terminal nodes, they have only a data value and a pointer to the record where that value is stored.

Values for the indexed data item are in sorted order *within* a node. Node occurrences are perhaps best explained by example. A B-tree for alphabetically indexing stock symbols in Byer's file is shown in Figure 10–15. This is just one possible form of a B-tree for this data. A different form is discussed shortly.

In Figure 10–15, the level 0 index contains the symbols F (for Ford) and TONY (for Tony Lama). Here, the first digit of the index pointer indicates the level in the hierarchy, and the second is a sequence number. The primary key value 1175 to the right of Ford means that the symbol F occurs in the record with primary key 1175 (Ford's record). The index pointer between F and TONY means that symbols alphabetically following F are in index 12. TONY is found in the record with primary key 1767. The fact that TONY is the last symbol in the level 0 index indicates that symbols following TONY are found in the index to the right of TONY, index 13.

FIGURE 10–15   A B-Tree of Order 2 and Height 2 for Stock Symbol
This B-tree has at most three stock symbols at each leaf because it is of order 2. It is of height 2 because it has two levels. To find the pointer to (primary key of) Intel's (INTL) record, first the level 0 index is searched. INTL is not in the level 0 index, so the search continues to level 1. Since INTL is less than TONY, the index preceding TONY is fetched (12) and searched sequentially until INTL is found. A fetch is then issued for the record occurrence with primary key 1231 to get Intel's data.

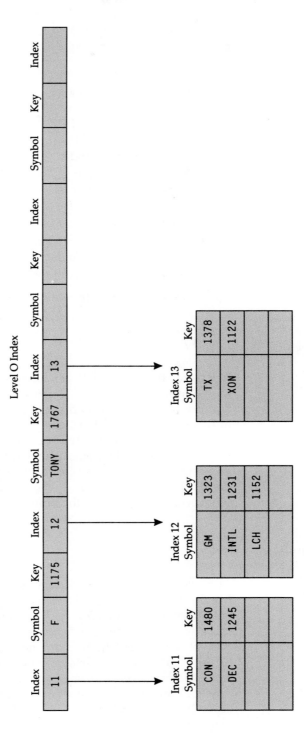

Finding Unique Values in a B-Tree

To illustrate how a specific (unique) record occurrence is located in a B-tree, assume a query requesting Intel's data with this form:

```
SELECT *
FROM STOCKS
WHERE Symbol = "INTL"
```

The primary key of Intel's record can be found by following the steps below.

1. Fetch the level 0 index.
2. Search the index until a symbol greater than INTL occurs. This happens when INTL is compared to TONY, because INTL is greater than F but less than TONY.
3. Fetch index 12.
4. This is a terminal node, so search it sequentially until INTL is found. (If it is not found, then it does not exist in the database.)
5. Fetch the record with primary key 1231.

This search takes only three disk accesses, so it is rather efficient.

Accessing B-Trees in Sequential Order

The B-tree in Figure 10–15 can also be used to fetch records in sequence by the indexed data item. To fetch records in sequence, we start at the leftmost terminal node and sequentially fetch the records for that node. In this example, we fetch Conoco's record (CON) first, then DEC's. Next, we move to the parent index of the leftmost terminal node, which in the example is the level 0 node. We fetch the record for Ford (F), then follow the index pointer to the right of Ford to index 12 and fetch its records sequentially (GM, INTEL, and LCH). Finally, we return to the level 0 index, get TONY's record, follow the pointer to index 13, and fetch TX and XON.

The Order of a B-Tree

Another B-tree for the stock symbol is given in Figure 10–16. This B-tree has three levels and thus has a height of 3. Notice that there is space for only two symbols at each node, whereas the tree in Figure 10–15 has space for three. The root node (level 0 index) of Figure 10–16 has one symbol value, one key, and two index (child) pointers. The root node of Figure 10–15 contains two symbol values, the same number of keys, and three indexes. These properties of B-trees can be generalized into a concept known as the **order** of the tree. The B-tree in Figure 10–15 is of order 2 and that of Figure 10–16 is of order 1. B-tree creation and maintenance algorithms ensure that B-trees of order n have the following general properties:

FIGURE 10–16   A B-Tree of Order 1 and Height 3 for Stock Symbol
Since the B-tree is of order 1, there are at most two symbol entries at each level other than the root. The tree has three levels, so its height is 3. A search for INTL is satisfied immediately because INTL is in the level 0 index. To find XON, the pointer to index 12 to the right of INTL is followed, then the pointer to index 24 is followed. Index 24 is a terminal node, so it is searched sequentially to find XON.

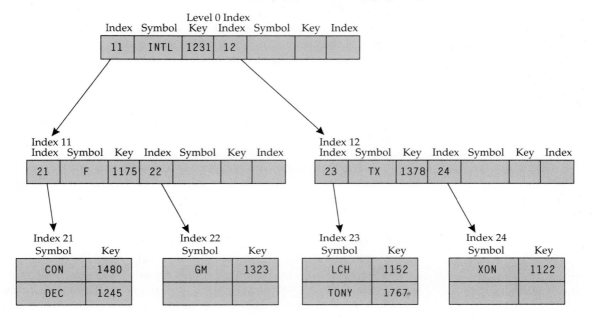

1. Each path from the root node to a terminal node (leaf) has the same length.
2. The root node can have from 1 to $2n$ data values and from 2 to $2n + 1$ children (the number of children is the number of data values plus 1).
3. Nonroot nodes can have from n to $2n$ data values.
4. Nonroot nodes other than terminal nodes can have from $n + 1$ to $2n + 1$ children (the number of data values plus 1).

When these properties are satisfied, it has been shown that processing with B-trees is quite efficient.

B-Trees and the Virtual Storage Access Method (VSAM)

Examination of B-tree indexes in Figures 10–15 and 10–16 suggests that the indexed data value might just as well be the primary key of the record as a secondary key. If the keys are then storage addresses instead of primary keys, the B-tree may be used to support a type of primary access method (other primary access methods are discussed in Appendix A). IBM has developed a powerful access method, the **Virtual Storage Access Method (VSAM),** based on this approach. Even though

VSAM is a primary access method, it is discussed here because it is based on B-trees and is a good illustration of how B-trees can provide access based on either primary or secondary keys.

VSAM is designed for direct access devices, but unlike ISAM it is not limited solely to disks and is said to be "hardware-independent." Therefore, VSAM terminology refers not to tracks and cylinders but to the more general **control interval** and **control area.** A control interval corresponds roughly to a block on disk storage and is a portion of the storage medium containing a collection of records. A control area consists of a collection of control intervals.

When a VSAM file is created, records are stored in sequential order by primary key. Initially, each control interval is only half full, providing space for new records. In addition, vacant control intervals and areas are reserved for database growth. This vacant space, **distributed free space,** is spread throughout the storage medium. The existence of distributed free space simplifies and speeds up the record insertion process because in most cases records do not have to be rearranged or stored in overflow areas when insertions are made.

If insertions have filled a control interval, then another insertion results in an overflow. Instead of having the usual overflow area, VSAM handles this by moving half of the records from the full interval to an empty interval. This is called a **control interval split.** Pointer chains are established to maintain sequential record order. If an entire control area would overflow, a **control area split** is performed. This approach reduces the need to reorganize the file, as must be done with ISAM. After many insertions, however, it may be necessary to reorganize VSAM files to obtain satisfactory performance.

As mentioned previously, a form of B-tree index is maintained to provide random access to records in VSAM files. VSAM actually has two types of indexes. The **sequence set** is an index that corresponds to the track index of an ISAM file. It contains an entry for each control interval, giving the highest key of the records stored in the interval. This is illustrated in Figure 10–17.

B-tree indexes constitute the **index set,** which is analogous to cylinder indexes in ISAM. The index set may be up to three levels (B-trees with a height of 3). A one-level index for primary keys in Byer's stock file is shown in Figure 10–17, and a two-level index is given in Figure 10–18. For purposes of illustration, only one record has been stored in each control interval. The indexes are searched as described above.

REPRESENTING RELATIONSHIPS BETWEEN RECORDS

As discussed in the first chapter, data relatability is one of the main goals of database management systems. Indeed, the principal distinguishing feature of the database approach is its ability to represent relationships *between* records. Conventional (nondatabase) systems treat files as independent, unrelated entities. In marked contrast, database systems emphasize interrecord relationships.

FIGURE 10–17   One-Level VSAM Indexes for Byer's Stock Data
Record occurrences are stored in control intervals. A group of control intervals (here four intervals) constitutes a control area. Each control area has a table in the sequence set that indicates the highest key value in
each control interval of that control area. The pointers in the index set point to tables in the sequence set.

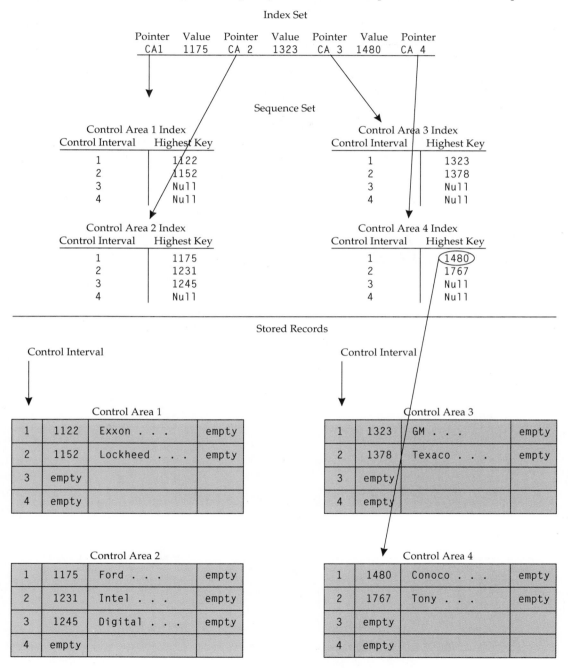

FIGURE 10–18   A Two-Level VSAM Index for Byer's Stock Data
Level 0 index pointers indicate to fetch the level 1 index. Level 1 pointers indicate which
sequence set to fetch.

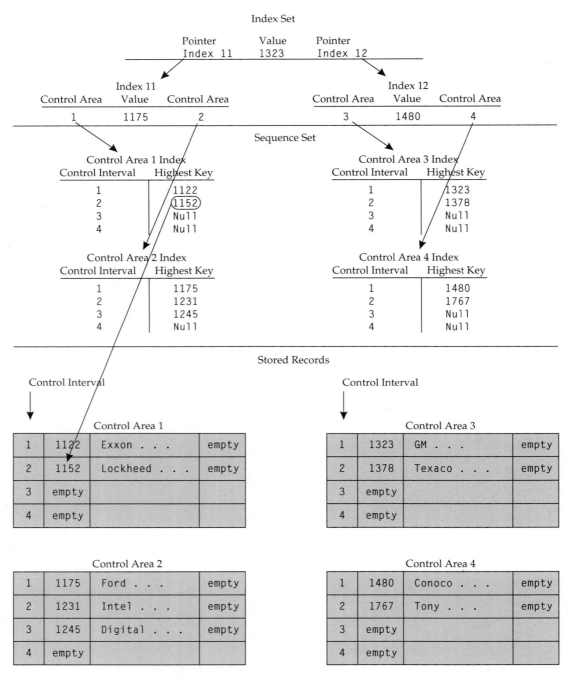

This emphasis is perhaps most vividly evident with data structure diagrams (associated with the CODASYL approach), where arrows reflect interrecord associations. Nevertheless, such relationships are equally important in relational systems. In relational systems, however, interrecord relationships are reflected at the logical (user) level by the data itself via attributes in different relations sharing a common domain. At the physical level, pointers may be used to represent such relationships, but the user does not have to be aware of this. Pointers are traversed and maintained automatically by the system without user intervention.

Because data structure diagrams make interrecord associations more explicit, the representation of these relationships is discussed in this chapter. Linked lists, inverted lists, and B-trees can all be used to support interrecord relationships.

This discussion is highly simplified. We do not consider representing relationships with B-trees, and none of the algorithms necessary to maintain relationships have been presented. One must not conclude that maintaining such information in database systems is a simple matter; it is not. References at the end of the chapter present a good discussion of the relevant algorithms.

Inverted Lists and Interrecord Relationships

To illustrate the inverted list representation of data structure diagrams, suppose that Byer wants to save the daily closing price for stocks in his database and to maintain a history of quarterly earnings and dividends. He has developed the data structure diagram in Figure 10–19 to represent this situation.

Identifying information for each company is maintained in a Company Record. The information on daily closing prices is maintained in a Daily Closing Price Record, and dividends and earnings are maintained in a Dividends and Earnings Record. There is a one-to-many relationship between Company Records and Price Records, as there is between Company Records and Dividends and Earnings Records.

FIGURE 10–19
Data Structure Diagram for Daily Closing Prices and Dividend and Earnings History

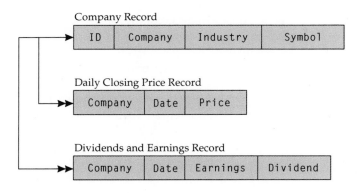

FIGURE 10–20
Company and Closing Price Data for Conoco and Exxon
To facilitate the explanation, each Daily Closing Price Record occurrence has been given a Record Index.

```
Company Record Occurrences
ID          Company      Industry        Symbol
1480        Conoco       Oil             CON
1122        Exxon        Oil             XON

     Daily Closing Price Record Occurrences
Company      Date         Price        Record Index

Conoco       8/20/88      150.000          01
Conoco       8/21/88      150.500          02
Exxon        8/20/88      112.000          03
Exxon        8/21/88      113.000          04
```

FIGURE 10–21
Inverted List Representing Relationships between Company Records and Price Records

```
Owner               Member Record
Record              (Daily Closing Price)
Conoco                   01, 02
Exxon                    03, 04
```

It is a simple matter to use inverted lists to maintain information on such relationships. Suppose, for example, that we have the data on Company Records for Conoco and Exxon and their daily closing prices as shown in Figure 10–20. Here, both Conoco and Exxon are associated with two Price Records each, as shown by the common values in the Company attribute for each record. For simplicity, Daily Closing Price Records have been given an index, as might be done in an ISAM approach. These indexes are used to represent the relationship between Company Records and Daily Closing Price Records.

The inverted list in Figure 10–21 can be used to represent these relationships. Here, we have a table with the company (Owner Record) in the first (leftmost) column and the indexes to its price records (Member Record) in the second column. It is a simple matter to search the Company column to find a particular stock and then use the indexes in the Price Record column to fetch its price records. A similar approach can be taken to represent the Dividends and Earnings data.

Linked Lists and Interrecord Relationships

The interrecord relationships in Figures 10–20 and 10–21 can also be represented with linked lists or chains. This is perhaps the most common way of handling such relationships in CODASYL implementations. This may be done by adding a field to Company Records that contains a pointer to the first Daily Closing Price Record owned by that company (see Figure 10–22). Conoco's Company Record, for example, has a pointer to record 01 in the Price Record file. Similarly, the Price Record

The User's View

Users want rapid response times for queries. They dislike waiting for a computer system to provide data. Waiting can be a costly waste of valuable personnel time.

Providing rapid, flexible access to data is a complex problem depending on several factors. Among these are the users' queries, the frequency with which these queries arise, and the retrieval (secondary) keys employed.

Efficient physical design depends heavily on these factors, which should be isolated during information requirements. Users must be encouraged to participate fully in requirements analysis to ensure that the physical implementation efficiently supports their needs. ■

---

file has a pointer field (Next Record) to the next record in the list, record 02. Record 02 is the end of the list and its pointer points back to Conoco's Company Record by using company ID, which is presumed to be key of Company Records. Records in the two files can be distinguished in this case by the fact that Company Records have four-digit indexes, while Price Records have two-digit indexes. A list is also maintained for Exxon's Price Records.

CHAPTER SUMMARY

Two of the primary distinguishing features of the database approach are the representation of secondary keys and relationships between records. Linked lists, inverted lists, and B-trees provide methods for satisfying these requirements.

FIGURE 10–22 **Linked List Representing Relationships between Conoco's Data**
The pointer from Conoco's Company Record points to its first Price Record, which points to the second Price Record, which points back to the Company Record.

Company Record Occurrences

ID	Company	Industry	Symbol	First Price Record
1480	Conoco	Oil	CON	01
1122	Exxon	Oil	XON	03

First member

Daily Closing Price Record Occurrences

Owner pointer

Company	Date	Price	Record Index	Next Record
Conoco	8/20/88	150.00	01	02
Conoco	8/21/88	150.00	02	1480
Exxon	8/20/88	112.00	03	04
Exxon	8/21/88	113.00	04	1122

METROPOLITAN NATIONAL BANK

You should now consider the types of data structures that would be best suited to support different aspects of the model you have developed thus far. Prepare a report comparing the different approaches to representing secondary keys and discuss the advantages and disadvantages of each. Also, suggest how relationships between records in your model can be supported. You may want to refer to Appendix A to review information concerning storage devices. ■

Linked lists consist of pointer chains embedded in the stored records themselves. Rings are a form of linked list in which the last record in a chain points back to the first. This arrangement permits entering the list and processing at any record. Multilists occur when more than one list is defined over the same file, as when several different items are used as secondary keys. Two-way linked lists or bidirectional chains have pointers in both forward (next) and backward (prior) directions.

Inverted lists are pointers stored in index tables independent of the stored records. Because the data in indexes can be manipulated to satisfy a query, inverted lists often provide more efficient query processing than linked lists.

B-trees are a type of hierarchical data structure similar to ISAM indexes. Nonterminal nodes of a B-tree index have sets of data values, pointers to records containing those data values, and pointers to indexes for values less than and greater than each value in the node. Terminal nodes have data values and pointers only.

These methods may be used to provide efficient, flexible access to stored data records to satisfy user queries quickly.

Questions and Exercises

1. Define the following terms:
   a. linked list
   b. ring
   c. two-way linked list
   d. forward pointer
   e. backward pointer
   f. multilist
   g. inverted list
   h. B-tree
   i. height of a B-tree

2. What is the difference between dense and nondense lists?

3. Prepare a linked list (descending order) for the Earnings data in Figure 10–1.

4. Verify that all the records in the list in Question 3 must be accessed to satisfy the following SQL query:

```
SELECT *
FROM STOCKS
WHERE Earnings < 2.00
```

5. Prepare a two-way list for the Earnings data in Figure 10–1.

6. Verify that the query in Question 4 is more efficiently processed with backward pointers.

7. Prepare a linked list (descending order) for the Dividends data in Figure 10–1.

8. How many records must be accessed if the Dividends chain in Question 7 is used to process the SQL query:

```
SELECT *
FROM STOCKS
WHERE Earnings > 2.00
AND Dividends < 0.60
```

9. Prepare a two-way linked list for the Price data in Figure 10–1.

10. Convert the linked lists for Earnings (Question 3), Dividends (Question 7), and Prices (Question 9) to rings.

11. Prepare inverted lists (ascending order) for Earnings and Dividends in Figure 10–11 and verify the results.

12. Prepare an inverted list (ascending order) for the Price data in Figure 10–1.

13. If the inverted lists in Questions 11 and 12 are used, how many data records must be accessed to satisfy the query:

```
SELECT *
FROM STOCKS
WHERE Earnings > 1.50
AND Price < 150.00
```

14. How many data records must be accessed if the query in Question 13 is an OR rather than an AND?

15. Prepare an ascending order B-tree for the Earnings data in Figure 10–1.

16. Describe, step by step, what a database management system would do in using the B-tree in Question 15 to satisfy the SQL query:

```
SELECT Company, Earnings
FROM STOCKS
ORDER BY Earnings ASC.
```

17. Prepare an ascending order B-tree for the Dividend data in Figure 10–1.

18. How many data records would be accessed if the B-tree in Questions 15 and 17 were used to process the SQL query:

```
SELECT *
FROM STOCKS
WHERE Earnings > 1.00
AND Dividends < 0.50
```

19. Define the following terms related to VSAM:
    a. control interval
    b. control area
    c. control interval split
    d. control area split

       e. distributed free space

       f. sequence set

       g. index set

20. Show how linked lists could be used to represent the relationship between Company Records and Dividends and Earnings Records in Figure 10–19 (use the Earnings and Dividend data in Figure 10–1).

21. Show how inverted lists could be used to answer Question 20.

For Further Reading

Korfhage, Robert R., and Norman E. Gibbs. *Principles of Data Structures and Algorithms with PASCAL.* Dubuque, Iowa: Wm. C. Brown, 1987. A thorough treatment of data structures with creation and maintenance algorithms in PASCAL.

Teorey, Toby J., and James P. Fry. *Design of Database Structures.* Englewood Cliffs, N.J.: Prentice-Hall, 1982. Covers both physical and logical design considerations.

Wiederhold, Gio. *Database Design.* 2nd ed. New York: McGraw-Hill, 1983. A readable and comprehensive discussion of both storage devices and data structures, including mathematical formulas for performance analysis.

TRANSACTION-BASED ISSUES IN DATABASE MANAGEMENT

Some of the more technical aspects of database management are examined in this chapter. We present material covering construction and management of data repositories, approaches to implementing security, methods for recovering from catastrophic events and minor errors, and means for managing concurrent access to database records in a database system.

DATA REPOSITORIES

Throughout this text, we have made reference to the data dictionary component of a database system. In fact, the term *data dictionary* is becoming dated. Because of the increasing complexity of this component and the programs required to manage it, we refer to it here using the more current term: the **data repository system.** This term includes the repository and all software that makes it available to users in the organization.

In some cases, the data repository system is a separate component of the database management system. The repository is a separate file, and separate database utility programs exist to maintain the data repository. Such is frequently the case in older database management systems, and the repository will be called the *data dictionary* in the documentation for these systems. In current approaches to database design, computer assisted software engineering (CASE) tools support development of repositories directly from the data models of the system. Also, newer, relational approaches automatically create, update, and maintain tables that provide the data repository capabilities that are discussed below. The data repository does not exist separately from the database, and there are no special utilities for maintaining this information in these relational environments.

The data repository system provides different types of support to different persons in the organization (see Figure 11–1). For management, the data repository system represents a rigorous model of the

FIGURE 11–1   Data Repositories Play Many Roles in an Organization

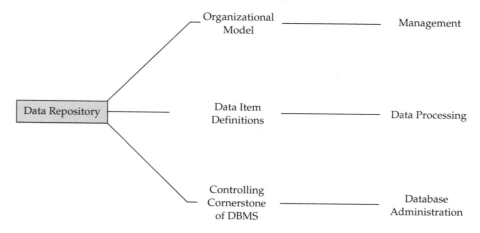

information requirements of the organization. When connected to a graphic data model, as in many CASE tools, the repository provides a comprehensive documentation component of the organization's information processing activities. As such, many writers suggest that the data repository should be developed even before a database management system has been selected (or built). (CASE tools ensure this design activity.)

For data processing professionals, the data repository contains the approved organizational definition for data items. The data repository is also a source of information for developing external schemas for applications. In the more advanced CASE tools, the data repository system supports automatic generation of data item descriptions and processing code needed by applications programs. At least one company claims that their CASE tool can generate 80 percent of the code required for business processing from the information stored in its graphic data model and associated data repository.

For the database manager, the data repository system is the central controlling mechanism—the cornerstone of all operations—in the database system. By forcing all processing to conform to the specifications stored in the data repository, the database manager ensures the database remains in a consistent state.

Components of the Data Repository System

The data repository system consists of two major components. The **data repository** is a depository of fundamental data about the database. The **data repository control program** is the software used to maintain the data repository. Each is discussed briefly below.

The Data Repository. The data repository is a database about the database. The contents of a data repository entry from the TOTAL database management system (by Cincom Systems) is shown in Figure 11–2. Minimally, the data repository is a uniform, formal mechanism that contains the names of all data elements in the system and data

FIGURE 11–2
Possible Data Item Descriptions in a TOTAL Database Management System Data Repository
(TOTAL is a product of Cincom Systems International.)

```
—name
—description
—associated TOTAL record code (if any)
—date created
—security level
—data type
—length
—position in record or TOTAL segment
—position of decimal point
—name of TOTAL file in which element can be found
—file type (TOTAL or non-TOTAL)
—number of repetitions of element
—password
—aliases
```

navigation information. The data repository should also contain information about system-related data items, such as important system parameters (number and size of buffers, latest revision data, number of users). In many cases, the data repository contains much more.

The data repository may contain information regarding the source of the data for each entity in the database. Data that maps the usage of each data item is sometimes also maintained; for example, the data repository may list where a data item occurs as an input, as a calculation, or as a report item.

Most data repositories maintain validation information regarding acceptable ranges for a valid occurrence of the data item. The units of measurement, as well as any scaling value needed to transform the data for other purposes, are stored in the data repository. The data repository also contains the dimensions of the data item. A data item named *net income*, for example, may be maintained "quarterly." The data repository reflects such conventions.

Some repositories are capable of distinguishing between "current," "proposed," and "no-longer-used" data items. These data repositories should also maintain the dates of a data item's change of status.

Security attributes can also be maintained in the data repository. As discussed in Chapter 4, one level of security is provided at the external schema level—items that do not appear in a particular external schema are not available to the user of that schema. Additional security mechanisms can be implemented in the data repository to control ad hoc retrievals.

The Data Repository Control Program. The data repository control program is a set of specialized routines for maintaining the data repository. These routines may be embedded within the database system and hence may not always exist as a separate program. When this occurs, the operations we now discuss are usually restricted to a specific class of user. For practical purposes, these operations can be considered a separate subsystem of the database system.

In a CASE environment, the control routines are embedded in the CASE tool. Thus, all users of the CASE tool control the maintenance of the repository. This access does not cause problems because these CASE tools typically generate the code for the system. Consequently, changes in the repository are automatically reflected in the system implementation.

The data repository control program is primarily concerned with maintaining the data repository. This program is used to add, delete, or modify data repository entries. Authorization to use the data repository control program must be restricted to the highest-level managers of the database system.

The data repository control program can also be used to generate cross-reference information from the data repository. This program can also provide supplemental database system documentation by formatting information in the data repository into a predefined report format. One of the more sophisticated uses of a control program, for example, is to generate a report that documents the extent to which modifications to the data repository impact the database system. If the data repository contains detailed information regarding data element usage, this report can be constructed by collecting all of the information for a given data element in the repository.

Developing a Data Repository

The process of developing a data repository revolves around the development of the two components, the data repository and the data repository control program. The development of the data repository control program is a standard problem of software design and implementation. As such, we do not discuss it in detail. If the database system is being purchased, this component is typically part of the purchase.

On the other hand, the data repository is unique to the database system. We discuss the development of this component in some detail, using our familiar information-requirements–logical design–physical design model to guide the discussion. Additionally, all of the phases described in this discussion are automatically embedded in the design process when CASE tools are used. The data repository development process is summarized in Table 11–1.

The Data Repository during the Information-Requirements Phase. During the information-requirements phase, the data repository design is primarily concerned with establishing standards to be used in conjunction with the data repository. The format of the data repository is established at this time. Standard abbreviations such as "$000" for "thousands of dollars," "ST" for "street," and "#" for "pounds" are determined at this stage.

Coding conventions are also established during this phase. Time values are standardized as either twelve-hour or twenty-four–hour (military) time. Dates are standardized as either "month/day/year," "year/month/day," or some other format. Codes for data items such as "sex" are established as either "M/F" or a numeric code.

As major modules in the database system—such as financial, marketing, and production applications—are identified, a convention is

TABLE 11–1   Data Repository Tasks and Database Design

Database Design Phase	Data Repository Task
Information requirements	Establish format Standardize abbreviations Standardize codes Identify base elements Identify synonyms
Logical design	Identify and reduce redundancy Identify logical groups Identify relationships
Physical design	Refine entries Add references to storage devices

developed for identifying data elements as being components of these applications. There will undoubtedly be cases where the same data item is used in different applications. A major task at this stage is to find these **synonyms,** determine their sources, and standardize their names.

Because a major feature of database systems is that data elements are shared, we must distinguish between data elements that are fundamental to a particular module ("owned" by a module) and data elements that are not. **Base data elements** are fundamental to a module; a data element such as production volume, for example, is probably a base data element to the production module, although it may be needed for calculations in a financial module.

As an example of coding base data elements, all data items used in the financial reporting application's balance sheet report could be coded as "FIN-RPT-BS" (Financial Report: Balance Sheet). Items used as inputs to this report could be coded "FIN-INP-BS" (Financial Input: Balance Sheet). A tentative format for data elements can be established at this stage also.

All data elements should be defined at this stage. A definition *must not* describe how a data element *should be used,* only what that data element represents. The data element date of birth, for example, should not be defined as "used to verify patient's identity." The proper definition is "defines the date of birth of a patient."

The Data Repository during the Logical Design Phase.   At the logical design phase, the data repository is ready for final organizational details. The fact that the organization's data requirements have been collected into a single place makes organizing the data much easier, though still difficult.

First, a pass is made through the data repository in an attempt to locate any unwanted redundancy. The database designers should question any data items that appear to be redundant. The definitions of each data item can now be reviewed as another check for redundancy; determining that "client code" and "project code" are synonyms may be difficult from just the names, but if the two have the same definition, the redundancy can be identified.

Logical relationships are added to the data repository at this stage. Logical groupings of data items into records or files may now be accomplished. Data items that appear on the same reports or input forms may be identified and aggregated at this time.

The Data Repository during the Physical Design Phase.   During physical design of database system development, the final entries can be made into the data repository. Some data repositories maintain information regarding the storage medium on which the data item resides. Also maintained may be access time requirements for different classes of users.

The physical design of the data repository is also determined at this time. In very small systems, it may be feasible to keep the data repository in main memory. In most systems, however, the data repository must be carefully implemented using appropriate data structures to ensure efficient access.

Types of Data Repository Systems

The extent to which a data repository system controls access to the database varies from system to system. We briefly discuss the three main categories of data repository systems.

Passive Data Repository Systems. Data repository systems that have no control over database system access are called **passive data repository systems.** They are also known as **free-standing repositories.** Passive systems are completely decoupled from the database system of the organization (see Figure 11–3). Such independence can be either an advantage or a disadvantage. On the positive side, a passive data repository system provides all of the documentation advantages of any data repository system and does not have to be reconstructed if the organization decides to change database systems. On the negative side, a passive system does nothing to impose the advantages of standardization inherent in a data repository system on the database system.

Passive systems are less complicated to construct and maintain. As a result, they are less expensive. This characteristic makes them attractive to organizations that wish to begin organizing their data before the actual selection or implementation of a database system.

Active Data Repository Systems. A data repository system that controls access to the database system is an **active data repository system.** These systems are also known as **integrated repository systems.** Active systems are an integral part of the database system, as indicated in Figure 11–4. Repositories developed by CASE tools are almost always integrated repositories. All processes that access the database must interact with the active data repository system. Applications programs get data item descriptions from the data repository system. Schemas are generated and mapped through the data repository system. Even system software accessing the database draws on the data repository system in an active data repository system environment.

The active data repository system enforces the advantages of the rigor and formalism of the database system approach through this extensive control. By controlling the processes accessing the data, the system controls the data.

FIGURE 11–3
A Passive Data Repository System Has No Effect on Database Operations

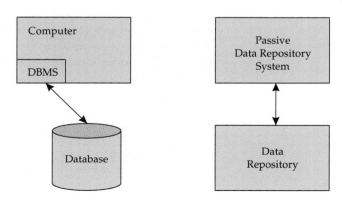

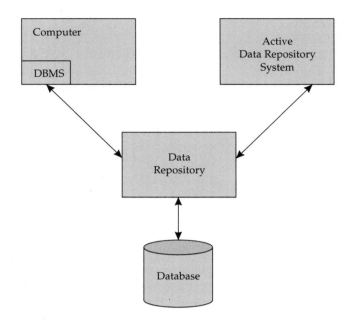

Potentially Active Data Repository Systems. A third category of data repository systems is the **potentially active data repository system.** A potentially active data repository system is a passive system that is capable of performing active control of database accesses (Figure 11–5). Potentially active data repositories are also called **partially integrated repositories.** Administrative routines and processes must be developed to enforce active control in this type of system. A policy (and supporting software) requiring applications programs to be validated using the current data repository is an example of supplemental administrative routines.

Relational Data Repositories

In hierarchical and CODASYL systems, data repositories (data dictionaries) were originally maintained as separate components of the database management system. In some cases, separate data repository management systems were developed for creating and updating the contents of the data repository. Only the database administrator would have access to this software. Usually, this software had a unique set of commands that only the database administrator knew. With the advent of relational systems, however, the data repository component changed conceptually.

A fundamental concept in the relational approach is that *all* of the system has relational characteristics. This concept implies that the data that occurs in a relational database management system data repository should also be maintained using relational database management techniques. In other words, the data repository data is maintained in tables

FIGURE 11–5
A Potentially Active Data Repository System Can Be Made to Control Database Operations

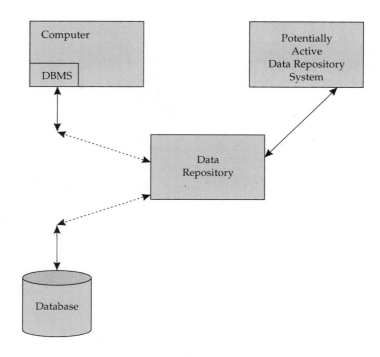

and is accessed using relational data manipulation (relational algebra, relational calculus, or SQL). There is no special program for data repository maintenance. In fact, in most relational systems today the data repository information is constructed automatically by the database management system. The database administrator does not need to know any special commands to manipulate the data repository. The data repository data, however, is accessible only by the database administrator.

We will consider the data repository information maintained by the Oracle database management system as a typical example of a relational data repository. Because Oracle uses SQL as a data manipulation language, the data repository information can be accessed by users and the database administrator using SQL. Some of the information can only be accessed by the database administrator.

Oracle maintains a number of tables that contain data repository information. The CATALOG table contains attributes for each table name, the table creator, the table type, and a table identifier. The COL table maintains data about the columns in the tables in the database. The attributes of COL include the table name, column number, column name, column type, column width, column scale, and whether null values are allowed. A table named VIEWS contains data about views that have been created, and a table named INDEXES contains information about indexes that have been defined in the database. The SYSTABAUTH table indicates access authority granted by or to users. The STORAGE table contains information about the storage used by a table. All of these tables are available to users and can be accessed in read-only mode.

The database administrator has access to two additional tables. SYSSTORAGE contains information that is characteristic of the internal schema and describes the internal storage of tables. SYSUSERAUTH contains user passwords and general access authorizations for users.

DATABASE SECURITY

Database security is so critical that any oversight on the part of the database administrator could lead to immediate failure of the database system, possibly even total and irreversible destruction. The data repository is capable of controlling almost every aspect of data access in the database system. Still, in many circumstances, security measures in addition to those available through the data repository are warranted.

The concept of security relates not only to a user's ability to access particular data items, but also to any person's ability to gain access to the physical database system facilities. Each of these is an important aspect of database administration. Examples of each type are given in Figure 11–6.

Auditing Database Systems

Controlled access is a fundamental concept that underlies the notion of security. Administrative controls appear in many forms. Organizational controls are implemented through organizational structure and the delegation of authority. Operational controls are defined in operational policies and procedures. **Auditing** is a process of examining and assessing the reliability and integrity of information-providing systems. When a database system is "under control," one expects the information provided to be reliable.

The techniques for auditing database systems that have been developed by the accounting profession provide the database administrator with a set of guidelines for maintaining control over the database environment.

All appropriate control mechanisms relevant to any other information-providing system are relevant to database systems. However, the database environment contains unique aspects that require additional

FIGURE 11–6
Security in an Information Management System

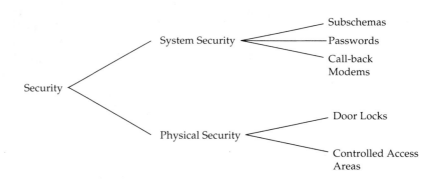

consideration. The American Institute of Certified Public Accountants (AICPA) (1982) has identified three broad areas in database systems where controls are very important.

A database system provides extensive update and access capabilities that may not be available in a nondatabase environment. **Update and access control** is one area of specialization identified by the AICPA. The primary focus of update and access control is retrieval, update, and concurrent access functions. Database systems should allow users to access and modify only those data items that they are authorized to access and modify. Users should be protected from the problems of concurrent access described below. A database system that provides these capabilities meets the general requirement of having sufficient update and access controls.

An inherent characteristic of database systems is that data, software, and hardware are shared. A second area of control identified by the AICPA is **coordination of activity control.** There is a need to ensure that shared resources are properly coordinated. Database systems should enforce varying levels of control over data items. Rules governing shared data should reflect the concerns of the user for whom the shared data item is most critical. Descriptions of shared data items must be maintained in a manner that ensures consistent interpretation by all users of the data item. Finally, shared data may be used at different times by different users. The database system should enhance the coordination of shared data usage to the extent that all users operate with consistent data during a given operating period. A database system that meets these criteria is considered to have sufficient coordination of activity control.

Another characteristic of database systems is that the resources of the database system may be concentrated in one (or a few) location(s). Hence, **concentration of resources control** is also necessary. One aspect of this area of control is that the physical database resources must be made secure. A second aspect is that the physical database structures (that is, indexes) must also be secure. There should be no possibility of an unauthorized modification of these structures. A third concern is that many functions in the organization depend on the database system functioning properly. Adequate back-up and recovery procedures address this concern.

Database systems may compromise a fundamental tenet of accounting control: separation of duties. An integrated database system has the capability to support a wide range of processing tasks, and, consequently, combining these tasks into one large task is an attractive idea. However, segregation of operations is a fundamental way of maintaining control. Shipping and billing procedures, for example, could be accomplished by the same department in an integrated database environment, but this would be an unwise combination of duties. An unscrupulous employee might ship a product to a friend and not bill the friend for the product (or falsify the billing record).

There are a number of ways that duties may be separated in a database environment. Source documents should originate and be authorized outside of the database administrative function. Individual functional areas supplying data to the database system should be held responsible for the accuracy of the data. The database administration function should not be allowed to authorize transactions that manipulate assets outside of the data processing environment.

The database system relies on just a few key personnel in some cases. The database administration function should have adequate procedures to deal with the risks of turnover, human error, and malicious behavior, as discussed in this chapter. A database system that meets these criteria is considered to have adequate concentration of resources control.

System Security

Just as an organization controls access to its cash, so too must it prevent unauthorized access to its data. Imagine how tempting it would be for someone to access a bank's database system and erase the outstanding balance amount on a large loan. Or consider the implications of unauthorized access to a national government's defense database systems.

Access to data items in a database system is typically controlled through the subschemas a user is allowed to use. Data items can be hidden from a user's view by omitting them from a subschema definition (see Chapters 3, 4, and 9), but this should be considered only a first step toward database system security. Measures should be incorporated that deter any unauthorized access to the database system.

Password changes should be required periodically and automatically by the database system. Stories abound of persons gaining illegal access to database systems by guessing or stealing the password of other users. In these cases, the password has usually been the name of a spouse or child, or perhaps a favorite recreation of the authorized user. Some organizations have been so lax in their attitude toward database system security that they have no passwords at all. This is an obviously unacceptable situation in all but the most trivial database system environments.

The Access Matrix Approach.   One method used to enforce security in database systems is an access matrix. An **access matrix** provides a concise way of representing the entities in the database and the persons (or applications) using the database. The database entities are frequently called **objects** in an access matrix, and persons (or applications) accessing the database are called **subjects.**

Table 11–2 shows an example of an access matrix for a database system. Subjects represent database users. Objects correspond to database items. The table entries indicate the privileges a particular subject has when accessing a particular object; the warehouse supervisor, for example, may update inventory levels in the database but has no access to salary information. (Implementation of an access matrix is particularly straightforward in a relational database system.) This basic approach may be extended to handle more complex situations. A logical database, a record, or a field in a record can be listed as an object.

TABLE 11–2   An Access Matrix for Controlling Access to Data

| | Objects | | | | |
| | Inventory | | Employee | | |
Subjects	Item Name	Stock Level	Name	Title	Salary
Vice President	READ	READ	ALL	ALL	ALL
Personnel	NONE	NONE	ALL	ALL	ALL
Warehouse Supervisor	ALL	ALL	READ	READ	NONE

Table 11–3   An Access Matrix with an Embedded Access Rule

| | Objects | | | | |
| | Inventory | | Employee | | |
Subjects	Item Name	Stock Level	Name	Title	Salary
Vice President	READ	READ	ALL	ALL	ALL
Personnel	NONE	NONE	ALL	ALL	ALL
Warehouse Supervisor	ALL	ALL	READ	READ	READ where Title = "clerk"

TABLE 11–4a   Equivalent Subject Profile for the Access Matrix in Table 11–2

Vice President	Inventory Record: READ; Employee Record: ALL
Personnel	Employee Record: ALL
Warehouse Supervisor	Inventory Record: ALL; Employee. Name, Employee.Title: READ

A second extension of the access matrix is the embedding of access rules within the matrix, as in Table 11–3. This access matrix contains a rule specifying the condition on which salary information is available to the warehouse supervisor. This rule indicates that the warehouse supervisor may access salary information only for warehouse clerks.

Profile Approaches.   One drawback to the access matrix approach is that the matrix can become very large and be very sparse when a large number of users (subjects) or data items (objects) exists. Such a matrix wastes storage space and may be inefficient to process. An alternative approach lists the authorizations that users have. A **subject profile** is a listing of all of the objects that a user may access. Table 11–4a shows the subject profiles that correspond to the authorizations listed in Table 11–2. When an object is omitted from a subject profile, the subject has no access to that object. Table 11–4b illustrates the object profiles for the authorizations in Table 11–2. An **object profile** indicates which

TABLE 11–4b   Equivalent Object Profile for the Access Matrix in Table 11–2

Inventory Record	Vice President: READ; Warehouse Supervisor; ALL
Employee.Name	Vice President, Personnel: ALL; Warehouse Supervisor: READ
Employee.Title	Vice President, Personnel: ALL; Warehouse Supervisor: READ
Employee.Salary	Vice President, Personnel: ALL

subjects can access this object. The object profile also includes the access authorization for this subject.

Data Encryption.   Another level of protection from unauthorized access to data is provided by **data encryption,** a process that converts the characters of the data from a meaningful sequence into an apparently random sequence. The name "Jones," for example, could be encrypted into "XPQDR." Many encryption algorithms exploit the fact that certain characters are not printable. Including these characters in the encryption process makes listings or displays of encrypted data nearly useless, since nonprintable characters appear as blanks. Encryption is supported directly in the CODASYL model (see Chapter 9). It is also a common technique in microcomputer environments, where data on floppy disks is particularly vulnerable to unauthorized access. The inverse process, which returns the data to its original form, is known as **data decryption.**

Although most computer systems provide a variety of techniques for securing data, there are almost always "holes" somewhere in the system. Encryption may be used to protect against someone finding such a hole and accessing data. Encryption is frequently used in databases and is also used to encode tables of passwords and to encode messages being transmitted between nodes in a network.

Most data encryption is accomplished by means of an **algorithm** for converting one character to another, along with a specific parameter of the algorithm known as the *key*. The **key** is used to determine how the transliteration will occur. This approach allows one algorithm to generate many different encryptions of data by changing the key. The algorithm may be public knowledge, but the key must be kept secret. Often, the algorithm specifies not only the change of characters (that is, "J" is replaced by "Q") but also a change in the sequence of the letters. Breaking a code thus becomes more than just determining the correct character correspondence; one must also determine how the sequence is changed. Double encryption, where encrypted data is encrypted a second time, is also used.

We will illustrate a simple encryption algorithm that has an interesting property. The same algorithm encrypts and decrypts the data. The algorithm uses the EXCLUSIVE OR function on bits to determine the encrypted bit pattern. EXCLUSIVE OR operates on two bits as follows:

If both bits have the same value, then the result is 0.
If the bits have different values, then the result is 1.

Now, consider the encryption of the letter C. The EBCDIC bit pattern for C is 10100011. If we use 01110111 as the key for our algorithm, then we obtain 11010100 as the encrypted C bit pattern. This pattern is obtained by using EXCLUSIVE OR to determine each bit by examining the corresponding bits in C and the key. If we apply the algorithm and the same key to the encrypted bit pattern, we will obtain 10100011. This is the original C bit pattern. As a matter of fact, we can use double encryption with two key values and can obtain the original bit pattern by reapplying the keys *in any order*. You might now understand that EXCLUSIVE OR is also called *symmetric sum*.

Encryption does not provide absolute security. If the key is not protected, the encrypted data is no safer with the encryption than without it. Although a simple substitution of one character for another in English provides 26 possible keys, making computation of all of the possible keys infeasible, the structure of the language provides other clues. The character E occurs quite frequently, while Z does not. Hence, an intelligent decryption process would use the frequency of the letters in the language to guide its search for the real key.

Even when one cannot decrypt values, unauthorized data access may occur. Suppose a database administrator determines the organization cannot afford to incur the overhead associated with encrypting data. He or she might decide that the next best action is to encrypt the passwords of the database users. That way, even if someone manages to access the password information, it is protected. If the encryption algorithm is known, the unauthorized user might still be able to determine the passwords. One approach is to encrypt a dictionary, using the encryption algorithm, then match the encrypted passwords to the encrypted dictionary entries. When a match is found, the dictionary provides the decrypted password. Many encryption algorithms are published and are well known. And, someone may have access to the database software and may have managed to extract the encryption routines. Thus, this scenario is quite real. For these reasons, users should be encouraged to use passwords that are not actual words.

Because many database systems use data compression (removal of unnecessary characters) to reduce storage space, encryption can be performed at the time of compression with little overhead. Encryption is usually implemented in the hardware of the system to increase the efficiency of the encryption process. For example, the National Bureau of Standards has developed an algorithm known as the Data Encryption Standard. This algorithm is typically implemented in hardware and is well known. Security is maintained by maintaining the secrecy of the encryption key.

Other Security Techniques. Another method of deterring unauthorized access is to incorporate security features that require certain actions by the user that only an authorized user can perform. These include answering special questions or performing a calculation that only the authorized user is prepared to do.

All attempted accesses to the database system should be recorded on a device accessible only to the database administrator. Some systems automatically invalidate a user authorization after some number (three to five) of consecutive unsuccessful attempts to gain access to the system. When this occurs, the user must personally arrange to have the authorization revalidated. This prevents unauthorized persons from writing a program to try all possible passwords to gain access to a system.

Because unauthorized access is often gained through telephone facilities, special measures can be applied here, too. Many database systems now have an automatic "call-back" feature. When a user accesses the system via a telephone and is identified as an authorized user, the system disconnects the telephone connection and calls back the authorized user at a predetermined number. With this protection, unauthorized access via a valid user identification code also requires calling from a specific telephone. This is unlikely.

Physical Security

Security of the facilities and hardware is also an important aspect of database system security. At a minimum, physical access to the hardware supporting a database system should be limited to the members of the database administration function who require access. A few examples help emphasize this point.

One company that now expends a great deal of effort to implement system security learned the importance of physical security the hard way. One evening the building's clean-up crew entered the room containing the computer hardware in order to wax the floor. The buffer used to shine the floor in these situations generates considerable static electricity. The cleaning person barely touched the computer cabinet with the buffer, but that was adequate for the static charge to be transferred to the computer. The charge disrupted the disk controller in the middle of an update to the disk, causing one area of the disk to become inaccessible. Unfortunately, that disk area contained the only copy of a new system being developed. The accident resulted in the loss of six months of work.

Another company lost the use of a computer in a similar accident. This time, the cleaning crew unplugged a computer in order to clean the floor around it. This caused some damage to the disk drives attached. The worst damage occurred, however, when the persons responsible for operating the computer attempted to restart the computer. The cleaning crew had unknowingly plugged the computer into an electrical outlet that supplied twice as much voltage as the computer could handle. As soon as the machine was started, most of the internal components of the computer were burned.

Cleaning crews are not the only instigators of situations in which the integrity of a database system is compromised. Another example brought to our attention involved a new employee. The employee went into a dark computer room where he could not find the light switch. The switch he found felt like a light switch, so he pressed it. Unfortunately, this switch was installed as a manual way to control fires in

FIGURE 11–7   Causes of Disaster in an Information Management System

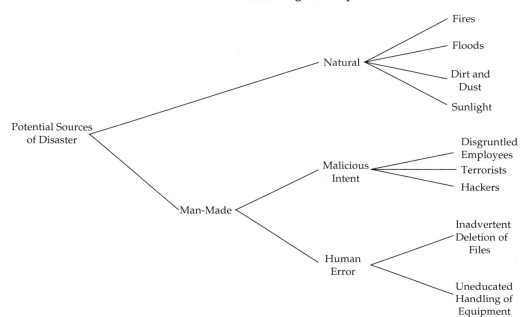

the computer room. All of the hardware shut down immediately, and the room began to fill with halon. Halon is a substance that will smother fires. Several days were required to clean the room and bring the hardware back on-line. Figure 11–7 shows other potential sources of problems.

As these examples indicate, oversights of physical security can be very costly. Physical security is implemented in the obvious ways, via locks and controlled access areas. Most organizations now routinely place combination locks on all doors leading to the database system hardware area. This is supplemented by locks on all disk and tape filing cabinets. Halon switches are usually covered to prevent inadvertent use.

In larger organizations, identification tags are required for access to controlled areas. These tags frequently have a magnetic strip across the back that is read when the tag is inserted into special locking devices. If the owner of the tag is authorized to enter the controlled access area, the door unlocks; otherwise, access is denied.

Natural disasters such as fires, floods, and earthquakes may cause extensive damage to a database system. Even if there is not a fire in the immediate area of the computer hardware, a fire nearby may activate sprinklers in the room housing the hardware, causing water damage. Air-conditioning failure may cause the database system hardware to overheat, and improper filtration may lead to damage caused by dust or dirt in the air.

Strategies for recovering from disasters caused by fire and flooding usually include special facilities. Fire control systems can be altered to use some type of chemical rather than water to extinguish a fire in the computer facility. The risk, of course, is that database system personnel could be hurt by the chemicals in the event of a fire. Consequently, they must be well trained in procedures for getting out of a room equipped in this manner.

Notably, magnetic tape is relatively undamaged by temperatures less than approximately 300°F. Fireproof cabinets are a good investment, since the likelihood is greater that a tape will be damaged by fire than by heat. Flood damage can obviously be controlled by placing the information management system facilities somewhere other than the basement of a building. Other sources of damage to a database system can be averted through the use of equipment that monitors the area housing the hardware. These devices monitor the room temperature, humidity, and airflow. They can be constructed in a way that will warn database users that the system is about to shut down as well as alert the database administrator that a problem has occurred.

Of course, damage may also be caused maliciously by disgruntled employees or customers. This is one reason that many organizations no longer house their database system hardware in rooms surrounded by glass walls. In the past, organizations were eager to display their computer hardware as a representation of progress. Now, organizations realize that glass walls are easily penetrated, permitting costly destruction of equipment. Government-related database systems must be increasingly concerned with terrorist attacks, too.

A final form of physical security that is almost universally overlooked involves the proper disposal of trash. Destroying every piece of output generated by a database system is not usually necessary. However, many organizations are becoming increasingly concerned about the printed documents leaving the organization via the garbage can. These documents may contain proprietary information or the secrets to a patented formula. In the worst case, they may contain information regarding user identification and passwords.

The database administrator cannot be responsible for everyone's trash, just as he or she cannot be expected to constantly monitor every employee's efficiency. This is another area where the administrator must act as an educator, impressing on the organization the need to act responsibly. The database administrator should, however, provide some type of paper-shredding facility to properly dispose of printed material that could be used to breach the security of the database system.

Finally, there is always the possibility of inadvertent destruction of important database system files by persons with authorized access. Humans make mistakes, and expecting database system personnel to be perfect is unreasonable.

To protect a database system from malicious or inadvertent physical destruction, all of the security measures discussed above should be implemented, within the constraints of a cost-benefit analysis. Although no one can prevent natural disasters, one can prepare for them. One of the database administrator's most important tasks is to have a plan and a set of procedures to be executed in the event of any disruption in the normal operation of the database system.

Provisions should be made with the hardware and software vendors of the database system components that allow the organization access to equipment needed in the event of a disaster. Of course, the hardware and software are useless without the proper data, so periodic copies of important files must be securely stored away from the main database system installation.

Thus far, we have been discussing the worst-case scenario. Being prepared for the smaller disasters that occur more frequently is also important. These "small disasters" are typically the inadvertent destruction of files and the more common daily interruptions of the system.

DATABASE RECOVERY

The examples discussed above concerning physical security have shown that accidents may result in losses of information or even the use of hardware in a database system. When data is lost in a database system, it must be recovered. Recovery techniques vary according to the scope of the data to be recovered. In some cases, the entire database must be recovered. In other cases, only a single value in the database must be recovered.

At some time, each of us has probably deleted a file that we did not really intend to destroy. Can you imagine the effect of inadvertently destroying a bank's file of customer account information? (How about your university deleting all of your academic records?) It happens, and, since it happens, database administrators go to great lengths to provide procedures for recovering from these accidents.

The simplest way to recover from situations in which files have been lost inadvertently is to load a copy of the lost files into the system. The time at which the last copy of the database (which is assumed to be error-free, or consistent) was made is known as a *checkpoint.* Checkpoints may occur whenever there is no activity on the system. Typically, the database system is constantly being modified, so that such a static copy of the database system files is rarely available. There must, therefore, be some way of recovering all of the modifications that have been made since the last checkpoint.

To fully appreciate the complexity of the process, we can examine the possible states in which a transaction (a series of database operations that performs some task) may exist relative to a checkpoint and a system failure:

1. Transaction begins and ends before the checkpoint and the system failure.
2. Transaction begins before the checkpoint and ends before the system failure.
3. Transaction begins before the checkpoint but is not completed before the system failure.

4. Transaction begins after the checkpoint and ends before the system failure.

5. Transaction begins after the checkpoint, but it is not completed before the system failure.

Techniques for Transaction Recovery

The foregoing discussion provides some insight into the complexity of recovering a single database value that has been changed by a transaction. Transaction recovery techniques address situations in which only a subset of a file (possibly just a single value) must be recovered.

Before discussing transaction recovery techniques in detail, we need to define several concepts. First is the concept of a *transaction* itself, alluded to above. A **transaction** is a logical unit of work in a database environment. It may be composed of a group of physical operations (such as access, read, add, then store) that collectively define a logical operation on the database. Consequently, more than one *physical* database operation may be necessary to define a *logical* operation on the database (in this case, an update).

When a transaction has been completed successfully, it is ready to be **committed** to the database. Some database systems allow users to embed a command within a transaction that signals that the effects of the transaction should be committed. Most database systems handle this process automatically.

Of course, transactions do not always complete successfully. For example, a user may initiate a transaction that attempts to modify a database item that the user only has permission to read. Sometimes a user stops a transaction after realizing that the transaction contains an error, as when an incorrect amount is added to an account balance. A transaction that does not complete successfully is said to **abort.** Whenever a transaction aborts, any changes to the database that the transaction made before aborting must not be allowed to be committed to the database. Some transactions may depend on the results of other transactions. The failure of a transaction can therefore result in the need to keep other transactions from committing.

Transaction Logging.   A number of techniques have been developed to manage the effect of transactions on a database. One approach is to create a **transaction log** of the effects of the transactions. Transaction logs contain information that identifies the transaction and data about the changes made in the database. The transaction log is maintained on a storage device other than the one containing the database. This approach prevents a single hardware problem (such as a disk-head crash) from affecting both the database and the transaction log.

We will illustrate logging approaches to transaction recovery with the following possible situation. Consider a mail order retailer who maintains a large warehouse of goods that are purchased by customers and shipped from the warehouse. Suppose a customer orders a patio set (a table and four chairs). There are two physical operations that compose the single logical operation that we might call "shipping the patio set to the customer." First, the patio set shipped to the customer is no longer in the warehouse. Second, the patio set has been sent to the customer. The inventory information and the customer information must be updated to reflect this shipment.

The physical operations in a transaction for shipping the patio set might be logically represented as shown in Figure 11–8a. If a system failure occurs before the transaction is finished, the database may not be in a consistent state. Specifically, problems exist if the failure occurs after the inventory record is written and before the customer record is written. If the transaction is restarted when the system resumes operation, then *another* unit will be "removed" from inventory. If the organization "hopes for the best" and assumes that the transaction terminated completely before the system failure, then the customer record is inaccurate. Either situation is clearly unacceptable.

Let us assume that there are 63 patio sets in inventory before the customer's order is filled. The transaction log in Figure 11–8b would be constructed for this transaction. The entries in the transaction log are called **after-images.** They reflect the value of the data item after the transaction has modified it. After the transaction commits, then the database may be physically updated. If the system ever fails, then all transactions for which a commit entry exists in the transaction log can be applied to the database by simply applying the values in the transaction log. If no commit exists for a transaction in the transaction log, then the transaction must be restarted.

A variation of this approach updates the database directly, but maintains before-values as well as after-values in the transaction log. A

FIGURE 11–8a
The Physical Operations in a Transaction

```
TRANSACTION T0:
READ INVENTORY RECORD FOR PATIO SETS
REDUCE NUMBER ON HAND BY 1
WRITE INVENTORY RECORD FOR PATIO SETS
WRITE CUSTOMER RECORD INDICATING PATIO SET IS SHIPPED
```

FIGURE 11–8b   **Transaction Log with After-Images**

```
TRANSACTION T0:                          START T0
READ INVENTORY RECORD FOR PATIO SETS
REDUCE NUMBER ON HAND BY 1
WRITE INVENTORY RECORD FOR PATIO SETS    T0,PATIO SET:NOH, 62
WRITE CUSTOMER RECORD INDICATING PATIO
        SET IS SHIPPED                   T0,CUSTOMER:PATIO
                                                     SET,1
                                         COMMIT T0
```

FIGURE 11–8c   Transaction Log with Before- and After-Images

```
TRANSACTION T_0:                               START T_0
READ INVENTORY RECORD FOR PATIO SETS
REDUCE NUMBER ON HAND BY 1
WRITE INVENTORY RECORD FOR PATIO SETS          T_0,PATIO SET:NOH, 63,
                                               62

WRITE CUSTOMER RECORD INDICATING PATIO
        SET IS SHIPPED                         T_0,CUSTOMER:PATIO
                                                              SET,0,1
                                               COMMIT T_0
```

before-value is the value of the database item before the transaction has modified it. The transaction log for our example would change as shown in Figure 11–8c. Here, the first value in each log entry is the value of the data item before modification, and the second value is the value after modification. If the system fails after the commit, then the transaction is "redone" by applying the after-values. If the system fails before the commit, then the effects of the transaction (if any) are "undone" by applying the before-values to the database. After the before-values are applied, the transaction is restarted.

Notice that in either case a system failure during the recovery process does not cause a problem. The recovery process is restarted as if no subsequent failure occurred. The operations used in the recovery process described above are called *idempotent*. The effect of applying them repeatedly is the same as applying them only once.

The database administrator is faced with two concerns when transaction logs grow. First, the recovery process grows longer. Second, subsequent transactions must search the transaction log for the most recent database values. This search takes more time. The database administrator must determine how frequently the transaction log will be merged with the physical database. The decision must consider desired response time, database volatility, and transaction volume.

After data values are recovered, transactions illustrated in Figure 11–9 will fall into one of three categories. The first transaction should not be considered, because the effects of this transaction were recorded when the last known correct record of the database was made. The second and fourth transactions must be redone because their effects were not recorded in the database. The third and fifth transactions must be undone because they may require data from transactions of the second or fourth type.

Transactions are undone by processing the transaction log backward and restoring the first before-image of a record in the log. After all transactions have been undone, transactions that must be redone are begun. This occurs by processing the transaction log forward and reapplying all of the transactions. These two operations are sometimes called **roll-back** and **roll-forward,** or **backward recovery** and **forward recovery.** When the forward recovery is complete, new transactions may be considered.

FIGURE 11–9
**Potential States of
a Transaction Relative
to Checkpoint and
System Failure**

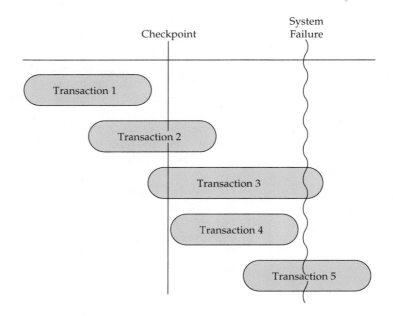

The transaction-logging approach can be applied at the transaction level, too. A transaction may be partitioned into smaller logical units separated by explicit commands to commit the intermediate results to that point. This approach allows a transaction to be recovered should the transaction fail. In this case, the transaction may be started from the last commit within the transaction, thus saving unnecessary processing time and overhead.

Memory Management.   An alternative to the transaction-logging approach described above is memory management. Memory management approaches are based on maintaining tables of indexes that indicate the parts of the database currently being processed in primary memory. Memory management techniques are sometimes called **shadowing** techniques because they rely on the existence of a copy of part of the database in memory and a "shadow" copy of the same part on a secondary storage device.

When a transaction alters a database value, the portion of the database affected is brought into main memory if it is not already resident. When this portion comes into memory, a table of the currently resident portions of the database (again on a separate storage device) is updated to reflect the disk address of the database segment that just entered. After a transaction is committed, the portion of the database that has been changed may be written to the storage device containing the database and the entry for this portion of the database deleted from the table.

At any point during the processing of transactions, a valid copy of the database always exists on the storage device being used (usually a disk). Consequently, another way of recovering from a transaction failure is simply to maintain a table (on another disk) of the portions of the database that are resident in main memory. Should a transaction fail, the memory management table indicates the location of the portion of the database to load to undo the effect of the aborted transaction.

Should a system failure occur before the update in memory is completed, the table can be brought into memory and used to recover the entire database. All database segments listed in the table are read, which restores the database to a point just prior to the failure. Transactions in process when the system failure occurred are restarted, and the system may proceed with processing. The roll-back and roll-forward procedures associated with transaction logging are not required.

Differential Files and Careful Replacement.   One aspect of the shadowing approach just discussed is that over a period of time the database becomes scattered over the storage device on which it resides. This situation occurs because new copies of portions of the database are created every time a transaction is committed. This may lead to a deterioration of processing. An alternative method for managing transactions is to commit the changes of a transaction to a separate file called a **differential file.** Should a transaction fail in a system using this approach, the effect of the transaction is never written in the differential file. Obviously, the database is unaffected by a transaction failure in this case as well. The database is updated by periodically merging the differential file with the database.

A drawback to this approach is that the differential file must be searched for changes to database items as transactions are processed. In other words, once a transaction that changes the value of a data item in the database is committed, any future transactions that access the same data item must search the differential file to access the current value for the data item. Hence, processing may deteriorate if the time between successive merges of the differential file and the database becomes too long.

A variation of the differential file approach is called **careful replacement.** In this approach, only the changes affected by a single transaction are accumulated in a differential file. These changes are then applied as the transaction commits. This solves the problem of searching the differential file for modified data items.

Issues in Selecting a Database Recovery Technique

Several issues are relevant in preparing database recovery techniques. How often should complete copies of the database system files be made? This depends on the nature of the organization's work and the size of the files being copied. Organizations that do not depend on absolutely correct information in their daily use of the database system may find that weekly copies of database system files are sufficient. For example, a group of dentists sharing a database system that contains information on their patients may be willing to risk losing one week's updates to the database system in order to save the cost of making daily copies. Organizations that are dependent on accurate daily information are not willing to take this risk. Airlines, for example, require absolutely accurate information regarding flight reservations. They cannot risk losing a week's worth of updates.

Which data should be copied? Copying all data in the system may be prohibitively expensive and time-consuming. In such a case, copying on a daily basis only those data values that have changed may be preferred, with a complete copy of the database system files made on the weekend. Another approach used in environments where users are computer literate is to provide a special area, or library, where users can place data to be protected. Only data in this area is copied daily and can be recovered with at most a one-day lag. Other data may be archived weekly in this scheme.

CONCURRENT ACCESS IN DATABASE SYSTEMS

Database systems are models of organizations. As we have noted on several occasions, the database exists to support decision making, which implies that the data in the database is intended to be used. While the database is being used, however, a situation may arise in which two (or more) transactions require the same piece of data. **Concurrent processing** is a term used to describe this situation.

Depending on how the data is used, concurrent processing may lead to a problem in the database.

Types of Concurrency Problems

Three types of concurrency problems can be identified. Figure 11–10 illustrates concurrent access to a database listing current stock levels of a part stored at a central warehouse. A transaction reflecting the reductions to inventory of the part for the day is to be processed. Notice that

FIGURE 11–10
Database Retrievals that Occur While the Database Is Being Modified Result in Inconsistent Analyses

Time	Update Transaction	Database Inventory Level	Read Transaction
0		1000	
1	Read inventory record		
2	Inventory level = 1000		Read inventory record
3	Deduct 120 units Inventory level = 880		Inventory level = 1000
4	Replace inventory record		
5		880	

FIGURE 11–11
Uncoordinated Modifications to the Database Result in Lost Updates

Time	Update Transaction	Database Inventory Level	Update Transaction
0		1000	
1	Read inventory record		
2	Inventory level = 1000		Read inventory record
3	Deduct 120 units Inventory level = 880		Inventory level = 1000
4	Replace inventory record		Deduct 80 units Inventory level = 920
5		880	Replace inventory record
6		920	

any other transaction accessing this data prior to completion of the update obtains inaccurate values. This type of concurrency problem is called the **inconsistent analysis problem.**

Figure 11–11 shows a second type of problem. In this example, two transactions are intended to modify the warehouse inventory levels concurrently. Whichever transaction is committed last destroys the effect of the other transaction. This is known as the **lost update problem.**

Figure 11–12 illustrates the **uncommitted dependence problem.** In this case, a transaction reaches a logical conclusion but is not committed to the database. As discussed earlier, such a situation can occur because another part of the transaction contains an error that causes the transaction to abort or because the user initiating the transaction decides to abort the transaction.

Methods for Dealing With Concurrency Problems

Concurrency problems have been studied in great depth and continue to be an exciting research area. We limit our discussion to three of the most well developed of the many approaches to concurrency problems. Each of these methods enforces *serialization:* the condition that the transaction execute in a serial, or sequential, manner. The methods differ in the manner in which transactions are forced to wait for an opportunity to execute.

Locking Mechanisms.   Perhaps the most widely used approach to handling concurrency problems is with a **locking mechanism.** Locking mechanisms work to prevent more than one transaction from accessing a data object. Figure 11–13 illustrates a locking mechanism applied to

FIGURE 11–12
**Updates that Are Ulti-
mately Aborted Lead to
Inconsistent Analyses**

Time	Update Transaction	Database Inventory Level	Read Transaction
0		1000	
1	Read inventory record		
2	Inventory level = 1000		
3	Deduct 120 units Inventory level = 880		
4	Replace inventory record		
5		880	Read inventory record
6	Transaction error occurs— abort update		Inventory level = 880
7		1000	

FIGURE 11–13
**Locking Can Prevent
Inconsistent Analysis**

Time	Update Transaction	Database Inventory Level	Read Transaction
0		1000	
1	Lock inventory record		
2	Read inventory record		
3	Inventory level = 1000		
4	Deduct 120 units Inventory level = 880		Inventory record locked—wait
5	Replace inventory record		Inventory record locked—wait
6	Release inventory record	880	Inventory record locked—wait
7			Lock inventory record
8			Read inventory record
9			Inventory level = 880

the inconsistent analysis problem shown in Figure 11–10. When the first transaction accesses the inventory records for updating, these records are "locked" to prevent access by any other transaction. Hence, the second transaction is automatically put into a "wait" condition until the first transaction commits. When the first transaction commits, the lock is removed and the inventory records are available to other transactions.

Locking works in a similar way to prevent lost updates and uncommitted dependencies. Figure 11–14 illustrates prevention of a lost update. One transaction locks the inventory records while it updates them. On successful completion, the transaction releases the lock and the second transaction begins. The second transaction also applies a lock to the records to prevent another update transaction from causing problems.

FIGURE 11–14
Locking Can Coordinate Concurrent Updates

Time	Update Transaction	Database Inventory Level	Read Transaction
0		1000	
1	Lock inventory record		
2	Read inventory record		
3	Inventory level = 1000		
4	Deduct 120 units Inventory level = 880		Inventory record locked—wait
5	Replace inventory record		Inventory record locked—wait
6	Release inventory record	880	Inventory record locked—wait
7			Lock inventory record
8			Read inventory record
9			Inventory level = 880
10			Deduct 80 units Inventory level = 800
11			Replace inventory record
12		800	Release inventory record

Figure 11–15 illustrates prevention of an uncommitted dependence problem. Here, the lock is released when the transaction aborts. Because the updates caused by the first transaction are not written to the database, the second transaction begins with correct data.

Locking mechanisms may also *cause* problems in their attempt to solve concurrency problems. Figure 11–16 presents one such situation. In this example, two transactions are each competing for two sets of records. The first transaction locks the inventory records while the second transaction locks the employee records. The second transaction attempts to access the inventory records, but they are locked by the first transaction. This puts the second transaction into a wait condition. Meanwhile, the first transaction is attempting to access the employee records, which are locked by the second transaction. This puts the first transaction into a wait condition. Each transaction is waiting for the other to release a locked resource, so neither transaction can finish.

FIGURE 11–15
Locking Can Prevent Inconsistent Analysis Caused by Uncommitted Updates

Time	Update Transaction	Database Inventory Level	Read Transaction
0		1000	
1	Lock inventory record		
2	Read inventory record		
3	Inventory level = 1000		
4	Deduct 120 units Inventory level = 880		Inventory record locked—wait
5	Replace inventory record		Inventory record locked—wait
6	Transaction error occurs— abort update	880	Inventory record locked—wait
7		1000	Inventory record locked—wait
8	Release inventory record		Inventory record locked—wait
9			Lock inventory record
10			Read inventory record
11			Inventory level = 1000

FIGURE 11–16
**Locking Can Create
Deadlock Situations**

Time	Transaction 1	Transaction 2
1	Lock inventory record	Lock employee record
2	Read inventory record	Read employee record
3	Employee record locked—wait	Inventory record locked—wait
4	Employee record locked—wait	Inventory record locked—wait
·	·	·
·	·	·
·	·	·

This situation is called a **deadlock** (also known as a **deadly embrace**). The only way to resolve such a situation is to abort one of the transactions and restart it later. This allows the locked records to be accessed by other transactions. The choice of a transaction to abort can be made in many ways. Some systems abort the transaction that started last; others abort the transaction with the fewest (or largest) number of locked resources.

Deadlock situations may be recognized by cycles in a graph of transaction dependencies, as shown in Figure 11–17. Each node in the graph represents a transaction, and each arrow represents dependence. A **cycle** exists if it is possible to trace through the graph beginning and ending at the same node. Any time a cycle appears in the graph, a deadlock condition exists. The deadlock condition is corrected by removing a node in the cycle, which implies aborting a transaction.

The effect of locking mechanisms varies with the level of data (attribute, entity, entity class, or database) locked. This level of locking is referred to as **granularity.** Locking at the attribute (or field) level (fine granularity) generates fewer waiting situations than locking at the record level (coarser granularity), since locking a record necessarily locks all fields within the record.

Time-Stamping.   A second approach to solving the problems of concurrent access is **time-stamping.** With this approach, each record is "stamped" with the last time the record was read and updated. This gives each record a time when it is considered "effective." Transactions are not allowed to invalidate an effective time by applying a new time stamp to a record that is earlier than the existing time stamp for that record. A transaction that attempts to invalidate an effective time is aborted and restarted later.

In Figure 11–18, for example, the first transaction is assigned time t_q as the effective time for records it modifies. This transaction accesses an inventory record and verifies that the time stamp on the record (t_o) is earlier than the transaction time stamp (t_q). At time t_o, the inventory record is accessed and stamped effective at time t_q. Meanwhile, a second transaction has been assigned time t_p as its effective time. The second

FIGURE 11–17
Cycles in Resource Allocation Graphs Indicate Deadlock Situations

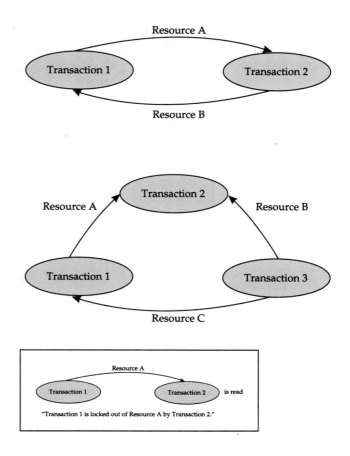

transaction also attempts to access the inventory record. But in this case, because t_p is earlier than t_q, the second transaction is aborted. The earlier time stamp assigned to the second transaction would have invalidated the first transaction. The second transaction must be assigned another time at which to become effective, in this case t_r. Because t_r is later than t_q, the inventory record may be accessed at time t_q and the second transaction completed.

Time-stamping forces serialization by ensuring that conflicting transactions do not operate concurrently. It does not lead to deadlock situations, as locking mechanisms may.

Preanalysis and Transaction Classes. Another approach to concurrency problems involves preanalysis of transactions. Transactions that exist in the same transaction class are run sequentially to ensure that no concurrency problems arise. A **transaction class** is a group of transactions that reads the same set of data items, called a **readset,** and writes the same set of data items, called a **writeset.** Transaction classes conflict if the writeset of one intersects the readset or writeset of the other. Once conflicting transaction classes have been identified, locking, time-stamping, or some other method can be used to prevent concurrency problems.

FIGURE 11–18
Time-Stamping
Coordinates Concurrent
Processing

Transaction 1	Transaction 2
Assign a time for update to be effective: t_q	
Access inventory record at t_n	Assign a time for update to be effective: t_p
Time-stamp the inventory record with t_q	Access the inventory record at t_o
Modify the inventory record	Next time inventory record will be effective is t_q, which is after t_p, so abort this transaction
Release the inventory record	Assign a time for update to be effective: t_r
	Access the inventory record at t_q
	Inventory record is effective so continue update
Note: Assume $t_n < t_o < t_p < t_q < t_r$, where $<$ means "is earlier than."	

Preanalysis does not lead to deadlock situations. Analysis must be efficient, however, to prevent incoming transactions from being delayed.

PERFORMANCE MONITORING

Evaluation of database system efficiency is the database administrator's responsibility. Although database system users can be expected to inform the database administrator if the system becomes too inefficient, such information can come far too late.

The database administrator must determine the standards of evaluation to be used in the organization. These standards depend on the nature of the business of the organization. As mentioned earlier, acceptable response times may vary from department to department within an organization.

There are several tools at the disposal of the database administrator for evaluating database system performance. Database systems typically contain special **performance monitor routines** that assist in system evaluation. These routines are special utilities that record statistics such as the number of disk accesses, the amount of time used by the CPU, the amount of time used by the input/output channel, and the amount of primary memory used by a particular application. If applications spend

The User's View

Most of the topics discussed in this chapter are apparent to users only through the policies that govern the use of the database system. Indeed, a primary goal of database systems is to isolate users from the technical aspects of database systems use.

Most users do not need to know how an active data repository system manages access to the database. Most users need know only that one of the functions of the data repository system is to provide users with the organization's formal, standardized description of the data used in organizational decision-making processes. The data repository system provides an authoritative reference for all data-related questions about information in the organization.

Certainly, most users are little concerned with how a database system handles concurrent access problems, as long as they are handled. Users who understand why concurrent access can lead to problems are more likely to be tolerant of being temporarily locked out of a data item, so users should be informed of these types of processes. However, the technical aspects of resolving these problems are unnecessary information for most end-users.

Security may be the most visible aspect of database administration covered in this chapter. As with concurrent access, informing users why the security policies being enforced are for the good of the organization may go a long way toward user understanding and tolerance. Of course, *how* security measures are implemented should definitely remain in the domain of the database administrator to avoid compromise.

Technical aspects of recovery measures are also of little concern to most users. As long as some recovery process exists to protect them satisfactorily, users will be satisfied. Certainly, no recovery procedure gives instantaneous and complete reconstruction of a database system, but users are usually very satisfied when any lost data is recovered with minimal effort on their part. ∎

---

an inordinate amount of time using the CPU, then a more powerful CPU may be needed for that system. Alternatively, the efficiency of the applications may require examination. Efficiency can be improved by examining the navigation paths and the indexing schemes relevant to the application. If applications just take a long time to run but are not making heavy use of the CPU, then the system may be overloaded. In this case, the database administrator should look at the peripherals of the system. Secondary storage devices and controllers should be examined to determine if more are needed or whether they can be used more efficiently.

In some cases, the needs of the organization may have changed significantly since the current data schemas were developed. This case arises when the organization has gone through a period of rapid expansion or has diversified into new areas. This type of change may require a restructuring of the schemas used in the database system.

CHAPTER SUMMARY

Technical aspects of database administration have been presented in this chapter. These topics provide insight into some of the nonmodeling aspects of database system design.

Data repository systems are composed of two components, a data repository and a data repository control program. The data repository

METROPOLITAN NATIONAL BANK

Because MetNat is a bank, great care has been taken to make the main office and branch facilities physically secure. MetNat's philosophy toward security has always been to maintain slightly more security than is believed to be necessary. This philosophy extends to the computer-based systems as well.

Consumers are protected by law against unauthorized access to any credit information on a customer. As you might expect, credit data is considered very sensitive information at MetNat. The next phase of your project is to develop a scheme for access protection. You should identify the access privileges for each table in your relational implementation. In some cases, you may want to consider access rights at the attribute level. Use SQL GRANT and VIEW commands to specify these access rights.

Recovery from system failure is of vital concern to MetNat's board of directors. Since so many of the bank's services depend on information systems being on-line, MetNat is willing to incur significant costs to maintain a high level of service quality. MetNat believes that archive and recovery issues also warrant careful consideration. Of course, all costs in this area must be justified by the benefits, but MetNat's management will authorize any reasonable expense in this area.

Investigate the costs of off-line storage technology. Prepare a report estimating the cost of investing in this technology. You will need to estimate the volume of data that will be stored. You can make this calculation by multiplying the number of accounts, loans, credit card holders, and employees by the size of these records. Then multiply this result by the number of credit card and bank account transactions and by the size of the transaction records you defined earlier in the project.

Concurrency protection is needed in all database environments in which several users have concurrent access to the database. A critical issue here is the level of concurrency protection needed. Are problem situations due to concurrent access likely given the types of access described in earlier chapters? If so, should concurrency protection be implemented at the field, record, or database level? Does one method provide better protection than another?

Address each of these issues in a report format. You may want to review the MetNat scenarios in earlier chapters for guidance. Prior policy issues should be reflected in any suggestions you make in this report. Relate each recommendation to your implementation design as much as possible, suggesting explicit methods and giving examples based on your design. ∎

system provides a central, formal description of all data used in the daily processes of the organization. A passive data repository system is a data reference system that does not control access to the database system. Active data repository systems provide reference and control.

Security is an important aspect of database systems. Many disasters can be avoided by implementing appropriate security measures. When security is breached, a portion or all of the database may be lost. Recovery methods are necessary to restore lost data. Transaction logging is a commonly used method that employs roll-back and roll-forward techniques to provide database recovery. Memory management techniques, which do not require roll-back and roll-forward methods, may also be used.

Concurrent access to databases is one aspect of control that even active data repository systems are unable to address. Concurrent access may lead to problems of inaccurate data. Locking, time-stamping, and preanalysis of transactions are methods for addressing the problems of concurrent access.

Questions and Exercises

1. What are the two components of a data repository system? What role does each play?

2. What types of tasks occur at each stage of data repository development?

3. Explain why data repository development should occur in phases. Why not just wait until the database is almost completed before developing a data repository that matches the database?

4. What are the three types of data repository systems? Describe a situation in which each is adequate to support the needs of an organization.

5. Compare and contrast the security and recovery needs of database systems for the following: a lawyer, a defense contractor, a neighborhood grocer, a university records office, a city police department, a dentist, a psychiatrist, a state senator, a committee managing the campaign of a candidate for the U.S. presidency, a library, and a book publisher.

6. For one of the situations described in Question 5, create a hypothetical access matrix for controlling access to the database.

7. How do an organization's size and purpose influence the amount of security that should be incorporated in the database system?

8. Discuss database system recovery procedures. How do the organization's size and purpose affect the need for back-up copies of data in the database system?

9. For one of the situations described in Question 5, write a policy statement concerning the frequency of making back-up copies of the database. Include an explanation for your decision.

10. Describe a situation in which three transactions are deadlocked due to locking mechanisms.

11. Draw a resource allocation graph depicting the situation described in Question 10. Where is the cycle in your graph?

12. Describe the transaction-logging approach to database recovery.

13. How does the time-stamp approach enforce serializability?

14. Create an example that demonstrates a transaction-logging

approach to database recovery. Show the state of the database (1) before the system failure, (2) after any aborted transactions are cleared, and (3) just before system restart.

15. How does database recovery using a memory management technique differ from database recovery using a transaction-logging technique?

16. Create an example that demonstrates a memory management approach to database recovery. Show the state of the database (1) before the system failure, (2) after any aborted transactions are cleared, and (3) just before system restart.

17. Suppose that as a database administrator you establish the following policy: Only the database administrator, the assistant database administrator, and the tape librarian will have access to the computer room and be allowed to mount tapes on the tape drives. You then learn that some of your best system analysts are upset about their loss of access to the computer room. These employees have college degrees in computer science and are offended that they cannot mount tapes as needed. They complain that you are unnecessarily adding red tape that will degrade their performance. How do you respond?

18. Write a memorandum addressing the situation in Question 17.

For Further Reading

Data repository system development is discussed in: Leong-Hong, B. W., and B. K. Plagman. *Data Dictionary/Directory Systems*. New York: John Wiley & Sons, 1982.

Van Duyn, J. *Developing a Data Dictionary System*. Englewood Cliffs, N.J.: Prentice-Hall, 1982.

The following article discusses an extension of the data repository concept: Dolk, Dan R., and Robert A. Kirsch. "A Relational Information Resource Dictionary System." *Communications of the ACM* 30, no. 1 (July 1987), pp. 48–61.

The classic reference for details on implementing a secure database system environment is: Fernandez, E. B.; R. C. Summers; and C. Wood. *Database Security and Integrity*. Reading, Mass.: Addison-Wesley Publishing, 1982.

Some "novel" security techniques are presented in: Botting, Richard. "Novel Security Techniques for On-Line Systems." *Communications of the ACM* 29, no. 5 (May 1986), pp. 416–17.

Broader security issues are discussed in the following articles:

Lapid, Y.; N. Ahituv; and S. Neumann. "Approaches to Handling 'Trojan Horse' Threats." *Computers and Security* 5, no. 3 (September 1986), pp. 251–56.

Rutledge, Linda S., and Lance J. Hoffman. "A Survey of Issues in Computer Network Security." *Computers and Security* 5, no. 4 (December 1986), pp. 296–308.

Wood, Charles C. "Establishing Internal Technical Systems Security Standards." *Computers and Security* 5, no. 3 (September 1986), pp. 193–200.

Wood, Charles C. "Security Modules: Potent Information Security System Components." *Computers and Security* 5, no. 2 (June 1986), pp. 114–21.

Material on concurrent processing and resolution of the problems associated with it can be found in:

Casanova, M. A. "The Concurrency Problem for Database Systems," *Lecture Notes in Computer Science,* Vol. 116. Berlin: Springer-Verlag, 1981.

Chan, M. Y., and F. C. D. Chan. "Database Concurrency Control Using Read/Write Set Information." *Information Systems* 11, no. 4 (1986), pp. 319–22.

Hsu, Meichun, and A. Chan. "Partitioned Two-Phase Locking." *ACM Transactions on Database Systems* 11, no. 4 (December 1986), pp. 431–46.

Thomasian, Alexander, and I. K. Ryu. "Analysis of Some Optimistic Concurrency Control Schemes Based on Certification." *Proceedings of the ACM Sigmetrics Conferences on Measurement and Modeling of Computer Systems* 13, no. 2 (August 1985), pp. 192–203.

More details on memory management approaches to transaction recovery are in: Korth, H. F., and A. Silberschatz. *Database System Concepts.* New York: McGraw-Hill, 1986.

Excellent general references on these technical topics and others are:

Date, C. J. *An Introduction to Database Systems.* 4th ed. Reading, Mass: Addison-Wesley Publishing, 1986.

Stamper, David. *Business Data Communications.* Menlo Park, Calif.: Benjamin/Cummings, 1986.

V

ADVANCED DESIGN ISSUES

12

DISTRIBUTED DATABASE MANAGEMENT SYSTEMS

Acompany with a central corporate headquarters and regional or district field offices will typically have some data that is important to all offices and other data that is important only to specific regional offices. Similarly, a company may have corporate headquarters in one city and major production facilities in several other cities. Corporate data will be in each of these locations in these scenarios, and each location will probably have a database management system that supports its operations. Ideally, a database user at any corporate location should be able to access any data item anywhere in the organization's database without regard to its location. Distributed database management systems (DDBMSs) have been evolving to satisfy this objective since large corporations first began using database technology.

Consider a large organization with a corporate headquarters in one city and several regional headquarters in other cities across the nation (Figure 12–1). A DDBMS could have a central database facility at the corporate headquarters and smaller database systems facilities at the regional headquarters. The regional installations could be used for localized database processing tasks such as payroll, inventory management, and marketing activities. These regional systems could also be used as remote stations for interacting with the central corporate computer.

There is another reason that DDBMSs are a natural fit for organizations. Finding an organization that has totally compatible hardware throughout its operations is extremely rare. One typically finds IBM computers in some locations, DEC computers in other locations, Hewlett-Packard or UNISYS computers in still other locations, and so forth.

FIGURE 12–1   Distributed Corporate Operations Require Distributed DBMSs

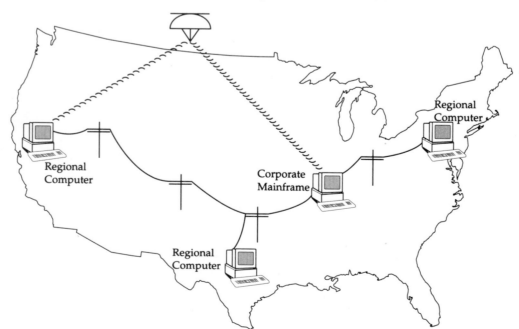

If we assume that all locations are running the same database management system, then the DDBMS allows the data to be shared as long as the various installations are communicating with each other. This assumption that all systems are running the same DBMS software is called the **homogenous system assumption.** We'll discuss the ramifications of this assumption later in the chapter.

In this chapter, we will first review the major technologies used to implement distributed systems. Then we will discuss how problems such as recovery and concurrent processing are handled in a DDBMS. We'll look at some of the advantages and disadvantages of DDBMS approaches, and then we'll provide some managerial considerations to remember as you evaluate this technology.

CLIENT/SERVER ARCHITECTURES

When computers are connected, some relationship between the machines must be defined so that the processing can be coordinated. A very practical relationship that has evolved is the **client/server architecture** (Figure 12–2). We can think of one machine as requesting some information (the client) and the other machine as providing the information (the server). Once this relationship is established, one needs only define the protocols for signaling that a request is being made or serviced, whichever the case may be.

The protocol translation is handled by a front-end processor[1] on the server system. The front end, also called a **gateway,** translates the request into a query suitable for the server system, executes the request on the server system, and then responds to the network with the results. Ideally, the server system responds with information in the proper format for the client's system. The client system's gateway is responsible for receiving the response from the network.

There are several advantages to successful implementation of the client/server architecture. First, the physical separation of the systems allows each local DBMS to be truly independent of any other computer hardware and operating system. Because the local DBMSs need be compatible only with the communications channel, they can be replaced without modification of the system.

A second benefit is the potential for supporting multiple "host" processors. The gateways between the hosts can handle all of the necessary translations to another host's language (or internal representation). Hence, flexibility exists on both sides of the gateway, and major changes in other components of the information management system do not require any modification of the database.

---

[1]Here terminology differs. Some authors refer to all processing related to the client as *front-end processing* and all processing related to the server as *back-end processing.* Other authors refer to processing that is *received* by either system as *front-end processing* and processing that is *disseminated* by either system as *back-end processing.*

FIGURE 12–2
Client/Server Architecture

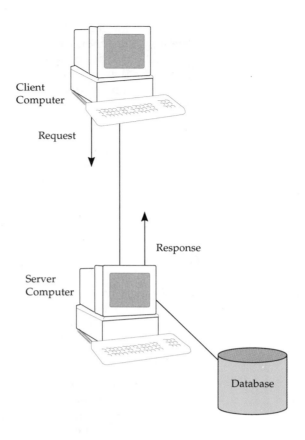

Because each local DBMS has a separate processor, it is insulated from problems caused when some other host in the system fails; if another system stops processing (for example, because of a power failure), the local database is unaffected.

Building more power into the communications channels makes other processing scenarios feasible. One can implement a type of parallel processing by instructing several local databases to process the same query. Or several local databases can process different queries on the same database. Or combinations of these processes can be used.

NETWORK TOPOLOGIES

The DDBMS concept is implemented with many technologies. Although typically discussed in terms of geographically dispersed nodes in a system, DDBMSs are becoming more and more associated with smaller databases that may be connected by local area networks (LANs). Whether connecting databases across a continent or across a street, each of these approaches has its place in a distributed database environment. As a manager, one of your duties will be to obtain more training in these areas so that you can evaluate each approach in light of your organization's specific needs.

A distributed database environment may include any combination of mainframe, minicomputer, and microcomputer workstations that are interconnected. The interconnection of the computing facilities is called the **network.** The connections may be called **links.** The computing facilities in any location are generally referred to as a **node.** The network allows users at any node to access and manipulate data at any other node. The network must provide communications hardware and software that link the interacting nodes. Several node arrangements have been implemented.

Star networks, shown in Figure 12–3, connect all nodes to a central computing resource. This arrangement is often used when the central facility is large relative to the other nodes in the network. For example, a company in a large city might have a large computer in the corporate

FIGURE 12–3   Star Network Arrangement

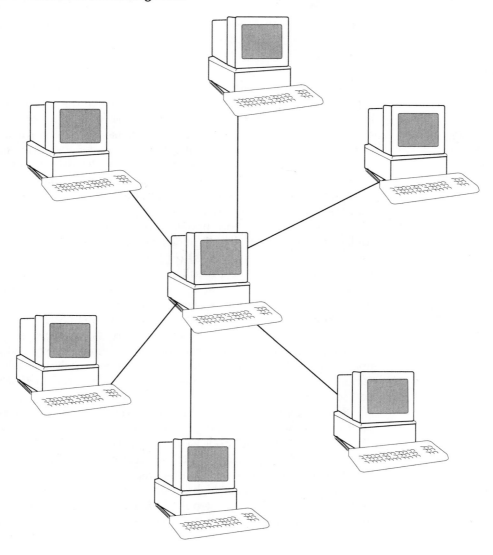

FIGURE 12–4a
Fully Connected Mesh
Topology

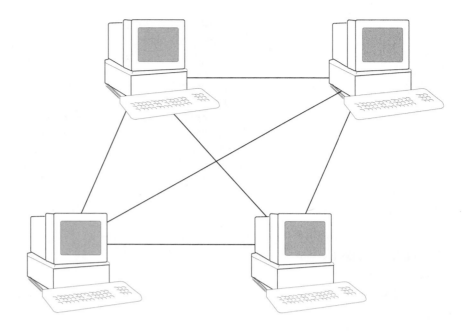

headquarters and smaller microcomputer-based workstations at branch offices in the suburbs. Alternatively, the nodes in the star network might be minicomputers that act as data repositories for multiple workstations at the branch offices. The star network relies heavily on the availability of the central computer. If it fails, then the nodes lose processing capabilities related to corporate functions. The nodes can still execute local processing, however. Star networks are sometimes called **tree networks.** When pictured as a tree, the central node is the root of the tree and the other nodes are leaves in the tree.

Mesh networks allow nodes to be interconnected with any other nodes in the system. If all nodes are connected to all other nodes, the network is **fully connected** (Figure 12–4a); otherwise, it is **partially connected** (Figure 12–4b). A fully connected network provides the most complete protection against a system failure that would prevent any type of global transaction processing. If any node or link in the network fails, another path to the destination node can be found. Fully connected networks are very reliable, but also very expensive. A corporation must have significant costs associated with a node or link failure to justify the cost of maintaining a fully connected mesh network. Partially connected mesh networks are more likely to be used in most business environments.

Ring networks connect nodes in a circular fashion, as illustrated in Figure 12–5. Each node in the network is connected to the next node in the network. The "last" node in the ring is connected to the "first" node. The ring topology provides protection against one failure in the system, but may not provide protection against more than one failure. For example, if a single node or link fails, then communications between nodes can be routed away from the failed node. If a second node fails more than one link beyond the first node that failed, then one part of

FIGURE 12–4b   Partially Connected Mesh Topology

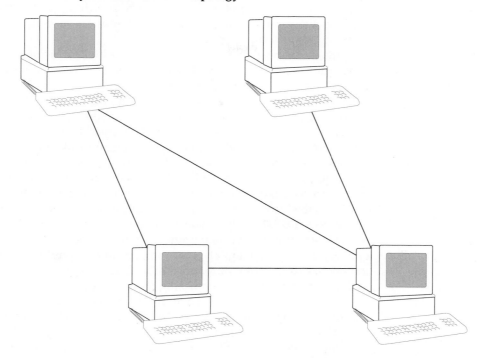

FIGURE 12–5   Ring Network Topology

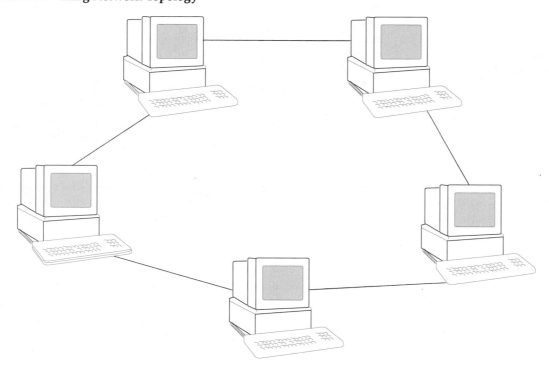

the network is isolated from the other part of the network. When this situation occurs, the network is said to be **partitioned** until such time as the network recovers from the failure. Networks may also become partitioned in mesh topologies.

Bus networks (Figure 12–6) have a different structure from the topologies we have discussed thus far. The bus network has nodes connected to a central cable that supports communications. The nodes "tap into" the cable for communications capabilities. The reliability of the central cable is crucial to the network's reliability.

A number of other terms are often used in distributed database environments. **Public data networks** typically link geographically dispersed processors, terminals, and other equipment via telephone lines. Any equipment that can be interfaced with the national telephone network can take advantage of this system. Public data networks provide fairly reliable, low-cost data communications capabilities. **Public branch exchanges (PBXs)** are local star networks. Digital telephone systems are at the heart of public branch exchange systems. Analog voice signals are converted to digital signals, allowing greater throughput. Another advantage is that public branch exchanges use the same cables for voice and data transmission, eliminating the need for two sets of cables.

Local area networks (LANs) are interconnected systems capable of communicating with each other. As the name implies, these networks typically serve to connect systems in a localized area, such as systems on several floors in an office building or in several buildings on a college campus. The technology that implements LANs currently has about a 10-kilometer (6.25 miles) limitation. This distance limitation can be overcome by placing intermediate **booster nodes** or **repeaters** along the bus

FIGURE 12–6
Bus Network Topology

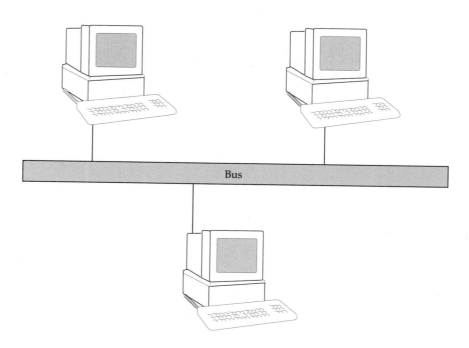

(see Figure 12–7). LANs typically use dedicated cables and consequently can have relatively high transmission speeds.

There are several methods of supporting the actual communication that occurs between network nodes. The star network topology typically relies on the central node to **poll** the other network nodes for processing needs. When a noncentral node indicates communication needs to occur, the central node receives the communication, processes it, and sends results to the node later. In mesh, ring, and bus topologies, data is typically transmitted in **packets.** In mesh and ring networks, the packets are examined as they circulate through the network. When a packet reaches a node for which it is destined, the node receives it and processes it. In bus arrangements, the packets flow through the bus and each node receives packets from the bus.

Several approaches are used to determine which node may use the network at any given time. Polling approaches resolve this issue by dedicating the network to nodes when the node requests permission to

FIGURE 12–7
Local Area Network (LAN)
with Booster

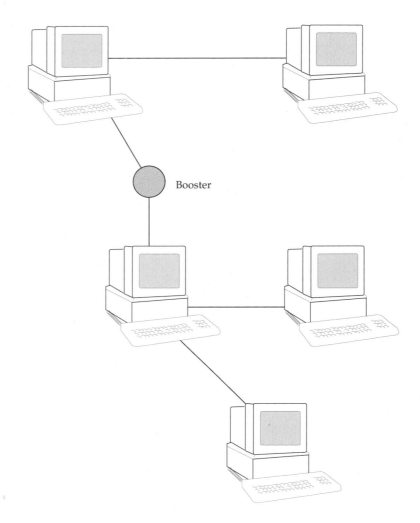

Booster

send a communication. Another approach is called **token passing.** A special signal, called a **token,** is passed from node to node around the network. Whichever node has the token also has control of the communications on the network. When this node completes its transmission, it puts the token back in the network for another node to capture. Nodes that need to use the communication capabilities must wait until control of the token is obtained. A third approach is based on a **reservation** system. In this approach, nodes request use of the network and rely on the network to provide the node with sole network access. When the node is finished, the reservation is canceled and another node may use the network.

Some networks are implemented in a manner that allows nodes to transmit communications whenever desired. The nodes and the network must detect when more than one node is attempting to transmit data simultaneously. A common approach taken in the **Ethernet** bus network system has the nodes checking the bus before and during any transmission to the bus. If the node detects the bus is in use before it begins transmission, the node delays its transmission. Since two or more nodes could possibly begin bus communication simultaneously, nodes also check for bus use during communication processes. Simultaneous communications are called **collisions,** and also cause the nodes to cease transmitting and delay communications.

DISTRIBUTING THE DATA IN DISTRIBUTED DATABASE ENVIRONMENTS

A distributed database environment places computers where problems and work are located and data where it is used. Determining where the computer hardware and software should be located is usually easy, but determining where data should be located can be difficult. A distributed database environment requires the data in the system to be *shared* between the nodes in the system. This data may be either *replicated*—duplicate copies of data are distributed throughout the system—or the data may be *partitioned*—the database is divided into parts that are distributed among the nodes.

Replicated data is shown in Figure 12–8. When data is replicated, the reliability of the system increases since a node or link failure in the system does not prevent access to data. However, more data storage is required than would be necessary if the data was not replicated. Also, updating any particular data item becomes a more complicated process because the update must occur in multiple locations.

When data is partitioned, the scheme for partitioning the data must be developed. On the one hand, partitioning data saves storage requirements. On the other hand, there is a cost associated with transmitting data from one node to another in order to satisfy database queries. Thus, careful consideration must be given to the characteristics of the database processing that will occur when deciding what data to replicate and

FIGURE 12–8   Replicated Data

```
Data at the Detroit Corporate Office:

EMPLOYEES
ID          Name      Department    Title           Awards

32172391    Smith     Accounting    Admin. Assistant    —
38474623    Baker     Accounting    Admin. Assistant    —
94847393    Jones     Production    Foreman             QC
98387344    Lopez     Accounting    Manager             —
83762921    Finch     Production    Technician II       Safety
12827393    Balboa    Production    Technician I        —


Data at the Dearborn Plant:

EMPLOYEES
ID          Name      Department    Title           Awards

32172391    Smith     Accounting    Admin. Assistant    —
38474623    Baker     Accounting    Admin. Assistant    —
94847393    Jones     Production    Foreman             QC
98387344    Lopez     Accounting    Manager             —
83762921    Finch     Production    Technician II       Safety
12827393    Balboa    Production    Technician I        —
```

what data to partition. Often, some combination of replicated and partitioned data best meets the needs of the organization.

In a relational database environment, there are several ways in which the data may be partitioned. A specific table might be partitioned by placing some rows at one node and other rows at some other node. This approach is called **horizontal partitioning.** Figure 12–9a shows the data from Figure 12–8 partitioned horizontally. If the Dearborn plant is primarily a production plant and the corporate office is primarily concerned with administration and there is little need for data on the two functional areas to be shared, then this partitioning may provide significant efficiencies.

An alternative approach partitions the table by placing attributes at different network nodes. This approach is called **vertical partitioning.** Figure 12–9b shows the data from Figure 12–8 partitioned vertically. If the awards maintained in the database are primarily production awards, then partitioning this data out to the Dearborn database may be a good decision. In some cases, a table may first be vertically partitioned, and then the attributes will be horizontally partitioned.

When horizontal partitioning is used, the original table can be reconstructed by performing a union operation on all of the partitions. Horizontal partitioning can always reconstruct the original table. Vertical partitioning, however, may be done in a manner that prevents reconstructing the original table. If key attributes are replicated in the

FIGURE 12–9a   Horizontally Partitioning the Data from Figure 12–8

```
    Data at the Detroit Corporate Office:

    EMPLOYEES
    ID          Name      Department     Title              Awards

    32172391    Smith     Accounting     Admin. Assistant   —
    38474623    Baker     Accounting     Admin. Assistant   —
    98387344    Lopez     Accounting     Manager            —


    Data at the Dearborn Plant:

    EMPLOYEES
    ID          Name      Department     Title              Awards

    94847393    Jones     Production     Foreman            QC
    83762921    Finch     Production     Technician II      Safety
    12827393    Balboa    Production     Technician I       —
```

**FIGURE 12–9b
Vertically Partitioning the
Data from Figure 12–8**

```
    Data at the Detroit Corporate Office:

    EMPLOYEES
    ID          Name      Department     Title

    32172391    Smith     Accounting     Admin. Assistant
    38474623    Baker     Accounting     Admin. Assistant
    94847393    Jones     Production     Foreman
    98387344    Lopez     Accounting     Manager
    83762921    Finch     Production     Technician II
    12827393    Balboa    Production     Technician I


    Data at the Dearborn Plant:

    EMPLOYEES        ID           Awards

                     94847393     QC
                     83762921     Safety
                     12827393     —
```

partitions, then join operations can be used to reconstruct the original table. When the key attributes are omitted, the partitions cannot be recombined. Some systems, however, will append identifiers to the tuples in the partitions that identify the original table from which the data was partitioned. The system can then reconstruct the original table, although this operation will not be accomplished through data manipulation via relational algebra.

Users should be unaware of details such as what data items are replicated and how data has been partitioned. Ideally, a distributed database environment allows a user to interact with programs and data stored anywhere in the system without knowing or seeing the details of the interaction. When transactions can be executed without concern for where the data being manipulated is stored, the system exhibits **location transparency. Replication transparency** exists when transactions may be executed without explicit concern for how many occurrences of the data item exist. Users cannot be kept totally isolated from these aspects. If a node or link failure occurs in a distributed database management system that has partitioned data, then subsequent attempts to access data at the unavailable node will be detected. Users will be required to delay their processing until the node becomes available again.

In an ideal situation, the data has been replicated and partitioned in a manner that all local database transactions can be satisfied without requiring any data to be communicated from one node to another. As you might expect, the ideal situation rarely occurs. When, for example, two tables must be joined and each table resides at a different node in the system, several decisions must be made. One table might be sent to the other node and processing continued at that node. Alternatively, transmitting the *other* table to the *other* node might be more cost-efficient (in terms of communication costs and response time).

An alternative approach, used frequently, constructs a result known as a **semijoin.** Suppose the data in Figure 12–10 must be joined, where the CUSTOMER information resides at one node in the network and the ORDER information resides at another. This operation might be required in order to mail out billing invoices from the regional sales office. Since the join will occur over the customer ID attribute, only this attribute will be transmitted to the node containing the customer data. Joining this attribute with the customer data effectively selects the tuples from the customer data for which order data exists. After this join occurs, the result is transmitted to the regional office, and the order information can be joined with this result to prepare the billing offices. This approach has minimized the amount of customer data that must be transmitted from one node to the other.

CONCURRENCY MANAGEMENT IN DDBMSS

DDBMSs must resolve concurrent access issues in the same manner that centralized database management systems must. The problems are more complex, however, because conflicting transactions may be executing at different nodes.

If data is replicated, then a transaction at one node in the system may "spawn" more transactions in other parts of the system. We must now deal with the concept of a **global transaction** and a **local transaction.** The global transaction is the initial transaction that a user submits. It is global in the sense that the user wants the data and should be able to access the data regardless of where it resides in the

FIGURE 12–10   Data at Two Nodes to Illustrate a Semijoin Operation

```
CUSTOMER
ID    Name                   Address              Credit Limit

101   Philip Smith           123 Apple St           1200.00
102   Samuel Adams           296 Maple Ave          1200.00
239   Bayard Wynne           12 Broning St           800.00
233   Robert Davis           2253 Rayado St         1500.00
298   Bala Shetty            1301 29th St           1800.00
185   Deron Walker           712 Stanton Rd         1900.00


ORDER
ID    Item                   No. Ordered          Unit Cost

102   Weston Grill                1                   29.95
102   Barbecue Rack               1                    9.95
102   Salad Bowl Set              1                   14.95
233   Dynamo Disks                3                   21.95
298   Gateway Men's Suit          2                  695.00
298   Oryx Reversible Belt        1                   29.95
```

system. This global transaction will generate possibly multiple transactions that are local to specific database systems in the distributed system (Figure 12–11). Each of these local transactions must supply some piece of the information required to satisfy the global transaction. The method for resolving concurrent accesses must also consider how replicated items, global transactions, and local transactions will be treated.

In general, the method chosen to manage concurrent access can be implemented on one central computer or the method may be distributed over the system. When a single, centralized approach is taken, the algorithm is typically simpler. The node that manages the concurrent processing activities need not be the node where a data item is physically stored. However, using a centralized computer to manage all of the concurrent processing needs (such as requests for locks) can be inefficient and slow as the number of transactions increases. The centralized approach also makes the entire system very reliant on the computer managing the concurrent processing. If this computer fails, the entire system is without a means to manage the concurrent processing.

Locking mechanisms can be used in distributed systems, and several approaches based on locking have been developed. When a centralized approach is taken, all requests for locks are directed to the central computer, which either grants or denies the request. If the lock is granted, the central node sends a message to all nodes containing the data item being locked that the lock has been applied. When the transaction is committed, the central node sends another message releasing the lock.

When the concurrent processing management is distributed, each node has a locking management program. Whenever a lock is needed,

FIGURE 12–11 Updated Data from Figure 12–8 after Spawned Transaction

```
Transaction:

UPDATE Awards = Safety
WHERE ID = 12827393

Modifies the data at the Detroit Corporate Office:

EMPLOYEES
ID          Name      Department    Title              Awards

32172391    Smith     Accounting    Admin. Assistant   —
38474623    Baker     Accounting    Admin. Assistant   —
94847393    Jones     Production    Foreman            QC
98387344    Lopez     Accounting    Manager            —
83762921    Finch     Production    Technician II      Safety
12827393    Balboa    Production    Technician I       Safety


But for consistency, the system must also spawn the same
transaction for the data at the Dearborn Plant:

Transaction:

UPDATE Awards = Safety
WHERE ID = 12827393

EMPLOYEES
ID          Name      Department    Title              Awards

32172391    Smith     Accounting    Admin. Assistant   —
38474623    Baker     Accounting    Admin. Assistant   —
94847393    Jones     Production    Foreman            QC
98387344    Lopez     Accounting    Manager            —
83762921    Finch     Production    Technician II      Safety
12827393    Balboa    Production    Technician I       Safety
```

the locking management program sends a message to all other nodes requesting the lock. Each node that can apply the lock does so and responds to the node that sent the original message. If all nodes respond that the lock may be applied, the transaction begins. If some nodes cannot apply the lock, the other locks are released and the transaction is delayed.

In practice, many algorithms require that only a majority of the nodes containing replicated data must be locked for a transaction to continue. This approach reduces the occurrence of deadlock situations. For example, suppose three transactions begin that request a lock on the same data item. Assume the data item is replicated at seven nodes, and assume that the first transaction has a lock at four nodes while the second and third transactions have locks at two nodes each. If locks are required at all nodes, then all three transactions will be delayed and restarted. If only a majority of locks are needed, the second and third transactions will be delayed and restarted, but the first transaction will be allowed to continue.

Deadlock situations can be difficult to detect in a distributed system. One must detect not only deadlocks at a particular node, but also deadlocks occurring across nodes. Figure 12–12 illustrates an example of a distributed deadlock situation. Here, four transactions are in progress. Transaction 1 at the Chicago location has a locked inventory record that transaction 2 in Chicago needs. Thus, transaction 2 is waiting on transaction 1. Transaction 3, at Dallas, is waiting on transaction 2 to complete because transaction 2 is a local transaction spawned by transaction 3. Transaction 3, however, locked a shipping record that transaction 4, also in Dallas, needs. So transaction 4 is also in a waiting state. Unfortunately, transaction 4 was spawned by transaction 1. Thus, transaction 1 will not complete until its local transaction, transaction 4, completes. This deadlock cannot be detected by looking only at the local database systems. Distributed locking therefore requires that some node maintain a global view of the concurrent process management.

Locking mechanisms require considerable overhead in a distributed system, since each occurrence of an item to be locked must be locked in multiple nodes throughout the system. The system could be overwhelmed by the messages necessary just to apply the locks. In spite of this drawback, locking is the most widely used concurrency management technique in distributed database environments. Time-stamping is a good approach for resolving concurrency problems in a distributed database environment. The message traffic is reduced to the time-stamp information that includes node information in a distributed system. However, the time stamp must now reflect both node and systemwide values. Typically, a global time stamp clock is maintained as well as a

FIGURE 12–12   **A Distributed Deadlock Situation**

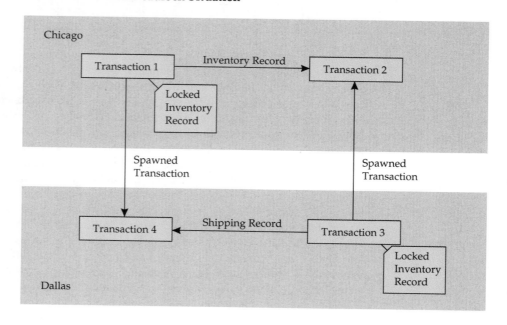

local one at each node. The global time stamp and the local time stamp are concatenated to form a single time stamp for any data item being accessed. When a node identifier is added to the time stamp, then the time stamp is guaranteed to be unique. Also, as noted in Chapter 11, deadlock situations do not occur.

RECOVERY IN DDBMSS

As we noted earlier, a transaction in a DDBMS may generate transactions at other nodes. For example, suppose the credit limit for a customer is maintained at both the corporate headquarters and at a local regional database node. If the regional office increases the customer's credit limit, the transaction to accomplish this task must also generate a similar transaction at the corporate node. Should either transaction fail, the database will be in an inconsistent state if the effect of the other transaction is not removed from the database. The transactions generated by a transaction are called *subtransactions*.

Distributed commit management is required to monitor the state of transactions in a DDBMS. All subtransactions must send a commit message to the commit manager in order for any change to be committed to the database. If any subtransaction fails, then the original transaction is aborted and must be reexecuted later.

A DDBMS must also contend with node failures and link failures. These failures are easy to recognize, since they are characterized by absence of communications across the network. The system can be recovered if the nodes execute local recovery processes as described in Chapter 11.

A more difficult problem is how to manage subtransactions that become isolated on partitioned nodes due to link failures. In other words, while the subtransaction was processing, the node became partitioned from the rest of the network due to one or more link failures. In this case, the subtransaction may successfully complete and be ready to commit, but it does not receive any message from the commit management process requesting its status.

A subtransaction in this state is called **blocked.** When subtransactions do not receive messages from transaction management processes such as the commit manager within prespecified time limits, they are assumed to be blocked. The subtransactions then send specific messages out to recovery management processes requesting instructions on what to do next. Based on the response received from the recovery management process, the subtransaction may abort or commit.

THE NETWORK REPOSITORY

Because each node in the system interacts with other nodes, a distributed database requires a data repository adapted for the network environment. The network repository provides information supporting navigation through the network, much as a data repository supports navigation through a single database. This repository will contain information about where data items are located, whether they have been partitioned or replicated. The network repository will also contain synonyms used by nodes for data items that are replicated in the system. Network repositories typically contain information about the origin of the data item, that is, which node generated the first occurrence of the item.

As with any other data in the distributed environment, the network repository could be replicated or partitioned. Again, complete replication requires significant overhead whenever the network repository must be updated, since the update occurs in multiple places. Complete partitioning requires significant overhead communication costs associated with determining where an item resides in the system.

The typical network repository maintains information about the origin site (sometimes called the *birth site*) of each data item. However, since data items may be moved from one location to another, each local repository also contains information about the location of any item that originated at this location but currently resides at another location. In this manner, the DDBMS will not have to search throughout the system for a particular data item. It will look first at the network repository to determine where the item originated and attempt to locate the item at that node. If the item is not there, the local repository will contain the current location. Thus, at most two locations must be polled to locate a data item.

ADVANTAGES OF DISTRIBUTED DATABASE ENVIRONMENTS

There are many potential advantages to the distributed database approach. Data entry tends to be greatly improved in a distributed environment because the local site tends to be more familiar with the data than the central corporate office. Obvious mistakes that might not be detected at a central location are recognized and corrected.

Another advantage is that small database processing tasks can be completed on the local equipment without incurring the communications costs involved in a strictly centralized environment. Communications costs are further reduced if only summary information need be transmitted to the central processing location rather than unprocessed, detailed data.

The response time may be faster at the local site. Distributed databases also reduce the workload on the central computing facility. The greatest advantage in management's eyes may be a perception that local database processing costs are controllable. Local managers often feel that they have little control over the costs involved when processing is performed by a central corporate facility. In distributed systems, the processing is under local control.

DISADVANTAGES OF DISTRIBUTED DATABASE ENVIRONMENTS

A distributed database system has disadvantages, too. One disadvantage is that economies of scale may be lost. Large computers tend to process information faster than smaller ones, so the local computers may take longer to accomplish the data processing at the local site. Increased costs in replicating hardware, software, and data may offset savings in communications costs.

All of the control problems associated with microcomputers discussed in earlier chapters are also possible in a distributed database environment. In particular, unnecessary duplication of design and programming activity may occur at the local sites; for example, the same payroll application would probably work at all sites in the organization. And although distribution may improve management at the nodes, overall management of the distributed facilities from the corporate center becomes complex.

Database systems are no less complex in a distributed database environment. Local managers may not have the technical expertise needed to manage the database system and its equipment. Thus, a local staff may be needed. This situation can pose special problems of its own. The local staff may be small, making it particularly difficult to cope with absences for sickness or vacation. Also, local staff may perceive that no opportunities for professional growth exist, leading to high turnover rates. And even if the local staff is satisfied, the central staff may perceive local staffs as a threat to their job security.

A WORD ABOUT THE HOMOGENOUS SYSTEM ASSUMPTION

We noted at the beginning of this chapter that we were assuming all nodes in the distributed system are executing the same DBMS software. We will now consider what additional activities must occur if we relax this constraint, thus allowing **heterogeneous DDBMSs.**

For a start, each DBMS must be able to determine what data items are under control of other DBMSs. This evaluation implies that each data repository format is known to other systems. This property is necessary to access data at other nodes in the system. Each client DBMS must also know the command structure of the other DBMSs in order to construct a data manipulation command that the server DBMS can process. All of the versions of SQL currently on the market contain small differences. These differences help define that product's market niche, but they also confound efforts to communicate across systems. Once the result is created, the server DBMS must also know the client's internal storage format so that the results can be communicated to the client system.

At a deeper level, the client and server systems must be communicating very specific information regarding concurrent processing and recovery. The concurrent processing techniques must be understood by

The User's View

Many of the characteristics that have been described are extremely critical for successful implementation and use of a distributed DBMS. For example, consider for a moment what would happen if the user was required to locate database items in a DDBMS. Let's take a simple case where a bank needs to transfer $50 from one bank account to another. Assume there are only two DBMSs in the system, one in New York and one in Boston. Suppose the money is to be transferred from account 3504964 to 3508837.

There are four cases that the bank must consider. Both accounts could be on the New York system. Both accounts could be on the Boston system.

The 3504964 account could be on the New York system and the 3508837 account could be on the Boston system. Or the 3508837 account could be on the New York system and the 3504964 account could be on the Boston system. If there were three possible locations, then there are nine potential combinations of account location. In general, there will be n^2 potential combinations, where n represents the number of locations. Major metropolitan area banks may have more than 30 branch offices. Programming a trivial transaction to transfer $50 from one account to another becomes an overwhelming task in this situation. ■

---

both systems in order to prevent the problems discussed in Chapter 11. There are often subtle differences in the algorithms used by DBMSs to implement various locking schemes, even when each one claims to be implementing the same algorithm. The task of coordinating a locking scheme on one system and a time-stamping approach on another is significant. Each system's logging activity must be similarly correlated.

Without discussing any of the technical details, we have outlined a great deal of translation and coordination activity. At least two events must occur before heterogeneous DDBMSs will become common. First, we will probably need to see still greater increases in generally available raw computing power before such translations can occur in real time. Second, the benefit to the DBMS manufacturers to interface with other DBMSs must exceed the costs of building the gateways to do it.

CHAPTER SUMMARY

A distributed database management system allows database users to access data anywhere in a network of databases without regard to any of the details associated with the data distribution. Distributed DBMSs, or DDBMSs, naturally mirror today's complex organizations. Organizations are frequently composed of geographically dispersed elements. Since databases are needed throughout an organization, database management systems must support local as well as organizationwide information processing.

A logical model for explaining the relationships between computers in a network is the client/server architecture. The client machine requests information and the server machine provides it. The problem of handling communication between the machines is handled by a gateway. Client/server arrangements and gateways are flexible methods for

Metropolitan National Bank

The following memorandum has just come to your office:

Metropolitan National Bank
Main Office: 8200 Northwest Parkway
Lincoln, Texas 79402–8297
MEMORANDUM

TO: All Employees
FROM: Board of Directors
SUBJECT: Merger with First Commerce Bank of the Southwest

We are pleased to announce that negotiations have been completed that will result in the acquisition by MetNat of the First Commerce Bank of the Southwest. As you are probably aware, First Commerce Bank's headquarters are in Tanner, Texas. First Commerce will be renamed Metropolitan National Bank–Tanner. We expect to begin a gradual process of reorganizing MetNat–Tanner so that it will become the first fully integrated member of what we hope will be a growing MetNat family of banks. This reorganization is expected to take 12 to 18 months. Your department vice president will be giving you specific directions regarding how MetNat–Tanner's operations will be integrated with ours. In the interim, please join us in extending a heart-felt welcome to our new colleagues in Tanner.

As you might expect, successful integration of the two banks will require successful integration of the supporting information systems. Here is some information you have been able to collect:

Tanner is a metropolitan area roughly equal in size to Lincoln. MetNat–Tanner is a bank of similar size to MetNat, but it has not emphasized a customer service orientation as MetNat has. MetNat–Tanner grew substantially in the early and mid-1980s by offering very attractive rates of return on money market accounts and securities such as certificates of deposit. (You suspect that these rates have contributed somewhat to the bank's weakened financial strength.)

MetNat–Tanner actually has had larger information processing needs than MetNat. MetNat–Tanner currently services approximately 50,000 checking accounts, 40,000 savings accounts, and 60,000 money market accounts. MetNat–Tanner has approximately 10,000 commercial loans and 7,000 personal loans outstanding. MetNat–Tanner also issues a bank credit card. However, the credit card has a rather high annual fee ($90) and an equally unattractive annual percentage (21 percent), so the bank has only around 10,000 card holders.

MetNat–Tanner operates seven branch offices. The staffing at these offices is minimal, typically only a branch manager and one or two tellers. Applications for loans and/or new accounts may be made at the branch offices, but the paperwork is forwarded to the central office and processed there.

The organizational structure of MetNat–Tanner is similar to MetNat's, with the following exceptions. Credit card operations are handled in a separate department, called credit card operations. This department is managed by a manager of credit card operations. There are two employees in this department.

No distinct marketing function exists. Each individual department is responsible for its marketing needs. This activity is typically managed by the vice president of the department. Similarly, MetNat–Tanner has no customer service representatives. Customer inquiries are handled on an ad hoc basis by the appropriate department. Also, MetNat–Tanner has no financial planning group available to its customers, and no safe deposit boxes are available either.

The data file contents and bank statements issued by MetNat–Tanner are almost identical to MetNat's files and statements. The computer operations are run by a manager of computer services. She has three assistants who support all of the operating system and application programming required at MetNat–Tanner. The computer services department has approximately a six-month backlog of application program work to address.

The board of directors has determined that all First Commerce Bank credit cards should be replaced with MetNat credit cards as soon as possible. The transition period will extend over three months. During this period, all current First Commerce Bank credit card holders will be reviewed and issued a new MetNat credit card with a credit limit equal to their current limit. Credit card bills will contain a statement indicating First Commerce cards will be valid for only one month following the issuance of the new card. After that time, the First Commerce card will be invalid. To encourage use of the new card, the higher First Commerce Bank interest charges will continue to be assessed to the First Commerce card.

The board of directors plans the following structural changes for MetNat and MetNat–Tanner. MetNat's executive vice president will manage MetNat–Tanner until a new person can be found to fill this role. The new chief executive position at MetNat–Tanner will be at the executive vice president level, reporting to the president of MetNat Bank in Lincoln.

The credit card operations department at MetNat–Tanner will be consolidated into the loans administration department at MetNat. All credit card operations will subsequently be directed from MetNat's Lincoln office. The marketing function will be removed from the special services department and designated a separate department. The new marketing department will be located at MetNat and will service both MetNat and MetNat–Tanner. A financial planning group and a customer service group will be developed at MetNat–Tanner. These groups will be in the new special services department at MetNat–Tanner.

All human resources operations will also be handled at the Lincoln office. The existing MetNat–Tanner human resources personnel will be extended offers to move to Lincoln, or given six weeks of severance pay and assistance in locating new employment. The board of directors is delaying any decision regarding the MetNat–Tanner computer services operations pending your input regarding how to best structure these operations.

Your task is to determine how to best distribute the data in the new combined organization. Provide relational schema descriptions that indicate how the data is replicated and/or partitioned between the two nodes. Determine the staffing needs required to support the distributed system and provide some rationale for where you locate the support staff. ■

supporting communication between computers, even if they are different brands.

Several network topologies have evolved to support distributed processing. Star networks connect all nodes to a central computing resource. Star networks rely on the central computing resource, as any failure there causes the entire system to fail. Mesh networks allow nodes to be interconnected with any other nodes in the system. If all nodes are connected to all other nodes, the network is fully connected; otherwise, it is partially connected. Ring networks connect modes in a circular fashion. Bus networks connect nodes to a central cable that supports communications. The nodes tap into the cable for communications capabilities. Local area networks are interconnected systems that typically serve to connect systems in a localized area, such as systems on several floors in an office building or in several buildings on a college campus.

There are several methods of supporting the actual communication that occurs between network nodes. Polling is used when a central computer controls the distributed functions. Packets of information are typically passed from node to node in a network. The token-passing approach uses a special packet of information to indicate which computer has control of the network. A common approach taken in the Ethernet bus network system has the nodes checking the bus before and during any transmission to the bus.

A distributed database environment places computers where problems and work are located and data where it is used. The data may be replicated or partitioned. When data is replicated, the reliability of the system increases since a node or link failure in the system does not prevent access to data. However, more data storage is required. Partitioning data saves storage requirements, but there is a cost associated with transmitting data from one node to another in order to satisfy database queries. Partitioning may be horizontal, vertical, or both.

DDBMSs must resolve concurrent access issues in the same manner that centralized DBMSs must. The problems are more complex, however, because conflicting transactions may be executing at different nodes. If data is replicated, then a transaction at one node in the system may spawn more transactions in other parts of the system. Locking is a widely used approach to concurrency management in a DDBMS. However, deadlock situations may go undetected on a local level, requiring global deadlock detection strategies.

Rollback and recovery also become more complex in a distributed environment. Distributed commit management is required to monitor the state of transactions in a DDBMS. All transactions spawned by a user's original transaction must send a commit message to the commit manager in order for any change to be committed to the database. If any spawned transaction fails, then the original transaction is aborted and must be reexecuted later. Handling node and link failures only adds to the complexity of recovery management.

Because each node in the system interacts with other nodes, a distributed database requires a data repository adapted for the network environment. The typical network repository maintains information about the origin site of each data item. However, since data items may be moved from one location to another, each local repository also contains information about the location of any item that originated at this location but currently resides at another location. In this manner, the

DDBMS will not have to search through more than two nodes for a particular data item.

There are many potential advantages to the distributed database approach. Data entry tends to be greatly improved. Obvious mistakes that might not be detected at a central location are recognized and corrected. Local database processing tasks can be completed on the local equipment without incurring the communications costs. The response time may be faster at the local site. The processing is under local control.

A distributed database system has its disadvantages, too. Economies of scale may be lost. Increased costs in replicating hardware, software, and data may offset savings in communications costs. And although distribution may improve management at the nodes, overall management of the distributed facilities from the corporate center becomes complex.

Questions and Exercises

1. Define *distributed database management system*.
2. What is the homogenous system assumption? How realistic is it? Contact three or four departments (or colleagues) at your university to determine the validity of the homogenous system assumption there.
3. Describe the client/server architecture model. What is a *gateway*?
4. What advantages does the client/server approach provide?
5. Describe a star network. What is the principal disadvantage of the star network topology?
6. Describe a mesh network. How does it differ from a star network? What is the principal advantage of the mesh network topology?
7. Describe a ring network. How can a ring network become partitioned? What problems exist when a ring network is partitioned?
8. Describe a bus network. How does it differ from other network topologies?
9. Describe a local area network. Find one in your university and determine how far apart the boosters are.
10. Describe the token-passing approach to network communications.
11. Describe two ways that data can be distributed in a DDBMS. What are the advantages and disadvantages of each?
12. Describe horizontal and vertical partitioning.
13. Consider the following situation. A corporation has three major corporate offices: one in Los Angeles, one in Dallas, and one in Baltimore. It needs to maintain employee information (name, address, salary, title, ID number) on all employees in all locations. Eighty percent of the information processing in the

organization is on a local basis. The remaining processing requires information from all three locations. Should the data be replicated or partitioned? If you choose partitioned, would you partition horizontally or vertically?

14. What is *location transparency*? Why is location transparency desirable?

15. What is *replication transparency*? Why is it desirable?

16. Suppose the following data exists at two locations in a DDBMS.

ID	Employee	Address	City
1234	John Smith	12 Apple St.	Canton
2837	Ian Baker	10 Downing St.	Canton
3874	Calvin Hobbs	222 Jump St.	Ogden
2928	Jim Nkomo	188 Delta Ave.	Trenton

ID	Name	Date
1234	Client Service	7/8/90
1234	Quality Control	5/19/88
1234	Innovative Idea	6/12/88
3874	Quality Control	6/20/89

Assume you want the names and addresses of award winners. Describe a semijoin operation to obtain this result.

17. What is a *global transaction*? What is a *local transaction*? Under what circumstances must a global transaction spawn local transactions?

18. Describe the "majority locking" approach to concurrency management in a DDBMS.

19. Describe a deadlock situation in a DDBMS. Will deadlocks always be detectable at the local level?

20. How does a network repository determine the location of a data item in a DDBMS?

21. What are the advantages and disadvantages of DDBMSs?

For Further Reading

Aspects of distributed database systems are discussed in Didising, David. "The Case for Decentralized Control of Data Processing." *The Office*, September 1984, pp. 51–54.

Dowgiallo, Ed. "The Art of Distribution." *DBMS*, March 1989, pp. 41–52.

Gligor, V. and R. Popescu-Zeletin. "Transaction Management in Distributed Heterogeneous Database Management Systems." *Information Systems* 11, no. 4 (1986), pp. 287–89.

Gray, Jim. "Transparency in Distributed Processing." *Database Programming and Design*, March 1988, pp. 46–52.

Holbrook, Robert. "Distributed RDBMSs Put Opportunities Online." *Business Software Review*, June 1988, pp. 46–53.

Mohan, C.; B. Lindsay; and R. Obermarck. "Transaction Management in the R* Distributed Database Management System." *ACM Transactions on Database Systems* 11, no. 4 (December 1986), pp. 376–96.

Sexton, Walter. "DDP Can Be Used to Implement Office Automation." *Data Management,* July 1984, pp. 47–48.

Stamper, D. A. *Business Data Communications.* Menlo Park, Calif.: Benjamin/Cummings, 1986.

Strehlo, Christine. "Mastering the Shared Database." *Personal Computing,* December 1988, pp. 121–25.

Triner, Michael. "The High Road to Host Connectivity." *PC Tech Journal,* January 1989, pp. 85–94.

Walsh, M. E. *Database and Data Communications Systems: A Guide for Managers.* Reston, Va.: Reston, 1983.

Yannakakis, M. "Deadlock Freedom (and Safety) of Transactions in a Distributed Database." *Journal of Computer and System Sciences* 33, no. 2 (October 1986), pp. 161–78.

13

Other Approaches to Database Management

Selected concepts and technologies that are just beginning to be realized in database environments are examined in this chapter. As a manager, you will always need to be aware of the new developments in your field of expertise. You may be evaluating this technology in the near future.

DATABASE ISSUES IN COMPUTER-INTEGRATED MANUFACTURING

Computer-integrated manufacturing (CIM) has been described as the integration of computer-aided design and engineering (CAD/CAE), computer-aided manufacturing (CAM), and production management through group technology principles by means of a common information system. Such an information system is supported by heterogeneous and distributed databases containing engineering, manufacturing, and management data. CIM information systems constitute a challenge to existing database technology because new database capabilities are needed to support CIM applications.

The life cycle of a product typically involves several phases: market analysis, product conceptualization, research and development, product design, product manufacturing, and product testing. These phases are highly interrelated and considerable amounts of information are shared among them. CIM attempts to integrate these phases needed in the production environment to increase the competitive advantage of the manufacturing firm.

Computer-integrated manufacturing (CIM) is defined as the use of database and communication technologies to integrate the design, manufacturing, and business functions of a factory. In a broader sense, CIM systems involve the combination of different technologies: expert systems, simulation-based decision aids, databases, communications, and, if it is to be used in operations, instrumentation and control systems. In conservative terms, CIM means computer assistance in all functions of the production process. Ideally, CIM is the complete automation of the factory, with all processes being executed under control of computers that use digital information to tie the processes together.

Among the advantages of CIM are greater flexibility, shorter product life cycles, greater product quality, better equipment utilization, and less labor costs. Moreover, CIM reduces the human component of manufacturing and thereby relieves the process of its most error-prone ingredient.

Historically, the introduction of computers into factories has occurred in a bottom-up fashion. Individual design and manufacturing processes have been automated without concern for compatibility between them. This information systems development process has yielded "islands of automation," that is, individual automated applications unable to communicate. As we discussed in Chapter 1, information systems based on this approach are unable to share, relate, and integrate data from different sources. Communication based on an effective and efficient information management system is thus the key to CIM integration. Information must be available when and where it is required and throughout all the organization.

Database Management Systems for CIM

Without effective information management, the necessary level of automation and control required by CIM would not be possible. Therefore, data management is a major concern for CIM.

Currently, most computerized manufacturing applications are developed the way old data processing systems were built: They are designed and written using conventional file management techniques. Data is stored and retrieved using data structures that fit specific applications. Data is shared among applications by providing an interface that converts the output file of one application to the input file format of another. As we have discussed earlier, maintaining this data sharing approach is very inefficient. Many interfaces must be developed, and whenever an application input or output file changes, the corresponding interface must be modified. Furthermore, data translation requires processing time.

Manufacturing organizations have often developed information systems while focusing on specific applications. This development methodology has several disadvantages, including:

1. The computer is the most critical and expensive resource; thus, emphasis is put on optimizing the physical storage and retrieval of the system.
2. Applications are tightly dependent on specific hardware and software configurations.
3. Applications are developed based on initial statements of requirements, and evolution through prototyping is typically not supported.
4. Each application is developed independently of all of the other related existing and future applications.

This approach contributes to major problems for an integrated CIM system. In complex applications such as the ones in CIM, a prototyping environment is very attractive. Prototyping allows users to experiment and provide feedback to the information system's developers. The complexity of modern manufacturing environments makes it unlikely that users will know exactly what is needed in an information system before it is developed. Moreover, optimizing computer resources for specific applications may result in suboptimal solutions in the global context of CIM.

Still, the development of independent applications is the most serious threat to an integrated CIM system. For CIM, the development of information systems must be based on an integrative methodology using a database as the core of the CIM system. The "architectural foundation" methodology provides an example of such methodology. This methodology is based on the design of an organizationwide strategic data architecture that serves as an underlying guide for all systems development. This approach positions the database of the firm as the center of the CIM system development, and thus avoids incompatibility for the integration of applications.

If a database constitutes the core of an organization's information system, then it represents a key component for the manufacturing integration process. However, existing DBMSs generally lack the power to support CIM applications satisfactorily.

The principal shortcoming of current general-purpose DBMSs rests in the descriptive capabilities of their underlying data models. The hierarchical, the network, and the relational data models generally lack the expressive power needed to represent semantics. As a result, some application-specific database systems, such as RIM, IPIP, DBS/R, and GLIDE, have been developed. Object-oriented databases systems, discussed later in this chapter, have also been developed to address this problem. The Semantic Database Model, also discussed in this chapter, was developed to address the need for better semantic representation in data models.

A DBMS suitable for CIM must be able to support all the factory's manufacturing functions. These functions can be classified into four categories: design, manufacturing, process planning, and production management.

Design involves the use of computer software and hardware to aid in the creation, management, and testing of product designs. The terms *computer-aided design (CAD)* and *computer-aided engineering (CAE)* are used to designate the use of computer support during the design stage.

Manufacturing consists of the use of computer technology to control and operate manufacturing equipment. It involves numerical control centers, robotics for materials and manufacturing operations, and flexible machining systems. The term *computer-aided manufacturing (CAM)* is often used to refer to the use of computers in supporting this activity.

Process planning constitutes the link between the design phase and the manufacturing phase of a product. Given a part design, process planning determines the sequence of operations required to produce it. You might encounter the acronym CAPP, which stands for computer-aided process planning, used in this activity.

Production management (PM) corresponds to a set of computer-based application systems that provide a continuous flow of information among all related planning, execution, and control centers. It involves forecasting, master scheduling, material requirements planning, production scheduling, inventory control, and cost accounting.

A CIM database can be visualized as the integration of design databases, manufacturing databases, and business-oriented production management databases all operating in a distributed environment. Each of these databases imposes data modeling and data management requirements different from the ones associated with traditional business data processing requirements (information systems to which current DBMSs were developed). These differences in requirements are discussed in the next sections.

Design Database Requirements

The design phase, in which CAD and CAE are used, imposes a series of data modeling and data management requirements that differ from the traditional business data processing requirements supported by current DBMSs. Requirement differences exist in the design objects' structure and version control, database retrieval, database transactions and concurrency control, database consistency enforcement, database response time, and recovery scheme.

Design Objects. A design object is represented by structural data and functional data. The structural data describes the physical configuration of the design. The functional data describes the analytical properties or behavioral aspect of the design.

The structural configurations of design objects, referred to as *product structures* or *bills of material* are usually assemblies of parts that are themselves composed of smaller parts. Such assemblies constitute a hierarchical structure and are referred to as *composite objects* or *complex objects.* These objects, not database tuples, are the units of retrieval and storage, and are the basis for enforcing semantic integrity upon the modification, insertion, and deletion of component objects. Traditional DBMSs do not fully support these needs.

The product structure of a part also involves its geometric definition. The geometry of a part can be represented by a two-dimensional wire-frame model, or a three-dimensional solid model. Three-dimensional solid models, which can be classified in constructive solid geometry (CSG) and boundary representation (B-rep), are dominating the CAD/CAM sector. The CSG approach involves solid primitives and a set of basic operations that are combined on a tree structure to build up a complex solid geometry object. In the B-rep approach, the boundaries of the solid are explicitly defined by various types of surfaces, whose boundaries are in turn defined as curves. DBMSs used for CAD/CAE must support at least one of the existing geometry representation schemes.

Version Control. Because of the tentative nature of the design process, each iteration may contain several apparently correct refinements at a given point in time. Designers usually choose one alternative and proceed until they complete the design. If the result is unsatisfactory, they back up and pursue another alternative. This implies that several current and past descriptions of a design object must be stored in the database. Current DBMSs do not meet the data modeling requirements arising from the iterative, tentative, and multistage nature of the design process.

In dealing with CAD databases, one must be aware that:

1. CAD involves several design descriptions, with designs moving from abstract specifications to progressively more concrete ones.
2. Given a design in one representation, designers typically experiment with various implementation alternatives, such as different technologies, design algorithms, or design constraints.

3. For each alternative, multiple versions of a design are generated to ensure correctness and optimize performance.

The problem of managing this complex environment of design descriptions is referred to as **version control** and has been studied for CAD applications and software development. Description requirements evolve constantly during the life cycle of a design. Therefore, the DBMS should support data evolution.

Design Retrieval.   Design retrieval is another area of interest in CAD systems. Design retrieval allows engineers to find design and engineering data about existing designs. Design retrieval is one of the most obvious benefits of data sharing. The person using a CAD database may want a design that satisfies current requirements or a similar design that requires only minor modifications. For such a purpose, assistance is needed in searching, matching, and understanding the functionality of the design descriptions.

Some researchers suggest that a design retrieval system can be implemented using a classification and coding scheme, a DBMS, and a user interface that allows the user to ask questions to find similar designs. Others argue that an automated design librarian is also needed to provide intelligent services through the use of artificial intelligence inference techniques such as default or nonmonatomic reasoning, plausible reasoning, and logical or deductive reasoning. If this second route is pursued, the DBMS that supports the design phase must be able to store knowledge bases as well as databases (see Chapter 14).

Transactions and Concurrency Control.   A CAD environment requires a significantly different model of transaction from the one we developed in Chapter 11 for typical data processing applications. Traditional database management transactions typically involve a short interaction with the database that preserves its consistency. We have seen that concurrency control based on the notion of serialization is adequate in these situations.

Unfortunately, this well-understood model is not applicable to CAD. Since CAD transactions are of longer duration and involve conscious decisions of human designers, making transactions wait until conflicting transactions terminate or having the system back out all updates to the database if a transaction fails is highly undesirable.

The environment of CAD applications consists of a public system that manages the database of stable design data and a collection of private systems connected to it. Each private system manages the private database of a designer. Initiated in a private database, a CAD transaction consists of:

1. Checking out the design data from the public system and their insertion into the private database.
2. Reading and writing in the private database.
3. Checking in updated design data to the public database.

A large design effort is typically partitioned into a number of projects that induce a partitioning of the database into a number of mostly nonoverlapping partitions. In this environment, concurrency control based on the concept of cooperating transactions that constitute hierarchies of client/server transactions is attractive.

Database Consistency. Enforcing database consistency is also different. In addition to the traditional referential and domain constraints checked by conventional DBMSs, design applications must satisfy some design constraints. Katz (1983) mentions three classes of consistency constraints for design applications. *Conformity constraints* ensure consistency between the specification and the implementation of a design part. *Composition constraints* ensure the correct cooperation of subparts to form a part. *Equivalence constraints* ensure different representations of a design part are in fact equivalent. In contrast to the traditional constraints, some design constraints cannot be enforced automatically by the DBMSs since design tools must be involved.

Additionally, two types of environmental consistency constraints are addressed (see Dittrich et al., 1986, and Ketabchi and Berzins, 1987). *Local consistency* exists when a description does not violate any built-in or user-defined constraint applicable to that description, without regard to its relationships with other descriptions. Locally consistent descriptions are checked into the public database as new alternatives or versions. *Global consistency* is the same concept generalized over the entire database. Global consistency is currently enforced through a lengthy validation process.

Response Time. Commercial DBMS are not fast enough to support simulators and interactive design tools needed in CIM environments. Two primary deficiencies exist. First, access paths in CAD applications follow the connectivity of real-world objects, not the logical structures reflected in existing database models. Second, commercial DBMSs are optimized for high transaction commitment throughput that lowers the response time to intermediate design transactions. In the CAD environment, a designer would be glad to sacrifice response time when saving a design in return for faster design editing capabilities.

Recovery Scheme. Given the long duration of CAD transactions, limiting the recovery scheme to a partial rollback of active long transactions is desirable. Moreover, standard logging techniques may not be adequate to implement a CAD system due to the overhead of logging design object data and to the length of CAD transactions.

Process Planning Database Requirements

The ideal CIM system is one in which the engineer designs a part on an interactive graphical terminal, stores this design data in a database, and then uses this data automatically to generate a program that is downloaded to a host computer for subsequent implementation on a machining center. This environment requires a link between the design phase and the manufacturing phase of a product. The interface between CAD and CAM is referred to as *process planning*.

Process planning is the means for determining the sequence of machining operations needed to produce a part that satisfies design specifications. Process planning generates information required to support the following manufacturing activities: detailed machine scheduling, tool requirements, cost calculations, numerical control programming, and the generation of work orders for the shop floor.

Manual process planning is highly labor intensive, and its effectiveness is highly dependent on the expertise of the process planner. There are two approaches to computer-aided process planning (CAPP): the variant approach and the generative approach.

The **variant approach** relies on a concept known as *group technologies*. Group technologies determines families of parts and assigns standard process plans to them. This process identifies, based on a code, parts that should be manufactured similarly. This code includes part material, shape, features, and the process for the production of these features.

If the standard process plans are stored in a database, the group technologies coding scheme allows for their search and reuse. Variant CAPP systems allow retrieving process planning data and editing standard process plans. Such a group technology retrieval system can provide manufacturing engineers with benefits similar to the ones provided to the design engineers by a design retrieval system. As before, reusability is the key to lower costs and shorter lead times. However, in manufacturing, additional advantages exist. Work cells can be designed, and production can be efficiently scheduled based on the group technology classification scheme.

The **generative approach** to CAPP has the ability to generate specific process plans for specific parts without relying on standard process plans. Generative CAPP systems are artificial intelligence-based systems that start with the geometry, material types, and machinability data of the part and emulate the process planner's logic. These systems rely on a database combined with a knowledge base. They present major research problems; geometric and technological knowledge management, feature recognition, and knowledge base acquisitions.

Much of the technical data used in both variant and generative CAPP systems lacks precision. This situation occurs partly because the parts in the CAD database normally do not match the exact specifications of the object being designed and partly because the properties of materials or components in the CAM database are determined by experimental and test measurements. Therefore, the true data typically consists of ranges instead of simple values. Complex indexing techniques and retrieval by ranges are processes needed to assist CAPP that are not efficiently supported by conventional DBMSs.

Manufacturing Database Requirements

CAM is the application of computer and communications technologies to enhance manufacturing by linking numerical control machines, using robots and automated material handling systems, monitoring the production process, and providing automatic feedback to control operations.

Manufacturing Database Objects.   *Numerical control (N/C)* refers to the use of computers to generate the commands needed to run machine tools. CAM databases should support the generation of N/C programs. In order to support N/C program generation, CAM databases must be able to represent the relationships between the geometry of a design and its detailed machining process.

The management of N/C programs through a DBMS can also enhance CAM. Storing the N/C programs on the CAM database makes it easier to implement fast setups by sending the corresponding N/C program version to the N/C machine through a computer network. It also allows more efficient N/C program updating. However, this imposes additional requirements to the DBMS: the storage and manipulation of N/C programs.

Events and Time Modeling.   Process control involves the on-line monitoring of the production processes to obtain feedback information. This information is used for quality control and to minimize stoppages in production. As part of the process control, shop floor data is collected to describe the status of entities such as machines, machine operators, work orders, and tools and to record the occurrence of events such as the initiation and completion of a work order, a machine breakdown, and so forth. Conventional DBMSs lack the expressive power to model events. Conventional databases model the dynamic real world as a snapshot at a particular point in time. Updating the state of a database is performed by using data manipulation operations such as insertion, deletion, or replacement, which take effect as soon as they are committed. In this process, past states of the database are discarded.

Enhancements to database models have been introduced to model time. Three categories of enhanced data models have been proposed: rollback, historical, and temporal databases (Snordgrass, 1987). **Rollback databases** store all past states of the database as it evolves. These states are indexed by transaction time. Rollback databases record the update history rather than the real-world history. **Historical databases** record the time in which a state correctly models reality. Historical DBMSs cannot "roll back"; they only store the current knowledge about the past. **Temporal databases** support both transaction time and valid time. They record the progression of states of an enterprise over an interval of time. The lack of an adequate means to model time in the traditional DBMSs raise serious problems for the use of conventional DBMSs for CIM.

Alerters.   Since management by exception is a natural way to monitor an automated production process, CIM requires the automatic recognition of relevant events and the automatic triggering of appropriate operations when an event occurs. This is not supported currently by commercial DBMSs. With conventional DBMSs, the database is a passive collection of data. To determine whether an event has occurred, an external query or application program must be executed. Research in event recognition has generated the concept of *active databases* that include alerters.

Alerters can be used to enforce state constraints. Like integrity constraints, an alerter monitors the database for certain conditions. On each condition, an alerter performs an associated action, such as sending a warning message or causing side effects in other database objects. Alerting differs from conventional exception handling in that it aims to provide almost immediate warnings, and possibly take immediate actions, rather than issuing periodic reports. Alerters may be event driven, such as the initialization of a work order, or may be time related, as with maintenance schedules. DBMSs for CAM should support both event-driven and time-related alerters.

Response Time.   In business-oriented applications, the time gap between real events and database updates may be tolerable sometimes. In traditional business-oriented applications, a poor response time might lead to an irritated user; in CIM, it can mean damage to in-process parts or even damage to expensive machinery and the consequent stoppage of production.

Fast response is required from a CIM database since most CIM operations are executed in an on-line or a real-time mode. In order to implement a real-time DBMS, some problems must be addressed: the feasibility of main memory database management, an aggressive policy for resource allocation, and the integration of new operating system primitives to an active, time-constrained DBMS. These problems are exacerbated by the fact that the storage requirements of a CIM database can be in the order of several tens of gigabytes.

Production Management Database Requirements

Production management applications manage data from sales, forecasting, inventory, human resources, suppliers, procurement, costs, and so on. Production management functions have been traditionally automated successfully as business-oriented applications. As such, conventional DBMSs are able to adequately support their information management and retrieval requirements. Consequently, this is the only area of production where the use of DBMSs has been the rule rather than the exception.

However, CIM requires a higher level of intelligence from its computer support. The CIM ideal, the factory of the future, will operate autonomously as a goal-directed system, one that receives rich sensory input from the environment, compares this input against its expectations, chooses among a variety of possible actions, and acts accordingly through manipulators to alter the environment in order to reach the assigned goal. This adaptive behavior requires an intelligent information system. Databases capable of supporting such an intelligent information system need to manipulate knowledge and to model time for the allocation of resources.

Conclusions

CIM information systems constitute a challenge to existing database technology. To be suitable for CIM applications, a DBMS must be able to support all the firm's manufacturing functions. A DBMS for CIM should be able to support: (1) multiple users in a distributed environment, (2) on-line and real-time applications, (3) schema evolution for a highly dynamic environment, (4) representation and fast retrieval of complex relationships, (5) storage and manipulation of programs, spatial and geometric data, range values, and knowledge, (6) version control, (7) time modeling, (8) enforcement of complex integrity constraints, (9) detection of events through alerters and triggers, and (10) concurrency control mechanisms suitable for the design and the manufacturing environments.

Data models used in conventional DBMSs do not have the expressive power needed for CIM applications. Multiple research efforts are currently carried out to overcome their limitations. Object-oriented database management systems (OODBMSs), discussed next, are prominent candidates for CIM applications.

OBJECT-ORIENTED DATABASES

In the first part of this book, we presented the basics of data modeling. The foundation of our approach was accurate and detailed models of entities that would be represented in the database being designed. In Chapter 3, we defined an entity as a conceptual representation of an object. A new approach to database management, called **object-oriented database management,** places great emphasis on modeling objects (entities). In order to understand this approach, however, we must first examine a larger issue known as the **object-oriented paradigm.** This paradigm defines the fundamental concepts of object-oriented approaches in general. Thus, an object-oriented database should be consistent with the underlying paradigm. (You may have also heard of object-oriented programming languages. These languages should also adhere to the tenets of the object-oriented paradigm.)

Object-Oriented Paradigm Concepts

The object-oriented paradigm (OOP) has many characteristics. In fact, the paradigm is still being defined. Unlike the relational approach to database management, which has a strong and well-grounded theoretical basis, object-oriented approaches have no underlying theory that drives their development. The first systems that become widely accepted will probably define the de facto standard. Many database researchers argue that the lack of a theoretical base is a major flaw in the object-oriented paradigm.

However, specific characteristics can still be identified in OOP approaches. OOP extends the basic concept of modularity that has been developed since the mid-1960s. In an OOP approach, the focus is on describing entities instead of describing processes. Although processes are defined, they are defined indirectly through the actions of the objects in the system. In an object-oriented system, an object is defined for each entity that will be represented. All aspects of the entity are incorporated into the description of the object. Thus, the object is defined in a manner that "behaves" like the entity being modeled. This approach leads to systems that directly model applications.

Objects have a public interface, which is the set of operations, called *methods*, applicable to the object. Methods are implemented in the object's private memory and may access variables stored in the private memory. For example, a Customer object might have a method defined as Credit-Rating, which calculates the customer's current credit rating. How this method is implemented is unknown to other objects. An object consists of an encapsulated representation (state) and a set of messages (operations) that can be applied to the object. This approach separates the object user from the object implementation. (We have seen this concept before; it is used to separate external schemas from internal schemas.)

Since processes are not defined in an OOP system, another means for creating action in the system must exist. Object-oriented systems perform computations by passing *messages* between active objects. The messages indicate to the receiving object which of the object's methods should be executed. In some cases, the execution of the method results only in a change in the internal state of the object (that is, a change in the object's private memory). In other cases, the receiving object may send a value back to the object that sent the original message. As an example, consider again a financial application. The application might have Customer objects sending debit and credit messages to Account objects. The Account objects might maintain Accounts-Receivable and Accounts-Payable objects.

Frequently, different objects may have very similar processes. For example, a banking system may have many types of Account objects. There may be fixed-interest–bearing accounts, money market accounts, and special accounts that earn a premium interest rate. These accounts are *specializations* of the more general Account class. New object subclasses may be defined in terms of an existing Account object class. In other words, Fixed-Interest-Account, Money-Market-Account, and Premium-Account could be defined as subclasses of the Account class.

Each Account object has some behaviors that are identical regardless of the Account class. Examples are methods that calculate when a deposit is made. When these methods are defined in the Account class, the Fixed-Account, Money-Market-Account, and Premium-Account subclasses *inherit* the methods. Thus, these methods need to be defined only once in the Account class, and the subclasses will understand messages that request these methods as long as the method is not redefined in the subclass.

On the other hand, the interest calculation in each of these sub-classes is slightly different. We would prefer to define a different interest calculation in each subclass to reflect the characteristics of the account. Each subclass can have a method named Calculate-Interest, because the method defined in the subclass will be used to respond to a message. **Polymorphism** is the name given to the characteristics of allowing different classes to have methods with the same name.

Although no theory exists, OOP researchers draw a distinction between systems that implement less than encapsulation, polymorphism, and inheritance. Encapsulation can be found in many simulation languages. Thus, encapsulation by itself does not indicate an object-oriented system. Systems that provide encapsulation and inheritance are called object-based systems by OOP research purists. The ADA programming language is considered object-based. Object-oriented systems provide encapsulation, polymorphism, and inheritance.

IRIS—An Object-Oriented Database System

Hewlett-Packard Laboratories has developed an object-oriented database named IRIS. IRIS illustrates how the object-oriented paradigm works when it is applied in the database setting. IRIS has been developed to meet the needs of new and emerging database applications such as supporting office automation, integrating with computer-aided design and computer-aided manufacturing systems, and supporting knowledge-based systems. These applications require new technologies because the entities that must be modeled in the database frequently cannot be represented well in traditional relational or network database systems. For example, CAD/CAM applications are typically graphical, and existing database systems do not provide very good support for storing, indexing, and manipulating graphical images.

The IRIS system can be described in three components. First an **object manager** handles the object-oriented aspects of the system. Second, several IRIS **interfaces** have been developed for flexible interaction with IRIS. Third, a **storage manager** controls the storage and retrieval of the data.

The IRIS Object Manager. The object manager provides object-oriented support for schema definition, data manipulation, and query processing. Entities in the application domain are modeled as objects. Each object is given a unique object identifier (OID), which it retains regardless of the values of the object's attributes. (This is similar to the database key that is associated with records in a CODASYL system.) The OID provides a more robust means for maintaining referential integrity, and thus provides an advantage over approaches in which the records may only be referenced by their attribute values. In fact, when an object is deleted in IRIS, all references to the object are deleted as well.

Objects are classified by **type.** A type is similar in concept to the generic entity concept described in Chapter 2. In IRIS, types are arranged in a type hierarchy. A type may have multiple parent types, called **supertypes,** and multiple child types, called **subtypes.** An object may be associated with more than one type. Figure 13–1 illustrates these concepts. The type object is at the top of the hierarchy; all types are subtypes of object.

Rather than associate properties with objects, IRIS takes the approach of associating **functions** with types. An object property is actually a function defined with the type. A function has an object as an argument and may return an object as a value. Consequently, functions may be applied to objects only if the object is associated with the type on which the function is defined. Types inherit functions from supertypes and pass functions along to subtypes.

Different functions may be defined on different types and have identical names. In this case, the function name is overloaded. IRIS uses the most specific type function whenever an overloaded function is applied to an object. If a most specific type cannot be determined, user-defined rules are used to determine which function to invoke. Functions may return single or multiple values.

IRIS Interfaces.   Objects and types are manipulated as shown in the following examples. These examples illustrate the Object SQL (OSQL) that has been developed to be used with IRIS.

The following command could be used to establish the Person type in Figure 13–1.

FIGURE 13–1   Sample IRIS Object Type Structure

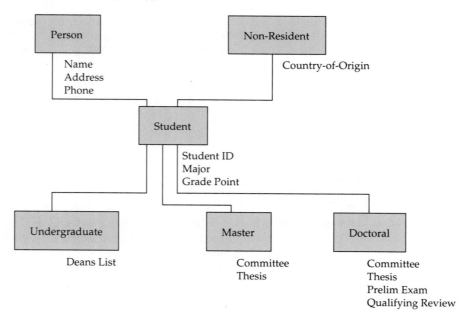

```
Create type Person
   (name Charstring required,
   address Charstring,
   phone Charstring);
```

The following command could be used to create the Student type in Figure 13–1:

```
Create type Student subtype of Person, Nonresident;
```

Persons could be added to the database with the commands:

```
Create Persons (name, address, phone) instances
Fraser ('Mike Fraser', '1982 Apple Cart Way',
   '555-7263'),
Ross ('Tim Ross', '8171 Masai Trail', '872-2928'),
Flores ('Benito Flores', '88 Sanchez Road',
   '657-9125');
```

We can add the Student type to all persons in the database with the command:

```
Add type Member (Student) = p for each Person p
   where p = Member (Person);
```

We can add the fact that Tim Ross is a nonresident student with the command:

```
Add type Nonresident to Ross;
```

The command:

```
Remove Member (Student) = Fraser;
```

removes the Student type from Mike Fraser, but the Person type is still associated.

A delete command is used to remove all information related to a type or an object. For example:

```
Delete type Undergraduate
```

will cause the type Undergraduate to be deleted. It will also cause all functions with Undergraduate as an argument to be deleted. Instances of Undergraduate, however, still exist in the database. They just will no longer have the Undergraduate type associated with them.

For flexibility in developing routine applications, IRIS supports interfaces to object-oriented programming languages. IRIS also supports a graphics-based interface and interfaces to programming languages such as C.

The IRIS Storage Manager.   A powerful aspect of object-oriented databases is *version control*. Version control allows the evolution of an object to be maintained in the database. IRIS supports version control by creating a generic instance and generic and specific references to controlled objects. A **generic instance** of an object has properties that are consistent across all versions of the object. A **generic reference** is a reference to the generic instance. A **specific reference** is a reference to a particular version of the object. In a CAD/CAM application, maintaining versions of the design of an automobile part could be beneficial in documenting decisions related to the design.

The data in the IRIS system is stored in a relational database. It provides access and update capabilities to a single relation at a time. It also provides transaction management, backup and recovery, and concurrent processing support.

Advantages of Object-Oriented Database Systems

Object-oriented database approaches have several advantages. First, once an object is defined, it may be reused in any application that requires it. Employee objects might be used in worker scheduling applications, payroll applications, project management applications, and so on. Second, implementation can be driven directly from data-flow diagrams. Functional decompositions of systems may not be needed. Third, messages can be passed from any object, triggering many operations that can be executed concurrently. Thus, concurrent (or parallel) processing is supported naturally in an object-oriented environment. Fourth, objects can reside anywhere in a system. The object-oriented approach is very amenable to a distributed database design. Of course, the system must know where each object resides, but this information can be stored in the network repository management facilities (see Chapter 12). Finally, since object-oriented databases directly model application environments, users should be better able to communicate system requirements and validate system implementations.

OBJECT-ORIENTED DATA MODELING USING THE SEMANTIC DATABASE MODEL[1]

Recently, object-oriented approaches have been proposed as a new method for data modeling. **The semantic database model, or SDM,** although not originally introduced as an object-oriented tool, is a good tool for object-oriented data modeling. SDM also stresses the entities that occur in the database.

SDM was originally designed to retain as much of the semantics, or meaning, that underlie database assumptions as possible. The SDM approach, in which descriptions and constraints may be explictly included in the definitions of entities, was developed to address this perceived deficiency in graphical approaches such as E-R models. The SDM approach is capable of much more detailed data description than we present here. Our discussion is only an overview.

---

[1]This section may be omitted without loss of continuity.

The SDM developers observed that a good logical description should support several means of expressing the same entity. This feature is attractive because many times the same entity is seen in different ways in an organization. Consider the case of an employee working on a particular project: The employee can be described as an attribute of the project (current worker on the project), or the project can be described as an attribute of the employee (current assignment).

One of the most practical benefits of SDM is that it provides a formal document in a standard format. SDM is similar to pseudocode in that it provides a basic set of concepts with which to work, but is flexible in the way the concepts can be combined. The general format of an SDM entity description is shown in Figure 13–2.

Basic SDM Concepts

To illustrate the fundamental SDM concepts, we will consider the needs of the Home Theater Company. Home Theater rents video cassette recorders and tapes. Home Theater's management has decided that a

FIGURE 13–2
General Template for an SDM Description

```
ENTITY_CLASS_NAME
   description:
      duplicates (not) allowed
      interclass connection:
   member attributes:
      Attribute_name
         description:
         value class:
         inverse: Attribute_name
         match: Attribute_name of ENTITY_CLASS_NAME
            on Attribute_name
         derivation:
         single valued
         multivalued (with size between_and_)
         may not be null
         not changeable
         exhausts value class
         no overlap in values
   class attributes:
      Attribute_name
         description:
         value class:
         derivation:
         single valued
         multivalued (with size between_and_)
         may not be null
         not changeable
   identifiers: Attribute_name (+ Attribute_name
         + ...)
```

database system will enable the company to serve its customers better. Management foresees this system providing answers to questions about selection, rental prices, and availability to customers. Management also believes the system will provide more control over inventory and better estimates of the demand for certain categories of tapes.

Data regarding video cassette tapes, video cassette recorders, and customers can begin to meet management's needs. Data for the recorders and tapes can address inventory issues. Demographic data about customers, combined with data regarding the types of tapes that are typically rented, can provide information about consumer demand.

Entity and Attribute Representations.   Each of these entities (video cassettes, video recorders, and customers) will be represented as SDM **entity classes** using the format shown in Figure 13–2. An entity class represents a collection of similar entities. Entity class names are written using small capital letters. Individual entities in an entity class are called **class members** and their characteristics are called **member attributes.** Member attribute names begin with a capital letter.

Movie title, category (drama, comedy, and so on), and rental price are shown as attributes of the CASSETTES entity class in the Home Theater database model (Figures 13–3 through 13–7). Video cassette recorders are classified by manufacturer and serial number, so these attributes are listed in the VCRS entity class. The CUSTOMERS entity class contains attributes that describe customers and the items each has rented.

In SDM, attributes are assumed to be single-valued unless the word *multivalued* is included after the attribute. An example of a single-valued attribute is the member attribute Brand in the VCRS entity class in Figure 13–3. A recorder is made by only one manufacturer.

A multivalued attribute in the CUSTOMERS entity class (Figure 13–4) is Current__tapes. A customer can rent more than one tape. If there is a limit on the number of tapes a customer can rent, the attribute

FIGURE 13–3
SDM Description for VCRs
Note the relationship to CUSTOMERS via the Checked__out__to attribute.

```
VCRS
   description: Only video cassette recorders rented
      from this store are included.
   duplicates allowed
   member attributes:
      Serial_number
         value class: VCR_SERIAL
         no overlap in values
      Brand
         value class: BRAND_NAMES
      Checked_out_to
         value class: CUSTOMERS
         inverse: Current_recorder
   identifiers: Serial_number
```

FIGURE 13–4
SDM Description for
CUSTOMERS **of Home**
Theater
Note the relationship to
CASSETTES via the
Current_tapes attribute.

```
CUSTOMERS
   description: Only customers that have rented
      equipment in the past three months are
      included.
   member attributes:
      Customer_number
         value class: CUSTOMER_NUMBERS
         mandatory
         not changeable
      Name
         value class: PEOPLE_NAMES
      Preference
         value class: MOVIE_TYPES
      Current_tapes
         value class: CAT_NUMBERS
         multivalued
         match: Catalog_number of CASSETTES on
            Held_by
      Current_recorder
         value class: VCRS
         inverse: Checked_out_to
   identifiers: Customer_number
```

size may be constrained by specifying the phrase *with size between__ and__*, where constant values are specified in the blanks. (There is no such constraint specified by Home Theater; it does not want to limit how many tapes its customers rent.)

Often, some attributes of entity classes are required to have a value. Typically, these attributes are **identifiers** and are used to distinguish one entity class member from another. Attributes which must have a value are called *mandatory*. Other times, attributes may assume null values. A null value is *not* the same as a zero or blank field. A null value implies that the value for the field is not known or is not applicable. Perhaps a customer owns a video recorder and only wants to rent tapes. In this case, a null value for Current_recorder in CUSTOMERS is valid. Since every VCR should have a serial number, Serial_number is mandatory.

Some attribute values should never be changed; for example, Serial_number in VCRS. There is no reason to modify this attribute value, except to correct an error. Attributes with this characteristic are specified as **not changeable.**

A member attribute can be required to be **exhaustive,** too. This term means every value of the attribute must occur somewhere in the database. The Recorder_used attribute of CASSETTES is exhaustive, because Home Theater only rents tapes for which it also supplies a recorder for viewing the tape. In other words, all possible values of Recorder_used (in this case only VHS and BETA) exist in the database.

A member attribute can also be described by the phrase **nonoverlapping,** which means that two entities have no values in common. Another way of putting this is that each attribute value is used only once. Serial__number of vcrs is nonoverlapping, because two VCRs should not have the same serial number.

SDM allows the definition of **class attributes** that maintain general information regarding the entity class. Typical class attributes are totals, averages, and minimum and maximum values. These are attributes that describe the class in general, but not necessarily any class member in particular.

Domains are defined by value classes. A **value class** may be an entity class or a name class. In vcrs, for example, the value class of Checked__out__to is customers. customers is an entity class. This use of an entity class indicates that information required about the customer that has rented a VCR can be obtained by accessing the customers data. Composite attributes are also represented by defining the value class as another entity class. This entity class contains the attributes that make up the composite attribute.

A name class, on the other hand, is used to define atomic values. Name classes (see Figure 13–5) are typically listed at the end of an SDM description. **Name classes** describe the set of acceptable values that an attribute may assume in terms of certain primitive concepts such as strings, integers, reals, numbers, and yes/no values. strings are characters; integers are values without a fractional part; reals are numbers that have a fractional part; numbers are numeric values that are not intended for arithmetic and may contain characters; yes/no values are Boolean.

One-to-One Relationships.　One-to-one relationships are not explicitly represented in SDM, but may be inferred by examining entity and attribute definitions. That a VCR can be rented to only one customer at a time is implied by the single-valued default of the Rented__to attribute in vcrs.

One-to-Many Relationships.　A one-to-many relationship exists between customers and the cassettes they may rent. This relationship can be inferred by the multivalued designation of Current__tapes in customers. This relationship is also designated by a **match clause.** In matching, the value for a member attribute in one entity class is determined by first finding a member attribute in a second entity class that has the first attribute as its value; the value of a third attribute then becomes the value of the attribute in the first entity class. The match in Figure 13–4 guarantees that the value for Current__tapes in customers is the same as the value for Catalog__number in cassettes (Figure 13–6) for a particular customer.

Many-to-Many Relationships.　A many-to-many relationship would be inferred through the use of two multivalued attributes.

FIGURE 13–5
Name Classes
Note the use of exact
formats where possible.

```
BRAND_NAMES
   interclass connection: subclass of STRINGS where
      value is 'BETA' or 'VHS'.
CAT_NUMBERS
   interclass connection: subclass of STRINGS where
      format is ANNNNN; A is either 'S' for SONY or
      'B' for BETAMAX, NNNNN is a five digit positive
      number.
CUSTOMER_NUMBERS
   interclass connection: subclass of INTEGERS where
      value is positive.
MOVIE_NAMES
   interclass connection: subclass of STRINGS where
      length is less than 50 characters where
      specified.
MOVIE_TYPES
   interclass connection: subclass of STRINGS where
      value is 'COMEDY', 'DRAMA', 'SCI-FI', or
      'CHILDREN'.
PEOPLE_NAMES
   interclass connection: subclass of STRINGS where
      length is less than 30 where specified.
POSITIVE_NUMBERS
   interclass connection: subclass of INTEGERS where
      value is positive.
PRICES
   interclass connection: subclass of REALS where
      format is a positive number 99.99.
VCR_SERIAL
   interclass connection: subclass of STRINGS where
      length is eight characters and value is stamped
      on each machine.
```

Other Relationships

Inverses.   A database designer must always be concerned that the design does not adversely affect the database system's ability to meet users' needs by being one-sided. There are, for example, two ways of expressing a recorder rental: from the store viewpoint and the customer viewpoint. These two views provide an example of an SDM **inverse** relationship. The member attribute Rented__to in the VCRS entity class has an inverse, which is Current__recorder in CUSTOMERS (see Figures 13–3 and 13–4). The inverse designation means the value for Rented__to for a particular member in the VCRS entity class is the same as those members in the CUSTOMERS entity class whose value of Rented__to is that member. An example makes this usage clearer: Bill Fraser is a member of the CUSTOMERS entity class who has rented a video recorder.

FIGURE 13–6
SDM Description for the
Base Class of CASSETTES

```
CASSETTES
   description: Pre-recorded video cassettes
        available at all stores in the franchise in
        this city are included.
   duplicates allowed
   member attributes:
      Title
         value class: MOVIE_NAMES
         may not be null
         not changebale
      Recorder_used
         value class: MOVIE_NAMES
         may not be null
         not changeable
      Recorder_used
         value class: VCRS
         exhausts value class
      Category
         value class: MOVIE_TYPES
      Catalog_number
         value class: CAT_NUMBERS
      Rental_price
         value class: PRICES
      Held_by
         value class: CUSTOMERS
   class attributes:
      Total_inventory
         value class: POSITIVE_NUMBERS
         derivation: number of members in CASSETTES
      Total_outstanding
         description: Total number of tapes currently
              rented.
            Calculated by an application program using
            information in Current_tapes in CUSTOMERS.
         value class: POSITIVE_NUMBERS
      Total_available
         value class: POSITIVE_NUMBERS
         derivation: Total_inventory — Total_out-
         standing
   identifiers: Catalog_number
```

The inverse relationship indicates that a video recorder is held by (Rented__to) a customer (Bill Fraser). An inverse establishes a binary relationship between member attributes.

Is this data redundancy? No, because SDM is a *logical* design tool. The inverse specification allows designers to view one event in more than one way without requiring the physical implementation to have multiple data occurrences. SDM clarifies that these relationships exist and that all should be maintained.

Derivation.   Whenever a relationship between member attributes can be specified in a formula, the formula can be represented explicitly in the SDM description. The term **derivation** is used to denote this relationship. Class attributes are frequently derived attributes, since class attributes are often totals or extreme (maximum or minimum) values. The attribute value might be derived by the database software, or by an application program. Again, SDM is used to incorporate the information into the database design. It is not important (from the logical design standpoint) how the value is calculated.

Generalization and Specialization.   SDM also supports generalization and specialization concepts. Base and nonbase classes are used to define these relationships. A **base class** is a class that can exist independently of other classes. A **nonbase class** is defined in terms of another class. An **interclass connection** is used to define the relationship between base and nonbase entity classes. The existence of an interclass connection in a class description indicates the class is nonbase.

   In the Home Theater database, categories of movies have been created using interclass connections. These categories are comedy, drama, and so forth (see Figure 13–7). Once again, be sure to note that this approach does not imply data redundancy. It only makes explicit the need to access the data via these different categories.

DEDUCTIVE DATABASES

One of the drawbacks of current database approaches is that the database remains essentially a passive reservoir of data. There must still be some intervention on the part of an intelligent being to build relationships between data items using common definitions. For example, how might we construct a database system that can start with "facts" such as:

   John is the father of Bob

and

   Bob is the father of Sue

FIGURE 13–7
**SDM Description for the
Nonbase Class of** DRAMAS

```
DRAMAS
   interclass connection: subset of CASSETTES where
      value of Category is DRAMA.
   member attributes:
      Suitable_for_children
         description: Indicates whether subject may be
            inappropriate for children.
      value class: YES/NO
```

and deduce:

John is the grandfather of Sue.

We are interested in reviewing some of the approaches that are being used in the design and development of deductive databases. Artificial intelligence (AI) languages are being used to build these types of databases. These languages operate on the notion of *inferring* conclusions (or loosely, "proving" them) based on stated "facts." Thus, in order to understand the AI approaches, we will first briefly review some of the notions of logic and theorem proving.

Logic as a Basis for Deduction

We must first define the primitive operations: NOT, AND, OR, and IMPLICATION.

Our logic will be two-valued: true and false (Boolean).

If p is a term that has a Boolean value, then NOT p has the opposite Boolean value.

If p and q are terms in our language, then p AND q is defined as:

p	q	p&q
T	T	T
F	F	F
T	F	F
F	T	F

and p OR q is defined as:

p	q	pVq
T	T	T
F	F	F
T	F	T
F	T	T

An important concept in logic is *implication*. Implication has the form: if p then q. If p and q are terms in our language, we will define implication as:

p	q	p→q
T	T	T
F	F	T
T	F	F
F	T	T

This truth table occasionally troubles students. First, we can show that this truth table is equivalent to the one for:

NOT (p AND (NOT q))

Let us consider an example:

If it is sunny, then I am playing golf.

An equivalent way of stating this proposition is:

> It is not the case that it is sunny and I am not playing golf.

Here, p is "it is sunny" and q is "I am playing golf."

The first line indicates "it is sunny" and "I am playing golf." Both parts are true, so certainly the entire statement should be considered true.

The second line indicates "it is not sunny" and "I am not playing golf." This is more easily seen from the equivalent statement:

> It is true that it is not the case that it is not sunny and I am not playing golf.

The third line indicates "it is sunny" and "I am not playing golf." Since I am not playing golf, the entire statement should be considered false. I am not playing golf, so we should not conclude that I am playing golf.

The fourth line indicates that "it is not sunny" and "I am playing golf." Since I am playing golf, we should conclude that I am playing golf. Thus, we conclude that the statement is true. Or equivalently,

> It is true that it is not the case that it is not sunny and I am not playing golf.

Another way that this is taught is that *anything* can be concluded if you start with a false premise.

These definitions can be used to solve rather perplexing problems.

> Suppose that Bob does not wish to visit Sue, unless Sue wishes Bob to visit her; and Sue does not wish to visit Bob if Bob wants to visit her, but Sue does wish to visit Bob if Bob does not want to visit her.

We can convert these statements to logical propositions and then ask the question, "Can we conclude that Bob wants to visit Sue?"

If p stands for "Bob wants to visit Sue" and q stands for "Sue wishes to visit Bob," we have:

> (NOT p) OR q
> ($p \rightarrow$ NOT q) & (NOT $p \rightarrow q$)

We wish to determine which of the following is a tautology (always true):

> ((NOT p) OR q) AND (($p \rightarrow$ NOT q) & (NOT $p \rightarrow q$)) $\rightarrow p$

or

> ((NOT p) OR q) AND (($p \rightarrow$ NOT q) & (NOT $p \rightarrow q$)) $\rightarrow$ NOT p

It turns out that the second truth table evaluates to all T's, and thus we conclude that Bob does not want to visit Sue.

If neither truth table had all T's, we would conclude that the premises were not strong enough to answer the question. On the other hand, if both truth tables were all T's, a contradiction must exist in the premises. They do not describe a valid reality.

Prolog

You may be wondering how we can get to deductive databases from the brief overview of logic above. As we noted earlier, artificial intelligence languages are being used to build these types of databases. Prolog is one such language. Prolog takes the basic notion of *implication*, turns it around, and allows you to program the following concept:

q is true, if it can be shown that p is true.

Or:

q is a goal that can be satisfied, if p is a goal that can be satisfied.

Prolog has two basic concepts: facts, and facts that are conditional on other facts. Facts that are conditional on other facts are called *rules*. For example, we might have:

```
father (John, Bob).
```

which means John is the father of Bob. And:

```
father (Bob, Sue).
```

which means Bob is the father of Sue.

Prolog then allows queries like:

```
father (X, Bob).
```

A Prolog query such as this is answered with the response:

```
X = John
```

Similarly:

```
father (John, X)
```

is answered:

```
X = Bob
```

So a Prolog fact with a variable acts like a query.

Then we might add the rule:

```
grandfather (X, Z) if father (X, Y) and father (Y, Z).
```

Depending on the dialect of Prolog being used, these might be written as:

```
grandfather (X, Z): father (X, Y), father (Y, Z).
grandfather (X, Z): mother (X, Y), father (Y, Z).
```

This rule states it can be deduced that X is the grandfather of Z if it can be shown that X is the father of Y and Y is the father of Z.

If we then entered:

```
grandfather (X, Z).
```

Prolog would determine that father (John, Bob) can satisfy the first "goal," and father (Bob, Sue) can satisfy the second goal, so setting

X = John and Z = Sue satisfies the grandfather goal. So the response would be:

```
X = John, Z = Sue
```

If the goal cannot be satisfied, the response is *no*.

Backtracking.   Prolog can find multiple answer to queries, because it has the ability to back up and retry different facts to determine whether these facts can solve the query. For example, if we enter;

```
father (X, Bob).
```

we will get the response:

```
X = John
```

with the cursor left at the end of John. If we then enter a semicolon (;), Prolog will automatically search for another fact that satisfies the query and we will get the response:

```
X = Bob
```

A subsequent semicolon will generate the response *no*, which indicates there are no other solutions.

Lists.   In most applications, lists of values need to be manipulated. A Prolog list has the form [value1 value2 value3 . . . valueN]. The notation [X|Y] assigns the first value of the list to X and a list containing values 2 through N to Y: in other words:

```
X = value1
Y = [value2 value3 . . . valueN]
```

X is called the *head* of the list, Y is called the *tail* of the list.

In the following rule, the underscore stands for a value that we don't care about. See if you can interpret how the following rule works:

```
member (X, [X| Y]).
member (X, [_| Y]) :—member (X, Y).
```

This rule states that a value is a member of the list if it is the value of the head of the list, or if it is a member of the tail of the list.

The rule would work as follows;

```
member (a, [a, b, c, d]).
```

Here, the first rule would be satisfied, since *a* is the head of the list.

```
member (c, [a, b, c, d]).
```

Here, the first rule would fail, so Prolog would search for another way to satisfy the goal. It would find the second rule, so internally it would process:

```
member (c, [_|[b, c, d]]) :— member (c, [b, c, d]).
```

To solve this goal, Prolog would try to determine if member (c, [b, c, d]) can be satisfied. The first rule fails, so Prolog would try to solve:

```
member (c, [_|[c, d]]) :- member (c, [c, d]).
```

Now the first rule would succeed, because *c* is at the head of the list.

This rule illustrates the notion of *recursion*. A rule is recursive if it uses itself to solve a goal.

A Deductive Database in Prolog

Consider the following data stored as Prolog facts.[2]

```
employee (adams, 1001, finance, senior_consultant,
    [stock_market, investments]).
employee (baker, 1002, accounting,
    senior_accountant, [stock_market]).
employee (clarke, 1003, accounting,
    senior_consultant, [investments,
    stock_market]).
employee (dexter, 1004, finance, junior_consultant,
    [taxation]).
employee (early, 1005, accounting,
    junior_consultant, [management, taxation,
    investments]).
manager (kanter, 1111, finance).
manager (yates, 1112, accounting).
project (23760, yates, new_billing_system, 1000,
    10000).
project (28765, baker, common_stock_issue, 3000,
    4000).
project (26713, kanter, resolve_bad_debts, 2000,
    1500).
project (26511, yates, new_office_lease, 5000,5000).
```

To determine the manager of the finance department, we would query:

```
manager (X, Y, finance).
```

The system would respond X = kanter, Y = 1111. If we were uninterested in the value for identification number, we could replace the Y with a __. The __will match any value.

For example, suppose we want to know who is adams's manager. The following Prolog query is constructed:

```
employee (adams, _, X, _, _) and manager (Y, _, X).
```

Prolog will first search for an employee fact that contains adams in the first argument. It will ignore the second, fourth, and fifth arguments, but will assign the value of the third argument (finance) to X. Next, Prolog will search the manager facts with the value of X being finance.

---

[2]Prolog dialects handle spaces between terms differently. We avoid the issue here by using the underscore character.

It will find the fact for kanter has the third argument of finance. The first argument kanter is assigned to Y, and the second argument is ignored. The response is:

```
X = finance, Y = kanter
```

As a final example, suppose we want to know what employees have both stock market and investment skills. You'll note that the skills are not always listed in the same order and that there may be any number of skills. Therefore, we cannot construct a query that depends on matching values, as we have thus far.

We need to create a query that searches the data for an answer. If we reformulate the query as: "What employees have both investments and stock market in their list of skills," the approach becomes clearer. The query we need is:

```
employee (X, _, _, _, L) and member (investments, L)
         and member (stock_market, L).
```

This query starts with information about an employee's skills as associated with the variable L. Then, the member rule discussed earlier is used to determine whether investments and stock_market are members of the list of skills. The Prolog system will only return values of X for employees whose list of skills L contains both skills.

NATURAL LANGUAGE DATABASE PROCESSING

The cost of hardware in computer systems has decreased tremendously while hardware performance has increased. Unfortunately, similar results cannot be described for software. Software costs, primarily the costs associated with employing skilled professionals to construct software systems, continue to rise. Furthermore, increasing demands for applications have created a backlog of software applications to be developed by a limited number of professionals, driving costs even higher.

One strategy that has been proposed to address the growing number of required applications while maintaining a lower cost is to provide nontechnical computer users with means for directly accessing data in database systems. Natural language processing is one such strategy. In **natural language processing,** computing systems understand and operate with language as spoken or written by humans. Research in natural language processing has been considerable over the past three decades. In this section, we discuss some of the major aspects of this new technique in a database environment.

Arguments for and against Natural Language Processing

The appeal of providing a natural language interface to a database system is such that an interface requires little or no learning on the part of the potential database user. After all, the user's ability to understand the language being used, say English, is a reasonable assumption in most cases. Learning to program in COBOL, PL/1, or some other high-level language, on the other hand, clearly incurs a cost. Even learning the data manipulation languages such as SQL and QBE (see Chapters 7 and 8) is a more costly effort than speaking or writing in one's natural language. Natural language has essentially no start-up cost associated with it; users bring the skill of communicating with them.

Critics of a natural language approach focus on the observation that a language such as English has too many instances of ambiguity. Critics also note that English contains "fuzzy" words such as "almost"—words with meanings difficult to implement in a computer program. Finally, many times, a partial sentence is sufficient in natural communication because listeners can provide missing information from the context of earlier parts of the conversation. This is a special complication for computer implementation.

Syntactic and Semantic Knowledge

Two concepts that are illustrated every time language is understood are *syntax* and *semantics*. **Syntax** represents the rules that govern the way words are presented in an understandable form—the way words are combined to form phrases, clauses, and sentences. **Semantics** is a matter of word meanings and of the way words are combined to express concepts. A brief example helps clarify these terms:

> It is a matter of syntax that "Boy blue the is" is not a properly constructed sentence, whereas "The boy is blue" is. It is a matter of semantics that "She is a bachelor" is a misuse of words.

These concepts are applied in natural language processing in database systems as well. **Syntactic knowledge** is a user's skill with a particular interface language. **Semantic knowledge** is the user's knowledge of the environment modeled by the database. A natural language interface may best support the decision-making activities of users with low syntactic knowledge and high semantic knowledge in a given situation.

Research Challenges in Natural Language Processing

Several obstacles must be overcome before natural language processing can gain currency. The following examples demonstrate the range of tasks a successful natural language interface must accomplish.

A statement can be made in many different ways. This phenomenon is called **range of expression.** Consider, for example, the following four requests, each of which could be used to get a reasonable set of information from a database system:

> Provide a list of names of all airline flights for Omega Airways that have Dallas as a destination.
> Print the names of all Omega Airways flights going to Dallas.

> What are the Omega flights to Dallas?
>
> Omega Dallas flights.

The first expression is information rich and unambiguous. The others provide decreasing levels of information and require increasing understanding of the context of the situation. The last query is quite terse indeed. Yet, each of these examples could be interpreted by a human and hence should be able to be processed by a natural language interface.

The following example demonstrate words ambiguity. The word *and* in this example has four different meanings. This phenomenon is called **lexical ambiguity.**

> Print the age of Bennett and Thames.
>
> Whose age is between 25 and 50?
>
> For plant one and plant two employees, print the name, title, and
>   salary of anyone who is between 25 and 50 and is a foreman.

The first statement demonstrates how *and* can mean *logical or.* The translation indicates that the query does not want data for an employee named Bennett and Thames, but rather data for employees whose name is either Bennett *or* Thames. The second statement shows how *and* could mean *through.* The last statement demonstrates that *and* can have several meanings in the same query.

One of the most difficult problems to address in a natural language system is **pronoun reference.** Consider the following sequence of questions:

> List all of the secretaries.
>
> Which of them work in the finance department?
>
> Which of them work in the marketing department?
>
> Which ones are under 30 years old?

The first query establishes the subject of discussion. The second query contains the word *them,* which clearly relates to the first query and means "the secretaries." The third query is not as clear, since in fact it does not refer to the query immediately preceding it, but rather to the first query. The last example is ambiguous beyond resolution. In systems providing only a *written* interface, spelling may cause problems. A good approach is to preprocess all queries to verify that the words in the query are known to the system. A spelling checker may be incorporated to address this need.

Another problem that arises when dealing with *spoken* natural language processing is that different people do not pronounce words identically. Even the same person does not pronounce a word the same way on different days, or at different times in the same day. A system processing voice input must be able to recognize the inputs regardless of the speaker's intonations.

There is also a problem with diction. The phrase *could you* is frequently pronounced "kudyew", as if it were a single word. When words are not distinctly enunciated, they are difficult to isolate and identify.

This difficulty adds to the storage problem, since storing phrases like *could you* as well as *could* and *you* becomes necessary.

In spite of these problems, however, natural language processing (written and spoken) is still a worthwhile area for investment of time and energy. Because a database models a specific domain, a natural language processing interface can exploit this fact to reduce or eliminate some problems. A natural language interface for an airport database system, for example, should recognize that the word *plane* means *airplane*. This system should not try to process this as the word *plain*, which could be a place or a characteristic.

The human voice is still the easiest and most natural interface we have. Natural language processing promises to increase productivity tremendously by taking advantage of this fact. Some systems capable of natural language processing are ROBOT (Harris, 1980), USL (Ott and Zoeppritz, 1980), and INTELLECT (developed as Artificial Intelligence Systems). These systems address many of the issues discussed above.

Systems capable of processing natural language are very sophisticated. These systems require knowledge about language to perform successfully. Systems that use still greater levels of knowledge, called *expert systems,* are discussed next.

EXPERT SYSTEMS

Expert systems are computer systems that have been designed to perform tasks that are normally done by a human expert—such tasks as medical diagnosis, electrical circuit design, mathematical analysis, and geological analysis. Given the time required to develop expertise in these areas, such expert systems are exceedingly valuable.

The most important characteristic of an expert system is that it is supported by a database of knowledge. This type of database is commonly called a **knowledge base.** A second major characteristic of an expert system is that it contains some method of inferring new knowledge from the contents of its knowledge base. The inference mechanism is called an **inference engine.**

Initial efforts at building expert systems were aimed at constructing general-purpose problem-solving systems. Most of these efforts were only marginally successful. As a result, many researchers began to work on narrow, problem-specific domains. Some of the early expert systems are SAINT (Slagle, 1961), a system for symbolic mathematics, and DENDRAL (Buchanan et al., 1969), a system to analyze mass spectrographics and other chemical data to infer the plausible structures of an unknown compound.

The past decade has witnessed the emergence of several expert systems. MYCIN (Shortliffe, 1976) addresses the problem of diagnosing and suggesting treatments for infectious blood diseases. PROSPECTOR (Duda et al., 1979) discovers ore deposits from geological data. HEARSAY-II (Erman, 1980) is a speech-understanding system. EL (Stallman and Sussman, 1977) analyzes electrical circuits.

Expert systems differ distinctly from conventional data processing systems. The main difference is that in most expert systems the knowledge of the domain is separated from the procedures that manipulate the knowledge, rather than appearing implicitly as part of the program code.

Expert systems differ from general decision support systems (discussed in Chapter 14) in that the former employ knowledge about their own inference processes and provide explanations or justification for conclusions reached. Perhaps the most important distinction is that expert systems are capable of "learning." They are high-performance systems (producing high-quality results) with domain-specific problem-solving strategies.

The experience from the early systems brought to focus three major areas of expert systems research—knowledge acquisition, knowledge representation, and knowledge utilization. **Knowledge acquisition** is the process of extracting knowledge from human experts to determine how they perform their activities. **Knowledge representation** is the means of conceptually representing knowledge in a computer-based system. **Knowledge utilization** is the process of applying the appropriate knowledge to a problem situation.

Experts perform a wide variety of tasks. Although the domains may be very different, there are fundamental types of tasks performed by experts. Each type requires some support through data manipulation. We discuss expert tasks briefly to expose the difficulties of expert reasoning and the design implications of each type of task.

Interpretation is the analysis of data to determine its meaning. The main requirement of the task is to find consistent and correct interpretations of the data. Although it is important that systems of analysis be rigorously complete, data is often full of errors, thus imposing a need to work with partial information. The interpreter must be able to identify uncertain or incomplete information and assumptions and to explain the interpretation.

An expert system could draw the data to be interpreted from a database system, as when economic data is interpreted in terms of trends. But trends are not always obvious. So, while the database may provide an efficient means for storing the data, the expert system must be relied upon for interpretation.

Diagnosis is the process of finding fault in a system based on interpretation of error-prone data. The requirements of diagnosis include those of interpretation. An understanding of the system organization and the relationships and interactions between subsystems is necessary. The key problems are that (1) faults can be masked by the symptoms of other faults, (2) faults can be intermittent, (3) diagnostic equipment itself can fail, and (4) some data about a system is inaccessible, expensive, or dangerous to retrieve.

The database component of a diagnosis system supplies the data required to test or validate relationships stored in the knowledge base. In this manner, the database becomes an active participant in the process of diagnosing any irregularities in the system being modeled.

Monitoring means continuously interpreting signals and activating alarms when intervention is required. A monitoring system must recognize alarm conditions in real time, and it must avoid false alarms. Alarm signals are context-dependent and imply variation in signal expectations with time and situation.

Monitoring obviously relies on data. The database system provides the natural base of data required to support the monitoring process. As the process becomes more critical, the database system must be designed to ensure maximum efficiency.

Prediction is the forecasting of the future from a model of the past and present. Prediction requires reasoning about time. Adequate models of how the environment changes over time are necessary. There are four key problems with prediction: (1) it requires the integration of incomplete information; (2) it must account for several possible futures; (3) it must make use of diverse data; and (4) it may be contingent on nearer but unpredictable events.

Systems drawing on stock market data, for example, must include some amount of predictive capability to issue automatic buy and sell orders. The systems also use monitoring and interpretation techniques to support the financial trading industry.

Planning is the preparation of a program of action to be carried out to achieve goals. Because planning involves a certain amount of prediction, it has the requirements of prediction. Other requirements include staying within constraints, achieving goals with minimum resources, and recognizing new opportunities resulting from change. Key problems include coordinating all those involved in implementing the plan, preparing contingencies for facing uncertainty, identifying critical factors, coping with interactions among subgoals, and adjusting plans according to feedback from prior actions.

A database system supports these activities in several ways. The data repository typically contains minimum and maximum bound specifications for data items, so some planning constraints are handled already. The data repository can be enhanced to categorize data items by their utilization in alternative plans. Similarly, a scale indicating the importance of a data item can be maintained in the data repository. All of these measurements can be maintained automatically by the system.

Design is the development of specifications to create objects that satisfy a set of requirements. It has many of the same requirements as planning. Key difficulties are (1) in large problems, the consequences of design decisions cannot be assessed immediately; (2) constraints generated by multiple sources may have no theory for integration; (3) breaking large problems into small subproblems in order to cope with complexity may create problems of interaction between subproblems; (4) large designs involve many design decisions, and it becomes difficult to assess the impact of a change in part of the design; (5) modifying a design to avoid suboptimal points can be difficult; and (6) techniques to reason approximately or qualitatively about shape and spatial relationships are not well known.

Many of the problems associated with design processes are solved by effective management of data. The database system must be capable

METROPOLITAN NATIONAL BANK

MetNat's senior management will soon be taking a planning retreat: a meeting at a location away from daily operations in which major planning issues for the bank are discussed. One of the topics to be discussed is the future of MetNat's information system.

One goal of the planning retreat is to determine a plan for incorporating microcomputer technology into the bank's operation. The board of directors has indicated the following broad topics it would like to have you discuss at the meeting:

Where should microcomputers be integrated into the bank's existing information system? Why?

How might the database system be more accessible to bank customers via personal computers located in customers' homes? How might the database system be more accessible to bank customers via simple telephone technology? What risks are involved regarding bank security if the bank utilizes these technologies?

In what areas might artificial intelligence technology such as expert systems be integrated into the bank's information system? What benefits might be gained?

You should develop a report that responds to these issues. Be sure to address the issue of how advancing technology will affect daily operations at MetNat. How would you recommend the bank monitor technological advances? What trends in the database industry might impact the bank's operations? For each trend you describe, include a discussion of MetNat's potential for exploiting this development. You should also include explanations of why a trend will have no impact on MetNat's database operations, if appropriate. ∎

of maintaining relationships, as large systems are decomposed into smaller ones. The database also provides means for data manipulation to evaluate new constraints.

Expert systems have been developed under each category of expert task. Expert systems that integrate these tasks are called **expert control systems.** Problems addressed by control systems include business management, battle management, and mission control.

CHAPTER SUMMARY

Many ways exist to extend the database concept in order to achieve greater efficiency and effectiveness in organizations. We have seen in this chapter how these extensions are not only desirable, but necessary to support certain types of organizational processes. The manufacturing environment presents many challenges to database processing. These challenges exist because the nature of the data, frequently in the form of design specifications and process models, is very different in substance from the factual data more commonly stored in organizational databases.

One approach to extending the traditional database models is embedded in the object-oriented paradigm. This approach emphasizes objects as the basic building blocks of systems. Objects are encapsulated representations of entities. Objects have a private memory and a public interface. Classes of objects have common characteristics, but subclasses can have features that distinguish the subclass from the parent class.

Several innovations in database processing are currently being developed. Some systems are able to understand written or spoken language. This type of processing is known as natural language processing. Natural language processing has been effective as an interface for database management systems.

Although a system that is capable of natural language processing demonstrates somewhat intelligent behavior, expert systems are the most advanced systems currently being developed. Expert systems are usually designed to solve problems in narrowly defined problem domains, although much research is under way to extend the capabilities of expert systems to broader domains. Expert systems require an efficient database interface to perform expert tasks.

Questions and Answers

1. Create a drawing that embodies the design of your classroom. What are the attributes that might be important to an architect that would want to access this design?

2. Assume you are an architect that has been hired to add built-in VCR facilities into your classroom. Create a drawing that reflects the current design of your classroom. Now indicate what attributes are important to you. If you answered Question 1, explain any differences.

3. Create a map that shows how you get from your home (or dorm) to your first class of the week. What are the attributes that might be important to a campus planner that would want to access this design?

4. Create a list of events that occur when you leave your home (or dorm) to go to your first class of the week. What are the important attributes of these events? What exceptions can occur to change the events?

5. Describe the origin of the object-oriented paradigm. What software development technique contributed to the development of object-oriented approaches?

6. How is information communicated between objects?

7. What is encapsulation? How is encapsulation related to the general concept of data independence?

8. Give an example of two object classes, one of which inherits a method from the other.

9. What is polymorphism? Give an example.

10. What advantage would an object-oriented database system have over a relational database system in an office environment?

11. What were the motivations for the development of SDM?

12. What is the difference between an SDM class attribute and a member attribute?

13. List five characteristics of a member attribute and discuss them.

14. Add addresses (street, city, state, and zip code) and telephone numbers to the SDM description for CUSTOMERS in Figure 13–4. How did you define the member attribute zip-code? How would you define the member attribute Telephone-number?

15. Modify the SDM description for CASSETTES in Figure 13–6 to include information on actors and actresses that appear in a movie.

16. Explain the difference between an SDM inverse relationship and an SDM matching relationship.

17. Explain the difference between an SDM base class and an SDM nonbase class.

18. How does a deductive database differ from a relational database?

19. What role does logic play in deductive databases?

20. Transform the data from Figure 6–1 into Prolog facts.

21. Consider the following Prolog facts about managers at a major accounting firm:

```
manager (12394, Smith, 1.2, [gas,
    telecommunications]).
manager (83736, Finch, 0.8, [banking, acquisi-
    tions, gas]).
manager (83887, Dexter, 2.3, [telecommunications,
    banking]).
manager (27762, Fraser, 2.2, [non-profit,
    government]).
manager (28736, Johnson, 1.3, [utilities, gas,
    non-profit, banking]).
```

The arguments have the following meanings: identification number, name, revenue generated in millions, list of industries of expertise. Write a Prolog rule that will provide the names of managers that have generated more than $1.0 million in revenue and have gas industry expertise.

22. Discuss the two types of knowledge that exist in a database environment relative to database interfaces.

23. Describe three peculiarities of natural language communication that must be addressed in a natural language processing system.

24. What is a natural language processor and what are its advantages and disadvantages?

25. What is the difference between a knowledge base and a database?

26. What is an expert system? Describe its characteristics.

27. Describe the types of problems for which expert systems have been developed. What characteristics do these problems have in common?

28. List the types of tasks performed by experts and give an example of an expert that performs this type of task.

29. Which of the approaches discussed in this chapter do you think will make the largest impact on the way organizations conduct their business activities? Why?

30. Which of the approaches discussed in this chapter will be the most difficult to manage? Why?

For Further Reading

Gabriela Marin contributed the primary source for our section covering database issues related to computer integrated manufacturing:

Marin, Gabriela. "The Challenge of Computer-Integrated Manufacturing to Database Technology." Presented at the Southwest Decision Sciences Conference, Houston, TX, 1990.

Additional information on the role of databases in computer-integrated manufacturing can be found in the following articles:

Bancilhon, F., and W. Kim. "Transactions and Concurrency Control in CAD Databases." *IEEE International Conference on Computer Design: VLSI in Computers.* New York, October 1985, pp. 86–89.

Bancilhon, F.; W. Kim; and H. F. Korth. "A Model of CAD Transactions." *Proceedings of the 11th International Conference on Very Large Databases.* 1985.

Banerjee, J.; W. Kim; H. J. Kim; and H. F. Korth. "Semantics and Implementation of Schema Evolution in Object-Oriented Databases." *Proceedings of the ACM SIGMOD'87 Annual Conference.* San Francisco, May 1987, pp. 311–22.

Batory, D. S., and W. Kim. "Modeling Concepts for VLSI CAD Objects." *ACM Transactions on Database Systems* 10, no. 3 (September 1985), pp. 322–46.

Cornelio, A., and S. B. Navathe. "Database Support for Engineering CAD and Simulation." *Second Conference on Data and Knowledge Systems for Manufacturing and Engineering.* Gaithersburg, Md., October 1989, pp. 38–47.

Dayal, U. "The HiPac Project: Combining Active Databases and Timing Constraints." *SIGMOD Record* 17, no. 1 (March 1988), pp. 51–70.

Dittrich, K. R.; A. M. Kotz; and J. A. Mulle. "An Event/Trigger Mechanism to Enforce Complex Consistency Constraints in Design Databases." *SIGMOD Record* 15, no 3 (September 1986), pp. 22–36.

Gaines, B. R. "Structure, Development, and Applications of Expert Systems in Integrated Manufacturing." In *Artificial Intelligence Implications for CIM.* A. Kusiak, ed., New York: Springer-Verlag, 1988, pp. 117–61.

Groover, M. P., and E. Simmer. *CAD/CAM Computer Aided Design and Manufacturing.* Englewood Cliffs, N.J.: Prentice Hall, 1984.

Hartzband, D. J., and F. J. Maryanski. "Enhancing Knowledge Representation in Engineering Databases." *IEEE Computer,* September 1985, pp. 39–48.

Ho, W. P. C.; Y. H. Hu; and D. Y. Y. Yun. "An Intelligent Librarian for VLSI Cell Databases." *IEEE International Conference on Computer Design: VLSI in Computers.* New York, October 1985, pp. 78–81.

Katz, R. H. "Managing the Chip Design Database." *IEEE Computer* 16 (December 1983), pp. 26–36.

Kemper, A.; P. C. Lockemann; and M. Wallrath. "An Object-Oriented Database System for Engineering Applications." *Proceedings of the ACM SIGMOD '87 Annual Conference.* San Francisco, May 1987, pp. 299–310.

Ketabchi, M. A., and V. Berzins. "Modeling and Managing CAD Databases." *IEEE Computer,* February 1987, pp. 93–101.

LeMaistre, C., and A. El-Sawy. *Computer Integrated Manufacturing: A Systems Approach.* New York: UNIPUB/Kraus International Publishers, 1987.

Lorie, R. A., and W. Plouffe. "Complex Objects and Their Use in Design Transactions." *ACM SIGMOD/IEEE Engineering Design Applications,* 1983.

Maier, D. "Making Database Systems Fast Enough for CAD Applications." In *Object-Oriented Concepts, Databases, and Applications.* eds. W. Kim and F. H. Lochovsky. New York: Addison-Wesley Publishing, 1989.

Mills, M. C. "Obstacles to Computer-Integrated Manufacturing." In *Computer Integrated Manufacturing Handbook.* eds. Eric Teicholz and Joel N. Orr. New York: McGraw-Hill, 1987, pp. 25–52.

Milner, D. A., and V. C. Vasiliou. *Computer-Aided Engineering for Manufacture.* London: McGraw-Hill, 1987.

Nobecourt, P.; C. Rolland; and J. Y. Lingat. "Temporal Management in an Extended Relational DBMS." *Proceedings of the 6th British National Conference on Databases.* July 1988, pp. 87–123.

Ranky, P. *Computer-Integrated Manufacturing.* Englewood Cliffs, N.J.: Prentice Hall, 1986.

Scheer, A. W. *CIM: Computer Steered Industry.* New York: Springer-Verlag, 1988.

Sidle, T. W. "Weakness of Commercial Database Management Systems in Engineering Applications." *Proceedings of the 17th ACM Design Automation Conference.* 1980, pp. 57–61.

Smith, F. J. and L. C. Emerson. "Indexing Technical Data in a Materials Database." *2nd Conference on Data and Knowledge Systems for Manufacturing and Engineering.* Gaithersburg, Md., October 1989, pp. 12–18.

Snordgrass, R. "The Temporary Query Language TQuel." *ACM Transactions on Database Systems* 12, no. 2 (June 1987), pp. 147–98.

Swyt, D. A. "CIM, Data and Standardization within the NBS AMRF." In *Computer Integrated Manufacturing: Communication/Standardization/Interfaces.* eds. Thomas Bernold and Walter Guttropf. New York: Elsevier–North Holland Publishing, 1988, pp. 27–39.

Teicholz, E. and J. Orr. *Computer Integrated Manufacturing Handbook.* New York: McGraw-Hill, 1987.

Vernadat, F. "Artificial Intelligence in CIM Databases." In *Artificial Intelligence Implications for CIM.* ed. A. Kusiak. New York: Springer-Verlag, 1988, pp. 255–98.

More information on object-oriented approaches can be found in:

Kim, W. "A New Database for New Times." *Datamation,* January 15, 1990, pp. 35–42.

Kim, W. "Object-Oriented Databases: Definition and Research Directions." *IEEE Transactions on Knowledge and Data Engineering* 2, no. 3 (September 1990), pp. 327–41.

Kim, W. and F. H. Lochovsky, ed. *Object-Oriented Concepts, Databases, and Applications.* New York: ACM Press, 1989.

Zdonik, S. B., and P. Wegner. "Language and Methodology for Object-Oriented Database Environment." *Data Types and Persistence.* New York: Springer-Verlag, 1988, pp. 155–71.

For more information about expert systems, see:

Chandler, J. S., and T. P. Liang. *Developing Expert Systems for Business Applications.* Columbus, Ohio: Merrill, 1990.

Harmon, P., and D. King. *Expert Systems.* New York: John Wiley & Sons, 1985.

Natural language processing is described in the following articles:

Erman, L. D.; F. Hayes-Roth; V. Lesser; and D. Reddy. "The HEARSAY-II Speech-Understanding System: Integrating Knowledge to Resolve Uncertainty." *Computing Surveys* 12, no. 2 (1980), pp. 213–53.

Harris, L. "ROBOT: A High-Performance Natural Language Interface for Data Base Query." In *Natural Language-Based Computer Systems,* ed. L. Bloc, Munich: Macmillan, 1980.

Johnson, Tim. "NLP Takes Off." *Datamation,* January 15, 1986. pp. 91–93.

Ott, N. and M. Zoeppritz. "An Experimental Information System Based on Natural Language." In *Natural Language-Based Computer Systems,* ed. L. Bloc, Munich: Macmillan, 1980.

Turner, J. A.; M. Jarke; E. A. Stohr; Y. Vassiliou; and N. White. " Using Restricted Natural Language for Data Retrieval: A Plan for Field Evaluation." In *Human Factors and Interactive Computer Systems.* Norwood, N.J.: Ablex Publishing, 1982.

Other research issues in database systems are found in:

Berstein, P. A. "Future Directions in DBMS Research: The Laguna Beach Participants." *SIGMOD Record* 18, no. 1 (March 1989), pp. 17–26.

Codd, E. F. "Extending the Relational Database Model to Capture More Meaning." *ACM Transactions on Database Systems* 4 (1979), pp. 397–434.

Goodhue, D. L.; J. A. Quillard; and J. F. Rockart. "Managing the Data Resource: A Contingency Perspective." *MIS Quarterly* 12, no. 2 (June 1988).

Hodges, P. "A Relational Successor?" *Datamation,* November 1, 1989, pp. 47–50.

Paradice, D. G. "The Role of Memory in Intelligent Information Systems." *Proceedings of the 21st Annual Hawaii International Conference on Systems Sciences* 3 (1988), pp. 2–9.

Other citations in this chapter are:

Buchanan, B. G.; G. L. Sutherland; and E. A. Feigenbaum. "Heuristic DENDRAL: A Program for Generating Explanatory Hypotheses in Organic Chemistry." In *Machine Intelligence,* Vol. 5, eds. B. Meltzer and D. Michie. Edinburgh: Edinburgh University Press, 1969.

Duda, R. O.; J. G. Gasching; and P. E. Hart. "Model Design in the PROSPECTOR Consultant System for Mineral Exploration." In *Expert Systems in the Micro-Electronic Age,* ed. D. Michie. Edinburgh: Edinburgh University Press, 1979.

Shortliffe, E. H. *Computer-Based Medical Consultations: MYCIN.* New York: American Elsevier, 1976.

Slagle, J. R. "A Heuristic Program That Solves Symbolic Integration Problems in Freshman Calculus. Symbolic Automation Integrator (SAINT)." Ph.D. Report 5G-0001, Lincoln Laboratory, Massachusetts Institute of Technology, 1961.

Stallman, R., and G. J. Sussman, "Forward Reasoning and Dependency Directed Backtracking in a System for Computer-Aided Circuit Analysis." *Artificial Intelligence* 9 (1977), pp. 135–96.

14

DATABASE SYSTEMS FOR MANAGEMENT DECISION-MAKING

In previous chapters, we have emphasized the treatment of data as an organizational resource to be made available for managerial decision-making. Database management systems provide the tools for doing this. Database systems may also be used as part of larger systems called *decision support systems*. A decision support system (DSS) helps a manager use both data and quantitative models to make decisions in unstructured or semistructured situations. A situation is **unstructured** if the manager has no well-specified procedure or algorithm for making the decision. A **structured situation** is just the opposite.

For example, it is easy to "decide" what a customer's bill should be on a revolving charge account. Thus, customer billing is a structured situation. On the other hand, it may be very difficult to decide whether to introduce a new product line—this is an unstructured decision. Decision support systems are oriented toward the more difficult category—unstructured decisions. As we shall see, databases to support unstructured decisions may have considerably different characteristics than those supporting more-structured situations. First, we will examine the DSS environment and then discuss how databases are different for that environment.

DECISION SUPPORT SYSTEMS

Managerial decisions are often based on some kind of model. The model may be no more than a simple **decision rule** or **heuristic** (rule of thumb) that exists only in the manager's mind, or it may be a highly complex set of mathematical equations.

An example of a simple heuristic to determine a firm's research and development (R&D) budget is:

The R&D budget should be 10 percent of last year's net profit.

A database system can easily support this kind of a simple heuristic if it contains last year's net profit as a data item.

A more complicated set of rules might be:

If net profit was normal last year, then the R&D budget should be 10 percent of net profit.

If net profit was above normal last year, then the R&D budget should be 12 percent of net profit.

If net profit was below normal last year, then the R&D budget should be 8 percent of net profit.

Again, decisions based on the set of rules above can be supported by a database system, since the rules depend on a data item in a database: net profit. Note, however, that it is up to the manager to decide which rule applies, since a conventional database system does not know whether net profit is normal, above normal, or below normal. Selection of the appropriate decision rule depends on the manager's judgment on whether last year's net profit was "normal" or not. (Of course, precise rules could be established for determining this as well.)

As a third example of a set of rules for determining a firm's R&D budget, consider the following case in which the rules are based on net profits for the *next* year:

> If net profit next year is expected to be normal, then the R&D budget should be 10 percent of forecasted net profit.
>
> If net profit next year is expected to be above normal, then the R&D budget should be 12 percent of forecasted net profit.
>
> If net profit next year is expected to be below normal, then the R&D budget should be 8 percent of forecasted net profit.

This set of decision rules is considerably different because it requires a *forecast* of net profit for the next year. The kind of database systems we have been concerned with in this book contains historical and current data, not forecasts. Of course, forecasts are often based on mathematical or statistical models that require historical data. Thus, as suggested in the previous chapter, a database system can provide the data on which to base such forecasts. The modeling component of the DSS provides the forecasting model.

Mathematically based forecasts are not without error, however, and they may not take all relevant factors into account. Thus, human judgment must be used to interpret and adjust the forecast. Managerial judgments such as these are based on *knowledge* of the organization and its environment. This knowledge is not included in database systems and is seldom found in computer systems at all.

The examples above are designed to illustrate the point that even though many management decisions require the use of data, data alone is not sufficient to make the decision. In addition to data, decision rules, mathematical models, managerial knowledge, and human judgment are all important factors in making management decisions. The DSS concept, first proposed in the early 1970s, has evolved to take these diverse factors into account in developing computer-based systems to augment managerial decision-making.

Decision support systems were initially defined as consisting of database management systems combined with mathematical modeling systems to provide powerful, flexible tools for quantitative analysis of management decisions. More recently, the DSS concept has been extended by incorporating ideas from expert systems and cognitive psychology, which deals with how people solve problems and make decisions.

As discussed in Chapter 13, expert systems try to capture expert knowledge of the problem domain, or specific problem area, and use that knowledge to make decisions. Knowledge is stored as a separate entity called a *knowledge base*, which is analogous to the database in a database system. In a database system, the database management system is a complex program that manipulates the database. In an expert system, the inference engine is a complex program that manipulates the knowledge base. Data in databases tends to be numeric, with some character data. Information in knowledge bases is more qualitative or textual in nature, and inference engines may use **qualitative reasoning** rather than quantitative models to reach decisions.

There is already a clearly observable trend toward the development of DSSs that integrate databases, knowledge bases, mathematical models, and expert system inference engines into integrated systems for management decision-making. The potential impact of these DSSs is tremendous. Because of the intimate reliance of these systems on databases, students of database systems should be familiar with the DSS concept. In the remainder of the chapter, we explore DSSs in some detail. First, we examine historical developments in DSS. Then, we look at more-recent developments in DSS, which attempt to incorporate concepts from artificial intelligence and expert systems, and we explain how those developments relate to database systems and management decision-making.

HISTORY OF THE DECISION SUPPORT SYSTEM CONCEPT

The term *decision support system* was popularized as a result of an article by Gorry and Scott Morton in 1971. While there is no clear consensus on a precise definition of DSSs, the DSS literature characterizes them as:

1. Interactive computer-based systems.
2. Facilitating the use of quantitative models and ad hoc queries in an integrated fashion.
3. Emphasizing flexibility and adaptability with respect to changes in the environment and decision-making approach of the user.
4. Generally targeted for upper-level managers to help in solving unstructured or semistructured problems.

Gorry and Scott Morton integrated the work of Robert Anthony (1965) and Herbert Simon (1960), work that is fundamental to an understanding of the concept of management decision support.

Anthony's Managerial Activities

Anthony categorized managerial activity into strategic planning, management control, and operational control. **Strategic planning,** usually performed by upper management (see Figure 14–1), involves activities such as determining organizational goals and long-range strategies for how those goals will be achieved. This might, for example, include the addition of a new product line and plans for manufacturing and marketing the new line. Strategic planning activities involve a long planning horizon (several years) and are typically unstructured. Designing a database to support such activities is difficult because it is difficult to

FIGURE 14–1
Anthony's Category of
Management Activity

anticipate what decisions will have to be made, much less what information will be needed. The relational approach is normally used in a DSS database because of the flexibility relational query languages provide in retrieving and manipulating data. Characteristics of databases in a DSS environment will be discussed shortly.

Managerial control in Anthony's scheme, the primary activity of middle management, consists of steering the organization toward the goals set in the strategic planning process. The time horizon is generally one year or perhaps somewhat longer. Activities include budgeting and resource allocation, monitoring the operation of the organization for problems, and correction of the problems when possible. These activities may be supported by a typical management information system built around an integrated database. Information requirements here are better defined and can be supported by either a network or a relational approach.

Operational control, the lowest level in the Anthony hierarchy, is concerned with the day-to-day operation of the organization. Example tasks include assigning personnel to projects or tasks, overseeing the execution of tasks, and reporting results to middle management. Many of these tasks involve well-defined data processing operations such as billing and inventory control.

Simon's Decision Types

Simon (1960) described managerial decisions as either programmed or nonprogrammed. These terms are not meant to imply that **programmed decisions** are computerized, but rather that well-specified procedures exist to handle them. They involve decisions such as the billing example and heuristics described previously. Programmed decisions may not be computerized, but they are readily computerizable.

Nonprogrammed decisions are those that are new, novel, or so complex that no well-specified procedures have been developed for handling them. Examples of such decisions include mergers and acquisitions, addition of new product lines, and location of new plants or warehouses. It is difficult to automate such decision processes, but aspects of them are computerizable. A database system may very well contain information useful in such decisions.

Gorry and Scott Morton's Framework

Gorry and Scott Morton combined Anthony's and Simon's categories, using the terms *structured, semistructured,* and *unstructured* instead of *programmed* and *nonprogrammed.* Their two-dimensional framework is shown in Table 14–1. Example applications are given for each category. Structured decision systems (SDS) (below the dashed line) deal with structured decisions, regardless of organizational level. In the original concept, DSSs, by definition, attack unstructured and semistructured problems.

DATABASES FOR DSS ENVIRONMENTS

Throughout most of this book, we have assumed that the situation in which a database system is being used or developed is relatively well-structured. In such cases, the design approach we have described is to perform an information-requirements analysis, a logical design, and a physical design. This is perfectly appropriate when information requirements can be specified rather accurately. However, in strategic planning activities and other relatively unstructured situations, a thorough specification of information requirements is often difficult to provide. Compare, for example, the information requirements to deal with a hostile takeover attempt or whether to enter a foreign market, with data needed for a payroll, billing, or inventory control applications. Clearly, the data needs for the latter applications are much more well defined than those for strategic decisions. Table 14–2 summarizes some of the differences in information requirements for strategic planning activities as compared to management control and operational control activities. Let us consider these differences in some detail.

TABLE 14–1   Gorry and Scott Morton's Two-Dimensional Systems Framework

	Strategic Planning	Management Control	Operational Control
DSS: Unstructured	Mergers	Career path management	Employee disputes
DSS: Semistructured	Long-range forecasting	Budgeting	Assigning people to projects
SDS: Structured	Dividend declaration	Vendor selection	Billing

TABLE 14–2   Characteristics of Information by Activity

Information Attribute	Strategic Planning	Management Control	Operational Control
Source	Largely external ⟶		Largely internal
Scope	Broad ⟶		Narrow
Detail	Aggregated ⟶		Specific
Time horizon	Future ⟶		Present
Precision	Good estimate ⟶		Precise
Access frequency	Infrequent ⟶		High

Adapted from G. A. Gorry and M. S. Scott Morton, "A Framework for Management Information Systems," *Sloan Management Review* 13, no. 1 (1971).

Planning Databases versus Control Databases

Since strategic planning deals with the relationship of the organization to its environment, much of the information required for this kind of activity comes from sources outside the organization. Information is needed on entities such as competitors, the industry as a whole, the economy, governmental regulations, technological developments, and consumer tastes and preferences. Much of this data may even be textual or anecdotal in nature, rather than numeric. It is difficult to anticipate all the different kinds of information that might be needed for strategic planning.

These information requirements contrast sharply to those of operational control. Take an inventory control system, for example. The latter requires largely internal information on inventory items, costs, stock on-hand, demand, and so forth. The data requirements are rather well defined, and readily available. Data for strategic planning often lacks the detail and precision required for control activities and may be aggregated for entire organizations, economies, or countries.

By its very nature, planning implies the need to anticipate the future, and thus is predictive in nature. Since prediction is not an exact science, we are forced to live with some margin of error in forecasts. Thus, the information for strategic planning not only comes largely from external sources, but also we may not need, nor even be able to provide, the degree of precision required in an application like payroll or billing. People want their pay checks and bills to be accurate. On the other hand, a 5 percent or 10 percent error in forecasting sales may not be calamitous.

Finally, strategic planning doesn't occur with the regularity or intensity of control activities. Whereas in a control-oriented application, there may be hundreds of thousands of transactions per day of the same type (say sales or airline reservations), the frequency of access to a strategic planning database may be much, much less, but the queries themselves may be of many different types. It is much more likely that users will be browsing through a planning database looking for relationships or clues, as opposed to looking for a specific inventory item or person in a control database.

Implications for Databases to Support Planning

The characteristics of strategic planning databases have important implications for database designers and developers. Since it is difficult to anticipate all the different kinds of data that may be needed for planning, a flexible and adaptable system is essential. We must be able to modify the structure of the database, adding tables or columns, and be able to access that data in unanticipated ways. Since the frequency of access is not great, efficiency is not nearly as important as effectiveness. That is, it is much more important to provide the right information rather than to provide it at minimum cost.

On the other hand, in a control database, efficiency may be critical. In an airline reservation system, for example, the same kind of access is performed thousands of times a day. A few milliseconds can be important in such cases. In a planning situation, a query may occur only once, so a few seconds or even minutes may not matter much.

In planning contexts, we must also support a wider variety of data types. Most data for control is numeric, interspersed with character data such as names, addresses, and product descriptions. Conversely, data for planning might well include articles from *The Wall Street Journal*, other newspapers, and trade journals. This information may require different methods of organization and different access methods. Much of this data may come from an outside party or "vendor" who provides access to it on the vendor's computer system. However, it is a common practice to download this data to a using organization's computer for local storage. Thus, the ability to integrate downloaded data with local systems becomes an issue.

The characteristics of planning data and the emergence of DSSs in the past few years may help to explain the movement to relational database systems. Relational systems are more suited to a DSS environment because they provide more-flexible access and tend to be more adaptable than network and hierarchical systems. Conversely, networks and hierarchies are very efficient in handling large quantities of data and high-volume access to relatively well structured databases. Since it is difficult to tune an operating system to handle both planning and control databases efficiently, many organizations have separate, but linked, facilities to support these different activities. The DSS and its planning database may reside on a minicomputer system designed for interactive browsing, while the control databases reside on a mainframe designed for high-volume access and many transactions. Since the DSS may require data from the organizational database on the mainframe, some type of telecommunications link is provided to give access to this data.

Since it is difficult to anticipate information needs in a planning environment, the approach to design advocated earlier in this text (that is, information-requirements analysis, logical design, and physical design) is not appropriate. Instead, an iterative and evolutionary approach is usually employed. This point will be discussed further after some other characteristics of DSS environments have been described to help you better understand the differences in DSS environments and structured environments.

DECISION-MAKING SYSTEMS

As indicated in Figure 14–2, **decision-making systems** are human/machine systems. Managers face decision problems and interact with DSSs to analyze those problems. Both the human and the computerized DSS may be viewed as information processors. The total capability of the system is the combined capabilities of the human and the computer. In the ensuing discussion, the human part of this system is considered first, then the computer part.

Human Information Processing

An understanding of the capabilities of humans as information processors is important in the design of DSSs. The Newell and Simon (1972) model of human information processing (discussed next) serves as a basis for examining the need for a computer information processor (the DSS) to help overcome human limitations.

The Newell-Simon model of the human information processor includes three different types of memory: long-term memory, short-term memory, and external memory (Figure 14–3). These, along with a processor (the brain) and input (the senses), enable people to process information.

Of particular significance to DSSs are the three types of memory and their respective capacities and limitations. Storage in long-term, high-capacity memory is thought by Newell and Simon to be in the form of symbols, structures, and images. Recall from long-term memory may be accomplished in terms of single symbol designations of quite large sets of stimuli. Considerable effort is required to store knowledge in long-term memory, but recall times are quite fast once stored.

Short-term memory has a quite small capacity, holding only five to nine symbols. These properties impose severe limitations on the ways humans can formulate and solve complex, semistructured problems. It is difficult or impossible for people to process complex problems because short-term memory is too small to hold the information necessary to

FIGURE 14–2
The Components of Decision-Making Systems
Managers are faced with decision problems and use DSSs to analyze those problems and arrive at decisions.

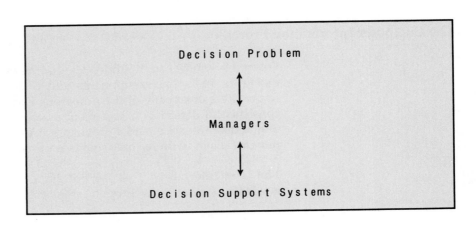

FIGURE 14–3   **The Human Information Processor**

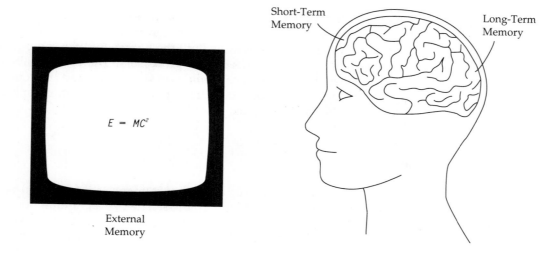

perceive the structure of the problem, while long-term memory has available only those strategies used frequently or recently.

External memory might be a pad of paper, a chalkboard, or, in the case of DSS, a computer system. External memory can be used very efficiently by people in problem-solving activities. This should be particularly true when the human is using a computer system as an external memory aid. Psychological and cognitive research indicates that humans differ in the way they use these memories to gather and process data: that is, they have different "cognitive styles." Some use a methodical, analytic approach to solve problems, while others are less structured in their approach, using trial and error, guessing, and heuristics.

There is considerable disagreement regarding the role of cognitive style in managerial decision-making. The main point as far as database systems and DSSs are concerned is that many different capabilities should be provided to support various approaches to decision-making—just as different user views of the same database should be provided. Not everyone needs the same data in a database system, and not everyone needs the same models in a DSS.

The Computer Information Processor

Figure 14–4 shows an expanded view of the computer-based DSS shown in Figure 14–2. The components and relationships as shown in this figure are a composite of the numerous existing DSS models. The DSS consists of a database management system, a model management system, a user interface, and a problem processor that links the other components. Each of these components is described below.

The User Interface.   The user interface of a DSS consists of the languages and other tools through which the user communicates with the

FIGURE 14–4
The Computer Information Processor or Decision Support System

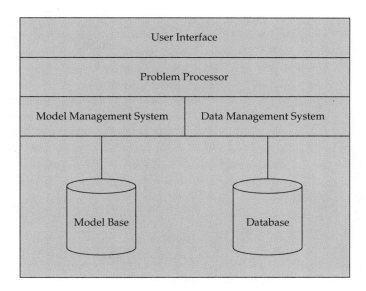

system. The IFPS modeling language, discussed below, is one example. The visual spreadsheet interface is another. Some systems use a command language like SQL (see Chapter 7); others use QBE (see Chapter 8). Most DSS researchers argue that a good system should provide several different interfaces to accommodate the various problem-solving styles of potential users. Providing several types of interfaces is, of course, expensive, and few packages do so at present.

The Problem Processor.   The user interface accepts input from the user, interprets (parses) it, and passes it to the problem processor for execution. The problem processor links the other elements of the system, extracting data from the database and models from the model base, executing models, and passing results to the user. To satisfy a user request, the system may only be required to extract data via the DBMS and pass it to the user with no further processing. On the other hand, it may have to extract a model and the data to run the model first, then run the model against the data, and finally present the results to the user.

   This can be a complex process, especially if the model base contains many sophisticated models and the database is large and integrated over several users. At the present time, most DSS packages do not have well-developed problem processors. A package may be able to find a model if the model's name is given by the user and run it against a set of data. The data may come from a file or perhaps even a fully implemented database system. Current packages may also be able to call routines written in ordinary programming languages such as FORTRAN, PASCAL, or C. That is about the limit of existing DSS technology.

More Comments on Data Management in a DSS Environment.   The DSS environment is characterized by a lack of structure and a great deal of uncertainty. In such an environment, it is difficult to anticipate queries that must be processed against a database. In addition, the queries that must be processed usually involve many secondary keys. Furthermore, there is generally little need for the massive updates that occur in transaction-oriented applications such as accounting systems or inventory processing.

Relational database systems are more suitable in a DSS environment than most network or hierarchical systems because they provide more flexible access to the database. Moreover, the relational approach provides more variety in the access languages available. Graphic languages like QBE provide a usable interface for visually oriented users. Command languages like SQL provide an alternative for people preferring Command Mode.

Relational algebra provides a procedural interface that might be preferred by systematic thinkers. Thus, most DSS software uses a relational approach to data management. Because this approach is described in detail in other chapters of the book, there is no need to discuss it further here.

The Model Base and Its Management System.   The model base is a collection of different kinds of mathematical models to use in different situations and for different functions. The model base, like the database, is a resource for planning and decision-making tasks. It may contain submodels, or "pieces," with which to build large, general-purpose, permanent models, user-defined models for ad hoc studies, or "canned" models for performing well-defined procedures. The need for forecasting models in the heuristics given at the beginning of the chapter is an example of the need for models in a DSS.

The model management system is designed to handle the model base in a manner analogous to database management systems' handling of data. The model management system should provide mechanisms for creating, cataloging, linking, integrating, and accessing the models in the model base. Unfortunately, model management systems have not developed to the point that all of these functions are fully supported. Many packages provide facilities for creating, cataloging, and accessing models, but virtually none provide powerful, generalized techniques for linking and integrating submodels.

DSS in a Microcomputer Environment.   Microcomputers provide an effective environment for delivery of decision support systems to users, especially when networked to larger machines supporting organizational databases. User interfaces on micros are often more "user-friendly" than those on larger machines. Micros may allow the use of a mouse or other input devices not readily available on mainframes, and usually support multiple windows and also provide better graphics capability.

In a networked environment, data can be downloaded to a micro and manipulated there by the user. This not only may make the data analysis task easier because of the better interface, but also relieves the mainframe of a computational burden. Thus the organization may benefit both from improved decision analysis, and from lighter load on its central computing resources.

Since you may not be familiar with mathematical modeling in general or DSS models in particular, we will describe a DSS modeling package in the next section. The package described below is the interactive financial planning system (IFPS), originally developed by Execucom Systems Corporation. It is one of the most popular DSS modeling packages. The main point to keep in mind during this discussion is that **DSS models are adaptable, which forces changes in the database from which they derive data.**

The Interactive Financial Planning System. As its name implies, IFPS is oriented toward planning rather than control activities. We have previously described planning as an unstructured process. Planning involves many vagaries and uncertainties because it involves looking into the future rather than the present or past (as in most control activities). Thus, a modeling language to support planning processes must provide the ability to deal with uncertainty. IFPS provides several mechanisms for handling uncertainty, but the most innovative (at the time of its introduction) is the WHAT IF capability. WHAT IF is used interactively to test the sensitivity of an IFPS model to changes in parameter values. For example, the user might wish to ask: "What if the interest rate is 10.0 percent instead of 11.5 percent?" The example described next illustrates the WHAT IF process.

An IFPS model is listed in Figure 14–5. An interactive editor is available to enter models in this form. This is a spreadsheet-type model that generates projected income statements for five years into the future. The model is designed to evaluate the profitability of a potential new product.

Line 1 of the listing in Figure 14–5 indicates that the model will have five columns with the labels 1988, 1989, . . . , 1992. Lines 2–4 cause the title "Income Statement" to be printed. Line 5 defines a variable or row called VOLUME. In the first column, VOLUME takes the value of the variable VOLUME ESTIMATE. The value for VOLUME ESTIMATE is defined in line 27. (Notice the nonsequential nature of data value assignments. This is a general characteristic of IFPS models.) In all subsequent columns, the value is the previous value of VOLUME times 1.045. This simple type of recursion is commonly used in defining column values in IFPS and is used again in line 6, for example. Lines 7–10 are self-explanatory. Line 11 is a call to an IFPS built-in subroutine for straight-line depreciation. INVESTMENT, SALVAGE, and LIFE are input values to the routine, and DEPRECIATION is the sole output.

The remainder of the model is self-explanatory, with the possible exception of IRR in line 23, which is a procedure to compute internal rate of return given cash inflow as the first argument and cash outflow as the second.

Assume that the user has logged into the machine, invoked IFPS, and loaded the model in Figure 14–5 by giving IFPS the model name. As illustrated below, IFPS prompts for input with a question mark. Here,

FIGURE 14–5   IFPS Income Statement Model

```
 1 COLUMNS 1988—1992
 2 *
 3 *    INCOME STATEMENT
 4 *
 5 VOLUME = VOLUME ESTIMATE, PREVIOUS VOLUME ESTIMATE * 1.045
 6 SELLING PRICE = PRICE ESTIMATE, PREVIOUS SELLING PRICE * 1.06
 7 SALES = VOLUME * SELLING PRICE
 8 UNIT COST = .85
 9 VARIABLE COST = VOLUME * UNIT COST
10 DIVISION OVERHEAD = 15% * VARIABLE COST
11 STLINE DEPR(INVESTMENT,SALVAGE,LIFE,DEPRECIATION)
12 COST OF GOODS SOLD = VARIABLE COST + DIVISION OVERHEAD + DEPRECIATION
13 GROSS MARGIN = SALES — COST OF GOODS SOLD
14 OPERATING EXPENSE = .02 * SALES
15 INTEREST EXPENSE = 15742,21522,21147,24905,21311
16 *
17 NET BEFORE TAX = GROSS MARGIN — OPERATING EXPENSE — INTEREST EXPENSE
18 TAXES = TAX RATE * NET BEFORE TAX
19 NET AFTER TAX = NET BEFORE TAX — TAXES
20 *
21 INVESTMENT = 10000,125000,0,100000,0
22 *
23 RATE OF RETURN = IRR(NET AFTER TAX + DEPRECIATION,INVESTMENT)
24 *
25 * DATA ESTIMATES
26 TAX RATE = .46
27 VOLUME ESTIMATE = 100000
28 PRICE ESTIMATE = 2.25
29 SALVAGE = 0
30 LIFE = 10
END OF MODEL
```

Source: "IFPS Tutorial" (Austin, Tex.: Execucom, June 1980).

the user responds with SOLVE and has asked for ALL solve options. ALL means display the values for all variables (rows) in the model. A list of variable names can be substituted for the word ALL, and only the values for these rows will be displayed. The simple dialogue generates the output in Figure 14–6.

```
? SOLVE
MODEL INCOME VERSION OF 03/15/88 13:11—5 COLUMNS 21
  VARIABLES
ENTER SOLVE OPTIONS
? ALL
```

To illustrate WHAT IF analysis, assume that the user wants to examine the impact of an initial VOLUME ESTIMATE of 150,000 units and a price of $2.10. The dialogue to do this is:

```
? WHAT IF
WHAT IF CASE 1
ENTER STATEMENTS
? VOLUME ESTIMATE = 150000
? PRICE ESTIMATE = 2.10
```

FIGURE 14–6 **Output from the IFPS Model in Figure 14–5**

INCOME STATEMENT	1988	1989	1990	1991	1992
VOLUME	100000	104500	109202	114117	119252
SELLING PRICE	2.250	2.385	2.528	2.680	2.841
SALES	225000	249232	276075	305808	338743
UNIT COST	.8500	.8500	.8500	.8500	.8500
VARIABLE COST	85000	88825	92822	96999	101364
DIVISION OVERHEAD	12750	13324	13923	14550	15205
DEPRECIATION	10000	22500	22500	32500	32500
COST OF GOODS SOLD	107550	124649	129245	144049	149069
GROSS MARGIN	117250	124584	146829	161759	189675
OPERATING EXPENSE	4500	4985	5521	6116	6775
INTEREST EXPENSE	15742	21522	21147	24905	21311
NET BEFORE TAX	97008	98077	120161	130738	161589
TAXES	44624	45115	55274	60139	74331
NET AFTER TAX	52384	52962	64887	70598	87258
INVESTMENT	100000	125000	0	100000	0
RATE OF RETURN			.0007	.0073	.1776
DATA ESTIMATES					
TAX RATE	.4600	.4600	.4600	.4600	.4600
VOLUME ESTIMATE	1000000	100000	100000	100000	100000
PRICE ESTIMATE	2.250	2.250	2.250	2.250	2.250
SALVAGE	0	0	0	0	0
LIFE	10	10	10	10	10

Source: "IFPS Tutorial" (Austin, Tex.: Execucom, June 1980).

```
? SOLVE
MODEL INCOME VERSION OF 03/15/88 13:11—5 COLUMNS 21
   VARIABLES
ENTER SOLVE OPTIONS
? ALL
```

This dialogue causes IFPS to recalculate the model with the new values and display the new results in the same format as illustrated above.

The IFPS EXPLAIN Feature. IFPS provides a unique feature based on artificial intelligence to help explain the results obtained by running a model. This is known as the EXPLAIN feature. EXPLAIN commands are given in "seminatural language," in the sense that natural language phrases can be used, but in a restricted fashion. We discuss three EXPLAIN commands—WHY, OUTLINE, and CONTINUE.

OUTLINE is used to depict the structure of a model based on relationships between one variable in the model and all other variables that affect it either directly or indirectly. It is based on the fact that the relationships between variables can be depicted as a tree or hierarchy with the selected variable as the root node. Because many terminals and personal computers do not have graphics capability, the structure is displayed, not in node-arc form, but in the form of an outline.

To illustrate, suppose we want to know which variables have a direct or indirect influence on DIVISION OVERHEAD in the model in Figure 14–5. The command:

```
OUTLINE DIVISION OVERHEAD.
```

generates this information, resulting in the following output:

```
DIVISION OVERHEAD
.VARIABLE COST
..UNIT COST
..VOLUME
...VOLUME ESTIMATE
```

The only variable having a direct influence on the root variable DIVISION OVERHEAD is VARIABLE COST. This is the only variable appearing in the equation defining DIVISION OVERHEAD in line 10 of Figure 14–5. VARIABLE COST, in turn, is influenced by VOLUME and UNIT COST, which are indented one level to indicate an indirect influence on the root variable. Similarly, VOLUME is affected by the value of VOLUME ESTIMATE, which is indented another level. The OUTLINE command is useful in gaining an understanding of the relationships among variables in a model and may also be useful in debugging a model.

The WHY command is used to get an explanation for the results obtained from a model. The explanation is based on the structure of the model as depicted above in the OUTLINE command. Suppose, for example, that we notice that DIVISION OVERHEAD went up between 1988 and 1989 and we want to know why. The following command answers this question:

```
WHY DID DIVISION OVERHEAD GO UP IN 1989?
```

In answering this question, IFPS uses the **path of influences** visually depicted in the previous OUTLINE result. This is not really a difficult question; IFPS would respond with something like this:

```
DIVISION OVERHEAD WENT UP IN 1989 BECAUSE VARIABLE
    COST WENT UP IN 1989.
```

We may trace the path of influences with the CONTINUE command. For example, the command:

```
CONTINUE
```

results in output such as:

```
VARIABLE COST WENT UP IN 1989 BECAUSE VOLUME WENT UP
    IN 1989.
```

These are simple examples of the use of EXPLAIN commands. If you try to manually create the output of an OUTLINE command for NET AFTER TAX, you can see how complex the structure of a relatively simple model is. The explanations also become more complicated because several variables may have an impact on the target variable. Even more, some of these variables can cause the target variable to increase while others cause it to decrease.

Many variations of the commands discussed above are available. These can be helpful in clarifying the structure and results of a complex model.

This discussion barely scratches the surface of the features of IFPS. Other features include a report generator, more-sophisticated forms of sensitivity analysis, risk analysis, an optimization subsystem, and goal seeking. In goal seeking, the system is given a target value for a goal variable such as net profit and a variable to manipulate to achieve the goal. IFPS works backward from the target value to determine the value of the adjustment variable that yields the target. A microcomputer version of IFPS has similar capabilities, including a visual interface such as that of LOTUS 1–2–3. Several other packages, including MODEL, EMPIRE, and INGOT, have similar features.

Researchers are studying the possibility of using other artificial intelligence techniques in DSS software. The objective is to create a system that knows enough about relationships among variables in the organization's environment (problem domain) to actually construct models, determine data necessary to run the models, fetch that data, run the model, and explain the results to the user.

The integration of expert systems techniques into database systems and DSSs is another area under heavy investigation. One possible architecture for a system integrating database, decision support, and expert systems is given in Figure 14–7. The concepts of *knowledge representation* and *explanation* (as in the IFPS EXPLAIN feature) are taken from expert systems. Managerial knowledge about the problem is captured and stored in the knowledge base. The knowledge base may very well contain heuristics or decision rules (such as those in the R&D examples at the beginning of the chapter). This knowledge is referred to as **procedural knowledge,** for it involves "how to" determine whatever is in question.

FIGURE 14–7
Architecture of a System Integrating Database, Decision Support, and Expert Systems

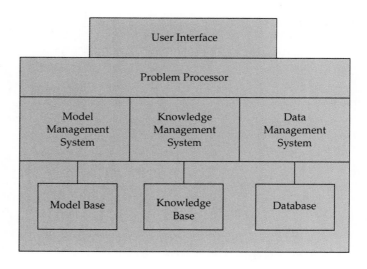

Data such as numeric or textual values for data items in the database are referred to as **declarative knowledge,** because they declare or state facts about the world. The inference engine (the problem processor in the present case) supplies declarative knowledge to the heuristics to solve problems and make decisions in the problem domain.

In the case of the R&D budget heuristics given earlier, the system would use models from the model base and data from the database to make the required forecasts. The forecast would then be run through the heuristic in the knowledge base and the budget would be determined. WHAT IF and EXPLAIN features could be used to explore the results of various future scenarios and to gain a better explanation of how different variables might impact the amount of the R&D budget. Unfortunately, such systems are still in the laboratory stage of development.

To understand how DSSs are used in organizations, it is necessary to see how a DSS is used in organizational decision-making processes. The next section describes the organizational decision-making process and where a DSS fits into each step of the process.

THE DECISION-MAKING PROCESS AND DSS

There are a number of different ways of describing the decision-making process. Simon's (1960) well-known model is suitable for our purposes. The model postulates three phrases: intelligence, design, and choice (Figure 14–8). *Intelligence* is used in the military sense; in this phase, the environment is scanned for situations requiring decisions. *Design* refers to the development of alternative ways of solving problems. *Choice* refers to the analysis of alternatives and implementation of the one that seems

FIGURE 14–8
Simon's Model of the Decision-Making Process

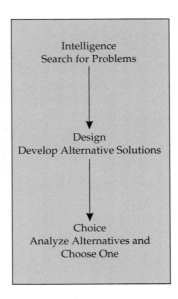

Intelligence
Search for Problems

Design
Develop Alternative Solutions

Choice
Analyze Alternatives and
Choose One

best. Each of these phases, along with the relevance of DSSs in this context, is described next.

Intelligence

The initial step in the intelligence phase is often referred to as **problem finding** or **problem recognition.** This step involves searching the environment for conditions requiring a decision. Raw data is obtained (perhaps using a query language such as SQL or the output of a report generator) and examined for clues that may identify problems.

A second step in this phase, called **problem formulation** or **problem structuring,** occurs as more information is sought to define the problem more clearly. This early stage of decision-making has the potential for affecting the direction of all succeeding phases. During this step, the decision-maker forms a "mental model" of the problem.

The mental model reflects the manager's understanding of the problem structure. *Problem structure* refers to the variables occurring in the problem and how they interact. The qualitative representation of the problem thus formed strongly affects the domain of possible solutions. Research has shown that computer graphics are useful in assisting in the problem-structuring process. A technique called **structural modeling** has proven useful in depicting and communicating the user's perception of a problem's structure. An example structural model is shown in Figure 14–9. This diagram shows the relationships between variables affecting DIVISION OVERHEAD in the IFPS problem (see Figures 14–5 and 14–6). Boxes represent variables, and arrows represent relationships. A system with graphics capability makes it feasible to display the output of an OUTLINE command in this form.

FIGURE 14–9
Structural Model of DIVI-SION OVERHEAD in the IFPS Problem

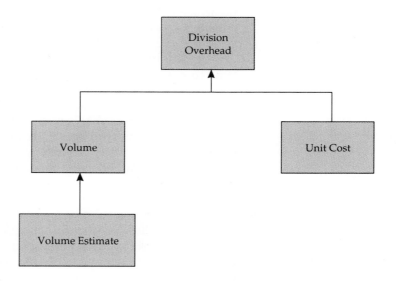

Design

In the design phase, data is manipulated to invent, develop, and analyze various possible solutions or courses of action. The mental model of the problem developed in the intelligence phase may be converted to a quantitative model using the modeling system of the DSS. Data for the model is assembled and manipulated to develop various alternatives. Because numerous alternatives may be available, unfeasible or inappropriate ones may be screened out before the choice phase is entered.

Choice

The main tasks in the choice phase are to evaluate possible alternatives and to select the best one. The perception of "best" depends on the decision-maker's perspective. The problem processor provides the tools to access data and models and to assist in a thorough analysis of alternatives. These may include extensive use of WHAT IF and other forms of sensitivity analysis. Once this analysis is complete, the best alternative is chosen for implementation.

Although the decision-making process is here characterized as sequential, it is less clearly so in practice. The activities of intelligence, design, and choice are interlaced and repetitive, and they take place within a dynamic decision-making environment. A DSS should support all aspects of this process.

DATABASE DESIGN IN A DSS CONTEXT

Because the DSS environment is unstructured and information requirements are difficult to anticipate and specify, traditional design approaches do not work well for designing databases in a DSS context. In most instances, DSS design is iterative and evolutionary.

The design process usually begins with the user and analyst working together to define the structure of a relatively small, tractable problem. To ensure the user's cooperation and commitment to the project, the problem should be one of importance to the user. Graphic techniques such as those of structural modeling may be useful at this time.

The analyst uses the DSS software package to construct a mathematical model of the problem (if that is appropriate) and to define queries necessary to satisfy information needs for the problem. Access to the data required to support these models and queries is then provided via existing organizational databases or new ones designed specifically for this application. As mentioned earlier, access to databases external to the organization may also be required.

When the first version of the application is running (which should be in a few days or weeks), the user is trained to run the system. As the user gains experience with the DSS, the analyst and user continue to work together to refine and extend it. New features may be added to

THE USER'S VIEW

Surveys of IFPS users indicate that 80 to 85 percent are managers and financial planning analysts who build and modify their own models rather than rely on professional management information system (MIS) personnel. This approach requires that users have some training in model building, but it brings them much closer to the computerized form of the problem and often results in greater user satisfaction.

By eliminating the intermediary or DSS analysts, communication problems about what the system should do are also eliminated. Users often seem much more satisfied with systems of their own making than with large-scale systems developed by centralized data processing shops.

This method is not without cost; DSS packages are expensive and usually not as efficient in the use of computer resources as are other kinds of software. Overall, however, costs may well be reduced by reducing or eliminating the need for professional MIS personnel in some applications.

Another problem brought about by this proliferation of "end-user computing" (users programming their own applications) is that DSS applications and transaction-oriented applications such as inventory and billing do not coexist well on the same machine and operating system. For that reason, many organizations acquire separate machines to support DSS users. These machines and their software are supported in information centers staffed by personnel independent of the central data processing shop.

If separate machines are used, they should be linked together, for DSS applications may require data from organizational databases residing on central machines. This approach provides the best of both worlds—large mainframe computing for transaction-oriented applications and user-oriented DSS computing, usually on interactive minicomputers or microcomputers linked to the mainframe. ■

---

provide additional information or present information in a more usable form. Thus, the DSS is adapted to changing needs over time and extended to new aspects of the problem.

This adaptive design may essentially never be completed. As the users gain experience with the DSS, they may be able to take over the whole process, freeing the analyst to work with other, less-experienced users and new problems.

Clearly, this kind of environment requires a flexible database system that is easy to use and modify. The database must continually be adapted as users learn more about the situation and build that knowledge into the system. It is vastly different from a typical control-oriented application, and, as described earlier, often requires different hardware, operating systems, and database management systems. Again, relational systems tend to be more suitable for these situations. Database analysts working in these environments must realize that DSS models and databases will constantly be changing in structure and content, and be prepared to incorporate those changes into the data management system.

CHAPTER SUMMARY

A decision support system combines data management technology and model management technology to support managerial decision-making in the presence of unstructured or semistructured problems. Because

METROPOLITAN NATIONAL BANK

The integrated database system that you have designed should provide reports in a timely fashion and support the routine managerial aspects of the organization. However, more information could be obtained from the data if the system provided more tools for decision-making support.

The MetNat president and vice presidents would like to know whether additional branch offices should be built. They also need to determine where these new branches should be located. The decision needs to be made in a timely manner. Acquiring the land needed can take 6 to 12 months, grading the land can take several weeks, and actual construction may take 6 to 10 months, depending on the size of the office.

The decision to build a new branch is not a trivial one. An analysis of use of existing office space, rather than purchasing land and building at a new location, is always conducted. If a decision is made to build a new office, the negotiations to purchase the land can be quite demanding, as the bank typically only considers prime locations.

The bank's senior management also would like to get more use from existing data in the database system. The marketing department should be able to identify trends in customer demographics that suggest new customer service strategies and/or new products. The loans administration department should be able to analyze loan data to determine the characteristics of good and bad loan risks. The special services department needs to be able to forecast market rates so that the bank can offer competitive interest rates while maximizing profit.

You should prepare a proposal of enhancements to the existing database system that can address these issues. You have great latitude in terms of the suggested additions to the system. You may propose anything you wish, as long as you can give some indication of the types of components required to implement your suggestions and some indication of the potential benefits. ■

such problems are not well specified, information requirements and processing requirements are extremely difficult to anticipate. This environment requires adaptability and flexibility in its supporting software.

DSS software generally relies on relational database management and powerful modeling languages such as IFPS. These tools yield systems that can be adapted to the different preferences and problem-solving styles of various users. They also readily augment the limited information-processing capabilities of the human mind. Because these tools are flexible, they are well suited to the iterative, adaptive design process essential in a DSS environment. In the future, even more powerful systems based on techniques developed in the field of artificial intelligence may be expected. These techniques are now beginning to bear fruit in an organizational development.

Questions and Exercises

1. Describe the major components of DSSs and the principal functions of each.

2. Why is the relational model generally preferred in a DSS environment?

3. Describe R. N. Anthony's management planning and control categories.

4. Describe H. A. Simon's management decision categories.

5. Describe G. A. Gorry and M. S. Scott Morton's combination of Anthony's and Simon's categories into a two-dimensional framework and give an example of a decision for each cell.

6. Describe the human mind as an information processor and explain how computers can be used to augment human information processing.

7. Show the terminal dialogue necessary to do a WHAT IF analysis using the IFPS model in Figure 14–5; assume that SALVAGE is $10,000 and LIFE is eight years.

8. Why is a typical information-requirements analysis–logical design–physical design approach unsuitable in a DSS database environment? Describe a better approach.

9. Define the term *heuristic* and explain the role of heuristics in decision-making. Give three examples of heuristics.

10. Describe the function of the problem processor in a DSS.

11. Describe the role of the user interface in a DSS.

12. Define the terms *model base* and *model management system*, and describe their roles in a DSS.

13. Define the terms *procedural knowledge* and *declarative knowledge*, and give three examples of each.

14. Define the terms *intelligence, design,* and *choice* as used in H. A. Simon's description of the decision-making process.

15. What is meant by the term *problem structure*? How does structural modeling graphically portray problem structure?

16. What would line 10 of the IFPS model in Figure 14–5 be if DIVISION OVERHEAD was 20 percent of variable cost?

17. What would line 21 of the IFPS model in Figure 14–5 be if the investment started at $10,000 and increased 10 percent each year? (Don't enter the numbers here, but use a statement like the one in lines 5 and 6.)

18. What command would you use to get an outline for the variable operating expense in Figure 14–5? What would the output of the command be?

19. Draw a structural model of the outline in Question 18.

20. What command would you use to have IFPS explain why

operating expense went up in 1989? What would the output of this command look like?

21. How would you get a more detailed explanation of the results in Question 20, and how would IFPS use the outline in Question 18 to give this explanation?

For Further Reading

Anthony, R. N. "Planning and Control Systems: A Framework for Analysis." Boston: Harvard Business School, 1965. A classic study of managerial roles.

Courtney, J. F.; D. B. Paradice; and Nassar Ata Mohammed. "A Knowledge-Based DSS for Managerial Problem Diagnosis." *Special Issue of Decision Sciences on Expert Systems and Decision Support Systems* 18, no. 3 (Summer 1987), pp. 373–99. Applies expert systems concepts to diagnosing management problems in a DSS context.

Gorry, G. A., and M. S. Scott Morton. "A Framework for Management Information Systems." *Sloan Management Review* 13, no. 1 (1971). The paper that coined the term *decision support system*.

"IFPS Tutorial." Austin, Tex.: Execucom, June 1980.

Newell, A. N., and H. A. Simon. *Human Problem Solving*, Englewood Cliffs, N.J.: Prentice-Hall, 1972. A monumental study of human problem solving.

Paradice, D. B., and J. F. Courtney. "Dynamic Model Construction in a Managerial Advisory System." *Journal of Management Information Systems* 3, no. 4 (Spring 1987), pp. 39–53. Shows how knowledge of problem structure can be used by an expert system to dynamically build models and provide advice to managers by using those models.

Simon, H. A. *The New Science of Management Decision*. New York: Harper & Row, 1960. A classic work defining programmed and nonprogrammed decisions.

Simon, H. A. *The Shape of Automation for Men and Management*. New York: Harper & Row, 1965. Extended the idea of programmed and nonprogrammed decisions.

APPENDICES

APPENDIX A
STORAGE MEDIA AND
ACCESS METHODS

In this appendix, we describe various storage devices and generic techniques for organizing and accessing the data stored on those devices. Most, but not all, students taking database courses have already covered this material; it is included here in an appendix for those unfamiliar with these topics and those desiring a review.

FUNDAMENTAL CONCEPTS OF STORAGE MEDIA

In computer systems, individual data items, such as employee numbers, social security numbers, and addresses, are organized into logical records. Logical records may be thought of as all the data items corresponding to some entity such as a person, an inventory item, or a product. The terms *attribute* and *field* are sometimes used as synonyms for *data item*.

The term *record occurrence* or just *record* is used to describe a specific instance of data values for a record type. Record occurrences of the same logical type, such as employee records, student records, or customer records, are stored together in files. Figure A–1 shows a file containing logical records with stock market data for several companies. A logical record consists of all the data items for one company. The data items are ID number, Company, Industry, Price, and so on. This file is part of Byer Kaufman's portfolio management system described in Chapter 1 (you need not read Chapter 1 to understand the discussion here).

Record occurrences might be more accurately described as *logical record occurrences,* for they do not necessarily conform to the actual organization of data values in stored record occurrences in the computer system. This is an important distinction in the context of storage and access of data. One of the major concerns of this appendix is with the relationships between stored records and logical records. Before storage

FIGURE A–1 **Byer Kaufman's Stock Data**

ID	Company	Industry	Symbol	Price	Earnings	Dividends
1122	Exxon	Oil	XON	46.00	2.50	0.75
1152	Lockheed	Aerospace	LCH	112.00	1.25	0.50
1175	Ford	Auto	F	88.00	1.70	0.20
1231	Intel	Computer	INTL	30.00	2.00	0.00
1245	Digital	Computer	DEC	120.00	1.80	0.10
1323	GM	Auto	GM	158.00	2.10	0.30
1378	Texaco	Oil	TX	230.00	2.80	1.00
1480	Conoco	Oil	CON	150.00	2.00	0.50
1767	Tony Lama	Apparel	TONY	45.00	1.50	0.25

devices themselves are described, it is convenient to introduce some terms and concepts fundamental to all storage devices.

Primary Keys

In most business applications, a data item (or perhaps several data items in combination) is used to uniquely identify each record occurrence of a given type. This identifier is known as the *primary key* for that record. Student numbers in academic files and part numbers in inventory files are often used as primary keys. Stock ID number is the primary key in Figure A–1.

Primary keys provide a means of organizing and locating record occurrences. The access methods described in this appendix use primary key values as a way of locating record occurrences.

Data Storage Blocks

Storage space is divided into units called **blocks,** or **physical records.** A block is the smallest addressable unit of the storage device; that is, if just one character from a block is needed by an application, the entire block must be read and its contents transferred into main memory. Thus, the block size determines the amount of data transferred between main memory and a storage device in one read or write operation.

Some devices transfer a fixed amount of data on each operation and are said to have a fixed block size or fixed-length blocks. A card reader, for example, transfers the data from one card at a time into main memory. The once common IBM card consists of 80 columns, each of which may contain one character, so the block size of an IBM card is 80 characters. One card constitutes one block or physical record.

Other devices allow the size of the block to be determined by software (within some minimum and maximum size) and are said to have a variable block size or variable-length blocks. Magnetic tape systems allow variable block sizes. Many magnetic disk devices also allow variable block size, whereas others have fixed block sizes.

Some disk systems have a fixed segment of the disk referred to as a **sector.** Often, a block consists of a sector. However, the user may have the option of linking several sectors into one block. Thus, one or more sectors may be read or written in one input or output (I/O) operation. This is referred to as **sector addressing.** Sector addressing is common on diskette systems for microcomputers and is also used in many larger systems.

Buffers

If data is being read from a storage device, it must have some place to go in main memory. A **buffer** is a portion of main memory used for transferring data between memory and storage devices. Data is also stored in the buffer before it is transferred to the storage device in a write operation. Since the buffer is a portion of main memory, its size is under software control and is usually the same as the block size. Some database management systems rely on the operating system to manage buffering; others perform their own buffering.

In double buffering, two buffer areas are maintained for the same file. This method can greatly speed up processing because the contents of one buffer can be made available to the applications program (via the operating system) while I/O operations are conducted on the other. This reduces the amount of time that the applications program must wait for I/O operations to be performed. Proper management of buffer operations is important in developing an efficient system. However, buffer management is a rather complex subject that is beyond the scope of this text. Weiderhold (1983) provides a very readable discussion of this topic.

Record Blocking

In most applications, logical records are much smaller than the maximum capacity of a block. **Record blocking** refers to the common practice of storing several logical records in each block in order to provide efficient processing and efficient use of storage space. The number of records per block is referred to as the **blocking factor.** This is one way logical records and stored records may differ.

Storage Device Categories

Storage media may be divided into two general classes that depend on how physical records are located. One class, **sequential access devices,** are exemplified by card readers and magnetic tape drives. These devices access the "next" block on the storage medium (although tapes can be rewound or backspaced and some systems even allow reading the previous record in reverse). On sequential devices, all records are stored, one after another, in the order in which they are written to the file. To access any one record, all preceding records must be read. For all practical purposes, the only read instruction possible for sequential devices is "get the next block." Access to randomly selected individual records is thus slow, so sequential devices are seldom used for any operations other than backup or temporary storage in a database environment.

In most business applications, records to be stored in sequential files are first sorted on the primary key, then written to the file in that order. This allows access to the file in order by primary key. In Figure A–1, records have been sorted into ascending order by ID number.

The second device class, **direct access storage devices** (DASDs), is represented by magnetic disks. Similar to main memory, each block of a DASD has an address. The data in a block is directly (or "randomly") accessible if its address is known. This allows processing in any order without resorting to a sequential search of the file. Thus, a DASD may be used to support instructions such as "get the block at address n," when n is known. In addition, if the records are stored in primary key sequence, DASDs may also support sequential access. Because of such features, direct access media, especially disks, are used almost exclusively to store operating databases.

The Objective in Access Method Selection: Rapid Response Time

Response time is the elapsed clock time from the initiation of a request for data until that data has been delivered to the user. The main objective when selecting an access method is to minimize response time. Because the CPU operates much faster than storage devices, response time is fastest when the number of accesses to storage devices is minimized. Because most databases are stored on disk, minimizing response time boils down to minimizing disk accesses.

SEQUENTIAL DEVICES

Even though computer cards are virtually obsolete as a storage medium, we describe them here because they give a good visual example of the relationship between logical records and blocks. We then proceed to a discussion of magnetic tapes.

Cards

Card files are rarely used, and then almost exclusively for input. Their main use now is as a "turn-around document" in billing systems where the customer returns a portion of the card with his or her payment. This approach expedites input processing of payments.

FIGURE A–2 Card Layout for Byer's Stock Data
A card is one physical record or block. The data for one stock constitutes one logical record. Here, one logical record is stored on one block (card).

				Columns			
1-4 ID	5-15 Company	16-25 Industry	26-30 Symbol	36-40 Price	41-45 Earnings	41-45 Div	46-80 Unused
1122	Exxon	Oil	XON	46.00	2.50	0.75	

An 80-column IBM card is illustrated in Figure A–2, along with a logical record description for the stock file. The data from one card is transferred to main memory during each read operation, so a card constitutes one block. In this system, each card contains one occurrence of a logical record; however, several columns of the card are not used and thus some storage space is wasted. More commonly, the logical record is greater than 80 characters, thus requiring more than one card (block) for its storage.

Magnetic Tapes

Magnetic tape is the primary sequential access medium in use today. Because it is much slower than disks, tape is used primarily to keep backup or temporary copies of data stored on disk. Tape used for computer applications is similar to that used on an ordinary reel-to-reel tape recorder except that it is usually ½ inch wide. The length varies from 600 to 3,600 feet, with 2,400 feet being the most common.

Some microcomputer systems use cassette tapes for backup storage. Computer cassette tapes are similar to those for audio use but are usually of higher quality. A typical cassette tape is ¼ inch wide and 300 feet long and can store 100 million bytes of data (100 mb or 100 megabytes). Data bits are stored on one recording surface, called a **track** or a **channel,** which runs the length of the tape. A parallel track may be used to store addressing or timing information.

Most large-scale tape systems today record data on nine tracks, each track running longitudinally down the tape (see Figure A–3). Individual characters (bytes) are recorded crosswise using eight of the nine tracks. The ninth track is used for parity checking, as described shortly. The **density** of a tape is the number of bytes recorded per inch. Densities range from 200 to 6,250 bytes per inch (bpi).

FIGURE A–3
Nine-Track Magnetic Tape
A nine-track tape has eight tracks for data and one for parity checking. This tape is set for odd parity: The parity bits are set so that the sum down a "column" is odd.

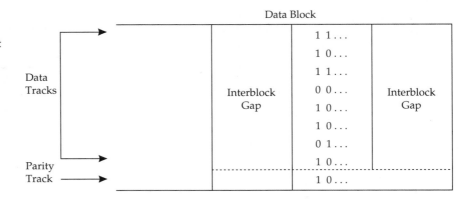

Physical records or blocks on a tape may be of variable length, within some minimum and maximum. Typical block sizes range from 5 bytes to 50 million bytes. The actual block length is determined by software and is under the programmer's control.

Blocks must be separated by an interblock gap, which allows the tape to reach the required operating speed so that reading or writing may be performed by the drive. Gaps are typically ½ or ¾ inch long, so if data blocks are small, most of the tape may be blank. This also slows input and output operations because pauses occur at each gap.

To make better use of the tape and to speed processing, many logical records are often grouped in memory and then written to a block. As mentioned previously, this is known as *blocking*; the number of logical records per block is called the *blocking factor*.

To illustrate the effects of blocking, a tape system utilizing ½-inch gaps recording 800 character blocks (10 cards) at 1,600 bpi would require 1 inch for each block (½ inch for the gap and ½ inch for the data). This is 12 blocks per foot. A 2,400-foot tape, then, could store 28,800 blocks or 23,040,000 characters. If instead 110 cards were put in each block (8,800 characters), then a block would require 6 inches of tape (a ½-inch gap and 5½ inches for data). The tape could hold only 4,800 of these larger blocks, but 422,400,000 characters—almost 20 times the amount in the previous case.

Over time, tapes can become damaged, dirty, or magnetically weak so that the data on the tape is no longer accurate. A technique known as **parity checking** is used to detect such errors. **Odd parity** means that the sum of the "on" bits across one position of the tape is odd; **even parity** means that the sum is even. The data itself is recorded on eight tracks of the tape using an eight-bit code. In an odd parity system, the ninth bit is set such that the sum of the "on" bits for the position is odd (see Figure A–3).

The tape drive is designed to set the parity bit for each position when the tape is written and to check the parity when the tape is read. Thus, if the tape is damaged or dirty, the system is usually (but not always) able to detect the problem and issue an error message.

Direct Access Storage Devices

Magnetic disk is by far the most common storage medium in database systems today. Good database design depends on an understanding of how to organize data on disks to get efficient performance from the system. Metal ("hard") disks are generally required for acceptable performance in a database environment, even on microcomputers. For very small applications, flexible ("floppy") disks may be suitable, although response times will slow. Floppies are often used for backup on small systems.

A rapidly increasing use of personal computers is to hold small portions of a large database that have been copied from a large mainframe system (downloaded), where the database is then manipulated on the user's personal workstation. Of course, data can be uploaded to the mainframe as well. This relieves the mainframe of much time-consuming processing of individual records.

Hard Disks

Hard disks are metal platters, the surfaces of which are divided into concentric circles called *tracks* (the same term used with tapes). Although the length of the tracks get smaller near the center of the disk, each track contains the same amount of data because bits are packed more densely near the center. Typical platter sizes are 5¼ inches for personal computers and 14 inches for large-scale systems. One surface of a typical disk is shown in Figure A–4.

The number of tracks per disk surface ranges from 15 to 600 for typical disk systems. Track sizes range from a few thousand to 50,000 bytes. The number of platters per unit may range from 1 to 200. Small-scale hard disk systems for personal computers may have capacities of 5 to 100 mb. Large-scale units may be capable of storing over 1 billion characters (a gigabyte). Several disk units may be strung together to store several billion characters.

FIGURE A–4
A Magnetic Disk Surface
Each ring represents a track on the disk surface. Each track is divided into blocks or sectors. Even though sectors of interior tracks are smaller, each contains the same amount of data because bits are packed more closely toward the center of the disk.

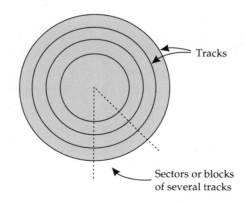

Tracks

Sectors or blocks
of several tracks

As with tapes, tracks are further divided into blocks. In some systems, the size of the block is fixed, giving fixed-length blocks or physical records; in other systems, block size is under software control. Like tapes, disk blocks are separated by gaps, and it is common practice to place several logical records in one block to reduce access time and avoid wasting storage space.

Usually, several disk platters are attached to a rotating spindle, similar to a stack of phonograph records except that the disks are fixed to the spindle and there is space between disks (see Figure A–5). In some systems, the platter assembly is called a **diskpack** because it may be removed and replaced with another pack, as tapes are on a tape drive. Thus, different packs may be used to store different files or databases, or for backup purposes. Diskpacks typically have from 1 to 11 platters.

In many disk systems, the platter assemblies are not designed for removal. One of the most popular nonremovable designs today is called a **Winchester drive.** In these devices, the platter assembly is enclosed in an air-tight, dust-free housing, which greatly increases the reliability and durability of the disks. Access is also faster than for comparable diskpacks, and recording densities are higher. Winchester drives are popular for microcomputers and are frequently found on larger systems as well.

The upper surface of the topmost platter and the lower surface of the bottommost platter are not used for recording data. Thus, if a disk unit consists of 16 platters, only 30 recording surfaces are available.

On **movable-head disk assemblies,** the most common technology, a read/write head exists for each usable surface. The read/write heads are all attached to one access assembly, which can move the head for a surface to any of its tracks. If, for example, the read/write head for a surface is located at its outermost track, then the read/write head for every surface is also at the outermost track. A **cylinder** consists of all

FIGURE A–5
A Movable-Head Disk Assembly
This assembly has seven platters and 12 read/write heads. Twelve surfaces are used for data storage. The access assembly moves the read/write heads to the desired cylinder. Any track in that cylinder may be read without further movement of the access assembly, reducing total access time.

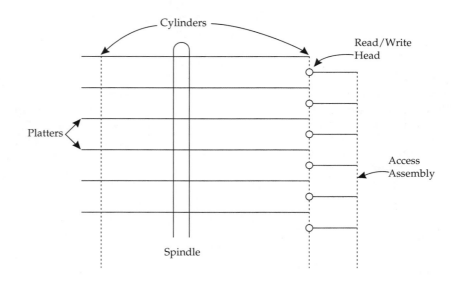

the corresponding tracks that can be read without moving the access assembly. To minimize movement of the access assembly (which takes time and slows response time), sorted files are first stored in all the tracks of one cylinder. When all the tracks of that cylinder are full, the access assembly moves to the next cylinder.

The speed of access assembly movement is called **seek time.** Maximum seek time occurs when the access assembly must be moved from the outermost to the innermost cylinder (or vice versa). Access times are usually expressed in terms of average seek time, which is maximum seek time divided by two. Average seek times typically range from 15 to 40 milliseconds for large-scale disks.

Fixed-head assemblies have a read/write head for each track, thus eliminating seek time. Because of the many read/write heads required, however, fixed-head assemblies are much more expensive than movable-head types.

Rotational delay is the time it takes for the desired block to rotate to the read/write head. As with seek time, average rotational delay is given by the maximum rotational delay divided by two. Average rotational delay times are typically 8 to 15 milliseconds.

The final factor affecting disk operating speed is the time it takes to transfer data to main memory and vice versa. This is called **transfer time.** Transfer time depends on the transmission rate and the amount of data in the block. Typical transfer rates are 1 million to 4 million bytes per second.

Total access time, the time required to move data from the disk to main memory (or vice versa), is the sum of seek time, rotational delay, and transfer time. Because a typical system can transfer a rather large data block in one millisecond or so, rotational delay and seek time tend to dominate the determination of total access time.

Floppy Disks

The surfaces of floppy disks are also divided into tracks. Many floppy systems further divide the track into fixed-length blocks called *sectors*. Each sector has an address, and its contents may be fetched directly by specifying the address. These floppies are thus sector addressable.

A floppy is said to be *formatted* if the markers indicating the beginning and end of each sector have been placed on the disk. Hard-sectored floppies have sector markers built in at the factory and may not be changed by the user. Soft-sectored floppies are formatted by the operating system and may be reformatted by the user.

Floppies typically come in either 8-inch, 5¼-inch, or 3½-inch sizes. Data storage capacities for 5¼-inch systems range from 180 kb (kilobytes) or 1,024 bytes to 1.2 mb and 3½-inch go up to 1.44 mb. Single-sided systems use only one side of the disk; double-sided systems use both. Single-density diskettes have 20 tracks per surface; double-density systems have 40. Floppy systems are much slower than hard disks, with average access times of 100 to 200 milliseconds.

FILE ACCESS METHODS

The terms **file access method** and **file organization** refer to the physical layout or structure of record occurrences in a file. File organization determines the way records are stored and accessed. The types of file organization discussed here are the sequential access method (SAM), the indexed-sequential access method (ISAM), and the direct access method (DAM). (Another access method, the virtual storage access method (VSAM), is discussed in Chapter 10 because it uses data structures known as B-trees, also discussed in that chapter.)

In sequential files, record occurrences are usually sorted on the primary key and physically arranged on the storage medium in order by primary key. If only sequential access is required, sequential media are suitable and probably the most cost-effective way of processing such files. In a database environment, it is rarely, if ever, the case that sequential access alone suffices.

In direct access files, an algorithm is applied to the primary key to compute the address at which the record is stored. This approach is suitable only for use with direct access storage devices.

In indexed-sequential files, record occurrences are sorted and stored in order by primary key on a DASD. In addition, a separate table called an *index* is maintained on primary key values to give the physical address of each record occurrence. This approach gives (almost) direct access to record occurrences via the index table and sequential access via the way in which the records are laid out on the storage medium.

Sequential Access Method

In sequential organization, record occurrences are referenced in the order that they are stored physically. Data stored on cards and tape are necessarily stored sequentially. Direct access devices such as disks may be, but are not necessarily, referenced sequentially. Some types of processing are best done through sequential access, even when direct access devices are used; such is the case when many records of a file must be accessed to satisfy a request for data.

We use the stock data in Figure A–1 to illustrate sequential access. Prices in this file are updated at the end of each week. New price data is first put into a sequential file on Byer's personal computer by downloading it from a company that maintains such information on a large, mainframe computer and sells it. The sequential file is used to update prices. Earnings per share and dividends change only every quarter, so these are updated by other means (discussed later).

Because every stock price is updated each week, disk accesses are minimized by arranging the file sequentially by ID number, even if it is stored on a movable-head disk. Once the heads are located at a cylinder, all the records in that cylinder can be accessed sequentially with no further movement of the access assembly.

For simplicity, assume that Byer uses a small double-sided, floppy disk system with fixed-length sectors of 128 bytes. Fixed-length logical records are of 60 bytes each. Each sector thus holds two logical record occurrences, with only eight bytes of unused space. Tracks contain four sectors, thus storing eight records. The cylinder consists of two tracks (one on each side of the disk) and so can hold 16 records.

Assume that, when the file is created, writing begins at cylinder 0, track 0, and sector 0 (0,0,0). The records for Exxon and Lockheed are stored at cylinder 0, track 0, sector 0; the records for Ford and Intel at cylinder 0, track 0, sector 1; the records for Digital and GM at (0,0,2), and so forth. When the sectors of track 0 are full, writing begins with sector 0 of track 1 (the other side of the disk).

Because the system uses fixed-length sectors of 128 bytes, a buffer size of 128 bytes is probably used. Double buffering is feasible because the buffer is rather small, even for a microcomputer.

This design provides efficient updating of Byer's stock data because sequential access minimizes movement of the read/write assembly. But what if Byer's system had to process queries such as "What were Texaco's earnings per share last quarter?" or "What is Digital's latest price?" If the file were large, finding the requested data would be slow in a sequential search. Indexed-sequential and direct access, discussed next, are designed to support efficient processing of such queries.

Indexed-Sequential Access Method

In the previous example, sequential updating of Byer's stock data is efficient because each stock is updated each week and must be accessed at least once to perform the update. Sequential access minimizes movement of the read/write assembly and provides efficient processing. However, processing queries for data about individual stocks or small sets of stocks is inefficient, because of the number of disk accesses required to find a particular stock if it is in the middle or end of the file.

Indexed-sequential access is especially well suited for problems such as this, in which record occurrences in a file must be accessed both sequentially (as in Byer's update problem) and directly (as in the query-processing problem). With ISAM organization, record occurrences are physically stored in sequence by primary key, but also an index or table associating primary keys to physical disk addresses is created as the file is created and updated when records are added or deleted. The index is usually stored on disk, along with the record occurrences themselves. Because the index would become quite large if an entry were made for each record occurrence, techniques for shortening the index have been devised. These techniques take advantage of the fact that more than one record usually fits into one block or sector.

ISAM Indexing. We illustrate ISAM indexes by reviewing the way words are indexed in a dictionary. To help people find words quickly, many dictionaries have a semicircular thumb slot where each letter of the alphabet begins. Each page has the first and last word on the page printed at the top. To find a word, one thumbs to the correct letter, then sequentially leafs through the pages by looking at the word index at the top of the page. When the word sought falls between the first and last word of the page, a sequential search of the page will produce the desired word.

ISAM indexes consists of three tables—a cylinder index, a track index, and a block index. The cylinder index contains an entry for each cylinder on which the file is stored. This entry gives the value of the largest (last) primary key stored in that cylinder (compare this to a dictionary page index giving the last word on each page). The track index gives the largest primary key value stored in that track, and the block or sector index gives the largest key in each block or sector. Figure A–6 shows the cylinder, track, and sector indexes for Byer's stock data and the floppy disk system described in the section on sequential devices. Most operating systems provide support for maintaining such indexes.

Suppose that we wished to find Texaco's record. Texaco has ID number 1378. Comparing this to the only entry in the cylinder index, we find that 1378 is less than the largest primary key on cylinder 0 (1767), indicating that 1378 is on that cylinder (which must be true because the file consumes less than one cylinder). Next, we search the track index for cylinder 0. Because 1378 is less than 1480, the highest value on track 0, we know that Texaco's record is on track 0. Finally, by examining the sector index for track 0, we find that Texaco is on sector 3. Thus, a read instruction may be issued for (0,0,3). When the data from this block is in main memory, it can be searched sequentially for the appropriate record.

FIGURE A–6   Cylinder, Track, and Sector Indexes for an ISAM Approach to Byer's Stock Data

Cylinder Index

Cylinder	Highest Key Value
0	1767

Track Index: Cylinder 0

Track	Highest Key Value
0	1480
1	1767

Sector Index: Track 0

Sector	Highest Key Value
0	1152
1	1231
2	1323
3	1480

Sector Index: Track 1

Sector	Highest Key Value
0	1767
1	null
2	null
3	null

Most operating systems provide support for ISAM files, and creating such files is rather easy from the application programmer's point of view. The steps in creating an ISAM file are as follows:

1. Create a sequential file sorted on the primary key.
2. Communicate to the host operating system that a new ISAM file is to be created.
3. If they are available, use utility programs to copy the sequential file to the ISAM file. If not, write a program to do the copy. The host operating system creates the required indexes during the file creation process.

Updating ISAM Files. Changing data (other than the primary key) in existing records in an ISAM file usually presents no problems. Byer's stock data, for example, must be updated weekly. Such updates would ordinarily be done using sequential processing in batch mode. But, for purposes of illustration, we update the file directly using on-line processing.

Suppose that we want to change Exxon's dividend from 0.75 to 1.00. We must find the block containing Exxon's data, bring it into the buffer, transfer the dividend to the applications program, change it, move it back to the buffer, and rewrite the block. This is not a complicated process; it can be implemented easily to support updates of earnings and dividends.

Suppose instead that we want to delete the record for Exxon because it is no longer held in the portfolio. If Exxon's record is removed from the file, an empty space is left where it once was stored unless all records following Exxon are moved up one location. Moving all records that follow Exxon would slow response time, which would be costly to the user. To avoid such a delay, most systems do not actually remove deleted records, they simply mark the record for later deletion. This may be done by adding a character to the record (say the first character) for use by the system. Active records might have a blank in this field; an asterisk or some other character could be used to mark records that were logically but not physically deleted. The deletion mark may be referred to as a **tombstone,** because it marks the location of "dead" records. This approach also allows for undeleting or reactivating records that may have been erroneously deleted but not yet physically removed from the file.

Inserting records into an ISAM file is somewhat more difficult because indexes must be updated and the proper sequence of the file must be maintained. Because it is inefficient to rewrite the file from the point of insertion, most systems have extra space associated with the file, called an **overflow area.** An overflow area is frequently provided for each cylinder so that the access assembly does not have to be moved to access the records in this area. The portion of storage where the original records are stored is called the **primary area.**

To describe how sequential record sequence is maintained when records are inserted into an ISAM file, it is necessary to explain the concept of *pointers*. A pointer is a value in one record that identifies a related record. ID numbers are used as pointers in our example to illustrate how logical record sequences are maintained in ISAM files after insertions.

When a record is inserted into the file, the insertion is done so as to maintain physical sequential order in the primary area with a pointer to the next record in sequence in the overflow area. This may involve transferring an existing record to the overflow area and replacing it with the new record in the primary area. A pointer embedded in the primary area indicates the location of the transferred record in the overflow area. The pointer in this case is the ID number of the next record in sequence in the overflow area. The pointer is set in a way that maintains sequential order by primary key.

To illustrate, assume that Byer wants to add Mesa Petroleum's stock to the file, using the ID number 1160. Mesa's record should therefore follow that of Lockheed. Because there is no space for Mesa's record, it is placed in the overflow area and a pointer in Lockheed's record is set to Mesa's address (see Figure A–7).

The sector index must also be updated so that the system can find Mesa's record. One method of doing this is to change the sector index to 1160 (Figure A–8). If a request is issued for Mesa's record, the system finds 1160 in the index for sector 0 and first looks for it in that sector. It is not found there, but the pointer in Lockheed's record is used to find it in the overflow area.

As another illustration, assume that a record for Control Data (ID number 1250) is to be added to the stock file. It logically fits between

FIGURE A–7   Byer's Stock Data with Pointer to Mesa's Record
Mesa's record caused an overflow at the primary, so it is stored in the overflow area and a pointer (its ID number) is set so that it can be found.

ID	Company	Industry	Symbol	Price	Earnings	Dividends	Pointer
\multicolumn{8}{c}{PRIMARY STORAGE AREA}

ID	Company	Industry	Symbol	Price	Earnings	Dividends	Pointer
1122	Exxon	Oil	XON	46.00	2.50	0.75	
1152	Lockheed	Aerospace	LCH	112.00	1.25	0.50	1160
1175	Ford	Auto	F	88.00	1.70	0.20	
1231	Intel	Computer	INTL	30.00	2.00	0.00	
1245	Digital	Computer	DEC	120.00	1.80	0.10	
1323	GM	Auto	GM	158.00	2.10	0.30	
1378	Texaco	Oil	TX	230.00	2.80	1.00	
1480	Conoco	Oil	CON	150.00	2.00	0.50	
1767	Tony Lama	Apparel	TONY	45.00	1.50	0.25	

OVERFLOW AREA

ID	Company	Industry	Symbol	Price	Earnings	Dividends	Pointer
1160	Mesa Petrol.	Oil	MESA	125.00	1.00	0.25	

FIGURE A–8   Cylinder, Track, and Sector Indexes after Mesa Petroleum (1160) Has Been Added to Byer's Stock File

The entry for sector 0 in track 0 has been changed to 1160, so the system will look for Mesa's record in track 0, sector 0. It will not be found there (see Figure A–7), but the system will follow the pointer to 1160 in the overflow area.

```
                              Cylinder  Index

                    Cylinder    Highest  Key  Value

                        0        |        1767


                      Track  Index:  Cylinder  0

                    Track    Highest  Key  Value

                        0        |        1480
                        1        |        1767


    Sector  Index:  Track  0                 Sector  Index:  Track  1

 Sector    Highest  Key  Value           Sector    Highest  Key  Value

    0            1160                        0            1767
    1            1231                        1            null
    2            1323                        2            null
    3            1480                        3            null
```

Digital's and GM's records. Because there is no space for the record, GM's record is moved to the overflow area and its previous location is overwritten with Control Data's record. A pointer is set in Control Data's record to the location of GM's record in the overflow area, as illustrated in Figure A–9. Notice that the sector index does not have to be updated in this case. GM still has the highest index in the track, at least logically. To find GM's record, however, the system must first search the sector where it expects to find GM and then follow the pointer to its record in the overflow area.

Reorganization of ISAM Files.   If many insertions and deletions have occurred in an ISAM file, access time may be slow because the system must bypass deleted records and follow pointers to inserted records. Furthermore, as overflow areas approach capacity, they must be "cleaned out" to make room for new insertions. The process of rewriting ISAM files to actually remove deleted records and move inserted records into their proper physical location is called **reorganization.** Vendors supply utility programs with operating systems supporting ISAM to perform file reorganization.

Performance Considerations with ISAM Files.   When accessed sequentially, ISAM files yield response times equivalent to those of sequential files. When more than about 15 to 20 percent of the records in a file must be accessed to satisfy a user request for data, sequential

FIGURE A–9   **Byer's Stock Data with Pointer to GM's Record**
Control Data's record caused an overflow in the primary area. GM's data is copied to the overflow area and replaced by Control Data's record in the primary area with a logical pointer (ID number) to GM's record.

PRIMARY STORAGE AREA

ID	Company	Industry	Symbol	Price	Earnings	Dividends	Pointer
1122	Exxon	Oil	XON	46.00	2.50	0.75	
1152	Lockheed	Aerospace	LCH	112.00	1.25	0.50	
1175	Ford	Auto	F	88.00	1.70	0.20	
1231	Intel	Computer	INTL	30.00	2.00	0.00	
1245	Digital	Computer	DEC	120.00	1.80	0.10	
1250	Control Data	Computer	CDC	80.50	0.25	0.00	1323
1378	Texaco	Oil	TX	230.00	2.80	1.00	
1480	Conoco	Oil	CON	150.00	2.00	0.50	
1767	Tony Lama	Apparel	TONY	45.00	1.50	0.25	

OVERFLOW AREA

ID	Company	Industry	Symbol	Price	Earnings	Dividends
1323	GM	Auto	GM	158.00	2.10	0.30

access provides faster response times than indexed access. This is due to the fact that the ISAM approach requires access to indexes as well as to the data itself. Time to access indexes may be minimized by copying the cylinder index into main memory when the file is opened and keeping it there until the file is closed. For large files, it is usually infeasible to keep more than a few track and block indexes in memory because of their size. Also, if many insertions have been made to the file, then overflow areas may have to be searched. This results in further disk accesses and increased response time.

The actual number of disk accesses can range from none to several. No accesses are required if the required indexes and data block already reside in main memory as a result of previous I/O requests. Several accesses are required if the track and block indexes must be read into main memory and then the required record fetched. On the average, about three accesses per record requested can be expected. To avoid disk accesses, some microcomputer systems copy as much of the database as possible to main memory when the DBMS is initiated.

A final technique for reducing response time with ISAM files is to use high-performance DASDs to store the indexes. For example, fixed-head disks may be used to eliminate seek time completely. An even more expensive option is the use of semiconductor devices that emulate disks. These have no moving parts and provide extremely fast access times when compared to disks. Whether the fixed-head disks or semiconductor devices are worth the extra cost depends on response time requirements.

Direct Access Method

Indexed-sequential access is suitable for Byer's stock data because his file must be accessed both sequentially and directly, and updating is done periodically. Up-to-the-minute information is not required. Many applications, on the other hand, require both on-line retrieval and on-line update to maintain the most current information possible. Stockbrokers, for example, need both rapid update and retrieval of stock price data. Airlines require rapid update and retrieval of passenger data, and automated teller machines require fast access to banking records.

Direct access to large ISAM files is slowed by the fact that the indexes and perhaps overflow areas must be searched before the desired record can be transferred to main memory. Even worse, update of ISAM files is slowed by the need to update indexes and pointers and to transfer records from primary to overflow areas.

The direct access method has been devised to satisfy the need to both update and retrieve data quickly. In this approach, an algorithm is used to compute the address of a record. The primary key value is the input to the algorithm, and the block address of the record is the output.

To implement the approach, a portion of the storage space is reserved for the file. This space must be large enough to hold the file plus some allowance for growth. Then, an algorithm that generates the appropriate address for a given primary key is devised. The algorithm is commonly called a **hashing algorithm** and the direct access method is referred to as **hashed access.** The process of converting primary key values into addresses is called **key-to-address transformation.**

More than one logical record usually fits into a block, so we may think of the reserved storage area as being broken into record slots sequentially numbered from 1 to n. These sequential numbers are called **relative record numbers, relative pointers,** or **relative addresses,** because they indicate the position of the record relative to the beginning of the file.

The objective of the hashing algorithm is to generate relative addresses that disperse the records throughout the reserved storage space in a random but uniform manner. This is graphically represented in Figure A–10. Records can be retrieved very rapidly because the address is computed rather than found through table look-up via indexes stored on a disk file.

Unfortunately, it is seldom possible to devise an algorithm that assigns each record to a block in such a manner that each record has a place in the storage area and no space is wasted. Usually, several key values map to the same relative address. A **collision** occurs if more than one record maps to the same block. Primary keys generating the same address are called **synonyms.** Because one block usually holds several records, collisions are only a problem when the number of records mapping to a block exceeds the block's capacity. To account for this event, most direct access methods also support an overflow area similar to that in ISAM procedures.

FIGURE A–10
**Dispersing Records in a
Reserved Area with a
Hashing Algorithm**
The hashing algorithm
converts the key value to
an address, and the
corresponding record is
stored at that address.

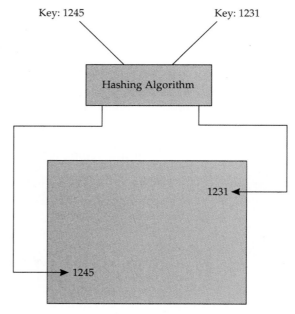

Reserved Disk Space

Hashing algorithms based on a technique called **prime number division** have proved to be effective in generating addresses that are rather uniformly distributed over the storage space. A prime number is a number that has no even divisor other than 1 and the number itself. For example, 3 and 5 are prime, but 4 is not. Tables of prime numbers are available, so generating them is not a problem.

If the primary key is a number, prime number division consists of dividing the primary key by a prime number (call it p) and using the remainder as the relative address of the record in the file. Remainders range from zero to $p - 1$. An algorithm is then devised to convert relative addresses to physical addresses.

Because the remainders (relative addresses) generated range from 0 to $p - 1$ and we want to allow room for growth, the prime number chosen as the divisor should be slightly larger than the number of blocks required to hold the file. For example, if the file consists of 5,000 records and only one record fits in a block, the prime number 5,501 might be chosen. This results in addresses in the range 0–5,500, allowing for 500 additional records to be added if the records are perfectly dispersed in the storage area (which they probably will not be). Thus enough storage space must be reserved for 5,501 records plus an overflow area. Direct access using prime number division is here illustrated with Byer's stock data from Figure A–1.

Assume that we have the same floppy disk system as in the sections on sequential and ISAM processing. One track holds eight logical records (two in each sector), so only one cylinder must be reserved to store the file. Assume that cylinder 0 has been reserved. This gives us space for 16 records, plenty for the 9 records Byer has plus room for an over-flow area and for new stocks that might be added.

For purposes of illustration, we use the prime number 13 as a divi-sor; it generates relative addresses between 0 and 12, which allows room for storing the records in the first seven sectors, leaving the last sector for overflow. Then, the relative address (call it R) for a stock is the remainder when the stock ID number is divided by 13. Exxon, for ex-ample, has the relative address 4, because $1,122/13 = 86$ with a remain-der of 4 ($R = 4$).

Next, the relative address must be converted to a physical address. Because all records are to be stored in cylinder 0, we do not have to generate a cylinder number. The track number T must be either 0 or 1 and may be given by the quotient when the relative address is divided by 8 (the number of records per track). This yields track numbers of 0 or 1. For Exxon, this yields track 0 ($4/8 = 0$ with a remainder of 4). Another way of saying this is:

$$T = \text{Integer part of } \frac{R}{8}$$

The sector number S is slightly more complicated and is given by the equation:

$$S = \text{Integer part of } \frac{R - (T \times 8)}{2}$$

For Exxon, this gives $[4 - (0 \times 8)]/2 = 2$ with a remainder of 0. The expression $T - (T \times 8)$ adjusts for the track on which the record is stored. The physical addresses generated by this formula for S are shown in Figure A–11.

Notice that Exxon and Ford have different relative addresses (4 and 5, respectively) but the same physical address (0,0,2). This causes no problem, because both records can be stored at the computed sector. The IDs of Digital, GM, and Conoco, however, all map to (0,1,1), creat-ing an overflow. If the records were added to the file in the order shown in Figure A–11, the overflow would occur when the attempt to write

FIGURE A–11
Relative and Physical Addresses for Byer's Stock Data
The collision formed by Digital, GM, and Conoco's records created an overflow at address (0,1,1). Conoco's record would be stored in an overflow area. GM's re-cord contains a pointer to the physical address where Conoco's record is actually stored.

Company	ID	Relative Address	Physical Address	Overflow Pointer
Exxon	1122	4	(0,0,2)	
Lockheed	1152	8	(0,1,0)	
Ford	1175	5	(0,0,2)	
Intel	1231	9	(0,1,0)	
Digital	1245	10	(0,1,1)	
GM	1323	10	(0,1,1)	(0,1,3)
Texaco	1378	0	(0,0,0)	
Conoco	1480	11	(0,1,1)	
Tony Lama	1767	12	(0,1,2)	

THE USER'S VIEW

Users generally do not care about the access method used to support their information needs. They want the information necessary to do their jobs and they want it in time to be useful. But if the analyst has chosen the *wrong* access method and response time is slow, users will certainly no-tice. Thus, the access method must be selected with care.

Effective selection of an access method de-pends on accurate determination of the informa-tion users need, and thus on clear information requirements and a good logical design. ■

Conoco's record was made (because Digital and GM would already be written). The simplest, but perhaps not the most efficient, way to handle this overflow would be to write Conoco's record in the next available space in the overflow area. Because no overflows have occurred previ-ously, Conoco's record would be the first stored at (0,1,3).

To find Conoco's record, the system would first use the primary key 1480 to generate the relative address 11. This address would then be converted to the physical address (0,1,1). The data at that sector would be fetched and searched sequentially for primary key 1480. Not finding Conoco's record, the system would automatically go to the overflow area and sequentially search it for 1480. Obviously, this would require several disk accesses if the overflow area were very large and the desired record were far down.

To mitigate this problem, the system may store a pointer to the first overflow record in the block generated by its primary key. The block where the first record is actually stored may then be fetched directly. This is illustrated in Figure A–11 by the overflow pointer to Conoco's record embedded in GM's Overflow Pointer field. The first record in the overflow area contains a pointer to the next record, and so on. This is one version of record chaining, which is discussed in Chapter 10.

Selecting an Access Method

Sequential access is more efficient than indexed-sequential or direct access because there is no processing overhead to maintain indexes and overflow areas, and read/write assembly movement is minimized. But sequential access alone is seldom, if ever, sufficient in a database envi-ronment, where random requests for individual records are a virtual certainty. Sequential access alone is ruled out, except for backup situa-tions and the like.

Because sequential updates are much more efficient than direct up-dates, indexed-sequential access is preferred to direct access whenever batch updating is feasible. Furthermore, whenever more than 15 to 20 percent of the records in a file must be accessed to satisfy a data request, sequential access is more efficient than direct access. Thus, indexed-sequential access is generally second to sequential access in overall efficiency.

If rapid update and retrieval are required, as for airline reservation systems or automated bank tellers, then direct access is the method of choice. Direct access provides rapid retrieval and update of individual records, but it fails to provide rapid batch processing because records are not in primary key sequence but scattered throughout the file.

APPENDIX SUMMARY

The objective in selecting an access method is to minimize response time while satisfying other requirements for security, integrity, and so forth. Most databases reside on disk storage, so disk access time dominates other factors affecting the rapidity of the system's response to data requests. Thus, response time is minimized when disk accesses are minimized.

The indexed-sequential and direct access approaches have been devised to provide flexible access to records. The use of these methods depends on the use of direct access storage devices. ISAM access is useful when batch updating or retrieval is acceptable. Direct access is useful when on-line updating is necessary.

Questions and Exercises

1. Define the following terms:
   a. block
   b. pointer
   c. fixed-length block
   d. sector
   e. buffer
   f. blocking
   g. blocking factor
   h. interblock gap
   i. track (disk and tape)
   j. cylinder
   k. seek time
   l. rotational delay
   m. transfer time
   n. total access time
2. What is the main objective in selecting an access method?
3. Where would the records for Texaco and Lockheed be located on the disk described in the section on the sequential access approach to Byer's stock data?
4. The prime number 13 left only one sector for overflow in the direct access approach to Byer's stock data. A choice of 11 would leave more room for overflow. Recompute the physical addresses using the algorithm given in the text and 11 as the divisor. How many overflows occur with this divisor?

5. Briefly discuss the differences in logical record occurrences and stored record occurrences.

6. Explain the concept of *double buffering* and describe how it speeds up processing.

7. Discuss the difference between sequential access devices and direct access devices.

8. What sequential device is found most often in a database environment, and for what is the device used?

9. How many characters may be stored on a typical IBM card?

10. Explain parity checking and how it is used to detect errors on magnetic tape.

11. Why is total access time faster on fixed-head assemblies than on movable-head assemblies?

12. Discuss how total access time is computed.

13. Why is sequential processing sometimes more efficient than random access processing?

14. Explain what is meant by reorganization of ISAM files. Why must ISAM files be reorganized?

15. Discuss factors influencing the performance of ISAM files.

16. In what circumstances are ISAM files most appropriate?

17. Describe the direct access method.

18. What is meant by the terms *hashing algorithms* and *key-to-address transformation?*

19. How many overflows can be handled in the direct access method?

For Further Reading

Teorey, Toby J., and James P. Fry. *Design of Database Structures*. Englewood Cliffs, N.J.: Prentice-Hall, 1982. A thorough treatment of data structures, access methods, and associated algorithms.

Wiederhold, Gio. *Database Design*, 2nd ed. New York: McGraw-Hill, 1983. A readable discussion of access methods and other physical design topics.

Appendix B
Sample Documents for the Metropolitan National Bank Scenario

Metropolitan National Bank
Main Office: 8200 Northwest Parkway
Lincoln, Texas 79402-8297
MONEY MARKET ACCOUNT

Page 1

Karen B. Silvermintz
2493 Rayado Ct.
Lincoln, TX 79411

Account Number: 3592594
Statement date: 5/30/91
Statement period: 4/30/91—5/29/91
SSN / Tax ID: 437-83-9939

Account Summary

To your previous balance of	1,753.60
You added 5 deposits for	5,585.68
You subtracted 35 withdrawals for	4,714.55
Giving you a current balance of	2,624.73
Number of days used for balances	34
Your average collected balance is	3,563.42
Your low balance occurred on 4-20 and was	1,753.60

Deposits and Other Additions

Date	Amount	Description
4-21	47.00	Deposit
4-21	626.40	Deposit
4-26	1,000.00	Deposit
5-02	3,896.02	Deposit
5-23	16.26	Money Market Interest Paid

Checks and Other Withdrawals

Date	Amount	Description
4-21	50.00	114 Jersey St. #2 Withdraw 4-21 Loc-A 0280/7437 Lincoln TX MNB
5-16	30.00	114 Jersey St. #1 Withdraw 5-16 Loc-A 0279/8715 Lincoln TX MNB
5-17	50.00	114 Jersey St. #1 Withdraw 5-17 Loc-A 0279/9424 Lincoln TX MNB
5-22	50.00	114 Jersey St. #2 Withdraw 5-22 Loc-A 0280/0354 Lincoln TX MNB

Metropolitan National Bank
Main Office: 8200 Northwest Parkway
Lincoln, Texas 79402-8297
MONEY MARKET ACCOUNT

Page 2

Karen B. Silvermintz
2493 Rayado Ct.
Lincoln, TX 79411

Account Number: 3592594
Statement date: 5/30/91
Statement period: 4/30/91—5/29/91
SSN / Tax ID: 437-83-9939

Chk	Date	Amount	Chk	Date	Amount	Chk	Date	Amount
2219	5-02	979.00	2251	5-03	28.00	2263	5-16	119.28
****			2252	5-08	21.73	****		
2241	4-22	94.00	2253	5-08	50.00	2266	5-19	203.00
2242	4-29	50.00	2254	5-08	50.00	2267	5-10	1,000.00
****			2255	5-09	50.00	2268	5-11	20.00
2244	4-26	15.52	2256	5-10	833.60	2269	5-17	15.50
2245	4-26	12.00	2257	5-12	70.00	2270	5-17	10.29
2246	4-26	17.21	2258	5-18	90.00	2271	5-18	46.76
2247	4-26	72.48	2259	5-12	34.12	****		
2248	4-27	29.01	2260	5-11	22.79	2273	5-22	29.90
2249	4-27	56.85	2261	5-11	79.32	2274	5-23	21.48
2250	5-02	219.91	2262	5-17	192.74			

Daily Balances

Date	Amount	Date	Amount	Date	Amount
4-20	1,753.60	5-03	5,699.04	5-17	3,049.61
4-21	2,377.00	5-08	5,577.31	5-18	2,912.85
4-22	2,283.00	5-09	5,527.31	5-19	2,709.85
4-26	3,165.79	5-10	3,693.71	5-22	2,629.95
4-27	3,079.93	5-11	3,571.60	5-23	2,624.73
4-29	3,029.93	5-12	3,467.42		
5-02	5,727.04	5-16	3,318.14		

Average Yield Rate   4.90
Year to Date Interest   73.87

Direct inquiries on this account to:

Metropolitan National Bank
Customer Service
8200 Northwest Parkway
Lincoln, TX 79402-8297

Metropolitan National Bank
Main Office: 8200 Northwest Parkway
Lincoln, Texas 79402-8297
SAVINGS ACCOUNT

Page 1

Karen B. Silvermintz
2493 Rayado Ct.
Lincoln, TX 79411

Account Number: 8474059
Statement date: 5/30/91
Statement period: 4/30/91—5/29/91
SSN / Tax ID: 437-83-9939

Account Summary
To your previous balance of 8,003.45
You added 2 deposits for 535.02
You subtracted 2 withdrawals for 105.00
Giving you a current balance of 8,423.47

Number of days used for balances 30
Your average collected balance is 7,933.45
Your low balance occurred on 5-10 and was 7,898.45

Deposits and Other Additions

Date	Amount	Description
5-29	500.00	Deposit
5-29	35.02	Interest Paid

Checks and Other Withdrawals

Date	Amount	Description
5-10	50.00	114 Jersey St. #2 Withdraw 4-21 Loc-A 0280/0053 Lincoln TX MNB

Chk	Date	Amount	Chk	Date	Amount	Chk	Date	Amount
0119	5-10	65.00						

Daily Balances

Date	Amount	Date	Amount	Date	Amount
4-29	8,003.45	5-10	7,898.45	5-29	8,423.47

Direct inquiries on this account to:

Metropolitan National Bank
Customer Service
8200 Northwest Parkway
Lincoln, TX 79402-8297

Metropolitan National Bank
Main Office: 8200 Northwest Parkway
Lincoln, Texas 79402-8297
CHECKING ACCOUNT

Page 1

Karen B. Silvermintz
2493 Rayado Ct.
Lincoln, TX 79411

Account Number: 3597622
Statement date: 5/30/91
Statement period: 4/30/91—5/29/91
SSN / Tax ID: 437-83-9939

Account Summary
To your previous balance of 2,753.60
You added 4 deposits for 4,185.68
You subtracted 35 withdrawals for 2,914.55
Giving you a current balance of 4,024.73

Your low balance occurred on 4-29 and was 2,629.93

Deposits and Other Additions

Date	Amount	Description
4-21	47.00	Deposit
4-21	226.40	Deposit
5-02	3,896.02	Deposit
5-23	16.26	Deposit

Checks and Other Withdrawals

Date	Amount	Description
4-21	50.00	114 Jersey St. #2 Withdraw 4-21 Location-A 0280 Lincoln TX MNB
5-16	30.00	114 Jersey St. #1 Withdraw 5-16 Location-A 0279 Lincoln TX MNB
5-17	50.00	114 Jersey St. #1 Withdraw 5-17 Location-A 0279 Lincoln TX MNB
5-22	50.00	114 Jersey St. #2 Withdraw 5-22 Location-A 0280 Lincoln TX MNB

Metropolitan National Bank
Main Office: 8200 Northwest Parkway
Lincoln, Texas 79402-8297
CHECKING ACCOUNT

Page 2

Karen B. Silvermintz
2493 Rayado Ct.
Lincoln, TX 79411

Account Number: 3597622
Statement date: 5/30/91
Statement period: 4/30/91—5/29/91
SSN / Tax ID: 437-83-9939

Chk	Date	Amount	Chk	Date	Amount	Chk	Date	Amount
4719	5-02	470.00	4751	5-03	28.00	4763	5-16	109.28
4720	4-21	17.50	4752	5-08	21.73	****		
4721	4-22	76.50	4753	5-08	50.00	4766	5-19	203.00
4722	4-29	50.00	4754	5-08	25.00	4767	5-10	500.00
****			4755	5-09	50.00	4768	5-11	20.00
4744	4-26	15.52	4756	5-10	72.60	4769	5-17	15.50
4745	4-26	12.00	4757	5-12	70.00	4770	5-17	10.29
4746	4-26	17.21	4758	5-18	15.00	4771	5-18	46.76
4747	4-26	72.48	4759	5-12	34.12	4772	5-22	75.00
4748	4-27	29.01	4760	5-11	47.79	4773	5-22	9.90
4749	4-27	56.85	4761	5-11	79.32	4774	5-23	21.48
4750	5-02	219.91	4762	5-17	192.74			

Daily Balances

Date	Amount	Date	Amount	Date	Amount
4-20	2,753.60	5-03	6,278.04	5-17	4,921.40
4-21	2,959.50	5-08	6,203.04	5-18	4,859.64
4-22	2,883.00	5-09	6,153.04	5-19	4,656.64
4-26	2,765.79	5-10	5,580.44	5-22	4,571.74
4-27	2,679.93	5-11	5,433.33	5-23	4,566.52
4-29	2,629.93	5-12	5,329.21		
5-02	6,306.04	5-16	5,189.93		

Direct inquiries on this account to:

Metropolitan National Bank
Customer Service
8200 Northwest Parkway
Lincoln, TX 79402-8297

Metropolitan National Bank
Main Office: 8200 Northwest Parkway
Lincoln, Texas 79402-8297
Loan Application

Name: Karen B. Silvermintz
Address: 2493 Rayado Ct.
     Lincoln, TX 79411
Home Telephone: (806) 328-7835
Taxpayer Identification Number: _437_ - _83_ - _9939_
Date of Birth: _9_ / _4_ / _65_

Loan Number: **23-38394**
Amount Requested: $12,300
Date Needed: 6/12/91
Loan period (months): 60

Employer
Northwest Electric Cooperative
3210 Roosevelt Highway
Lincoln, TX 79420
Telephone: (806) 874-2510
Supervisor / manager: Mr. Eldon Wright
Years at current employment: 6

Personal Reference:
William Stein
3254 Socorro Cir.
Lincoln, TX 79412
Telephone: (806) 325-8272

Monthly income: $3,250.00

List any other sources of income you would like to have considered:

_____

Home: Rent _____Own _X_   Monthly rent/mortgage: $743.86

Other monthly payments:
Automobile: _____   _____ : _____
_____ : _____   _____ : _____
_____ : _____   _____ : _____

MetNat Checking Account Number: 3597622
MetNat Saving Account Number: 8474059

Credit Cards:
VISA
Account Number: 4277-7282-9393-9801
Expiration date: 12/93
Average monthly balance: $500.00
AMERICAN EXPRESS
Account Number: 344627-723527-93
Expiration date: 6/93

OTHERS
Account Number:
Expiration date:
Average monthly balance:

MASTERCARD
Account Number: 7393-4840-4992-4302
Expiration date: 11/93
Average monthly balance: $500.00
DISCOVER
Account Number:
Expiration date:
Average monthly balance:

Account Number:
Expiration date:
Average monthly balance:

Prior MetNat loans (paid): 21-83748
Outstanding MetNat loans: None
Other paid loans: _____
Other outstanding loans: _____
Purpose for loan: New car purchase

Metropolitan National Bank
Main office: 8200 Northwest Parkway
Lincoln, Texas 79402-8297
Account Application

Name: Karen B. Silvermintz   Account Number: _____

Address: 2493 Rayado Ct.   Checking ___ Saving ___ Money Market $\underline{X}$

Lincoln, TX 79411   Date: 6/12/91

Home Telephone: (806) 328-7835

Taxpayer Identification Number: $\underline{437}$ - $\underline{83}$ - $\underline{9939}$

Date of Birth: $\underline{9}$ / $\underline{4}$ / $\underline{65}$

Joint account information (fill in only if others have access to this account):

Name	Relationship	Taxpayer ID	Date of Birth

Preferred account name: _____

Employer
Northwest Electric Cooperative
3210 Roosevelt Highway
Lincoln, TX 79420
Telephone: (806) 874-2510
Supervisor / manager: Mr. Eldon Wright
Years at current employment: 6

Monthly income: $3,250.00

Home: Rent _____ Own $\underline{X}$ Monthly rent/mortgage: $743.86

Do you desire an automated teller card? Yes: _____ No: _____

Metropolitan National Bank VISA
Main Office: 8200 Northwest Parkway
Lincoln, Texas 79402-8297

Page 1

Karen B. Silvermintz
2493 Rayado Ct.
Lincoln, TX 79411

Account Number: 3762-3873-9399-22
Statement date: 5/30/91
Statement period: 4/30/91—5/29/91
SSN / Tax ID: 437-83-9939

Account Summary

To your previous balance of	326.63
You made 12 purchases for	483.17
You had 0 cash advances for	0.00
You made 1 payment of	150.00
Your account was charged interest of	17.66
Giving you a current balance of	677.46
The monthly interest rate is	1.50%
Number of days used for balances	30
Credit limit	5,000.00
Available credit	4,322.54

Transaction Identifier	Posted Date	Purchase Date	Location	Amount
POER3948	5-03	5-03	HEAD BANGERS	33.45
OEIE3874	5-03	5-03	FAJITA RITAS	46.83
POYT8873	5-04	5-04	CASA DEL TACO	15.32
PIYY9820	5-04	5-02	K&G MENS STORE	195.90
RIHT8763	5-10	5-10	REGGIES	23.88
PEIF9288	5-12	5-10	AM/PM CLINIC	54.00
PEIE2736	5-14	5-14	APPLEBY'S	15.80
EOPP8277	5-17	5-17	REGGIES	20.47
PEEI8339	5-18	5-18	ACE SPORTSWEAR	12.98
EJUU3647	5-20	5-19	FRANK'S BAR & GRILL	22.54
ORIW8892	5-21	5-21	Q-MART	33.87
OPEE8203	5-22	5-22	YESTERDAYS	8.13

Direct inquiries on this account to:

Metropolitan National Bank
Customer Service
8200 Northwest Parkway
Lincoln, TX 79402-8297

Metropolitan National Bank
Main Office: 8200 Northwest Parkway
Lincoln, Texas 79402-8297

SAFE DEPOSIT BOX RENTAL & ENTRY RECORD

Name: Karen B. Silvermintz   Box Number: 304

Address: 2493 Rayado Ct.   Size: 5 x 5

Lincoln, TX 79411

Home Telephone: (806) 328-7835

3-01-91	Rental—12 months	15.00
3-01-91	Entry 12:32	
4-17-91	Entry 14:45	
4-20-91	Entry 10:29	

Metropolitan National Bank
Main Office: 8200 Northwest Parkway
Lincoln, Texas 79402-8297

TAX DEFERRED ANNUITY ACCOUNT

Page 1

Karen B. Silvermintz
2493 Rayado Ct.
Lincoln, TX 79411

Account Number: 83-3597622
Statement date: 5/30/91
Statement period: 4/30/91—5/29/91
SSN / Tax ID: 437-83-9939

Account Summary
Net Contract Contributions 35,667.41
Beginning Cash Surrender Value 35,744.99
Ending Cash Surrender Value 39,973.71
Total Account Value 43,474.68

Account	Date	Description	Transaction Amount	Fee	Total Transaction	Per Share Value	Number of Shares
Fixed	4-05-91	Payment	172.91	0.00	172.91	n/a	n/a
Growth	4-05-91	Payment	259.37	0.00	259.37	3.072	84.411
Market	4-05-91	Payment	172.92	0.00	172.92	1.815	95.248
Managed	4-05-91	Payment	259.37	0.00	259.37	1.986	130.580
Fixed	5-07-91	Payment	172.91	0.00	172.91	n/a	n/a
Growth	5-07-91	Payment	259.37	0.00	259.37	3.088	83.985
Market	5-07-91	Payment	172.92	0.00	172.92	1.826	94.695
Managed	5-07-91	Payment	259.37	0.00	259.37	1.983	130.795
Market	5-14-91	Shift	12,700.67 −	0.00	12,700.67 −	1.828	6,945.750 −
Special	5-14-91	Shift	12,700.67	0.00	12,700.67	2.792	4,548.286
Fixed	6-05-91	Payment	172.91	0.00	172.91	n/a	n/a
Growth	6-05-91	Payment	259.36	0.00	259.36	3.331	77.850
Managed	6-05-91	Payment	259.36	0.00	259.36	2.086	124.277
Special	6-05-91	Payment	172.93	0.00	172.93	2.949	58.633
Fixed	6-25-91	Acct Charge	0.00	6.08	6.08 −	n/a	n/a
Growth	6-25-91	Acct Charge	0.00	3.67	3.67 −	3.220	1.139 −
Managed	6-25-91	Acct Charge	0.00	7.53	7.53 −	2.051	3.670 −
Special	6-25-91	Acct Charge	0.00	7.72	7.72 −	2.869	2.690 −
Market	6-28-91	Shift	13,458.02	0.00	13,458.02	1.843	7,298.976
Special	6-28-91	Shift	13,458.02 −	0.00	13,458.02 −	2.922	4,604.229 −

Metropolitan National Bank
Main Office: 8200 Northwest Parkway
Lincoln, Texas 79402-8297
TAX DEFERRED ANNUITY ACCOUNT

Page 2

Karen B. Silvermintz   Account Number: 83-3597622
2493 Rayado Ct.   Statement date: 5/30/91
Lincoln, TX 79411   Statement period: 4/30/91—5/29/91
                                              SSN / Tax ID: 437-83-9939

Fixed
   Beginning Account Value . . . 9,729.48
   Deposits 518.73
   Contract Charges . . . . . . 6.08 −
   Appreciation/Depreciation . . 196.62
   Ending Account Value 10,438.75

Growth
   Beginning Account Value . . . 5,219.22 Unit value 3.053 Units 1,708.922
   Deposits 778.10
   Contract Charges . . . . . . 3.67 −
   Appreciation/Depreciation . . 457.30
   Ending Account Value . . . . 6,450.95 Unit value 3.301 Units 1,954.099

Market
   Beginning Account Value . . . 12,254.26 Unit value 1.813 Units 6,755.807
   Deposits 345.84
   Shifts 757.35
   Appreciation/Depreciation . . 105.37
   Ending Account Value . . . . 13,462.82 Unit value 1.844 Units 7,298.976

Managed
   Beginning Account Value . . . 11,675.29 Unit value 1.976 Units 5,908.185
   Deposits 778.10
   Contract Charges 7.53 −
   Appreciation/Depreciation . . 676.30
   Ending Account Value . . . . 13,122.16 Unit value 2.086 Units 6,290.167

Special
   Beginning Account Value . . . 0.00 Unit value 0.000 Units 0.000
   Deposits 172.93
   Shifts . . . . 757.35 −
   Appreciation/Depreciation . . 592.14
   Ending Account Value . . . . 0.00 Unit value 0.000 Units 0.000

Summary of Account Value by Contribution Source:
   Fixed 10,438.75
   Growth 6,450.95
   Market 13,462.82
   Managed 13,122.16
   Total 43,474.68

Metropolitan National Bank
Main Office: 8200 Northwest Parkway
Lincoln, Texas 79402-8297
VISA APPLICATION

Name: Karen B. Silvermintz

Address: 2493 Rayado Ct.

Lincoln, TX 79411

Home Telephone: (806) 328-7835

Taxpayer Identification Number: __437__ - __83__ - __9939__

Date of Birth: __9__ / __4__ / __65__

Loan Number: **23-38394**

Amount Requested: $12,300

Date Needed: 6/12/91

Loan period (months): 60

Employer

Northwest Electric Cooperative

3210 Roosevelt Highway

Lincoln, TX 79420

Telephone: (806) 874-2510

Supervisor / manager: Mr. Eldon Wright

Years at current employment: 6

Monthly income: $3,250.00

List any other sources of income you would like to have considered:

_____

Home: Rent _____ Own __X__   Monthly rent/mortgage: $743.86

Other monthly payments:

Automobile: _____ : _____   _____ : _____

_____ : _____   _____ : _____

MetNat Checking Account Number: 3597622

MetNat Saving Account Number: 8474059

Credit Cards:

VISA

Account Number:

Expiration date:

Average monthly balance:

AMERICAN EXPRESS

Account Number: 344627-723527-93

Expiration date: 6/93

OTHERS

Account Number:

Expiration date:

Average monthly balance:

MASTERCARD

Account Number:7393-4840-4992-4302

Expiration date: 11/93

Average monthly balance: $500.00

DISCOVER

Account Number:

Expiration date:

Average monthly balance:

Account Number:

Expiration date:

Average monthly balance:

Prior MetNat loans (paid): 21-83748

Outstanding MetNat loans: None

Other paid loans: _____

Other outstanding loans: _____

Requested credit limit: __$2,000__

GLOSSARY

Boldface words in the text are defined in the glossary.

aborted transaction   a **transaction** that is not allowed to have its effects applied permanently to the database. See also **committed transaction.**

access flexibility   allows for easy retrieval of selected items in a database and presentation of that data in a variety of formats.

access matrix   one method used to enforce security in database systems. An access matrix provides a concise way of representing the entities in the database and the persons (or applications) using the database. The database entities are frequently called **objects** in an access matrix, and persons (or applications) accessing the database are called subjects. See also **object profile, subject profile.**

active data repository system   a **data repository system** that controls access to the **database management system.**

after-image   values of database items stored in a **transaction log** after **transactions** have executed. See also **before-image.**

aggregation   refers to collecting possibly different **entities** into a single more abstract entity concept in order to refer to the collection by a single term.

algorithm   a defined sequence of operations. Also, a component of a **data encryption** process.

alias   an alternative name for a **data item.** Often established when different users refer to the same data item by different names.

American National Standards Institute (ANSI)   a board composed of government officials, aca-demics, and industry experts that sets standards in many areas.

ANSI   see **American National Standards Institute.**

attribute   a property of an **entity.** Also, a column in a **relation.**

auditing   a process of examining and assessing the reliability and integrity of information-providing systems.

authorization identifier   a code that identifies users that have access to the database.

automatic insertion status   in the **CODASYL** model, a way of specifying that, whenever a record occurrence is added to the database, the **database management system** establishes the record occurrence as a member of a set occur-rence that has been preselected by the **run unit;** that is, the applications program is responsible for selecting the proper set occurrence *before* the record is transferred to the database manage-ment system for addition to the database. See also **manual insertion status.**

B-tree   a form of data structure based on hierar-chies. B-trees are balanced in the sense that all the terminal (bottom) nodes have the same path length to the root (top) node.

backward pointer   see **prior pointer.**

backward recovery/forward recovery   see **roll back/roll forward.**

balanced B-tree   B-trees are balanced in the sense that all the terminal (bottom) **nodes** have the same path length to the **root** (top) **node.**

base class   in the **Semantic Database Model,** an **entity class** that can exist independently of other classes. See also **nonbase class.**

base data elements   data items that are fundamental to a particular applications module.

base relation   a **relation** that can exist independently in a database.

before-image   values of database items stored in a **transaction log** before **transactions** have executed. See also **after-image.**

bidirectional list   see **two-way list.**

binary relation   a **relation** with only two **attributes.**

binary search   an efficient search algorithm. In this technique, the value sought is first compared to the value in the middle of the list. This comparison indicates whether the value sought is in the top or the bottom half of the list. The value sought is then compared to the middle entry of the appropriate half. This comparison indicates which fourth the value is in. Then the value is compared to the middle of that fourth, and so on until the desired value is found or the list cannot be further divided.

block   the smallest addressable unit of space on a storage device. The block size defines the **physical record** size.

blocked transaction   a **transaction** that cannot **commit** because it cannot receive the proper signal from the **network** management facilities. See also **partitioned network.**

blocking factor   the number of **logical records** per **block.**

booster node   a special processor that resends signals on a network to overcome transmission limitations in hardware.

Boyce-Codd normal form   is satisfied when **third normal form** is satisfied and all **determinants** in the data structure are also **candidate keys.**

buffer   a portion of main memory used to facilitate the transfer of data to and from main memory and a secondary storage device.

bus network   an arrangement of processors in which each **node** is connected to a central cable that supports communications.

candidate key   an **attribute** or collection of attributes that uniquely identifies a **tuple.**

cardinality   the number of **tuples** in a **relation.**

careful replacement   a variation of the **differential file** approach in which only the changes affected by a single **committed transaction** are accumulated in the differential file.

channel   see **track.**

CASE Tool   see **Computer Assisted Software Engineering (CASE) Tool.**

checkpoint   a point in time when a database is known to exhibit **data consistency.**

class attribute   in the **Semantic Database Model,** a characteristic of an **entity class.**

class member   in the **Semantic Database Model,** individual **entities** in an **entity** class.

client/server architecture   a conceptual relationship between multiple processors in a **network** in which one machine requests information (the client) and another machine provides the information (the server).

closure   a characteristic of **relational algebra** that requires operations on a relation (or several relations) to always produce another relation.

CODASYL   Conference on Data and Systems Languages. An ANSI committee that sets standards for data processing.

collision   simultaneous communications in a **network** environment. Also, a situation in which more than one data object **hashes** to a particular address.

committed transaction   a **transaction** whose effects are ready to be applied permanently to the database. See also **aborted transaction.**

composite attribute   formed by combining simpler **attributes** into a single attribute.

composite entity   an **entity** being modeled is composed of characteristics of each of the contributing entities. Composite entities result from **many-to-many relationships.**

Computer Assisted Software Engineering (CASE) Tool   a design support system used to automate and standardize the design process of complex information systems.

computer-integrated manufacturing (CIM) the use of database and communication technologies to integrate the design, manufacturing, and business functions of a factory.

concatenated key a **primary key** composed of two or more **attributes.**

concentration of resources control one form of control specified by the AICPA. A system that exhibits this type of control has effective security, back-up, and recovery features. See also **coordination of activity control** and **update and access control.**

conceptual level of data refers to the ANSI conceptual model that defines three levels of data. The middle level in the architecture is the **conceptual level.** The conceptual level represents the union of all the user views at the **external level.** Thus the conceptual representation is an integrated **view** or **schema** of the entire database. At this level, the representation of data still reflects human views of data. See also **external level of data** and **internal level of data.**

conceptual schema see **logical schema.**

concurrent processing occurs when multiple users are processing the same record during the same time interval.

condition box in **Query By Example (QBE),** a special area used to define constraints used in queries.

control area in the **Virtual Storage Access Method,** consists of a collection of control intervals.

control area split occurs when half of the **control intervals** in a full **control area** are moved to an empty control area in order to create more free space within the control area.

control interval in the **Virtual Storage Access Method,** corresponds roughly to a block on disk storage and is a portion of the storage medium containing a collection of records.

control interval split occurs when half of the records in a full **control interval** are moved to an empty control interval in order to create more free space within the control interval.

constraint a rule or condition that must be satisfied in a database.

coordination of activity control one form of control specified by the AICPA. A system that exhibits this type of control ensures that shared resources are properly coordinated. See also **concentration of resources control** and **update and access control.**

currency indicators in the **CODASYL** model, special registers used to determine **navigation paths.** These registers contain the **database keys** of the most recently accessed **record occurrences** for each **record type** and **set type** in the **subschema** invoked by the **run unit.**

cycle a circular logical relationship, or a path through a transaction dependency graph which begins and ends at the same node.

cylinder the area in a **diskpack** defined by a specific track location on multiple disk platters.

data numbers, words, names, and other symbols that can be stored in a computer system.

data aggregate in the **CODASYL** model, a named collection of data items. These may be arrays or groups of **attributes** that occur more than once for an **entity.**

data decryption a process that converts encrypted data from an apparently random sequence of symbols (characters) into a meaningful sequence. See also **data encryption.**

data definition language (DDL) a language used to translate the **logical schema** into a software schema for the database management package in use.

data dictionary see **data repository.**

Data Division in a CODASYL DBMS, the part of a COBOL program can have an optional Renaming Section to specify aliases for **records, sets,** and **data items.** It must have a Record Section specifying records to be accessed.

data encoding see **data encryption.**

data encryption a process that converts data from a meaningful sequence of symbols (characters) into an apparently random sequence. See also **data decryption.**

data integrity exists when data values are correct, consistent, and current.

data item a field to be stored in a database. This corresponds to an **attribute** of an **entity.**

data management see **information management.**

data manipulation language (DML) commands that may be embedded in applications programs to add, retrieve, or change database values.

data redundancy occurs when one piece of **data** is stored in more than one place in an information system.

data relatability the ability to establish logical relationships between different types of **records,** usually in different files.

data repository a facility containing data item definitions, their internal storage characteristics, and their relationships to other data items. Often called a **data dictionary** in older **database management systems.**

data repository control program the software used to maintain the **data repository.**

data repository system includes the **data repository** and all software that makes it available to users.

data security processes that protect data from unauthorized access and from accidental or intentional damage or destruction.

data shareability exists when different users or user groups can use the same (nonredundant) **data.**

data structure the manner in which relationships between data elements are represented in the computer system.

data structure diagram a common graphical technique for presenting the **entities** and relationships in a database.

data subentry describes each **data item** in a **CODASYL schema** record description.

database highly integrated sets of files shard by users throughout an organization.

database administrator the person (or group of people) responsible for the design, development, and administration of a **database system.**

database analyst an information technology worker who uses database technology to design systems satisfying the requirements specified by an **information analyst.**

database application programmers programmers that write programs in high-level languages such as COBOL or PL/1 to perform the data processing activities required to support the module.

database key in the **CODASYL** model, a unique value automatically assigned by the **database management system** to a record when it is entered into the system. The database key is unique and is used to determine the location of each record on the storage devices of the system.

database management system (DBMS) a commercial software package designed to provide the basis for building database systems.

database package prewritten database software. See **database management system.**

database system an integrated collection of databases along with users who share the databases, personnel who design and manage databases, techniques for designing and managing databases, and computer systems to support them. The main goal of database systems is to provide managers with information so that they can make effective decisions about how to run the organization.

database system master plan details the ultimate structure and contents of the database system. It should indicate the database system's role in realizing organizational goals. This plan should be developed prior to database implementation.

DBMS see **database management system.**

DDL see **data definition language.**

deadlock a situation in which database processing stops because **transactions** are waiting on each other to unlock resources. See **locking.**

deadly embrace see **deadlock.**

decision-making system a system capable of making a decision.

decision rule A policy or model used to determine a course of action. See also **heuristic.**

decision support system (DSS) an information system designed to provide information for managerial decision making in cases where the decision is **ill-structured** or **semistructured.**

declarative knowledge knowledge of facts. See also **procedural knowledge.**

decomposition dependence a partitioning of relations characterized by **join dependence.**

degree the number of **attributes** in a **relation.**

deletion anomaly occurs when the removal of one logical **entity** results in loss of information about an unrelated logical entity. See also **modification anomaly.**

dense list a **linked list** embedded within a **file** in which most of the **records** in the file are included in the list.

density a measure of the amount of **data** stored on a storage device.

derivation in the **Semantic Database Model,** a relationship between **member attributes** that can be specified in a formula.

derived relation see **view.**

determinant refers to a **data item** that, if the value is known for this data item, then the value of a second data item is also known.

diagnosis the process of finding fault in a system based on **interpretation** of error-prone data.

difference a **relational algebra** operation that identifies tuples that occur in one **relation** but not in another.

differential file a separate file containing the changes of **committed transactions.**

direct access storage device a storage device on which **records** may be stored physically in any order. Processing may also occur in any order. See also **sequential access storage device.**

diskpack a removable set of disks.

distributed free space vacant storage space spread throughout a storage medium.

DML see **data manipulation language.**

domain the set of potential values that a **data item** may have.

domain dependence the values for an **attribute** must come from a specific **domain.**

domain-key normal form is satisfied if every **constraint** on a **relation** can be inferred by knowing the set of **attribute** names and their underlying **domains,** along with the set of **keys.**

DSS see **decision support system.**

effective systems systems that provide correct, current information that is relevant to the decision at hand.

efficient systems systems that perform a task in a cost-effective manner.

entity any **object,** tangible or intangible, about which **data** will be stored in a database.

entity class in the **Semantic Database Model,** a collection of **entities.**

entity integrity a **constraint** requiring that once the **primary key** is established, no change may be made that corrupts the ability of the **primary key** to uniquely identify a tuple. This constraint guarantees access to all data.

Entity-Relationship Model (E-R Model) the most common approach to logical database specification. A graphical method of representing **entities, attributes,** and relationships.

equi-join see **join** and **theta-join.**

E-R Model see **Entity Relationship Model.**

error status variables in the **CODASYL** model, special registers used to maintain values indicating various conditions that may arise in the **user work area** while processing a **data manipulation language** statement.

essential data structure a **data structure** that is required to convey information.

essentiality see **essential data structure.**

Ethernet a specific bus architecture used in distributed systems.

even parity in **parity checking,** the requirement that the number of bits in a **track** be an even number. See also **odd parity.**

exhaustive in the **Semantic Database Model,** this term means every value of the **attribute** must occur somewhere in the database.

existence dependent the existence of one **entity** depends on the existence of another entity in a relationship. See also **weak entity.**

expert system a highly specialized information system constructed to make analyses comparable to a human expert. See also **inference engine** and **knowledge base.**

expert control system an **expert system** that integrates **interpretation, diagnosis, monitoring, prediction,** and **planning** tasks.

external level of data   refers to the ANSI conceptual model that defines three levels of data. The external level is closest to the users of the system and refers to the way users view the data. This level is closely related to a **user view** and a **subschema**. See also **conceptual level of data** and **internal level of data**.

4GL   see **language generations**.

fifth generation language   see **language generations**.

fifth normal form   is satisfied when **fourth normal form** is satisfied and the data relationships embodied in the **data structure** cannot be reconstructed from data structures containing fewer data items. If the data structure can be decomposed only into smaller records that all have the same key, then the data structure is in fifth normal form.

file   a collection of **records**.

file access method   the procedure through which records are located. Determined by the physical layout or structure of the **records** in a **file**.

file organization   see **file access method**.

first generation language   see **language generations**.

first normal form   is satisfied when a **data structure** can be represented as a flat file structure.

fixed-head disk assembly   a **disk** which contains a read/write head for each **track**. This approach minimizes **seek time**. See also **movable-head disk assembly**.

fixed retention class   a **CODASYL retention class** that requires a record occurrence, once it has been connected to or stored in an occurrence of a **set,** to remain a member of that set occurrence as long as it exists in the database.

foreign key   an **attribute** defined on the same domain and logically related to a **primary key** in a **relation**.

forward pointer   a **pointer** to the next record in a linked list.

fourth generation language (4GL)   see **language generations**.

fourth normal form   is satisfied when **Boyce-Codd normal form** is satisfied and either (1) a

data structure contains no multivalued dependencies or (2) all its multivalued dependencies are also functional dependencies.

free-standing data repository   see **passive data repository**.

full functional dependence   exists when **functional dependence** exists between a data item and all of the data items in a set of data items and functional dependence does not exist between the data item and any proper subset of the set of data items.

fully connected   an arrangement of processors such that all processors are connected to all other processors. See **partially connected**.

fully relational system   a **relationally complete system** that also supports **entity integrity** and **referential integrity**.

function   in some object-oriented systems, a function is an **attribute** or property of an **object**.

functional dependence   exists between two data items in a **data structure** if the value of one data item implies the value of a second data item.

gateway   a processor that translates requests in **client/server architectures** into queries suitable for the server system, executes the request on the server system, and then responds to the **network** with the results.

generalization/specialization   refers to the relationship that can occur when very similar **entities** exist in a database. **Generalization** refers to the collection of these entities as a whole (the general characteristics that make them similar). **Specialization** refers to them individually (the characteristics that make them different). See also **aggregation**.

generative approach   one approach to computer aided **process planning** in which planning is based on new designs generated specifically to manufacture a product.

generic instance   in an object-oriented system, an object description that has properties that are consistent across all versions of the object. There is one generic instance of an object for the set of all versions of the object. See also **generic reference** and **specific reference**.

generic reference in an object-oriented system, a reference to the **generic instance.** See also **specific reference.**

global transaction in a **network,** the initial **transaction** that a user submits. It is global in the sense that the user wants the data and should be able to access the **data** regardless of where it resides in the system. See also **local transaction.**

granularity the level of **locking** applied in a database. **Data-item** level locking is representative of fine granularity; **record**-level locking is considered more-coarse granularity.

graphic language a high-level language that displays pictures of relations; the user fills in the appropriate attribute with an example of the desired data. See also **Query By Example (QBE).**

hashed access the process of accessing a **record** using **hashing.**

hashing a method of calculating the location of a **record** in a **file.**

hashing algorithm the sequence of instructions used to accomplish **hashing.**

head the first record in a **linked list.**

height the number of levels in the hierarchy of a **B-tree.**

heterogeneous DDBMS a **network** of computer systems containing different hardware and software at some or all of the **nodes.** See also **homogeneous system assumption.**

heuristic A generally useful policy to follow in a situation in order to determine a course of action. A heuristic is often called a rule of thumb.

hierarchical database model an approach to database management based on **tree** structures.

hierarchical sequence an ordering of the records in an **IMS** database system. The hierarchical sequence is a result of both the value of a designated **sequence field** in each segment and the relative positioning of the segment in the hierarchical structure.

hierarchical sequence key a special value associated with each **segment** occurrence in an **IMS** database. A segment's hierarchical sequence key value is a code identifying its **segment** type code and sequence key value, prefixed by the hierarchical sequence key value for its parent.

historical database a database that models time by recording the time in which a state correctly models reality. Historical DBMSs cannot rollback; they only store the current knowledge about the past. See also **rollback database** and **temporal database.**

homogeneous system assumption the assumption that all systems in a distributed processing system are running the same **database management system** software.

horizontal partitioning an approach to distributing data in a **network** in which the **data** in a **relation** is divided by placing some rows at one **node** and other rows at some other node.

ID dependent entity an **entity** that cannot be uniquely identified without considering identifying **attributes** of another entity.

Identification Division in a CODASYL DBMS, this part of a COBOL program names the **subschema,** the **schema** from which it is derived, and the **privacy key** to unlock the schema if necessary.

identifier in the **Semantic Database Model,** an **attribute** used to distinguish one **entity class member** from another.

ill-structured problems problems that cannot be solved using a well-defined algorithm.

IMS (Information Management System) a database management system developed by IBM based primarily on a hierarchical approach to data management.

inconsistent analysis problem occurs during **concurrent processing** when invalid values are processed because a **transaction** accesses data while another transaction is updating that data. See also **lost update problem** and **uncommitted dependence problem.**

index set in B-trees, high level pointers into the **tree.**

inference engine a process for manipulating a **knowledge base.**

information useful **data.**

information analyst an information systems worker who works closely with users of information to carefully define information requirements and to structure these requirements into a logical form.

information center   an organizational unit that typically is dedicated to providing user services related to information processing.

information management   The task of managing organizational data and data processing functions.

information requirements analysis   work done with users to define information needs.

insertion anomaly   occurs when the insertion of data about one logical **entity** that requires the insertion of data about an unrelated logical entity. See also **modification anomaly.**

insertion class   in the **CODASYL** model, determines what happens when a record is added to the database. See **automatic insertion status** and **manual insertion status.**

integrated data repository   see **active data repository.**

integrated system   a collection of software modules, typically including word processing, spreadsheet, and database capabilities, that provides a means to easily transfer data or text from one module to another.

interclass connection   used in **SDM** to define the relationship between **base classes** and **nonbase classes.**

interface   the link between a user and a computer system, or the link between two computer systems or a computer system and a programming language.

internal level of data   refers to the ANSI conceptual model that defines three levels of data. The lowest level in the architecture is the **internal level.** The internal level corresponds to the actual representation of data within the computer system and the methods used to access the data. This level may also be referred to as the **physical level,** for it specifies how the data is represented physically in the storage devices of the machine. See also **external level of data** and **conceptual level of data.**

interpretation   the analysis of data to determine its meaning.

intersection   a **relational algebra** operation that generates a **relation** that contains only **tuples** that appear in both relations.

inverse   a means of specifying a relationship in **SDM** that will be viewed conceptually from more than one viewpoint.

inverted list   an index table of **pointers** stored separately from the data **records** rather than embedded in pointer fields in the stored records themselves.

join   a **relational algebra** operation that takes the result of the **product** operation and retains only **tuples** where the value for a specific **attribute** matches in each **relation.** This is also known as a **natural join** or **equi-join.** See also **maybe-join** and **theta-join.**

join dependence   a constraint that requires a relation to be the join of its projections.

key   usually synonymous with **primary key.** Also, a component of a **data encryption** process.

key dependence   implies that no changes to the relation that would result in the key no longer being a unique identifier of tuples in the relation are allowed.

key-to-address transformation   the process of converting **primary key** values into physical addresses on a storage device. See also **hashing.**

knowledge acquisition   the process of extracting knowledge from human experts to determine how they perform their activities. See also **knowledge base, knowledge representation,** and **knowledge utilization.**

knowledge base   a database of facts and rules for deriving facts.

knowledge representation   the means of conceptually representing knowledge in a computer-based system. See also **knowledge base, knowledge acquisition,** and **knowledge utilization.**

knowledge utilization   the process of applying the appropriate knowledge to a problem situation. See also **knowledge acquisition, knowledge base,** and **knowledge representation.**

LAN   see **local area network (LAN).**

language generations a method of classifying programming languages. The first generation is machine (binary) language; the second, assembly language; and the third, programming languages such as COBOL, FORTRAN, PASCAL, or BASIC. Fourth generation languages (4GL) are very high level **query languages** and **data manipulation languages**. Fifth generation languages are artificial intelligence languages such as LISP and Prolog.

lexical ambiguity refers to how a word can have multiple meanings in **natural language processing**.

link a connection between processors in a **network**.

linked list a collection of records connected by **pointers**.

local area network (LAN) a **network** of computer systems in relatively close proximity to each other, typically in the same building.

local transaction a **transaction** that executes on a specific processor. See also **global transaction**.

location transparency exists in a **network** when **transactions** can be executed without concern for where the **data** being manipulated is stored in the system.

locking a method for resolving the problems that occur during **concurrent processing**. Records are "locked" and cannot be accessed by **transactions** during a specific time interval.

locking mechanism an implementation of **locking**.

logical data independence exists when the **external schemas** are independent of changes to the **logical schema**. One user may wish to change or add a user view, which changes the **conceptual level of data,** but this should have no impact on other users and their **views**.

logical database design the development of **schema** and **subschema** definitions.

logical organization the way data is organized in terms of the logical relationships between the **entities** represented in the database.

logical pointer a **data item** in one **record** that is used to locate an associated record. See also **pointer, physical pointer,** and **relative pointer**.

logical record the **data** associated with an **entity**. There may be several logical records in a **block**. See also **record blocking**.

logical schema the description of the database at the **conceptual level of data**.

loss decomposition a partitioning of relations during normalization characterized by **loss projections**.

loss projection a **projection** of a **relation** that produces spurious information when the projections are **joined**.

lost update problem occurs during **concurrent processing** when invalid values are processed because two **transactions** are intended to modify the database during the same time interval. Whichever transaction is **committed** last destroys the effect of the other transaction. See also **inconsistent analysis problem** and **uncommitted dependence problem**.

management information systems information systems designed to help control the organization. These systems derive much of their **information** by summarizing and abstracting **data** from transaction processing systems. They tend to be report oriented; standard reports are produced periodically (weekly, monthly, or annually) for use by middle managers to support tasks such as budget decisions and personnel assignments.

managerial control the primary activity of middle management, it consists of steering the organization toward the goals set during **strategic planning**. See also **operational control**.

mandatory in the **Semantic Database Model, attributes** that must have a value.

mandatory retention class a CODASYL **retention class** that requires once a record occurrence is connected to an occurrence of a **set**, it must be a member of some occurrence of that set as long as it exists in the database.

manual insertion status in the **CODASYL** model, a way of specifying that the applications program is responsible not only for selecting the appropriate **set** occurrence but also for explicitly establishing membership in that set occurrence. See also **automatic insertion status**.

manufacturing   the process of making products from raw materials.

many-to-many relationship   a relationship in which many instances of an **entity** of a given type are associated with many instances of another type.

match clause   a means of specifying a relationship between **entities** in the **Semantic Database Model (SDM).** With this approach, the value for a member attribute in one entity class is determined by first finding a member attribute in a second entity class that has the first attribute as its value; the value of a third attribute then becomes the value of the attribute in the first entity class.

maybe-join   a definition of the **join** operation in **relational algebra** that can accommodate the existence of **null values.**

member attribute   in the **Semantic Database Model,** a characteristic of a **class member.**

member record type   the record type participating in the "many" side of the **one-to-many relationship** embodied in a **CODASYL set.**

member subentry   describes each member record type participating in a **CODASYL set.**

membership class   in a CODASYL DBMS, the membership class of a record type in a set determines whether the DBMS or the applications program is responsible for maintaining the proper owner-member relationships when records are added to or removed from the database. See also **insertion status** and **retention status.**

mesh network   an arrangement of processors in a manner that allows **nodes** to be interconnected with any other nodes in the system. See **ring network** and **star network.**

message   information passed between **objects** in the **object-oriented paradigm.** They indicate to the receiving object which of the object's **methods** should be executed.

method   a public interface maintained by an **object** in the object-oriented paradigm, which is the set of operations applicable to the object.

minimally relational system   a **tabular system** that supports only the **selection, projection,** and **join** operations of **relational algebra.**

modification anomaly   occurs when mistakes in inserting, deleting, or modifying records are a consequence of the database design. See also **insertion anomaly, deletion anomaly,** and **update anomaly.**

monitoring   continuously interpreting signals and activating alarms when intervention is required.

movable-head disk assembly   a **disk** which contains a single read/write head for each usable surface. The read/write heads are all attached to a single movable assembly that moves all of the heads simultaneously. See also **fixed-head disk assembly.**

multilist   several **linked lists** that are defined over the same **file.**

multivalued attribute   an **attribute** that may have more than one value at any time.

multivalued dependence   occurs when one value of a data item determines a collection of values of a second data item.

name class   in the **Semantic Database Model,** a special form of **entity class** that defines a **domain.**

natural join   see **join.**

natural language processing   processing written or oral human communications.

navigation path   a means for accessing records in a **database management system** by following **pointers** embedded in the database.

network   a conceptual relationship between **entities** in which **many-to-many relationships** occur. Also, an interconnection of computing facilities. See **mesh network, ring network,** and **star network.**

next pointer   see **forward pointer.**

node   a **record** in a tree. Also, the computing facilities in any location in a **network.**

nonbase class   in the **Semantic Database Model,** an **entity class** defined in terms of another class. See also **base class.**

nondense list   a **linked list** embedded within a **file** in which most of the **records** in the file are not included in the list.

nonoverlapping   in the **Semantic Database Model,** this term means the values of an **attribute**

for any two entities have no values in common. In other words, each attribute value is used only once.

nonprogrammed decision a decision for which well-specified decision-making procedures do not exist. See **programmed decision, structured situation,** and **unstructured situation.**

normal forms criteria that define the levels of normalization. There is a sequence of normal forms, each one adding more **constraints** to a **data structure** as one progresses from the first set of criteria, called **first normal form,** through the highest set, called **domain-key normal form.**

not changeable in the **Semantic Database Model,** an **attribute** that cannot be modified except to correct an error.

null value a special value that represents one of two cases: the actual value is unknown or the attribute is not applicable.

object an entity.

object manager a component of an object-oriented system that administers and controls the **objects** in the system.

object-oriented database management a **database management system** approach that places great emphasis on modeling **objects.**

object-oriented paradigm a definition of the fundamental concepts of object-oriented approaches.

object profile a listing of all of the **subjects** that may access a particular **object.**

occurrences table in an **inverted list,** a table (column) containing the primary key for the record in which that value occurs. See also **values table.**

odd parity in **parity checking,** the requirement that the number of bits in a **track** be an odd number. See also **even parity.**

one-to-many relationship a relationship in which one instance of an **entity** of a given type is associated with many instances of another type.

one-to-one relationship a relationship in which one instance of an **entity** of a given type is associated with only one instance of another type.

operational control concerned with the day-to-day operation of the organization. See **managerial control** and **strategic planning.**

optional retention class a **CODASYL retention class** that allows membership to be canceled for a **member record** in a **set.**

order a value that constrains the number of entries at each level of a **B-tree.**

overflow area an additional area of storage on a disk used to hold **records** after the **primary area** becomes full.

owner record type the record type participating in the "one" side of the **one-to-many relationship** embodied in a **CODASYL set.**

packet a unit of data transmitted in a distributed system.

parity checking a technique for detecting errors in the way **data** is stored on a storage device. The technique involves counting the number of bits in a **track.** See also **even parity** and **odd parity.**

partial participation constraint occurs when a relationship can exist without at least one instance of each of the entities involved participating in the relationship. See also **total participation constraint.**

partially connected an arrangement of processors in which all processors are not connected to all other processors. See **fully connected.**

partially integrated data repository see **potentially active data repository.**

partitioned network a network that has two or more unconnected parts.

passive data repository system a **data repository system** completely decoupled from the **database management system.**

path of influences in the Interactive Financial Planning System (IFPS), a list of the data items that impact (i.e., influence) the value of a particular data item.

PBX see **public branch exchange.**

performance monitor routines special utilities that record statistics such as the number of disk accesses, the amount of time used by the CPU, the amount of time used by the input/output channel, and the amount of primary memory used by a particular application.

physical data independence   exists when the **logical schema** is independent of changes in the **internal schema.** The way the data is actually stored or accessed in the system can be changed without requiring a change in the logical schema.

physical database design   establishes exactly how the data in a database will be organized and stored on the storage devices.

physical organization   the way the data is organized and stored on storage devices.

physical record   the **data** stored in a **block.**

physical pointer   a **data item** in a **record** that gives the actual address of an associated record in the storage system. See also **pointer, logical pointer,** and **relative pointer.**

planning   preparing a program of action to achieve goals.

pointer   a data item that indicates the location of a record. The record may be in another file. Pointers may be data items accessible by users or they may be maintained internally by the **database management system.**

polling   a process in which one processor systematically communicates with other processors in a distributed system to determine whether these processors have information to send over the **network.**

polymorphism   a characteristic of the **object-oriented paradigm** that allows different classes to have **methods** with the same name.

potentially active data repository system   a **passive data repository system** that is capable of performing active control of database accesses. Administrative routines and processes must be developed to enforce active control in this type of system.

preanalysis   a method of resolving the problems that occur during **concurrent processing.** This approach analyzes conflicting **transaction classes.**

precompiler   vendor-developed programs that convert programs with embedded **data manipulation language** commands into programs with only standard statements of the host language.

prediction   forecasting the future from a model of the past and present.

primary area   the area of a disk in which records are first placed. See also **overflow area.**

primary key   a **candidate key** selected to be the key of a **relation.**

prime number division   a process for calculating the address of a record in which the **primary key** is divided by a prime number and the remainder is used for the address.

prior pointer   a **pointer** to the prior record in a **linked list.**

privacy key   a value, typically a password, that corresponds to the **privacy lock** specified in a **CODASYL schema, subschema, record, set** or **data item.**

privacy lock   in the **CODASYL** model, a password or user-written procedure applied to a **schema, subschema, record, set,** or **data item.** See also **privacy key.**

problem finding   the process of searching for a situation requiring a decision.

problem formulation   the process of determining the structure of a problem. It occurs as more information is sought to define a problem more clearly.

problem recognition   see **problem finding.**

problem structuring   see **problem formulation.**

procedural knowledge   knowledge of a process. This type of knowledge is sometimes called "how to" knowledge. See also **declarative knowledge.**

process planning   the sequence of operations needed to manufacture a product. See **manufacturing.**

product   a **relational algebra** operation that constructs a new **relation** by combining all of the **tuples** in two relations horizontally. It connects each tuple of one relation with all tuples of a second relation, combining all of the **attributes** into the resulting relation.

production management   management of the operations needed to manufacture a product. See **manufacturing** and **process planning.**

program maintenance   modification of existing programs to satisfy changing information requirements.

programmed decision   a decision for which well-specified decision-making procedures exist. See **nonprogrammed decision, structured situation,** and **unstructured situation.**

projection a **relational algebra** operation for choosing specific **attributes** from a **relation.**

pronoun reference a problem in **natural language processing** involving the process of establishing the referent of a pronoun in an earlier sentence.

prototype the first version of a system, or the act of developing the first version of a system.

public branch exchanges (PBX) a local area **star network.**

public data network an arrangement of processors that typically links geographically dispersed processors, terminals, and other equipment via telephone lines.

QBE see **Query By Example.**

qualitative reasoning judgment based on analysis of nonquantitative concepts.

Query By Example a graphics-based, relational **data manipulation language** interface.

query language a special **data manipulation language** designed to access and manipulate data with a few simple commands.

range of expression refers to the multiple ways that a thought can be communicated in **natural language processing.**

readset a set of data items read by a class of **transactions.**

record blocking occurs when several **logical records** are stored in a **block.**

record occurrence the set of data values for one instance of a **record type.**

record subentry describes the record name and the record's **privacy locks** in a **CODASYL schema.**

record type a collection of logically related data items. See also **record occurrence.**

recovery the process of using logs and backup copies to recreate a damaged database.

recursive relationship occurs when an **entity** exists in a relationship with itself.

recursive set a **CODASYL set** in which the **owner record** type and the **member record** type are the same.

referential integrity a constraint requiring values of a **foreign key** to either match a **primary key** that exists in the database or be a **null value.** This rule ensures that if another **tuple** is referenced in the database, then that tuple exists.

relation a two-dimensional table with several specific characteristics that is the only essential **data structure** in the **relational model of data.**

relational algebra a set of operators for manipulating entire **relations.** Relational algebra is considered a procedural approach to data manipulation because the user must specify in a specific order how the relational algebra operators will be used.

relational calculus a set of operators that provide great flexibility in manipulating the data in **relations.** These operators are said to be nonprocedural because the user only specifies what the desired data is, not how to get it.

relational model of data an approach to data management based on two-dimensional tables called **relations.**

relationally complete system a **tabular system** that supports all the operations of **relational algebra.**

relative address see **relative record number.**

relative pointer a **data item** in a **record** that indicates the position of an associated record in a **file** by giving its position relative to the beginning of the file. See also **pointer, logical pointer,** and **physical pointer.**

relative record number a method of indicating the position of a record by numbering records from 1 to n as they are entered into the system.

reorganization the process of rewriting a **file** in order to remove records marked for deletion (see **tombstone**) and place inserted records into their proper location.

repeater see **booster node.**

replication transparency exists in a **network** when **transactions** may be executed without explicit concern for how many occurrences of the **data** item exist.

report generator programming languages with special commands for creating headings, titles, rows, columns, sums, and other elements frequently found in reports. The programming of reports is often greatly simplified by using such facilities.

reservation   an approach to controlling simultaneous use of a communications channel by computer systems in a **network**. A system wishing to use the channel makes a request and is given sole access to the channel.

response time   the elapsed clock time from the initiation of a request for **data** until that data has been delivered to the user.

restriction   a special case of **selection** defined in **relational calculus** in which the value of an **attribute** is compared to a specific value—this is called **restriction**.

retention class   in the **CODASYL** model, one of several means for specifying how **member records** are retained in **sets**. See **fixed retention class, manual retention class,** and **optional retention class.**

ring   a **linked list** in which the **tail** is connected to the **head**.

ring network   an arrangement of processors such that each processor is connected to another processor in a circular fashion. See **mesh network** and **star network.**

roll back/roll forward   a method of database **recovery**. **Transactions** are undone by processing the transaction log backward and restoring the first **before-image** of a **record** in the **transaction log.** After all transactions have been undone, transactions that must be redone are begun. This occurs by processing the transaction log forward and reapplying all of the transactions.

rollback database   a database that models time by storing all past states of the database as it evolves. These states are indexed by transaction time. Rollback databases record the update history rather than the real world history. See also **historical database** and **temporal database.**

rotational delay   the time required for desired **data** to rotate to the read/write head of a disk. See also **seek time** and **transfer time.**

run unit   an executing application in a **CODASYL database management system.**

SQL   see **Structured Query Language.**

schema   defines an integrated database by describing all the **data items** and relationships in the entire database.

screen generator   programming language with special commands for creating forms on a terminal screen. Users fill in these forms to retrieve, modify, or add data to the database. These facilities simplify the process of capturing data and making it readily accessible to users.

SDM   see **Semantic Database Model.**

second generation language   see **language generations.**

second normal form   is satisfied when **first normal form** is satisfied and all nonkey data items are **fully functionally dependent** on the primary key.

sector   an addressable portion of a disk. It often corresponds to a **block.**

sector addressing   the ability to access a **sector.**

seek time   the amount of time required to move a read/write head on a disk to the proper **track.** See also **rotational delay** and **transfer time.**

segment   a record in an **IMS** database. See also **hierarchical sequence.**

selection   a **relational algebra** operation for choosing specific **tuples** from a **relation.** In **relational calculus**, the term **selection** is reserved for the case in which the value of an **attribute** is compared to the value of another attribute.

Semantic Database Model (SDM)   a logical database modeling approach.

semantics   how words and word meanings are combined to express concepts. See also **syntax.**

semantic knowledge   knowledge of "meaning," knowledge needed for interpretation of statements in a language. See also **syntactic knowledge.**

semijoin   a **network** approach to performing the **join** operation in **relational algebra.**

semistructured problems   see **ill-structured** problems.

sequence field   a special field in **IMS** databases used to maintain the **hierarchical sequence.**

sequence set   contains an entry for each **control interval** in the **Virtual Storage Access Method**

giving the highest key of the records stored in the control interval.

sequential access storage device a storage device on which **records** must be stored physically in the order they are written onto the device. Processing requires that the records be accessed in the same order they were stored. Thus, to process the nth records, the preceding n-1 records must be read. See also **direct access storage device.**

serialization the condition that **transactions** behave as if they execute in a serial, or sequential, manner.

set a **one-to-many relationship** used in the CODASYL approach to database management.

set subentry describes the set in a **CODASYL schema.**

set type in the **CODASYL** model, a named, two-level, hierarchical relationship between record types. The parent node in the hierarchy is called the **owner record** type, and the child nodes are called **member record** types.

shadowing an approach to database **recovery** that relies on the existence of a copy of part of the database in memory and a "shadow" copy of the same part on a secondary storage device.

singular set a **CODASYL set** that has a special **owner record** called SYSTEM. This construction is used to process records sequentially. The desired sequential record is the **member record.** See also **set type.**

software schema the schema representation used in a particular **database management system** implementation.

sorted list a set of **records** maintained in a particular order.

specific reference in an object-oriented system, a reference to a particular version of an **object.** See also **generic reference.**

spreadsheet system spreadsheet software.

SQL see **Structured Query Language.**

standardization common definitions of data items, in terms of both the precise definition of a data item name and its storage format in the database.

star network an arrangement of processors in a manner such that all **nodes** are connected to a central computing resource. See **mesh network** and **ring network.**

storage manager a component in an object-oriented system that controls the storage and retrieval of data associated with objects.

strategic planning involves activities such as determining organizational goals and long-range strategies for achieving them. See also **managerial control** and **operational control.**

structural modeling a process of modeling a system using **nodes** connected by **links** (called arcs in structural modeling).

Structured Query Language (SQL) the standard query language for relational database systems.

structured situation one in which a well-specified procedure or algorithm exists for making a decision. See **unstructured situation.**

subject typically, a user of a database system. A subject may also be an application program.

subject profile a listing of all of the **objects** that a user may access.

subschema defines a particular subset, or **view,** of a **schema.** In a **CODASYL** database, a sub-schema is a subset of a given schema and cannot overlap schemas.

subtype in a generalization / specialization relationship, a subtype is the more specialized **entity type.** See also **supertype.**

supertype in a generalization / specialization relationship, a supertype is the more general **entity type.** See also **subtype.**

synonym see **alias.**

syntactic knowledge the knowledge required to construct valid combinations of words into a statement in a language. See also **semantic knowledge.**

syntax the rules that govern the way words are presented in an understandable form. How words are combined to form phrases, clauses, and sentences. See also **semantics.**

tabular system a system that supports only tables as **data structures** and does not support any of the operations defined in **relational algebra.**

tail the last record in a **linked list.**

temporal database a database that models time by supporting both transaction time and valid time. Temporal databases record the progression of states of an enterprise over an interval of time. See also **historical database** and **rollback database.**

ternary relation a **relation** with only three **attributes.**

theta-join the more general definition of the **join** operation in **relational algebra.** Theta-join replaces the **constraint** that specific **attributes** must match (that is, be equal) with the more general constraint that some relationship, represented by the Greek letter theta, must exist between these attributes. When "=" is substituted for θ, the comparison is equality and the theta-join is called an **equi-join.**

third generation language see **language generations.**

third normal form is satisfied when **second normal form** is satisfied and a **data structure** contains no **transitive dependencies.**

threaded list see **multilist.**

time stamping a method for resolving the problems that occur during **concurrent processing.** With this approach, each record is "stamped" with the last time the record was read and updated.

token passing a process for controlling communications in a **network** of distributed processors. A special signal, called a token, is passed from node to node around the network. Whichever node has the token also has control of the communications on the network. When this node completes its transmission, it puts the token back in the network for another node to capture. Nodes that need to use the communication capabilities must wait until control of the token is obtained.

tombstone a special mark in a file denoting a record that has been deleted.

total access time the total time required to locate and move data from a storage device to main memory and vice versa. It equals **seek time** plus **rotational delay** plus **transfer time.**

total participation constraint occurs when a relationship cannot exist without at least one instance of each of the entities involved participating in the relationship. See also **partial participation constraint.**

track the band in which **data** is stored on a tape or disk.

transaction a logical unit of work in a database environment. It may be composed of many physical operations on the database. See also **aborted transaction** and **committed transaction.**

transaction class a group of transactions that reads the same set of data items, called a readset, and writes the same set of data items, called a writeset. Transaction classes conflict if the writeset of one intersects the readset or writeset of the other.

transaction log a compilation of the physical operations that occur when **transactions** are executed.

transaction processing systems information systems designed to support the processing of "production" data, for example, for inventory maintenance, accounts receivable and payable, and other accounting functions.

transfer time the amount of time required to move data from a storage device to main memory and vice versa. See also **rotational delay** and **seek time.**

transformation language a high-level language that transforms input relations into the desired output relations. See also **Structured Query Language (SQL).**

transitive dependence exists when a **determinant** of a data item that is not a **candidate key** is in turn determined by a prior data item. (The data item in the middle of this relationship is not a **candidate key.**)

tree a **one-to-many data structure.**

tree network see **star network.**

tuple a row in a **relation.**

two-way list a **linked list** with **pointers** both forward to the next record and backward to the prior record in the list.

type a generic description of an **entity** or **attribute.**

unary relation a **relation** with only one **attribute**.

uncommitted dependence problem occurs during **concurrent processing** when invalid values are processed because a **transaction** reaches a logical conclusion but is not committed to the database. See also **inconsistent analysis problem** and **lost update problem**.

union a relational algebra operation for combining two **relations** vertically to form a third **relation**.

union compatible a **constraint** on some **relational algebra** operations that requires that the **relations** have the same number of attributes (have the same **degree)** and that the **attributes** in the corresponding columns assume values from the same **domain**.

update and access control one form of control specified by the AICPA. A system that exhibits this type of control allows users to access and modify data items they are authorized to access and modify, without concern for concurrent processing problems that may occur when other users are accessing the same data item. See also **coordination of activity control** and **concentration of resources control**.

update anomaly occurs when the modification of the information for one logical **entity** requires more than one modification to a **data structure**. See also **modification anomaly**.

unstructured situation one in which no well-specified procedure or algorithm exists for making a decision. See **structured situation**.

user interface the part of the system that provides for communication with the person using the system.

user view the subset of data seen by an individual user or group of users with similar needs.

user work area a portion of main memory allocated to **run units** for transferring data values between application programs and the database.

value class a **domain** in the **Semantic Database Model**.

values table in an **inverted list,** a table (column) containing the data item that has been "inverted" or rearranged. See also **occurrences table**.

variant approach one approach to computer aided **process planning** in which planning is based on the degree of variation from a standard required to manufacture a product.

version control a method for maintaining evolving forms of a data object.

vertical partitioning an approach to distributing data in a **network** in which the **data** in a **relation** is divided by placing some columns at one **node** and other columns at some other node.

view A subset of a database available to a particular user. Also, a **relation** that is constructed from other relations.

Virtual Storage Access Method (VSAM) a powerful access method developed by IBM based on the **B-tree** approach.

VSAM see **Virtual Storage Access Method**.

weak entity an **entity** whose existence depends on another entity.

Winchester drive a type of nonremovable **diskpack**.

writeset a set of data items written by a class of **transactions**.

INDEX